AF571878

The Critical Temper

The Critical Temper

Interventions from The New Criterion *at 40*

EDITED BY
ROGER KIMBALL

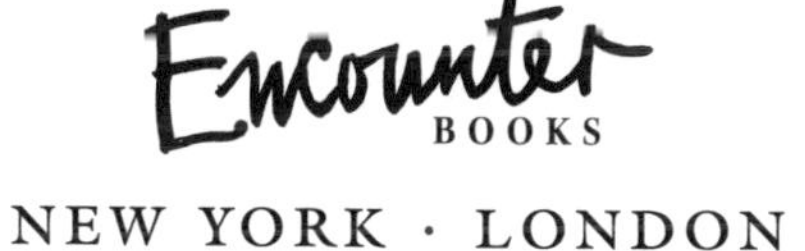

NEW YORK · LONDON

First American edition published in 2021 by Encounter Books, an activity of Encounter for Culture and Education, Inc., a nonprofit, tax-exempt corporation.
Encounter Books website address: www.encounterbooks.com

Manufactured in the United States and printed on acid-free paper. The paper used in this publication meets the minimum requirements of ANSI/NISO Z39.48—1992 (R 1997) (*Permanence of Paper*).

FIRST AMERICAN EDITION

LIBRARY OF CONGRESS CATALOGING-IN-PUBLICATION DATA

Names: Kimball, Roger, 1953– editor.
Title: The Critical Temper: Interventions from The New Criterion at 40 / by Roger Kimball, [editor]
Other titles: Critical temper (New criterion) | New criterion (New York, N.Y.)
Description: First American edition. | New York: Encounter Books, 2021. | Includes bibliographical references and index. |
Identifiers: LCCN 2021016467 (print) | LCCN 2021016468 (ebook) | ISBN 9781641772174 (hardcover) | ISBN 9781641772181 (ebook)
Subjects: LCSH: Culture. | Arts.
Classification: LCC NX60.C747 2021 (print) | LCC NX60 (ebook) | DDC 700—dc23
LC record available at https://lccn.loc.gov/2021016467
LC ebook record available at https://lccn.loc.gov/2021016468

1 2 3 4 5 6 7 8 9 10 20 21

CONTENTS

IV. DISCRIMINATIONS

Foreword

SOME FIFTEEN YEARS AGO, in the foreword to *Counterpoints: 25 Years of The New Criterion on Culture and the Arts*, our founding editor, Hilton Kramer, and I began by recalling T. S. Eliot's reflections on what prompted him to start *The Criterion*, the quarterly magazine that ran from 1922 to 1939. Looking back in the 1940s, Eliot wrote that he and his colleagues had intended *The Criterion* to be partly a means of fostering "common concern for the highest standards of both thought and expression" and partly a means of discharging "our common responsibility … to preserve our common culture uncontaminated by political influences." That comes close to describing our abiding ambition with *The New Criterion*. In the editorial note introducing our first issue in September 1982, we wrote that

> Today … the prevailing modes of criticism have not only failed to come to grips with such tasks, they have actually come to constitute an obstacle to their pursuit. A multitude of journals of every size and periodicity—quarterlies, monthlies, fortnightlies, weeklies, and even the daily papers to the extent that they concern themselves with matters of the mind—lavishes upon the life of culture a vast amount of attention. Yet most of what is written in these journals is either hopelessly ignorant, deliberately obscurantist, commercially compromised, or politically motivated. Especially where the fine arts and the disciplines of high culture are concerned, criticism at every level—from the daily newspaper review of a concert or a novel to the disquisitions of critics and scholars in learned journals—has almost everywhere degenerated into one or another form of ideology or publicity or some pernicious combination of the two. As a result, the very notion of an independent high culture

and the distinctions that separate it from popular culture and commercial entertainment have been radically eroded.

A lot has changed in the nearly four decades since those words appeared. But the fundamental threats to our culture that were identified there have only become more entrenched and insinuating. With *The Critical Temper*, we offer a generous sampling of essays that represent the range of *The New Criterion*'s response to the cultural challenges and opportunities of our times, a response that we have organized under the rubrics "The fate of freedom," "Reputations reconsidered," "Appreciations," and "Discriminations." In addition, we have included, as a polemical interlude, a small sampling of the Notes & Comments that begin every issue. Taken together, the fifty-five essays in this volume aspire to live up to Eliot's definition of the vocation of criticism as "the common pursuit of true judgment."

In his poem "At the Grave of Henry James," W. H. Auden spoke of the "Resentful muttering Mass," its "ruminant hatred of all that cannot/ Be simplified or stolen" and "its lust/ To vilify the landscape of Distinction." James dedicated his career to opposing that hatred of complexity and lust for leveling. From the beginning, *The New Criterion* has understood its vocation in similar terms. "All will be judged," Auden declared in the last stanza of his elegy for that master of discrimination. For us, the imperative of judgment, of criticism, has revolved primarily around two tasks.

The first is the negative task of forthright critical discrimination. To a large extent, that means the gritty job of intellectual and cultural trash collector. In that note to our inaugural issue, we spoke of applying "a new criterion to the discussion of our cultural life—a criterion of truth." The truth was, and is, that much of what presents itself as art today can scarcely be distinguished from political sermonizing, on the one hand, or the pathetic recapitulation of Dadaist pathologies, on the other. Mastery of the artifice of art is mostly a forgotten, often an actively disparaged, goal. At such a time, simply telling the truth is bound to be regarded as an unwelcome provocation.

In the university and other institutions entrusted with preserving and transmitting the cultural capital of our civilization, kindred deformations are at work. Pseudo-scholarship propagated by a barbarous reader-proof prose and underwritten by the destructive imperatives of "woke" identity politics is the order of the day, increasingly as much in the corporate as the academic world. From its earliest days, *The New Criterion* sallied forth onto this cluttered battlefield determined not simply to call attention to the emperor's new clothes, but to do so with wit, clarity, and literary panache. We acknowledge that these have been hard times for the arts of satire and parody. With increasing velocity, today's reality has a way of outstripping yesterday's satirical exaggeration. Nevertheless, *The New Criterion* has always been distinguished by its effective deployment of satire, denunciation, and ridicule—all the astringent resources in the armory of polemic—and that is one of the things that has enabled the magazine to live up to Horace's injunction to delight as well as instruct.

But *The New Criterion* is not only about polemics. An equally important part of criticism revolves around the task of battling cultural amnesia. From our first issue nearly four decades ago, we have labored in the vast storehouse of cultural achievement to introduce, or reintroduce, readers to some of the salient figures whose works have helped weave the great unfolding tapestry of our civilization. Writers and artists, philosophers and musicians, scientists, historians, controversialists, explorers, and politicians: *The New Criterion* has specialized in resuscitating important figures whose voices have been drowned out by the demotic inanities of pop culture or embalmed by the dead hand of the academy.

It is worth noting that our interest in these matters has never been merely aesthetic. At the beginning of *The Republic*, Socrates reminds his young interlocutor, Glaucon, that their discussion concerns not trifling questions but "the right conduct of life." We echo that admonition. *The New Criterion* is not, we hope, a somber publication, but it is a serious one. We look to the past for enlightenment and to art for that humanizing education and ordering of the emotions that distinguish the man of culture from the barbarian.

Allan Bloom once observed that a liberal education consists in knowing and thinking about the alternative answers to life's perennial questions. Today, when some of history's less savory alternatives are once again on the march, the claims of culture—and criticism, which keeps culture vital—are particularly exigent.

In the note introducing our twentieth-anniversary issue, we quoted two passages from Evelyn Waugh. They are as relevant today as they were in 2001. The first, written near the end of Waugh's life, concerned Rudyard Kipling's view of culture. Kipling, Waugh wrote, "believed civilization to be something laboriously achieved which was only precariously defended. He wanted to see the defenses fully manned and he hated the liberals because he thought them gullible and feeble, believing in the easy perfectibility of man and ready to abandon the work of centuries for sentimental qualms."

In the second passage, written three decades earlier, Waugh dilates more fully on this theme. Barbarism, he wrote in 1938,

> is never finally defeated; given propitious circumstances, men and women who seem quite orderly will commit every conceivable atrocity. The danger does not come merely from habitual hooligans; we are all potential recruits for anarchy. Unremitting effort is needed to keep men living together at peace; there is only a margin of energy left over for experiment however beneficent. Once the prisons of the mind have been opened, the orgy is on. . . . There is no more agreeable position than that of dissident from a stable society. Theirs are all the solid advantages of other people's creation and preservation, and all the fun of detecting hypocrisies and inconsistencies. There are times when dissidents are not only enviable but valuable. The work of preserving society is sometimes onerous, sometimes almost effortless. The more elaborate the society, the more vulnerable it is to attack, and the more complete its collapse in case of defeat. At a time like the present it is notably precarious. If it falls we shall see not merely the dissolution of a few joint-stock corporations, but of the spiritual and material achievements of our history.

We wrote this only a few weeks before the terrorist attacks of 9/11. In the years since, we have often returned to Waugh's prescient observations: "Conservative" means wanting to conserve what is worth preserving from the ravages of time and ideology, evil and stupidity. In some plump eras, as Waugh says, the task is so easy we can almost forget how necessary it is. At other times, the enemies of civilization transform the task of preserving culture into a battle for survival. That, we believe, is where we are today. And that is one reason that *The New Criterion*'s effort to tell the truth about culture is as important today as it was in 1982. *The Critical Temper*, a wide-ranging chrestomathy of essays published during the last fifteen years, provides a record of *The New Criterion*'s recent contribution to this imperative task.

Foreword

From its beginning, *The New Criterion* has been a collaborative enterprise, not least a collaboration between editors and writers. As the list of contributors to this volume shows, we have been particularly fortunate in attracting some of the most vital critical talent of our time to our cause, and we are pleased to have this opportunity to acknowledge our gratitude to the many writers who, for meager recompense, have provided so much insightful and gracefully written commentary.

I want also to acknowledge my gratitude to the staff of *The New Criterion*, past and present, who over the years have made this dream a reality. Benjamin Riley, our Managing Editor, and Andrew L. Shea, our Associate Editor, were particularly helpful in assembling this book and seeing it through the complexities of production. James Panero, our Executive Editor, and Isaac Sligh, our sometime Hilton Kramer Fellow and now an Assistant Editor, were also indispensable in helping to put this anthology together.

Finally, I would like to acknowledge our gratitude to the many individuals and institutions that, for well-nigh forty years, have underwritten our efforts and made *The New Criterion* possible. I would like in particular to thank The Lynde and Harry Bradley Foundation, the late, great John M. Olin Foundation, the Sarah Scaife Foundation, the late Donald Kahn, Virginia James, the Kleinschmidt Family Foundation, and that prolific and ubiquitous philanthropist Anonymous. Without their stalwart support, and the support of many other generous benefactors, neither *The New Criterion* nor *The Critical Temper* would exist.

RK
May 2021

INTRODUCTION

Hilton Kramer & the critical temper

Roger Kimball

> No one, if he could help it, would tolerate the presence of untruth in the most vital part of his nature concerning the most vital matters. There is nothing he would fear so much as to harbor falsehood in that quarter.
> —PLATO, *The Republic*, Book II

PROSE. Many of the recollections that followed Hilton Kramer's death, age 84, on March 27, 2012, dilated on the nature of his prose. "Clarity" usually came towards the top of the list. George Orwell somewhere likened good prose to a transparent window pane. It revealed what it was about without calling attention to itself. It disappeared in rendering the thing it described. Hilton's prose displayed that Orwellian clarity. Not only did you always know where you stood reading an essay by Hilton Kramer, you knew exactly where he stood, too. And you knew precisely what he thought about the subject under discussion.

You might suppose that is the least you should ask for from a writer of critical prose. You would be right. It is the least you should be able to ask for. The disappointing thing is how rarely you get it. You always got it from Hilton. Column after column, essay after essay, year in and year out for more than forty years, Hilton delivered the goods about art, literature, politics, and cultural life generally. He was not only remarkably clear in his writing, he was also prodigiously productive. The four plump compendia of his critical writings—*The Age of the Avant Garde* (1973), *The Revenge of the Philistines* (1985), *The Twilight of the Intellectuals* (1999), and *The Triumph of Modernism* (2008)—contain only a portion of his published work. Until illness silenced him in the last decade of his life, Hilton was an indefatigable as well as an articulate observer of the cultural scene.

Yet another oft-noted aspect of Hilton's writing was its intelligence. You might disagree with Hilton's judgments—many did, and vehemently—but you always knew what his judgments were and you had confidence (assuming you were smart yourself) that he knew whereof he spoke. That, of course, only added insult to injury for those who disagreed with him. Hilton's range, not only in art history but also in the history of ideas, was formidable. It was also practical. Back in the 1980s, I wrote an essay about the philosopher Arthur Schopenhauer, the grand panjandrum of pessimism. Hilton read it and instantly saw that it lacked something essential. Today, Schopenhauer's philosophy has been relocated to off-site storage in the university. But back in the early decades of the twentieth century it exercised a broad and mesmerizing appeal. It features prominently in Thomas Mann's great novel *Buddenbrooks*, for example, something I didn't know but that Hilton did. I read the novel, rewrote the essay, and found that the Thomas Mann connection brought everything into focus.

The point is that Hilton's engagement with ideas was the opposite of academic. He liked to quote a remark by the British writer Ernest Newman, for decades the music critic for the London *Times*: "journalist," said Newman, is a term of contempt applied by writers who are not read to writers who are. Between the academic and the journalistic approach to ideas, Hilton embraced the latter. It was not a matter of popularity or currency. Nor was it a matter of rigor (though academics like to pretend that it is). It was a matter of the proper application of ideas to the metabolism of life.

There was yet another characteristic of Hilton's prose that struck many of his readers. Leaf through the recollections and you find plenty of references to his clarity and intelligence. You will also discover another quality that people struggled to get a handle on. Some called it "severity." In fact, Hilton praised as often as he deprecated. But he was famously reputed to be a "severe," "acerbic," or "judgmental" critic. The last adjective always puzzled me. What manner of thing would a "non-judgmental," i.e., a non-critical, i.e., a non-discriminating, critic be? Hilton liked to quote Walter Bagehot in this context: "The business of the critic," said Bagehot, "is to criticize." One of Hilton's favorite stories involved the movie director and actor Woody Allen. Back when Hilton worked at *The New York Times*, he happened to be seated next to

Allen one night at a dinner. He asked whether Hilton ever felt embarrassed when he encountered socially artists he'd written disparagingly about. Without missing a beat, Hilton replied, No, why should I be embarrassed? They made the crappy art. I just described it.

Hilton's response was both witty and innocent—witty, because it was a riposte unanswerable, innocent because it was only on his way home from the event that Hilton remembered he had written a negative review of *The Front*, a piece of left-wing agitprop about the Hollywood blacklist, in which Woody Allen acted.

For a critic, making judgments, distinguishing good from bad, better from worse, is the name of the game. It was a game at which Hilton excelled. Many recollections noted the "confidence" or "authority" that his writing exudes. "Mandarin" was another favorite epithet. All those descriptions circle around what I think was a central—maybe the central—quality of Hilton's work as a critic: a ferocious allegiance to the truth of experience.

That quality is much rarer than you might suppose. It is a multifaceted attribute, as much a matter of temperament, of character, as it is a matter of conscious deliberation. It colors not just one's critical judgments but also one's whole approach to the vocation of criticism, which, as Matthew Arnold said of literature, is in its highest sense a "criticism of life." Criticism is a serious business because life is a serious business. "Serious," I hasten to add, does not mean "somber." It certainly does not mean "academic." It does mean that tone is more than a cosmetic resource. It is a matter, at bottom, of respect, of dignity. Seriousness is compatible with humor, but not with frivolity. "No one," said Plato, "would tolerate the presence of untruth in the most vital part of his nature concerning the most vital matters." Hilton's unwavering, instinctive commitment to the truth underlay his whole practice as a critic. The quality of that commitment helps explain why he regarded himself as a modernist.

"Modernism" is a word with many meanings. As Hilton understood the term, it describes not just a particular style or period of art but an attitude towards the place of culture in the economy of life. This may be the place to say a word about abstract art. Hilton is sometimes regarded as a champion of abstract art. It would be more accurate, I believe, to say that he was a champion of good art, by which I mean art that, whatever its genre or technical prowess, was palpably true to our experience of life. An inventory of Hilton's criticism shows that he wrote as often, and as enthusiastically, about figurative as about abstract art. Unlike Clement Greenberg, he never thought (as Greenberg wrote in 1959) that "the very best painting, the major painting, of our age is almost exclusively abstract." If modernism, as Hilton put it, remains "the only really vital tradition that the art of our time can claim as its own," it was not because of its association with abstract or other "experimental" forms of art. It was because modernism recognized that traditional sources of spiritual nourishment had been irreversibly complicated. The "melancholy, long, withdrawing roar" of the "sea of faith" that Matthew Arnold descried in "Dover Beach" was now an inextricable part of our cultural inheritance. Preserving or reclaiming what was vital in that inheritance, and adapting it honestly to the vagaries of new experience, was the high and serious task of cultural endeavor. Hilton loathed everything that traveled under the banner of postmodernism not because it was "playful" (as was sometimes said) but because it betokened a terrible cynicism about the whole realm of culture, which is to say the realm of human engagement with the world. Postmodernism, said Philip Johnson, doyen of the genre, installed "the giggle" into architecture. He was right. But that giggle bespoke not the laughter of joyful affirmation but the rictus of a corrosive and deflationary snideness, a version of nihilism. It is not always easy to distinguish the two. That was part of Hilton's genius: an unerring instinct for the fraudulent.

What was probably Hilton's most original achievement in this regard was his definitive anatomy of the Alexandrian quality of today's "avant-garde" (the scare quotes are requisite). "The Age of the Avant-Garde," first published in *Commentary* in 1972, is one of his most ambitious and most important contributions to this task. The central insight of that essay concerns what Hilton elsewhere called "the institutionalization of the avant-garde." It used to be that the Salon looked to the past and resisted aesthetic innovation. The Salon of today insists on the *appearance* of innovation and forgets the past. As Hilton shows, this situation is not new. If it gained majority status in the 1960s, it has been with us, in essentials, since the 'teens, when the Dadaist crusader Marcel Duchamp unveiled his "ready-mades" and impishly offered them to the public as works of art.

As Hilton noted, what happened to Dada set an ominous precedent.

Among other things, it demonstrated the extent to which the outrageous can be trivialized by being institutionalized: assimilated into the predictable cycle of museum exhibitions, curatorial safekeeping, and critical commentary. The cultural situation that Hilton dissected—and it is still very much *our* situation—is defined largely by the aftermath of the avant-garde: by all those "adversarial" gestures, poses, ambitions, and tactics that emerged and were legitimized in the 1880s and 1890s, flowered in the first half of the twentieth century, and that live a sort of posthumous existence now in the frantic twilight of postmodernism.

In part, our present situation, like the avant-garde itself, is a complication (not to say a perversion) of our Romantic inheritance. The elevation of art from a didactic pastime to a prime spiritual resource, the self-conscious probing of inherited forms and artistic strictures, the image of the artist as a tortured, oppositional figure: all achieved a first maturity in Romanticism. These themes were exacerbated as the avant-garde developed from an impulse to a movement and finally into a tradition of its own.

The problem is that the avant-garde has become a casualty of its own success. Having won battle after battle, it gradually transformed a recalcitrant bourgeois culture into a willing collaborator in its raids on established taste. But in this victory were the seeds of its own irrelevance, for without credible resistance, its oppositional gestures degenerated into a kind of aesthetic buffoonery. In this sense, the institutionalization of the avant-garde—what Clement Greenberg called "avant-gardism"—spells the death or at least the senility of the avant-garde. Look around at a museum or art gallery near you and you will see what I mean.

Hilton recoiled in almost visceral distaste from untruth. I don't just mean that he didn't like lies, though I do mean that. There was something more. His practice as a critic could seem startling because of its moral force. At first blush, it might seem paradoxical that his criticism regularly displayed a moral component. After all, Hilton was a critic who emphasized the autonomy of aesthetic experience. He always gave priority to first-hand experience. He prized connoisseurship, and his criticism, like Ruskin's (Hilton greatly admired John Ruskin), dwelt on the evidence of the work itself, not on any extrinsic narrative festooned around the work. That is why he reacted with such contempt when, back in the 1980s, the social scientist Edward Banfield suggested that museums relinquish the art objects in their possession to the lucrative art market and replace them with reproductions—"high quality" reproductions, he stressed, though perhaps not too high. "If one is willing," Banfield wrote,

> to settle for copies that are "excellent" (meaning that no one but an expert can detect a difference with the naked eye), the cost will be less. And if one is willing to have copies that are just "very good" (meaning that an experienced and careful viewer gets almost as much aesthetic satisfaction from them as from an original) the cost will be lower still.

Yes, and as Hilton points out, "the costs—in dollars, anyway—would be lower still if we just chucked art out of our lives altogether." Mr. Banfield's book was called *The Democratic Muse*, but in fact his proposal was not only profoundly anti-aesthetic but anti-democratic to boot. What this "ghastly intellectual fraud" entailed, Hilton observed, was a policy of "reproductions for the plebs, originals for the rich."

Some of Hilton's readers were taken aback by the passion of his critical responses. "Ghastly intellectual fraud" is pretty severe. And Edward Banfield, it is worth noting, was a political conservative, someone with whom Hilton would have agreed on many other topics. Some found Hilton personally intimidating as well as rhetorically astringent. "I only met him once," a friend wrote me the day he died, "and I was appropriately terrified." I don't believe the terror really was appropriate. Hilton could be a formidable polemicist, but in person he tended to be quite mild, even jovial. He was a commanding raconteur with a large library of amusing stories. He did not suffer fools gladly, or—now that I think back on it—in any other way. Yet he was engaging company. But from the very beginning of his career Hilton called things exactly as he saw them. He did not temper his disapprobation—nor his praise, come to that—to suit the politesse of any establishment. Which brings me back to the moral pressure of Hilton's critical writing, a feature that was as evident in his writing about painting as it was in his writing about politics. Hilton understood that at bottom the aesthetic is deeply implicated in our moral life. In this, he was like one of his culture heroes, Henry James. James's exquisite dissections of human emotion and motivation play out on a canvas of great moral urgency. Just so, Hilton's embrace of the aesthetic escaped the aridity of arts-for-art's-sake aestheticism because it was rooted in a larger vision of life. He insisted on the integrity of aesthetic experience because the aesthetic, the experience of beauty and its filiations with our life as moral beings, is a fundamental part of human nature. From the beginning of his career, Hilton celebrated art and literature—and the tradition of humanistic endeavor generally—not as an escape from but a revelation of reality.

This was evident already in his first major foray in criticism, an attack on Harold Rosenberg's once-famous idea of "action painting." The piece, which appeared in *Partisan Review* in 1952, put the twenty-four-year-old Hilton Kramer on the map. Rosenberg pretended to peer deeply into the existential engine room of art. In fact, as Hilton put it in a later reflection on Rosenberg, he substituted talking about the psyche of the artist for talking about the work of art. "This shift of critical focus away from the artist's completed work," Hilton wrote,

> had an effect quite the opposite of what was intended. It alienated the visual realities of painting from the crux of the discussion, leaving the audience free to regard the creation as being little more than the psychological residue of the artist's personal crisis. In making the existential component not only dominant but all-encompassing, Mr. Rosenberg succeeded in reducing Abstract Expressionist painting to a cultural datum utterly discontinuous with the art history that actually produced it.

Hilton freely acknowledged Rosenberg's prowess as a phrasemaker, his intelligence, the "vivacity" of his prose. What he deprecated was the void that opened up between his verbal lucubrations and the art that was his ostensible subject.

In the realm of culture, that void is filled by sentimentality, kitsch, or some other species of untruth to experience. In the realm of politics, the compact between mendacious fantasy and power fabricated illusions that could be as murderous as they were false. Hilton's recognition of this truth nourished his uncompromising anti-Communism and his allergy to the myriad intellectual and moral deformations that allegiance to Communism begat. In a review of Anne Applebaum's magisterial *Gulag: A History*, Hilton recalled his uneasiness about Hannah Arendt's essay "The Concentration Camps," which he had read when it appeared soon after the war. "The horror of the concentration and extermination camps," Arendt wrote, "can never be fully embraced by the imagination for the very reason that it stands outside of life and death.... The fear of the absolute Evil which permits of no escape knows that this is the end of dialectical evolutions and developments." Come again? What, besides imparting a bit of Teutonic owlishness, could Arendt have meant by standing "outside of life and death"? Where did "dialectical evolutions and developments" come into the story? It is one of the great if harrowing virtues of Applebaum's book that it regards the monumental horror of the Gulag with unblinking concreteness. It was a matter not of "standing outside life and death" but of death and degradation *tout court*, on an industrial scale. There were no dialectics at play, only the diabolism of human, all-too-human evil.

The Left has always had trouble coming to terms with the enormity of Communism. The tincture of perverted idealism that somehow clings, even now, to that utopian fantasy has licensed all manner of mendacious posturing, especially among intellectuals. Always there was an exemption, an excuse, a bit of moral equivalence on hand to paper over its inescapable, freedom-blighting viciousness. Publication of Aleksandr Solzhenitsyn's *Gulag Archipelago* in the 1970s ought to have put paid to that forever. It didn't. Hilton quotes George Steiner, who reviewed the book in 1974 for *The New Yorker*. "To infer," wrote Steiner, "that the Soviet terror is as hideous as Hitlerism is not only a brutal simplification but a moral indecency." Recalling this passage in 1991, Hilton noted that

> Steiner's sense of moral indecency ... has probably been modified by recent events in Russia and Eastern Europe. The noise of all those Lenin monuments being toppled must have reached even his reclusive ears. Yet it is important to recall attacks of this kind, which always had less to do with the realities of Communism and the Soviet system than with the need to uphold the pieties of Left-liberal orthodoxy, if we are to understand the assaults still to come on the writers who insisted on telling the truth about the longest reigning tyranny of the twentieth century.

It's no wonder that during his long exile in Cavendish, Vermont, when Solzhenitsyn decided to grant an interview to *The New York Times*, the only reporter he would agree to talk to was Hilton Kramer. Not the Russia experts, not the political reporters or editorialists: only the chief art critic, but one whose reputation for truth-telling preceded him.

The spectacle of toppled Lenins reminds me of a story Hilton liked to tell about his visit to the Soviet Union in 1967. He was part of a platoon of *New York Times* reporters sent to cover the fiftieth anniversary of the Bolshevik revolution. That sojourn resulted in lots of emetic celebrations of Soviet "achievements," but not from Hilton. Like the rest of the *Times* contingent, Hilton was closely shepherded by Intourist handlers (i.e., KGB agents) but he managed a few off-roster meetings. There was the poet who, living in garret-like penury, was engaged in the illicit activity of translating Wallace Stevens (talk about counter-revolutionary literature!). Hilton threw his hosts into confused panic when he asked to meet the artist who supervised the production of the statues of Lenin that were then ubiquitous in the totalitarian state. They hadn't anticipated such a request. What was this wily American up to? After considerable hemming and hawing the interview was approved and Hilton was driven to the factory that disgorged the totemic figures. There were hundreds of plaster and stone Lenins in various states of completion—gigantic oversize Lenins for your town square and diminutive Vladimirs suitable for desk or mantelpiece. Hilton toured the facility, asked the usual polite questions, and then was ushered into the artist's office where there was the obligatory green baize table and large flask of vodka. A couple of drams later he quietly asked a devastating question. Were there up-and-coming young artists available to keep this great revolutionary tradition alive? No! The artist banged the table and let loose a torrent of lamentation about how difficult it was. The younger generation had no interest in the Revolution. They had been seduced by bourgeois individualism. It was almost impossible to find young artists to carry on his work. The story all but wrote itself.

Hilton's habit of frankness was of inestimable value in my own career. I first met him in the spring of 1983. I was then a graduate student at Yale, but, like Balthazar at that famous feast, I had seen the writing on the wall. The academic option, which had once seemed so attractive, was, like an item on a computer menu, grayed out. I had looked into *The New Criterion*, then in its first year of publication, and liked what I saw. Armed with an introduction from my Greek tutor in college, I made a date to have lunch with Hilton. We met at the Century Association in New York. It was an impressive engagement for a twenty-something refugee from the People's Republic of Yale. As Hilton knew, I was hoping for a job at *The New Criterion*. None was available at the time, but there were plenty of opportunities for writing. In short order, I had my first assignment, a review of a book about William James by Jacques Barzun.

In due course—slightly overdue course, if truth be told—I turned in a piece about twice as long as assigned. Hilton printed the whole thing, thus paving the way for the hundreds of pieces, signed and unsigned, I have contributed to *The New Criterion* over well-nigh thirty years.

It was only much later that I learned from Hilton that my review of the book by Jacques Barzun had been the source of some consternation. For one thing, I had been pretty hard on the pragmatism of William James, and by implication on Jacques Barzun, who apparently was not pleased. Was there a more eminent personage in academic life than Jacques Barzun? I doubt it. And who was Roger Kimball? The insouciance of youth rarely calculates eminence. Even more shocking, in some circles, was the criticism I offered of a latter-day pragmatist, Richard Rorty. At the time, there was a feeling that Rorty, an academic star, might harbor pro-American, even conservative sentiments. He soon dispelled that illusion, revealing himself to be a chummy nihilist of decidedly left-wing opinions. But for one shining moment many conservatives cherished the hope that here, at last, was a prominent academic they could call their own. One very distinguished conservative commentator wrote to Hilton to complain about my piece. Hilton responded by defending the essay and promptly giving me another assignment.

I said earlier that, reading Hilton, you always knew where he stood. It was that way in person, too. For a writer, that is a gift of incalculable value. If you're an editor, it is the easiest thing in the world to distribute indiscriminate praise. You please your interlocutor and save yourself a world of intellectual labor. Hilton's praise was never indiscriminate. He did every writer the courtesy of taking their work as seriously as they ought to have taken it. Like Montaigne, he understood that admonition and correction were among the highest offices of friendship. This made Hilton as great a teacher as he was an editor. In another age, he might well have had a distinguished academic career. But the implosion of higher (and, by now, of lower) education in this country—its dumbing down, its politicization, its emancipation from any real engagement with human realities—rendered that impossible.

The pedagogical habit was woven deep into Hilton's make up. Anyone who knew him well would at some point hear the story of how he got his name. The loathsome Gore Vidal—whose only real distinction is having been found repugnant by not one but two cultural giants, William F. Buckley Jr. as well as Hilton—liked to refer to Hilton as "the Tel Aviv Hilton," thus simultaneously revealing his anti-Semitism as well as his malign fatuousness. In fact, Hilton owes his name to Miss Hilton, a grade-school teacher in Gloucester, Massachusetts, where he grew up. When one of his older brothers was home sick for some months, she came daily after school to tutor him, free of charge. Imagine a public school teacher doing that today! Hilton's brother got well; he didn't have to repeat the year; and Hilton's parents, when he was born, named the newest Kramer Hilton in honor of her. I have no doubt that the spirit of Miss Hilton lived on in her namesake. I like to think a bit of Miss Hilton, and of Hilton Kramer, too, somehow persists in young James Hilton Kimball. One friend of ours asked whether we named our son after the author of *Lost Horizon* and *Goodbye, Mr. Chips.* No flies on that novelist, but, no, it was after the non-fabulizing Hilton. RIP.

May 2012

I. The fate of freedom

Leninthink

Gary Saul Morson

Lenin was more severe.
—VYACHESLAV MOLOTOV
the only senior official to work for both Lenin and Stalin, when asked to compare them.

Lenin "in general" loved people but . . . his love looked far ahead, through the mists of hatred.
—MAXIM GORKY

When we are reproached with cruelty, we wonder how people can forget the most elementary Marxism.
—LENIN

BEYOND DOCTRINE

AN OLD SOVIET JOKE poses the question: What was the most important world-historical event of the year 1875? Answer: Lenin was five years old.

The point of the joke, of course, is that the Soviets virtually deified Lenin. Criticism of him was routinely referred to as "blasphemy," while icon corners in homes and institutions were replaced by "Lenin corners." Lenin museums sprung up everywhere, and institutions of every kind took his name. In addition to Leningrad, there were cities named Leninsk (in Kazakhstan), Leninogorsk (in Tatarstan), Leninaul (in Dagestan), Leninakan (in Armenia), Leninkend, Leninavan, and at least four different Leninabads. On a visit to the Caucasus I remember being surprised at seeing Mayakovsky's famous verses about Lenin inscribed on a mountaintop: "Lenin lived! Lenin lives! Lenin will live!" The famous mausoleum where his body is preserved served as the regime's most sacred shrine.

As we approach the 150th anniversary of Lenin's birth, understanding him grows ever more important. Despite the fall of the Soviet Union, Leninist ways of thinking continue to spread, especially among Western radicals who have never read a word of Lenin. This essay is not just about Lenin, and not just Leninism, the official philosophy of the USSR, but also the very style of thought that Lenin pioneered. Call it Leninthink.

Lenin did more than anyone else to shape the last hundred years. He invented a form of government we have come to call totalitarian, which rejected in principle the idea of any private sphere outside of state control. To establish this power, he invented the one-party state, a term that would previously have seemed self-contradictory since a party was, by definition, a part. An admirer of the French Jacobins, Lenin believed that state power had to be based on sheer terror, and so he also created the terrorist state.

Stephen Pinker has recently argued that the world has been getting less bloodthirsty. The Mongols, after all, destroyed entire cities. But the Mongols murdered *other* people; what is new, and uniquely horrible about the Soviets and their successors, is that they directed their fury at their *own* people. The Russian empire lost more people in World War I than any other country, but still more died under Lenin. His war against the peasants, for instance, took more lives than combat between Reds and Whites.

Numbers do not tell the whole story. Under the Third Reich, an ethnic German loyal to the regime did not have to fear arrest, but Lenin pioneered and Stalin greatly expanded a policy in which arrests were entirely arbitrary: that is true terror. By the time of the Great Terror of 1936–38, millions of entirely innocent people were arrested, often by quota. Literally no one was safe. The Party itself was an especially dangerous place to be, and the NKVD was constantly arresting its own members—a practice that was also true of its predecessor, the Cheka, which Lenin founded almost immediately after the Bolshevik coup.

NKVD interrogators who suspected they were to be arrested often committed suicide since they had no illusions about what arrest entailed. They had practiced exquisite forms of torture and humiliation on prisoners—and on prisoners' colleagues, friends, and families. "Member of a family of a traitor to the fatherland" was itself a criminal category, and whole camps were set up for wives of "enemies of the people." Never before had such practices defined a state.

For good reason, many have traced these practices to Lenin's doctrines. In his view, Marx's greatest contribution was not the idea of the class struggle but "the dictatorship of the proletariat," and as far back as 1906 Lenin had defined dictatorship as "nothing other than power which is totally unlimited by any laws, totally unrestrained by absolutely any rules, and based directly on force." He argued that a revolutionary Party must be composed entirely of professional revolutionaries, drawn mainly from the intelligentsia and subject to absolute discipline, with a readiness to do literally anything the leadership demanded.

These and other disastrous Leninist ideas derived from a specific Leninist way of thinking, and that is what this essay focuses on. I know this way of thinking in my bones. I am myself a pink diaper baby and I remember being taught this way of thinking, taken for granted by all right-thinking people. Memoirs of many ex-Communists, from David Horowitz to Richard Wright, confirm that, more than doctrines, it was the Leninist style of thought that defined the difference between an insider and an outsider. And that way of thought is very much with us.

WHO WHOM?

> Introduce at once mass terror, execute and deport hundreds of prostitutes, drunken soldiers, ex-officers, etc.
>
> —Lenin's instructions to authorities in Nizhnii Novgorod, August 1918

Lenin regarded all interactions as zero-sum. To use the phrase he made famous, the fundamental question is always "Who Whom?"—who dominates whom, who does what to whom, ultimately who annihilates whom. To the extent that we gain, you lose. Contrast this view with the one taught in basic microeconomics: whenever there is a non-forced transaction, both sides benefit, or they would not make the exchange. For the seller, the money is worth more than the goods he sells, and for the buyer the goods are worth more than the money. Lenin's hatred of the market, and his attempts to abolish it entirely during War Communism, derived from the opposite idea, that all buying and selling is *necessarily* exploitative. When Lenin speaks of "profiteering" or "speculation" (capital crimes), he is referring to every transaction, however small. Peasant "bagmen" selling produce were shot.

Basic books on negotiation teach that you can often do better than split the difference, since people have different concerns. Both sides can come out ahead—but not for the Soviets, whose negotiating stance John F. Kennedy once paraphrased as: *what's mine is mine; and what's yours is negotiable.* For us, the word "politics" means a process of give and take, but for Lenin it's we take, and you give. From this it follows that one must take maximum advantage of one's position. If the enemy is weak enough to be destroyed, and one stops simply at one's initial demands, one is objectively helping the enemy, which makes one a traitor. Of course, one might simply be insane. Long before Brezhnev began incarcerating dissidents in madhouses, Lenin was so appalled that his foreign minister, Boris Chicherin, recommended an unnecessary concession to American loan negotiators, that he pronounced him mad—not metaphorically—and demanded he be forcibly committed. "We will be fools if we do not immediately and forcibly send him to a sanatorium."

Such thinking automatically favors extreme solutions. If there is one sort of person Lenin truly hated more than any other, it is—to use some of his more printable adjectives—the squishy, squeamish, spineless, dull-witted liberal reformer. In philosophical issues, too, there can never be a middle ground. If you are not a materialist in precisely Lenin's interpretation, you are an idealist, and idealism is simply disguised religion supporting the bourgeoisie. The following statement from his most famous book, *What Is to Be Done?*, is typical (the italics are Lenin's): "The *only* choice is: either the bourgeois or the socialist ideology. There is no middle course (for humanity has not created a 'third' ideology, and, moreover, in a society torn by class antagonisms there can never be a non-class or above-class ideology). Hence to belittle the socialist ideology *in any way, to turn away from it in the slightest degree*, means to strengthen bourgeois ideology." There is either rule by the bourgeoisie or dictatorship of the proletariat: "Every solution that offers a middle path is a deception ... or an expression of the dull-wittedness of the petty-bourgeois democrats."

Contrary to the wishes even of other Bolsheviks, Lenin categorically rejected the idea of a broad socialist coalition government. He was immensely relieved when the short-lived coalition with the Left Socialist Revolutionaries collapsed. Immediately after seizing power he declared the left-liberal Kadets "outside the law," leading to the lynching of two of their ex-ministers in a Petersburg Hospital. He would soon arrest

Mensheviks and the most numerous group of radicals, the Socialist Revolutionaries, famed for countless assassinations of tsarist officials. We think of show trials as Stalinist, but Lenin staged a show trial of Socialist Revolutionary leaders in 1922.

By the same token, Lenin always insisted on the most violent solutions. Those who do not understand him mistake his ideas for those of radicals like the anarchist Peter Kropotkin, who argued that violence was permitted *when necessary*. That squishy formulation suggests that other solutions would be preferable. But for Lenin maximal violence was the default position. He was constantly rebuking subordinates for not using enough force, for restraining mobs from lynchings, and for hesitating to shoot randomly chosen hostages.

One could almost say that force had a mystical attraction for Lenin. He had workers drafted into a labor army where any shirking or lateness was punished by sentence to a concentration camp. Yes, Bolsheviks used the term concentration camp from the start, and did so with pride. Until economic collapse forced Lenin to adopt the New Economic Policy, he demanded that grain not be purchased from peasants but requisitioned at gunpoint. Naturally, peasants—Lenin called recalcitrant peasants "kulaks"—rebelled all over Russia. In response to one such "kulak" uprising Lenin issued the following order:

> The kulak uprising in [your] 5 districts must be crushed without pity.... 1) Hang (and I mean hang so that the *people can see*) *not less than 100* known kulaks, rich men, bloodsuckers. 2) Publish their names. 3) Take *all* their grain away from them. 4) Identify hostages .... Do this so that for hundreds of miles around the people can see, tremble, know and cry .... Yours, Lenin. P. S. Find tougher people.

Dmitri Volkogonov, the first biographer with access to the secret Lenin archives, concluded that for Lenin violence was a goal in itself. He quotes Lenin in 1908 recommending "real, nationwide terror, which invigorates the country and through which the Great French Revolution achieved glory."

Lenin constantly recommended that people be shot "without pity" or "exterminated mercilessly" (Leszek Kołakowski wondered wryly what it would mean to exterminate people mercifully). "Exterminate" is a term used for vermin, and, long before the Nazis described Jews as

Ungeziefer (vermin), Lenin routinely called for "*the cleansing of Russia's soil of all harmful insects, of scoundrels, fleas, bedbugs—the rich*, and so on."

Lenin worked by a principle of anti-empathy, and this approach was to define Soviet ethics. I know of no other society, except those modeled on the one Lenin created, where schoolchildren were taught that mercy, kindness, and pity are vices. After all, these feelings might lead one to hesitate shooting a class enemy or denouncing one's parents. The word "conscience" went out of use, replaced by "consciousness" (in the sense of Marxist-Leninist ideological consciousness). During Stalin's great purges a culture of denunciation reigned, but it was Lenin who taught "A good communist is also a good Chekist."

THE ABBEY OF THÉLÈME

A special logic governs the Leninist approach to morality, legality, and rights. In his famous address to the Youth Leagues, Lenin complains that bourgeois thinkers have slanderously denied that Bolsheviks have any ethics. In fact,

> We reject any morality based on extra-human and extra-class concepts. We say that this is a deception .... We say that morality is entirely subordinated to the interests of the proletariat's class struggle.... That is why we say that to us there is no such thing as a morality that stands outside human society; that is a fraud. To us morality is subordinated to the interests of the proletariat's class struggle.
>
> When people tell us about morality, we say: to a Communist all morality lies in this united discipline and conscious mass struggle against the exploiters.

In short, Bolshevik morality holds that whatever contributes to Bolshevik success is moral, whatever hinders it is immoral.

Imagine someone saying: "my detractors claim I have no morals, but that is sheer slander. On the contrary, I have a very strict moral code, from which I never deviate: *look out for number 1*." We might reply: the whole point of a moral code is to *restrain* you from acting only out of self-interest. Morality begins with number 2. A moral code that says you must do what you regard as your self-interest is no moral code at all.

The same is true for a code that says the Communist Party is morally bound to do whatever it regards as in its interest.

Rabelais' pleasure-seeking utopia, the Abbey of Thélème, was governed, like all abbeys, by a rule. In this case, however, the rule was an anti-rule: *Fay çe que vouldras*, "Do as you wish!" People were to be restrained from yielding to any restraints. Ever since, such self-canceling imperatives have been called *Thelemite commands.*

Bolshevik legality was also Thelemite. If by law one means a code that binds the state as well as the individual, specifies what is and is not permitted, and eliminates arbitrariness, then Lenin entirely rejected law as "bourgeois." He expressed utter contempt for the principles "no crime without law" and "no punishment without a crime." Recall that he defined the dictatorship of the proletariat as rule based entirely on force absolutely unrestrained by any law. His more naive followers imagined that rule by sheer terror would cease when Bolshevik hold on power was secure, or when the New Economic Policy relaxed restrictions on trade, but Lenin made a point of disillusioning them. "It is the biggest mistake to think that NEP will put an end to the terror. We shall return to the terror, and to economic terror," he wrote. When D. I. Kursky, People's Commissariat of Justice, was formulating the first Soviet legal code, Lenin demanded that terror and arbitrary use of power be written into the code itself! "The law should not abolish terror," he insisted. "It should be substantiated and legalized in principle, without evasion or embellishment."

So far as I know, never before had the law prescribed lawlessness. Do as you wish, or else. Lenin had ascribed the fall of the Paris Commune to the failure to eliminate all law, and so the Soviet state was absolutely forbidden from exercising any restraint on arbitrary use of power. Indeed, officials were punished for such restraint, which Lenin called impermissible slackness and Stalin would deem lack of vigilance.

The same logic applied to rights. On paper, the Soviet Constitution of 1936 guaranteed more rights than any other state in the world. I recall a Soviet citizen telling me that people in the USSR had absolute freedom of speech—so long as they did not lie. I recalled this curious concept of freedom when a student defended complete freedom of speech except for hate speech—and hate speech included anything he disagreed with. Whatever did not *seem* hateful was actually a "dog-whistle."

As far back as 1919, Soviet parlance distinguished between purely formal law and what was called "the material determination of the crime." A crime was not an action or omission specified in the formal code, because every "socially dangerous" act (or omission) was automatically criminal. Article 1 of the Civil Code of October 31, 1922, laid down that civil rights "are protected by the law unless they are exercised in contradiction to their social and economic purposes." Like the "material" definition of crime, the concept of "purposefulness" (*tselesoobraznost'*) created a system of Thelemite rights: the state was absolutely prohibited from interfering with your rights unless it wanted to.

LENINSPEAK

Lenin's language, no less than his ethics, served as a model, taught in Soviet schools and recommended in books with titles like *Lenin's Language* and *On Lenin's Polemical Art*. In Lenin's view, a true revolutionary did not establish the correctness of his beliefs by appealing to evidence or logic, as if there were some standards of truthfulness above social classes. Rather, one engaged in "blackening an opponent's mug so well it takes him ages to get it clean again." Nikolay Valentinov, a Bolshevik who knew Lenin well before becoming disillusioned, reports him saying: "There is only one answer to revisionism: smash its face in!"

When Mensheviks objected to Lenin's personal attacks, he replied frankly that his purpose was not to convince but to destroy his opponent. In work after work, Lenin does not offer arguments refuting other Social Democrats but brands them as "renegades" from Marxism. Marxists who disagreed with his naive epistemology were "philosophic scum." Object to his brutality and your arguments are "moralizing vomit." You can see traces of this approach in the advice of Saul Alinsky—who cites Lenin—to "pick the target, freeze it, personalize it."

Compulsive underlining, name calling, and personal invective hardly exhaust the ways in which Lenin's prose assaults the reader. He does not just advance a claim, he insists that it is absolutely certain and, for good measure, says the same thing again in other words. It is absolutely certain, beyond any possible doubt, perfectly clear to anyone not dull-witted. Any alliance with the democratic bourgeoisie can only be short-lived, he explains: "This is beyond doubt. Hence the absolute necessity of a separate ... strictly class party of Social Democrats.... All this is beyond the slightest possible doubt." Nothing is true unless it is absolutely, indubitably so; if a position is wrong, it is entirely and irredeemably so;

if something must be done, it must be done "immediately, without delay"; Party representatives are to make "no concessions whatsoever." Under Lenin's direction the Party demanded "the dissolution of *all* groups *without exception* formed on the basis of one platform or another" (italics mine). It was not enough just to shoot kulaks summarily, they had "to be shot on the spot without trial," a phrase that in one brief decree he managed to use in each of its six numbered commands before concluding: "This order is to be carried out strictly, mercilessly." You'd think that was clear enough already.

No concessions, compromises, exceptions, or acts of leniency; everything must be totally uniform, absolutely the same, unqualifiedly unqualified. At one point he claims that the views of Marx and Engels are "completely identical," as if they might have been incompletely identical.

Critics objected that Lenin argued by mere assertion. He disproved a position simply by showing it contradicted what he believed. In his attack on the epistemology of Ernst Mach and Richard Avenarius, for instance, every argument contrary to dialectical materialism is rejected *for that reason alone*. Valentinov, who saw Lenin frequently when he was crafting this treatise, reports that Lenin at most glanced through their works for a few hours. It was easy enough to attribute to them views they did not hold, associate them with disreputable people they had never heard of, or ascribe political purposes they had never imagined. These were Lenin's usual techniques, and he made no bones about it.

Valentinov was appalled that both Lenin and Plekhanov, the first Russian Marxist, insisted that there was no need to understand opposing views before denouncing them, since the very fact that they were opposing views proved them wrong—and what was wrong served the enemy and so was criminal. He quotes Lenin:

> Marxism is a monolithic conception of the world, it does not tolerate dilution and vulgarization by means of various insertions and additions. Plekhanov once said to me about a critic of Marxism ... : "First, let's stick the convict's badge on him, and then after that we'll examine his case." And I think we must stick the "convict's badge" on anyone and everyone who tries to undermine Marxism, even if we don't go on to examine his case. That's how every sound revolutionary should react. When you see a stinking heap on the road you don't have to poke around in it to see what it is. Your nose tells you it's shit, and you give it a wide berth.

"Lenin's words took my breath away," Valentinov recalls. I had the same reaction when I first heard a student explain that a view had to be wrong simply because it was voiced on Fox News.

Opponents objected that Lenin lied without compunction, and it is easy to find quotations in which he says—as he did to the Bolshevik leader Karl Radek—"Who told you a historian has to establish the truth?" Yes, we are contradicting what we said before, he told Radek, and when it is useful to reverse positions again, we will. Orwell caught this aspect of Leninism: "Oceania was at war with Eastasia; therefore Oceania had always been at war with Eastasia."

And yet the concept of "lying," if one stops there, does not reach the heart of the matter. In *The Death of Ivan Ilyich*, Tolstoy remarks that, contrary to appearances, the hero was not a toady. Rather, he "was attracted to people of high station as a fly is drawn to the light." A toady decides to toady, but Ivan Ilyich had no need to make such a decision. In much the same way, a true Leninist does not decide whether to lie. He automatically says what is most useful, with no reflection necessary. That is why he can show no visible signs of mendacity, perhaps even pass a lie detector test. La Rochefoucauld famously said that "hypocrisy is the tribute that vice pays to virtue," but a true Bolshevik is not even a hypocrite.

Western scholars who missed this aspect of Leninism made significant errors. For example, they estimated the size of the Soviet economy by assuming that official figures were distorted and made appropriate adjustments. But as Robert Conquest pointed out, "they were not distorted, they were invented." The Soviets did not find out the truth and then exaggerate; they often did not know the truth themselves. In *Nineteen Eighty-Four*, Winston Smith hears that fifty million pairs of boots were produced that year and reflects that, for all he knows, no boots at all were produced. Orwell, who never studied the Soviet economy, grasped a point that escaped experts because he understood Leninthink.

PARTYNESS

Lenin did not just invent a new kind of party, he also laid the basis for what would come to be known in official parlance as "*partiinost'*," literally Partyness, in the sense of Party-mindedness. Arthur Koestler understood part of *partiinost'* when he described a Communist confessing to fantastic crimes because loyalty to the Party trumped everything else.

If the Party needed one to confess to spying for the Poles, Japanese, and Germans at the same time, while conspiring with Trotsky to murder Stalin and spread typhus among pigs—all while one was already in prison—a true, party-minded Bolshevik would do so.

In his celebrated "Catechism of a Revolutionary," the nineteenth-century terrorist Sergei Nechaev—whose story inspired Dostoevsky's novel *The Possessed*—writes that a true revolutionary "has no interests, no habits, no property, not even a name. Everything in him is wholly absorbed by a single, exclusive interest, a single thought, a single passion—the revolution." Nechaev and his contemporary Pyotr Tkachov established a particular tradition of revolutionaries, to which Lenin traced his lineage. The true Party member cares for nothing but the Party. It is his family, his community, his church. And according to Marxism-Leninism, everything it did was guaranteed to be correct.

Trotsky, forced to reverse one of his positions to conform to the Party line, explained:

> None of us desires or is able to dispute the will of the Party. Clearly the Party is always right.... We can only be right with and by the Party, for history has provided no other way of being in the right.... [I]f the Party adopts a decision which one or other of us thinks unjust, he will say, just or unjust, it is my party, and I will support the consequences of the decision to the end.

Even this much-quoted statement does not get *partiinost'* quite right, since, immediately after affirming that history guarantees the Party's infallibility, Trotsky speaks of supporting the Party even when it is wrong. His ally, the prominent Bolshevik Yuri Pyatakov, did better. When Valentinov happened to meet Pyatakov in Paris, he reproached him for cowardice in renouncing his former Trotskyite views. Pyatakov replied by explaining the Leninist concept of the Party:

> According to Lenin, the Communist Party is based on the principle of coercion which doesn't recognize any limitations or inhibitions. And the central idea of this principle of boundless coercion is not coercion itself but the absence of any limitation whatsoever—moral, political, and even physical, as far as that goes. Such a Party is capable of achieving miracles and doing things which no other collective of men could achieve.... A real Communist ...

> [is] a man who was raised by the Party and had absorbed its spirit deeply enough to become a miracle man.

Pyatakov grasped Lenin's idea that coercion is not a last resort but the first principle of Party action. Changing human nature, producing boundless prosperity, overcoming death itself: all these miracles could be achieved because the Party was the first organization ever to pursue coercion *without limits*. In one treatise Stalin corrects the widespread notion that the laws of nature are not binding on Bolsheviks, and it is not hard to see how this kind of thinking took root. And, given an essentially mystical faith in coercion, it is not hard to see how imaginative forms of torture became routine in Soviet justice.

Pyatakov drew significant conclusions from this concept of the Party:

> For such a Party a true Bolshevik will readily cast out from his mind ideas in which he has believed for years. A true Bolshevik has submerged his personality in the collectivity, "the Party," to such an extent that he can make the necessary effort to break away from his own opinions and convictions, and can honestly agree with the Party—that is the test of a true Bolshevik.
>
> There could be no life for him outside the ranks of the Party, and he would be ready to believe that black was white, and white was black, if the Party required it. In order to become one with this great Party he would fuse himself with it, abandon his own personality, so that there was no particle left inside him which was not at one with the Party.

Did Orwell have this statement in mind when O'Brien gets Winston Smith to believe that twice two is five? In 1936 Pyatakov asked the Party secretariat to censure him for not having revealed his wife's Trotskyite connections. To prove his *partiinost'*, he offered to testify against her and then, after her condemnation, shoot her. Pyatakov was himself shot.

THE NATURE OF LENINIST BELIEF

Partyness does not entail merely affirming that black is white but actually believing it. The wisest specialists on Bolshevik thinking have wondered: what does it mean to believe—truly believe—what one does not believe?

Leninthink

Many former Communists describe their belated recognition that experienced Party members do not seem to believe what they profess. In his memoir *American Hunger*, much of which is devoted to his experiences in the American Communist Party, Richard Wright describes how he would point out that the Party sometimes acted contrary to its convictions, or in the name of helping black people, actually hurt them. What most amazed Wright was that he usually could get no explanation for such actions at all. "You don't understand," he was constantly told. And the very fact that he asked such questions proved that he didn't. It gradually dawned on him that the Party takes stances not because it cares about them—although it may—but because it is useful for the Party to do so.

Doing so may help recruit new members, as its stance on race had gotten Wright to join. But after a while a shrewd member learned, without having been explicitly told, that loyalty belonged not to an issue, not even to justice broadly conceived, but to the Party itself. Issues would be raised or dismissed as needed.

My mother left the American Communist Party in 1939 in response to the Hitler–Stalin pact, but her friends who remained were able, like Pyatakov, to turn on a dime. One morning *The Daily Worker* followed *Pravda* and described Nazis as true friends of the working class; the next, nothing too strong could be said against them. Crucially, and as Orwell dramatized in *Nineteen Eighty-Four*, there was never an admission that any change had taken place.

When it suddenly dawned on them that issues were pretexts, Wright and some others like him faced a choice. Usually, however, there was no sudden realization and so no choice was required. I speak from memory now. What happens is something like this: when a criticism of the true ideology is advanced, or when embarrassing facts come out, everyone learns a particular answer. One neither believes nor disbelieves the answer; one demonstrates one's loyalty by saying it. It is interesting to be present when the answer is still being rehearsed. Gradually, one acquires a little mental library of such canned answers, and the use of them signals to others in the know that you are one of them. If this process took place often enough in childhood, the moment of decision lies in the remote past, if it ever happened at all. For those who joined as adults, there is social pressure to accept one more explanation. Imagine not accepting today's charge against Trump or Chick-fil-A. Why stop now? Wright is unusual in that for him the process became acute and demanded he address it.

In his history of Marxism, Kołakowski explains some puzzling aspects of Bolshevik practice in these terms. Everyone understands why Bolsheviks shot liberals, socialist revolutionaries, Mensheviks, and Trotskyites. But what, he asks, was the point of turning the same fury on the Party itself, especially on its most loyal, Stalinists, who accepted Leninist-Stalinist ideology without question? Kołakowski observes that it is precisely the loyalty to the ideology that was the problem.

Anyone who believed in the ideology might question the leader's conformity to it. He might recognize that the Marxist-Leninist Party was acting against Marxism-Leninism as the Party itself defined it; or he might compare Stalin's statements today with Stalin's statements yesterday. "The citizen belongs to the state and must have no other loyalty, not even to the state ideology," Kołakowski observes. That might seem strange to Westerners, but, "it is not surprising to anyone who knows a system of this type from within." All deviations from the Party line, all challenges to the leadership, appealed to official ideology, and so anyone who truly believed the ideology was suspect. "The [great] purge, therefore, was designed to destroy such ideological links as still existed within the party, to convince its members that they had no ideology or loyalty except to the latest orders from on high .... Loyalty to Marxist ideology as such is still—[in 1978]—a crime and a source of deviations of all kinds." The true Leninist did not even believe in Leninism.

THE OTHER FOOT

I know of no other political ideology that entails such a conception of belief. When I was a young associate professor teaching in a comparative literature department, whose faculty were at each other's throats, I remarked to one colleague, who called herself a Marxist-Leninist, that it only made things worse when she told obvious falsehoods in departmental meetings. Surely, such unprincipled behavior must bring discredit to your own position, I pleaded.

Her reply brought me back to my childhood. I quote it word-for-word: "You stick to your principles, and I'll stick to mine." From a Leninist perspective, a liberal, a Christian, or any type of idealist only ties his hands by refraining from doing whatever works. She meant: we Leninists will win because we know better than to do that. Even Westerners who regard themselves as realists have only taken a few baby steps towards a true Leninist position. They are all the more vulnerable for imagining they have an unclouded view.

Recently Attorney General William Barr asked how his critics would have reacted had the FBI secretly interfered with the Obama campaign: "What if the shoe were on the other foot?" From a Leninist perspective, this question demonstrates befuddlement. In his book *Terrorism and Communism*, Trotsky imagines "the high priests of liberalism" asking how Bolshevik use of arbitrary power differs from tsarist practices. Trotsky sneers:

> You do not understand this, holy men? We shall explain it to you. The terror of Tsarism was directed against the proletariat.... Our Extraordinary Commissions shoot landlords, capitalists, and generals .... Do you grasp this—distinction? For us Communists it is quite sufficient.

What is reprehensible for them is proper for us, and that's all there is to it. For a Leninist, the shoe is never on the other foot because he has no other foot.

THE SPECTRUM OF AWARENESS

When I detect Leninist ways of thinking today, people respond: surely you don't think all those social justice warriors are Leninists! Of course not. The whole point of Leninism is that only a few people must understand what is going on. That was the key insight of his tract *What Is to Be Done?* When Leninism is significant, there will always be a spectrum going from those who really understand, to those who just practice the appropriate responses, to those who are entirely innocent. The real questions are: Is there such a spectrum now, and how do we locate people on it? And if there is such a spectrum, what do we do about it?

There is no space to address such questions here. My point is that they need to be asked.

October 2019

The scab & the wound beneath

Victor Davis Hanson

An overriding theme of the historian Thucydides' monumental history of the Peloponnesian War (431–404 B.C.) is the fragility of civilization. In extremis, when both the elites and masses lose their thin veneer of culture, society can turn feral quickly. During a horrific war, plague, or revolution, even a wealthy and sophisticated civilization such as that of the classical Greek city-states regresses in a second to its innate state. And what follows from these natural and man-made disasters is not pretty. Still, these calamities can be tragically instructional. Hypocrisies arise. Pretexts vanish. Fundamental but forgotten truths, easily masked in times of calm, reemerge. From Thucydides' warnings, we can glean that even suburban elites in Range Rovers can in a day be reduced to tugging over toilet paper rolls at Whole Foods.

During the twenty-seven-year-long Peloponnesian War, Athens, the most liberal and confident of some 1,500 Greek city-states, proved the readiest to butcher prisoners and civilians. And it did so en masse at Mytilene, Scione, and Melos. Thucydides noted that during the plague of 430–29, the most virtuous of Athenians ("especially the case with such as made any pretensions to goodness") perished along with the selfish. Indeed, their courage in abandoning social distancing to aid the infectious sealed their doom ("honor made them unsparing of themselves in their attendance in their friends' houses").

Throughout the savage revolution on the island of Corcyra (Corfu), honesty of language and moderation in politics were among the first casualties. And once the violence and body count mounted, extremism in thought and action followed:

> Words had to change their ordinary meaning and to take that which was now given them. Reckless audacity came to be consid-

> ered the courage of a loyal ally; prudent hesitation, specious cowardice; moderation was held to be a cloak for unmanliness; ability to see all sides of a question, inaptness to act on any.

The historian's diagnosis of Corcyrean social malaise could be aptly applied to our current war being waged over vocabulary: whether it is impolite to say "Wuhan virus," or whether we need euphemisms like "shelter in place" for quarantine or "social distancing" for "anti-social avoidance."

Of course, in historical terms, COVID-19 may prove a rookie virus in comparison to the still mysterious infection—typhus, smallpox, or typhoid?—that wiped out one quarter of the Athenian population along with its iconic sexagenarian leader Pericles. He was the architect of the very wartime strategy of forced withdrawal inside the walls of Athens that birthed the plague in the first place and took his life.

The Athenian disease promptly revealed that the city of Socrates, Sophocles, and Euripides was all too human. The desperate threw the corpses of friends and family on the pyres of others, often while still aflame:

> sometimes getting the start of those who had raised a pile, they threw their own dead body upon the stranger's pyre and ignited it; sometimes they tossed the corpse which they were carrying on the top of another that was burning, and so went off.

At such times, the majestic Parthenon on the Acropolis or Sophoclean tragedy in the Theater of Dionysus or three hundred triremes at the Piraeus became irrelevant. Recounting the even worse plague of 541–42 A.D. that ended the Byzantine emperor Justinian's dreams of reconstituting the Roman Empire, the court historian Procopius describes scenes in Constantinople that come right out of contemporary New York: "During that time it seemed no easy thing to see any man in the streets of Byzantium.... And work of every description ceased, and all the trades were abandoned by the artisans, and all other work as well, such as each had in hand."

Wartime and plague-stricken Athens, the most refined of cities, turned the most brutish. Rural and inward Sparta, home of the supposedly duller wits with little cultural enrichment from the wider Aegean, remained more or less true to its traditional mores, avoiding the plague and the panic that the epidemic birthed among coastal and cosmopolitan Athens.

In times like these, for once it was deemed wiser to live in Sparta or in rural Utah than in the bustle of cosmopolitan Athens or Manhattan.

Thucydides' accounts of the plague, the savage factionalism at Corcyra, the mass executions at Mytilene and Melos, and the disaster at Syracuse all remind us that what is considered normal in calm can be rendered absurd instantly in the cauldron of panic and death. Last month I saw what seemed to be a stylishly dressed woman in a Lexus buying toilet paper from her car window in the parking lot of a local Walmart from someone who appeared homeless, a social interaction rare in healthier times.

The pernicious coronavirus tore off an American scab and revealed suppurating wounds beneath. Take the central actor of this plague, China. For much of the twenty-first century, the American establishment's foreign policy toward China, to the degree it was even formalized, was ethically and logically bankrupt. Yet the status quo remained unquestioned, given it rested on a rare alignment of both progressive and commercial self-interests.

Of course, Americans in general have had a long romance with China. They were never colonialists in China, at least in the manner of the Europeans. Over fifteen million Chinese, our erstwhile allies, were killed in World War II, many brutally slaughtered by our enemies, the Japanese.

More recently, Mao Zedong, arguably the most lethal mass murderer of the twentieth century—perhaps a greater killer than Attila the Hun, Genghis Khan, Tamerlane, Hitler, Stalin, and Pol Pot combined—held an attraction for the New Left of the 1960s. His cherubic smile, worker's cap, peasant dress, cool aphorisms, and hatred of running-dog capitalists once captivated student protestors. Even Barack Obama's acting White House communications director, Anita Dunn, in 2009 still swooned that Mao was one of her two favorite political "philosophers":

> And then the third lesson and tip actually come from two of my favorite political philosophers, Mao Tse-Tung and Mother Teresa—not often coupled with each other, but the two people that I turn to most to basically deliver a simple point, which is, you're going to make choices. You're going to challenge.

More recently for the Left, China has become empathetic as the classic long-suffering "other"—as opposed perhaps to the less sympathetic discriminated-against Chinese-Americans applying to Ivy League colleges. Beijing is guilty of interning roughly one million Muslim Uighurs, all but wiping out the culture of Tibet, destroying vestigial democracy in Hong Kong, and forging a new Silk Road imperialism in Africa and Asia. This is to say nothing of their systematic patent and copyright infringement, pollution, and currency manipulation. And yet liberals have been hesitant to fault China for these legal injustices and civil rights violations.

Indeed, in the present crisis, China is now praised for its supposedly more successful reactions to the very virus that it spawned than the remedies of the Trump administration. We are learning that the Left accepts and finds politically useful the ridiculously constructed data issued by the Chinese communist government. That fact is known to Beijing, which in turn might explain why it keeps promulgating outright lies about virus fatalities that are embarrassing to all but the American Left.

Hillary Clinton, for example, on March 27 retweeted a *New York Times* story with the headline "The U.S. Now Leads the World in Confirmed Coronavirus Cases. Following a series of missteps, the nation is now the epicenter of the pandemic." She added her own snarky editorial quip: "He did promise 'America First.'"

Aside from her apparent indifference to American dead and ill being used as a source of embarrassment to the American government, Clinton must have also known that the United States was *not* the leader in the world in actual deaths or cases, given that by mid-March the Chinese government had simply declared that the virus all but over in its 1.4-billion-person population, and claimed falsely that there were few, if any, new cases or deaths. Such myths were necessary to shift blame for Beijing's culpability in spreading the virus by fraudulently claiming credit for first eliminating the contagion. Clinton further knew that in terms of deaths per million, a 330-million-person America was not "first," given that almost all European countries, with the exception of Germany, had suffered a far higher fatality to population rate.

Chinese money has been far more influential in warping American politics than were the supposedly colluding Russians who ran some Facebook ads to stir up chaos in 2016 and may have spent a few million dollars in salting misinformation. By the time the virus abates, there may indeed be Chinese "collusion" in this election year, as the media and the Left parrot the Chinese Communist Party's conspiracy theories and fantasies about the virus, ones deemed mutually efficacious in ensuring that the purported Sinophobe Donald Trump is not reelected. It would be no exaggeration to suggest that the Chinese communists and the American Left hate Trump equally.

The viral panic has reminded Americans of all sort of anomalies. Some 360,000 Chinese students serve as money-makers for American colleges and universities at a time of higher education's financial crisis. Certainly, the art of charging Chinese students full freight for a college education has proved far more lucrative for campus administrators than trying to squeeze out more money from American students currently over $1.5 trillion in collective student debt. One realization of the crisis is that students can continue their courses online and at a distance—without the need of diversity and inclusion czars, and without receiving refunds for their tuition fees, which were predicated on a full, in-person college experience.

When Donald Trump announced on January 31 travel restrictions on foreigners entering the United States from China, he was blasted as racist and xenophobic by many of the now-withdrawn Democratic 2020 presidential candidates—most of whom eventually grew quiet or supported the measures. His references to the "Wuhan" and "Chinese" virus supposedly proved his bias—in a way unlike China's own use of the former adjective and the long-standing practice of labeling infections by their places of origin.

Joe Biden's staff scrambled to explain the candidate's earlier demagoguery surrounding the restrictions by claiming he was really outraged by Trump's reference to a "Chinese" virus—oblivious that Biden's attack on the measures predated Trump's reference to the origins of the virus. Still, many wondered how and when Biden would inevitably try to square the circle of blasting Trump's travel restrictions by later agreeing with them. And he tried just that on April 4 by insisting a once racist and xenophobic prohibition would have been enacted even earlier by a President Joe Biden, given that he knew it likely would have saved thousands of lives. Perhaps Biden meant he would have banned in early January all Chinese from arriving at U.S. airports and yet not called them Chinese? In sum, China, for a variety of economic, cultural, and historical reasons, was given a pass by the Left in a way that many monsters in the Middle East, for instance, have usually not been.

Corporate "conservatives" likewise have manipulated China's special status. How otherwise could American companies so easily and without censure have outsourced key production in rare earth metals, medical supplies, high-tech military applications, and pharmaceuticals? As a result, in the post-virus world, there may be no more smears of "protectionism," "nationalism," and "nativism," but rather embarrassed silence about the globalist rhetoric that veneers what is really just self-interest at the expense of one's fellow citizens.

How could a Democratic presidential candidate, the multibillionaire corporate mogul Michael Bloomberg—for a brief moment the great Democratic hope to stop socialist Bernie Sanders and to replace an enfeebled Joe Biden—claim to Americans, as he did in a 2019 interview, that President Xi Jinping is "not a dictator. He has to satisfy his constituents or he's not going to survive"? How could Bloomberg craft multibillion-dollar investment schemes to capitalize Chinese companies while simultaneously not allowing his own *Bloomberg* reporters to faithfully report stories that show the Chinese Communist Party in a negative light?

The Bloomberg viral ironies did not end there. During his campaign, his prior folk wisdom emerged in a series of embarrassing videos of past sermons. In one, he lectured an Oxford audience about the banality and rote of farming, ancient and modern, claiming that he "could teach anybody to be a farmer." Information technology, Bloomberg insisted, required "a lot more gray matter." During the lockdowns in Manhattan, the country did not need any more multibillionaires with brains full of "gray matter" capitalizing Chinese communist government companies, but instead needed innovative farmers—you could call them "anybodies"—to keep sending a sheltered-in-place America the most diverse, safe, plentiful, and cheap food in the world.

The apparently consensually led China touted by Bloomberg has lied about the birth, origins, spread, and infectiousness of COVID-19; sent over one million of its citizens into U.S. airports after Beijing knew that the virus was communicable; had countless more circumvent U.S. restrictions; falsely declared that the U.S. military created the virus; threatened to cut off shipments of medical supplies produced in China by U.S.–Chinese joint ventures; and caused several thousand American deaths while causing trillions of dollars' worth of economic damage.

Remember, before the epidemic, Donald Trump was attempting to recalibrate U.S.–Chinese commercial relations via punishing tariffs that had already rattled the communist government, which was suddenly eager for a more compliant president approved by the Council on Foreign Relations. Perhaps Americans will come to their senses when the virus subsides. They might not tolerate a country that harvests human organs, sells bats and live scorpions in wet markets for medicinal purposes, and controls Iowa's supply of ventilators, California's N95 particle masks, or Detroit's ampicillin. If, in the past, the profit-minded multimillionaire stars of the NBA seemed deluded in their loud appreciation of the Chinese communist government—and more so by their equally loud disdain for their own elected president—in the future such appeasement will seem not just naive, but perhaps even repugnant or near-treasonous.

Not having control of the supply of needed medical appurtenances and medicines may be the Boomers' version of the Greatest Generation's waking up on December 8, 1941, and realizing that there was nothing in the American arsenal comparable to the Japanese Mitsubishi A6M "Zero" fighter or Type 93 "Long Lance" torpedo—and would not be for the months of hard fighting and dying ahead. Likewise, Beijing now enjoys enormous advantages in the short term as it inventories all the ways the American military, government, and consumers are China-dependent. Whether China has woken a sleeping giant in the manner of the earlier Japanese, or just a purring kitten, remains to be seen. One test will be whether we begin to recalibrate key American industries or unleash Adam Schiff to conduct yet another congressional investigation against his nemesis Donald Trump.

Before the epidemic, critics of globalization could not convince our best and brightest that enriching autocracies by asymmetrical trade policies would not eventually turn China into Jackson Hole or Palm Beach. Doubters of America's China policy complained that running up staggering American trade deficits with China would hardly lure China into the family of nations—at least in the manner of Barack Obama, who in 2014 once boasted that his new outreach initiatives with Beijing, *inter alia*, would "help affected countries to strengthen capacity-building on health and epidemic prevention so as to place the epidemic under control as soon as possible." How has China's envisioned "epidemic prevention" and "control" worked out?

The virus also exposed the absurdities of transnational utopianism more generally. For decades, the European Union has been held up by progressives as a model that had ossified old national rivalries and chronic European wars. The original and inspired European Common Market, in comparison, appeared to elites as a Neanderthal effort of only haphazardly integrating a few autonomous European economies. In contrast, the European Union would create an economic colossus comparable to the United States. But it would be guided by postmodern humanitarianism, sustained by wind and solar energy, and defended by heralded "soft" power. In fact, it was soon run and financed by a new Germany that increasingly sounds as we would expect an old Germany to sound.

Nonetheless, boundaries were to disappear. A common currency and common protocols would create a European new man. All-knowing, all-wise technocrats in Brussels and Strasbourg would adjudicate what exactly qualified as a banana on Crete. But then suddenly something happened to pan-European ecumenicism. The virus arrived and most of Northern Italy turned into something nightmarish, right out of Boccaccio's *Decameron*. Spain began to suffer a viral death rate of over 2,500 fatalities per million population, as if it were the beginning of 1348 rather than of 2020.

Borders slammed and have remained shut. The much-lauded Schengen Area Agreement that had abolished all passport control and border checkpoints among twenty-five European countries—a postmodern pact often contrasted with the supposedly paranoid and premodern U.S. border wall with Mexico—was suspended in a few minutes.

What was to be the fate of so-called undocumented migrants who sought an enlightened European refuge from the horrors of Africa and the Middle East? The logic of Camus' *La Peste* took over. Interned in Turkey and Greece, the migrants were now quarantined and treated as suspect illegal aliens that should go home to North Africa.

Did German banks step up to relax repayment schedules to their near-bankrupt Mediterranean brothers, hit hardest by the virus? In the euphemistic language of the German Chancellor Angela Merkel, the notion of issuing "corona bonds" was not "the view of all E.U. countries." Translated, that meant E.U. brother nations with cash and fewer dead were certainly not going to lend money to E.U. nations without it but with more dead.

Surely medical supplies such as ventilators and masks were common

E.U. property, a humanitarian version of the common Euro that reflected pan-European brotherhood? Not quite, as the ancient creed of every nation for itself supplanted the European Convention on Human Rights before the European Union announced a transnational medical stockpile. Germany abruptly stopped all shipments of key medical supplies before later opening up exports. It tightened its borders. It turned back French shoppers who had skipped across to hoard at better-stocked German supermarkets. The virus should remind Europe that if a war ever came, any E.U.-abiding country that shared its arsenal and headed for the front would suffer the fate of the virtuous citizens in the plague chronicles of Thucydides and Procopius who died first.

The United Nations did little more than pass resolutions praising itself for its singular efforts to control the virus. In the key first weeks of the outbreak, when the death and destruction might have been somewhat contained, the UN medical appendage, the World Health Organization, proved little more than a Chinese megaphone. Indeed, it helped spread the contagion rather than arrest it. The organization's director-general, Tedros Adhanom Ghebreyesus, assured the world that there was little threat from the Chinese virus. Director Tedros is not a medical doctor, a first for the WHO. He had no international health management experience. His chief recommendation might have been that he was non-Western and had come to the UN post from his government sinecure as a health minister in Ethiopia, itself perhaps predicated on his past service in the Tigray People's Liberation Front.

Tedros's résumé may help explain why the UN mouthpiece so readily assured the world that the virus was not transmissible between humans, that it was largely already contained by China, and that Donald Trump's all-important January 31 travel restrictions stopping foreigners from entering the United States from China (a heavy contributor both to the WHO and to Ethiopia) was not just unnecessary but would "have the effect of increasing fear and stigma, with little public health benefit."

Prior Trump initiatives now seem prescient. Donald Trump's controversial efforts in the pre-virus days to call out China for systematic Chinese mercantilism and serial cheating and lying, to secure U.S. borders, to issue travel bans on countries that had no quantifiable passport control, and to greenlight experimental and off-label drugs for near-terminal patients proved requisites for the policies he quickly enacted to fight the spread of the virus. Most of Trump's initiatives were initially blasted by the very foreign and domestic censors who soon quietly advocated adoption of them.

So the virus confirmed what many Americans had long suspected at home as well. "Trump Derangement Syndrome" was no longer a Republican talking point, but was exposed as a psychosis with real consequences for the entire country. In the initial weeks of January, when Trump was told by the WHO, the Centers for Disease Control, Dr. Anthony Fauci, and most foreign and American leaders that the virus, like the earlier Chinese-born SARS virus, was containable, the President, like they had at times, compared it to a bad flu. But by January 31 he had reversed course earlier than many of his future critics, rejected the earlier insistence of experts that xenophobia, racism, and chauvinism, and not the virus, were the real enemies, and issued travel restrictions—the one step that stopped some fifteen to twenty thousand Chinese nationals from arriving daily into the United States, including on direct flights from ground zero in Wuhan. Altogether over a million Chinese had arrived in October, November, December, and January. After the restrictions were enacted, many more found ways to enter the United States on connecting flights from non-embargoed nations in Europe and Asia.

No matter. House Speaker Nancy Pelosi claimed Trump's response to the virus had been "deadly" and later added, "As the president fiddles, people are dying." At about the same time, she tried to delay passage of a joint congressional bailout bill intended to keep endangered small business and the unemployed afloat as she scrambled to insert funding for the Kennedy Center and Planned Parenthood.

By the end of March, Pelosi was hinting about desires for something akin to impeachment 2.0 and a commission similar to the 9/11 investigation. Such a Star Chamber would supposedly find Trump criminally naive in not reacting earlier to the epidemic. In that context, perhaps the coronavirus was supposed to do what the Twenty-fifth Amendment, the Emoluments Clause, Stormy Daniels, the Mueller "dream team," and impeachment had not—derail the Trump presidency before the November 2020 election.

On the Alinskyite assumption that progressives project their own vulnerabilities onto their opponents, it was quickly noted that Pelosi herself, almost four weeks *after* the Trump travel restrictions, had visited San Francisco's Chinatown, indeed as late as February 24, to encourage

Americans to come there and shop: "That's what we're trying to do today is to say everything is fine here. Come because precautions have been taken. The city is on top of the situation."

The whines of other Trump critics—such as the New York Mayor Bill de Blasio—that Trump was late to the anti-corona effort, at least in comparison to their own performances, are not to be believed either. De Blasio in mid-March, six weeks *after* the Trump travel restrictions were announced, had urged New Yorkers to go out and enjoy the city: "If you love your neighborhood bar, go there now because we don't know what the future holds."

Pre-virus, some suspected that the entire agenda and energy of the American Left was focused on destroying the Trump presidency at any cost and by any means necessary. During the epidemic this was confirmed, and this hatred was shown to have national consequences. When evidence prompted Trump to let the public know that old drugs like hydroxychloroquine and azithromycin were often efficacious in treating particular patients infected with coronavirus, reporters sought to persuade Americans that such off-label uses had no utility and were dangerous—even if they had to stoop to find someone unhinged who drank fish-tank cleaner, clearly marked unfit for human consumption, to prove that a non-potable chloroquine derivative cleaning agent provided confirmation of "Dr." Trump's malpractice.

Almost daily, the reactions to the virus revealed how surreal pre-virus America had insidiously become. On March 28, the governor of Rhode Island announced that the state's law enforcement officers would stop cars, check license plates, and knock on doors to ferret out citizens who had come from New York State—a type of surveillance of U.S. citizens that has rarely been applicable to millions of aliens who have entered and resided illegally in the United States.

Because of worry about overcrowded jails and infectious prisons, some criminals throughout the nation were given early parole—even as our elite erupted in a fight over whether to allow gun stores to remain open. Rumors abounded that those without any prior firearm experience were among those inquiring how to buy handguns. Despite claiming to be the watchdog of American civil liberties, it was the Left that hammered Trump to employ the Defense Production Act to nationalize American companies by fiat. Mostly Democratic mayors urged strict surveillance of shelter-in-place compliance and threatened stiff fines for offenders, sometimes to be ratted out by snitches.

What has made the U.S. reaction to the virus so different from the response to the 2009 H1N1 epidemic that eventually infected 60.8 million, hospitalized 274,304, and may have killed 12,469? Why did we not similarly shut down the country during the bad flu season of 2017–18 that had killed *more than* 60,000 Americans, put nearly a million in the hospital, and may have likewise infected over 60 million? The answer? Lots of both logical and illogical reasons. The coronavirus was, we were reminded ad nauseam, not influenza. It was more contagious and could become more lethal.

Perhaps. But when one excepts health workers of all ages who were subject to enormous and repeated initial viral load exposures at work, along with those over the age of sixty-five with concomitant pulmonary, diabetic, cardiac, or malignant complications, the toll of COVID-19 may in the end prove comparable to, or less than, some of the totals of 2009 and 2017–18.

What terrified the world in general, and America in particular, were media-driven reports of occasional excruciating symptoms and sudden death among a small percentage in good health that overshadowed the fact that the majority of the infected had mild or few symptoms. News blared about the less than 0.5 percent of the infected non-elderly who died and ignored the 99.5 percent under sixty-five who had recovered. The media hyped models that showed biblical plague rates of death in the coming weeks, never returning to such prognostications when they were proven fallacious if not hysterical a few weeks later.

So there was also initially not just little data about the infection, but awful data. Modelers worked only from known cases and supposedly known deaths to terrify the world with projections of 3 percent death rates of the infected and predictions of two million Americans and a half-million Britons to die. In truth, those already recovered from the virus, or carrying it without symptoms, were likely much more numerous than those who felt ill or were exposed enough to request testing and had proved positive. Moreover, even the numerators in the arithmetic of death were never uniformly defined, since no one seemed to know how to calibrate deaths *from* or deaths *with* the virus. Yet in the Thucydidean logic of panic, it made sense for the media, for some on the front lines of medical care worried about supply shortages, and for politicos to count those who died with toxic help from COVID-19 as dying only from it.

Issues such as prior herd immunities established earlier than the falsified dates of the outbreak supplied by Beijing also likely invalidated the initial tabloid warnings of experts. By April, some increasingly appeared more like astrologers than statisticians. Modeling had consequences. For example, on March 12, the Ohio Republican Governor Mike DeWine and Dr. Amy Acton, the director of his state's health department, declared on shaky grounds that one hundred thousand Ohioans probably were at the time infected (e.g. 1 percent of Ohioans "has it") at a moment when there were five known cases, under a theory known as "community spread." If one were to collate the then-current lethality rates per known cases of infection—which Acton admittedly did not do—such a staggering number of those *actively* infected would imply for the state's more than two million residents over sixty-five that about two thousand five hundred were perhaps already doomed. The governor and his director also warned that cases were likely to double every six days in Ohio before peaking in late April or May. As I write in early April, twenty-four days later, Ohio has reported a total of 4,043 known cases and 119 reported COVID-19 deaths. The doomsday scenario suggested more than 1.6 million infected Ohioans (one hundred thousand doubling four times) and perhaps forty thousand dead or dying (at a 2.5 percent rate of known cases). That was with no social shutdown, a now-unverifiable proposition since Ohio swiftly moved to enact a lockdown.

Little has been reported about the way that the scientific models factor in the effect of common-sense social distancing and increasing herd immunity, both of which have been effective in slowing the virus's spread. Instead, the American people are treated to worst-case scenario predictions that don't factor in the reality on the ground. Meanwhile, off-label drug treatments, new medical protocols, and plain old experience in handling patients—with news of far more rapid introductions of effective new drugs—are continuing to offer hope of a swifter-than-predicted recovery. Sophisticated statisticians oddly seem unsophisticated in failing to account for the human mobilization and response to warnings of mass death—which they had helped encourage, perhaps on the logic that the pessimist is never faulted.

After all, if a public health official errs on the side of caution in times of plague, she saves lives; if she is right in implying mass casualty over the next twenty-four days, she is prescient. In contrast, the optimist is proven correct only because of the pessimist's bleak warning that changed behaviors, but if wrong is tantamount to a murderer. If an optimist had countered on March 12 that even in the unlikely event that 100,000 were infected in Ohio, many of them would not even know it, and never need hospitalization, she would have lost either way: only Acton's warning had prompted action which later *made* the optimist's skepticism look warranted.

Another contributor to the ongoing hysteria has been the idea that China has lied about the origins and nature of the virus, which has only led to paranoia. There are legitimate questions to be asked about the virus's origins, given the presence of a Chinese military level-four virology lab proximate to ground zero of both the SARS and COVID-19 viruses.

Then there was the elephant in the room of Donald J. Trump and the 2020 election. In America and the world at large, the media has reported on the spread of the virus in terms of Trump's own reaction to it. Various internet global clocks of infections and deaths by country and state ticked hourly, as if scorecards to assess relative efficacies. For a cynic, the subtext of the entire reportage, here and abroad, was that the more America might become terrified of a Spanish flu–style wipe-out, the longer the shutdown was required, the more the economy sank into recession, and the more it was unlikely to recover its lost robustness before the November election, and thus the more likely the coronavirus would at last appear as the coup de grace where all other blows to Trump had failed. The co-generators of international news, Europe and China, were both invested in seeing Trump discredited and defeated, and the result was the strange collusionary effect of American media progressives quoting chapter and verse both Chinese communist propaganda and European Union pontifications.

The media has not hesitated to call coronavirus the "Trump virus," while Scott Stringer, the New York City comptroller, said that Trump had "blood on his hands." This besmirching was joined by willful misrepresentations, such as that Trump had called the viral outbreak a "hoax," when he clearly was referring to the lie that he had done nothing to combat the epidemic. Trump supposedly in its initial appearance had uniquely downplayed the new coronavirus as a mere flu, when most at the time, from the WHO to the CDC, was urging us not to panic, given the virus would likely resemble a bad flu year. Again, it is still not clear whether the coronavirus in fact will prove more lethal than, say, the 2017–18 flu outbreak.

Trump, in his alleged climate-denialist fashion, was again reportedly at war with "science," when in truth he and his administration have encouraged almost all the suggestions of his advisors Drs. Fauci and Birx such as social distancing, sheltering in place, and the wearing of masks in public places. Those two doctors are now under suspicion from the Left that they have become enablers of the Trump agenda.

Had Trump *not* been president, had he *not* just been impeached, had he *not* previously galvanized resistance to Chinese mercantile piracy, had China *not* lied about the virus, had it *not* originated in Wuhan, had it *not* been a new sort of virus, had we *not* yet been in a globalized world of instant communications and cheap and easy intercontinental travel, had the media *not* been 90 percent negative in its prior reporting on Trump, had it *not* been an election year in 2020, and had Trump's popularity *not* spiked but crashed during the epidemic—then the hysteria might have been prevented, and the United States might have reacted with care and concern but without the veritable destruction of its economy and the human damage that it entailed.

But those were too many "had nots." Epidemics and the reactions to them, ancient and modern, do not allow much margin of error. And so it has been too in our time of plague.

May 2020

The Sixties at 40

Peter Collier

OVER THE YEARS I've gotten rid of most of the embarrassing evidence—the photos of us on Telegraph Avenue giving the clenched fist salute while wreathed in choking teargas; the North Vietnamese flag that hung in my front window all those years; the pistol I bought because we all believed that the FBI was coming for us. But one item from the Sixties I've kept—a commemorative comb brought back from Hanoi by Tom Hayden after one of his trips there to support General Vo Nguyen Giap's shrewd perception that the war would not be won in the jungles of Vietnam but on the streets of America.

The comb is machine-cut out of the metal of a downed U.S. aircraft. It is about five inches long, in the shape of an F-105. There are patches of white paint on the unfinished side. A cockpit and insignia have been stamped on the shinier front. Just above the teeth are inscribed these words: "The American Pirates 1,100th plane shot down in North Vietnam."

When Hayden gave it to me the comb seemed a jaunty symbol of an invincible peasant nationalism, and a challenge to us, Hanoi's American irregulars, to step up the struggle. When I look at it now, of course, I wonder about the American who piloted the plane out of which this macabre artifact was made. Did he survive the crash? Was he killed by members of the local militia soon after parachuting to the ground, like so many U.S. airmen? Did he make it to the Hanoi Hilton and survive the barbaric captivity there?

The comb has been on my mind particularly during this fortieth anniversary of 1968, which those who continue to believe that a terrible beauty was being born back then often refer to as an *annus mirabilis.* The Latin phrase is usually followed with a breathless catalogue of the events that took place when the whole world was watching: Tet, LBJ's withdrawal, My Lai, the seizure of Columbia University, the assassinations of King and Kennedy, the student uprising in Paris, the Democratic convention in Chicago, and so on.

There are always omissions from this list of wonders. One of them is the iconic photo taken on February 1, 1968, showing a bullet fired at close range by South Vietnamese police commander Nguyen Ngoc Loan into the right temple of Viet Cong Nguyen Van Lem exiting on the other side of his skull. Along with the photo taken four years later of nine-year-old Phan Kim Phuc roasting from napalm as she ran naked down a highway in the Central Highlands, this is the most evocative image of the war. But both photos, starkly black and white in meaning back in the day, have since taken on a grayer coloration. Lem was executed not out of the mad random bloodlust that is supposed to have touched everything related to the U.S. presence in Vietnam, but because he was captain of a terrorist squad that had just massacred the family of one of Loan's deputy commanders. And Kim Phuc, after all the skin grafts and years of being displayed as a propaganda doll in Havana and other revolutionary venues, finally made her way to Canada, converted to Christianity, and stood in quiet opposition to the Vietnamese government.

That's the problem with these ritualized celebrations of the Sixties: they show only part of the picture. I recently happened on a brief article in *The Chronicle of Higher Education* by Jay Parini, a Professor of English at Middlebury College, which repeated what has now become the giddy conventional wisdom about this having been a time characterized by "a feeling of freedom from old pieties and a sense of fresh potential." Every time I see this sentiment, more a recitation than an actual thought, I'm reminded of the statement sometimes attributed to that insufferable old charlatan Timothy Leary: people who remember the Sixties weren't really there.

That this was a time simply of spunky homegrown prometheans making performance art out of transgression and mournfully sincere young idealists who wanted nothing more than to give peace a chance is a Soviet socialist realist view. Behind such people stood a smaller cadre of heavy hitters with an agenda: to force the transition from American Mischief to American Mayhem by whatever means necessary; to make treason of the heart evolve in timely fashion into treason of the deed. The relationship between the two groups, the soft- and hardliners, was analogous to one James Burnham had seen in an earlier time when he said that the difference between the liberals and the Communists was that the Communists knew what they were doing.

The hardcore Left knew what it was doing in the Sixties. But it forgot not long after. During the small aperture for second thoughts about the era that occurred in the mid-1980s, my friend David Horowitz and I, apostates from The Movement, tried to provoke a discussion about what that Left had done and meant and what remained after it flamed out in histrionics and impotence. In response, a stone wall.

But the omission of ideas has consequences, too. When his "authoritative" advocacy history of the era first appeared, for instance, Todd Gitlin forgot to mention how the Black Panthers had developed into a sort of New Left–sanctioned Murder Inc. operating out of the Oakland ghetto. It is not surprising that a few years later, David Hilliard, the former "chief of staff" of the Panthers and the only leader left standing after the deaths of Huey Newton (1989) and Eldridge Cleaver (1998) and Bobby Seale's wise decision to trade revolution for the barbecue business, was running a successful enterprise leading Potemkin bus tours to all the Oakland landmarks associated with the Panthers' "civil rights" triumphs. ("Stop 2: Traffic Signal, corner of Market and 55th. A small cadre of armed Black Panthers stopped motorists and personally escorted children across the busy intersection. Installation of the traffic signal begun Aug. 1, 1967.") Local school districts now sign their children up for this educational experience in "community organizing."

Because it is still so unassimilated—"a cadaver," soixante-huitard André Glucksmann recently said, from which people of all political points of view break off chunks at will—the Sixties continues to shadow our politics like a mean dog. John Kerry got bit when he cluelessly decided to "report for duty" in 2004. More recently the Sixties lunged at Barack Obama in the person of the Reverend Jeremiah Wright, negrifying him when he wanted to be post-racial and ideologizing him when he wanted to be post-partisan, and ending abruptly his attempt to hope-a-dope an electorate desperate to believe.

If Wright's rancid ideas about *Amerikkka*, right out of the Sixties Black Power play book, were not burden enough, Obama also had to account for Billy Ayers, who helped found Weatherman out of SDS after a series of carcinomic political cell divisions had gorked that organization.

This nihilistic group, which took its name from Bob Dylan's line "You don't need a weather man to know which way the wind blows," inspired some opposition from the *ancien régime* of the New Left (one of whose members famously said, "No, and you don't need a rectal thermometer to know who the assholes are"). But in constantly "upping the ante," Weatherman expressed the temper of the time. And no one in the group better embodied the era's penny-ante Neitzscheanism than Ayers himself. ("Guilty as hell, free as a bird, America's a great country" was how he summarized his life in the Sixties and after in a talk with me and David Horowitz not long after emerging from the terrorist underground and heading toward the tenure track at the University of Illinois.)

There is justice in Obama's plaintive objection that he was, after all, in knee pants in the years when Weatherman was on its little bombing spree. All he knew about Ayers was the conventional wisdom about all such unreconstructed "activists" from the Sixties: that they are solid progressives with social consciences who, like the candidate himself, believe in change. Indeed, given the way the era is portrayed by Professor Parini and all the others, why should Obama have thought anything else?

Hillary Clinton was also blindsided by the Sixties, although in a slightly more roundabout way. The hit came from Obama-supporter Tom Hayden, who as the New Left's acknowledged Everyman, was uniquely qualified to pronounce the anathema. After Hillary's victory in Pennsylvania, Hayden reminded readers of *The Nation* of her own "roots in the Sixties"—how she had chaired a Yale Law school movement against the Vietnam war; joined the defense of Bobby Seale during his New Haven murder trial in 1970; and, after law school, spent her summer vacation in the Bay Area working in the fellow-traveling law firm of Robert Treuhaft, which specialized in defending Black Panthers during their war against the cops. Then, having finished this little exercise in Sixties redbaiting, Hayden stipulated that these causes she had once espoused were, of course, "noble," and charged that she had betrayed her former self by dissing a man, the Rev. Wright, "who represents the very essence of the black radicals Hillary was associating with in those days."

Staining her with the Sixties and then rubbing in that stain by accusing her of betraying the Sixties: it was one of those sinuous intellectual maneuvers that shows why Irving Howe once said of Hayden that he gave opportunism a bad name.

A whiff of this opportunism accompanied Hayden to Berkeley when he arrived in the miracle year of 1968. (What was he *thinking* when he showed up teary-eyed at Bobby Kennedy's funeral at a time when the rest of The Movement was contemptuous of RFK for co-opting dissidents back into the System, the same charge that had led to the New Left's defamation of Martin Luther King as an "Uncle Tom" in the months before his assassination?)

But there was no denying that Hayden was the Movement's indispensable man—co-author of the Port Huron Statement, Magna Carta of the New Left; a freedom rider in Mississippi in the dangerous early civil rights days; a community organizer in the Newark ghetto when it exploded in a bloody riot in 1967 (and the author of the lengthy essay on that event in *The New York Review of Books* whose front-page illustration showed the recipe for a Molotov cocktail); leading representative of the Movement in its shuttle diplomacy with Hanoi and promoter of the notion that what was happening there was nothing more or less than "rice roots democracy"; architect of the riots at the Democratic convention in Chicago.

Whatever his quirks, Hayden had certainly been there, done that. And by 1969, with revolution now so palpably in the air that *Newsweek* had a cover story considering its possibility in America, he had become one of its canniest tacticians. He helped design the People's Park riots that spring and conceived the idea of turning places like Berkeley, Cambridge, and Madison into "liberated zones" which would hook up virtually in a revolutionary America with the Black Panthers, who did not have white radicals' qualms about "picking up the gun," functioning as a vanguard "Americong."

Over the next couple of years, as the revolution got more serious rhetorically and more fantastical as a practical possibility, Hayden helped form an affinity group called the Red Family. It was very much influenced by Weatherman, whose "heavier the better" antics were causing status anxiety among old New Leftists and a bit of organizational penis envy as well. The Red Family talked revolutionary violence and did some target practice in the Berkeley Hills led by one of its members, a man whom Hayden eulogized as their "Minister of Defense" after his early death from cancer. But most of the group's energy was directed inward in self-lacerating sessions about the doomed-in-advance imperative to smash monogamy and whether or not it was "bourgeois privatism" to close the door when using the bathroom.

In 1971, some members of the Red Family made a high-profile trip to North Korea to praise the living hell that Kim Il Sung had created there. By this time Hayden had been expelled from the collective for transgressing against the ban on charismatic leadership and had moved to Southern California where he eventually met and married Jane Fonda, whom he directed in her greatest role as Hanoi Jane. They had a son, Troy, purportedly named after Nguyen van Troi, the Vietcong martyr who had tried to assassinate then–Secretary of Defense Robert McNamara when he visited Vietnam in 1966. They pooled their talents in building an "economic democracy movement" and in getting Hayden elected to public office so that he could function as "an outsider on the inside."

He won a seat in the California legislature in 1982, and served both in the Assembly and Senate until 2000, when he was term-limited out. He and Jane divorced. Adrift in the new century, he entered a Harold Stassen–like period when he became a perennial political candidate, running unsuccessfully for Governor of California and mayor and city councilman of Los Angeles. He wrote about his Irish heritage and about Native Americans. Then he was gone from the spotlight he had sought for close to four decades. (But not forgotten: in an episode of *The Simpsons*, Homer, trying to make sense of an odd-shaped piece of a jigsaw puzzle, muses, "This is either an old coconut or Tom Hayden." And next year, he will be portrayed in a film about the Chicago Seven trial to be directed by Steven Spielberg, although the script apparently focuses on Abbie Hoffman, the unsheathed id of the Sixties, who once told me that he regarded Hayden, always somberly preoccupied with his selfhood, as something of a drag.)

I am recalling all this now and wondering how this past will turn out because Hayden's latest book, *Writings for a Democratic Society*, happened to arrive in the mail shortly after his piece bludgeoning Hillary appeared in *The Nation*. A collection of his writing since his days as editor of the *Michigan Daily* in the late 1950s, the book is a legacy project for the author and the Movement he helped create, a sustained exercise in case-making for the Sixties and its earnest effort to make democracy "participatory," and an attempt to identify pieces of that past in his and our present. The fact that the book is published by City Lights Books, whose big hits were the Beat classics *Howl* (1956) and *Coney Island of the Mind* (1958), and that the most recent pieces were first written for blogs and internet sites rather than publications like *The New York Review*, requires an explanation: the "mainstream media" now marginalizes him, Hayden says, making two misstatements in one sentence, because "the spectrum of what's considered legitimate editorial opinion has drifted far to the right since the Reagan and Bush eras, even when public opinion moves to the left."

Hayden's own picaresque tale is only hinted at in this book, although (or because) he is very interested in re-inflating his old heroic persona. He reprints the Port Huron Statement in its entirety and confesses that he still feels the existential yearnings and need for authenticity that made this document a generation's call to arms. Comparing himself to James Baldwin, he writes, "I have found it necessary to embrace my alienation as the only way to discover radical traditions usually hidden from white Americans. Otherwise I would have adjusted to the system's relentless demands long ago and as a writer would be a stranger to my own estrangement."

He sees his life as divided into three movements. First was "youthful radical idealism"; then came the "purposeful and pragmatic" electoral years; and finally today's "reflective period" when his work turns back toward the "social movements and large concerns of my youth." Reconnecting with the meaning of the Sixties, he says, not only brings symmetry to his life, but "is important to social movements of the future and the suppression or distortion of that meaning is vital to the conservative agenda."

Billy Ayers said in the notorious interview about his underground days (that had the bad luck to run in *The New York Times* on the morning of 9/11) that "we didn't do enough." (Did he mean by this that the bombs he and his wife Bernardine Dohrn set off in trash cans in the empty bathrooms of Federal buildings should have been deployed instead in crowded areas?) Hayden, though, feels that we did just fine. He summarizes the accomplishments of the Sixties as follows: "American democracy became more participatory. Political access and power was redistributed.... New issues and constituencies were recognized in public policy.... The war in Vietnam was ended and the Cold War model challenged. The Sixties gave birth to new technologies, including the personal computer."

This last point sounds like an editorial suggestion from Al Gore; the others, at minimum, need a warning that things may seem larger than they actually are when seen in the rear view mirror of history. And this take on the Sixties is bound to leave some of the era's aging true believers in cognitive dissonance. If these moderate accomplishments were all we were aiming for, why did we spend so much time back then in our seamy Berkeley apartments glorifying the homicidal maniac Che Guevara, pushing the theory of repressive tolerance, and attacking the myth of the vaginal orgasm? Was all that quivering attention paid to revolution and were all those clandestine nighttime meetings to determine where to hide the Panthers' guns so the cops wouldn't find them just a dumbshow to achieve these paltry reformist ends?

Writings for a Democratic Society tries to be a forward-looking book, not a nostalgic one. So, if democracy was "in the streets" in the Sixties, where is it in the new century? Still there, according to some of the more recent pieces in the collection—especially in the anti-globalization movement ("Seattle was bigger than Chicago," Hayden writes, bestowing the highest praise possible on the fight against the World Trade Organization). It is in places he has visited as an unreconstructed internationalist: Chiapas with Subcomandante Marcos and the Zapatistas ("the latest manifestation of the same dream" dreamed in the Sixties); Bolivia with Evo Morales (who is "writing a new Bolivian diary" like the one Che wrote for "the indigenous people" here when he organized his guerrilla base). And of course Cuba, whose leaders, he finds on a visit to Havana, continue wryly to endure "Yanqui imperialism."

But Hayden's causes and the lifeless way he espouses them suggest that the Sixties has suffered a fate worse than death as its anarchic brio dissolves into a glutinous mixture of revisionism, political correctness, multicultural clichés, and progressivism. Then there is the popular-fronting solidarity—with affirmative action, queer studies, animal rights, and the fight to save endangered species; solidarity too with a "spirituality" that is one part Greenpeace and one part Pelagius, evoking a "sense of reverence and kinship toward the inherent worth of the natural world"; and most solemnly, solidarity with Native Americans. This last incidentally allows Hayden to complete the tape loop joining old and the new: "Ho Chi Minh should be viewed less like Joseph Stalin and more like Sitting Bull."

The man who negotiated with world historical figures such as Madame Binh and Pham Van Dong now engages in solidarity meetings in the Middle East under the auspices of Code Pink with the likes of Cindy

Sheehan. He extracts this weird causation from the shock and awe of 9/11: "Osama bin Laden set the stage for a political shift to the right by targeting civilians." Even the idea that the personal is political, one of the cherished principles of the Sixties, has become a wizened concept: "One of my fantasies is to mobilize heart patients like myself to demand the legalization of coca for medical purposes.... [This] blow against the drug war would be hugely beneficial to Bolivia."

Some things Hayden has gotten right, of course. One of them is that "the final stage of the Sixties, the stage of memory and museums, is underway." But this raises a question. When the exhibits are finally installed, will there be a place for that comb he brought home from a foreign war in the good old days when we were all so bad?

June 2008

Prophecies of democratic leveling

Jacob Howland

Søren Kierkegaard considered the primary human good to be individual freedom: the freedom to judge for oneself, to speak and act for oneself, and to come to be oneself in the fullness of one's concrete particularity. "The good cannot be defined at all," he wrote in *The Concept of Anxiety* (1844). "The good is freedom. The difference between good and evil is only for freedom and in freedom, and this difference is never *in abstracto* but only *in concreto*." The goodness of the natural world resides in the harmonious abundance of existing beings—this improbable lily, that joyful bird—each of which earnestly inhabits no more or less than its allotted place and time, spontaneously expressing, within these limits, its own rich particularity. The goodness and meaning of human life similarly consists in the irreducible particularity of individuals and communities—families, congregations, nations—that arise in freedom and are sustained by freedom.

As early as the 1840s, however, Kierkegaard warned that late modernity is animated by a crushing spirit of abstraction that poses the gravest threat to the human good. The Hegelian philosophy that dominated the age's intellectual culture, he observed in *Concluding Unscientific Postscript* (1846), was of no use to actually existing human beings; it spoke absurdly "of speculation as if this were a man or as if a man were speculation," and would perhaps someday find its "true readers" among "inhabitants of the moon." But such philosophical lunacy was the least of the matter. Long before the revolutionary followers of Marx and Engels brought Hegel's systematic science down from the heavens and settled it in the cities of men in a malignantly inhuman form—the reductive ideology of dialectical materialism—Kierkegaard prophesied the inevitable destruction of individual character and passion through an inherently reflective social process of "leveling." The present age, he wrote in

Two Ages (1846), is democratically "oriented to equality" and marked not by "the happy infatuation of admiration but the unhappy infatuation of envy," a "censorious" passion that wants to "stifle" and "degrade" individual excellence rather than to emulate it. A constant bane of human existence, envy is particularly destructive in the present age because "the abstraction of leveling is related to a higher negativity: pure humanity." Late-modern leveling, Kierkegaard predicted, would destroy all organic structures that mediate between living individuals and the bloodless abstraction of humanity as such. Nothing—no person, institution, or even "national individuality"—will be able to halt what he calls the "spontaneous combustion of the human race."

Kierkegaard's bleak prediction was fulfilled in the twentieth century by the totalitarian regimes of Lenin, Stalin, Mao, and their many lesser imitators, which collectively sacrificed as many as one hundred million people to their ideologically purified Idea of Man. Victims and students of communism have not failed to affirm Kierkegaard's intuition that human freedom, meaning, and particularity are inseparably interwoven, as well as his warning about what the philosophical positivist Auguste Comte promoted as the "religion of humanity" (as Daniel J. Mahoney informs us in his new book, *The Idol of Our Age*): a scientific, morally progressive substitute for the worship of the transcendent God of the Bible.

What constitutes "the freedom, the soul of an individual life," Vasily Grossman wrote in *Life and Fate* (written 1960, published 1988 in the USSR), the greatest novel of the Soviet era, "is its uniqueness." And because "the only true or lasting meaning of the struggle of life lies in the individual, in his peculiarities and his right to these peculiarities," the proper purpose of "human groupings" is "to assert everyone's right to be different, to be special, to think, feel, and live in his or her own way." The philosopher Chantal Delsol amplifies these thoughts in *Unjust Justice: Against the Tyranny of International Law* (2008): "If being loses its specificity, it loses its dignity. The biblical anthropology, and later that of Christendom, ties the value of being to its unique singularity. Any unity that sought to dissolve these singularities would ipso facto abolish its own value. This is why God prefers a harmony to a unity." And in *Hope Abandoned* (1974), the sequel to her literary memoir *Hope Against Hope* (1970), Nadezhda Mandelstam—the widow of the poet Osip Mandelstam, who died in the Gulag—observes that "The house in which a man lives has grown out of his native soil and merges with the landscape: it is made out of the timber and the clay produced by that particular soil and no other." These authors sing in harmony. They teach us that one cannot make a human home in the frozen sky, for no matter how dense and leaden the theoretical principles of political constructivism may be, such materials will not keep us warm.

In what used to be known as the Free World, this lesson has not so much been forgotten as never learned at all. Thirty years after the Soviet Union's collapse, the specter of ideological leveling in the name of humanity continues to haunt the democracies of the West by means Kierkegaard also anticipated in *Two Ages*:

> For leveling really to take place, a phantom must first be raised, the spirit of leveling, a monstrous abstraction, an all-encompassing something that is nothing, a mirage—and this phantom is *the public*. Only in a passionless and reflective age can this phantom develop with the aid of the press, when the press itself becomes a phantom.

Press and public today largely coalesce and dissolve, according to their own unerring logic, in cyberspace—an ethereal realm that is itself everywhere and nowhere. The psychologically compressive emptiness of these monstrous phantasms of authoritative judgment produces souls that are pinched and flat. Disdainful of the precious accumulated traditions and local conditions of the human world—the rich soil that alone nurtures robust individuality—such souls willingly conform to sterile ideological artifacts and other empty mass constructions. Kierkegaard asserted that leveling in the name of the "infinite abstraction" of pure humanity would in modern times be "correlative to fate in antiquity." He foresaw with terrible clarity the inevitable emergence of great masses of deracinated individuals who know not who they are or what they do: people who "run nameless through the innumerable multitude" (in the words of *The Sickness Unto Death*, 1849), living in ignorance of their true and unrepeatable names.

Kierkegaard was not the only nineteenth-century prophet of democratic leveling. Alexis de Tocqueville visited the United States in the early 1830s, hoping to find an antidote to the kind of despotism, as he wrote in *Democracy in America* (1835), that "is particularly to be feared in ages of democracy." Tocqueville envisioned a time when citizens would be kept in "perpetual childhood" by a government of "schoolmasters" who "relieve them from the trouble of thinking and all the cares of living," a government that "extends its embrace to include the whole of society." Burdened by "a network of petty, complicated rules that are both minute and uniform," even "men of the greatest originality and the most vigorous temperament" would be unable to "force their heads above the crowd." Individuals would nevertheless willingly submit to being collared like dogs, because they "see that it is not a person, or a class of persons, but society itself which holds the end of the chain."

Tocqueville's worries have proven to be well founded. And while the enormous nanny state he so perceptively foresaw exercises a relatively benign form of democratic despotism, real ideological hardness draws closer by the day. In the academy, the old social calculus of class, race, and ethnicity favored by both Marxists and National Socialists is again in vogue, updated to include gender, sexual orientation, disability, body type, and other categories in which inequality, and therefore presumptive oppression, may be ferreted out. An all-purpose tool of moral judgment and social policy, this zero-sum reckoning treats the phenomena of freedom only in the aggregate. It crudely predetermines guilt and innocence, and reduces individual thought and action to points on a probability curve. More broadly, the political parties, media outlets, international organizations, multinational technology corporations, charitable foundations, and cultural and educational institutions whose efforts to promote "soft" Tocquevillian despotism have recently been met with popular resistance in the United States and Europe increasingly resort to the chastising orthodoxy of political correctness. Acting in the name of what Grossman called the "Good with a capital 'G'"—an abstraction, he adds, that can produce "greater evil than evil itself"—the new orthodoxy does not argue with nonconforming individuals, but seeks to take words from their mouths and put others in them. So far, professors, writers, artists, performers, and others who refuse to wear the bit, or who have been exposed for having done or said things that run afoul of current dogma, have *only* been publicly shamed, de-platformed, financially harmed, and in some cases forced to abandon their careers. Who expects matters to end there?

What's past is prologue. While the tyrants of antiquity were not ideological revolutionaries, they practiced leveling with a primitive directness that returned on an industrial scale under Fascism and Communism.

The quintessential Greek tyrant was Periander of Corinth (d. 585 B.C.), of whom Herodotus relates a memorable tale in his *Histories* (*ca.* 420 B.C.). Having just come to power, Periander sent a messenger to Thrasybulus, the tyrant of Miletus, for advice about how to proceed:

> Thrasybulus led the man who had come from Periander outside the town and into a field sown with grain. While they walked together through the crop, Thrasybulus kept questioning and cross-examining the messenger about the reason for his arrival from Corinth, and whenever he saw one of the stalks extending above the others, he would cut it off and cast it away, until he had in this manner destroyed the finest and most flourishing part of the crop.... [Returning to Corinth] the messenger said that Thrasybulus had given no advice at all, and that he was amazed that he had been sent to a man who was clearly not in his right mind and who destroyed his own possessions; and then he reported everything he had seen Thrasybulus do. Periander understood the meaning of what Thrasybulus had done and perceived that he was advising him to murder the prominent men of the city.

Herodotus's story impressed no less a mind than Livy, for he tells it again in his *History of Rome*, this time about the notorious Tarquins: Sextus, who had just gotten control of the city of Gabii, and his father, Tarquin the Proud, whose overthrow at the end of the sixth century birthed the Roman republic.

> The king, as if absorbed in meditation, passed into the garden of his house, followed by his son's envoy. There, walking up and down without a word, he is said to have struck off the heads of the tallest poppies with his stick. Tired of asking questions and waiting for an answer, the messenger returned to Gabii, his mission, as he thought, unaccomplished. He reported what he had said himself and what he had seen. Whether from anger, or hatred, or native pride, the king, he said, had not pronounced a single word. As soon as it was clear to Sextus what his father meant and what was the purport of his silent hints, he rid himself of the chief men of the state.

The ancient historians present leveling in its simplest and purest form, that of direct tyrannical oppression. Whether maddened by envy and hatred or motivated merely by cold self-interest, all tyrannies, ideological or otherwise, seek to destroy the good and the beautiful: the most nourishing human grain and the loveliest human blossoms. For they know that individuals who publicly lay claim to the goodness of their freedom—people of real moral stature, who in dangerous times continue to speak, think, and act for themselves—especially endanger their rule.

Kierkegaard's study of antiquity informed his understanding not only of democratic leveling, but of its particular connection with reflective abstraction. His dissertation, *The Concept of Irony with Continual Reference to Socrates* (1841), drew heavily on Aristophanes and Plato, two Athenian contemporaries who understood that democracies are particularly susceptible to ideological leveling in the name of equality. Aristophanes' *Assemblywomen* (*ca.* 390 B.C.) depicts a matriarchal dystopia that comically foreshadows Tocqueville's vision of a smothering and infantilizing government. The play is an extreme realization of the rage for equality: women take power, seize private property and redistribute it in equal shares from a common store, abolish families, and eliminate—or rather, reverse—discrimination on the basis of age or beauty (any man may have sex with any woman, provided that he first satisfies all others who request his services, starting with the oldest and ugliest ones).

The fate of Socrates was probably even more important than Aristophanes' comedies in shaping Kierkegaard's intuitions about democratic leveling. A few years before the philosopher was put to death in 399 B.C., he was targeted by the oligarchy known as the Thirty Tyrants that came to power in Athens in the immediate aftermath of the Peloponnesian War, a long and wasting conflict into which the city had been drawn by the imperial ambitions of Periclean democracy. Led by Plato's older cousin Critias, the Thirty practiced a politics of aristocratic purity. According to the speechwriter Lysias (whose brother Polemarchus they murdered), the Thirty proposed "to purge the city of unjust men, and to turn the rest of the citizens toward virtue and justice." Over the course of their eight-month rule in 404–03, they arrested, robbed, and exiled their political opponents and put to death roughly fifteen hundred Athenians. When Socrates criticized the regime, the oligarchs made it illegal to teach the "art of speech" and forbade him to associate with anyone under the age of thirty. After the Athenian democrats returned from exile to overthrow the oligarchy, they, too, sought to purge their opponents. Suspecting Socrates of having influenced Critias—the two are together on three occasions in the Platonic dialogues—they denounced him as a religious and social pollution (*miasma*) and engineered his execution for the crimes of impiety and corrupting the young.

The trial and death of his teacher gave Plato ample material for reflection. Plato's *Euthyphro* and *Apology* (both set in 399) sketch a vivid portrait of a now all-too-familiar public type: the young radical democrat who scorns traditional values and practices; whose thinking is highly schematic and confined to empty abstractions; whose inflated self-perception manifests itself in envy and resentment; and who seeks personal advancement by attacking nonconforming individuals and groups. All of these attributes are shared by a matched pair of ignorant, arrogant men: Socrates' accuser Meletus and a crank named Euthyphro. Taken together, these defective characters depict a brave new kind of political actor born in the restored democracy of post-war Athens—and destined, apparently, to be reborn repeatedly in late modernity.

The *Euthyphro* takes place at the courtroom where Socrates has come to answer the preliminary indictment by someone "young . . . and unknown" he seems never even to have met ("they call him Meletus, I believe"). Socrates instructs the Athenians at his trial that it is noblest "not to restrain others, but to equip oneself to be the best possible." But it is always easier to blame others than to improve oneself, and the philosopher is a natural target. He tells Euthyphro that his philanthropic practice of freely sharing his thought with anyone he meets has aroused the Athenians' spirited opposition.

When Euthyphro asks what charge he faces, Socrates tells him with characteristic irony that Meletus's indictment is "not ignoble":

> For that one, as he maintains, knows in what way the young are being corrupted, and who are the ones corrupting them. And he may be someone wise, and, looking down upon my ignorance, he is coming to accuse me before the city as before his mother on the ground that I am corrupting those of his own age. And he alone among the politicians seems to me to begin correctly. For it is correct to care first for the young in order that they may be as excellent as possible, just as it is fitting for a good farmer to care first for the young plants, and after this for the others. And more-

over, Meletus is perhaps first purging us, the corrupters of the young shoots, as he claims. Then after this it is clear that, having taken care of the older ones, he will be responsible for the most and greatest good things for the city, as is likely to happen for one beginning from such a beginning.

Herodotus's vigorous grain-stalks have here become weeds that stunt and embitter the Athenian sprouts—actually a single weed, for Meletus claims in the *Apology* that Socrates is the sole corrupter of the young. This is in some respects an apt image, for weeds, like philosophers, are undomesticated and spring up spontaneously. Yet the "not quite full-bearded" Meletus, whose name roughly translates as "Mr. Care," is somehow not a tender shoot but a wise farmer!

In fact, Meletus wants to be treated as if he were both. Socrates' description of Meletus deftly exposes the internal contradictions of a politically ambitious type of character one may find on any college campus today. Meletus's apparent conservatism as a defender of traditional religious belief is less relevant in this context than his radical opposition to socially unorthodox speeches and deeds. He wrongheadedly advocates a legal solution to a crisis of civic and ethical education that he himself exemplifies. Hauling Socrates to court, he accuses him "as before his mother"; he regards the city as an *in loco parentis* authority that will protect him and his vulnerable young peers from harmful speech. At the same time, he aspires to be recognized not only as a mature and fully independent individual, but also as the source of the greatest good for the city. If he is to elevate himself in the public eye, he must publicly destroy another human being, rousing against him the community's collective power to shame and make a scapegoat of another. As Meletus makes clear in the *Apology*, he proposes to cure the city's ills by removing from its midst the "most polluted" individual who is the sole source of its moral infection. In advocating this solution, however, he lays claim to wisdom that he does not possess. Socrates easily shows at his trial that Mr. Care "never cared" about the Athenians' well-being.

The sympathetic Euthyphro is quick to compare himself to Socrates. Both, he asserts, are envied for their special knowledge of divine matters: just as Socrates invites slander because he claims to be counseled by a divine voice, he himself is unjustly ridiculed as a madman whenever he utters prophecies in the Athenian Assembly. But while Euthyphro deplores Meletus's indictment, he fails to notice how similar he is to Socrates' accuser. His statement that Meletus is "doing evil to the city, beginning from the hearth" is an unselfconscious projection that perfectly describes his own deeds.

Euthyphro proudly observes that he has come to the court to indict "someone whom in prosecuting I again seem to be mad." Socrates is shocked to learn that he has charged his father with homicide; respect for ancestral authority was a cornerstone of ancient piety, and he naturally assumes that the victim must have been a relative. But Euthyphro, whose name means "Straight Thinker" as well as "Instant Mind," is a man of inflexible principle. With quasi-scientific exactitude, he asserts that a homicide must be prosecuted "even if the killer shares your hearth and table. For the pollution is the same if you knowingly associated with such a man, and do not purify yourself as well as him by proceeding against him in a lawsuit." Asked whether he doesn't fear that he himself may be acting impiously in prosecuting his father, he replies that he wouldn't "be any different from the many human beings, if I didn't know all such things precisely." Like Meletus, Euthyphro hungers for recognition—Socrates bitingly remarks that no one "even seems to see you"—and it soon becomes clear that he, too, hopes to make a name for himself and settle scores by indicting an old man.

Euthyphro says that his father's crime took place on the island of Naxos, where his family was farming. If so, it must have occurred before 404, when the Spartans took control of the Cyclades. Euthyphro has been biding his time in a way that is inconsistent with his supposed concern for religious pollution. "A laborer of mine," he tells Socrates, got drunk and slit the throat of a slave; his father tied up the man and threw him in a ditch while he sent to inquire of the exegete, an expounder of Athenian religious law, what he should do. Naxos is roughly a hundred miles by sea from Athens, and the man died of hunger and exposure before the messenger returned. Euthyphro's real motives are clear enough from this story. It was a family slave whose throat was slit, but it was *his* hired man that his father killed. What is more, he is himself an expert in matters of piety; what need, then, to consult an exegete? By prosecuting his father in a court whose special jurisdiction concerns sacred matters, he intends publicly to establish his claimed expertise while avenging these paternal insults.

But things do not go well for Euthyphro in his conversation with

Socrates. Like the wings of Icarus, his boasts melt into air under the light and heat of Socratic scrutiny. His ostensible science of piety turns out to be the unprincipled or *ad hoc* practice of giving the gods whatever they want, whenever they want it. It is nothing but the utterly conventional "art of commerce" (as Socrates puts it) first described in Homer's *Iliad*: the slavish gratification of great amoral powers in the hopes of currying favor or at least avoiding destruction. All that is left of Euthyphro's fine talk of justice toward gods and men is shameful nakedness: the indignant self-assertion of a young know-nothing who, failing to obtain the respect he craves but has not earned, is prepared to make criminal the religious practices of the older generation and to tear apart his family. He would have made a fine commissar.

The *Apology* and *Euthyphro* anticipate several crucial political developments of the twentieth century. Seen against the backdrop of the Athenians' successive purges of socially corrupting elements, Euthyphro's spurious knowledge of pollution and purification looks like a rudimentary version of the ideological pseudoscience that has justified the widespread "cleansing" of undesirables in every totalitarian regime since the foundation of the USSR. And viewed in connection with Euthyphro's attack on traditional practices and beliefs, Meletus's attempt to present himself as caring for the city's future by zealously protecting its exclusive power to inculcate young minds prefigures the progressivist propaganda that substitutes for education in all ideological tyrannies. Meletus condemns Socrates for impiety, but in fact hopes to eclipse the Athenian gods by usurping their traditional role as the source of "the most and greatest good things for the city." He thus also offers an inchoate (if unsuccessful) example of the strategy by which leaders like Stalin and Mao would become the human equivalent of pagan deities, adored for their paternalistic benevolence in cults of personality that were especially popular in youth organizations like the Komsomol and Mao's Red Guard.

Plato's dialogues are also distant prophecies for the twenty-first century. Democratic leveling thrives in an atmosphere of ignorance and fear. Such was the case in Athens, which by 399 had largely become the "wretched theatocracy" deplored in Plato's *Laws*. The justice system provided a form of social welfare: Athenian juries were huge (Socrates' had 501 members) and included many regulars who depended on the modest remuneration of a few obols per day—and who enjoyed the spectacle of defendants pleading for mercy. Socrates declares in the *Apology* that one should be governed by justice rather than shame, and he repeatedly asks the jurors not to shout; by turns cowed and riled up by public opinion, many are evidently incapable of calmly attending to his defense of the philosophical life. Like one "fighting with shadows" (including all who have anonymously maligned him in the past), he confronts a multitude of indolent souls whose uncritical capitulation to decades of slander places them beyond the reach of rational persuasion.

The absence of mediating political structures in the direct democracy of ancient Athens amplified the destructive effects of cowardice, envy, resentment, and intellectual slackness. Paradoxically, modern media has the same effect as ancient immediacy: the internet, itself a wretched theatocracy, not only rewards these vices but weaponizes them. In that electronic wasteland, moral condemnation is a blood sport, and libelous flash mobs are drawn to the merest suggestion of heterodoxy like hammers to nails. (In the exemplary case of the Covington Catholic teenagers, the ritual identification of social pollution and its purgation through scapegoating was performed by a monstrous fusion of press and public.) But while individual responsibility dissipates in a crowd, especially in the faceless ones of cyberspace, so does individual visibility. This fact perversely encourages extremism in the service of compelled conformity, as the Euthyphros and Meletuses of the present age can hope to achieve the recognition they crave only by outdoing others in their enthusiasm for ideological purity and moral scourging.

Democratic leveling cannot take place unless a people (*demos*) is already on low ground. Socrates' final public act was to point out that this was the case in Athens. It is just as much the case today, although we lack anyone of his stature to say so. But even when there is no one above us to absorb the blows, it may still be better to be a nail than a hammer. Grossman, who forever regretted the moment of abject weakness in which he signed a letter denouncing Jewish doctors on the cooked-up charge of plotting to kill Stalin, writes in *Life and Fate* that "everything in the world is insignificant compared to the truth and purity of one small man." If the witness of the poets does not steel us for whatever lies ahead, perhaps the prophecies of the philosophers will help, just because they dispel the illusion of individual control in an epoch of democratic leveling. For if everyone is fated to be under the hammer eventually—as millions of passionate Bolsheviks and Maoists discovered when the State's blank and pitiless gaze fell on *them*—then let us resolve right now to be judged by the amount of force it takes to pound us down.

March 2019

Liberalism vs. humanism

James Piereson

WRITING FORTY YEARS AGO in *The New Industrial State*, John Kenneth Galbraith called on academics and intellectuals to seize the mantle of national leadership which at that time (he said) was in the hands of a bipartisan coalition of corporate managers, union officials, and machine politicians. Galbraith feared that these conventional leaders had defined the goals of the industrial system too narrowly in terms of production, consumption, and employment when in fact a much broader vision was needed to direct the goals of the new economy toward aesthetic, artistic, and intellectual interests such that the lives of the American people might be elevated above mere work and consumption. Noting their growing influence within the Democratic Party and the increasing activism of students and faculty, Galbraith concluded that the colleges and universities of the nation were well-positioned to exercise political leadership in the name of those humane ideals that were expressed in the academic curricula and research programs of the time.

While Galbraith sought to harness academic humanism to the purposes of liberal politics, campus radicals tried to do something similar to augment the influence of the "New Left." In the Port Huron Statement, written in 1962, the founders of a new campus organization, Students for a Democratic Society, decried the loss of meaning and humane ideals in a consumer-driven economy. "The goal of man and society," the students wrote, "should be human independence: a concern not with image but with finding a meaning in life that is personally authentic." They wished to raise deep questions that their elders had brushed aside in their headlong pursuit of money and comfort: What is really important? Can we live in a different and better way? If we wanted to change society, how would we do it?

The radicals, too, astutely zeroed in on the university as (in their words) "a potential base and agency in a movement for social change." They viewed the university in nakedly political terms as a far better institutional base for their movement than a new political party. For one thing, the campus archipelago that stretched across the nation was home to both liberals and socialists as well as to millions of young people yearning for "change." These would be the key constituent groups for a new Left. For another, the university ethos gave a wide berth for political activity. "The University," the radicals said, "permits the political life to be an adjunct to the academic one." There was nothing to stop professors or students from becoming spokesmen and activists for the new politics. The young radicals asserted that "meaning" had to be found, not through study and reflection, but through political action.

That the university might be seized as a base for a political movement or that the humanistic ideals of the academy might be projected outward into the political process—these were novel and surprisingly compelling conceptions which together suggested that the academy had come of age as a partner in the institutional coalition that governed post-war America. Such propositions also pointed toward a reformulation of liberal doctrine away from the older emphasis on economic growth that held together the New Deal coalition. Both liberals like Galbraith and the student radicals seemed to agree that the time had come for a new emphasis in liberal thought on cultural, humanistic, and quality of life issues that had not previously been viewed in political or partisan terms. For both liberals and radicals, the university would play a key role in guiding this reformulation and in giving it political expression.

Much of what the liberals and radicals called for in the 1960s eventually came to pass, albeit in the rough-edged way by which history is made. Galbraith's idea of using the university to elevate national politics backfired in spectacular fashion, but the vision of turning it into a base for liberal and left-wing politics was soon achieved against only weak resistance from more traditionally minded academics. With their broader political aims blunted, however, the surviving reformers who settled into academic careers were forced to reformulate their ideological notions into academically acceptable modes of study. As they did so, as they pushed questions of race, gender, and multiculturalism to the forefront of the academic agenda, they unwittingly chased away those ideals of humanism and humanistic study which, according to liberals like Galbraith and the student radicals, had conferred on the university a degree of moral legitimacy that other institutions lacked. As political liberalism and radicalism advanced on the campus, humanism receded at a nearly identical pace.

Humanism is the name given to the various intellectual movements that have developed since the Renaissance which emphasize the secular achievements of man in the fields of art, literature, philosophy, and politics, using as starting points and models for study the civilizations of ancient Greece and Rome. Though humanism originally developed out of Medieval Christianity, its main purpose then and afterwards was to demonstrate the dignity and creative power of man. The major intellectual movements that shaped the modern world, including most especially the Renaissance and the Enlightenment, arose out of humanist ideals. Reason, science, free inquiry, the power of the human intellect—these have been the watchwords of humanist movements through the centuries. Humanists have always pointed to the highest human achievements in order to promote understanding of what is great and noble in human affairs and to encourage efforts at emulation. Humanism—or the *humanities*—has long found a home in the great universities of Europe and North America. Indeed, those institutions have developed over several centuries as instruments for spreading the ideals of humanistic study. Until quite recently, the ideals of the university have been indistinguishable from those of humanism.

Liberal conceptions have now replaced traditional humanistic ideals in defining both the form and substance of the American university. Liberal ideals like freedom of choice, equality among all groups and fields of study, tolerance of disparate viewpoints and lifestyles, diversity, and compassion have pushed aside the older humanistic ideals of the structured curriculum, classical studies, mastery of ancient languages, the great books of western civilization, the aristocracy of the intellect, and the republic of letters. Important historical figures or impressive works of art and literature which were once held up by humanists as models for emulation and aspiration are now viewed in terms of a "hermeneutics of suspicion" which unmasks the hidden political interests they claimed to represent. Since these interests are always framed in terms of money or power or some similarly dishonorable calculation, such an approach has the pedagogical effect of reducing every subject of study to a common moral level. The point of these exercises is to establish equality as the conceptual prism through which all subjects must be viewed. This is a vision of equality—equality with a vengeance—that grows out of contemporary liberalism but which cannot be reconciled with the humanities as traditionally studied or with the ideals of classical humanism.

It is hard to know if the eclipse of humanism on the campus is but a temporary setback for a venerable philosophy or if it marks the end of an intellectual tradition that for centuries provided the rationale and purpose for advanced academic study.

The rise of liberalism as a counter-ideal has brought the university more into line with the norms of democracy and equality that are widely influential within American society at large—a development which (surprisingly enough) may have augmented its legitimacy in the eyes of parents, public officials, and philanthropists who are called upon to provide it with resources and students. From this point of view, humanism appears as an obstacle to the fulfillment of liberal goals both on the campus and in the wider polity since those who defend the traditional humanities are immediately portrayed as enemies of equality and democracy. For this reason, the academic revolutions of the past half-century may prove difficult to reverse or to modify.

At the same time, humanism has long been thought to be a necessary educational adjunct to liberal political doctrine. Beginning in the late 1600s, liberalism advanced as a political theory because it defined "liberty" as the individual's right to choose his own way of life, primarily in the area of religion but also as time passed in an expanding field of activities. Liberalism set the individual free but did not provide instruction as to how he should live or how he should order his private conscience. As followers of a revolutionary doctrine and one that sought to limit the reach of government, early liberal thinkers were forced to look to classical traditions for instruction in important civic matters such as war, statecraft, and citizenship. For most people, religion filled the void opened up by liberalism in the area of private life and morals. Humanism did so as well for those who pursued advanced academic studies or who may have harbored political or literary ambitions. Liberalism, it was understood, was not the same as the liberal arts. However powerful it may have been as a political doctrine, liberalism (like science) was thought to be insufficient as a general guide to life and thus in need of support from other sources and traditions of thought.

This awareness of the limits of liberalism is one source of the calls we hear today for a revival of the humanities in higher education. It also accounts for the wide readership gained by books critical of the academy like Allan Bloom's *Closing of the American Mind*, Roger Kimball's *Tenured Radicals*, and Harold Bloom's *The Western Canon*. Such works, while routinely dismissed by college presidents and deans as reactionary tracts out of step with the times, point to a permanent problem in liberal thought that cannot be overcome by further reforms in the direction of more democracy, equality, and freedom on the campus. Such books, and the responses to them, have raised the main question—whether humanism is in fact an obstacle to the fulfillment of liberal ideals or a complementary philosophy that can supply them with a measure of content and purpose.

The latest call for a revival of humanism comes from Anthony T. Kronman, a distinguished professor of law at Yale University, who (like many others) laments the loss of purpose in undergraduate education. The title of his highly useful and provocative volume, *Education's End: Why Our Colleges and Universities Have Given Up on the Meaning of Life*, contains a deliberate irony that points at once to the enduring "ends" of higher education as well as to the terminal destination at which our academic institutions now appear to have arrived. The whole point of a college education, in his view, is to encourage reflection about the purposes of life, but it is also obvious that academics no longer regard this as central to their mission. In keeping with his title, Professor Kronman seems alternately hopeful that such ends might be restored to the curricula of our colleges and deeply pessimistic that the strong countercurrents at work in the academy can ever be overcome.

The reader has to admire Professor Kronman for subordinating his interests in professional education in order to make a case for the vital role played by the traditional humanities in the undergraduate curriculum. That such a case has to be made by a law professor is perhaps a sign that it can no longer be made by professors of history, literature, classics, or philosophy. One also has to admire the author for the strong words that he attaches to the various academic fads and practices which have led to the eclipse of the humanities, calling them "ruinous," "deadening," "destructive," "disastrous," "impoverished," "deformed," and "mistaken." At the same time, perhaps to counterbalance these strong words, he takes pains to present the case in a manner least likely to offend the academic gate-keepers who control the flow of ideas into the campus, refraining especially from chalking up the crisis in the humanities to the political upheavals of the 1960s (as other critics have done).

Professor Kronman reflects back nostalgically to his undergraduate years in the mid-1960s at Williams College where he was exposed to something resembling a humanistic education that explored questions of the meaning of life. Such a "quest for meaning" led the young Kronman, like other students of the time, to take a year-long leave of absence from college to work as a community organizer in Chicago under the auspices of Students for a Democratic Society. Disappointed in what he was able to accomplish in that role, he returned to Williamstown to engage the questions of meaning by a different route. In a seminar on "Existentialism," where he encountered authors like Kierkegaard and Sartre, he discovered something important that subverted his radical presumptions, namely "that the meaning of life is a subject that can be studied in school." Thus as a young man he managed to frame a central question of the modern age: whether ultimate meaning is to be found in politics or in study and reflection undertaken by the individual.

In his view, our colleges and universities took the wrong path when they jettisoned humanism in the 1960s in favor of the politicized doctrines that have ever since held sway within humanities departments. These doctrines are weak and mistaken in the academic setting precisely because they do not allow students to engage those ultimate questions that captivated him as an undergraduate. Professor Kronman advocates a return to the secular humanism of that earlier period, which he defines as "the exploration of life's mysteries and meaning through the careful but critical reading of the great works of the literary and philosophical imagination." This was a twentieth-century version of humanism which replaced the older humanistic focus on Greece and Rome with an emphasis on the continuity of Western civilization from those early sources to the influential works of the modern age. His view of humanistic education embodies an outlook advanced decades ago by Robert Maynard Hutchins, one of his predecessors as dean of Yale's Law School, who wrote, "The tradition of the West is embodied in the Great Conversation that began in the dawn of history and continues to the present day." Like Hutchins and his colleague Mortimer Adler, Professor Kronman is an advocate of an education in the great books.

Professor Kronman suggests that the modern research university played a complex role first in the development of secular humanism and, later, in its destruction. In the years following the Civil War, the American university was reorganized along the lines of the "German" model which asserted the autonomy of the professor to teach and to conduct research free from control by religious or secular authorities. The research model also introduced the concept of the graduate school into higher education. The research university, which was dedicated to the discovery of new knowledge, thus replaced the traditional antebellum college which emphasized humanistic studies but which also placed these studies in the service of religious faith. This era, which ran from roughly 1870 into the 1960s, was something of a golden age for the American university because it was a time in which the humanities were liberated from religion but not yet subordinated to science and specialization. The humanities were thus able to carve out an independent role at the center of the undergraduate curriculum against the twin challenges from religion and science.

He parts company with critics like Bloom and Kimball, however, in asserting that the collapse of secular humanism was caused not by political movements that invaded the campus in the 1960s, but instead by the relentless advance of the research ideal that caused academics to abandon the large issues of humanistic learning for narrower (yet meaningless) subjects more amenable to scientific study.

While the scientific approach may have been crucial to the advance of knowledge about nature and the physical world, it proved a disaster when applied to the humanistic fields which could not be cut up into researchable parts without compromising their main purpose. The point of the humanities, after all, was to understand life from the broadest possible vantage point. The narrow specialization which is an integral part of the scientific enterprise worked against the ideal of a "great conversation" extending from the ancient Greeks to modern times.

Thus by the end of the 1960s the humanities were compromised beyond redemption by the emphasis on research and publication. Intellectually curious students could no longer find answers to the vexing questions of life and politics in their courses in philosophy, literature, and history which were increasingly given over to questions raised by the research disciplines. Into this void flowed the "ruinous" and "destructive" concepts and modes of study that we associate with the contemporary university. All of these doctrines, from multiculturalism to race and gender studies, pointedly dispute the continuity of Western civilization or even that such a civilization ever existed in the first place outside the minds of a handful of humanists. These approaches, moreover, systematically attacked the assumptions of humanism yet accommodated the demands of research, a tactic which was essential to their success. At the same time, these approaches were able to invade and subvert the humanities only because the research ideal had already emptied them of content.

One might easily dispute Professor Kronman's account of the sequence of events by which the humanities were overtaken in the 1960s. The research ideal, while certainly detrimental to humanism, cannot finally be blamed for bringing on to campus the radical ideologies that have done so much damage to the humanities. The most destructive upheavals of the 1960s took place precisely on those campuses where the liberal arts had been given the most serous attention. At no institution in the post-war era, for example, were humanism and the great books taken more seriously than at Columbia University in New York City. Columbia was, after all, academic home to an eminent group of humanists, including Lionel Trilling, Jacques Barzun, Gilbert Highet, Moses Hadas, along with others too numerous to mention. All were associated in one way or another with the ideals of secular humanism that Professor Kronman rightly celebrates. Columbia was known for its pioneering introductory course, Contemporary Civilization, that had long been a requirement for incoming freshmen. It enjoyed a well-earned reputation as an international center for academic humanism. Yet in 1968 radical students took over the campus, with the tacit support of many faculty and students not actively involved, demanding an end to the war in Vietnam, a moratorium on campus expansion to adjoining neighborhoods, and a more "relevant" education than the one then being offered. It was one of the loudest shots fired in the campus wars of the time—and one of its effects was to bring to an end the tradition of humanism for which Columbia was well known.

The collapse of academic humanism has now left a generation of undergraduates intellectually adrift in a sea of nihilism, relativism, and political correctness. Professor Kronman believes that the rise of religious fundamentalism here and abroad is one consequence of the failure of the academy to address the ultimate questions from a secular point of view. Whatever its weaknesses, fundamentalist religion at least provides answers to the questions of life's meaning that every thinking person must consider. These answers are flawed, in Mr. Kronman's view, because they approach the crisis of meaning from the standpoint of dogma rather than reason and because they represent a flight from reality rather than an engagement with it. Humanism (in his view) is superior to fundamentalism, and to religion in general, because it alone equips us with the resources of intellect and reason needed to face up to that crisis with honesty and composure.

Professor Kronman ends his book on a hopeful note, declaring that the age of political correctness will soon end and that the humanities will begin to recover from the abject state to which they have fallen. There is little evidence to justify that faith, as he acknowledges, other than the fact that since things cannot get much worse, they are bound to get better. One hopes this will be the case. If humanism is to advance, however, it must do so in the face of two well-entrenched adversaries: political correctness on the one side and research specialization on the other. As of now, its troops on campus are still too few to win this fight.

Yet Professor Kronman is able to point to some favorable straws in the wind. There is, first of all, the Directed Studies Program at Yale where he now regularly teaches and which offers a rigorous series of courses for freshmen in the great books of philosophy, literature, and politics. This is an elective rather than a required course of study, but it attracts far more applicants than can be accommodated within the current roster of courses. St. John's College continues to offer a complete four-year curriculum in the great books and has little difficulty filling its classrooms with able and highly motivated students. Some small colleges, more the exceptions than the rule, still maintain traditional core curricula. Other institutions, at the initiative of faculty members, have begun to offer courses of study in Western civilization, the ideals of the American founding, the history of liberty and free societies, or various combinations of the above. So far such concentrations have been offered on an elective basis for students who wish to pursue a traditional curriculum. Fledgling programs in Western civilization are now being developed at several major institutions, including the University of Texas, with others soon likely to follow. These programs will give students an opportunity to "vote with their feet," as it were, and to send signals to administrators about the kinds of courses they wish to take and the kinds of faculty who should be hired. There is a clear awareness among many college teachers today that the degree of specialization found in graduate studies should be kept from spreading to the undergraduate curriculum.

Humanism is thus in the process of being brought back into the academy through accommodations made with the reigning ideals of student choice, the open curriculum, and faculty freedom to teach the courses they choose. Humanism, which once shaped the academy, is today being presented as an option for consideration by students and faculty on a par with every other field of study. This is progress of an important kind and it no doubt represents the only effective strategy available for those wishing to restore content to the humanities, since there is little prospect today for restoring the traditional core curriculum in the humanities that was once standard fare at leading colleges and universities. At the same time, the need for such a strategy highlights the inescapable fact that in the contemporary university humanism and liberalism are at odds with one another and that, for the time being, the latter holds a decided advantage.

It is encouraging and not a little surprising to read such an urgent call for a revival of the humanities as the one set forth by Professor Kronman—and even more so because of the case he makes for humanism as an instrument for discovering the meaning of life. Humanism has been advanced and defended in various ways in the past, but not often in modern times on these particular grounds. Sartre said that "existentialism is a humanism" because it demanded courage from the individual to face a world without meaning. There were others, like Erich Fromm, who said that "Marxism is a humanism" because it promised to end the alienation of man from himself, though the life of the individual had no meaning outside the process of history. According to both accounts, man does not discover but rather makes his own meaning through action and choice—and shapes his own character through the struggle with existence. Perhaps it is true that academics gave up on teaching about the meaning of life because they were finally convinced by these doctrines that there was no such meaning to be found.

The question today, as at times in the past, is how and under what circumstances the humanities might be revived or reformulated. The past offers little in the way of guidance, since we are unlikely very soon to follow the paths of Christian or Classical humanism charted by the likes of Erasmus or Goethe. The revival of the traditional great books curriculum now underway at several institutions is a welcome step in the right direction. Yet what really needs to be recovered is not so much a curriculum but an older understanding of a liberal political order which said that the real friends of liberty and equality are those who remind us of the limits of those ideals. Humanism in its different varieties fills a void by pointing to the human ends which the ideals of liberty and equal rights are unable to prescribe. In that way humanism can counterbalance some of the defects of a democratic order, "propping us up on the side that we lean."

May 2008

A sketch of democracy

Aleksandr Solzhenitsyn

FOR TWO MONTHS already there had been an invitation waiting for me from the Canton of Appenzell to attend the ceremony of their cantonal elections, and the editor-in-chief of the *Neue Zürcher Zeitung*, Fred Luchsinger, had urged that this was something I absolutely must not miss, and now he drove [my wife] Alya and me there.* My departure for Canada was planned for Monday, and the elections being on Sunday, I could still make the ceremony. Appenzell is a small mountain canton in eastern Switzerland; in fact, there are two Appenzells—two half-cantons—a Catholic and a Protestant one, that had separated from one another. We had been invited to the Catholic one. On the way there, as we passed the people walking toward the town hall (in Appenzell one goes to elections on foot—not doing so is considered inappropriate), it was impossible not to notice that the men were all carrying swords, a sign of the right to vote, which women and the young do not have. People were arriving from all directions, also walking over the meadows (the law in Appenzell states that prior to Election Day you can walk over a meadow, but afterward the grass must be allowed to grow untrampled). Many of the young men and women were wearing an earring in one ear.

The Catholic Mass was drawing to a close, the church crowded to overflowing, and around the altar hung the ornate flags of the different communes of Appenzell. From the windows of the brightly painted chalets along the main street long banners with strange designs, symbols, and images of animals were draped. Those who were invited into the town hall first put down their arms there, and then placed their black cloaks over them. Then six standard-bearers in traditional uniform carried their banner to the head of the procession, accompanied by young pages, also in uniform. The officials and the guests of honor marched in procession, one slow step at a time, along the street lined by townspeople, while groups of onlookers were leaning out of all the windows. I was met by everyone with the greatest enthusiasm, as if I was their own countryman who was returning home famous, whereas I would have thought that in this distant canton they would never have even heard of me. (They welcomed me not only as a writer, but as a champion fighting against evil, which the chief magistrate of the canton, the Landammann, also said in his speech.)

A provisional wooden platform had been set up on the square for all the officials, a dozen or so, who lined up on it and stood there throughout the entire ceremony in their black cloaks, their heads bare. The town square was filled with a dense crowd of *stimmberechtigte Männer*—men with the right to vote—they too with swords at their sides, their heads bare, some gray, some reddish, some white; but they were all wearing everyday clothes. The women had gathered somewhere beyond the edges of the crowd or were standing on balconies and at windows. Young people were sitting as best they could on the slanted roofs, while a photographer was picturesquely straddling a roof's gable. The chief magistrate of the canton, Landammann Raymond Broger, with grayish fuzz on his head, his face intelligent and energetic, gave a speech that filled me with wonder. If only Europe could lend its ears to its half-canton Appenzell! If only the rulers of the big nations could adopt such ideas!

For more than half a millennium, the Landammann said, our community has not significantly changed the forms by which it has governed itself. We are led by our conviction that there is no such thing as "general freedom," but only various individual freedoms, each associated with our obligations and self-restraint. On an almost daily basis, the violence of our times proves to us that the guaranteed freedom of person or state is impossible without discipline and honesty, and it is precisely on such grounds that our community has managed to perpetuate its incredible vitality through the centuries. Our community never gave itself over to the folly of total freedom, and never made a pact with inhumanity with the view of making the state almighty. There cannot be a rational functioning state without a dash of aristocratic and even monarchic elements. It goes without saying that in a democracy the ultimate judgment in all important issues falls to the people, but a people cannot be present on a daily basis to run the state. And the government must not rush to cater to the changeable popular vote just so that its rulers will be re-elected, nor must it give misleading speeches to sway the voters, but must move against the current. In deed and in truth the government's task is to act the way a reasonable majority of the people would act if they knew everything in all its details, which is becoming increasingly impossible under the growing civic overload. It therefore remains for us to elect the best possible individuals to guide and govern us, and to give them all necessary confidence. Democracy without mettle, democracy that seeks to grant rights to each and every individual, degenerates into a democracy of servility. The soundness of a system of government does not depend on the perfection of the articles of a constitution, but on the ability of leaders to bear its burdens. We sell democracy short if we elect weak individuals to its government. It is in fact the democratic system, more than any other, that requires a strong hand able to steer the state along a clear course. The crises that society is currently facing were not triggered by the people, but by their governments.

This was no ordinary April, meanwhile, but the April of 1975, a dangerous moment for the West (though the West was barely aware of it), the United States having fled Indochina. Only ten days before the election at Appenzell the naive Western press had reported: "The people of Phnom Penh have welcomed the Khmer Rouge with joy."

Therefore, on this April day it was a great surprise to hear on this sunny town square—in such a remote corner of the world, and yet at the very center of Europe—a warning of the extent to which the general danger had increased in the past year, to hear how horrifying America's behavior was in abandoning its Indochinese allies, and how horrifying was the fate of the South Vietnamese people who were fleeing their Communist "liberators" in droves. In the face of this tragedy, the Landammann continued, we ask ourselves with great concern whether America will remain loyal to its alliance with Europe, a Europe unable to fend off Soviet aggression on its own but expecting American support as if it were guaranteed. Particularly throughout the Vietnam War, anti-Americanism has grown in Europe; consequently, we must assume that in the future America will not come to the defense of any state that does not strive to protect itself. Europe must prove without delay that it is prepared to make great sacrifices and come together in an effective way.

The Landammann then criticized Switzerland for considering exorbitant its military spending that was 1.7 percent of the national budget, after which he spoke about the economy and how Switzerland was no longer a fairytale country.

After this speech and more words of welcome to his guests, the Landammann took off the large metal chain he was wearing on his chest, a symbol of his power, and gave it to the man standing next to him on the platform along with some sort of baton, and quickly left the podium. That was that. He had served out his term.

Another official, however, stepped up to where he had just been standing, and proposed that Broger be reelected for another term as Landammann. The official called for a vote, and the entire crowd of men assembled on the town square raised their hands in a single motion. The vote was not counted, the result being clear enough: Broger had been re-elected. (Here I had to suppress a chuckle: ha, democracy, *just like back home.*)

Broger returned to where he had been standing only moments before, and, raising his hand, repeated in a loud voice the oath read out by the speaker. He then put the chain on again and read out the oath for the assembled crowd to repeat, which the crowd did, the people swearing to the people!

The Landammann then began to proclaim the names of the members of his cabinet, at each name asking the crowd if there were any objections; there were none, though he seemed to be allowing only a second or two for anyone to object. I kept chuckling to myself: again *just like back home.* But I was quickly disabused. The first important law that the Landammann tried to introduce was the raising of taxes: the canton, he said, was struggling to meet its financial commitments. A rumble went through the crowd, the men conferring with one another. A speaker came up to the platform and spoke against the proposed law for five minutes. Then the Minister of Finance attempted to argue for the law, but the crowd again rumbled, voicing that it did not want to hear him out but wanted to vote. The Landammann called for a raising of hands: All those in favor?—only a few hands were raised. All those opposed?—there was a forest of hands. Hands had shot up with such energy that it was as if the crowd was flapping its wings, the vote having the force of conviction that does not exist in secret ballots. (Not to mention that there were daggers and swords hanging from every man's belt, though this was indiscernible in the crowd.)

The Landammann was quite downcast, and using, from what I could tell, his right of office, argued against the result and demanded a second vote. The crowd listened to him respectfully, but then voted as crushingly as before: taxes were not to be raised!

It was the voice of the people. The issue had been decided conclusively—without newspaper articles, television commentators, or Senate committees; this in ten minutes and for the whole year ahead.

The government now put forward a second proposal: the raising of unemployment benefits. The crowd shouted: "They should go work!" From the platform: "They can't find work!" The crowd: "They should keep looking!" There was no debate. The vote was again a crushing "no." The overwhelming majority was so unmistakable that there was no count of hands, the voters not even raising them long enough to be counted, though probably there never is a count, as the outcome is always clear enough to the eye.

There was then a third proposal put forward by the government: to admit as residents of the canton individuals, mainly Italians, who had lived in Appenzell for a number of years. There were about ten candidates. There was a separate vote for each one, and all of them, from what I could tell, were rejected as not sufficiently deserving, not accepted.

So no, this was definitely not the least bit *like back home*. Having unanimously re-elected their beloved Landammann, entrusting him with the formation of the kind of government he wanted, they immediately rejected all his major proposals. And now he is to govern! I had never seen or heard of such a democracy, and was filled with respect (especially after Landammann Broger's speech). This is the kind of democracy we could do with. (Were not perhaps our medieval town assemblies—the *veche*—very much like these?)

The Swiss Confederation, established in 1291, is in fact now the oldest democracy in the world. It did not spring from the ideas of the Enlightenment, but directly from the ancient forms of communal life. The rich, industrial, crowded cantons, however, have lost all this, conforming to Europe for many years now (and have adopted everything European from miniskirts to sexual *poses plastiques*). But in Appenzell, on the other hand, much has been kept as of old.

How great is the diversity of the Earth, and how many unknown, unseen possibilities it offers us! There is so much for us to think about for a Russia of the future—if we are only given the chance to think.

The following morning I flew to Canada, in a mood both anxious and excited. On the one hand, I was leaving with the idea of never returning (taking with me many personal things and some of my manuscripts), of finding a home in the harsh Canadian wilds, withdrawing entirely, turning away from the world that was tearing at me, and doing nothing but write and write. I no longer wanted to go somewhere to a house in the country to get away for just a week, but wanted to stay in my own home without interruptions. I was already fifty-six years old, but the main thrust of my work on *The Red Wheel* still lay ahead of me. I had to be careful that my life, with its intensity and all its outward successes, did not suddenly find itself having failed in its main task.

On the other hand, these were the fiery days of Vietnam's capitulation, and neither America nor Europe seemed to realize how much the foundations of their future were shaken in those days. The Landammann of Appenzell had, to the extent that he could, spoken courageously and openly to the continent of Europe, but who would hear him? I had spent a frenzied year in Europe, unable to strike root anywhere, unable to settle down, always on the move—and what was it that I had actually said beyond publishing *Archipelago*? Of course, it was more than enough for those who could understand, but were there really that many people in Europe who dared understand? And when I had been in France—did I manage to say all that much? My true duty is to my work, and it is in no way an attempt to shield myself when I state that I am not a politician: I do not want to be dragged into never-ending political debates, into a series of issues that to me are redundant—what I want is to choose my issues and when I will discuss them. My temperament leads me not to remain aloof, to hide in the wilderness, but on the contrary to enter the densest crowd and shout with the loudest voice.

In the next few hours this contradiction was resolved as follows: flying across the ocean, permanently as I thought, I wrote during the seven-hour flight a first draft and then a fair copy of my article "The Third World War?"

How could one fail to see? First Eastern Europe had been given to Communism on a silver platter, now East Asia, and no one was stopping Communism from advancing into the Middle East, Africa, and Latin America. Fearing a new great war, one can easily hand over the entire planet. How difficult it is, when living in prosperity, to be resolute and make sacrifices!

Aware as I was of the unreliability of the Canadian postal service that was forever on strike, I gave my letter containing the article to the Swiss steward for him to take back to Switzerland that same day.

And there already, beneath the wings, lay America.

September 2018

* Aleksandr Solzhenitsyn (1918–2008) won the 1970 Nobel Prize in Literature. These pages, written in 1978, describe Solzhenitsyn's visit to the Swiss half-canton of Appenzell in April 1975, on the eve of his first departure for North America. They were excerpted from his memoir, *Between Two Millstones, Book 1: Sketches of Exile, 1974–1978*, translated by Peter Constantine, and reprinted with permission from the University of Notre Dame Press, © 2018 by University of Notre Dame.

Bad ideas never die

David Pryce-Jones

To have a pen is to have a war, or in Voltaire's elegant wording of this aphorism, "qui plume a, guerre a." Never quite sure who might take offense at what he'd exposed, he took the precaution to live close enough to the Swiss frontier to make a dash for it if he had to. From his day to ours, this war inherent in writing has had the simplest of objectives, which is to get hold of public opinion either by describing things as they are, or by trying to prevent things being described as they are. Any infringement or limitation of discussion, any attempt at imposing a version of reality, is a sure sign that someone, some group, or some interest is pushing for privilege. In a random example that could be reproduced any day of the week, the President of Estonia was reported in a newspaper quite rightly complaining that Russian aggression against Ukraine was directed against liberal democracy, free speech, the freedom of the press, tolerance, and the rule of law, all of which he summed up as a "civilizational argument."

A fierce round in the war Voltaire considered a permanent feature in the to-and-fro of human affairs has recently been fought in London. A number of journalists had found out how to hack telephone calls, and were listening in on the private conversations of all sorts of people in the news, and then putting into print what they had eavesdropped. A young girl had disappeared, and the hacking of her mobile gave rise to false hope that she might be found when in fact she had been murdered. In the view of much of the public, free speech may be all very well, but its invasive practice in a case of this kind was evidently immoral. Tabloids feeding off distress and scandal had to be taught manners. Writers of tendentious columns uninvolved in the business of hacking delighted in scourging writers of tendentious columns accused of malpractice and brought to court. With the exception of a few loose cannons like John

Wilkes and Horatio Bottomley, British journalists have not been jailed. Several have received prison sentences for hacking. The editor of the large circulation newspaper under whose auspices most of the hacking had occurred claimed to have known nothing about it, and amid general astonishment was believed by the jury and acquitted.

Freedom of speech comes under attack from several directions. English libel laws play fast and loose with reality by severely restricting the full and truthful description of things as they are. A Saudi millionaire, for instance, was able to use the courts to stop publication of information about him that the public had every right to know. So-called hate speech is defined widely enough to impose outright prohibition on comment, and a telephone call from someone who deems himself offended by a chance remark about his religion or ethnicity is enough to involve the police. As a result of the furor about hacking, Lord Leveson, a prominent judge, was appointed to inquire into "the culture, practices and ethics of the British press." A report of 1,987 pages came up with recommendations that would in effect give politicians ultimate control over freedom of speech. Prime Minister Cameron jibbed, but the shadow of censorship is passing over the country. Like illnesses, bad habits are infectious; in the United States, the First Amendment, hitherto a reliable defender of freedom, also needs defending. Democrats have proposals for investing Congress in certain circumstances with blanket authority to censor newspapers and television reports, to ban books and films, and imprison people for their opinions.

Assorted British fifteen-minute celebrities, in the main actors and singers, have formed a pressure group to suppress what may be said about them. One who has a figurehead role in public life is Max Mosley. The son of the British fascist Sir Oswald Mosley, he participated in a sadomasochistic orgy with several prostitutes. A tabloid had been tipped off, presumably by one of the prostitutes. The whole to-do was then filmed in secret and sensationalized in print as a Nazi fantasy. A vociferous Mosley went to court to deny any element of Nazism and came up with the defense that what had occurred was between consenting adults in private. "Hacked Off," the title the group gives itself, advocates strong data protection laws, along with the introduction of Continental-type laws to protect privacy, otherwise expressed more realistically as "the right to be forgotten." Evidently here is a specious appeal for privilege. All imaginable behavior has to be indulged, free from shame and scandal, secure from the reach of comment.

In the present age, ideology has defined reality. Similar authoritarian measures were practiced in Germany and the Soviet Union and their conquered satellites: the suppression of books by burning or otherwise, compulsory membership of a writers' union instructed to permit or veto publication, the confiscation of a life's work as described for instance in Vitaly Shentalinsky's *The KGB's Literary Archive*, exile, and the ultimate penalty of death in a concentration camp for those with or without reputations alike.

To speak briefly from my own experience, as a student at the time I was allowed to attend a conference in Geneva of the Congress for Cultural Freedom. This forum had been set up by private initiative and CIA sponsorship in order to have political and cultural argument at the requisite intellectual level. The Soviet spokesman was Ilya Ehrenburg, by then an international celebrity, reputed to have a long history of survival behind him. Rumor had it that when Stalin started his post-war campaign against Jews, Ehrenburg stood up to him. Gesticulating as he spoke on this occasion, looking angry and apparently sincere, Ehrenburg denounced American and European public intellectuals as capitalist lackeys, lickspittles, and what have you. There was a certain amount of embarrassment in the hall. At lunch, he hurried over to sit with these unregenerate capitalists and talk to them in French about mutual friends, especially publishers and translators of his books. Hypocrisy was his tribute to reality.

"Freedom of speech" was the title of a conference organized in 1978 by Fritz Molden in the Austrian mountain village of Alpbach where he lived. A Wehrmacht soldier in occupied France, he had overheard German scientists discussing the V1 and V2 missiles due to be launched from Peenemünde. Taking his life into his hands, he had traveled to Switzerland in 1943 to give this intelligence to Allen Dulles and the OSS. I read the paper I'd been invited to write. The next speaker was Marcel Reich-Ranicki, famous in Germany for treating literary criticism as though he was a sergeant-major marching off the parade-ground everyone who got the drill wrong. In a falsetto voice, he started to parody my oh-so-English boy's view that free speech is an absolute that should never be compromised. Behind him on the platform, the Polish poet Zbigniew Herbert suddenly leaned forward and told him in the coarsest German to shut his trap and sit down. Reich-Ranicki broke off in mid-sentence. Afterwards I asked Zbigniew how he came to have the power to stop such a man in his tracks. He explained that by the time he had finished his first book of poems, the Communists had taken Poland over, and the Party would decide whether or not to publish this work. Reich-Ranicki, the apparatchik in charge, judged that Zbigniew's background and life-story did not fit the Communist version of reality. Telling Zbigniew that he would never be published, he advised him instead to do something socially useful like driving a tram, which Zbigniew did for a number of years. Defecting to Germany in due course, Reich-Ranicki had kept secret his past as a Party censor; and exposure of it would reveal him as an untrustworthy hypocrite.

And now swathes of the Muslim Middle East are replacing reality with ideology. Not just the leader-writers but the Friday preachers in the mosques are briefed what line to take. Speech is an aspect of policing. Setting up the Islamic Republic of Iran, Ayatollah Khomeini gave assurances that "there would be freedom of expression, pen, and views for all," whereupon he issued his fatwa condemning to death Salman Rushdie, someone not even in his jurisdiction, for his novel *The Satanic Verses*. Copies of the book were ceremonially burnt in several countries. One among thousands who have fallen victim is Hashem Shaabani, a thirty-two-year-old poet and an ethnic Arab from the Iranian province of Khuzestan. Arrested for his opinions, he explained in a letter from prison that he had always rejected violence: "I have tried to defend the legitimate right that every people in this world should have ... to live freely with full civil rights. I have never used a weapon ... except the pen." Shortly afterwards he was hanged as an "Enemy of God," an extension of Enemy of the People, the charge invented as a death sentence by Robespierre and the Committee of Public Safety.

Writing a blog advocating civil rights was "insulting Islam" in the case, also exemplary, of Raif Badawi, a Saudi in his early thirties. Acquitted of apostasy for which he would have been hanged, he was sentenced to ten years in prison, a thousand lashes, and a fine of over a quarter of a million dollars. The Turkish Prime Minister for a decade and currently the Turkish President, Recep Tayyib Erdoğan has his hands full remaking the country in his Islamist image. Falsely charging that the military was conspiring to seize power, he had 300 senior officers, the Chief of Staff in the lead, rounded up and kept in prison. Turkey is second only to China in the numbers of journalists serving prison sentences essentially because they do not share Erdoğan's sense of reality.

Radjaa Abu Dagga is a journalist sent by his employers in France to cover the latest clash between Hamas and Israel. A French national of Palestinian origins, he could call on members of his family still living in Gaza. He observed for himself that Hamas was firing missiles from crowded urban sites. Compelling local Gazans to be human shields, Hamas was playing fast and loose with Palestinian lives. To prevent Abu Dagga from publicizing this crucial and damning fact, Hamas concocted an elaborate conspiracy that he was collaborating with Israel, "objectively" at least.

Accused of such collaboration, a contested number of Gazans—anywhere between thirty and 120—have been summarily executed in public, and Abu Dagga was fortunate not to be one of them. Interrogated in a hospital that served as a protected Hamas command and control center, he was expelled from Gaza. Five or six other journalists had also witnessed the deliberate placing of human shields around missile launch pads but all were intimidated by Hamas to stay silent even when they were back at home. Protesting, the Foreign Press Association blasted Hamas's methods as "blatant, incessant, forceful, and unorthodox." But still it worked. In this completely inverted version of reality, Israeli countermeasures are made to take the blame for the inhumanity of Hamas.

American presidents and British prime ministers go out of their way to assert that Islam is a religion of peace, and that the violence now raging in Muslim countries is a perversion of the faith by a few fanatics. This is the familiar abuse of free speech to manufacture an alternative reality. President George W. Bush found it in him to say even after 9/11 that Islam "is a faith based on love, not hate ... [with] commitment to morality, and learning, and tolerance." Muslim extremists in his view had hijacked this ideal. President Obama in his Cairo speech in June 2009 said he knew that "Islam has always been a part of America's story" since its founding. Repeating himself this year, he spoke of the achievements of American Muslims in "building the very fabric of our nation and strengthening the core of our democracy." Names and examples, please.

The Istanbul Process looks like one of those initiatives that keep diplomats occupied to no meaningful end. Not so: under this aegis, the fifty-six Muslim states that form the Organization of Islamic Cooperation have held a series of closed-door conferences with the aim of extracting privileges from the West. Hillary Clinton and Catherine Ashton, at the time respectively U.S. Secretary of State and the European

Union representative for foreign affairs, were in attendance at these conferences, giving the impression that they were eager to compromise over an issue with which they should properly have had nothing to do. In particular, the United Nations Human Rights Council, no friend of the West or of free speech, passed a resolution misleadingly named "Defamation of religion." On the basis of this resolution, the OIC is attempting to internationalize Islam's blasphemy laws. Anyone who then questions or discusses Islam could be accused of blasphemy and therefore risks being sentenced to death. Along much the same track of putting out of bounds the discussion of controversial or politically incorrect topics, the European Union already treats critical observations about ethnicity as equivalent to blasphemy, as Bob Dylan discovered when he told an interviewer that "the Serbs can sense Croatian blood" and had to answer to a tribunal for it.

Willingness to negotiate the principle of free speech is a surrender of the pass. The pen has to hold the line in the permanent war against the falsification of reality.

January 2015

Dependence Day

Mark Steyn

IF I AM PESSIMISTIC about the future of liberty, it is because I am pessimistic about the strength of the English-speaking nations, which have, in profound ways, surrendered to forces at odds with their inheritance. "Declinism" is in the air, but some of us apocalyptic types are way beyond that. The United States is facing nothing so amiable and genteel as Continental-style "decline," but something more like sliding off a cliff.

In the days when I used to write for Fleet Street, a lot of readers and several of my editors accused me of being anti-British. I'm not. I'm extremely pro-British and, for that very reason, the present state of the United Kingdom is bound to cause distress. So, before I get to the bad stuff, let me just lay out the good. Insofar as the world functions at all, it's due to the Britannic inheritance. Three-sevenths of the G7 economies are nations of British descent. Two-fifths of the permanent members of the UN Security Council are—and, by the way, it should be three-fifths: The rap against the Security Council is that it's the Second World War victory parade preserved in aspic, but, if it were, Canada would have a greater claim to be there than either France or China. The reason Canada isn't is because a third Anglosphere nation and a second realm of King George VI would have made too obvious a truth usually left unstated—that the Anglosphere was the all but lone defender of civilization and of liberty. In broader geopolitical terms, the key regional powers in almost every corner of the globe are British-derived—from Australia to South Africa to India—and, even among the lesser players, as a general rule you're better off for having been exposed to British rule than not: why is Haiti Haiti and Barbados Barbados?

And of course the pre-eminent power of the age derives its political character from eighteenth-century British subjects who took English ideas a little further than the mother country was willing to go. In his sequel to Churchill's great work, *The History of the English-Speaking Peoples*, Andrew Roberts writes:

> Just as we do not today differentiate between the Roman Republic and the imperial period of the Julio-Claudians when we think of the Roman Empire, so in the future no-one will bother to make a distinction between the British Empire–led and the American Republic–led periods of English-speaking dominance between the late-eighteenth and the twenty-first centuries. It will be recognized that in the majestic sweep of history they had so much in common—and enough that separated them from everyone else—that they ought to be regarded as a single historical entity, which only scholars and pedants will try to describe separately.

If you step back for a moment, this seems obvious. There is a distinction between the "English-speaking peoples" and the rest of "the West," and at key moments in human history that distinction has proved critical.

Continental Europe has given us plenty of nice paintings and agreeable symphonies, French wine and Italian actresses and whatnot, but, for all our fetishization of multiculturalism, you can't help noticing that when it comes to the notion of a *political* West—one with a sustained commitment to liberty and democracy—the historical record looks a lot more unicultural and, indeed (given that most of these liberal democracies other than America share the same head of state), uniregal. The entire political class of Portugal, Spain, and Greece spent their childhoods living under dictatorships. So did Jacques Chirac and Angela Merkel. We forget how rare on this earth is peaceful constitutional evolution, and rarer still outside the Anglosphere.

Decline starts with the money. It always does. As Jonathan Swift put it:

> A baited banker thus desponds,
> From his own hand foresees his fall,
> They have his soul, who have his bonds;
> 'Tis like the writing on the wall.

Today the people who have America's bonds are not the people one would wish to have one's soul. As Madhav Nalapat has suggested, Beijing believes a half-millennium Western interregnum is about to come to an end, and the world will return to Chinese dominance. I think they're wrong on the latter, but right on the former. Within a decade, the United States will be spending more of the federal budget on its interest payments than on its military.

According to the CBO's 2010 long-term budget outlook, by 2020 the U.S. government will be paying between 15 and 20 percent of its revenues in debt interest—whereas defense spending will be down to between 14 and 16 percent. America will be spending more on debt interest than China, Britain, France, Russia, Japan, Germany, Saudi Arabia, India, Italy, South Korea, Brazil, Canada, Australia, Spain, Turkey, and Israel spend on their militaries *combined*. The superpower will have advanced from a nation of aircraft carriers to a nation of debt carriers.

What does that mean? In 2009, the United States spent about $665 billion on its military, the Chinese about $99 billion. If Beijing continues to buy American debt at the rate it has in recent years, then within a half-decade or so U.S. interest payments on that debt will be covering the entire cost of the Chinese military. This year, the Pentagon issued an alarming report to Congress on Beijing's massive military build-up, including new missiles, upgraded bombers, and an aircraft-carrier R&D program intended to challenge American dominance in the Pacific. What the report didn't mention is who's paying for it. Answer: Mr. and Mrs. America.

Within the next five years, the People's Liberation Army, which is the largest employer on the planet, bigger even than the U.S. Department of Community-Organizer Grant Applications, will be entirely funded by U.S. taxpayers. When they take Taiwan, suburban families in Connecticut and small businesses in Idaho will have paid for it. The existential questions for America loom now, not decades hence. What we face is not merely the decline and fall of a powerful nation but the collapse of the highly specific cultural tradition that built the modern world. It starts with the money—it always does. But the money is only the symptom. We wouldn't be this broke if we hadn't squandered our inheritance in a more profound sense.

Britain's decline also began with the money. The U.S. "Lend-Lease" program to the United Kingdom ended with the war in September 1946. London paid off the final installment of its debt in December 2006, and the Economic Secretary, Ed Balls, sent with the check a faintly surreal accompanying note thanking Washington for its support during the war. They have our soul who have our bonds: Britain and the world were more fortunate in who had London's bonds than America is seventy years later. For that reason, in terms of global order, the transition from Britannia ruling the waves to the American era, from the old lion to its transatlantic progeny, was one of the smoothest transfers of power in history—so smooth that most of us aren't quite sure when it took place. Andrew Roberts likes to pinpoint it to the middle of 1943: One month, the British had more men under arms than the Americans; the next month, the Americans had more men under arms than the British.

The baton of global leadership had been passed. And, if it didn't seem that way at the time, that's because it was as near a seamless transition as could be devised—although it was hardly "devised" at all, at least not by London. Yet we live with the benefits of that transition to this day. To take a minor but not inconsequential example, one of the critical links in the post-9/11 Afghan campaign was the British Indian Ocean Territory. As its name would suggest, it's a British dependency, but it has a U.S. military base—just one of many pinpricks on the map where the Royal Navy's Pax Britannica evolved into Washington's Pax Americana with nary a thought: from U.S. naval bases in Bermuda to the Anzus alliance down under to Norad in Cheyenne Mountain, London's military ties with its empire were assumed, effortlessly, by the United States, and life and global order went on.

One of my favorite lines from the Declaration of Independence never made it into the final text. They were Thomas Jefferson's parting words to his fellow British subjects across the ocean: "We might have been a free and great people together." But in the end, when it mattered, they were a free and great people together. Britain was eclipsed by its transatlantic offspring, by a nation with the same language, the same legal inheritance, and the same commitment to liberty.

It's not likely to go that way next time round. And "next time round" is already under way. We are coming to the end of a two-century Anglosphere dominance, and of a world whose order and prosperity many people think of as part of a broad, general trend but which, in fact, derive from a very particular cultural inheritance and may well not survive it. To point out how English the world is is, of course, a frightfully un-English thing to do. No true Englishman would ever do such a ghastly and vulgar thing. You need some sinister rootless colonial oik like me to do it. But there's a difference between genial self-effacement and contempt for one's own inheritance.

Not so long ago, Geert Wilders, the Dutch parliamentarian and soi-disant Islamophobe, flew into London and promptly got shipped back to the Netherlands as a threat to public order. After the British Government had reconsidered its stupidity, he was permitted to return and give his speech at the House of Lords—and, as foreigners often do, he quoted Winston Churchill, under the touchingly naive assumption that this would endear him to the natives. Whereas, of course, to almost all members of Britain's governing elite, quoting Churchill approvingly only confirms that you're an extremist lunatic. I had the honor a couple of years back of visiting President Bush in the White House and seeing the bust of Churchill on display in the Oval Office. When Barack Obama moved in, he ordered Churchill's bust be removed and returned to the British. Its present whereabouts are unclear. But, given what Sir Winston had to say about Islam in his book on the Sudanese campaign, the bust was almost certainly arrested at Heathrow and deported as a threat to public order.

Somewhere along the way a quintessentially British sense of self-deprecation curdled into a psychologically unhealthy self-loathing. A typical foot-of-the-page news item from *The Daily Telegraph*:

> A leading college at Cambridge University has renamed its controversial colonial-themed Empire Ball after accusations that it was "distasteful." The £136-a-head Emmanuel College ball was advertised as a celebration of "the Victorian commonwealth and all of its decadences."
>
> Students were urged to "party like it's 1899" and organisers promised a trip through the Indian Raj, Australia, the West Indies, and 19th century Hong Kong.
>
> But anti-fascist groups said the theme was "distasteful and insensitive" because of the British Empire's historical association with slavery, repression and exploitation.
>
> The Empire Ball Committee, led by presidents Richard Hilton and Jenny Unwin, has announced the word "empire" will be removed from all promotional material.

The way things are going in Britain, it would make more sense to remove the word "balls."

It's interesting to learn that "anti-fascism" now means attacking the British Empire, which stood alone against fascism in that critical year between the fall of France and Germany's invasion of Russia. And it's even sadder to have to point out the most obvious fatuity in those "anti-fascist groups" litany of evil—"the British Empire's association with slavery." The British Empire's principal association with slavery is that it abolished it. Before William Wilberforce, the British Parliament, and the brave men of the Royal Navy took up·the issue, slavery was an institution regarded by all cultures around the planet as as permanent a feature of life as the earth and sky. Britain expunged it from most of the globe.

It is pathetic but unsurprising how ignorant all these brave "anti-fascists" are. But there is a lesson here not just for Britain but for the rest of us, too: When a society loses its memory, it descends inevitably into dementia. As I always try to tell my American neighbors, national decline is at least partly psychological—and therefore what matters is accepting the psychology of decline. Thus, Hayek's greatest insight in *The Road to Serfdom*, which he wrote with an immigrant's eye on the Britain of 1944:

> There is one aspect of the change in moral values brought about by the advance of collectivism which at the present time provides special food for thought. It is that the virtues which are held less and less in esteem and which consequently become rarer are precisely those on which the British people justly prided themselves and in which they were generally agreed to excel.
>
> The virtues possessed by Anglo-Saxons in a higher degree than most other people, excepting only a few of the smaller nations, like the Swiss and the Dutch, were independence and self-reliance, individual initiative and local responsibility, the successful reliance on voluntary activity, noninterference with one's neighbor and tolerance of the different and queer, respect for custom and tradition, and a healthy suspicion of power and authority.

Within little more than half a century, almost every item on the list had been abandoned, from "independence and self-reliance" (some 40 percent of Britons receive state handouts) to "a healthy suspicion of power and authority"—the reflex response now to almost any passing inconvenience is to demand the government "do something." American exceptionalism would have to be awfully exceptional to suffer a similar expansion of government without a similar descent, in enough of the citizenry, into chronic dependency.

What happened? Britain, in John Foster Dulles's famous post-war assessment, had lost an empire but not yet found a role. Actually, Britain didn't so much "lose" the Empire: it evolved peacefully into the modern Commonwealth, which is more agreeable than the way these things usually go. Nor is it clear that modern Britain wants a role, of any kind. Rather than losing an empire, it seems to have lost its point.

This has consequences. To go back to Cambridge University's now non-imperial Empire Ball, if the cream of British education so willingly prostrates itself before ahistorical balderdash, what then of the school system's more typical charges? In cutting off two generations of students from their cultural inheritance, the British state has engaged in what we will one day come to see as a form of child abuse, one that puts a huge question mark over the future. Why be surprised that legions of British Muslims sign up for the Taliban? These are young men who went to school in Luton and West Bromwich and learned nothing of their country of nominal citizenship other than that it's responsible for racism, imperialism, colonialism, and all the other bad -isms of the world. If that's all you knew of Britain, why would you feel any allegiance to Queen and country? And what if you don't have Islam to turn to? The transformation of the British people is, in its own malign way, a remarkable achievement. Raised in schools that teach them nothing, they nevertheless pick up the gist of the matter, which is that their society is a racket founded on various historical injustices. The virtues Hayek admired? Ha! Strictly for suckers.

When William Beveridge laid out his blueprint for the modern British welfare state in 1942, his goal was the "abolition of want," to be accomplished by "cooperation between the State and the individual." In attempting to insulate the citizenry from the vicissitudes of fate, Sir William succeeded beyond his wildest dreams: want has been all but abolished. Today, fewer and fewer Britons want to work, want to marry, want to raise children, want to lead a life of any purpose or dignity. Churchill called his book *The History of the English-Speaking Peoples*—

not the English-Speaking Nations. The extraordinary role played by those nations in the creation and maintenance of the modern world derived from their human capital.

What happens when, as a matter of state policy, you debauch your human capital? The United Kingdom has the highest drug use in Europe, the highest incidence of sexually transmitted disease, the highest number of single mothers; marriage is all but defunct, except for toffs, upscale gays, and Muslims. For Americans, the quickest way to understand modern Britain is to look at what LBJ's Great Society did to the black family and imagine it applied to the general population. One-fifth of British children are raised in homes in which no adult works. Just under 900,000 people have been off sick for over a decade, claiming "sick benefits," week in, week out, for ten years and counting. "Indolence," as Machiavelli understood, is the greatest enemy of a free society, but rarely has any state embraced this oldest temptation as literally as Britain. There is almost nothing you can't get the government to pay for.

Plucked at random from *The Daily Mail*: A man of twenty-one with learning disabilities has been granted taxpayers' money to fly to Amsterdam and have sex with a prostitute. Why not? His social worker says sex is a "human right" and that his client, being a virgin, is entitled to the support of the state in claiming said right. Fortunately, a £520 million program was set up by Her Majesty's Government to "empower those with disabilities." "He's planning to do more than just have his end away," explained the social worker.

> "The girls in Amsterdam are far more protected than those on U.K. streets. Let him have some fun—I'd want to. Wouldn't you prefer that we can control this, guide him, educate him, support him to understand the process and ultimately end up satisfying his needs in a secure, licensed place where his happiness and growth as a person is the most important thing? Refusing to offer him this service would be a violation of his human rights."

And so a Dutch prostitute is able to boast that among her clients is the British Government. Talk about outsourcing: given the reputation of English womanhood, you'd have thought this would be the one job that wouldn't have to be shipped overseas. But, as Dutch hookers no doubt say, lie back and think of England—and the check they'll be mailing you.

After Big Government, after global retreat, after the loss of liberty, there is only remorseless civic disintegration. The statistics speak for themselves. The number of indictable offences per thousand people was 2.4 in 1900, climbed gradually to 9.7 in 1954, and then rocketed to 109.4 by 1992. And that official increase understates the reality: many crimes have been decriminalized (shoplifting, for example), and most crime goes unreported, and most reported crime goes uninvestigated, and most investigated crime goes unsolved, and almost all solved crime merits derisory punishment. Yet the law-breaking is merely a symptom of a larger rupture. John O'Sullivan, recalling his own hometown, said that when his grandmother ran a pub in the Liverpool docklands in the years around the First World War, there was only one occasion when someone swore in her presence. And he subsequently apologized.

"The past is a foreign country: they do things differently there." But viewed from 2010 England the day before yesterday is an alternative universe—or a lost civilization. Last year, the "Secretary of State for Children" (both an Orwellian and Huxleyite office) announced that 20,000 "problem families" would be put under twenty-four-hour CCTV supervision in their homes. As the *Daily Express* reported, "They will be monitored to ensure that children attend school, go to bed on time and eat proper meals." Orwell's government "telescreen" in every home is close to being a reality, although even he would have dismissed as too obviously absurd a nanny state that literally polices your bedtime.

For its worshippers, Big Government becomes a kind of religion: the state as church. After the London Tube bombings, Gordon Brown began mulling over the creation of what he called a "British equivalent of the U.S. Fourth of July," a new national holiday to bolster British identity. The Labour Party think-tank, the Fabian Society, proposed that the new "British Day" should be July 5th, the day the National Health Service was created. Because the essence of contemporary British identity is waiting two years for a hip operation. A national holiday every July 5th: they can call it Dependence Day.

Does the fate of the other senior Anglophone power hold broader lessons for the United States? It's not so hard to picture a paternalist technocrat of the Michael Bloomberg school covering New York in CCTV ostensibly for terrorism but also to monitor your transfats. Permanence is the illusion of every age. But you cannot wage a sustained ideological assault on your own civilization without profound consequence. Without serious course correction, we will see the end of the Anglo-American era, and the eclipse of the powers that built the modern world. Even as America's spendaholic government outspends not only America's ability to pay for itself but, by some measures, the world's; even as it follows Britain into the dank pit of transgenerational dependency, a failed education system, and unsustainable entitlements; even as it makes less and less and mortgages its future to its rivals for cheap Chinese trinkets, most Americans assume that simply because they're American they will be insulated from the consequences. There, too, are lessons from the old country. Cecil Rhodes distilled the assumptions of generations when he said that to be born a British subject was to win first prize in the lottery of life. On the eve of the Great War, in his play *Heartbreak House*, Bernard Shaw turned the thought around to taunt a British ruling class too smug and self-absorbed to see what was coming. "Do you think," he wrote, "the laws of God will be suspended in favor of England because you were born in it?"

In our time, to be born a citizen of the United States is to win first prize in the lottery of life, and, as Britons did, too many Americans assume it will always be so. Do you think the laws of God will be suspended in favor of America because you were born in it? Great convulsions lie ahead, and at the end of it we may be in a post-Anglosphere world.

January 2011

Morals & the servile mind

Kenneth Minogue

I AM IN TWO MINDS about democracy, and so is everybody else. We all agree that it is the sovereign remedy for corruption, tyranny, war, and poverty in the Third World. We would certainly tolerate no different system in our own states. Yet most people are disenchanted with the way it works. One reason is that our rulers now manage so much of our lives that they cannot help but do it badly. They have overreached. Blunder follows blunder, and we come to regard them with the same derision as those who interview them on radio and television. We love it that our rulers are—up to a point—our agents. They must account to us for what they do. And we certainly don't live in fear, because democracy involves the rule of law. Internationally, democracies are by and large a peaceful lot. They don't like war, and try to behave like "global citizens." There is much to cherish.

Yet it is hard to understand what is actually happening in our public life under the surface of public discussion. An endless flow of statistics, policies, gossip, and public relations gives us a bad case of informational overload. How does one tell what is important from what is trivial? The sheer abundance of politics—federal, state, and local—obscures as much as it illuminates. The first clarifying step must be to recognize that "democracy" in the abstract misleads us. Living in a democracy—and it is lived experience that must be our theme—becomes a different thing in each generation. Something that benefits us in one generation may no longer be a benefit in the next. Experiencing twenty-first-century democracy is radically different from what our ancestors cherished in 1901. Rising levels of prosperity, for example, change many responses. For, as Plato noted, constitutions are made out of human beings: as the generations change, so will the system.

My concern with democracy is highly specific. It begins in observing the remarkable fact that, while democracy means a government accountable to the electorate, our rulers now make *us* accountable to *them*. Most Western governments hate me smoking, or eating the wrong kind of food, or hunting foxes, or drinking too much, and these are merely the surface disapprovals, the ones that provoke legislation or public campaigns. We also borrow too much money for our personal pleasures, and many of us are very bad parents. Ministers of state have been known to instruct us in elementary matters, such as the importance of reading stories to our children. Again, many of us have unsound views about people of other races, cultures, or religions, and the distribution of our friends does not always correspond, as governments think that it ought, to the cultural diversity of our society. We must face up to the grim fact that the rulers we elect are losing patience with us.

No philosopher can contemplate this interesting situation without beginning to reflect on what it can mean. The gap between political realities and their public face is so great that the term "paradox" tends to crop up from sentence to sentence. Our rulers are theoretically "our" representatives, but they are busy turning us into the instruments of the projects *they* keep dreaming up. The business of governments, one might think, is to supply the framework of law within which we may pursue happiness on our own account. Instead, we are constantly being summoned to reform ourselves. Debt, intemperance, and incompetence in rearing our children are no doubt regrettable, but they are vices, and left alone, they will soon lead to the pain that corrects. Life is a better teacher of virtue than politicians, and most sensible governments in the past left moral faults to the churches. But democratic citizenship in the twenty-first century means receiving a stream of improving "messages" from politicians. Some may forgive these intrusions because they are so well intentioned. Who would defend prejudice, debt, or excessive drinking? The point, however, is that our rulers have no business telling us how to live. They are tiresome enough in their exercise of authority—they are intolerable when they mount the pulpit. Nor should we be in any doubt that nationalizing the moral life is the first step towards totalitarianism.

We might perhaps be more tolerant of rulers turning preachers if they were moral giants. But what citizen looks at the government today thinking how wise and virtuous it is? Public respect for politicians has long been declining, even as the population at large has been seduced into demanding political solutions to social problems. To demand help from officials we rather despise argues for a notable lack of logic in the *demos*. The statesmen of eras past have been replaced by a set of barely competent social workers eager to take over the risks of our everyday life. The electorates of earlier times would have responded to politicians seeking to bribe us with such promises with derision. Today, the *demos* votes for them.

Our rulers, then, increasingly deliberate on our behalf, and decide for us what is the right thing to do. The philosopher Socrates argued that the most important activity of a human being was reflecting on how one ought to live. Most people are not philosophers, but they cannot avoid encountering moral issues. The evident problem with democracy today is that the state is pre-empting—or "crowding out," as the economists say—our moral judgments. Nor does the state limit itself to mere principle. It instructs us on highly specific activities, ranging from health provision to sexual practices. Yet decisions about how we live are what we mean by "freedom," and freedom is incompatible with a moralizing state. That is why I am provoked to ask the question: can the moral life survive democracy?

By "the moral life," I simply mean that dimension of our inner experience in which we deliberate about our obligations to parents, children, employers, strangers, charities, sporting associations, and all the other elements of our world. We may not always devote much conscious thought to these matters, but thinking about them makes up the substance of our lives. It also constitutes the conditions of our happiness. In deliberating, and in acting on what we have decided, we discover who we are and we reveal ourselves to the world. This kind of self-management emerges from the inner life and is the stream of thoughts and decisions that make us human. To the extent that this element of our humanity has been appropriated by authority, we are all diminished, and our civilization loses the special character that has made it the dynamic animator of so much hope and happiness in modern times.

It is this element of dehumanization that has produced what I am calling "the servile mind." The charge of servility or slavishness is a serious one. It emerges from the Classical view that slaves lacked the capacity for self-movement and had to be animated by the superior class of masters. They were creatures of impulse and passion rather than of reason. Aristotle thought that some people were "natural slaves." In our democratic world, by contrast, we recognize at least some element of the "master" (which means, of course, self-managing autonomy) in everyone. Indeed, in our entirely justified hatred of slavery, we sometimes think that the passion for freedom is a constitutive drive of all human beings. Such a judgment can hardly survive the most elementary inspection of history. The experience of both traditional societies and totalitarian states in the twentieth century suggests that many people are, in most circumstances, happy to sink themselves in some collective enterprise that guides their lives and guarantees them security. It is the emergence of freedom rather than the extent of servility that needs explanation.

Servility is not an easy idea with which to operate, and it should be clear that the world we live in, being human, cannot be fully captured in ideal structures. But in understanding Western life, it is difficult to avoid contrasting courage and freedom on the one hand with servility and submission on the other. We think of freedom as being able to do what we merely want to do, but this is a condition cherished no less by the slave than by the master. When the cat's away, the mice will play! Here is the illusion that freedom is merely having a lot of options available. What freedom actually means is the capacity not only to choose but also to face the consequences of one's choice. To accept employment, to marry, to join a cause, to sustain a family, and so on, all involve responsibilities, and it is in the capacity to sustain self-chosen responsibilities, the steadiness to face up to the risks and inevitable *ennui* inseparable from a settled life, that we exhibit our freedom. And its essence is that each individual life is determined by this set of chosen commitments and virtues (whatever they may be) rather than by some set of external determinants or regulations. Independence of mind requires thinking one's own thoughts: poor things many of them may be, but they are our own, and we have found some reasons for thinking them.

The problem about identifying servility in our modern Western societies results from the assumption that freedom and independence are admirable, and their opposites not. Hence the strong human tendency to trade off freedom for some other condition of things—money, security, approval—must take on the appearance of a virtue. A further problem with servility is that its opposite might seem to be a swaggering parade of one's own independence, but this is just as likely to be a cover for a servile spirit. Since the essence of servility is dependence of mind, independence is compatible with situational caution, as in the case of the assistant to Lord Copper in Evelyn Waugh's *Scoop*, who responds to whatever idiotic remark his press baron employer might make with the words "Up to a point, Lord Copper." Wariness, tact, and hypocrisy are inevitable elements in the comic conditions of modern bourgeois life, and their significance is never obvious, even to those indulging them.

The real opposite of servility is individualism, as it has long been understood in European thought. But the very word "individuality" itself is often confused with egoistic self-interest and the pursuit of mere impulse. One needs to tread with delicacy in using any of the common words in this area. In our time, the structural rigidities that have emerged from the basic ideas of social justice and of vulnerability in contemporary society constitute a new world of servility, but the essentials of the condition were recognized nearly a century ago by Hilaire Belloc. His slightly eccentric diagnosis of the condition remains acute even in our time. The issue is how we judge the character of society. As he writes: "Society is recognized as no longer consisting of free men bargaining freely for their labor or any other commodity in their possession, but of two contrasting statuses, owners and non-owners." It is a world in which the servile seek security in avoiding the risks of life, even at the sacrifice of their freedom. And it cannot easily be recognized in action.

The social conditions of the servile mind are much less elusive than the personal. That they consist in welfare dependency has been widely recognized—even governments themselves find the resulting costs, crime, and apathy of such programs intolerable. But servility is also evident in the state's concern to protect any set of people from prejudice, offense, or danger to self-esteem. Immigrants in earlier times did not need, and many would have regarded as demeaning, the current apparatus designed to protect supposedly vulnerable people. Courage and resilience did for these people what the state now does for their successors. Such legislation, in protecting people from victimhood is, paradoxically, simultaneously an education in how to be a victim.

One of the collateral corruptions of this situation is that control must often be exercised not against those who commit whatever offense is in question, but against those who might, at the convenience of lawyers and the state, be made accountable. An employer, for example, may become accountable for sexual harassment committed by an employee because he has not provided what appears to be known as a "safe environment" for women. Employers are much more satisfactory targets for legislation and litigation, a version of the idea of "deep pockets." More generally, the duty not to offend the vulnerable classes in speech has been codified as the amorphous thing called "political correctness." As disposing of the power not only to rebuke, but also to enforce by penalties, such codification makes the codifiers our masters. We must obey less in deference to the law than from the demand to regard "correctness" as a moral virtue. To legislate opinion is itself to create a servile relationship. Codification of this kind destroys the freedom to respond to each other (within the law) as we choose.

And if it should seem that invoking servility as characterizing some of the conduct of modern Westerners is excessively dramatic, let me observe that we do actually have a vocabulary that recognizes slavishness in the everyday life of our societies. It happens, for example, when we call someone a toady, creep, wimp, careerist, or some other such denigration. Indeed, our vocabulary reveals a variety of ways in which we recognize tendencies which are quite precisely servile. Any failure to perform a public duty unless some private benefit is given, for example, is an exercise in corruption, and such corruption is a derogation of the moral life characteristic of the slave. Again, our common moral disapproval of "greed" characterizes those who go beyond the capitalist drive for the best deal, in order to gain something to which they are not entitled. This judgment implicitly invokes the charge of allowing reason to be overpowered by impulse. But of course, servility has much more evident characteristics. Let us bring them out by a contrast.

The European societies that became democracies in the course of the last two centuries understood themselves as associations of self-moving individuals. Rich and poor alike made their own arrangements within a civil society containing a large and increasing range of associations: social, charitable, religious, mutually supportive, unionized. These associations expressed that capacity for spontaneous institutional creativity which so impressed visitors to Europe, and especially to Anglophone countries. The crucial mark of independence was the ability to generate the resources needed for life without dependence on governmental subsidy, and it constituted "respectability." No doubt it was sometimes easier for the rich to sustain such independence, but moral character was the crucial point. The respectable poor in the nineteenth century recognized themselves, and were recognized by others, as having a proud sense of their independence.

The major change from the late nineteenth and early twentieth century is thus one in our very conception of society itself. In Europe, and even to some extent in the United States, it has become less an association of independent self-moving individuals than an association of vulnerable people whose needs must be met and sufferings mitigated by the power of the state. The idea of "vulnerability" has become such a cannibal of meanings that it has now acquired a remarkable range. The victims of crime were evidently vulnerable; in modern usage, however, the perpetrators of crime have also become vulnerable. The reason underlying this remarkable semantic development is that "society itself" has failed in its duty to instill decency and integrity in those who have turned to violence and crime. Here we have the most direct possible challenge to the basic idea of moral agency.

It is considerations of this sort that lead me to assimilate the moral order of Western societies in some degree to that of the slaves of the ancient world. We must today as citizens accommodate ourselves to increasing regulation and dependence on authority even to the point of falling in with the correct opinions. The moral world of the classical individualist emerged from the coherence of self-chosen commitments. His basic duty was to his own conception of himself. Contemporary moral life by contrast is marked by a greater involvement of external elements. It is not only that states regulate ever wider areas of life so that even family life becomes subject to demands for compliance. It is also that we have learned to pick up signals about respectable opinion from the responses of others—a feature of modern life that the sociologist David Riesman (in *The Lonely Crowd*) called "other directed."

"Democracy" is central to this change in our condition not because it "causes" the change, but because most changes in our moral and political sentiments will sooner or later be recommended and justified as some form of democracy. What causes what in social life is so complicated that we can hardly be sure of any particular connection; we only ever grasp parts of it. Technology and economic enterprise, the secularization of life, changing opinions, new moral tastes—many such things are implicated in these changes. But the drive to equalize the conditions of a population, to institute something called "social justice," to make society a model of "inclusion"—all such things will eventually be advanced as an element of "democracy." Household democracy is men and women equally sharing the burdens of running the household. It may also involve granting children a vote on family matters. Educational democracy consists in switching resources to the pupils currently less capable of getting good results. No remnants of hereditary constitutions are safe from this homogenizing steamroller: democratization is the most dramatic of all the corruptions of constitutionality in which separation and balance are to be replaced by a single ideal believed to solve all problems. The moral life can no more be isolated from this drive than anything else. It too must be democratized. And the result is to destroy individual agency.

Our inherited moral idiom is thus being challenged by another, in which individuals find their identifying essence in supporting public policies that are both morally obligatory and politically imperative. Such policies are, I suggest, "politico-moral." Such an attitude dramatically moralizes politics, and politicizes the moral life. It feeds on our instinctive support for good causes. Yet it also suggests that the most important sign of moral integrity, of decency and goodness, is not found in facing up to one's responsibilities, but in holding the right opinions, generally about grand abstractions such as poverty and war. This illusion might well be fingered as the ultimate servility.

Some might think that morality is of little significance, because it is merely the subjective values people adopt. No doubt sexual mores in our times are in a state of massive confusion, but no one believes that doctors can choose about putting the interests of the patient first, or accountants may legitimately make up the figures, or friends betray us. The current muddle between subjectivism about morals and dogmatism about rights, for example, merely conceals the semantic changes by which the moral is being transposed into the manipulable, leading to a gullible acquiescence in the projects of governments. These semantics cannot help but attract philosophical interest. And the philosopher had better start by observing that what we recognize as our "culture" is merely the surface of our lives, the debris left behind from our moral responses in times past. It is out of date even as it is recognized. We never step into the same culture twice.

At the end of a period of civil strife, as Tacitus tells us, Augustus Caesar established peace and security in Rome during the long period in which he ruled, ending in 14 A.D. Augustus carefully preserved the constitutional structures inherited from the republican period. Rome was still, in a sense, at the height of its power. When he died, however, the Romans discovered that a new system had quietly come into being: they had acquired a master. And what they also learned was that almost insensibly, over the long reign of Augustus, they had learned the moral practices needed for a sycophantic submission to such a figure.

The fate of the Romans under Tiberius, who followed Augustus, was alarming beyond anything even imaginable in our time, but we should not forget the broader lesson: that over long stretches of time, the moral changes that take place only become evident in the light of some unexpected crisis. It is a lesson that ought to make us wary of our easy-going and liberated ways. Our world is infinitely benign, and we are in no immediate danger of falling into the distractions and treacheries that afflicted the early days of Rome under the Principate. But we should never forget that moral change never ceases, and it takes place below, and often deeply below, the surface of a culture.

June 2010

The wisdom of "The Federalist"

Harvey Mansfield

THE WISDOM OF the American Founders does not come to us in authoritative phrases such as "Confucius says" or in what we have unfortunately come to call our "values," but mostly in the form of a Constitution. The Constitution has been best explained to us in *The Federalist*, a series of papers first written for New York newspapers by three defenders of it—Alexander Hamilton, John Jay, and James Madison. These papers contain arguments against opponents of the Constitution intended for the immediate debate over its ratification in that state in 1787–88 and also for a wider audience in the future who would read them as a book. They were neither official statements of the meaning of the Constitution nor private interpretations but somewhere in between, and, over the years, they have acquired a semi-official status both from the prominence of their authors and the quality of their explanations.

The Constitution is intended to make and maintain a free people, so it consists mostly of powers and procedures of institutions rather than goals that would tell a free people what it must do. That might seem to allow a people free to live by its "values." I put the word in quotation marks to indicate disdain for a term that Publius, the shared pseudonym of the authors of *The Federalist*, never used and would have rejected. "Values" is a recent verbal noun indicating that your goals are yours or your group's and exist by virtue of your valuing. They are particular to you and changeable when you change—for no reason you can cite. Having no reason behind them, values make no claim on the attention or agreement of others; one must either bow to them or get out of the way.

The Federalist, however, is avowedly based on political science that has a solid foundation in a permanent and fixed conception of human nature. The constitution it explains is the first actual constitution (as opposed to imaginary ones in the books of philosophers) to be based on political science, and Publius announces on the first page that the new American Constitution proposes to make an "experiment for mankind" to see whether a republic can actually be "good government" in practice as well as imagination. America will be exceptional rather than unique: exceptional in being the first to make a republic work, to prove its point by its success, thus to lead the way—rather than unique because of its values or circumstances. American exceptionalism is so far from parochialism ("British buns are best") as to tout its success to other peoples by demonstrating to them that a republic, or what we today call a liberal democracy, is a viable choice for them, not a chimera.

Political science based on human nature is capable of progress (not just change) by making new discoveries, such as those Publius finds in "modern" (i.e. sixteenth- to eighteenth-century) political science, to which the American Constitution adds a few of its own. Unfortunately, political science today consists of the study of facts without reference to values ("value-free"), which means that you supply your own values to its analysis—which means in turn that it is based on the values that practicioners bring to it. It is relative to the times, not timeless, a structure of complicated mathematical artifice built to stand on shifting sands. For the most part it accepts the "living constitution" of the Progressives, particularly Woodrow Wilson. He thought that the Constitution was an eighteenth-century document based on the Newtonian science of action and reaction and should be replaced in its animating idea by an organic, developing constitution inspired by the Darwinian science of evolution. Progressives like Wilson say they believe in progress, but they have no way to define it because they have no fixed end toward which it might evolve. They ask for a constitution that does not know where it is going, a constitution of aimless "change."

By contrast, *The Federalist* knows where it is going. What is most impressive about the political science behind it is the introspection it shows into the congenital weaknesses of republics. *The Federalist* is a partisan polemic against the Anti-Federalists, the opponents of the new Constitution. They were republicans absorbed in the defense of republics against their two great enemies, monarchy and aristocracy. They were conscious that they had just fought for their liberty against Great Britain, which was a mix of popular government with monarchy and aristocracy, and they were on the lookout for any trace of such enemies lurking in the proposed Constitution—monarchy in the executive or aristocracy in the Senate and the judiciary. They had no care for the weaknesses of republics, amply revealed in the sorry history of republics, which features instability, inaction, and surrender to tyranny. Recent experience in the Revolution and afterward had produced a situation called by Publius "almost the last stage of national humiliation" (*Federalist* 15).

America, however, was a country with a "republican genius." There was no danger from partisans of non-republican regimes because the American Tories had been chased out during the Revolution. In fact, the main danger identified in *The Federalist* was one of too much reliance on the republican tradition that called for small size, a homogeneous people, and government as close to the people as possible. The utopian theories behind the tradition that *The Federalist* disparaged were republican theories far distant from the realities of politics and human nature. It insisted, rather, that republicanism be held to the standard of "good government," meaning government that works, one that provides the energy and stability that are requirements of all government, and one that cannot be wished away with the assumption that republicanism is good in itself.

Among the republican weaknesses due to enthusiasm were: lack of a strong executive, arising from distrust of monarchy and resulting in an inability to act decisively, especially in foreign affairs; representatives valued for resembling their constituents rather than their disinterestedness; an obsolete view of federalism as demanding a league of independent states rather than a national government layered on top of state governments; no understanding of the positive role of ambition in government; and reliance on mere responsiveness in government rather than on the virtue of responsibility, which permits government to take the initiative, to take charge in a crisis, and to plan for the long term. And above all these faults, the Anti-Federalist republicans had no recognition of, let alone solution for, the most outstanding defect of republics heretofore, the problem of majority faction.

Republicans had previously understood faction as coming from a minority, an individual, or an oligarchy opposed to the majority. But the true danger comes from a *majority* that wants to do wrong, because the majority's actions and demands appear to accord with the republican principle of majority rule. A faction as defined by *The Federalist* is a number of citizens, whether a minority or a majority, united by passion or interest contrary to the rights of other citizens or against the permanent and aggregate interests of the community. This definition conveniently comprises the rights-based and utilitarian concepts often thought to be incompatible by today's political theory. Our political science is unable to recognize the problem of majority faction because this definition of it is not value-free or beyond dispute; it requires a value judgment as to what is against others' rights and what is for the public good. Making such judgments is what citizens do every day but what political scientists, keeping their distance from citizens, believe they must never do. With this modesty—or is it obtuseness?—they forswear the possibility of becoming as relevant, important, and beneficial to their country as the authors of *The Federalist*.

The Federalist's solution has two parts: the principle of "extend the sphere," so as to make a large republic, and "auxiliary precautions" within the government. The large republic is more diverse and more moderate than a small one, making it more difficult to put together a majority than when the people are homogeneous and think alike. The republican principle still demands a majority, but, in this case, it has to be composed of heterogeneous parts. Because it is more difficult to secure, it is less likely to be based on an "impulse," and thus factious. But it is not enough to make the government representative of the people; one must also divide the government in its structure by means of the separation of powers within government and federalism between the state and national governments. A divided structure enables and compels government to check itself, in addition to maintaining public accountability. The people may be inattentive to the task of holding their representatives to account, but the latter will be supplied with ambitious motives to keep a vigilant watch over their rivals.

The word "precautions" implies that checks within the government are intended mainly to prevent mischief, and that is how they are presented at first. Yet, as the argument of *The Federalist* proceeds, the three separated powers acquire the positive function of improving republican government by encouraging the diverse contributions of legislating, executing, and judging to "good government." Power is not only one thing, as we imply when saying that power checks power. There are different kinds of power—the generalizing of a legislator, the quickness and initiative of an executive, the sober legality of a judge—that need to be kept separate in order to make their full contribution to the whole of republican government. The Anti-Federalists opposed the American

Constitution because they thought it both too complex and too "consolidated," two opposite criticisms.

Publius wanted complexity for the sake of safety and consolidation (in the executive) for the sake of energy. Republican government needs both safety and energy, which one learns by being compelled to measure the requirements of republican government against those of good government. Publius assures us that any government will gain the favor of the people by providing them with good administration. Thus, when holding republican government to the standard of good government, *The Federalist* shows political science how to get its recommendations accepted by the people at the same time that it raises the sights of republicans towards the best. What starts as being necessary to survive—restrictions on republicanism—ends up as what is necessary to excel—improvements to republicanism. The new Constitution will be safer because, having addressed the non-republican standard of good government, it works better than all previous republics.

Then what is, exactly, a constitution—to be both republican and successful? "Constitution" has two meanings: limited government and a way of life. A constitution secures limited government when it is above ordinary government in order to limit it (*Federalist* 53). The constitution is held to be a fundamental law superior to the ordinary law because the constitution is made by the people and ordinary law is made by the legislature. This means that the constitution can be changed only by recourse to the people, as when the American Constitution was ratified, whereas ordinary law can be changed by the legislature.

So in the first meaning of constitution there is a hierarchy from top to bottom: First is the people, or "We the People" as the preamble to the American Constitution has it. Second comes the constitution, which has been constituted by the people, not in accordance with a higher law, nor by natural law, but in the act of constituting. John Locke, the semi-official philosopher of the Constitution (even more so than the "celebrated Montesquieu"), indicates that the word "constitution" is a verbal noun, the result of "constituting" (cf. "values"). The activity of constituting may be guided by an end, such as securing liberty, but the activity defines the constitution. Its end is not sovereign at the top of the hierarchy. Third, the legislature—that is, the legislative process that includes the executive and judiciary—established by the constitution makes the ordinary laws. And fourth come the people as citizens, who obey the laws and elect the legislature.

Thus the people are both the top and the bottom of the hierarchy; this is the magic of constitutional government. The people are sovereign, but they do not rule. Governments fashioned in this way are limited, and are constitutional; if not, they are unconstitutional. (A pretended constitution like that of the Soviet Union in 1936 does not count, for a written constitution must supply means by which the separate powers can be effective as checks.) A limited constitution cannot maintain its limits by what *The Federalist* calls "parchment barriers," limitations written on fancy paper that have no constitutional means of enforcement.

Yet it does not seem that "constitutional means" are enough to secure enforcement of limits on government. Must there not exist a way of life that demands liberty be secured and supports limits on government to that end? In this view, the constitution becomes not just a means but also an end, part of the republican way of life. So understood, the American Constitution would come in time to be "venerated," a requirement that Publius sets down in *Federalist* 49. In 1787–88 the Constitution was ratified by the people; it was their choice. Now, however, despite the airy fancies of certain professors, it seems inconceivable that the American people would abandon their Constitution and choose another. It has now become their most valuable common possession, the one that forms them. This is constitution in a second meaning, not explicit in *The Federalist*, as forming a way of life; it is constitution as structure, used in the way one speaks of a person's strong or weak biological constitution. In this sense, every country has a constitution, though it may be strong or weak, just or unjust.

The American Constitution seems to be a constitution in both senses. It has certain innovations of political science, such as the strong executive mentioned above, which enforce limitations on the legislature. But the demonstration that a republic is improved by a strong executive has perhaps influenced the American way of life as well: think of the very many instances of one-man rule by presidents and CEOs in the private sphere—even including universities—an otherwise surprising phenomenon in a republican country like America. Another example would be the way in which the Anti-Federalists, the defeated opponents of the Constitution, were nonetheless brought into the Constitution (in the second meaning) by the passage of the Bill of Rights. All this was done by one man, one could say with slight exaggeration, for James Madison is known as the "Father of the Constitution," but he was also the Father of the Bill of Rights in the First Congress. Today the Constitution is known more for the Bill of Rights that the Anti-Federalists wanted than for the more important structure of government that they unsuccessfully opposed.

Above all, the second meaning of constitution brings out the greatness of America in showing the world that a republic can succeed in being both popular and free. Americans are the can-do people, practical in their idealism, often impatient, sometimes hasty. The Constitution appeals to this desire for greatness with its use of political ambition: "Ambition must be made to counteract ambition," says *Federalist* 51. The Constitution, we know, is also based on self-interest in its reliance on the diversity of interests in a large republic. But ambition is a mixture of self-interest and honor. Why honor? Because it may not be in your interest to expose yourself to the trials and troubles of ambition. The Constitution presupposes, and demonstrates, that human beings can govern themselves rather than living as victims of historical forces or slaves to their passions. All liberty depends on political liberty, on the "honorable determination ... to rest all our political experiments on the capacity of mankind for self-government" (*Federalist* 39).

In what sense, then, does the Constitution produce limited government? No government can ignore necessities that might compel it to violate its laws; one can readily imagine military or other emergencies requiring stringent actions that might make liberties look like mere peacetime luxuries. The Constitution includes a "necessary and proper" clause in the powers of Congress, which is given a vigorous, expansive interpretation in *Federalist* 33. There, it almost seems that everything proper to do is necessary and everything necessary is proper. The Constitution, we have seen, brings necessity within itself, making everything necessary to do constitutional. It does not adopt the squeamish attitude that *this* is constitutional because it is moral and *that* is necessary to do outside the Constitution, hopefully when no one is looking. Ignoring necessity leads to ruin or to hypocrisy. If you leave necessity outside the Constitution, your principles shrivel to your wishes—your "values."

Minimal necessity becomes maximal when a republic is held to the standard of good government. Good government is not perfect, because government itself is a "reflection on human nature." Human nature is always the same, and human beings will always need government. There will be no perpetual peace, as Kant has it, and no "spontaneous order," in the theory of Friedrich Hayek. Good government consists in the rule of law, together with necessary exceptions to the rule of law.

Limited government, therefore, must be big or expandable enough to meet unpredictable necessities that may arise. Government cannot be kept small by forbidding it to do what it must do. But it can be limited to what is necessary to maintain self-government. Limited government needs to be limited not in its powers but in scope: to activities that secure liberty without usurping it. *The Federalist* is concerned to make free government strong, and it does not comment on the danger of Big Government that we face today, as Tocqueville was to do half a century later in *Democracy in America*. But both books regard political liberty as the crux of all liberty, the standard by which to measure the success of a free society.

In *The Federalist*, human nature is fixed but the Constitution is not. The Constitution is open to interpretation, but it can be amended or replaced only by the people. Nor is republican government fixed; it is open to choice by the people, to partisan dispute, to the differences between liberals and conservatives. The Constitution, therefore, is not a guarantee of good government; it is not a machine that runs itself. Each generation has the responsibility to make it a success, and the wisdom of the Founders is more a challenge to choose freely and well than a solution we have merely to accept.

February 2011

The Founders' priceless legacy

Myron Magnet

HOWEVER UNFASHIONABLE to say so at the moment, the American Founding is one of the noblest achievements of the Western Enlightenment. It created something breathtakingly new in history: a self-governing republic that protects the right of individuals—not serfs, not subjects, but equal citizens before the law—to pursue their own happiness in their own way. Who could have imagined that such a triumph would come under the violent attack that now seeks to deny and besmirch it? Whether it flies the banner of The 1619 Project, Black Lives Matter, or Critical Race Theory, the new anti-Americanism condemns the Founding Fathers' project as conceived in slavery, not liberty, and dedicated to the proposition that we can never be equal citizens with equal rights.

It is a militant anti-Americanism, too. Like the iconoclasm of the most violent English Puritans, who smashed the faces off the carved saints and angels in one sublime medieval church after another, or of the French *sans-culottes*, who dug up and desecrated nine centuries of royal bodies from their tombs in the Abbey of Saint-Denis, defacing for good measure the statues of the Old Testament kings on the façade of this first great Gothic building, today's anti-Americanism seeks to pulverize and obliterate our national past as something too offensive and obscene to have existed.

The current upheaval is the latest paroxysm of a cultural revolution that has gained momentum for half a century or more, and its trajectory from the universities to popular culture is too well known to need repeating. What I want to discuss here is the precious value of our inheritance from the Founding Fathers that today's vandals want to destroy. If they succeed—since history, even our own, doesn't always go forward and upward, despite the claims of the so-called "progressives"—we will find ourselves in a new Dark Age of constraint and superstition.

At the heart of the Founding was a thirst for liberty. In announcing our national freedom from imperial domination, the Declaration of Independence began by asserting our right to *individual* liberty. For the Founders, that liberty was not some vague abstraction. They understood it concretely, as people do who've suffered its opposite. They grasped it like those Eastern Europeans who once lived under Communist tyranny, for instance, or like Jews who survived the Holocaust.

Remember that the Plymouth Pilgrims were only the first of many who came to America to escape religious persecution. Hard as it is to believe today, British law once forbade non-Anglican Protestants from worshiping freely, and it barred them from the great universities and from political office for holding and professing the wrong beliefs. In response, thousands of Congregationalists, Presbyterians, Baptists, Quakers, and others fled. They brought with them their Dissenting tradition of governing their own congregations, and hiring and firing their own ministers—in other words, they brought to these shores a political culture of self-government. Moreover, because they were accustomed to reading the Bible and feeling free to judge its meaning for themselves—to believing that they had a direct relation to God and his word independent of any worldly institution or authority—they also brought a deeply rooted culture of individualism and personal responsibility. For them, the individual and his conscience, his freedom of thought and belief, were preeminent.

The longtime New Jersey governor and signer of the Constitution, William Livingston, for instance, wrote to readers of his hugely influential mid-eighteenth-century journal, *The Independent Reflector*, that it was "the countless Sufferings of your pious Predecessors for Liberty of Conscience, and the Right of private Judgment" that drove them "to this country, then a dreary Waste and barren Desert." One such exile for the right to think and believe for oneself was his own Presbyterian grandfather.

John Jay, our first chief justice, grippingly recalled how his grandfather, a French Protestant, returned from a foreign trading voyage to find his family and neighbors gone. Their homes were occupied by soldiers, their church destroyed, their savings confiscated. While he'd been abroad, he learned, France had revoked its toleration of Protestants. Only by luck did he sneak aboard a ship and sail away to freedom in the New World. Two of Jay's other grandparents similarly had to flee anti-Protestant persecution, one from Paris and one from Bohemia. Jay's son and biographer recounts this proudly; it was a living family tradition.

As Edmund Burke warned his fellow members of parliament four weeks before Lexington and Concord, when it was already too late, "All protestantism ... is a sort of dissent," but American Protestantism "is a refinement on the principle of resistance; it is the dissidence of dissent, and the protestantism of the protestant religion." Whatever might be the differences among the American Protestant sects, they all agree, he said, "in the communion of the spirit of liberty," so don't push them.

Long before Emma Lazarus wrote about the huddled masses yearning to breathe free, George Washington noted that, for "the poor, the needy, & the oppressed of the Earth," America was already what he called "the second Land of promise." This Promised Land offered, said James Madison, "an Asylum to the persecuted and oppressed of every Nation and Religion."

In fact, for Madison—trained at Princeton by the radical Scottish-born Presbyterian minister John Witherspoon—it was red-hot outrage over a remnant of religious oppression in the New World that drove him into a political career. Virginia, where Anglicanism was still the official, established religion until the Revolution, had jailed a group of Baptist preachers for their unorthodox religious writings. If you aren't free to think your own thoughts and believe your own beliefs, fumed Madison, you aren't free, period, since freedom is seamless. And as a practical matter, there can be no progress, either material or moral, without intellectual freedom. So when the twenty-five-year-old revolutionary took part in drafting Virginia's Declaration of Rights, he rejected its original provision for religious toleration. It's not government's business to "tolerate" somebody's belief or not. You are unconditionally free to think whatever your reason convinces you is true, government or no government—and that's what the Declaration of Rights ended up saying.

After Independence, Madison shepherded through the Virginia Legislature the Statute of Religious Freedom that Jefferson, then serving as ambassador to France, had drafted. No one can deny, Jefferson's statute declared, echoing Milton's sublime *Areopagitica* and prefiguring Mill's *On Liberty*,

> that truth is great and will prevail if left to herself; that she is the proper and sufficient antagonist to error, and has nothing to fear from the conflict unless by human interposition disarmed of her natural weapons, free argument and debate; errors ceasing to be dangerous when it is permitted freely to contradict them.

Madison would never use Jefferson's high-flown language, but he would certainly agree with his friend's sentiment that "I have sworn upon the altar of god, eternal hostility to every form of tyranny over the mind of man." These Virginia neighbors knew what it meant to individuals and to a whole culture to have to parrot an official orthodoxy, or else shut up—and they knew what further physical tyrannies such unfreedom of belief could unleash, as Milton had seen when he visited the aged Galileo, imprisoned for saying the Earth revolved around the sun. All history teaches this simple and obvious truth about freedom of thought and speech, but can one find a college administrator or newspaper editor with the courage to say this to politically correct mobs howling down unorthodox speakers or writers today? Today's slogan seems to be: speak power to truth.

The Founders' conception of liberty rested on their Lockean political philosophy, which got diffused throughout the colonies by journals like William Livingston's—ones that John Adams believed had created the real American Revolution, the decades-long revolution of sensibilities that sharpened the "principles, opinions, sentiments, and affections" of the colonists and ultimately led them to take up arms in 1775. At Princeton, Madison and his classmates were still quoting Livingston's articles twenty years after publication: talk about the political power of freedom of speech and of the press!

As Livingston paraphrased Locke, men are born free and equal into the State of Nature, endowed with rights to life, liberty, and property that come from nature "prior to all political Institution." But because fallen human nature is what it is—because the inborn "Depravity of Mankind" gives individuals a tendency to invade the "Person or Fortune" of their neighbors—"the Weak were a perpetual Prey to the Powerful" in the State of Nature. To "preserve to every Individual, the undisturbed Enjoyment of his Acquisitions, and the Security of his Person," Livingston wrote, men "entered into Society" and appointed magistrates, arming them with "the total Power" of the community to protect everybody's safety and property. Such was the origin of government.

This formulation contains several tightly compressed propositions that need unpacking. First, it includes a psychology. Men are not born with original virtue. They are not peaceful creatures, naturally living together in harmony, before the rise of capitalism or private property or racism sows strife among them. They come into the world with instinctive aggression that can lead them to oppress, rape, steal, and kill. "Man is a wolf to man," as Plautus put it, and such thinkers as Hobbes and Freud have quoted his epigram in drafting their own political philosophies.

Second, government is in essence a police power. On entering society, people authorize officials to protect their lives, liberty, and property, by force if necessary, against the predations of others. The fundamental civil right—a right guaranteed by government, that is—is to be kept safe in your home and streets.

Third, in the Founders' view, economic freedom is an inseparable component of liberty. In their Lockean political scheme, because your natural right to own the private property you have acquired or built is as absolute as your right to life and liberty, its protection by government is no less fundamental a civil right. You are free to accumulate it and do with it what you please, under government protection.

Fourth, government officials work for the citizens, not vice-versa. As Jefferson later put it, "Kings are the servants, not the proprietors of the people." If officials don't do the job government was instituted to do, or if they use the power that citizens have given them for any purpose beyond what the citizens have specified, they lose their legitimacy and, as Locke wrote and the Declaration of Independence emphasized, they can be fired. Government by expert administrators who supposedly know better than the people themselves was no part of their vision. As early as the Declaration of Independence, Jefferson was complaining that George III "has erected a Multitude of new Offices, and sent hither Swarms of Officers to harass our People, and eat out their Substance." Might as well be the EPA.

Moreover, because the money that pays officials and supports their activities comes from the property that they are hired to protect, Livingston argued that any "Tax ought to be considered as the voluntary Gift of the People, to be applied to such Uses, as they, by their Representatives shall think expedient." That's why, to make an up-to-the-minute aside, "Defund the police" is a logical incoherence. If there is no police power, there is no government, and hence no authority to collect taxes. "Defund the police" means dissolve the government.

Eighteenth-century English Whigs, also Lockeans, believed that their taxes were voluntary gifts, too, made through their elected representatives. Given England's corrupt electoral system and limited franchise, this was only a partial truth. But the American colonists, with no members of parliament, lacked even this shadow of consent. The Founding Fathers were deadly serious, therefore, when they said "Taxation without representation is tyranny!" It wasn't a metaphor when George Washington called the stamp tax and the tea tax the "most grievous and intollerable Species of Tyranny and Oppression, that ever was inflicted upon Mankind." The Continental Congressman Richard Henry Lee didn't think he was overwrought in comparing the taxes to "Egyptian bondage." In their explicitly stated view, the British government was stealing the property it was supposed to preserve.

In addition to their Lockean philosophy, the Founders had concrete historical reasons for their outrage over taxation without their consent. Their ancestors had planted a civilization in the New World wilderness on their own initiative and by their own efforts. They *did* build that!

Having forged prosperity out of wilderness, the Founders had a positive, optimistic vision of what economic liberty could achieve. It was a vision that George Washington nicely articulated. The "spirit of commerce," he noted, lies at the very heart of America's national character. How could it not, given that the country's first settlers were self-reliant, enterprising risk-takers even before they arrived? They had crossed the ocean seeking to live on their own terms and to make their own fortunes, and they created a culture of free enterprise that Washington believed should be vigorously nurtured.

Though a slave-owning Virginia planter, he was also a large-scale entrepreneur. He built a grist mill and a distillery, the latter of which became America's biggest, he set up a fishery that exported salt herring and shad internationally, and he speculated so successfully in land that he became one of the country's richest men. He had no patience with Jefferson's sentimentality about farming's moral superiority to manufacturing and finance. He had seen beyond mercantilism before the Revolution ended: yes, he remarked, Spain has rich colonial silver mines, but the truth is that "Commerce and industry are the best mines of a nation." He was the prime mover of a Potomac canal to serve as a highway for the trade of the Ohio country, and the conference he arranged at Mount Vernon for representatives of Virginia and Maryland to plan the canal led to the 1786 Annapolis Convention that in turn set up the Constitutional Convention the next year. His vision of America as "a Land of promise, with milk & honey," was a vision of opportunity for all.

As president, he fully backed Treasury Secretary Alexander Hamilton's financial program for fostering the entrepreneurial spirit and turning his dream of a land of plenty into a reality. You know the details of that plan—the funding of the national debt, the bank, the mint, all to create sufficient credit to exploit fully the vast resources of the new nation. It was the key accomplishment, after the Bill of Rights, of Washington's first term.

As important as Hamilton's economic vision was, though, his moral one was even more so. Why is it vital to have a highly developed, highly diversified economy?, he asked in his *Report on Manufactures*. The object is not just the production of more goods and services, but of human fulfillment in thinking them up and creating them. So while "a more ample and various field of enterprize" will certainly increase the wealth of the nation, it will also allow all "the diversity of talents and dispositions which discriminate men from each other" to develop to their fullest excellence. In a society with limited opportunity, he wrote, "minds of the strongest and most active powers for their proper objects … labour without effect, if confined to uncongenial pursuits." But "when all the different kinds of industry obtain in a community, each individual can find his proper element, and can call into activity the whole vigour of his nature."

To Hamilton, economics was soulcraft. As he put it, "To cherish and stimulate the activity of the human mind, by multiplying the objects of enterprise, is not among the least considerable of the expedients, by which the wealth of a nation may be promoted." To nurture human talent and realize human potential, to facilitate the pursuit of happiness: has the free enterprise system that is central to the Founding ever had a more magnificent defense? And when he came to set up the mint, Hamilton took care to issue coins of the smallest denominations, so that the humblest Americans could participate in the opportunity economy that this self-made immigrant framed.

It's a grim paradox that the Founders also valued liberty so highly because they lived amid slavery. Even the slave owners among them knew how obscenely unjust the institution was. "The whole commerce between master and slave," wrote Jefferson, "is a perpetual exercise of the most boisterous passions, the most unremitting despotism on the one part, and degrading submissions on the other." I needn't detail the toil, the sadistic punishments, the sexual exploitation, the break-up of families, the enforced ignorance, and the regulation of every aspect of life comprehended in Jefferson's decorous statement of the inhumanity of which human nature is capable.

In 1759, more than a century before the Civil War, Richard Henry Lee of Stratford Hall, later the president of the Continental Congress (and a cousin of the Stratford-born Robert E. Lee), made his maiden speech in the Virginia House of Burgesses. His message to his fellow slave-owners: *end slavery*. How can anyone who calls himself a Christian, he demanded, think that "our *fellow-creatures* . . . are no longer to be considered as created in the image of God as well as ourselves, and equally entitled to liberty and freedom by the great law of nature?"

Jefferson, who had written that all men are created equal and who had tried unsuccessfully at the age of twenty-six to persuade the colonial legislature to allow Virginians to free their slaves, wrote, in words that prefigure Lincoln's Second Inaugural,

> When the measure of their tears shall be full, when their groans shall have involved heaven itself in darkness, doubtless a god of justice will awaken to their distress, and by diffusing light and liberality among their oppressors, or at length by his exterminating thunder, manifest his attention to the things of this world, and that they are not to be left to the guidance of a blind fatality.

Like most of the Founders, he himself trusted the advance of Enlightenment to end slavery, but it was exterminating thunder that did the job, after all.

At any rate, when the young and pigheaded King George III began meddling in American affairs after decades of Britain's official policy of "salutary neglect" toward its New World colonies, the Founders had a ready explanation for his intentions. The king, concluded Washington in 1774, aimed "to make us as tame, & abject Slaves, as the Blacks we

Rule over with such arbitrary Sway"—a sentiment whose full implications it took the General a lifetime to grasp, before he left deathbed instructions to free his slaves. Even earlier, Richard Henry Lee's brother Arthur, who became one of the Revolution's foreign agents, declared, "I cannot Conceive of the Necessity of becoming a Slave, while there remains a Ditch in which one may die free." For such men, to repeat, liberty wasn't just a word. Choosing your beliefs, your thoughts, your job, your officials, your laws, your taxes; speaking your mind; being equal citizens before a law that was the same for all: how could they take these freedoms for granted?

Government, the Founders recognized, is a double-edged sword. You arm officials with the power to protect you, but those officials have the same fallen human nature as everyone else, so who is to say that they won't use that power to oppress you, as European governments oppressed the colonists' forebears? Even a democratic republic has to be run by imperfect men, and thus even it can turn into what Richard Henry Lee called an elective despotism. It's important to remember today the Founders' warning that the mere fact that you elect representatives to govern you is no guarantee of liberty. You will readily think of examples.

This danger worried the Founding Fathers constantly, and they struggled to protect their new government from it. Their first experiment was to make that government too weak to oppress them. But it was also too weak to do its chief job of protecting them. The war against Britain proved longer and harder than it needed to be, since the central government lacked authority to tax to pay soldiers or buy arms. With scanty funds, Washington's army starved and froze and died through the nightmare winters at Valley Forge, at Middlebrook, at Morristown. "To see Men without Cloathes to cover their nakedness," Washington wrote, "without Blankets to lay on, without Shoes, by which their Marches might be traced by the Blood from their feet, and almost as often without Provisions as with; Marching through frost and Snow, ... is a mark of patience and obedience which in my opinion can scarce be parallel'd." Yet they were willing to do this to uphold principles so lightly discarded today. That they won the war was a miracle, made possible by the second miracle of George Washington himself.

(Just as an aside, exploring Philadelphia years ago, I chanced upon Washington Square, an airy expanse with a marble monument at one end. Curious, I went to see what it was. A bronze statue of Washington guarded an everlasting light and a tomb, which read: "Beneath this stone rests a soldier of Washington's army who died to give you liberty." In fact, the two and a half acres of grass cover thousands more unknown soldiers who succumbed to wounds or disease. In June, some vandal desecrated the memorial with the spray-painted lie "Committed genocide.")

Well, when the Founders set out to write a new Constitution to give the federal government powers sufficient to its purpose, they did so with their hearts in their mouths. They strictly limited those powers to what they deemed absolutely essential, and they carefully spelled out what they were. They divided and subdivided power, and made each branch of government a check on the others, to guard against overreaching. They set frequent elections, gave the president a veto, and in turn made him and other officials subject to impeachment.

No one was more alive to the danger of democratic despotism than Madison. If an elected majority tramples rights to life, liberty, or property given individuals by nature or God, it is still despotism. In the most famous of the *Federalist Papers*, Number 10, Madison confronts the thought that—hold on—taxation *with* representation can be tyranny. "Those who hold, and those who are without property, have ever formed distinct interests in society," he writes. "Those who are creditors, and those who are debtors, fall under a like discrimination. A landed interest, a manufacturing interest, a mercantile interest, a moneyed interest … grow up of necessity in civilized nations, and divide them into different classes.… The regulation of these differing interests forms the principal task of modern legislation."

The heart of that task is taxation. "The apportionment of taxes on the various descriptions of property," Madison continued, "is an act which seems to require the most exact impartiality, yet there is perhaps no legislative act in which greater opportunity and temptation are given to a predominant party, to trample on the rules of justice. Every shilling with which they overburden the inferior number, is a shilling saved to their own pockets." And you can't count on enlightened statesmen, or morality or religion, to prevent such injustice. They won't.

Nor is unjust taxation the only "improper or wicked project" a democratic majority might cook up to trample the property rights of the richer minority, Madison noted. There could also be, he wrote, a "rage for paper money, for an abolition of debts, for an equal division of property." America had seen all of these, as either a threat or a reality, since the Revolution began. During the war, as Congress printed paper currency backed by nothing, inflation had soared. A dollar of gold or silver brought eight paper dollars at the start of 1779, forty-two at year's end. By then, George Washington wrote, "a waggon load of money will scarcely purchase a waggon load of provision." The General was all too aware that such inflation meant a huge transfer of wealth from creditors to debtors. Someone who long ago had bought six hundred acres from him "in the most valuable part of Virginia, that ought to have been pd. for before the money began to depreciate; nay years before the War," he complained, wanted to pay the debt in 1779 in paper money then worth no more than a year's salary for "a common Miller." Though fearful "of injuring by any example of mine the credit of our paper currency," Washington also feared that to accept the deal "is not serving the public but ... countenancing dishonesty."

As for the abolition of debts and the equal division of property, a year before the Constitutional Convention, an uprising called Shays' Rebellion gave the Founders an ominous glimpse of the property-rights invasions citizens could plot. Thousands of depression-squeezed, pitchfork-armed young farmers in western Massachusetts had tried to hijack guns from the Springfield armory to force the courts to close before judges could take their farms for tax delinquency or allow creditors to foreclose. Washington reported to Madison, quoting the Secretary of War, Henry Knox, that the rebels' "creed is, that the property of the United States has been protected from confiscation of Britain by the joint exertions of *all*, and therefore ought to be the *common property* of all." Washington's letter bristles with incredulous underlinings. Further, Knox had written him, "They are determined to annihilate all debts public & private." In that case, Washington demanded in his letter to Madison, "what security has a man of life, liberty, or property?"

Madison was just as aghast as Washington at the claim that the Revolution should bring about socialist, redistributionist *égalité*, beyond the equality of rights and equality before the law. The Founders aimed only for *liberté*. In fact, Madison insisted in *Federalist* 10, if you want liberty to pursue your own happiness in your own way, as Americans do, you are *bound* to have *in*equality, since people have different abilities and tastes. "From the protection of different and unequal faculties of acquiring property," he wrote, "the possession of different degrees and kinds of property immediately results." So the whole constitutional machinery of which he was the chief architect—the extensive republic comprising many competing and mutually opposing interests; the strictly limited, enumerated powers; the checks and balances of branch against branch, and legislative house against legislative house—all aimed to ensure that a government with the power to tax enough to fight wars effectively wouldn't be so strong that it would threaten the individual liberty and property it was instituted to protect. One of the main purposes of the Constitution, in other words, is to ensure that the unpropertied majority won't confiscate, by unjust taxation or any other means, the possessions of the propertied minority. That is what he meant by the tyranny of the majority. Thus the redistributionist welfare state of the New Deal and the War on Poverty is not an evolution from his vision but a repudiation of it, a body-snatching whose history I recount in *Clarence Thomas and the Lost Constitution* (Encounter Books, 2019).

As the Constitution's chief designer, Madison constructed his exquisitely balanced mechanism to work by the power of ambition countering ambition, and interest countering interest. A realist about human nature, he devised a government for ordinary men as they really were, not for prodigies of virtue. Perhaps because the Founders recognized that they had to work within the limits of human nature, instead of trying to change it, their revolution was the only great one that succeeded. Still, Madison conceded, there had to be at least a smidgen of virtue somewhere. If "there is not sufficient virtue among men for self-government," he wrote, then only "the chains of despotism can restrain them from destroying and devouring each other."

Washington was even more explicit about this, the last great Founding idea we need to protect: a democratic republic requires a special kind of culture, one that nurtures self-reliance and a love of liberty. Constitutions are all very well, the Founders often observed, but they are only "parchment barriers," easily breached if demagogues subvert the "spirit and letter" of the document. They can do this dramatically, in one revolutionary putsch, or they can inflict a death by a thousand cuts, gradually persuading citizens that the Constitution doesn't mean what it says but should be interpreted to mean something different, even something opposite. That's how the Framers' Constitution of limited and enumerated powers morphed into Woodrow Wilson's, FDR's, and Earl Warren's unlimited, so-called "living" one.

The ultimate safeguard against such usurpation is the vitality of America's culture of liberty. In his first State of the Union speech, Washington stressed this point, emphasizing a view universal among the Founders. The "security of a free Constitution," he said, depends on "teaching the people themselves to know and to value their own rights; to discern and provide against invasions of them; to distinguish between oppression and the necessary exercise of lawful authority; . . . to discriminate the spirit of liberty from that of licentiousness," and to unite "a speedy, but temperate vigilance against encroachments, with an inviolable respect for the laws." If citizens start to take liberty for granted, if their culture—molded by reporters and writers, preachers and teachers—starts to hold other values in higher esteem, then the spirit that gives life to the Constitution will flicker out. Americans, Washington advised, should guard against "listlessness for the preservation of natural and unalienable rights," for "no mound of parchm[en]t can be so formed as to stand against the sweeping torrent of boundless ambition on the one side, aided by the sapping current of corrupted morals on the other."

The Founders well understood, as John Adams had said, how crucial were the "principles, opinions, sentiments, and affections," of Americans to the character of our republic. That's why today's all-out effort to persuade us that America is the opposite of a shining city on a hill, that our Founding Fathers were self-interested and oppressive schemers rather than heroes, that our national enterprise has been shameful from the start, is so dangerous. For the boundless ambition, the lust for power, that Washington feared doesn't drive only the various radicals whose agitations have set our cities aflame. It also impels a powerful and ruthless competitor for world hegemony. We can't overcome these threats if we don't believe we have something precious, something worth defending. And we most emphatically have inherited just such a priceless and exceptional treasure.

November 2020

Patriotism, allegiance & the nation-state

Andrew Roberts

MIGHT I TAKE YOU BACK to the meeting of the Literary Club on the evening of Friday, April 7, 1775, which we know from Boswell's *Life of Johnson* took place in a tavern amongst "numerous company"? Other than Dr. Samuel Johnson, the other people we know to have been present were Johnson's friends Bennet Langton and the aristocrat Topham Beauclerk, as well as Sir Joshua Reynolds and Edward Gibbon. After discussing Addison's supposed lack of grasp of Italian, the non-appearances of wolves in the poems of Ossian, the differences between the Irish and Erse languages, and the effect of singing the ballad of "*Lilliburlero*" on the Glorious Revolution, the conversation got around to the subject of Patriotism. In one of his most famous remarks, Johnson "suddenly uttered, in a strong determined tone," the statement: "Patriotism is the last refuge of a scoundrel."

Now, all conservatives know well the following sentence, written by Boswell in the *Life*, though it is never quoted in the books of quotations, or by the Left which sees patriotism as the mere handmaiden to her bastard sisters nationalism, hyper-nationalism, and Fascism. What Boswell wrote of Johnson's remark was: "But let it be considered, that he did not mean a real and generous love of country, but that pretended patriotism which so many, in all ages and countries, have made a cloak for self-interest." As the conversation continued, Boswell said "that certainly all patriots were not scoundrels." This is no more than stating the obvious truth that although dogs have four legs, not every four-legged animal is a dog, so Boswell was asked—though not by Johnson—to name an exception, and Boswell named "an eminent person," whom John Wilson Croker assumes was Edmund Burke, because Boswell often ascribed the adjective "eminent" to Burke, "whom we all greatly admired."

Boswell's comment on Johnson's statement makes it clear, I believe, that the latter's general statement—which has done so much damage over the past two and a half centuries, especially coming from such a profound Tory—was in fact rooted in the specific, in particular his dislike of Lord North's ministry which lasted for twelve years from 1770 until 1782. "Sir," Johnson said of the person we can safely assume to have been Burke, who sat for Bristol as a Rockinghamite Whig, "I do not say that he is *not* honest; but we have no reason to conclude from his political conduct that he *is* honest. Were he to accept a place from this ministry, he would lose that character of firmness which he has.... This ministry is neither stable, nor grateful to their friends, as Sir Robert Walpole was."

Elsewhere in the six volumes of annotations to Boswell's *Life of Johnson*, edited by Hill and Powell in the 1930s, it seems clear that Johnson was referring not to patriotism in general, but to the false use of the term "patriotism" as employed by the faction led by John Stuart, Third Earl of Bute. That politician's program seems solely to have concentrated on trying to win office, and it seems to be of Bute that Johnson was employing the term scoundrel. So one of the phrases that we all know of Johnson's, which has been used to hang around the neck of anyone advocating a genuine love of country ever since, might have merely been a specific denunciation of a particular set of unscrupulous politicians, rather than the blanket condemnation of patriotism *per se*.

I should now like to jump forward two centuries from Johnson's dangerously all-embracing aphorism, from the London tavern of 1775 to a meeting of the Oakeshott Society in Dr. John Casey's set of rooms in Gonville and Caius College, Cambridge, in the Michaelmas term of my first year as an undergraduate, 1982. Noting that the new generation of Tory undergraduates were pro-American Thatcherites, as opposed to anti-American followers of Enoch Powell, John Casey asked us: Would we spy for the CIA if a Marxist-Leninist government of the U.K. left NATO and joined the Warsaw Pact? He asked the question only three years after Tony Benn had held senior Cabinet rank, and whilst the Trade Union movement was partly infiltrated by the Communist Party, so it was not so outlandish an idea as perhaps it sounds today.

To those of us who tried to argue that spying for the CIA did not constitute treachery against the United Kingdom, John was scathing, shooting down our arguments one by one on constitutional, ethical, moral, legal, and every other ground barring the political.

With the related issues of national identity, patriotism, and allegiance reappearing strongly since 9/11, I think it worthwhile to try to answer John Casey's conundrum a quarter of a century later, and, I hope, with more success than when I was a callow undergraduate. As a reactionary whose favorite hymn is the one the Church of England has tried to ban on grounds of hyper-nationalism, namely Sir Cecil Spring-Rice's sublime *I Vow to Thee My Country*, I was naturally disgusted when, during the opening of the London Olympics in August 2012, the Lancashire-born pop-singer Morrissey compared the national mood to that of Nazi Germany and asked if the country "has ever been quite so foul with patriotism?" (If he felt that way about the Olympics—with its opening ceremony presenting Britain's greatest achievement as having been the National Health Service—God knows how he had kept his sanity during the Diamond Jubilee.)

Yet that reference to Nazi Germany might be used as a springboard to ask a few more questions along the same lines as John Casey's in 1982. Should we consider the Stauffenberg plotters to be traitors when they attempted to assassinate their legally constituted head of state on July 20, 1944, the man President Hindenburg had chosen to be Chancellor of Germany under the German constitution as it stood in January 1933, and to whom they had all taken a personal oath of allegiance in 1934? In the same conflict, was Charles de Gaulle a traitor when he left France in June 1940 to take up arms against the legally constituted Vichy Government of France, as established by a vote of 569 to 80 with 10 abstentions in the National Assembly? Were the 7/7 plotters, who killed fifty-two innocent people on London's public transport system in 2005, also traitors, as well as murderers? How do we morally differentiate between Bashar al-Assad using violence to crush a rebellion of his own people today, using every power available to him, and Abraham Lincoln doing precisely the same thing between 1861 and 1865? Are the Free Syrian Army, and were the Confederates, traitors as well as rebels?

With Lincoln, we can argue that the president was duly elected by democratic constitutional means, a distinction that Assad clearly doesn't enjoy. Yet in a country that has never had much democracy, indeed in a region where, besides Israel and Turkey (and now, thanks to President George W. Bush, Iraq and Afghanistan), genuinely representative institutions are otherwise unknown, can we really just write off every non-democratic regime in the world as illegitimate and thus not worthy of its citizens' allegiance? If there is no historical tradition of holding meaningful elections in a country, or if, as in Saudi Arabia, those elections don't enfranchise 50 percent of the population, are we really saying that its leaders automatically and necessarily lack all legitimacy and thus the right to expect patriotic allegiance?

In his maiden speech in February 1901, as the Boer War was entering its most vicious phase, Winston Churchill ignored the ancient convention of avoiding contentious subjects and said, "If I were a Boer, I hope I should be fighting in the field." The Irish Nationalists cheered and Joseph Chamberlain commented, "That's the way to throw away seats," but it showed that he appreciated that enemies can be patriotic too. If I were an Iranian, I would one day want my country to possess the nuclear bomb, though obviously not now while it's ruled by Islamic fundamentalist terrorists who constantly threaten to use it.

Being conflicted about one's identity, where one's patriotism ultimately lies, is as old as the nation-state itself. Even worse has been the suspicion that others might be conflicted, when in fact they weren't. It was a source of discrimination against and persecution of English Roman Catholics from the Reformation to the mid-nineteenth century and of Jews in many lands throughout history, who were assumed to owe other allegiances, rather as the Sudeten Germans genuinely did at the time of the Munich crisis. We must, therefore, as a matter of simple decency as well as out of considerations of national security, get this right.

For national identity, patriotism, allegiance, and the nation-state are intimately bound up with each other, and what it means to be a good person, especially in a time of massive demographic flux. It will be interesting to see the psychological reaction of English-speaking Americans when, around the year 2050, America becomes mostly Spanish-speaking. Will Los Estados Unidos have the same levels and rights of allegiance, naturally carried over from those who had hitherto pledged allegiance to the same territory, albeit in a different tongue?

Britain has nothing like the American Pledge of Allegiance, and all attempts to introduce one are subjected to scoffing ridicule. Patriotism is supposed, somehow, to be imbibed with our mother's milk, even in a country that is taking on many of the melting pot aspects of the United States and has effectively stopped teaching the kind of history lessons needed to inculcate it. (Though I've high hopes that Michael Gove's educational reforms in England and Wales might reintroduce some aspects of narrative history, and we can escape the present situation in which 23 percent of British teenagers think that Winston Churchill was a fictional character and that Sherlock Holmes and Eleanor Rigby were real people.)

We know that the Left—especially in academia—considers patriotism and a sense of national allegiance to be a danger, a crime against the United Nations–run uniglobalism that is their ultimate goal for the planet. As we learn from Roger Kimball's *The Fortunes of Permanence*, an indispensable ur-text for modern conservatism, the philosopher Martha Nussbaum warns that "patriotic pride" is "morally dangerous"; that Amy Gutman of Princeton believes that it is "repugnant" that students be taught that they are, "above all, citizens of the United States" instead of members of what she calls a "democratic humanism"; and worst of all, that Richard Sennett of New York University has denounced "the evil of a shared national identity," while inevitably George Lipsitz of the University of California states that "In recent years refuge in patriotism has been the first resort of scoundrels of all sorts." Yet another ignorant misreading of Dr. Johnson's true meaning, flung against conservatives.

Yet in fact it can be shown—as it eloquently has been by David Pryce-Jones in his book *Treason of the Heart*—that when lack of patriotism is taken to its logical outcome, namely treachery, it can produce myriad forms of deep psychological disorder, but also that it often stems from personality defects too. From Tom Paine to Kim Philby, Pryce-Jones shows the profound moral and personal flaws in traitor after traitor, proving how they aren't just nasty pieces of work because they're traitors, but also that they were traitors because they were nasty pieces of work. Again and again treachery was not just the result of a belief in a higher loyalty than that to the nation-state, such as "the rights of Man" in Paine's case, or Marxism-Leninism in Philby's, but also of the traitors' own narcissism, alienation, perversity, viciousness, and inability to feel love—except a love for the act of betrayal itself. Pryce-Jones proves how the overlap between traitors and utter shits is simply too uniform to be coincidental, the shaded area of the Venn diagram between the two is so vast as almost to overwhelm the two subsets. Yet when we look at some of the people willing to betray the Soviet Union in the Cold War—Oleg Gordievsky, for example—we see a man suffused with love of his country, who was moreover personally admirable, and is rightly considered a hero.

So what conservatives need now is an overarching philosophy that explains these dichotomies, widens our understanding of why it is right to feel loyalty and patriotism in the West, but also why those who betrayed the USSR, or attempted to kill Hitler, or who are fighting against Assad today, are not traitors, except perhaps in the very narrowest of legal terms. We need to answer the age-old saw of when a terrorist becomes a freedom-fighter; why are the Minutemen and perhaps even the Stern Gang one thing, while al-Qaeda and the IRA are something quite different? We need, in effect, to answer John Casey's question of a quarter-century ago, which as you can see has troubled me ever since. Moreover, this theory can't simply concentrate on democracy, equality, free speech, and human rights, since people like Julian Assange and the so-called whistleblowers such as Clive Ponting will use that argument against us, and we will merely descend to the tedious postmodernist rowing over definitions of liberty.

The opening sentence of the *War Memoirs* of Charles de Gaulle—who was of course under sentence of death for treason for four years in France between 1940 and 1944—seems to me to offer the key for conservatives looking for an all-embracing theory encompassing the concepts of national identity, patriotism, allegiance, and treachery. It explains the reason why Lincoln was not a traitor, but also why Jefferson Davis was not either, why Stauffenberg was not a traitor, but why those Britons who went to fight for the Taliban against the forces of the Crown and wound up in Guantánamo Bay were and are, whereas George Washington, who also fought against the forces of the Crown, was not.

"All my life," wrote de Gaulle, "I have had a certain idea of France." This "certain idea" of the soul of his country existed quite separately from its legal entity. It was a concept of Frenchness that couldn't be defined, or at least not easily, but was nevertheless stronger than the votes of the National Assembly as it voted to dissolve the Third Republic in the auditorium of Vichy's opera house on July 10, 1940. De Gaulle's "certain idea" of France was certainly not rooted in concepts of democracy and free speech—though those of course were tangential aspects of it—but rather in the sacred blood, soil, religion, history, people, and essential Frenchness of France, the aspects that no other nation had.

French exceptionalism was never better put, and it of course immediately explains why Pétain and Laval were traitors to the true, real France, while de Gaulle was its paladin.

As de Gaulle went on to explain in his *War Memoirs*, his "certain idea" of France

> is inspired by sentiment as much as by reason. The emotional side of me tends to imagine France ... as dedicated to an exalted and exceptional destiny. Instinctively I have the feeling that Providence has created her either for complete success or for exemplary misfortunes.... In short, to my mind, France cannot be France without greatness.

Now, if we extend de Gaulle's concept to other countries in the world, conservatives will find that it works for us too. I could perfectly well spy for the CIA in a Communist Britain in the 1980s, because there is a "certain idea" of Britain rooted in her blood, soil, history, people, and essential Britishness that would have been effaced had she fallen to an anti-monarchist, atheistic, totalitarian creed like Marxism-Leninism. Claus von Stauffenberg was legally guilty as charged, but not guilty of betraying a "certain idea" of Germany, that of Beethoven and Schiller, which, as we've seen since 1945, is the true Germany. The Declaration of Independence, Bill of Rights, Constitution, and *Federalist Papers* are likewise the eloquent expressions of a "certain idea" of the nascent United States that absolves the American-born Founding Fathers from the charge of treachery.

Of course any "certain idea" has to be deeply rooted in knowledge of a country and its past, otherwise it is likely to become impossibly subjective and ultimately meaningless. The 7/7 bombers could argue, in our postmodernist, multicultural world, that their "certain idea" of Britain had nothing to do with Queen and Country, and everything to do with Islam and their interpretation of the Koran, and thus according to their "certain idea" their actions were not treacherous. That is again why history teaching in schools needs to be central to the curriculum—since only in that way can we refute such arguments—and we must support Michael Gove's efforts to return it to its rightful place in it.

Oleg Gordievsky was being true to the "certain idea" of the true Russia—the great soul of Mother Russia who was waiting to shrug off the Communist mantle after three-quarters of a century. Any brave souls who are today betraying the People's Republic of China are undoubtedly acting in accordance with the certainty that there is something far more ancient and noble in their "certain idea" of China than is represented by a Chinese Communist Party that attempted to root out Confucianism during the Cultural Revolution.

Once one appreciates that a "certain idea" of a country, an uplifting one representing its underlying true nature, is the concept to which its inhabitants also owe their allegiance over and above its present-day legal entity, then the rebels against Assad are not traitors, while Major Nidal Hasan, who carried out the Fort Hood shooting, most certainly is. No certain idea of American history, purpose, or experience can make his killing of American soldiers anything but an act of treachery to the United States.

That is also why, although it is possible to feel allegiance towards a United States of America if one is American, it is impossible for anyone to feel genuine loyalty or allegiance for a United States of Europe, or United Nations, or indeed any multi-national body. Allegiance must be rooted in the nation-state, which since the 1648 Treaty of Westphalia has been the basic building block governing advanced societies' makeup. One could feel allegiance for the Emperor Franz Josef's multiethnic Austro-Hungarian Empire, of course, but not for a soulless multinational entity like the European Union, and still less for an amorphous mass such as "The Planet" or "Mankind." One can have a "certain idea" for France or Britain or Spain or America, or even a new country like Syria or Jordan, but not for a group of countries. No one will be willing to fight and die for the European Union, and even those blue berets who fight and die for the United Nations do so with their own countries' flags on their shoulders. Part of the "certain idea" that one has for one's country is that it is indivisible. As George Canning put it at the time of the collapse of the Holy Alliance: "Things are back to a healthy state again; every nation for itself and God for us all!"

Charles de Gaulle was a clearly impossible human being; he was also a genius of sorts: to adopt Churchill's reference in his maiden speech, if I were a Frenchman I hope I would be a Gaullist. In his explanation for his treacherous actions in 1940, I see a way for conservatives to look at the seemingly complex issues of national identity, patriotism, and allegiance, and appreciate that, with common sense and a profound reverence for the past, especially for a country's soul, customs, and traditions, we can feel a "certain idea" of a country to which its citizens must remain true, quite apart from what the law might say. So, thirty years after he posed his question I can finally answer Dr. Casey by saying that I would have spied for the CIA against a Communist government of Britain, because any such entity would have already betrayed my "certain idea" of my country.

January 2013

The globalist legal agenda

Andrew C. McCarthy

HAVING ANNEXED CRIMEA as well as swaths of eastern Ukraine and Georgia, Russian strongman Vladimir Putin casts a menacing eye at the Baltics. His new favorite ally, Iran, violated President Obama's ballyhooed nuclear arms deal before the ink was dry, testing a new class of intermediate-range ballistic missiles designed to be tipped with the very nuclear warheads the mullahs deny coveting. Meanwhile, China flouts international law by constructing artificial islands to bolster its aggressive South China Sea territorial claims. In Europe, a Middle Eastern diaspora wreaks havoc on the continent, exploiting its generous laws on immigration and travel between countries while overrunning communities with Muslim settlers notoriously resistant to Western assimilation.

Rarely in modern history has the inadequacy of law to manage the jungle that is international relations been more starkly illustrated. Yet, according to the United States Supreme Court Justice Stephen Breyer, it is precisely law, as divined by judges, that can tame our tempestuous times. That the judiciary is the institution least competent and least politically accountable for the task is evidently no more an obstacle than the impotence of law itself.

Appointed to the High Court by President Bill Clinton twenty-one years ago, Justice Breyer has been a stalwart liberal—which is to say, a political "progressive" on a court that is increasingly political. He is refreshing nonetheless, even for those of us who recoil from his ideological bent, for his willingness to depart from the Court's custom of avoiding public debate. Like his colleague and philosophical counterpart Justice Antonin Scalia, Breyer is a frequent public speaker and occasional author on jurisprudential approaches to contemporary challenges. His newest book is *The Court and the World: American Law and the New Global Realities.*

The work has much in common with *Active Liberty*, Breyer's offering of a decade ago, which the Hoover Institution scholar Peter Berkowitz perceptively pegged as a rationalization of "judicial willfulness masquerading as judicial deference" to democratic self-determination. *The Court and the World* is similarly a call for judicial supremacy, this time under the guise of international "interdependence." The courts are once again pitched as an enabling agent of democratic choice, but on a supranational scale.

The world, though, is a very undemocratic place—though perhaps no more undemocratic than Supreme Court diktats that remove controversies like abortion and "same-sex marriage" from democratic resolution.

How to explain the difference between progressive pretensions to "activate" liberty—i.e., to vouchsafe "the right of all persons to enjoy liberty as we learn its meaning," as Justice Anthony Kennedy vaporously put it in imposing same-sex marriage on the nation—and progressive judging's actual effect of curtailing our freedom to live as we choose? This inversion of democracy, it turns out, flows naturally from Breyer's inversion of the judicial role—a philosophy of judging shared by a working majority of his Court, the bloc of five unelected jurists whose edicts control ever more of what was once democratic space.

"[O]ur American judicial system," he contends, should "see itself as one part of a transnational or multinational judicial enterprise." Inconveniently (but, alas, not insuperably), the only "judicial enterprise" licensed by the Constitution, from which federal judges derive their authority, is the protection of Americans from overreach by our government and the remediation of other harms inflicted by third parties in violation of laws enacted by our elected representatives.

Interpreting the law as written—an intellectual challenge that is vital to the rule of law even if not sufficiently stimulating for many a robed social engineer—is not so much an enterprise as a discipline. In our system, it is supposed to be the politically accountable branches that get to do the enterprising. Nor does the discipline of judging take on a "transnational or multinational" character merely because some small percentage of the parties implicated in legal disputes is of foreign extraction—even if, as Breyer rightly observes, modern technology has made the percentage larger by making the world smaller.

What does Breyer see as the objective of this global judicial enterprise? The advancement of "acceptance of the rule of law itself." This "rule of law," you'll no doubt be shocked to learn, bears an astonishing resemblance to the rule of *lawyers*—in particular, the judges along with the army of equally unelected transnational progressive lawyers who urge them on.

International law is especially fertile soil for growing this empire. It continuously discovers new legal rights—i.e., new progressive pieties that undermine national security, commerce, and bourgeois sensibilities—by the judicial ascertainment of "the general assent of civilized nations." And how do judges go about finding this "assent"? As Breyer matter-of-factly explains, they explore "the works of jurists and commentators who by years of labor, research, and experience, have made themselves particularly well acquainted with the subjects of which they treat."

Who needs Congress when we've got law professors?

The global "judicial enterprise" Breyer pioneers has done its greatest harm to our national defense. Tracing the history of the judiciary in wartime, Breyer invokes Cicero's aphorism, "*Silent enim leges inter arma*" ("When the cannons roar, the laws fall silent"), which is largely seen as our nation's default setting after the Constitution was adopted. This sensibly owed to the fact that the Constitution commits the conduct of warfare exclusively to the political branches. As late as the post–World War II period, Justice Robert Jackson—a giant in both the political and judicial realms—wrote for the Court:

> [T]he very nature of executive decisions as to foreign policy is political, not judicial. Such decisions are wholly confided by our Constitution to the political departments of the government, Executive and Legislative.... They are and should be undertaken only by those directly responsible to the people whose welfare they advance or imperil. They are decisions of a kind for which the Judiciary has neither aptitude, facilities, nor responsibility and have long been held to belong in the domain of political power not subject to judicial intrusion or inquiry.

Over time, nevertheless, the Court has disregarded this wisdom, a development Breyer lauds. The Court was ignored by President Lincoln when it attempted to invalidate his suspension of habeas corpus in response to dangerous insurrections by Confederate sympathizers. As Lincoln sagely put it, were the Court to have its way, "all the laws but one"—namely, habeas corpus, the right to judicial review of one's detention—would be eviscerated and the nation gravely endangered. Still, a pattern developed in which presidents were indulged in their wartime excesses—Wilson's World War I prosecutions of dissenters were particularly egregious. Civil liberties were then advanced by corrective judicial measures in the wake of war, when the crisis had passed.

Judicial passivity in wartime reached its nadir when the Court endorsed President Franklin D. Roosevelt's internment of 70,000 Americans of Japanese descent during World War II. Breyer is quite right to see the 1944 *Korematsu* decision as among the most shameful in American history. This, however, is because the abused persons were American citizens who were not shown to pose a threat and who were treated far more harshly than white American descendants of the other enemy states, Germany and Italy.

That is, the shame lies in the failure to protect non-belligerent Americans within the Court's jurisdiction. One might also take *Korematsu* as a cautionary tale about the Court's fallibility, and thus the folly of vesting it with too much power. Not Justice Breyer, though: he rationalizes the case into a summons to judicial wartime interventions on behalf of anyone anywhere—including the enemy overseas.

Thus: the War on Terror rulings. Beginning in 2004, Breyer and his progressive colleagues issued a series of decisions in which they endowed foreign enemy combatants, captured and held overseas during combat operations endorsed by Congress, with an American constitutional right to challenge their detention in court—notwithstanding that their only connection to the United States was to wage a terrorist war against her. The Court further invalidated efforts to try alien jihadist captives by military commission rather than civilian trial—notwithstanding that the use of military commissions traces back to the Revolutionary War.

The Court's usurpation of war powers denied to it by the Framers probably owes as much to our culture as to judicial imperiousness. In modern America, victory is no longer seen as the aim of warfare. With our objectives thus muddled, judicial action that compromises combat effectiveness but is portrayed as serving "human rights" is an easier sell. Moreover, our culture has eroded the privileges of citizenship and trembles at the prospect of being thought "Islamophobic." Consequently, it becomes possible to swallow the preposterous notion that the Constitution—by which Americans created a government for their protection—is intended to safeguard alien terrorists who mass-murder Americans while making war against our government's forces.

That said, the global "judicial enterprise" proceeds by undoing long-standing protocols of restraint, modesty, and deference to peer branches of government, as well as by giving American law extra-territorial application that would interfere with another country's conduct of its internal affairs.

Reading Breyer, one can be forgiven for assuming that it must simply be expected that judges should fabricate standards and meddle in governmental or business practices as necessary to reach "just" results. It would never dawn on us that the lack of standards and guidelines could signal areas into which Congress did not intend courts to intrude—or, indeed, that Congress has much to say about these matters at all—even though the Constitution makes it the master of the extent and scope of federal court jurisdiction.

For the most part, the Court thumbs its nose at Congress. In the War on Terror cases, it pleaded with Congress—in an opinion written by Breyer himself—to consult with President Bush rather than abide his unilateral resort to military detention without trial for alien terrorists. When Congress took up the justices' invitation and codified Bush's practices, the Court huffed and rejected them anyway. To bring terrorists into civilian court, it invoked a treaty (Common Article 3 of the Geneva Convention) even though treaties are political understandings between governments that do not create judicially enforceable rights. And even to bring the treaty into play, it had to pretend that the global War on Terror then being fought against alien enemies on foreign battlefields thousands of miles from the United States was somehow a conflict of a "non-international" character.

Similarly, in the "enterprise" to develop international judicial standards, the court invokes the once moribund Alien Tort Statute to resolve controversies that have utterly nothing to do with the United States—e.g., kidnapping and torture in Paraguay by the Paraguayan regime against Paraguayan citizens. To pull this off, the courts have extended beyond recognition the venerable "Law of Nations." Once reflective of a universal condemnation of piracy and crimes against diplomats, it now potentially applies to any act the judges decide should be universally condemned. And, as night follows day, it invites the judges of other nations to reciprocate: condemning American officials for actions taken in, or in defense of, the United States.

Breyer is thoughtful, amiable, accessible, and modest as one can be in advancing a supremacist program. It is almost easy to miss the casual radicalism of his underlying assumptions. He sees law as preferable to other compasses for governance—like, say, self-interest—because it is (or should be) a product of reason. But that is not the half of it. In a democracy, law reflects a singular species of reason: derived from a community's expression of its principles, from its charter and statutes by which the community declares what conduct should be forbidden, or at least regulated. The rule of law thus presupposes the existence of a community that sees itself as such, and consents to self-government as such.

Consequently, there can thus be no "rule of law" for the world. In addressing legal controversies with international dimensions, Breyer ruefully concedes that "there is no Supreme Court of the world." That, however, is beside the point. The intractable problem is that there is no "international community," globalist paeans to the contrary notwithstanding.

The world's menagerie of nation-states, federations, spheres of influence, sub-sovereign factions, insurgencies, and terror networks cannot constitute a community. Indulging the fantasy that it does is profoundly anti-democratic and hostile to individual liberty, the principle the Constitution most cherishes. Democracy and liberty must necessarily be degraded if they are to commune with authoritarian forms of governance.

So in the real world, we have conflict without community: constant competition among divergent peoples, their interests pursued by leaders accountable only to them—and often not very accountable at that. How do we arrive at consensus, or at least a *modus vivendi*, in international relations? By understanding that it is the domain not of law but of politics—diplomacy, alliances, espionage, economic pressure, and the specter or reality of force. As Justice Jackson recognized, international relations must be committed to the political branches because there are no overarching legal standards and enforcement mechanisms to govern it, no democratic representation to assure that all key decision-makers are politically accountable to the people whose lives are affected.

Of course the courts are vital, but in their place. That is not the place envisioned by Justice Breyer: global maestro. American courts, however, are a core component of our government and thus the servant, not the master, of our people. They ensure our rule of law. Thus fortified, it is the United States, not a congeries of jurists and international law professors, that remains the indispensable force for good in a troubled and dangerous world.

February 2016

II. Reputations reconsidered

The case of Stephen Greenblatt

Bruce Bawer

"FOR ME," Stephen Greenblatt once told an interviewer, "it had everything to do with the extraordinary place that Berkeley, California was. In the 1970s there was a sense of excitement, of disorder, of the dream of reconstituting the world—a sense that hierarchies were breaking down. It was a great institution for that." Greenblatt, who started his career at the institution in question, namely the University of California at Berkeley—and who now, having held since 2000 the title of John Cogan University Professor of the Humanities at Harvard, is by many accounts the most influential figure in academic literary studies—was referring to the birth of the so-called New Historicism, the "school" of criticism that he founded and that turned out to be his ticket to the top. He had been trained—at Pembroke College, Cambridge, and Yale—to be a New Critic, analyzing literary texts in a formal, dispassionate way with the goal of understanding what made them tick. But he was living, as he put it, in "an exuberant moment of generational insurgency," when some of his professors at Yale were starting to show an interest in "theory"—principally deconstructionism, that wonderful new import from France—and when he and some of his friends and colleagues at Berkeley, influenced by "the Marxist ferment of the late sixties," were "passionately reading [Walter] Benjamin and [Louis] Althusser," not to mention Michel Foucault and Raymond Williams.

Rejecting the New Criticism, Greenblatt and his crew, while unable to come to total agreement on anything so strict as a theory, decided that they shared certain attitudes and attributes, which he and Catherine Gallagher summed up as follows in *Practicing New Historicism* (2000): "the fascination with the particular, the wide-ranging curiosity, the refusal of universal aesthetic norms, and the resistance to formulating an overarching theoretical program." Literature, they affirmed, was

> not the path to a transhistorical truth, whether psychoanalytic or deconstructive or purely formal, but the key to particular historically embedded social and psychological formulations. . . . Where traditional "close readings" [in the New Critical mode] tended to build toward an intensified sense of wondering admiration, linked to the celebration of genius, new historicist readings are more often skeptical, wary, demystifying, critical, and even adversarial.

Greenblatt and company treated "culture as text"; they challenged such concepts as originality, genius, aesthetic merit, "the classics," the canon, and "major works" vs. "minor works"; and even as they sought to upend conventional approaches to literary criticism, they sought, too, to overturn what they saw as old-fashioned approaches to the telling of history, producing "counterhistories" that would amount to "assaults on the *grands récits* inherited from the last century."

If all this sounds rather vague, it's because it is. Greenblatt himself has admitted that the New Historicism "slightly resisted, and still resists, definition. If I simply say that it's about recontextualizing works, or resetting them in their cultural and historical moment, or treating them as objects of anthropological analysis—if I say any of those things, I slightly distort the origin and the impulse." He's even acknowledged that "New Historicism" was "a not particularly deeply thought-out term." The one thing that can be said with reasonable certainty about the New Historicism is that whatever it was meant to be, it was meant to be radical—a product, as well as an integral part, of the campus-centered youth rebellion of the day. "There was a moment within the discipline of literary criticism," Greenblatt has said, apparently unaware of just how embarrassingly callow it sounds, "in which it felt like a political act in itself, just to open the windows and bring other things to bear on literature." Yet there's a good deal of truth, too, in the British literary critic John Carey's suggestion that, for all their radical hype, many of the New Historicists were doing little more than "putting literature into its historical context"—something that had long been a standard element of literary criticism prior to the ascendancy of the New Critics in the mid-twentieth century. The chief difference was that New Historicists were at once insufficiently knowledgeable about history and insufficiently sensitive to literary merit.

Eager to spread their purportedly new, edgy, and impossible-to-define *modus operandi* to English departments far and near, Greenblatt and his colleagues founded a journal, *Representations*, that became their movement's flagship publication. Thus did Greenblatt help initiate the long, slow destruction of the serious study of literature in the American academy. Few people, if any, have played as significant a role in this process as he has—and few have profited from it as much, either professionally or financially. Academic fame came early: years before he had even coined the term New Historicism, Greenblatt had already come to embody—in the minds of colleagues who'd attended his guest lectures at universities on both sides of the Atlantic—a new breed of hustling, jet-setting, self-promoting English professor. (In David Lodge's 1975 novel *Changing Places*, a now-classic satire of cynical academic flim-flam artists, Greenblatt appears briefly under the name Sy Gootblatt.) Lucasta Miller has recalled that in 1988, when he spoke to a packed lecture hall at Oxford, he was a glamorous figure, "his flamboyant rhetoric, his energy and focus, even his elegant suit add[ing] up to something far removed from the tweedy understatement of the average Oxford don." A 1992 newspaper profile began as follows: "Berkeley's star English professor is the progenitor of 'the new historicism,' currently the hottest of the hot literary theories. Academics from Cambridge to Tokyo fly him in for lectures and hang on his analyses with a tenaciousness previously reserved for the mumblings of French philosophers."

Now seventy-three years old, Greenblatt has served as the President of the Modern Language Association; he's currently the general editor of both *The Norton Shakespeare* and *The Norton Anthology of English Literature*; and in addition to being perhaps the most celebrated humanities professor in America, he's also parlayed his academic celebrity into success with the general public, receiving (reportedly) at least one million-dollar advance, making the bestseller list, and winning the Pulitzer Prize, National Book Award, and last year's Holberg Prize from the Norwegian government (which included $735,000 in taxpayer funds). Yet throughout his career, he's been dogged by questions about his basic competence in several of the areas into which he's wandered. Camille Paglia said it plainly in a 2005 interview in which she lamented the supplanting of the New Criticism by the New Historicism: "the people practicing it, people like Stephen Greenblatt, they're not good historians. They're not erudite." To be sure, one point that should be made about the damage Greenblatt has done to literary studies is that he has done almost all of it indirectly: while his own work has certain merits and he writes in a style that is unquestionably more lucid than that of his theory-besotted contemporaries, the same cannot be said of most of his New Historicist protégés: as Miller has observed, Greenblatt's followers "employ dull, tautological abstractions—'the textuality of history and the history of textuality' for example" (that's a quote from the New Historicist Louis Montrose)—while "Greenblatt's own prose style is sinuous and lively." Sir Jonathan Bate, a Shakespearean at Oxford who considers Greenblatt a "clever critic" and gifted writer with "enormous panache" (yes, "panache") and an interest "in the diversity and oddity of historical forces," argues that Greenblatt's influence "is in a curious way at odds with what he really is himself. He's been followed by second-rate Marxists offering a crude model of literature being in the service of ideology."

Another point to be made about Greenblatt's influence is that it has spread beyond those who identify themselves as New Historicists and has helped shape—if that's the right word to describe something almost entirely shapeless—what is now known as Cultural Studies. As I wrote in my 2012 book *The Victims' Revolution*, Cultural Studies (the term was coined in 1964 by the British scholar Richard Hoggart) is "the soul of today's humanities—or is, rather, the empty space where that soul should be. In a time when the line between the humanities and social sciences is blurring, Cultural Studies is the prime location where that blurring is taking place." It makes sense that Cultural Studies has succeeded the New Historicism at the top of the humanities heap, because it's even more unserious, even more indefinable, even more open to *recherché* (not to say inane and capricious) topics of "study"; to an even greater extent than the New Historicists, the typical practitioner of Cultural Studies combines a breathtaking cultural and historical illiteracy with a tendency to lean on pseudo-radical tropes about Western imperialism and so forth. In sum, it's an intellectual and scholarly disaster. And its spiritual father is Stephen Greenblatt.

Originally a specialist in the twentieth century, Greenblatt soon turned his attention to Shakespeare and the Tudor era generally. In his first important book, *Renaissance Self-Fashioning: From More to Shakespeare* (1980)—he had previously published his undergraduate thesis on Waugh, Orwell, and Huxley, and his Ph.D. dissertation on Sir Walter

Raleigh—Greenblatt subjected the Bard and some of his contemporaries to a critical discussion focused on the New Historicist concept of "self-fashioning." The term became so trendy that it has its own Wikipedia entry: self-fashioning, the online encyclopedia informs us, describes "the process of constructing one's identity and public persona according to a set of socially acceptable standards" and reflects a "conscious effort to strive to imitate a praised model in society." *Renaissance Self-Fashioning* ("the book in which I first found my own voice") starts off interestingly enough, with an engagingly detailed analysis of *The Ambassadors*, a Holbein painting of two noblemen. The analysis doesn't read like the work of some academic who's bent on selling a new school of criticism but rather like something that could have been written decades ago by any intelligent art critic. From Holbein, however, Greenblatt shifts to Thomas More, and this is where things get odd: quoting short, obscure fragments of More's writing, Greenblatt interprets them in a way that involves a great deal of dubious speculation, and uses his interpretations to leap to conclusions not just about More himself but about the supposed centrality of "self-fashioning" to life in Tudor times. Greenblatt may be talking about literature and art, but only so that he can pontificate about identity-creation, social roles, and, ultimately, individuals' ways of dealing with the power structures of the societies in which they live.

Greenblatt goes on to read More's *Utopia*, very curiously, as an act of self-criticism. Try to follow this: what we would regard as the real More, based on what we know about his life, is, for Greenblatt, a "self-fashioned" More, a fake More, a factitious image self-consciously concocted and theatrically incarnated by More in order that he might thrive in Henry VIII's court and country. It is not in More's biography, then, but in *Utopia* that we can discover the lineaments of the *real* More: for in this book, writes Greenblatt, More imagined a society in which he would have been free to be his true self, and consequently truly happy. More's kind of "performance," we are meant to understand, was typical of the Renaissance, when people in a wide range of social positions, liberated from what Greenblatt views as lockstep medieval restrictions on personal self-presentation, grasped "the role of human autonomy in the construction of identity" and took advantage of it to devise their own public selves. But was the Renaissance really, as this might imply, a time of new individual "power" and "freedom"? No, says Greenblatt, because then, as in every era, the acts of "fashioning oneself and being fashioned by cultural institutions" were "inseparably intertwined," making people always and everywhere "remarkably unfree," the "ideological product[s] of the relations of power in a particular society."

Power, power, power: it's all familiar, and tiresome, postmodern schtick, of course. Fortunately, Greenblatt's thesis doesn't force itself on you on every page, and you don't have to buy into it to get something out of the book here and there. It's possible to read with pleasure, for example, such set pieces as the opening passage on Holbein, while fully discounting Greenblatt's argument about "self-fashioning," or, alternatively, seeing his thesis as somewhat valid in certain instances while recognizing at other points that it's being rather crudely forced upon the material. At times, indeed, one suspects that Greenblatt is pushing his thesis in order to preserve and enhance his street cred as a cutting-edge, Foucault-influenced academic, even as he's engaged in critical activities that are, to a considerable extent, thoroughly conventional.

Greenblatt continued down the same road in *Shakespearean Negotiations* (1988) and *Hamlet in Purgatory* (2001), although several critics did notice that the latter book indicated at least the beginning of a turn away from the New Historicism: having previously denigrated literary greatness and exalted ideology, Greenblatt now extolled the former and played down the latter (so much so that Robert Alter, reviewing the book in *The New York Times*, applauded Greenblatt for resurrecting exactly that which he and his acolytes had striven to undermine: "This sort of appreciation of the distinctive 'magical intensity' of the poetic imagination has been eroded by many of the recent fashions in literary studies"). Greenblatt pretty much completely jettisoned the New Historicism in *Will in the World: How Shakespeare Became Shakespeare* (2004), for which the Berkeley rebel-turned Harvard eminento reportedly collected that aforementioned million-dollar advance. Frankly (if not shamelessly) tailored to a general audience, it became a major bestseller; reading it, you'd never know that its author had founded a purportedly radical critical movement that questioned the very concept of literary greatness. For *Will in the World* isn't only a celebration of Shakespeare's greatness but a flight from radicalism by a patently cynical author who's determined to give middlebrow readers exactly what they want.

Now, as everyone knows, the challenge that has always confronted any would-be chronicler of the Bard's life is the lack of solid information about it. For that reason, all Shakespeare biographers have been obliged to speculate to a certain degree. But Greenblatt, eager to fill all the gaps in the narrative and thus provide his customers with a dramatic, novelistic tale in which the protagonist is as real as real can be, takes speculation to a new level. Colm Tóibín, noting in his review of *Will in the World* that "[a]lmost every step" Greenblatt takes in reconstructing Shakespeare's life "involves a step backward into conjecture and a further step sometimes into pure foolishness," provided an example from the book's early pages:

> Greenblatt discovers, for example, that Shakespeare's father in his official capacity was responsible for paying two groups of touring players who came to the town in 1569. Would the father "have taken his 5-year-old son to see the show?" Greenblatt asks. The answer is as emphatic as the question is banal: We do not know. In the following paragraph, nonetheless, Greenblatt writes as though Shakespeare had in fact attended the play. "His son, intelligent, quick and sensitive, would have stood between his father's legs. For the first time in his life William Shakespeare watched a play."

This placement in the reader's mind of a vivid image of the five-year-old Will watching his first play—an image with no basis whatsoever in the documentary record—exemplifies Greenblatt's procedure throughout this book. Drawing on equally scanty evidence, Greenblatt decides, among much else, that Shakespeare was a friend and follower of the Catholic martyr Edmund Campion and that he was obsessed with making money and accumulating property. Greenblatt spends half a page on a last will and testament that turns out not to have anything at all to do with Shakespeare but that simply mentions somebody else with a similar name. He drags into the book anecdotes and personal details about contemporaries whom Shakespeare "might have" met, events he "might have" witnessed, and so on, all with an eye to shaping an image of the playwright. Again and again, he serves up speculations built on speculations built on speculations: was Shakespeare's father a secret Catholic? If so, was he a Catholic for only part of his life, and Protestant for another part? Or was he, in some distinctive way that was perhaps anticipatory of later Anglicanism, "both Catholic and Protestant"? In any event, how much did his son know about—and share—his religious leanings? If

Shakespeare did know about them, or even share them, did this have anything to do with certain characterizations, settings, plots, and lines in this or that play?

Some of Greenblatt's biographical speculation, admittedly, seems reasonable enough and even helps illuminate Elizabethan life; too much of it, however, is much less valuable, and makes you wish you were reading about Shakespeare's plays instead of about the few scraps of public documents he and those close to him left behind (and not just reading about those documents, moreover, but reading about everything Greenblatt has decided to read into them). Repeatedly, and with wild abandon, Greenblatt does the very thing all of us were warned never to do when we studied literary criticism under the New Critics—he pulls out specific lines, incidents, and details of character from works by Shakespeare and uses them to draw all kinds of conclusions about the author's life. For instance, he attributes various devices in *Hamlet* (such as the use of a ghost) to sundry personal reasons ranging from Shakespeare's grief over his son's death to his supposed dissatisfaction over the abolition of the doctrine of purgatory under Queen Elizabeth. Greenblatt's discussion of *Hamlet* itself is often absorbing, but every time he tries to squeeze some biographical significance out of it, the effort feels strained and unconvincing.

Similarly, it's interesting when Greenblatt ponders "the centrality of wooing" in Shakespeare's works, the number of marriages in Shakespeare that are "forced upon one party or another," and the "terrifying" nature of the two truly strong marriages in Shakespeare's plays (Claudius and Gertrude and the Macbeths). But then he uses all this as a reason to speculate at length about Shakespeare's own marriage—and it just seems harebrained and boring. Shakespeare, he maintains, had "an overall diffidence in depicting marriages." Is it permissible to say of a pronouncement by Harvard's John Cogan University Professor of the Humanities that it sounds just plain silly? "It is difficult," asserts Greenblatt, "*not* to read his works in the context of his decision to live for most of a long marriage away from his wife." No, not that difficult, at least to anyone trained in the New Criticism. And there's more:

> Perhaps, for whatever reason, Shakespeare feared to be taken in fully by his spouse or by anyone else; perhaps he could not let

> anyone so completely in; or perhaps he simply made a disastrous mistake, when he [married at] eighteen, and had to live with the consequences as a husband and as a writer. Most couples, he may have told himself, are mismatched, even couples marrying for love; you should never marry in haste; a young man should not marry an older woman; a marriage under compulsion—"wedlock forcèd"—is a hell. And perhaps, beyond these, he told himself, in imagining *Hamlet* and *Macbeth*, *Othello* and *The Winter's Tale*, that marital intimacy is dangerous, that the very dream is a threat.

Yes—perhaps, perhaps, perhaps. The bottom line is that Greenblatt, for whatever reason, has decided that Anne Hathaway was a nasty piece of work and that Shakespeare's marriage to her was unhappy. Over to John Carey: *Will in the World* "would seem, to any self-respecting 1980s new historicist, so old-fashioned as to be feeble-minded." But the book's most sensational review came from Edinburgh University's Alastair Fowler, a top-flight Shakespearean, who thundered in the *Times Literary Supplement* that Greenblatt was giving his readers "toy history" and had "a mind quite innocent of English history."

But the controversy stirred up by *Will in the World* was nothing compared to that which erupted upon the publication of *The Swerve: How the World Became Modern* (2011). If in *Will in the World* Greenblatt had had the nerve to try to flesh out Shakespeare based on very little evidence, in *The Swerve* he did something even more audacious: he claimed to have uncovered the previously unrecognized secret of how the Middle Ages gave way to the Renaissance and, eventually, what we now think of as the modern world. The story he tells in *The Swerve* is that of Poggio Bracciolini, a Florentine monk, humanist, and bibliophile who worked for the Pope and who, while visiting a German monastery in 1417, ran across a copy of *De Rerum Natura* (*On the Nature of Things*) by Lucretius, the first-century B.C. Roman poet, which he took home with him, copied, and distributed. Lucretius's poem is an expression of Epicurean philosophy, which Greenblatt sums up in a couple of dozen statements, among them: "Everything is made of invisible particles." "All particles are in motion and in an infinite void." "The universe has no creator or designer." "Nature ceaselessly experiments." "The universe was not created for or about humans." "The soul dies." "There is no afterlife." "All organized religions are superstitious." Greenblatt would have us believe that Lucretius's philosophy was by far the closest the ancient world came to the mindset of people living today in secular liberal democracies, and that Poggio's discovery of *De Rerum Natura* set off the Renaissance and made the modern world possible. The title *The Swerve* refers to Lucretius's statement that "[e]verything comes into being as a result of a swerve" (*clinamen* in Latin), meaning "an unforeseen deviation from the direct trajectory." For Greenblatt, Poggio's discovery of Lucretius's book, and its impact on Western civilization, represented just such a swerve, turning Western civilization away from where it had been headed (i.e., "toward oblivion") and aiming it in the direction of modernity.

Like *Will in the World*, *The Swerve* received glowing reviews in general-audience publications and became a bestseller. It also won a Pulitzer Prize. It's a terrific read. The only problem with it is that it's a barefaced lie from beginning to end—drastically simplifying and distorting history for the sake of a gripping story. First of all, Greenblatt wants us to believe certain flatly untrue things about the Middle Ages—for example, that during that period everyone "turn[ed] away from reading and writing" and the culture of ancient Greece and Rome was essentially lost. On the contrary, books were revered and classical authors such as Aristotle, Virgil, and Ovid were a staple of scholarly studies. Likewise, Greenblatt depicts medieval Europeans as gripped by "a hatred of pleasure-seeking, a vision of God's providential rage and an obsession with the afterlife." But no one who's ever taken a course in medieval literature would buy that picture, and no respected historian has painted such an unequivocally dark view of the Middle Ages in generations.

Second, Greenblatt wants us to see Lucretius as the very model of modernity—a distant mirror, as it were, of our own contemporary selves and sensibilities. Yes, Lucretius wrote a number of things that atheists today would agree with, and he anticipated, sort of, some of the basic discoveries of modern physics. But in order to depict Lucretius as the father of the modern world, Greenblatt has to drop the very heart of Epicureanism down the memory hole. I'm referring to *ataraxia*, which for Epicureans meant cultivating a state of serenity in which one is emotionally impervious to absolutely everything, including the suffering and death of others. As Laura Saetveit Miles, a medievalist, wrote last year in a splendid takedown of *The Swerve*, Lucretius's poem "actually proposes an apathetic, anesthetized calm that is as incompatible with empathy, compassion, affection, bodily pleasure, or joyful happiness as it is with pain." Just as Alastair Fowler called *Will in the World* "toy history," so Miles accused Greenblatt, in *The Swerve*, of "dumbing down the complexities of history and religion" and "rewriting history to fit a detective story."

Third, what about Greenblatt's insistence that this philosophy, thanks to Poggio's discovery, spread around Europe and ultimately triggered the Renaissance? Quite simply, there's no evidence for it whatsoever. As John Monfasani, a professor at SUNY Albany, wrote, *The Swerve* "purports to tell us how the Renaissance began. Yet nowhere does it do so." Yes, noted Monfasani, there were fans of Epicureanism in the fifteenth century, but they learned about it from Cicero and others, not Lucretius. In any event, the works of the Skeptics, who had vastly outnumbered the Epicureans in classical Rome, played a far more significant role in shaping the Renaissance than Epicureanism did. Furthermore, several historians have pointed out that the very idea that Poggio "rescued" or "discovered" *De Rerum Natura* is absurd: two manuscripts of it, produced during the ninth-century "Carolingian Renaissance," existed, and still exist, in the library at Leiden University, and scholars before and after Poggio are known to have quoted from them.

Surely Greenblatt did enough homework to know all these things, but if he'd told us any of them, it would have ruined his story. And what kind of story is it to read? Miles herself admits to having been swept up by it, only to realize, upon finishing it and thinking about it, that she'd been taken in by a "dangerous" book. Same here. Greenblatt takes history, which in and of itself cannot help being fascinating when told well and honestly, and reduces it to a cheesy potboiler. How, you ask, can a purportedly distinguished Harvard professor lower himself to serving up such dishonest swill? Reading *Will in the World* and, especially, *The Swerve*, I couldn't help feeling that for somebody who had been at Yale when the Gallic smog of deconstruction was beginning to poison the New Haven air with its fashionable questioning of objective, absolute truth, and who at Berkeley had led a coterie of academic rebels determined not to build on known truths but to challenge received views (not, mind you, for the sake of truth, but for the sake of challenge itself), telling outright lies about history might not be all that big a stretch. It could be, quite simply, that the truth doesn't matter as much to Greenblatt as a good, rousing story.

This thought was still lingering in my mind when I dove into Greenblatt's newest product, *The Rise and Fall of Adam and Eve.* As it happens, the book opens with an autobiographical introduction in which he remembers recognizing, as a child, that something his family rabbi said was untrue. His immediate reaction was: "I have been lied to." But that incident also engendered a lifelong fascination with "the stories that we humans invent in an attempt to make sense of our existence." He has "come to understand," he writes, "that the term 'lie' is a woefully inadequate description of either the content or the motive of these stories.... Humans cannot live without stories." And one of those vital stories, he argues in *The Rise and Fall of Adam and Eve*, is that of the Garden of Eden—and his aim here is to chronicle the ways in which Jews and Christians have viewed Adam and Eve over the millennia.

It's a long slog. Greenblatt tells us about non-canonical ancient texts that expanded on the Genesis story of Adam and Eve; about early Christians who debated whether or not to accept that story as canonical; about Origen and other ancients who read it as symbolic; about the insistence by Augustine on its literal truth, an insistence that was inextricable from his own fixation on carnal sin; about Jerome's influential argument that Eve, not Adam, was responsible for the Fall, and that all women shared in her guilt; about the depiction of Adam and Eve in medieval art, especially that of Albrecht Dürer, who forged "the most influential contribution to the image of Adam and Eve"; and about *Paradise Lost*, which "forever transformed the ancient narrative," giving Adam and Eve "a more intense life ... than they had ever possessed in the thousands of years since they were first conceived."

From Milton, Greenblatt moves on, rather meanderingly, to the "tremors," in the Renaissance and afterwards, "that began to cause cracks in the Bible's origin story," compelling more and more Christians to view it as allegorical; to Voltaire's animus toward the Adam and Eve story; to the Mormons' insistence that Eden lay in the western United States; to Mark Twain's mockery of the Garden of Eden story; and—boom!—to the explosion that was Darwin. The book's long, anticlimactic final chapter finds Greenblatt in the jungle of Uganda, where he encounters chimpanzees and imagines that he is in some kind of Eden; this bemusing *envoi* is followed by not one but two appendices, the first of which compiles interpretations of Adam and Eve by figures ranging from Duns Scotus to John Calvin and the second of which brings together creation stories from ancient Egypt, Greece, Rome, Zimbabwe, Togo, and elsewhere.

I've read electrifying books about the Bible. This isn't one of them. From the opening sentence, one has the sneaking suspicion that one is in the presence of an author who has nothing fresh to say, is not genuinely charged up by his topic, and has selected it in the cynical hope of making a triumphant return to the bestseller list. From the introduction: "The story of Adam and Eve speaks to all of us. It addresses who we are, where we came from, why we love, and why we suffer. . . ." And so on, for pages. Greenblatt might as well be begging the reader to start skimming. It's mechanical, obvious, repetitive; the sense of awe and wonder feels thoroughly inauthentic. (From the first page of Chapter One: "We cannot know when someone, venturing to imagine how the universe and humankind came to exist, first told this story about what happened in the beginning to set our species on its course.") Like *Will in the World* and *The Swerve*, this is a work of potted history, a grab-bag of set pieces, combining borrowed scholarship with mostly unremarkable commentaries by Greenblatt that rattle on far longer than seems justifiable. Much of the book—notably the long biographical accounts of Augustine and Milton, the latter of which runs to over sixty pages—feels like sheer padding. Just as, in *Will in the World*, Greenblatt sought to find traces of Shakespeare's life in his plays and poems, he seeks here to read *Paradise Lost* as a poem largely informed by the events of Milton's own life; just as in *The Swerve*, the principal villains here are the medieval prudes who, after Augustine, saw the Adam and Eve story as primarily concerned with the sinfulness of sex, even in marriage, and used it as a cudgel with which to punish and oppress women.

As I read this book, I kept thinking of Jack Miles's *God: A Biography* (1995), not least because it was standing on a shelf a few feet away from me. Miles's book, I found myself thinking repeatedly, is everything Greenblatt's is not: a thrilling, revelatory account of the development of the image of God from the beginning of the Hebrew Bible to the end. Startlingly original, it's written with deep knowledge and with a palpable urgency, relish, and passion for the subject; when I first read it, it made me see the Hebrew Bible with new eyes, and over twenty years later its impact remains with me. Equally impressive, in its own way, was a recent YouTube talk about Adam and Eve by the Canadian psychology professor Jordan Peterson. Brilliantly, over the course of over two hours, he uncovered rich layers of meaning in the Eden story, bringing in psychology, physics, philosophy, evolutionary biology, and anthropology in ways that made profound sense and weren't in the least pretentious. It was mesmerizing. By contrast, after reading Greenblatt's book, I hardly know what to make of it. It feels—if I may be so blunt—like a gratuitous contrivance, a mishmash of second- and third-hand material that doesn't seem to add up to anything particularly coherent or compelling. If nothing else, it is yet more evidence that the founder of the New Historicism, that magnificent if half-baked fusion of ambiguity and radicalism that made his name, has put that childish enterprise behind him for good and continued to cultivate the middlebrow public that has made him rich. For all its defects, I have little doubt that, like its two immediate predecessors, *The Rise and Fall of Adam and Eve* will win major prizes, sell like hot cakes on the free market that Greenblatt and his Berkeley confrères started out despising, and affirm yet again his position at the forefront of the very institution, the academic humanities, for whose ongoing demise no one on the planet is more responsible than he.

September 2017

Ayn Rand: engineer of souls

Anthony Daniels

Love thy ego as thyself.
—Leonard Peikoff

My copy of *The Concept of Benevolence* by T.A. Roberts, in the series New Studies in Practical Philosophy, was deaccessioned from a university library. The librarian took advantage of the fact that it had not been borrowed since October 17, 1977, only four years after its publication, to disembarrass his institution of yet another book so uselessly cluttering up the library shelves. It was carefully endorsed with ugly withdrawal stamps to reduce its resale value to an absolute minimum. Perhaps the librarian was a follower of Ayn Rand, the apostle of selfishness, who did not want youth corrupted by stray thoughts of altruism. Going from the loan history of the book (and from my casual observations of British youth), there was never much danger of this, but it is always better to be safe than sorry and therefore to treat selfishness as if it were an endangered species.

Ayn Rand was never, in fact, much appreciated or very influential in Europe; at the height of her fame in America, where her books sold by the million, her name was not one to conjure with on the other side of the Atlantic. She was much read by middle-class young Indians of the time, however, as well as by Americans, and she is now coming back into fashion globally. I confess that enthusiasm for her is to me utterly mysterious, and the excellent new biography by Ann C. Heller, *Ayn Rand and the World She Made*, does not clear up the mystery but, rather, deepens it. Able and gifted people (not the least of them Alan Greenspan) were captivated both by her writings and her person, but the picture of Rand that emerges from Ms. Heller's book is all the more damning because the biographer is obviously fair-minded and, indeed, something of an admirer of her subject.

Clearly, Rand was a most remarkable person, admirer and detractor must agree. She was born in St. Petersburg in 1905 into a middle-class Jewish family that hovered uncertainly between prosperity and persecution, but that nevertheless managed to penetrate into the higher echelons of Russian society. (Vladimir Nabokov's sister was a childhood friend of Rand's.) The Bolshevik Revolution deprived the family of everything. They fled to the Crimea in the hope that the advancing White armies would restore their fortunes, but, with the final victory of the Reds, they returned home, to live—like everyone else—in sordid and oppressed penury. At the age of twenty-one, Rand (alone of her immediate family) managed to escape to America.

There, with a determination truly admirable and heroic, she transformed herself into a writer. Although she wrote in English, and her two most famous books are American in subject matter and location, she remained deeply Russian in outlook and intellectual style to the end of her days. America could take Rand out of Russia, but not Russia out of Rand. Her work properly belongs to the history of Russian, not American, literature—and nineteenth-century Russian literature at that.

Rand's virtues were as follows: she was highly intelligent; she was brave and uncompromising in defense of her ideas; she had a kind of iron integrity; and, though a fierce defender of capitalism, she was by no means avid for money herself. The propagation of truth as she saw it was far more important to her than her own material ease. Her vices, of course, were the mirror-image of her virtues, but, in my opinion, the mirror was a magnifying one. Her intelligence was narrow rather than broad. Though in theory a defender of freedom of thought and action, she was dogmatic, inflexible, and intolerant, not only in opinion but in behavior, and it led her to personal cruelty. In the name of her ideas, she was prepared to be deeply unpleasant. She hardened her ideas into ideology. Her integrity led to a lack of self-criticism; she frequently wrote twenty thousand words where one would do.

Rand believed all people to be possessed of equal rights, but she found relations of equality with others insupportable. Though she could be charming, it was not something she could keep up for long. She was deeply ungrateful to those who had helped her and many of her friendships ended in acrimony. Her biographer tells us that she sometimes told jokes, but, in the absence of any supportive evidence, I treat reports of her sense of humor much as I treat reports of sightings of the Loch Ness monster: apocryphal at best.

A passionate hater of religion, Rand founded a cult around her own person, complete with rituals of excommunication; a passionate believer in rationality and logic, she was incapable of seeing the contradictions in her own work. She was a rationalist who was not entirely rational; she could not distinguish between rationalism and rationality. Of narrow aesthetic sympathies, she laid down the law in matters of artistic judgment like a panjandrum; a believer in honesty, she was adept at self-deception and special pleading. I have rarely read a biography of a writer I should have cared so little to meet.

The Russian tradition to which Rand belongs is not that of Gogol, Turgenev, and Chekhov but that of Dobrolyubov, Pisarev, and Chernyshevsky: that is to say, of angry literary and social critics, pamphleteers and ideologues. She was neither fully a philosopher, nor fully a novelist, but something in between the two—the characters in her novels are not creatures of flesh and blood but opinions on legs, and her expository prose has the quality of speechifying. This is not to say that a woman of her intelligence and life experience had nothing interesting to say or no insights to convey. She did, on occasion, put things very well. She was often shrewd, seeing the dangers of statism very clearly, when few others did.

Rand's statement that racism is the lowest and most primitive form of collectivism is a striking apothegm. Likewise, she was among the first to appreciate that the notion of collective rights (a mirror image of racial discrimination) would "disintegrate a country into an institutionalized civil war of pressure groups, each fighting for legislative favors and special privileges at the expense of one another." This could hardly be expressed better; neither could her observation that "Even if it were proved ... that the incidence of men of potentially superior brain power is greater among the members of certain races than among the members of others, it would still tell us nothing about any given individual and it would be irrelevant to one's judgment of him."

Unfortunately, Rand's vices as a writer are never very far from her virtues. Not only does the above passage suggest that people are to be judged mainly by reference to their brain power, a very narrow and inhumane criterion, but she continues: "A genius is a genius ... and a moron is a moron, regardless of the number of morons who belong to the same race." This grates because one knows that she not only divides the world into creators and parasites with no intermediate category, but also because she never expresses any sympathy or understanding for the weak or ill, always referring to them with disdain at best and eugenicist hatred at worst. A moron is to be blamed for his own lack of intelligence.

Rand treats the physically ill as if their misfortunes were always their own fault, and a sign of their moral and human worthlessness. In *The Fountainhead*, for example, she compares "the bright, the strong, the able boys" of Ellsworth Toohey's class during his childhood with Skinny Dix, who "got infantile paralysis, and would lie in bed." This comparison is indicative of a truly loathsome and disgusting hardness of heart and lack of compassion as well as a crude intellectual error (made, no doubt, partly as a result of her loathing for Roosevelt—infantile paralysis does not affect the intelligence and therefore cannot be taken as a symbolic opposite of ability).

Rand's hardness of heart was not only confined to the page. There is a chilling account in the biography of how she treated her long-suffering husband, Frank O'Connor, when he suffered from dementia:

> She nagged at him continually, to onlookers' distress. "Don't humor him," she [said]. "Make him try to remember." She insisted that his mental lapses were "psycho-epistemological," and she gave him long, grueling lessons in how to think and remember. She assigned him papers on aspects of his mental functioning, which he was entirely unable to write.

This downright cruelty (as well as downright stupidity) derived from her overvaluation of supposed intellectual consistency in the conduct of daily life. She believed that it was more important to adhere to a principle than to behave well. Among her many bad ideas was the compatibility of all human desiderata, and that any conflict of a man's interests was merely the consequence of his not having thought through his situation sufficiently, and applied a fundamental and indubitable principle correctly and consistently. For Rand, there was no ambiguity in the world: if it is true that man has free will and is responsible for his conduct, it cannot also be that there is a condition such as dementia that robs a man of his capacity for choice. Hence her husband's lapses were willful and deliberate, to be corrected by Randian brainwashing. This is authentically horrible.

Rand's crude dichotomizing is evident throughout her work. Her rejection of compassion is Nietzschean in tone, seeing in pity merely an attempt by the weak and ill-favored to overcome the power and influence of the strong and healthy. But this is an elementary error. From the correct psychological insight that the allegedly compassionate sometimes use the existence of the weak and needy as a tool for their own social ascent and attainment of power—whole political parties, in almost every country, are founded upon this principle—it does not in the least follow that there are no people in need of assistance or that compassion for them is ipso facto bogus and a cover for the will to power. From the insight that government assistance to the unfortunate increases the number of the unfortunate, often imprisoning them in their misfortune, it does not follow in the least that it is right for human beings to be utterly callous and indifferent to the fate of the unfortunate. Human sympathy is, as Adam Smith himself pointed out, implanted by nature in the human breast, but Ayn Rand, to a greater extent even than Pharaoh, hardened her heart and expunged sympathy from it utterly.

Rand's hero-worship is also Nietzschean in inspiration. It is deeply unpleasant. She entirely lacks the literary ability to convey anything admirable, or even minimally attractive, about her heroes, who are the kind of people one would not cross the road to meet, though one might well cross it to avoid them. They partake fully of her humorless monomania and have all the human warmth of a praying mantis. We are told that they are geniuses, but their genius seems mainly to consist of an unswerving adherence to their own ideas.

Howard Roark is the architect-hero of *The Fountainhead*, but there is abundant evidence in the book that he is not a very good architect: his ideas are totally derivative and, furthermore, derivative of ideas that are themselves not merely worthless, but monstrous. Like his creator, he claims an originality that he does not have. Here he describes how a house may have what he calls "integrity":

> Every piece of it is there because the house needs it—and for no other reason. The relation of masses was determined by the distribution of space within. The ornament was determined by the method of construction, an emphasis of the principle that makes it stand.

This is pure, unadulterated Le Corbusier. Indeed, it could have been written by him. (Roark also praises Le Corbusier's favourite thing in all the world, reinforced concrete.) We all know what Le Corbusier led to; the very idea that a house "needs" things while the desires of human beings can be disregarded is one that would occur only to someone with a reptilian mind.

It is not altogether surprising that Roark lacks taste; Rand herself did, too. She called Bach and Mozart "pre-musical," preferring Tchaikovsky and even Lehár. She thought that Victor Hugo was the greatest novelist who ever lived. She ridiculed Rembrandt's "visual distortions." These judgments show her to have been seriously deficient in sensibility and discrimination across a wide range of important human activities: in fact, I cannot think of any field in which she showed proper aesthetic or intellectual judgment.

Humanity, according to Rand, is divided into heroes, creators, and geniuses on the one hand, and weaklings, parasites, and the feeble-minded on the other. Needless to say, the latter outnumber the former by a very wide margin, but only the former are truly human in the full sense of the word. But let us leave aside for a moment the empirical justification for such a sharp division of mankind into two categories: it never seems to occur to Rand that her classification does not provide a very strong rationale for the limited government and free market that she claims so strongly to admire. On the contrary, it would seem to justify the reign of philosopher-kings, though she claims also to hate Plato passionately.

Let us examine the "heroism" of Howard Roark as an example. Why is he a hero to be admired? In the book, Rand grants Roark the right to rape Dominique because of his status as a Nietszschean hero, an act which she would have found repellent and inexcusable if, say, his enemy Ellsworth Toohey, had committed it. Roark is a hero because, as a completely self-sufficient man, he sticks to his guns and never compromises; this means that he eventually manages to build a skyscraper according to his own conception and to none other. But why should this make him a hero, unless his skyscraper is of superior value? Heroism in pursuit of an undesirable end is not itself desirable, very much to the contrary. Unless what Roark builds has some social or aesthetic value, his heroism (actually, arrogance and pigheadedness) is itself worthless, indeed reprehensible.

It is odd that Rand should have chosen architecture as her battle-horse for radical individualism because, of all the arts and crafts, architecture is not—or rather, should not be—individualistic in any pure sense. Let me give a brief illustration. When I am in England, I live in a Queen Anne house in a church close which consists of Elizabethan, Jacobean, Queen Anne, and Georgian houses. I own my house and the land on which it stands outright, but this (in my opinion) does not give me the right, even if the law granted it, to knock my house down and build a brutalist construction of reinforced concrete in its place, however much it might be in my individual financial interest to do so. A single such construction would ruin the whole once and for all; where architecture is concerned, the public or collective interest really does exist.

Moreover, Rand fails to notice that, by the standards of the marketplace, Roark is a comprehensive failure and is prevented from being a success by market forces—all those supposed philistines who do not commission him, but retain instead the people whom he and Rand consider second-rate, philistine, and unoriginal. Either the marketplace is not always the source and proper judge of value, or Roark deserves his failure. Neither does Rand notice that, while she considers the skyline of New York to be mankind's highest architectural achievement (a debatable proposition), she also considers each individual building as being without merit, which is why New York needs Roark so badly.

These contradictions would not be very grave were Rand not so adamant that a wholly consistent and rational philosophy of life were possible, and that she herself had found it and propagated it in her books. Her combination of vehemence, moral fanaticism, and mediocrity as a thinker was very characteristic of the earnest journalistic tradition of Dobrolyubov, Pisarev, and Chernyshevsky. The only other tradition known to me that shares this unfortunate combination of characteristics is that of the German materialists of the second half of the nineteenth century such as Moleschott and Buchner.

In some respects, Rand is almost Soviet. Her habit of remaking the past in accordance with her wishes or needs of the present is most striking. The original edition of *Atlas Shrugged* was dedicated to Nathaniel Branden, a young man whom Rand deemed to be in apostolic intellectual succession to her until he displayed his irrational tendencies by refusing to continue a sexual liaison with her (a refusal she considered irrational despite their very considerable age difference). The dedication was removed from subsequent editions in the way that Trotsky and others were removed from Soviet photographs once they had fallen from favor. Perhaps the most significant sentence in Ms. Heller's biography is this from the preface: "Because I am not an advocate for Rand's ideas, I was denied access to the Ayn Rand Papers at the Ayn Rand Institute . . ."

Allied to this tendency to remodel the past was Rand's megalomaniac notion that moral philosophy had been nothing but a tissue of sentimental error until she came along. This is rather like the Stalinist view, Marxist in inspiration, that all was misery and exploitation until Stalin brought happiness into the world: Ethics and ethics laws lay hid in night; God said, Let Ayn Rand be, and all was light.

Like any Stalinist despot, Ayn Rand considered herself to be totally unprecedented and quite without parallel. Like Kim Il-Sung and Howard Roark, she sprang into the world with her philosophical genius fully formed, not needing any support from any other thinker, despite the fact that (in fact) no element of her thought was entirely original. For example, it was perfectly well known to Hobbes that power-seeking might be masked by alleged altruism and compassion; the fact that no man did or could love humanity was expressed by Hume as follows:

> There is no such passion in human minds, as the love of mankind, merely as such, independent of personal qualities, of services, or relation to ourself.

Hume, however, did not go on to draw the extreme conclusion (Russian in style) that, if one could not love humanity, one was condemned, or fortunate enough, to have to think only of oneself:

> Tho' it be rare to meet with one, who loves any single person better than himself; yet 'tis as rare to meet with one, in whom all the kind affections, taken together, do not over-balance all the selfish.

In her expository writings, Rand's style resembles that of Stalin. It is more catechism than argument, and bores into you in the manner of a drill. She has a habit of quoting herself as independent verification of what she says; reading her is like being cornered at a party by a man, intelligent but dull, who is determined to prove to you that right is on his side in the property dispute upon which he is now engaged and will omit no detail.

Her unequivocal admiration bordering on worship of industrialization and the size of human construction as a mark of progress is profoundly Stalinist. Where Stalinist iconography would plant a giant chimney belching black smoke, Randian iconography would plant a skyscraper. (At the end of *The Fountainhead*, Roark receives a commission to build the tallest skyscraper in New York, its height being the guarantor of its moral grandeur. According to this scale of values, the Burj Dubai would be man's crowning achievement so far.) Industrialists are to Rand what Stakhanovites were to Stalin: both saw nature as an enemy, something to be beaten into submission. One doesn't have to be an adherent of the Gaia hypothesis to know where this hatred of nature led.

Finally, Rand's treasured theory of literature, what she called Romantic Realism, is virtually indistinguishable from Socialist Realism:

> Since my purpose is the presentation of an ideal man, I had to define and present the conditions which make him possible and which his existence requires. I had to define and present the kinds of premises and values that create the character of an ideal man and motivate his actions.

Zhdanov could have written that, and it is hardly surprising that, as a result, Rand's heroes are not American but Soviet. The fact that they supposedly embody capitalist values makes no difference. Rand fulfilled Stalin's criterion for the ideal writer: she tried to be an engineer of souls.

Rand's fanaticism is Russian; philosophically, she resembles Bazarov in *Fathers and Sons*, but without his more attractive qualities. Nathaniel Branden was still Rand's sexual partner and intellectual eunuch when he wrote, with her complete nihil obstat, the following:

> There is no greater self-delusion than to imagine that one can render unto reason that which is reason's and unto faith that which is faith's. Faith cannot be circumscribed or delimited; to surrender one's consciousness by an inch is to surrender one's consciousness in total. Either reason is absolute to a mind or it is not—and if it is not, there is no place to draw the line, no barrier faith cannot

> cross, no part of one's life faith cannot invade: one remains rational until and unless one's feelings decree otherwise.

One doesn't know whether to remark more on the arrogance, self-delusion, or sheer ignorance of this. According to the passage above, the man who was probably the greatest scientist of all time, Sir Isaac Newton, was not rational. Ayn Rand was the only rational being in history. Of course, she was so intolerable that her sister, visiting her in the United States after decades of separation, couldn't wait to return to the Soviet Union. After reading Ms. Heller's book, I sympathize with her sister. Rand was the Chernyshevsky of individualism.

February 2010

The postmodern calculus

James Franklin

IN THE OLD DAYS—in the dawn of the Cold War—the Left was all for science. The Red Army was as keen to spirit German rocket scientists east as the Americans were to ship them to New Mexico. Atomic scientists wanting to share blueprints were accorded every facility. Sputnik scared the living daylights out of the Western world, and quite rightly. At the more theoretical end of ideological warfare, Marxism claimed to be a "scientific" analysis of economic reality. Neither the Stalinist Left nor its fellow travelers saw any conflict between their values and science itself: any failure of Soviet Science was not for want of trying but from the difficulties of pursuing science without free communication of results. In the last few decades, however, the Left in the West has moved in an entirely different direction. A large part of it has come to have a stand against science in principle.

It began with the abuse directed by the New Left of the Sixties against the "military-industrial complex." Western military power was, indeed, heavily indebted to science and its applications. But anyone who thought that Western power was a bad thing, as the Left did, had a choice about what attitude to take to science itself. It would have been most natural to say that science itself is an ideologically neutral means of discovering truth that could be applied for good or ill—the undesired use of it could be blamed on its misuse by militarists, capitalists, and "warmongers." And many on the left did say just that. With such people, it was, and remains, possible to conduct rational argument as to whether military spending is justified, what the risks are otherwise, and which wars are just.

But since Marx at least, the Left has always hankered after Theory, a desire to show that, on a "deeper" analysis, the forces of reaction are entangled in some kind of conceptual confusion or contradiction. Their "mistakes" arise from errors in their own theories. So the search was on for ways to "deconstruct" (to use a later term) the chief ideas underlying Western success: religion and constitutional democracy came first before the firing line; the rule of law, fine art, and the ideal of economic progress soon enough; and then, last and possibly hardest, science and its standards of objectivity. How could this be done?

Put yourself, for the moment, in the position of one of science's enemies. You are a *circa*-2000 Western humanistic intellectual raised in a culture of suspicion and you are "conflicted" about science. Perhaps you were not very good at it at school but have discovered a skill in spinning words. Perhaps you find science authoritarian because authoritative and you have a problem with authority figures. Perhaps you are indignant about Western science-based economic and military success for political reasons. Perhaps you are broke and need the money from whatever you can write fast. It doesn't matter what the causes of your animus against science are, because you won't be telling your public about them. What you want are reasons, or strategies, to mount an attack on science. What are the resources available to you?

The first three lines of attack come courtesy of the ancient sophist Gorgias of Leontini. He achieved a lucrative *succès de scandale* in the Athens of the fifth century B.C. by defending the propositions: "Nothing exists; if anything existed, it could not be known; if anything were known, it could not be communicated." There is plenty of life still in those. A modern formulation of his "Nothing exists" is to doubt whether there is any solid reality out there for science to know (or, at least, to label "naive" the assumption that there is such a reality). Gorgias's "nothing can be known" also reappears as the claim that even if there is some sort of reality out there, we cannot know what it is because we are trapped in our own evolutionarily determined brains/cultural understandings/specific historicities/reactionary educations. The modern reviver of Gorgias's third idea alleges that language is incapable of communicating any truth about objective reality, as it cannot refer directly to things and their properties.

Post-Greek thought has come up with another triple plan of attack, which may have seemed outré in the days when rationality itself was new and exciting. It is: to doubt the logical nature of the relation of evidence to conclusion, maintaining that the conclusions are "underdetermined" by evidence and hence that the gap must be filled by political decisions, wishful thinking, or similar; to confuse ethics with logic by taking the misuse of scientific discoveries as reasons to disbelieve the discoveries themselves; and to "put politics in charge," as Mao said—claim that the classifying of objects and the assertion of conclusions as true (why not say "absolutely true"?) is in itself authoritarian and patriarchal, hence deserving of opposition and "transgression."

When all of these ideas are put together in a blender the resulting purée has come to be called postmodernism and has now set into a fixture on the intellectual scene. The rest of us may well ask, is it a threat? It is unlikely that such speculations will make much impression on real science, which is pursued by people with a sound sense of rationality, with demonstrably effective results in the eyes of funding agencies. Unfortunately, however, people with such views have been given carte blanche to corrupt the minds of the young in humanities and education faculties. Before discussing that, let us look at the remarkable popular successes achieved by some of the leading anti-science writers.

The way forward was shown by the American philosopher of science Thomas Kuhn's phenomenally successful 1962 book, *The Structure of Scientific Revolutions.* Although Kuhn himself was not politically oriented, his book has been an essential source for many later attacks on scientific rationality. According to the *Arts and Humanities Citation Index*, which counts citations in academic articles, in the period 1976–83 the single most cited twentieth-century book was Kuhn's *Structure*, although the most cited twentieth-century *author* was Lenin (no surprises there). Interest in Kuhn's book has not waned. The *Index* is now online, and 554 citations are recorded in all Indexes (Arts and Humanities, Social Science, and Science) for 2007. To call the tone of most of these citations reverential would be an understatement. It is reported that *Structure* is Al Gore's favorite book, and William Safire's *New Political Dictionary* has an article on "paradigm shift," a phrase popularized by Kuhn, which reports both Bush (senior) and Clinton being much impressed with its usefulness. In very recent years, commentators as diverse as Clifford Geertz and George Soros have spilled ink on the book's importance.

To understand why *Structure* created such excitement in the "progressive" Humanities world, it is sufficient to understand what the Humanities crowd wants said about science. The answer is obvious: Kuhn's thesis is that scientific theories are no better than ones in the Humanities. Up to his time, philosophy of science had concentrated on such questions as how evidence confirms theories and what the difference is between science and pseudo-science, that is, questions about the logic of science. Kuhn declared logic outmoded and replaced it with history and politics.

The caricature of the thesis set out in *Structure* is as follows: a science, say astronomy, is dominated for a long period by a "paradigm," such as Ptolemy's theory that the sun and planets revolve around a stationary earth. Most work is on "normal science," the solving of standard problems in terms of the reigning paradigm. But anomalies—results the paradigm cannot explain—accumulate and eventually make the paradigm unsustainable. The science enters a "revolutionary phase," as a new paradigm (such as Copernicus's heliocentrism) comes to seem more plausible. Defenders of the old order, who cannot accommodate the change and usually cannot even understand the concepts in which it is expressed, gradually die out and the new paradigm becomes normal. The process repeats itself, *ad infinitum*. As Francis Fukuyama expresses it in *The End of History*:

> The cumulative and progressive nature of modern science has been challenged by Thomas Kuhn, who has pointed to the discontinuous and revolutionary nature of change in the sciences. In his most radical assertions, he has denied the possibility of "scientific" knowledge of nature at all, since all "paradigms" by which scientists understand nature ultimately fail.

As with many caricatures, one finds that the original consists of the caricature with the addition of qualifications that render it inconsistent (and the number of inconsistencies multiplies with the author's subsequent denials that he had meant to say anything so crude). The caricature, however, has a historical career considerably more vigorous than the original, whose qualifications dilute its appeal.

What the enemies of science particularly took from Kuhn was the substitution of the logic of science with its sociology. There is, of course, a respectable discipline of the sociology of science, which might inquire into peer pressures in the climate science community, how astrology manages to survive when it has no credibility, or why scientists are, on average, more male, immigrant, Jewish, and firstborn than the rest of the community. But the enemies of science are not interested in actual empirical inquiry. They wish, rather, to *replace* considerations of logic, such as the probability of theories on the evidence, with talk about sociological causes, such as patronage. The Left championed nurture in the nature-nurture controversy for similar reasons: if scientific theory or human nature is infinitely malleable by social causes, then one can blame any inequalities of outcome on political factors and promise to fix them through social engineering.

An exemplary version of this phenomenon was the "Strong Programme in the Sociology of Knowledge," or social constructivism, of the philosophers David Bloor and Barry Barnes. They proposed to replace all considerations of logic, of what scientific theories are reasonable, with considerations of sociology—that is, of what interests theories serve. Since science is practiced by people, they are convinced its explanation should be in the realm of causes acting on people, not in the realm of abstract reason. People, they think, can be acted on by their interests, or patronage, or the social milieu, but abstract facts like 2 + 2 = 4 do not act. Thus, explanations of how people, including scientists, think ought to be sociological.

This argument appears in various forms, mostly not very explicit: Bloor argues that observation "underdetermines" theory—that is, that several theories are logically compatible with any given body of observations—and concludes immediately that it must be social factors that determine which theory is chosen. He says that the "existence of nature" does not account for scientific theories and that simple "attention to nature" will not adjudicate their merits. He reserves particular hostility for the opinion that belief in reasonable theories is at least in part explained by their being reasonable, while mistakes require causal explanations; Bloor says sarcastically that this is an attempt to render science "safe from the indignity of empirical explanation." Barnes and Bloor write:

> Our equivalence postulate is that all beliefs are on a par with one another with respect to the causes of their credibility. It is not that all beliefs are equally true or equally false, but that regardless of truth and falsity the fact of their credibility is to be seen as equally problematic. The position we shall defend is that the incidence of all beliefs without exception calls for empirical explanation and must be accounted for by finding the specific, local causes of this credibility.

It must be emphasized that Bloor does not admit any possibility of cooperation between causes and reasons: explanation in terms of causes is quite different to that in terms of reasons, he says; if one is right, the other is wrong.

What is wrong with this argument is most clearly seen by comparing it with what an electronic calculator does. When we punch in 2 + 2, there are causes in the wiring that explain why 4 is displayed, but the fact that 2 + 2 really is 4 is also essential to the explanation: the calculator has been wired precisely so as to agree with the laws of arithmetic. The causes track the reasons. It is the same with brains and communities doing science. They have a natural aptitude for building on perception and other evidence so as to reach theories that are well-supported by the evidence, but individual emotional and political causes can either cooperate or interfere with that process.

The "Strong Programme" was British and easy enough to understand. Obscurity was joined to bad argument in the French-inspired movement loosely called "postmodernism." As is usual with Leftist errors, postmodernism is a moral posture before it is an invalid argument, but the combination of the two is essential to it. It is an attitude of suspicion—suspicion especially about claims of truth. So if postmodernists are asked "Aren't the claims of science just true, and some things objectively right and wrong?" the reaction is not so much "no, because," but "they're always doubtful, or relative to our paradigms, or just true for dominant groups in our society; and anyway, in whose interest is it to think science is true?"

Not only is postmodernism an attitude of suspicion, but it also one of unteachable suspicion. If one tries to advance good arguments for some truth claim, the postmodernist will be ready to "deconstruct" the concept of good argument as itself a historically conditioned paradigm of patriarchal Enlightenment rationality. Furthermore, the postmodernist *congratulates* himself morally on being unteachably suspicious. Being "transgressive" against established standards is taken as a good in itself, positioning the transgressor as a fighter against "oppression," prior to giving any reasons why established standards are wrong. In asking how to respond to postmodernism, it is especially important to understand that its motivation does not lie in argument but in the more primitive moral responses, resentment and indignation.

The core of the postmodernist position is a version of Gorgias's third thesis, that "if anything were known, it could not be communicated." It is an idea taken more directly by Jacques Derrida from the early twentieth-century founder of French structuralist linguistics, Ferdinand de Saussure, who claimed that the words of language do not get their meaning from any connection with reality but only from connection within language, its structure. In other words, "black" means the opposite of "white" but neither word has its meaning pinned down by the perceptual experience of black and white things. The effect of this line of thinking is to see language, in principle, as incapable of expressing truths directly about reality. Plainly, that is destructive of any pursuit of truth, scientific or otherwise.

Later postmodernists looked for ever more radical ways to undermine the relation of thought to reality. A popular choice of French guru was Gilles Deleuze, who went back for another bite of the Gorgian cherry with the thesis that if anything did exist, it didn't exist as a unity. He proposed what William Bogard calls "a philosophical ontology of Being as pure difference or becoming. Being, for Deleuze and Guattari, is that which differs from itself, in nature, always already, in itself, qualitatively different"—which is to say that "Deleuze and those of his generation sought to conceptualize both difference and becoming, but a difference and becoming that would not be the becoming *of* some being." Such a philosophy enables one to *congratulate* oneself on "resisting" any "totalizing" discourses such as science which naively speak as if there are coherent objects with persistent properties. As soon as anyone asserts that object A has property B, the Deleuzian is ready to attack the notions of both solid object A and continuing property B. Instead of things and properties there are only "virtualities," "potentials," "becomings."

The vast abstraction of such concepts as "difference" and "becoming" recalls an acute comment by Jean Curthoys in her book *Feminist Amnesia*, which traces the development of feminist theory from simple demands for equality in the 1960s to realms of abstraction divorced from reality. It is a process with close parallels to the development of Leftist theory on science. She writes:

> I am not sure that it is in fact much less crazy to think of political conflicts taking place between categories of "sameness" and "difference" or between "bourgeois formal logic" and "proletarian

> dialectical thought" than it is, say, to believe that one is being pursued by Hitler around one's local neighbourhood. But it does look a lot less crazy.

And maybe it keeps would-be revolutionaries off the streets. That is good for the streets but bad for the academic milieux and untrained young minds in which these idea-viruses breed.

Any discussion of scientific truth by postmodernists is bound to be negative, and any scientific terminology used in it will probably be ... well, take this example, from Deleuze's translator and English-language interpreter Brian Massumi:

> Just as "higher" functions are fed back—all the way to the subatomic (that is position and momentum)—quantum indeterminacy is fed forward. It rises through the fractal bifurcations leading to and between each of the superposed levels of reality. On each level, it appears in a unique mode adequate to that level. On the level of physical macrosystems analyzed by Simondon, its mode is potential energy and the margin of "play" it introduces into deterministic systems (epitomised by the "three body problem" so dear to chaos theory). On the biological level, it is the margin of undecidability accompanying every perception, which is one with a perception's transmissibility from one sense to another. On the human level, it is that same undecidability fed forward into thought, as evidenced in the deconstructability of every structure of ideas (as expressed, for example in Gödel's incompleteness theorem and in Derrida's *différance*). Each individual and collective human level has its own peculiar "quantum" mode; various forms of undecidability in logical and signifying systems are joined by emotion on the psychological level, resistance on the political level, the spectre of crisis haunting capitalist economies.... The use of the concept of the quantum outside quantum mechanics, even as applied to human psychology, is not a metaphor.

The Citation Indexes report an enthusiastic embrace of Massumi's ideas. Recent articles citing the book that contains this passage include such titles as "Aesthetics of intermediality" (*Art History*, June 2007), "Deleuze and space" (*Annals of the Association of American Geographers*, December 2007), "Caught in the terrains: an inter-referential inquiry of trans-border stardom and fandom" (*Inter-Asia Cultural Studies*, 2007), and "Broccoli and desire" (*Antipode*, November 2007).

Science itself has remained resolutely unaffected by these developments. Scientists just do not—cannot—think in terms of "difference" or "desire" when it comes to evaluating the evidence for global warming or trying to prove the Riemann Hypothesis. For real science, the whole enormous wave of sociological and postmodernist theory has been water off a duck's back. (There may be some problems with climate science, for example, but a tendency to postmodernism is not one of them.) The funding for any given field of study can be influenced by political forces that are outside the control of science, but there is little sign so far of postmodernist congressmen questioning scientific budgets.

Why should we care about these developments, if they are confined to an esoteric realm almost entirely quarantined from the real world? The real reason for anger has nothing to do with the possible effects. It is that the right human reaction to any cynical attack on the good, the true, or the beautiful, as such, is outrage. Take, for instance, the postmodernist attacks on art. The main character of Zadie Smith's novel *On Beauty* is the postmodernist art academic Howard Belsey, alleged expert on Rembrandt. Naturally, he is opposed to beauty. "What we're trying to … interrogate here," he drones, "is the mytheme of artist as autonomous individual with privileged insight into the human…. What are we signing up for when we speak of the 'beauty' of this 'light'?" Smith knows how to arouse our indignation. She shows Howard's lecture through the eyes of Katie Armstrong, a naive sixteen year old from the Midwest who "used to dream about one day attending a college class about Rembrandt with other intelligent people who loved Rembrandt and weren't ashamed to express this love."

As with Rembrandt, so with Newton. Newton's laws are among the high points of human achievement, in the same way as Rembrandt's portraits, but in the deparment of truth rather than beauty. Attempts to "interrogate" them, that is, refuse to look at them honestly, deserve our outrage first of all for their innate repulsiveness, irrespective of any bad effects they may have.

But if the perpetrators are then permitted to corrupt the natural good impulses of the young, they deserve double the outrage. For an academic salary pertaining to a named chair, add another 50 percent. And this, in fact, is one respect in which postmodernism in science does threaten serious consequences. Science and mathematics comprise a much larger portion of the school syllabus than art history and art appreciation. The education of teachers in those disciplines is, as the theorists say, a "contested site." Syllabuses that introduce education students to the nature of science take seriously social constructivist and postmodernist views, while rarely allowing students to see any straightforward defense of the rationality and objectivity of science and mathematics. Instead they recycle Kuhnian views, at best, or at worst promote opinions like the following, from *Educational Studies in Mathematics* (2004):

> The supposed apolitical nature of mathematics is an institutional frame that functions to sustain specific power structures within schools. This paper disrupts the common assumption that mathematics (as a body of knowledge constructed in situated historical moments) is free from entrenched ideological motives. Using narrative inquiry, the paper examines the ways in which novice mathematics teachers negotiate the intersection of curriculum and institutional politics.

Science cannot be defended from that kind of attack by scientists. It needs support from everyone who values reason.

September 2010

Guilt trip: Versailles, avant-garde & kitsch

Roger Kimball

> Ever and anon into the hearts of men sounds the enchanting whisper: "Ye shall be as gods." But humanity-worship is so profoundly inadequate to the true aspiration of man ... that it must end almost fatally in some form or other of individual or collective self-worship, and indeed it ends not infrequently in devil-worship pure and simple.
> —Étienne Mantoux

> What a vast difference there is between the barbarism that precedes culture and the barbarism that follows it.
> —Christian Friedrich Hebbel

In *Europe's Last Summer*, his brilliant book about the origins of the Great War, the historian David Fromkin dilates on the seductive beauties of the summer of 1914. It was, he notes, the most gorgeous in living memory. That serene balminess seemed an objective correlative of the rock-solid political and social stability that Europe had enjoyed for decades. To be sure, percipient observers discerned troubling clouds on the horizon. As far back as the 1890s, Otto von Bismarck predicted that "One day the great European War will come out of some damned foolish thing in the Balkans." And his anxiety was later echoed by many statesmen who regarded the extraordinary arms race in Russia and Germany and the Balkanization of the teetering Ottoman Empire with trepidation. In 1912, Helmuth von Moltke, then chief of staff of the German army, opined that war was "inevitable," and "the sooner the better." A world war, he admitted, "will annihilate the civilization of almost the whole of Europe for decades to come," but Germany would eventually have to confront an ever-strengthening Russia. Better now, when Russia was still fledgling and Germany was taut with Prussian vigor.

On the other side, there were plenty of soothing voices to point out that the world's increasing economic interdependence rendered any serious conflict "impossible"—that was the reassuring word one heard repeatedly. There had been no war among the Great Powers for nearly half a century, *ergo* the status quo would persist for decades, maybe forever. There would *always* be honey then for tea.

War was "inevitable." War was "impossible." Between the horns of that dilemma the world trod the mournfully contingent path of the actual.

When war did finally break out, it was greeted in many quarters as a lark, a holiday, a deliverance from the tedious routines of everyday life. Yes, there were some cautionary voices. "If war breaks out," warned Sir Edward Grey, the British Foreign Secretary, at the end of July, 1914, "it will be the greatest catastrophe that the world has ever seen." On August 3, when the German armies were swarming towards France and the "Rape of Belgium" was about to begin, he somberly predicted that "The lamps are going out all over Europe. We shall not see them lit again in our life-time."

But in early August, Grey's was a minority perspective. "We'll just pop over to France next week and be home by Christmas." That was the popular refrain. In Germany, the mood was triumphalist. Even a moralist like Thomas Mann welcomed the war as "a purification, a liberation, an enormous hope. The victory of Germany will be ... a victory of soul over numbers." "The German soul," Mann wrote, "is opposed to the pacifist ideal of civilization, for is not peace an element of civil corruption?" What contempt Mann had for the "nation of shopkeepers" across the channel.

Then in September came the first battle of the Marne. Its unprecedented slaughter exacted half a million casualties in a week. It is accounted a great victory for the Allies. But although it halted the German advance, it also paved the way for four years of that butchery by attrition that was trench warfare in the age of total war.

It is often said that the primary existential or spiritual effect of the war was disillusionment. Barbara Tuchman, for example, notes in one of her classic studies of the Great War that the war had many results but that the dominant one was "disillusion." She quotes D. H. Lawrence, who observed that "All the great words were cancelled out for that generation." Honor, Nobility, Valor, Patriotism, Sacrifice, Beauty: who could still take such abstractions seriously after the wholesale slaughter of the war?

But it's worth interjecting two points. First, it is sometimes said that the Great War, because of its body count, the tactics of its generals, the as-it-turned-out false promise that it was "a war to end all wars," was therefore meaningless. I submit that, on the contrary, it was instinct with significance. As David Fromkin put it at the end of *Europe's Last Summer*, "it was fought to decide the essential questions in international politics: who would achieve mastery in Europe, and therefore in the world, and under the banners of what faith."

Second, on the matter of culture, it is worth noting that most of the primary innovations in form and sensibility that we associate with that spirit of disillusionment predated the war. Picasso painted *Les Demoiselles d'Avignon* in 1907, ushering in decades of ugliness and assaults on the human form. We haven't recovered yet. Marinetti's Futurist Manifesto, with its gleeful "smear of madness" and its giddy "war-is-beautiful" apotheosis of speed, technology, and violence, appeared in 1909. "We want no part of it, the past," he shouted, giving voice to an entire movement that was sick and tired of bourgeois stability. Stravinsky's primitivist extravaganza, *Le Sacre du Printemps*—he had thought of calling it "The Victim"—was first performed in Paris to Diaghilev's carefully staged pseudo-riots in 1913.

There was a fair amount of posturing involved all around. Recalling Roger Fry's exhibition of some post-Impressionist paintings at the Grosvenor Gallery, Virginia Woolf famously said that "On or about December 1910, human character changed." That made the punters sit up and take notice. Was it true? It would be impolite to ask.

If there was a shift in artistic sensibility *because* of the war, I suspect that it had more to do with mood, with the quantum of braggadocio involved, than any formal innovation. Picasso, Marinetti, and early Stravinsky were brash gatecrashers. After the war the brashness evaporated, the energy turned rancid. "These fragments I have shored against my ruins," T. S. Eliot wrote at the end of *The Waste Land*, a poem whose title and suspended splinters of a shattered civilization seemed to epitomize the somber flirtation with nihilism, impotence, and polysyllabic despair that the Great War left in its wake.

Such signposts, I think, are pretty familiar. The sniggering, anti-art hijinks of Dada, the progenitor of so many bad things, belong here, as do the strenuous reactions and attempted recuperations of high modernism. What I'd like to do is step back and place the cultural consequences of the war in a broader context. This is where the promised theme of misplaced guilt, highlighted in my title, comes in.

One of the most famous books to emerge in the immediate aftermath of the war was John Maynard Keynes's *Economic Consequences of the Peace*. It was an instant bestseller. By 1924, it had been translated into eleven languages. (It is somehow appropriate that the other great bestseller that year was Lytton Strachey's *Eminent Victorians*: the spirit of Bloomsbury was riding high that year.) Keynes, the brilliant Bloomsbury economist whom the commentator David Frum percipiently called "the Nietzsche of economics," had been at the Paris Peace Conference in 1919 as a representative of the British Treasury. He quit in disgust because he thought the terms of the proposed peace treaty were too harsh. General Jan Christiaan Smuts, the South African delegate to the Conference, convinced him to write up his objections. *The Economic Consequences of the Peace*, which might just as well have been called "Don't Let's Be Beastly to the Germans," was the result. The book is not a novel. But it occupies a place in the hinterland between fact and fiction—of moralistic melodrama, say, what the public relations people might call a "docudrama": not true, exactly, but close enough to be described as "based on a true story."

This is not, I know, the usual opinion about this book. On the contrary, *The Economic Consequences of the Peace*, along with its 1922 sequel *A Revision of the Treaty*, is widely regarded as a prophetic work of genius. Keynes's searing moral indictment of Greed and Cruelty among the Allies, even more than his gloomy economic and political prognostications, sounded a gratifying note of moral superiority that was eagerly embraced by simpatico elites. They thrilled to the book's knowingness, its sarcasm, its literary polish no less than to its message. Indeed, *The Economic Consequences of the Peace* is a classic in the library of liberal hand-wringing. As such, its contentions are proposed not as arguments, but as taken-for-granted, inarguable truths about the world, in this case the historical realities of the post-war settlement and the succeeding political and economic situation.

Think about it. The one thing that *everyone* knows about the Treaty of Versailles is that, because of the overly harsh terms the Allies imposed upon Germany, it led directly to Hitler and World War II. An article in *The Economist* in 1999 epitomized this bit of folklore: The "final crime" of the Great War, the article proclaimed, was the Treaty of Versailles, which "would ensure a second world war."

As usual, Mark Twain came closer to the truth. It's not so much the things you don't know that get you into trouble, Twain wrote, as the things you do know that ain't so.

In fact, as the historian Andrew Roberts argues in his *History of the English-Speaking Peoples Since 1900*, there are good reasons for believing that the Treaty of Versailles ought to have been a good deal harsher than it was. Had it divided Germany into two parts, as happened after World War II, or perhaps returned it to its 1870 status of several independent principalities, or even had the Allies merely enforced its original terms, the world would probably have been spared Hitler and the horror of Nazism. There might well have been "no *via dolorosa* of Rhineland-Anschluss-Sudetenland-Danzig for Europe to walk between 1936 and 1939."

Roberts cites for support a neglected masterpiece in the history of polemic, Étienne Mantoux's book *The Carthaginian Peace, or the Economic Consequences of Mr. Keynes.*

Let me introduce you to Monsieur Mantoux. Born in 1913, he was a brilliant French economist. His experience with England started early. His father was a diplomat, and young Mantoux crossed the Channel six times with his family before war broke out in 1914. As a young man, he studied at the London School of Economics as well as in Paris. He joined the French Air Force in 1939 after Hitler invaded Poland. After the fall of France in 1940, Mantoux was unable to make his way to England and so went to Lyon to finish his dissertation. In 1941, he managed to travel on a Rockefeller Fellowship to Princeton's Institute for Advanced Study, where he wrote, in lapidary English, *The Carthaginian Peace.* In 1943, he returned to France, rejected the offer of an administrative post, and took up a position flying under General Leclerc. In April 1945, a scant week before Germany's surrender, he was killed in action outside a Bavarian village. He was thirty-two.

The "Carthaginian Peace" of Mantoux's title—what was that? Keynes several times charges that the Allies, and especially the French Prime Minister Georges Clemenceau, wanted to impose a "Carthaginian Peace" upon the defeated powers, in particular upon Germany. What did

Keynes mean? History provides two possibilities. There was the final Carthaginian peace at the end of the Third Punic War in 146 B.C. This was the fruit of Cato the Elder's repeated injunction "Carthago delenda est," "Carthage must be destroyed." The Romans burned the rival city to the ground, killed or sold into slavery the entire population and, legend has it, salted the fields. Only one bona fide Carthaginian monument from the once glittering city has come down to us, and that, appropriately enough, is a tomb.

That doesn't sound like the Treaty of Versailles, does it? Perhaps Keynes remembered the other "Carthaginian Peace," the peace treaty that followed the battle of Zama in 202 B.C. in which Scipio defeated Hannibal. The Romans appropriated most of Carthage's vessels of war, her overseas possessions, and exacted an indemnity of 4,000 talents.

Maybe that is the sort of thing that Keynes had in mind. As far as I know, he never said. But he did charge that the Treaty of Versailles sought "to weaken and destroy Germany in every possible way" and that it was "one of the most outrageous acts of a cruel victor in civilized history." Those who sign it, he said, "will sign the death sentence of many millions of German men, women, and children." The Germans, he claimed, would never be able to afford the reparations exacted by the Treaty. And as for all the provisions about the Rhineland and other territories, Keynes sniffed that the "perils of the future" lay not in "frontiers or sovereignties" but in "food, coal, and transport." As an aside, I might mention that Adolf Hitler, for one, would have been surprised to hear that.

Let's linger over that word "reparations." Can anyone hear the word straight any longer? Keynes's book took the word out of normal circulation and invested it with an aura of malignancy and unreality that persists to this day. But Germany started the war, which was fought almost entirely on foreign soil, and, along with the other Central Powers, it inflicted horrendous property damage and killed millions. As the historian Sally Marks points out, "France's ten richest industrial departments were only horrific ruins, over 1,000 square miles now a desert." German industry was intact. Why shouldn't Germany pay? Keynes claimed that the Allies sought to revenge themselves upon the Germans. But restitution is not revenge (even if it happens to be mistaken policy). It is merely justice.

Keynes predicted that if the treaty were put into effect, Europe would be threatened with "a long, silent process of semi-starvation, and of a gradual, steady lowering of the standard of living." It is true that certain aspects of the Treaty—regarding reparations, for example—were only haphazardly imposed. (Germany began reneging on its reparation payments within a year or two and stopped paying altogether in 1932.) But it was the territorial settlement of the Treaty, in which Germany lost more than 13 percent of its territory, that Keynes said would sharply "diminish the production of useful commodities" and lead to the starvation of those "millions of German men, women, and children." In fact, ten years later, Europe's production and standard of living were well above the pre-war level. Keynes predicted that the iron and steel output of Germany would diminish, but by 1927 it was producing nearly 30 percent more iron and 38 percent more steel than the record year of 1913. It was the same story with other commodities. Keynes initially warned that Germany could not afford to spend more than 20 billion goldmarks in reparations per year (in 1913, $1 equaled about 4.1 goldmarks). Hitler, by his own reckoning, spent seven times that much *every year* from 1933 to 1939 in rearming Germany.

And by the way, if you want to see what a genuinely harsh peace treaty looks like, you need only contemplate how Germany planned to treat the Allies if it had won—Britain, for example, was to be "squeezed to the uttermost farthing"—or turn to the Treaty of Brest–Litovsk that Germany imposed upon the Bolsheviks in 1918. Russia agreed to default on its financial commitments to the Allies. It ceded the Baltic States to Germany, other territory to the Ottoman Empire, and recognized the independence of Ukraine. Russia also agreed to pay 6 billion German goldmarks in reparations. Hostilities did end, but on terms that one might almost describe as Carthaginian.

Throughout *The Economic Consequences of the Peace*, Keynes was careful to don his economist's hat to supplement the moralist's mantle. Dilating on the wickedness of reparations, for example, he embroiders his discussion with various technicalities about the difficulties of transnational currency flows. But after 1939, the Germans found that wholesale expropriation, enslavement, and extermination more than overcame these little difficulties in extracting wealth from conquered peoples. The idea that France had anything to fear from Germany in the future, Keynes said in *A Revision of the Treaty*, was "a delusion." It would, he explained, be "many years" before Germany once again cast her eyes Westward. Germany's future "lies in the East." Any fears, he wrote in *Economic Consequences*, of "a new Napoleonic domination, rising . . .

from the ashes of cosmopolitan militarism" were but "the anticipations of the timid." Whew! Everyone can relax. It was almost as reassuring as the Kellogg–Briand Pact of 1928, that "General Treaty for the Renunciation of War as an Instrument of National Policy," which was signed by fifty countries, including Germany, Italy, and Japan. It was a monument to idealism, perhaps, but lacked the homely wisdom of Catherine the Great's observation that human skin is more ticklish than paper.

In another work, Keynes famously wrote that "Practical men, who believe themselves to be quite exempt from any intellectual influence, are usually the slaves of some defunct economist." Pondering what he wrote about the Treaty of Versailles, I believe I begin to understand what Baron Keynes meant. Perhaps this is the place to note how close Keynes was to the German parties of the Treaty. As Niall Ferguson points out in *The Pity of War*, Keynes was deeply attached to Carl Melchior, Max Warburg's right-hand man at the Hamburg Bank of M. M. Warburg & Co. He read parts of a draft of *Economic Consequences* to Melchior and Warburg, and apparently profited from their response. "Thanks to Dr. Melchior's clear explanation," the German Foreign Office official Kurt von Lersner recalled, "Herr Keynes ... is trying to find common ground with us." How nice. Posterity has not, Ferguson notes, appreciated "the extent to which Keynes was manipulated by his German friends" or "the extent to which he erred in his analysis of the consequences of the peace."

In 1929, at the end of the third and final volume of his book on the Great War, Winston Churchill noted that by 1940 there would be twice as many men of military age in Germany as in France. That was the sort of nubbly fact that prompted Clemenceau to observe that "We do not have to beg pardon for our victory." But that is precisely what Keynes wanted the Allies to do. One of the most notorious passages of the Treaty of Versailles was Clause 231, the so-called "War Guilt Clause," which required Germany and her allies to accept responsibility for all the damage and loss of life the war caused.

Keynes in effect reversed the direction of the guilt and, in an access of sentimentality that will be familiar to contemporary students of political correctness, made the perpetrators appear to be the victims and vice versa. It turns out that there is a moral variety of Keynesianism as well as the more familiar economic version. Mantoux aptly calls this transvaluation of values "meaculpism." It's an apt phrase. "Long before Hitler had made his appearance on the European scene," he notes sardonically, "meaculpists were agitating for revision of the Treaty." He continues:

> When concession after concession on the part of the Allies had finally been rewarded, most properly, by the National-Socialist Revolution, they never tired of complaining that Hitler was the consequence of Versailles and of the outrageous treatment meted out to the German Republic. But from that time onwards, they became more reluctant to see their Governments acceding to Germany's new moves. If only it had not been Hitler! How distressing to have to grant the demands of that bad man, when there were so many others to whom they could have conceded without the slightest inconvenience! But still ... it had to be done. Versailles, you see. And if anyone was likely to forget it, Hitler would soon remind him. Abuse of the "Diktat" was a favorite gag in his grandiose nerve-war. But now his invective sounded in many ears like some ghastly echo from *The Economic Consequences of the Peace*.

Munich, as Mantoux points out, represented the apex of meaculpism. But there were many smaller peaks: the fate of Czechoslovakia, for example. Hitler gobbled up the richest bit of it in 1938. Whitehall was distressed. Paris was worried. Objections abounded. But they counted for very little in the scale overbalanced by paralyzing meaculpism. Besides, what happened in Czechoslovakia was only a matter of frontiers and sovereignties. And had not the great Keynes taught us that the real perils of the future lay not in "frontiers or sovereignties," but in "food, coal, and transport"?

"Mankind," Étienne Mantoux observed, "is not a philanthropic institution." But the mea-culpism of Keynes and other well-meaning, left-leaning sages seems compelling only on the basis of a gigantic sentimentality about mankind, a faith in the goodness of man that would be touching were its results not so predictably malignant.

In a remarkable book called *Rites of Spring: The Great War and the Birth of the Modern Age*, the historian Modris Eksteins anatomizes the metabolism of the sentimentality that underwrites Keynes's embrace of guilt as an instrument of policy. Eksteins shows how sentimentality and a species of extravagant mythmaking mark the points of contact between avant-garde culture and burgeoning totalitarianism. This was especially true in Germany, the country that had advanced the radical program of the avant-garde most enthusiastically. England, by contrast, was a conservative power. Where Germany started the war to transform the world, England fought the war to preserve a world and the culture that defined it.

A key difference lies in the aestheticization of life: treating life, that is to say, as if it were a work of art devoid of human reality. On the continent, as the historian Carl Schorske put it in his classic study of *fin-de-siècle* Vienna, "the usual moralistic culture of the European bourgeoisie was ... both overlaid and undermined by an amoral *Gef ühlskultur* [sentimental culture]." This revolution in sensibility amounted to a crisis of morality—what the novelist Hermann Broch called a "value vacuum"—that quickly precipitated a crisis in liberal cultural and political life. "Narcissism and a hypertrophy of the life of feeling were the consequence," Schorske wrote.

> The threat of the political mass movements lent new intensity to this already present trend by weakening the traditional liberal confidence in its own legacy of rationality, moral law, and progress. Art became transformed from an ornament to an essence, from an expression of value to a source of value.

It was out of this hothouse atmosphere that Hitler, the serially disappointed art student in Vienna, was first formed. His heady experiences at the front during the war, where he was wounded at least twice, added purpose to the brew. His inconsolable rage at defeat finished the job.

Eksteins is right that the Weimar period, from 1918 to 1933, and the Third Reich, from 1933 to 1945, are "stages in a process" that began with the cultural underpinnings of the Great War and stretched forward to the end of the second war. Am I suggesting that Keynes was somehow implicated in the rise of Hitler? No, I'd say he was no more implicated than was the Treaty of Versailles. Partly because of his habit of sentimentalization, partly because of his addiction to economic melodrama and close attachment to some of the German principals, Keynes lent his enormous intellectual authority to a view of the Treaty and the post-war settlement that encouraged the conviction that, deep down, the victims were wrong to seek restitution from the aggressors. The popularity of that view—all right-thinking, i.e., left-leaning, people believe it to this day—made it impossible for the allies to invigilate the peace settlement effectively. And this failure encouraged the sorts of malignant fantasies that spread like wildfire through Germany in the Twenties and Thirties. These fantasies, Eksteins suggests, were deeply interwoven with the cultural ambitions of certain elements of the avant-garde. "Nazi kitsch," he argues, "may bear a blood relationship to the highbrow religion of art proclaimed by many moderns." It is here, I believe, that we touch upon some of the most telling cultural consequences of the Great War.

Let's pause to consider the term "kitsch." The word itself is mysterious. It seems to have its origins in the Munich art world of the late nineteenth century. But its etymology is controverted. One suggestion is that it is a German corruption of the English word "sketch." Visiting tourists would ask for a quick drawing, *eine Skizze*, of some bucolic, picturesque scene to take home as a souvenir. The saccharine result was often a species of kitsch.

But what is kitsch? The dictionary defines it as a "sweet, sentimental product of bad taste," "characterized by worthless pretentiousness," whose "distinguishing mark is untruthfulness." That is a first answer. But what does it mean to be "sentimental" in this sense?

We tend to think of sentimentality as extravagantly intense or overpowering emotion. Really, though, it is a kind of false or manufactured feeling. "Sentimentality," the poet Wallace Stevens observed, "is a failure of feeling." That is where the element of "untruthfulness" comes in. The intensity is a sign not of conviction but of spuriousness. As the critic Clement Greenberg put it, "Kitsch is vicarious experience and faked sensations."

The sentimentality of kitsch is a sign of its falseness. But it is also a sign of its extravagance. Unanchored to reality, sentimentality is naturally unbounded. Kitsch is a response to a failure or disintegration of cultural values. When the world no longer speaks meaningfully to us, we shout into the void and pretend the echoes come to us from on high.

The grandiosity of kitsch is in proportion to the existential poverty out of which it arose. In this context, it is worth noting a limitation of that dictionary definition of kitsch. The sentimentality of kitsch can be "sweet," but it can also be sour, malignant. Hence the phenomenon of Nazi kitsch. Whole books have been devoted to the subject. It was not confined to preposterous images of Hitler in gleaming armor astride a white steed and the like. It went much deeper. It was the aestheticizing not just of politics but of existence as a whole. "The German everyday shall be beautiful," insisted one Nazi motto.

Which brings us to the curiously amphibious nature of kitsch. Kitsch lives with one foot in the realm of aesthetics and another foot in the realm of ethics. Which is why to say that something is kitsch is to utter a judgment that is moral as well as aesthetic. The failure of kitsch is not just an artistic failing. There is an ethical dimension as well. Hermann Broch identifies kitsch as "the element of evil in the value system of art" and notes that "kitsch" describes not only certain works of art but also a certain attitude towards life. Again, the element of untruthfulness is key. "He who produces kitsch," Broch writes, "is not someone who produces art of meager value. He is not someone of little or no talent. He is definitely not to be judged according to the standard of aesthetics but is ethically depraved; he is a criminal who wills radical evil."

That may seem hyperbolic. We've certainly come a long way from corny genre scenes, paintings of puppies with big eyes, or pretentious, pseudo-classical hotel lobbies bedizened with colored lights. But Broch understands that kitsch rests on a fundamental refusal of reality, on an effort to counterfeit life, to replace reality with a species of narcissistic fantasy. The puppy with big eyes may seem innocent enough. But when extended to the whole of life and invested with the pathos of untrammeled fantasy, kitsch forms a brew that is toxic as well as infatuating. "Evil" is not too strong a word. Modris Eksteins does not mention Broch in *Rites of Spring*. But his understanding of the link between kitsch and evil is similar to Broch's. Kitsch is a sentimentalization of reality in response to cultural failure. The greater the failure, the more malignant the sentimentalization.

I noted earlier the contention that one dominant response to the Great War was "disillusion" and a repudiation of principles named by such lofty abstractions as Honor, Patriotism, Virtue, and Beauty. It is easy to find examples of that solvent at work. But in another sense, the response to the war, especially on the continent, and most particularly in Germany, was just the opposite: it was what we might call the re-enchantment, the re-illusioning, of the world by means of a wholesale embrace of empty abstractions. The re-enchantment was malign, to be sure, but it was also thoroughgoing. Nazism was the most poisonous effort. It was, as Eksteins puts it, "an attempt to lie beautifully to the German nation and to the world." This is where kitsch comes in. "The beautiful lie," Eksteins writes, is

> the essence of kitsch. Kitsch is a form of make-believe, a form of deception. It is an alternative to a daily reality that would otherwise be a spiritual vacuum.... Kitsch replaces ethics with aesthetics.... Nazism was the ultimate expression of kitsch, of its mind-numbing, death-dealing portent. Nazism, like kitsch, masqueraded as life; the reality of both was death. The Third Reich was the creation of "kitsch men," people who confused the relationship between life and art, reality and myth, and who regarded the goal of existence as mere affirmation, devoid of criticism, difficulty, insight.

It is important to note that the kitsch of Nazism was not only for committed Nazis. Writing in 1944, Mantoux observed that "the German people, as a whole, ... [have] been a willing, active, and satisfied partner—so long as things went well." Before Hitler's podium at those early rallies, the historian Joachim Fest observed, "the masses actually celebrated themselves." It is often suggested that Hitler was a product of the Depression, hyperinflation, or both. These may well have been enabling or exacerbating events. But there is an important sense in which Hitler, the avid painter and devotee of Wagner, was, as Eksteins puts it, more a "creature of the German imagination rather than ... of social and economic forces.... He was a mental construct in the midst of defeat and failure. The ultimate kitsch artist, he filled the abyss with symbols of beauty." The *Gesamtkunstwerk*, the "total work of art," that Hitler aspired to create involved more than a Wagnerian stage set: Germany as a whole was his stage. "From first to last," Eksteins writes, "the Third Reich was spectacular, gripping theater. That is what it was intended to be." Even when Allied bombing was devastating German cities, Hitler made the immediate reconstruction of theaters and opera houses a top priority. The mythmaking had to proceed unabated.

Eksteins concludes his book with a harrowing example of this malevolent deployment of kitsch. In the final days of the war, when the Russians were closing in on Berlin, most of the Nazi high-command retreated to Hitler's underground bunker. On May 1, Josef Goebbels had his six children injected with morphine. When they were unconscious, his wife Magda and Hitler's personal doctor crushed ampules of cyanide in their mouths.

A few days earlier, Magda had written a farewell letter to Harald Quandt, a son by a previous marriage. "Our splendid concept," she wrote,

> is perishing and with it goes everything beautiful, admirable, noble, and good that I have known in my life. The world which will succeed the Führer and National Socialism is not worth living in and for this reason I have brought the children here too. They are too good for the life that will come after us.... Harald, my dear—I give you the best that life has taught me: be true—true to yourself, true to mankind, true to your country—in every respect whatsoever.

Splendid. Beautiful. Admirable. Noble. Good. What can one say in response to this nauseating performance? The kitsch, as Eksteins observes, "continued to the very end."

In the final pages of *The Carthaginian Peace*, Étienne Mantoux recalls the remark of a New York taxi driver who said that the war would last longer than its duration. No one would have believed it in August 1914. But as we look around at the world we have inherited from that protracted conflict, we see that, as is so often the case, the paradoxical has turned out to be not contradictory but true. "What a vast difference there is," as the poet Hebbel observed, "between the barbarism that precedes culture and the barbarism that follows it."

September 2014

The problem with "Mockingbird"

Kyle Smith

WRITTEN FOR THE STAGE by Aaron Sorkin, *To Kill a Mockingbird* (at the Shubert Theatre) opened before Christmas, yet continues to be the sensation of the Rialto. On several occasions it has sold more than $2 million worth of tickets in a single week. There are only so many seats in a theater, so arriving at that gargantuan number requires charging $500 for the best seats, $275 for good ones. Finding a same-week ticket for as little as $200 is almost impossible. Rarely, if ever, in Broadway history has a non-musical created such a sustained frenzy.

Harper Lee's *To Kill a Mockingbird* (1960) is not just a classic but perhaps *the* classic text for the cohort that provides the biggest pool of potential Broadway ticket buyers: the affluent, well-meaning American liberals who define themselves above all other qualities as brave and righteous scourges of racism. Liberals name their children Atticus and Scout. (Well, maybe not Atticus anymore, but I'll get to that.) On the night I attended, theatergoers were taking selfies of themselves with the set in the background, eager to show the world they bore witness to this play. Yet the Bible, Torah, and Koran of American liberalism is, at its core, illiberal. Whether told as a novel, movie, or play, the story stands for the actual opposite of what it purports to stand for. Why don't liberals notice, or care? Because liberals don't actually believe in liberalism. What they believe is that their side is good, and they adore having their self-image projected back at them. The dramatic and thematic flaws of the work are obvious to a rational, adult eye, but *To Kill a Mockingbird* is written at a child's level, and childhood is when people tend first to encounter it. The book is therefore double-ring-fenced against clear-eyed analysis: it's about racism, and it's about childhood, and who are you to point out its failures, Mr. Critic, if not some kind of kid-hating racist?

There was a carnival atmosphere at the Shubert Theatre. Outside, a man with a small pushcart was selling buttons and other tchotchkes off a kiosk labeled "The Anti-Trump Bandwagon." Inside the theater, the souvenir stand sold T-shirts labeled "Consent is sexy" and "Patriarchy is a bitch." There was also a hooded sweatshirt for sale, labeled in large lettering "TRAYVON." Trayvon Martin, you will recall, tackled a man who had done him no harm whatsoever and repeatedly pounded his head into the pavement. He was shot in the chest for his attack. The man who killed him, George Zimmerman, was told by police that they had security-camera footage of the whole encounter. Zimmerman's response? "Thank God." Police knew Zimmerman's story was true immediately, yet prosecutors bowed to a howling mob of celebrities, pundits, and politicians and charged Zimmerman with murder. He was wrongfully put to trial, was in fact the victim of a gross injustice, because of his race. You would think the souvenir stand at a play about a race-based miscarriage of justice would be selling shirts emblazoned with the word "ZIMMERMAN." But that would only confuse the left-wingers paying to see this play. They are here to have their tribalism affirmed. The average ticket-buyer for *To Kill a Mockingbird* would have been delighted to join the mob calling for a completely unjustified trial for Zimmerman, then, after his acquittal, to join the mob that formed to demand Zimmerman unjustly be retried in a federal court on the same charge, albeit with the wording on the indictment changed slightly from "murdering Trayvon Martin by shooting him in the chest" to "violating Trayvon Martin's civil rights by shooting him in the chest." We can be thankful that the Justice Department, unlike the mob, saw no reason to disregard the double-jeopardy clause of the Fifth Amendment. It implicitly defended the importance of procedural correctness, unlike *To Kill a Mockingbird*.

To Kill a Mockingbird draws a diverse audience—young white people, middle-aged white people, and elderly white people. Why were there almost zero black people in attendance in a play about a miscarriage of justice carried out against a black man in 1934 Alabama? Later I will hazard a guess. Bob Ewell (Frederick Weller), the angry and violent racist who pushes his teen daughter, Mayella (Erin Wilhelmi), to make an obviously false charge of rape and assault against the black handyman Tom Robinson (Gbenga Akinnagbe), refers to blacks as animals—but so does the criminal defense attorney Atticus Finch (played with a refreshing minimum of showboating by Jeff Daniels). Mockingbirds don't do anything but sing their hearts out for us; that's why it's a sin to kill a mockingbird. Innocent, dumb, incapable of doing genuine evil: that is how we are meant to think of Tom Robinson, and by extension of black folk. Harper Lee's racists and anti-racists alike agree that blacks are inferior to whites; they disagree merely on whether they are more like wild animals or cute pets.

Sorkin has been praised for updating the story, but he really hasn't. The major difference is that he beefs up the character of Calpurnia (LaTanya Richardson Jackson), the black woman who has served as the family housekeeper going back generations. Sorkin has Calpurnia steer Atticus away from his view that no one, even a Klansman like Bob Ewell, is irredeemable. It seems unlikely that a black woman in Calpurnia's position would speak her mind so freely in 1934, but what is important to Sorkin is to capture a very 2019 emotional imperative on the left—the idea that it's crucial not merely to oppose bad things but also to make a show of anger about them, to denounce whole systems rather than just misbehaving individuals. Sorkin, who in his recent collaboration with Daniels, HBO's series *The Newsroom* (2012–14), offered a running fantasy of how news programs could have covered real events in a more nakedly partisan-progressive way, has nudged *To Kill a Mockingbird* away from Atticus's Southern gentility and a bit in the direction of woke columnists. In the bargain, it allows him to have a black character who does something other than suffer; Calpurnia is another stock figure, though, the wise black person bestowing enlightenment on whites.

Sorkin's source remains what it always was: a young-adult novel, with all of the oversimplification that goes with it. Sorkin does nothing to make the work more mature, more complicated for sophisticated adults. There are three kinds of people in Sorkin's play: white racists, white anti-racists, and kindly, innocent blacks. Reducing race relations to this schema was more forgivable in 1960, when the book was published, than it is today, but then again, for white progressives, it's still 1960. Priding themselves on their ability to weigh all the nuance and complexity in, say, human sexuality or the market economy, they adhere to a resolutely childlike vision of racial matters. Hence that TRAYVON hoodie: even as the disappointing facts dribbled out, the Left simply slotted the story of Martin's demise into this pre-existing story of racist white trash (Zimmerman), white saviors (the mob clamoring for Zimmerman's arrest), and innocent blacks in the middle. Martin, being black, could not possibly have done anything wrong. He was unarmed except for his Skittles, we were told. As if an unarmed person is incapable of committing assault. A photo of him looking like a cherub circulated widely, as if no young black male could be a criminal. Zimmerman was assigned the role of white racist because he had reported to the police a young black male, and because he had kept a wary eye on Martin. That it was perfectly understandable for a neighborhood watchman to watch the neighborhood could not be conceded by the woke mob. None of the white liberals who demanded Zimmerman be tried, then demanded he be convicted, then demanded he be re-tried, would waive the right to call the police upon sighting a suspicious stranger who happens to be a young black male. That it was racist for Zimmerman to call the police was an important fiction they told themselves (and screamed in public), a way to reassure themselves that they were so pure of heart that they would never, ever suspect an unknown young black male of anything.

Trite formulas may work fine as political slogans, but they don't take you very far in drama. Atticus Finch would be a much more convincing hero if he were more like Lyndon Johnson—a man who did much to advance civil rights but who was also a racist who habitually referred to black Americans with the nastiest racial slurs. *To Kill a Mockingbird*'s characters are merely billboards for racism and anti-racism positioned around the two wonderful blacks—noble, helpful, suffering Tom and wise, soulful Calpurnia. Far from being important tutelage on the price of racism in America, *To Kill a Mockingbird* is mere flattery for white progressives seeking reassurance about their moral stature in the universe—at the top of the order, stalwart opponents of the white trash but also above the blacks, who are not their equals but fragile, tender mockingbirds who require white protection. *To Kill a Mockingbird* is a story of white liberal self-congratulation. That may be why blacks aren't especially interested.

A more exacting drama would work in twists and doubts: if Tom were not entirely innocent, or if there were some ambiguity about whether he had carried out the attack, the courtroom drama might be gripping. But Tom lost the use of his left arm in a cotton gin accident many years ago and couldn't have choked Mayella with both hands nor hit her with his left fist. Somehow the citizens of the town where Tom is well known, and even the family for which Tom has repeatedly done chores, are unaware that his left arm is useless. He's been doing work for everybody for years with one arm and nobody noticed? Preposterous. A witness who takes the stand in Tom's defense about the arm injury is cross-examined about the defendant's character and drinking habits to impugn his credibility, as though any of that would matter: in a burg like Maycomb, where everyone knows his neighbors, everyone would already know about poor Tom's arm. Failing that, the mangled arm could simply be displayed to the jury. As a trial drama, *To Kill a Mockingbird* wouldn't pass muster in the writer's room of the most routine television courtroom saga.

Bob Ewell, the despicable bigot who beats up his daughter for behaving flirtatiously toward Tom, and who leads a Klan lynching party to attempt to break into the prison where Tom is being held, would be a more interesting character if he had some shred of psychological motivation for his ill will toward blacks—say, if he had been brutalized by a black man. The children in the play would have more dramatic weight if they, as products of their time, were infected with racism instead of being adorable little bonbons of childhood sweetness. (Think back to your earliest days: are kids really so sweet?) But any such adjustments that might make *To Kill a Mockingbird* a more effective drama would make it less like a banner of white liberal self-love, less like the narrative equivalent of a TRAYVON hoodie. When it emerged in Lee's long-delayed follow-up to *To Kill a Mockingbird*, *Go Set a Watchman* (2015)—which turned out to have been written before the sanctified novel that secured Lee's immortality but is set twenty years later—that Atticus, as late as his seventies, was actually a white supremacist, Lee's fans were aghast and hurt. Never mind that Atticus was closely based on Lee's own father, Amasa Coleman Lee, who was indeed a segregationist until nearly the end of his life. (Finch was her mother's maiden name.) How dare Lee let messy reality intrude into a children's fable about a plaster saint! How dare she introduce thorny and vexatious debate about race into their garden of race innocence! Atticus's fifty-five-year reign as the paragon of white liberal virtue was abruptly ended. As Randall Kennedy, a black academic, wrote in *The New York Times*, "*Go Set a Watchman* demands that its readers abandon the immature sentimentality ingrained by middle school lessons about the nobility of the white savior." To cling to immature sentimentality, though, is exactly what white progressives want. Adam Gopnik, writing in *The New Yorker*, seemed offended that *Go Set a Watchman* even exists, harrumphing that it "has not a single prefatory sentence to explain its pedigree or its history or the strange circumstance that seems to have brought it to print after all this time." The novel is now undergoing approximately the same fate as *The Godfather, Part III*: fans of its predecessor are simply choosing to pretend it never appeared. Hip Brooklyn parents are not going to be naming their boys Atticus in the future, though.

Few if any of *Mockingbird*'s progressive fans seem to have noted that, in its final act, it contradicts itself. The core of liberalism means granting your worst enemy the same rights, the same due process, that you would grant your brother. The worst enemy here is Bob Ewell, the violent death (possibly justified) of whom at the hands of Boo Radley goes uninvestigated because everyone involved—including, after some grumbling, Atticus Finch—agrees to participate in a lie and a cover-up about the circumstances of the racist's demise. It ought to fall to the legal process to decide whether Boo Radley is justified in killing Ewell, who is menacing the Finch children when Radley fells him with a knife. Instead, the sheriff announces he will preempt all inquiry by declaring that Ewell somehow killed himself, by falling on his own knife. A novel about the injustice of lynch mobs and race bias concludes, then, by arguing that sometimes legal procedure must be discarded in order to achieve some kind of rough justice. Ewell did great wrong to Tom Robinson, therefore he has forfeited his rights. He got what was coming to him for being a bad guy. Yet this is the same kind of tribal thinking that drives lynch mobs: forget due process, we know this guy is bad. *To Kill a Mockingbird*'s driving passion is not justice for all but an eye for an eye: "Let the dead bury their dead," the sheriff says. In other words, let's not get too hung up on whether murder was done here, it all evens out. That the reclusive, possibly mentally handicapped Boo Radley is, like Tom Robinson, described as an innocent "mockingbird" who enjoys special protection because of his intrinsically guileless nature, and cannot be judged by his actions like any other person, says much about the progressive mindset: animals, black people, and retarded people are all cast into the same basket. They're all helpless, all in need of crusading white liberals to look out for them.

The phrase "blind spot" is the new cliché among progressive pundits who wish to call someone a racist without actually using the word, which even they must notice has a tendency to pollute the air, to render further civilized discourse unlikely. *To Kill a Mockingbird* represents the blindness of progressivism. It has for more than fifty years been right there in plain sight as a totem of the patronizing, condescending, dehumanizing mindset of white liberals when it comes to race. Liberals don't see its dramatic flaws and don't see that its final message is damning rather than reassuring. They don't care, because what they want is a soothing balm and reassurance for their anguish about race. At the end of the performance, as I politely waited for the standing ovation to end, I noticed that many of the women around me were crying. It would never have occurred to me that such a transparent case of pandering could elicit such an emotional reaction, but then again I was left equally unstirred by the supposedly inspirational speeches of Barack Obama. People actually believed Obama was going to fundamentally transform the United States of America, to lift us to a higher level? We would become a better people by ticking the box next to his name? *To Kill a Mockingbird* was well ahead of the game. It proved that when you flatter white liberals with the idea that they're holy race saviors, you can get them to believe nearly anything.

September 2019

The denunciation machine

J. Christian Adams

On March 14 of this year, Morris Dees, the co-founder and chief trial lawyer of the Southern Poverty Law Center (SPLC), was fired. Nine days later, the president of the organization, Richard Cohen, resigned. This implosion of leadership came after rumors surfaced of a long-standing culture of discrimination, harassment, and employee mistreatment.

The SPLC began as a civil rights law practice in 1971 and later became a nonprofit organization devoted to various social justice initiatives. As the SPLC tells it, in the years since, the organizations has

> shut down some of the nation's most violent white supremacist groups by winning crushing, multimillion-dollar jury verdicts on behalf of their victims. It dismantled vestiges of Jim Crow, reformed juvenile justice practices, shattered barriers to equality for women, children, the LGBT community and the disabled, protected low-wage immigrant workers from exploitation, and more.

But consistency is not the SPLC's strong suit. Though the group was founded to fight racial discrimination, harassment, and the mistreatment of people because of immutable characteristics, we now know that the SPLC didn't practice internally what it preached publicly.

It's now clear that the organization's very name reflects the stack of falsehoods that has characterized its rise and fall. For starters, the organization is not focused exclusively on the South. And the poverty in the name clearly doesn't refer to Dees, who lives in extraordinary luxury, or even to the organization itself, which has become a fundraising machine (described by one employee as "the Poverty Palace").

Indeed, the Southern Poverty Law Center is little it professes to be.

Instead of protecting civil rights, it more closely resembles a shakedown outfit, engaging in attacks on those exercising First Amendment rights in ways that the SPLC—and the Left—disagrees with. The SPLC uses the favorite tool of leftist shakedown artists: exaggerated charges of racism and bigotry against some of their targets.

During my time as an attorney in the Civil Rights Division at the United States Department of Justice from 2005–10, I had occasion to cross paths with the SPLC. The first time was when one of my colleagues sent an email to all of the employees in the Justice Department Voting Section. The email provided a link to the latest SPLC "hate map" and suggested that Justice Department employees consult the map in regards to any state where they might already have a case. After all, if you can show bigots are active in an area, then the area must be bigoted, or so went the logic of the leftist bureaucrat who sent the email.

That email to the entire DOJ Voting Section, however, triggered a section-wide response from one employee who questioned relying on the SPLC's methodology and its biases in branding a particular group a "hate group." This was civil rights heresy, to question the SPLC. It was a short-lived debate, because, at the Justice Department, the SPLC was a source trusted by nearly all of the staff to aid their law enforcement efforts. The SPLC aligns ideologically with the left-leaning DOJ employees who make up the rank and file in the Civil Rights Division. To those employees I knew at DOJ who genuinely thought an America Nazi takeover might happen, the SPLC was a sentinel protecting us from the fascist uprising.

Fearmongering about fascist takeovers has been very good for business. In 2014, the SPLC raised $45 million, in 2015 $50 million, and in 2016 an astounding $132 million in contributions. Tax returns for the organization showed $6.7 million in 2015 investment income alone. The latest information shows net assets of the SPLC at $449,834,593. Remember, the SPLC is a charity under the Internal Revenue code and isn't supposed to be a cash-generating machine. Yet it has almost a half-billion dollars in reserve.

The SPLC also disclosed to the IRS that it fundraises in the Middle East, East Asia, and Russia, but the tax returns do not disclose the amount of money raised in those parts of the world, nor from whom. Recently, it has also been revealed that the SPLC is holding millions in offshore accounts.

To accumulate this pile of treasure over the years, the SPLC employed sharp elbows. Even other liberal civil rights groups have been taken aback by their shameless willingness to overstate any threat, jump on any bandwagon, and make any small piece of news into a crisis—all to drum up more donations. One former ACLU staffer told me that other liberal groups have noticed how the SPLC's fundraising campaigns crowd out dollars that could be used more effectively elsewhere by other groups.

The SPLC says it is "dedicated to fighting hate and bigotry and to seeking justice for the most vulnerable members of our society." It has a number of specific priorities under that umbrella: exposing and countering "hate and extremism," advocating for children and aliens, eliminating fines and bail, and relaxing other criminal penalties.

The way that the SPLC has differentiated itself from other leftist groups, however, is the self-styled "Hatewatch." The SPLC's core activity is to find so-called hate groups and individuals and to publicize their existence via the "hate map" and their list of extremists that were go-to resources of my Justice Department colleagues.

The SPLC hate map is a slick feature, offering lists of groups the SPLC doesn't like, organized by state and year. While you might expect all the targeted groups to be typical neo-Nazis or Klansmen, the truth is something else. Take two West Virginia organizations the SPLC labeled as hate groups in 2018: Warriors for Christ and ACT for America.

Warriors for Christ is essentially a Christian ministry run by a fundamentalist pastor, Rich Penkoski. After his ministry was labeled an "Anti-LGBT" hate group by the SPLC, Penkoski and his family became the recipients of plenty of hate themselves, some directed at his children. "They said things about coming to our home and doing the most brutal, awful things," Penkoski told a reporter for the Christian Action Network. Penkoski had to flee West Virginia for Tennessee; presumably the 2019 hate map will show that Warriors for Christ has moved states. But will it mention the threats and hate Penkoski's family received from people who trust the SPLC map?

ACT for America's website gives no more hint as to why it was labeled an "Anti-Muslim" hate group than the SPLC hate map does. Founded by Brigitte Gabriel, the organization claims to be the nation's "largest and most influential national security grassroots advocacy organization." It has sections supporting law enforcement, Israel, and the military.

Now ACT for America is fighting back. Their website has a page promoting another organization, SPLC Exposed, and states, "The discredited Southern Poverty Law Center has waged a war against ACT for America and every other national organization that espouses conservative viewpoint [*sic*] and values." Other groups are taking legal action, with more than sixty considering defamation lawsuits.

A large part of the SPLC map's insidiousness is that it offers no specific information about most of these groups. Perhaps some of the allegedly threatening groups captured by the hate map are merely crackpots with blogs—we don't know, because the map is curiously silent about the details of each organization. In most cases, the hate map doesn't provide information to substantiate its accusations of "hate" beyond mere tags designating a group as "White Nationalist," "Anti-LGBT," "General Hate," etc. The reader has to take the SPLC at its word or seek out further information independently of the map. Without context, the SPLC has the ability to make it seem like there are many more "hate groups" in the United States than there may actually be.

Of course, not every organization labeled as a hate group on the SPLC hate map is as harmless as the local Rotary International club. Some of them are indeed organizations with truly vile pedigrees, such as the Ku Klux Klan. The problem is that the SPLC isn't transparent about the decision to place a group on the list, and the results seem to have a lopsided ideological tilt.

Other groups ensnared in the SPLC hate map at one time or another include the H. L. Mencken Club, Jihad Watch, and the Young Americans for Freedom chapter at Michigan State University. What is more, such individuals as Ayaan Hirsi Ali, Charles Murray, Maajid Nawaz, Ben Carson, and Pamela Geller—to name just a few—have been at one time (or are still) listed as "extremists" by the SPLC.

This might be laughable if it weren't so tragic. On August 15, 2012, Floyd Lee Corkins II entered the offices of the Family Research Council, an organization dedicated to "faith, family, and freedom in public policy and the culture from a biblical worldview," opened fire, and shot a security guard before he was stopped from slaughtering FRC employees. He told the FBI he went there to "kill as many as possible and smear Chick-Fil-A sandwiches in the victims' faces." Corkins said he relied on the SPLC hate map to pick his target.

To keep up with the evolving definition of hate, the SPLC is now on the hunt for "male-supremacy" groups. "Rabid misogyny is now an integral part of America's hate scene," said Heidi Beirich, the director of the SPLC's "Intelligence Project." If you are surprised to hear of this new threat of male-supremacy hate groups and their dangerous campaign of misogyny, you are not alone. Even the SPLC can hardly find them. The hate map only identifies two male-supremacy groups in the entire nation: A Voice for Men in Texas and Return of Kings in Washington, D.C. Return of Kings professes to be a "blog for heterosexual, masculine men. It's meant for a small but vocal collection of men in America today who believe men should be masculine and women should be feminine."

As absurd as it might seem to raise the alarm about the "male-supremacy" movement by finding precisely two "male-supremacy" groups across the entire nation, the SPLC will ride this "woke" wave and fundraise off the threat. This is the standard operating procedure of the SPLC: exaggerate a threat and scare and provoke a subset of the population that is all too willing to believe in bogeymen. When the SPLC steps in to fight on their side, their pocketbooks open up.

Naturally, the SPLC website doesn't mention the hate-filled women's studies programs on campuses across America, where a burning animosity towards men is inculcated in young women by college professors. Perhaps the SPLC should consider nominating the women's studies program at Northeastern University for inclusion on its hate map. Suzanna Danuta Walters, the chair of their women's studies department, penned a 2018 *Washington Post* editorial entitled "Why can't we hate men?" She wrote to men:

> Don't run for office. Don't be in charge of anything. Step away from the power. We got this. And please know that your crocodile tears won't be wiped away by us anymore. We have every right to hate you. You have done us wrong.

Had a male-supremacist group written this garbage with the genders reversed, you can be sure the SPLC would have added a third male-supremacist outfit to their hate map.

Since the downfall of the SPLC leadership, the former SPLC staffer Bob Moser has written in *The New Yorker* about various instances of misconduct at the organization. He revealed that new female employees were warned about the tendencies of Dees and Cohen. Staffers would covertly share among themselves unflattering articles about race and sex discrimination at the SPLC. Moser described the SPLC as a "highly profitable scam."

After Dees and Cohen disappeared in the recent reckoning, Meredith Horton, the highest-ranking black attorney at SPLC, resigned due to "the hardships women and employees of color faced at SPLC." Employees signed letters of protest about systemic failures to address an environment of sexual harassment and racial discrimination. The letter alleged a culture of retaliation against anyone who questioned the behavior of Dees and the SPLC leadership.

The SPLC isn't saying much about the resignations. When a reporter for *The Daily Caller* asked Beirich and Maureen Costello, the SPLC's Director of Teaching Tolerance, what they knew about the lecherous behavior of the SPLC leadership, they threatened to call the police on the reporter. Others in the media who have previously relied on the SPLC aren't asking many questions. Few investigative journalists are drilling into the details of why Dees and Cohen are now gone.

Not only are most journalists not asking the right questions, some are still relying on the SPLC for stories and narratives. The SPLC still continues to be quoted and taken seriously. Tom Schuba at the *Chicago Sun-Times* cited SPLC hate-group designations for an April story entitled "How groups tied to white nationalists are targeting Chicago and Kim Foxx." Bess Levin, in an article for *Vanity Fair*, used an SPLC designation in her headline "Trump Wants Former 'Hate Group' Leader for Top Immigration Job." Levin sought to sink consideration of Julie Kirchner for a Department of Homeland Security post because she was the executive director of the Federation for American Immigration Reform. This is how it is intended to work. A once-credible civil rights organization denounces you. Others can then rely on the denunciation to smear you; smeared once, smeared forever. Fearful liberal donors write big checks. Repeat.

The SPLC has perfected ritualized denunciation. The power of the verb "denounce" is hardly understood in the free West, but in other regimes and political cultures, a denunciation carries the gravest consequence. One neighbor would denounce another, and the latter would vanish in the middle of the night. Denunciation has been a tool of the powerful to eliminate competition. Even the failure to censure those who were worthy of denunciation could be a crime.

Here, the SPLC has used this form of public criticism to deplatform, delegitimize, and kneecap individuals and organizations with whom they disagree. When the David Horowitz Freedom Center landed on the SPLC map, Visa and MasterCard decided they would stop processing donations made to them. Without the ability to accept online donations, an organization stands little chance of survival. Only after a loud public outcry, including by the leading voices in conservative media, was the Freedom Center able to reutilize financial services and credit card payment streams.

Groups vilified by the SPLC can count on the denunciation appearing in a prominent place on their Wikipedia page. The American Family Association's page says the "AFA has been listed as a hate group by the Southern Poverty Law Center." The Family Research Council? "In 2010, the Southern Poverty Law Center classified FRC as an anti-gay hate group." The David Horowitz Freedom Center? "The Southern Poverty Law Center (SPLC) has described the Center as a far-right organization."

Twitter, until April 2019, included the SPLC in its Trust and Safety Council, a group that already contains leftist organizations chosen to advise Twitter on how to police speech on their platform. The SPLC's role on the council was only terminated after the recent allegations of sexual and racial impropriety, not because of the years spent besmirching organizations with which it disagrees.

Give the SPLC credit. The founders built an effective fundraising machine that could raise hundreds of millions of dollars by exaggerating claims that America was filled with Nazis and dangerous conservatives. They succeeded in marginalizing groups that enjoy broad respect and espouse views that were mainstream only a decade ago. To tens of millions of Americans, for example, the pro-life American Family Association remains mainstream. But SPLC profits from deeply embedded psychological circumstances where fears open checkbooks. They've also managed to shake down major corporations, such as Google, Apple, and J. P. Morgan Chase, that feel compelled to demonstrate publicly their liberal bona fides.

Celebrations about the embarrassing demise of SPLC leadership should be short-lived and measured. Nothing about the behavior of Dees and Cohen undermines the SPLC business model in the long term.

The underlying machine hums on, searching for more organizations to denounce, sending out more email fundraising blasts warning of bigots coming to a town near you, and continuing to divide America along racial and religious lines.

June 2019

Beauty locked out

Alexander McCall Smith

JANE AUSTEN may have died in 1817, but sometimes we need to remind ourselves of the fact, such is the continuing enthusiasm for everything associated with her. Jane Austen societies and websites abound, and hardly a publishing season goes by without the publication of several new Austen pastiches. *Pride and Prejudice*, perhaps the most popular novel in the Austen canon, is regularly transplanted to new settings, working just as well, it seems, in Los Angeles or Amritsar as it does in rural England. The same is true of film: remakes of Austen titles are launched as soon as it is deemed decent to do so, while favorite versions are watched time and time again by their enthralled devotees. To talk of a Jane Austen cottage industry may sound somewhat hackneyed, but it is not far from the truth.

The reasons for the continuing popularity of Austen's novels is to be found partly in their essential merits and partly in the needs of those who respond to them. The novels are, of course, gems of human observation—encapsulations of the world within that the novelist herself referred to as "little bits of ivory." They satisfy the most fundamental requirement of literature: they engage the reader and maintain that engagement through the course of the novel. They are, in the view of their many devotees, just perfect.

It is not just Jane Austen's technical virtuosity, however, that accounts for her appeal. Her novels seem to fulfill a deeper need in today's readers: the yearning for an ordered and innocent world in which violence and conflict are absent. Of course we know those issues are there in the background; we are well aware—or should be—that the leisured world of the novels was based on cruelty and exploitation on a massive scale. The comfortable life of their protagonists did not spring from nowhere: there were distant slave plantations that kept European tables supplied.

We know that, yet in spite of that knowledge, the novels still cater to a need for calm, for gentleness in pace and attitude. They persist.

Not all authors have been as fortunate. Barbara Pym, who is viewed by some as being the twentieth-century answer to Jane Austen, enjoyed a considerable measure of success with her small-scale portrayal of rather timid lives. Then she fell victim to a changed *zeitgeist*; her publisher rejected a new novel. There followed a period of silence that was only ended a short time before her death when the disaster of that cold-shouldering was at last recognized. Her fault, it seems, was the lack of what is now referred to as "edge."

Pym's novels, like Austen's, deal with lives that are, in many respects, rather ordinary. They do not dwell on conflict, social dysfunction, or psychopathology. They contain no explicit violence; they do not portray people killing one another. They are quiet books. They would not do—at least for the literary establishment that kept the gates. For readers, of course, it might have been quite different: they might well have been content to go on appreciating Barbara Pym in the same way as they continued to enjoy Jane Austen, but for quite some time they were not to be given that chance.

Fifteen years ago, I sat down and wrote a novel set in Botswana, where I had lived for a short while some time before and which I had come to know and admire over many visits. I chose to set this novel, to which I gave the title *The No. 1 Ladies' Detective Agency*, there because I felt that there was something special about the southern African country that was worth portraying in fiction. The particular qualities I appreciated were peacefulness and, quite simply, goodness. In my view, Botswana was a good place—a place of harmony and stability in a region that had been wracked by division and conflict for years. It was, I thought, an extraordinary achievement on the part of the people there that they should have created such a well-run and successful state in a region where oppression and violence had been a daily reality for so long. It was also much to the credit of Botswana that it enjoyed unbroken democracy from the day of its independence in 1966, and that there had been very little corruption and, very significantly, no political prisoners.

The resulting novel was something of a pastoral. Although I chose to concentrate on the affairs of a small detective agency, there was, to begin with, no real crime in the story, the emphasis being on the depiction of place and on the day-to-day life of people whose lives were relatively uneventful. I wanted to portray Botswana as the country I had experienced when I lived there—one where courtesy and consideration were the keynotes of social interaction and where the practice of the traditional African communitarian values could still be witnessed. I knew that this picture of Botswana society was an incomplete one, and that alongside these positive features there were, of course, all the problems that any society faces: violence, exploitation, want, and so on. But while those things existed, I believed that they had been given excessive weight in writing about Africa and that most Western writers, when addressing their gaze to the continent, ended up writing yet another version of *Heart of Darkness*. Mr. Kurtz's cry, "*The horror, the horror!*" has echoed through a whole slew of novels since Conrad wrote his bleak book. There *was* good reason for that *cri de coeur*—and at times there still is—but it seemed to me that to dwell on it to the exclusion of any other focus is to misrepresent reality. It would be odd to avoid any mention of the raining down of bombs when writing about London during the Blitz, but would it not be equally odd to exclude any mention of the fact that ordinary life went on in the middle of all that? People had love affairs, drank pints of beer with friends, collected stamps, and went to the office, just as they always had. Ordinary life tends to go on even in the direst circumstances; the fact that it does is a matter for wonder and celebration.

Once *The No. 1 Ladies' Detective Agency* was completed, I submitted it to the publishers who had published my previous two books, a collection of short stories and a book of African folk tales. They initially agreed to publish, but then had second thoughts. Quite understandable: publishers get nervous about the market and are fully entitled to turn down books that they feel are too much of a commercial risk. In my case, though, it was not the prospect of loss that deterred them—they seemed more concerned that the book was too gentle, too lacking in "edge," too little concerned with violence, aggression, or dysfunction.

I responded to suggestions that I should include more grittiness, and I inserted into the novel a rather sinister case of witchcraft and an episode in which my heroine suffers physical abuse at the hands of a violent husband. It was not enough. The tone wasn't right. Scottish writers had to be tough and uncompromising, their eyes fixed firmly on all that was wrong, uncomfortable, and unresolved. The creation of a world in which the traditional virtues were practiced was not considered a worthy occupation of a contemporary writer.

Fortunately, my novel went to another firm of publishers who did not share that view. They were an exception, though, and when it came to finding a paperback home for the book in London, the same response seemed to prevail: too comfortable, too reassuring, too devoid of—there was no other term—edge. It was only when the book was imported into the United States that it was given the oxygen it needed and found an extensive readership.

I do not in any way blame those publishers for their response—indeed I still hold them in high regard. Publishers are inevitably tempted to follow fashion and to publish works that cater to prevailing expectations. But what the experience did for me was to make me think about the way in which a curious prejudice has developed against the depiction of visions of harmony and contentment, of the positive as opposed to the negative, of the functional rather than the deeply and disturbingly dysfunctional in some of the arts. Why is it that dystopia has replaced utopia to the extent that few self-respecting writers dare to pay the latter state more than a cursory visit? Is it because, quite frankly, for many people, probably the majority, the virtues have become boring and the only interesting material is to be found firmly located in the vices? The answer to both of these questions is probably yes, and that has certain worrying consequences for our culture and for the sort of life in society that our culture creates and nurtures.

Of course, there is a counterargument to this—and a fairly compelling one at that. If one looks at what is on offer in bookstores today the choice is overwhelming. Every sort of taste in fiction is liberally catered to, and new technology enables us to have it at the press of a button. The old restrictions of expensive print are gone. No longer are publishers the sole gate-keepers of what is available: if you want to publish something, you can always do it yourself, and it can be read by anybody, virtually anywhere, in the world. In such a world, limitations of choice are not a factor. If Barbara Pym were turned down today, then she would surely have found some niche, publish-on-demand company that would have made her work available.

In such circumstances, one might argue that no one vision of literature is likely to dominate; conditions are ideal for artistic pluralism—if you want contemporary Austenesque novels you will find them; if you want gritty *noir* mysteries, you can have those too. Can anybody really complain that the overall artistic climate is inimical to any particular vision? If there is no overall climate, but merely a wide selection of micro-climates, is there any issue to debate? I think there is. I believe that there are opinions and attitudes that can impose on the public a certain hegemony of approach. Even if there is a wide choice of voices available, there are certain institutions that can exercise significant control over what we get to read and see—there is, although they may be unwilling to admit it, a critical establishment that can be very influential in deciding who gets noticed and who wins prizes. If these institutions and individuals decide that a particular approach is to be favored, then you can be sure that that approach will have a very strong advantage in the literary marketplace, one far more likely to shape public taste.

For reasons on which one can only speculate, the view seems to have emerged that the real concern of the writer, the dramatist, and the screenwriter should be social dysfunction and individual turmoil. It is a curious phenomenon that rather skews literary and artistic output in a particular direction. I have already given the examples of the silencing of Barbara Pym and of the criticism I have received for dealing in my novels with constructive lives lived well. Another example comes from the world of British television. The BBC seems to be determined to concentrate its dramatic output on what it calls blue-collar drama. Such dramas—which amply satisfy the "edge requirement"—are clearly worth doing, but should they really crowd out other visions? Somehow the default position for television drama has become one in which dysfunctional, damaged lives are played out in circumstances of aggression, conflict, and often considerable psychopathology. What is viewed as middle-class drama—drama in which mild-mannered, ordinary people, or exceptional but stimulating and intelligent people, lead out their lives—is frowned upon and has little chance of an airing. It is very peculiar, and very limiting.

The defenders of this exclusive approach justify their position on the grounds that television—and fiction in general—should be about real people: it should reflect the true face of the society it purports to portray. This is the social realism argument, and it is a familiar one. Yet it is seriously flawed because it presumes that social reality has only one face: a damaged and dysfunctional one. In fact, in any given population, the vast majority of people lead lives that would be unrecognizable to the creators of the grim-spirited drama that claims to represent them.

Television producers do have to pay attention to Jane Austen. And, by and large, they hate her. Yet the fact of the matter is that Jane Austen pays the bills—every costume drama, no matter how corny and heated-up, tends to be wildly popular whatever the critics may say. That is because people want to be entertained in a positive way; they want to witness beauty; they do not want a diet of unrelieved gloom.

What has happened is that, in some of the arts, we have become so used to the portrayal of pathology that we assume that it is the only reasonable approach—that any more positive emphasis is naive, misleading, and, frankly, without real significance. The assumption is made, then, that all work of literary merit is going to have to be bleak in its outlook; anything else may have a function as mere diversion, but is not serious and will never be given the critical imprimatur. This ignores the fact that novels that are not about recalcitrant social problems or any other form of human suffering may make just as profound observations on what it is to be human as their miserable counterparts. Humor, for example, can be used to say a great deal about loneliness and vulnerability and may reach a far greater audience than the worthiest, heaviest treatment of those issues in the conventional—and largely unreadable—literary novel.

It is interesting that this creeping pathology does not appear to have infected music and the visual arts quite as much as it has the written word and drama. Composers, in particular, are free to write joyful music, and will not be condemned for failing to be gloomy. Painters, too, may produce works that are positive in tone without being accused of being too optimistic or unrealistic. It seems that it is only when we sit down to tell a story that we are expected to eschew optimism and an affirmative register if we wish to be taken seriously.

It could be that the reader, having come this far in the argument, is beginning to think that I overstate my case. I would certainly be wrong to make excessive claims for this argument, but if one is in any doubt about the overall tenor of much of our current entertainment, simply compare the typical offering of a day's television of, say, three decades ago with what is on offer today. How much more aggression, violence, and downright hostility there is on today's screens. How much conflict and social pathology there is in contemporary reality television; how much graphic violence, blood, and destruction there is on the larger screen. And, most significantly, how old-fashioned it sounds to point any of this out. The paradigm has shifted in favor of social dysfunction. Dystopia is what artists are now expected to preach; utopia is not an option for the serious artist. Beauty, once considered the goal of all the arts, including literature, is locked out.

Does it matter, as long as people are getting what they want? It matters greatly. Surely there is something unhealthy about an imaginative diet made up of visions of conflict and confrontation to the exclusion of anything positive. At least some writers need to be able to hold before their readers a vision of the positive without fear of being labeled Pollyannas. And perhaps our civilization would be better if we stopped entertaining ourselves a little less with images of destruction and death. Thanatos, be it remembered, along with his unpleasant siblings, destroys cities; Eros, with the positive gods that assist him, builds them.

What we need, then, is a rehabilitation of the positive, a re-evaluation of our automatic assumption that the only weighty concern of art should be that which is wrong. That which is affirmative, that which does not brood on the distorted and the vicious, which shows the positive possibilities of human nature, deserves its time too: not all the time, just its proper share.

September 2011

Confucian confusions

Eric Ormsby

IT WAS A SAD DAY for poetry when Ezra Pound discovered Confucius. Like some latter-day Don Quixote addled by tales of chivalry, Pound became enthralled by Confucian precepts, and though they never had any appreciable influence on his own thoughts or actions—he was the least Confucian of men—those precepts, or his version of them, scrambled his brains for the next sixty years. As A. David Moody tells it in the opening volume of his magisterial biography, the third and final volume of which has now appeared (*Ezra Pound: Poet: Volume III: The Tragic Years 1939–1972*), the encounter came about in October 1913 when Pound first read the *Analects* in French translation. He then moved on to Allen Upward's *The Sayings of Confucius* of 1904 and the die was cast. In China Pound believed he had found his "new Greece." Of course, Pound's discovery of China led to two of his finest—and most idiosyncratic—achievements as a translator: *Cathay* of 1915 and *The Classic Anthology Defined by Confucius* of 1954, the 305 odes he translated during his confinements at St. Elizabeth's hospital. These utterly original re-creations of ancient Chinese lyrics, in a manner and idiom all his own, are probably what he will best be remembered for in future years, and rightly so. As the late Simon Leys remarked,

> Pound had a mistaken idea of the Chinese language, but his mistake was remarkably stimulating and fecund as it was based on one important and accurate intuition. Pound correctly observed that a Chinese poem is not articulated upon a continuous, discursive thread, but that it flashes discontinuous series of images (not unlike the successive frames of a film).

He will probably not be long remembered for *The Cantos*, his baggy, rambling and tedious "epic," the tutelary spirit of which is the hapless Confucius. Discontinuous flashes may work in a brief lyric but they tend to sputter out in a long poem, and *The Cantos* runs to over 800 pages. Or, if remembered as other than a miscalculation of colossal proportions, it will probably be as a monument to ungovernable eccentricity, a sort of Watts Tower of modern verse.

Though Moody has written a masterful biography, as meticulous as it is broad-ranging, he never solves an abiding puzzle, despite valiant efforts: what exactly was the source of Pound's fixation on Confucius, of all available sages? Not one of the virtues delineated in the *Analects* applies to Pound, and least of all the Confucian virtue usually rendered as "humaneness."

"The noble person does not abandon humaneness for so much as the space of a meal" is one such precept, and yet, in page after page of Moody's biography, we find Pound not only abandoning humaneness but seemingly quite unaware of it. Again, the *Analects* tell us that "Being able to recognize oneself in others, one is on the way to being human" but Pound seems to have been temperamentally incapable of recognizing others or himself, let alone "oneself in others." Perhaps it was a simple case of the attraction of opposites, however strenuously Pound would have denied this. A nacreous self-immurement, oysterhood rather than humaneness, characterized virtually all his actions, especially during the war years and afterwards. And if the decades which this third volume covers were "the tragic years," as Moody's subtitle has it, well, they were certainly tragic for those millions of people all around him to whose fate Pound remained blithely oblivious. But perhaps the tragedy for Pound (though he remained blind to this as well) was that during these years he set about almost systematically, almost willfully, gutting his own great talent in the service of highly dubious objectives, both moral and aesthetic. Some of these would be comical if they were not so repellent: for example, Pound's imbecilic desire to "introduce the doctrine of Confucianism into Fascism" or his call for "the immediate need of Confucius" in Mussolini's Italy. His adherence to such ideas, with the concomitant corruption of language itself they entailed, ended up vitiating *The Cantos*. One could be forgiven for thinking of this tedious and vituperative work as more *Ranto* than *Canto*.

Though Moody is scrupulous in detailing Pound's words and deeds and does not shy away from the ugliest of them, he is also prone to mollifying if not excusing them. In his preface to Volume I, he describes his biography as

> the five-act tragedy of a flawed idealist and a great poet who, in a time of war, carried to excess his exercise of the rights and freedoms of a United States citizen, and who, in consequence, suffered the loss of both his freedom and his civil rights.

As if to reinforce this rosy depiction he sets as an epigraph to Part One of his third volume a citation from the First Amendment to the Constitution: "Congress shall make no law … abridging the freedom of speech." The implication is that Pound was a martyr to the exercise of free speech (perhaps echoing Pound's line in Canto 74, the first of *The Pisan Cantos*, "that free speech without free radio speech is as zero"). I find this disingenuous. No one disputed Pound's right to free speech; it was where and when he chose to exercise that right—by radio from fascist Italy, in 1941, during the war—that led to his indictment for treason in 1943. This emollient note crops up more than once in the third volume. Though Moody can criticize Pound's "twisty language" and deplore the "awful waste of Pound's gifts," he persists in invoking "his profound idealism, his utopian intentions." Pound's virulent anti-Semitism is presented as merely his "worst error," a pretty mild characterization of the poet's utter moral squalor in this regard. This "error" is on full display throughout Volume III, as when Pound rants against "the Italian-Jewified plutocratic press" or declares that "the British Empire was already rotted from inside by the Jews in London." Perhaps the most notorious instance occurs in the opening lines of Canto 52, written in 1939, with their evocation of "Stinkschuld/ paying for a few big jews' vendetta on goyim" and "better keep out the jews/ or yr grand children will curse you/ jews, real jews, chazims, and *neschek* … " As Moody explains, the name "Stinkschuld" was Pound's substitution for Rothschild after T. S. Eliot (not known for his philo-Semitism) pressured Pound to make the change; as Eliot put it, "if you remain keen on jew baiting, that is your affair, but the name of Rothschild should be omitted." Faber and Faber went on to publish *Cantos LII–LXXI* in which these lines appeared but were blacked out (they have been restored in the current Faber edition).

This was bad enough but worse was to come. Pound's praise of Hitler and of *Mein Kampf*, all gruesomely noted by Moody, makes for sickening reading. He went so far as, grotesquely, to compare Hitler with Joan of Arc (this, in an interview, mostly about Confucius, with a reporter from the *Philadelphia Record* in 1945), saying that "Adolf Hitler was a Jeanne d'Arc, a saint. He was a martyr. Like many martyrs he held extreme views." (For once Uncle Ez did not exaggerate.) Though Moody claims that Pound could not have known about the Holocaust or the concentration camps in the early 1940s (Why not? Others did.), he certainly knew about them after 1945. He also read *The Protocols of the Elders of Zion* with great enthusiasm, claiming that it was "an absolute condensation of history of the U.S.A. for the past fifty years." To the charge that they were forgeries, as they were, he remarked, "Certainly they are a forgery and that is the one proof we have of their authenticity.... The Jews have worked with forged documents for the past twenty-four hundred years." We are up against here what the Catholic Church (which Pound hated almost as much as the Jews) used to call "invincible ignorance," a phrase that perfectly epitomizes Ezra Pound during this period.

Sometimes Moody's indulgence of Pound goes too far. After the fall of Mussolini, whom Pound had long admired (and met with once), Moody remarks that Pound was "well aware of the stresses and dangers of the time" but that "his response to them was to hold on to and to assert all the more vehemently his visionary idea of a better world. He went on believing in the impossible." (You can almost hear the violins of "The Impossible Dream" tuning up in the background.) And what was this "better world"? Moody, rhetorically but also somewhat plaintively, asks, "But how could he have hoped to inculcate, all by himself, a Confucian ethic within, and via the media of, a Fascist-Socialist regime subject to Hitler's Nazism?" How indeed? It was an Orwellian nightmare if ever there was one. Moody is also inconsistent at times. He tells us that Pound was not a Fascist ("Confucian would be nearer the truth"), but then he quotes Pound himself stating "But I believe in Fascism and want to defend it." Such inconsistencies were rampant in Pound's own disordered mind and so it's no wonder if his biographer sometimes runs afoul of them.

Moody does his best to disentangle Pound's bizarre amalgam of

Confucianism, Fascism, and the U.S. Constitution, but his attempts never really convince (how could they in any case?). He is at his best, however, in describing Pound's post-war experiences, from his imprisonment at Pisa to the legal quagmire that ensued when he was returned for trial to the United States, and his thirteen-year confinement in St. Elizabeth's Hospital in Washington. At Pisa Pound was kept in what he called his "gorilla cage," an open-air cell with concrete floors, some six-by-six-and-a-half-feet in dimensions, with a tar paper roof over a timber frame. This has been seen as "inhumane" treatment; certainly it was no picnic, though Pound did have shelter and three-squares a day, unlike the millions of refugees and displaced persons swarming all over Europe. And he did have a typewriter which he used for composing his *Pisan Cantos*. As for the legal wrangles that followed his return to the United States, Moody is quite critical of Pound's lawyer, one Julien Cornell, and of Pound's old friend James Laughlin. He believes that Cornell, along with Laughlin, inveigled Pound into accepting a plea of insanity and that had Pound come to trial for treason, he would have been acquitted (since there had to be treasonable intent under the law). It seems clear, even from his account, however, that both men were trying to save Pound from the death penalty. The trouble with the insanity plea was that the confinement that resulted was indefinite and if Pound were found to be sane after all, he could again be brought to trial.

Again, there has been much hand-wringing about Pound's commitment to St. Elizabeth's. To judge from Moody's lengthy description, Pound suffered from loneliness and boredom but not much else in the asylum. He was swarmed with visitors, from old friends like T. S. Eliot and Marianne Moore to younger admirers such as Elizabeth Bishop, Charles Olson, and Mary Barnard, a fine if forgotten poet and classicist whom Pound encouraged. Here Pound fed his former obsessions; he was neither remorseful nor chastened. His anti-Semitic tirades against "the bacillus of kikism" prompted Marianne Moore, the wittiest of his visitors, to remark, "Profanity and the Jews are other quaky quicksands against which may I warn you? You have seen turtles or armadillos, possibly, when annoyed and I sometimes have to be one of them." Of course, not even an enraged armadillo could quell Pound's bigotry which now expanded to take in other targets. His most disturbing visitor was John Kasper, a violent white supremacist, who carried out private book-burnings of hated Jewish authors (Freud, Marx, Reich, and Einstein) and who engaged in "violent white racist resistance" after the Supreme Court struck down segregation, including suspected bombings—all with Pound's approval and encouragement. For Pound the Civil Rights Movement was "a Jewish-Communist conspiracy."

Moody also gives a good detailed account of the sordid brouhaha over the award of the Bollingen Prize to Pound in 1949, an account everyone who wants to plumb the sleazy depths of literary politics should read. No one came out with reputation unscathed from this imbroglio. The award was for *The Pisan Cantos*, extravagantly admired but—in my minority opinion at least—for all the wrong reasons: despite occasional beauties these cantos are as flawed and uneven as the rest.

This prompts me to ask: what went wrong with *The Cantos*? Pound spent some fifty years on the work and he certainly considered it his masterpiece. Moody devotes many pages in his biography to close and loving analysis of canto after canto. Taking his cue from Pound's remark that "It's music. Musical themes that find each other out," he makes a great effort to tease out the musical structure of individual cantos. Of Canto 31, for example, he remarks that it rhymes "not to the ear but to the understanding," this with reference to the opening phrase "Tempus loquendi,/ Tempus tacendi ... " which he says "rhymes" with the word "time" in the following line. This notion of what might be called "conceptual rhyme" is certainly interesting, but it isn't really persuasive; I don't think any reader, however sophisticated, would hear a rhyme between "tempus" in the Latin translation of Ecclesiastes and the English word "time." Pound was an excellent musician as well as a composer; he even wrote a highly original treatise on harmony. But there are harmonies and harmonies. A suite performed on a washboard and a kazoo may have harmony, and even counterpoint, but in the end the effect is one of cacophony.

Pound's greatest gift, it seems to me, lay in a kind of inspired ventriloquism. When he wrote in the voice of others, when he assumed what he called his *personae*, his masks, he could be both inimitable and magnificent. Whether adopting the voice of Propertius or the Seafarer or an anonymous Chinese woman, he wrote masterpieces that will be remembered and loved as long as English is spoken and read. But he seems to have required the scaffolding of another self, an alien and imagined self, to achieve this. In *The Cantos*, by contrast, he gives us the voice of

Uncle Ez himself; even the many quotations he strews liberally throughout the text somehow take on his droning accents. It is a voice by turns pedantic, preachy, faux-folksy, and yet strangely anodyne.

In a famous quip Gertrude Stein called Pound a "village explainer," adding "excellent if you were a village but if you were not, not." The village explainer is much in evidence, especially in his crackpot theories of economics. Amid the potted histories of Renaissance Italy and imperial China, amid the ranting and the slurs ("the total dirt that was Roosevelt") and the sheer windbaggery, there will, however, suddenly arise, as if miraculously, passages of stunning beauty. Marvelous as these are, they too often have the effect of accentuating the surrounding drabness of language and diction. Take this, for one example, from Canto 49:

> Autumn moon; hills rise about lakes
> against sunset.
> Evening is like a curtain of cloud,
> a blurr above ripples; and through it
> sharp long spikes of the cinnamon,
> a cold tune among reeds.
> Behind hill the monk's bell
> borne on the wind.
> Sail passed here in April; may return in October
> Boat fades in silver; slowly;
> Sun blaze alone on the river.

Even though this is pure *chinoiserie*, like all Pound's lyrical passages in *The Cantos*, that is, not really a landscape observed in itself but a stylized artifact of a landscape, it is exquisite. There are several such passages in the work, and all are quite lovely, but they do not really lighten or redeem its ponderous and deadening mass. The first dozen or so cantos are certainly magnificent too; they seem to announce a new kind of poetry, a new way of structuring verse. But as Pound's manias intensified, from the 1930s on, this bold prospect faded. Pound was an editor of genius (as *The Waste Land* attests). Why didn't he edit his own work with the brilliance he brought to Eliot's? The answer is all too painfully simple: Pound would have had to edit himself, and drastically, before moving on to the more technical labor of textual editing.

If no sympathetic impression of Pound the man emerges from Moody's pages—his inner life well concealed under torrents of rant—that is probably not Moody's fault. In fact, to judge from the biography, Pound seems not to have had much of an inner life; he seems to have been impervious to introspection. He seems never to have questioned or doubted and certainly never to have lacerated himself over his failings or his "errors." The only perceptible alteration lay in further distillations of the venom that consumed him. When he fell stubbornly silent from 1962 until his death in 1972, some took this as a form of remorse or even penance for his lifelong intemperance, his betrayal of the precision of language he had enjoined on his disciples. The evidence, based only on statements by Robert Lowell and Allen Ginsberg, interested parties both, is meager. But who knows? Maybe in his final silence he was pondering the adage of his master Confucius: "The humane person is cautious in his speech."

February 2016

Polemical interlude

NOTES & COMMENTS

On some uses of "but"

[W]hat Americans call "liberalism" is the ideology of Western suicide.
—JAMES BURNHAM, *Suicide of the West*

IN JANUARY 2015, *The New Criterion* featured an extensive symposium on "Free Speech Under Threat." Wide-ranging though the eight contributions to that special section were, the horrific massacres in Paris that month reminded us that there was still more to say.

Free speech does not exist in isolation. It is part of a constellation of freedoms that include, for example, the freedom to apostatize and the idea that all are equal before the law. Those ideas are, or were, bedrock principles in the modern secular West, but they are foreign to all major allotropes of Islam. Apostasy is a capital crime for Islam, in principle everywhere, in brutal fact in the Middle East, Africa, and elsewhere. Equality is also foreign to Islam, for which an assumed existential disparity between Muslim and infidel is central, as indeed is the disparity between man and woman.

In the aftermath of the Paris shootings, there was a lot of moralistic posturing about solidarity with the victims and the mightiness of the pen compared with the sword. As the Australian commentator Andrew Bolt pointed out, however, the journalists at *Charlie Hebdo* had fistfuls of pens. The brothers Kouachi had a couple of Kalashnikovs. That was all it took. As for the herds of "Je Suis Charlie" marchers in Paris and else where, it is worth noting how very few actual "Charlies" there were. It is one thing to carry a placard. It is another to take a stand by, for example, publishing a caricature of Mohammed. The *Jyllands-Posten*, which published the original "Danish Cartoons" in 2005, was not Charlie. They declined a request to reprint the images because, they said, "violence works." *The New York Times*, *The Daily News*, The Associated Press: neither they nor any other news outlet of note were Charlie either. At best, they published only pixelated images of the cartoons. The eminent free-speech lawyer Floyd Abrams, who defended the *Times* when it published The Pentagon Papers, wrote a disgusted letter to the *Times*, castigating it for its pusillanimity. (Publishing material damaging to the U.S. government is one thing: the Left applauds. Publishing material that might be personally risky is something else entirely.) As Gérard Biard, the editor-in-chief of *Charlie Hebdo*, observed on Meet the Press, by blurring the face of Mohammed, such papers "blur out democracy, secularism and freedom of religion and they insult the citizenry." (Some of his colleagues put it more bluntly: "We vomit on these people who suddenly say they are our friends," said one of the cartoonists.)

It is important to understand the place of free speech in the economy of Islam. In brief, there isn't any. This is something that the London-based Muslim cleric Anjem Choudary explained with admirable clarity in *USA Today* a few days after the Paris shootings. "Contrary to popular misconception," Choudary began, "Islam does not mean peace but rather means submission to the commands of Allah alone." Accordingly, "Muslims do not believe in the concept of freedom of expression, as their speech and actions are determined by divine revelation and not based on people's desires."

Choudary's exegesis is quite correct, embarrassing though it might be to the "Islam means peace" narrative. And he is ominously clear, too, about the implications of this view. "In an increasingly unstable and insecure world," he wrote, "the potential consequences of insulting the Messenger Muhammad are known to Muslims and non-Muslims alike." Choudary's point was that, at the end of the day, the bloodshed was France's fault. They knew what to expect. "Why," he asked, "did France allow the tabloid to provoke Muslims?"

While you ponder that amazing question, note how much overlap there is between *The New York Times*'s response to the Paris shootings and Choudary's. The *Times* omitted the free-speech angle, but in an editorial in the aftermath of the Paris shootings it came down hard on France. The "profiles" of the killers—i.e., the fact that they hailed from poor immigrant families—constituted "an indictment of the decades-long failure of France to address long-festering alienation and exclusion among too many Muslim immigrants" and their children. Three Muslim men murder nearly twenty people. The *Times* blames France.

Not all Muslims are as categorical as Anjem Choudary about free speech. Ekmeleddin Ihsanoglu, for example, the Secretary General of the Organization of Islamic Cooperation for a decade, put it this way: "Freedom of speech is one thing, but usage of your freedom should not be to offend others or advocate hate speech or provoke people to violence." Note that little word "but." Freedom of speech is one thing, but ... But what?

The Organization of Islamic Cooperation, which represents fifty-six Muslim countries plus the Palestinian Authority, has been a tireless advocate for the imposition of laws against blasphemy for years. As the journalist Asra Q. Nomani noted in a disturbing piece in *The Washington Post*, the OIC has underwritten "an honor corps that tries to silence debate on extremist ideology in order to protect the image of Islam. It meets even sound critiques with hideous, disproportionate responses."

Nomani, a secularized but devout Muslim, knows whereof she speaks. She's received death threats, been called a "Zionist media whore," and "many other unprintable insults." "Observant members of the flock," she observes,

> are culturally conditioned to avoid shaming Islam, so publicly citing them for that sin often has the desired effect. Non-Muslims, meanwhile, are wary of being labeled "Islamophobic" bigots. So attacks against both groups succeed in quashing civil discourse. They cause governments, writers and experts to walk on eggshells, avoiding important discussion.

Indeed, as the commentator Robert Blitt recently observed, the OIC has seen to it that *any* insult—which means any *perceived* insult—has to be suppressed. "Translated into practice," he notes, "this toxic vision breeds contempt for freedom of religion and expression, justifies the killing of Muslims and non-Muslims alike, and casts a pall of self censorship over academia and the arts." As Andrew C. McCarthy observed, "Islam need not be lampooned for caricatures to run afoul of sharia." *Any* description can call down the Mullah's wrath. So it was hardly surprising that, even as the crowds were parading around with their "Je Suis Charlie" placards, Oxford University Press announced that it was henceforth banning "pork-related material" from its children's books. Yes, that's right, say goodbye to characters like Piglet and Wilbur and the Three Little Pigs. A company press release said it was part of an effort to avoid offending "Jews and Muslims," but when was the last time the Jewish lobby complained about *Winnie the Pooh*? What was particularly nauseating was the justification offered by an OUP spokesman: "Many of the educational materials we publish in the UK are sold in more than 150 countries, and as such they need to consider a range of cultural differences and sensitivities." Do you see any such accommodation for, say, Buddhist or Christian sensitivities? No, "cultural differences and sensitivities" is the OUP's current translation of "Muslim intimidation."

Dear Reader: does this all sound surreal? It is surreal. But it is also, and increasingly, the way we live now. And it is worth noticing the large element of hypocrisy involved. "We Muslims, we never insult Christians, Jesus Christ, Moses," Ihsanoglu said in an interview, "nobody in our countries produces films mocking Jesus or Moses." It was about ten minutes after we read this that a headline from Italy caught our eye: "Muslims Destroy and Urinate on Virgin Mary Statue." We could produce many more examples. So could you.

The issue, however, is not only or even mostly about Islam and free speech. At the end of the day, the issue centers around the status of free speech in Western countries that gave birth to that indispensable auxiliary to political liberty. How's that faring? We've come a long way from 1964 and the "free speech movement" at Berkeley—about the same distance traversed in *Animal Farm* from "All Animals Are Equal" to "But Some Are More Equal than Others." Let us introduce you to Tanya Cohen, a feminist commentator who thinks that the U.S. needs to "get tough on hate speech through the law." *Through the law*, n.b. "I am a strong believer in the unalienable right to freedom of speech," Cohen wrote in a widely quoted (and widely mocked) column. She then lists some of the sorts of unpopular speech of which she approves ("pro-LGBT speech in Russia," for example) and concludes with this: "But"—there's that little word again—"but we must never confuse hate speech with freedom of speech." Cohen elaborates: Speech that "offends or insults in general, along with speech that voices approval of anti-democratic, anti-freedom, and/or totalitarian ideologies and propaganda for war" are among the things that do not get the Tanya Cohen seal of approval.

Note that both Cohen and Ihsanoglu avail themselves of the popular neologism "hate speech." The law has long had statutes against speech that incites violence, gratuitously crying "Fire" in a crowded theater, etc. "Hate speech" is like that other item in the lexicon of leftist redress, "social justice." It is a weapon masquerading as a moral imperative. The adjective is cognitively vacuous but emotionally charged: it injects an intoxicating dose of moral self-righteousness that clouds the head even as it sets the heart aflutter. Tanya Cohen, like Ihsanoglu, is "a strong believer in free speech," *but* not speech that "offends or insults in general," etc. In other words, she is a strong believer in free speech, except that she isn't.

The pathetic Tanya Cohen is hardly alone in the West in having given up on free speech. We pick her simply because she happened to be in the news. The Harvard student who wants to replace academic freedom with "academic justice" in order to outlaw research that justifies "oppression" is her soul mate, as is the Rochester Institute of Technology professor who believes that those who disagree with him about climate change should face jail. "I am for free speech, but not 'hate speech' / speech that offends Mohammed / speech that insults Greens / speech that mocks, satirizes, ridicules, and laughs at some PC icon," etc. Then you are not for free speech at all, and your "but" is merely a species of capitulation pretending to redemptive conceptual nuance. Free speech is by nature offensive speech, at least potentially. If it couldn't offend, if it couldn't insult, it also couldn't enlighten. Remember Molly Norris? She's the Seattle-based artist who in 2010 suggested denominating May 20 "Everybody Draws Mohammed Day." A contest to do just that duly followed. Then came the death threats. Norris was still in hiding, with an assumed identity, more than four years later. Her name popped up on al Qaeda's most wanted list in the jihadist magazine *Inspire*. The list also included Stéphane Charbonnier, the former, now the late, editor of *Charlie Hebdo*.

The epigraph from James Burnham's *Suicide of the West* that prefaces these remarks may seem hyperbolic. In what sense is liberalism "the ideology of Western suicide"? In the course of his analysis, Burnham quotes the nineteenth-century French writer Louis Veuillot. *Quand je suis le plus faible, je vous demande la liberté parce que tel est votre principe; mais quand je suis le plus fort, je vous l'ôte, parce que tel est le mien.* "When I am the weaker, I ask you for my freedom, because that is your principle. But when I am the stronger, I take away your freedom, because that is my principle." In other words, it's the old Leninist credo: demand freedom, toleration, and diversity when out of power; practice suppression, control, and elimination of opponents when in power. What is *our* principle? Anjem Choudary and his friends understand what they are about. Do we?

February 2015

Decline & fall: classics edition

For the study of classics, it is (if we may adapt Dickens) the best of times and the worst of times. It is the best of times because there are multiple popular initiatives, mostly outside the academy, introducing people young and old to the riches of Greek and Latin. There are even a few bright spots inside the academy, for example Princeton University's new Latin 110, a course taught entirely in Latin: the students and teacher do not speak in English *about* Latin but instead conduct the entire class in the ancient but still-living language. Impressive.

But such bright spots are few and far between. Indeed, even that class at Princeton has been castigated on Twitter for catering to students who are too "fit," too male, and probably too heterosexual. More and more, it seems, the study of classics—like the study of the humanities generally—has fallen under the spell of grievance warriors who have injected an obsession with race and sexual exoticism into a discipline that, until recently, was mostly innocent of such politicized deformations—largely, we suspect, because of the inherent difficulty of mastering the subject. (In this sense, classics is different from pseudo-disciplines like women's studies, black studies, LGBTQ studies, and the like, because classics can never be entirely reduced to political posturing. You actually have to know something.)

Consider the fate of *Eidolon*, an online journal that was started in 2015 to demonstrate the relevance of classics to modern life. It wasn't long before Donna Zuckerberg, the sister of the personal data magus and surveillance guru Mark Zuckerberg, engineered a palace coup and declared that henceforth *Eidolon* would "err on the progressive side," dedicating itself to "the spirit of bringing politics into Classics." Because, you know, the humanities have not been sufficiently tainted by signing up for every trendy progressive cliché going. From now on, Zuckerberg said, *Eidolon* would forgo objectivity—"often nothing more than a cover for upholding the status quo, and *to hell with the status quo*"—in its quest to become "a progressive, feminist publication with a commitment to social justice." And how was this goal to be achieved?

Well, this year, Zuckerberg noted, the magazine would aim to make sure that "at least [*at least*] 70 percent of our contributors be women and 20 percent of our writers be POC," i.e., "people of color," i.e., not white. (But isn't race merely a "social construction"? No, silly, that was last year.) And just how are those percentages going to be achieved? Well, going forward, *Eidolon* will ask people pitching stories for "demographics," i.e., are you black or white? Male or female? "I have no interest," Zuckerberg sermonized, "in providing bland and false reassurances that we only care about good ideas and good writing and not who our authors are." Who would doubt it? And what about merit? "[A]ppeals to merit," she said, are "often … white supremacist dog-whistles." So: "If you're white and we publish you, you will know, for maybe the first time in your career, that it was because of the merit of your idea and *not* because you're white."

We'd like to know if there are *any* cases of anyone anywhere being published in a classics journal *because* he (or even she) was white. Still, Zuckerberg's destruction of *Eidolon* as a serious journal does raise an interesting question about the level of masochism among white classicists, especially white male classicists. Why would anyone of that description who was not a masochist submit work to a journal that is self-confessedly hostile to them? Indeed, why would anyone not a masochist read it?

But the fate of *Eidolon* (which Zuckerberg shut down in 2020) is only one symptom of the toxic substitution of identity politics for humanistic learning in classics. An episode that took place at the annual Society for Classical Studies conference in January 2019 further dramatized the rot affecting the discipline.

These big academic conferences, in the humanities at least, are sad, repellent affairs. They are sad because one large contingent of attendees is composed of young, and often not-so-young, supplicants for an academic job, any job, anywhere. They are repellent partly because of the preening and posturing of the elect—the tenured and celebrity elite who glide through the hallways of whatever anonymous hotel is home to the event—partly because of the menacing aura of fatuousness that clings to most of the proceedings.

At the San Diego Marriott, a panel on "The Future of Classics" provided a notable example of the latter. Among the speakers was Dan-el

Padilla Peralta, a rising star in—well, we were going to say "classics," but that is not quite right. Yes, Padilla is an assistant professor of classics at Princeton, but to date his reputation has depended not on his work in classics but on his expertise in a species of grievance-mongering and racial complaint. As far as we can tell, his only published book is *Undocumented: A Dominican Boy's Odyssey from a Homeless Shelter to the Ivy League*. If there were truth in advertising, it should have been called *Illegal*, since it concerns Padilla's status as an immigrant from the Dominican Republic who, with his mother, overstayed his visa when he was a young boy.

To say that Padilla has a chip on his shoulder does not do justice to the exasperating potential of chips. There is no doubt that he is a clever man. Princeton not only accepted him as an undergraduate but also gave him a full scholarship out of its own funds (because federal money cannot go to people here illegally). He performed so well that he was the class salutatorian. After graduate work, he ascended to the Princeton faculty as a "target of opportunity" candidate. Such positions are not advertised, which is usually required by law, because there is a candidate in mind who fulfills some affirmative action goal. In other words, Padilla, in addition to his native gifts, is one lucky man. He has been given every preferment. Naturally, he is therefore especially bitter about the establishment that coddles him.

Readers of *The New Criterion*'s website may recall Dan-el Padilla Peralta. In 2017, he responded to an article by Solveig Lucia Gold called "The colorblind bard." Gold argued against the idea that Western civilization was the province of white men. On the contrary, it belonged, potentially, to all of us. It was a *universal* inheritance, not a parochial one.

This was too much for Padilla. For him, everything must be filtered through the scrim of race (although he is happy to add sex as a suppurating accessory). There are, he said, "centuries of whitewashing to rectify" ("whitewashing," get it, get it?). "Each and every" classics scholar, he said, has the "responsibility . . . to *race* the discipline." Forget about treating people as individuals. Forget about the idea that what matters is not the color of your skin but the content of your character. Padilla is an apostle of all race all the time.

This was the theme of "Racial Equity and the Production of Knowledge," Padilla's talk in San Diego. Tabulating the number of women and "people of color" published in major classics journals, he issued an anguished bulletin in the minatory, reader-proof argot so favored by left-wing academics today. Decrying the "hegemony of whiteness," he called for strategies to "decenter and displace white privilege and supremacy from its position of preeminence and priority in the discipline's self-image." According to him, "the most fundamental question for the future of knowledge production in Classics is this: how do we recognize, honor, and repair the silencing of the knowledge that people of color carry?" In fact, of course, every classics journal and every classics program in the Western world is on high alert, scouring the landscape for "people of color" they might employ, publish, and advance.

But that is not enough for Dan-el Padilla Peralta. He wants "reparative epistemic justice," i.e., the expulsion of whites from the discipline and (like Donna Zuckerberg) the end to colorblind assessment of merit. "[H]olders of privilege," he intoned, "will need to surrender their privilege. In practical terms, this means that … white men will have to surrender the privilege they have of seeing their words printed and disseminated; they will have to take a backseat so that people of color—and women and gender-nonconforming scholars of color—benefit from the privilege of seeing their words on the page." Should that not happen, he has said elsewhere, "all options for reparative intellectual justice—*including the demolition of the discipline itself* [our emphasis]"—should be kept open. In other words, institute a new regime of prejudice or we'll destroy classics.

This repugnant species of racial redress is par for the course in the fetid bubble of academia these days. But there were a couple of additional entertainments in San Diego. At one point, hotel security guards asked to see credentials for a couple of black attendees in working-class dress who were not displaying their badges. Horrors! Why were the badgeless white men not similarly accosted? Possibly because they acted and were dressed appropriately for the occasion. But Padilla and many other attendees were outraged by this instance of what Padilla called "racial profiling."

Then there was the *pièce de résistance*: question time after Padilla's talk. One woman, an independent scholar named Mary Frances Williams, had the temerity to defend Western civilization—how that stung!—declare that she was "not a socialist," and allegedly—*dictu nefas*—tell Padilla that he only got his job because he is black.

The hundred or so people in the room could not believe what they had just heard. The Twitterverse erupted in outrage. Williams herself was deemed to have violated a new interdiction against "harassment" and was ejected from the conference.

Now, Williams's observation was certainly impolitic. But was it inaccurate? "Only" is a strong word. But it appears to be the case that Padilla was the beneficiary of racial prejudice. So let us say that he was hired in part because he was black. He claims to have been outraged by the comment. But the irony is, in a much-reported whining response to the episode, he championed the idea of appointing people to academic positions because of their race. Since, he wrote,

> no one in that room or in the conference corridors afterwards rallied to the defense of blackness as a cornerstone of my merit, I will now have to repeat an argument that will be familiar to critical race scholars of higher education but that is barely legible to the denizens of #classicssowhite. *I should have been hired because I was black*: because my Afro-Latinity is the rock-solid foundation upon which the edifice of what I have accomplished and everything I hope to accomplish rests …

So there you have it. Not only was Padilla the beneficiary of racial preference. He proudly asserts that he *should have been* and that race is the "rock-solid foundation" of his work. Yet only he is allowed to acknowledge that.

As we have observed previously in these pages, "racism" is a neologism so recent that it wasn't in the Oxford English Dictionary in 1970. George Orwell noted in the 1940s that "fascist" was a content-free negative epithet, applied to anyone and anything of which one disapproved. "Racism" performs a similar disreputable function for the permanently aggrieved today. It is, we think, a question worth asking: why has racism emerged as the cardinal sin of our era, precisely at a moment when age-old bigotries have been laid to rest and institutions throughout our culture bend over backwards to cater to racial sensitivities?

Answering that is beyond our remit. But one thing is clear: the obsession over race (and exotic sexualities, too) has done more to disfigure our academic culture than all of the ancient bad prejudices we have overcome.

A CODA

We have long appreciated the admonitory wisdom contained in the observation that "things are always worse than they seem." Pathetic though that panel ostensibly devoted to "The Future of Classics" seemed to us when we first learned about it, it turns out that it, and the professional response to it, was far more cringe-making than we understood at the time.

We wrote about the event based on several reports, some of them eye-witness reports, but before the video of the panel had been released. This has now happened. The video is available on YouTube. We said that such academic events tend to be "sad and repellent." As the video shows, we understated the depressing reality of the situation.

The papers were bad enough, oscillating between the politically tendentious and self-congratulatory. Sarah Bond, now an Associate Professor of Classics at the University of Iowa, disparaged the great nineteenth-century Latinist Basil Gildersleeve for racism, bragged that she did not cite people of whom she disapproves, and suggested that her blog posts should count towards tenure. But the really repugnant part starts about forty-four minutes in when the question period opens. Multiple reports said that Mary Frances Williams, the brave but scared and hapless "independent" (i.e., jobless) scholar who put in a few words on behalf of Western civilization, had "shouted" the accusation that Dan-el Padilla Peralta had got his position at Princeton because of his race.

Only, Williams didn't shout that or anything else. Nor did she later "run" from the room, as at least one report stated. Although clearly ill-at-ease among the fancy people on the panel, she endeavored to make the case for the civilizing importance of classics. Here's what she said, in part:

> For thirty years I've heard you talk about the need for diversity and inclusiveness, and reaching out, doing "Women in Ancient Rome," and all sorts of other areas, which is fine, it's interesting, it's important .... But, maybe, we should start defending our discipline in-and of itself, and saying, it's Western civilization and it matters ... because it's the West.

It was at this point that Sarah Bond interrupted to inform Williams that "Western civilization" is "a construct ... that's complete construction."

Williams soldiered on, insisting that Western Civ was "important, particularly in its focus on liberty, democracy and freedom."

Take a look at the video: you can practically feel the contempt emanating from the panel, particularly from Associate Professor Bond who objected (speaking of shouting) "We *aren't* Western Civ!" We daresay that no one who witnessed her performance would have any doubts on that score.

For ourselves, we think Ms. Williams was right. Quoth she: "We're not? Then we might as well just shut down.... We don't have to only do Women's Studies, only do Ethnic Studies, only do a Balkanization of our field." She went on to underscore the intrinsic value of classics and offered the radical suggestion that Classics was worth pursuing for its own sake. "Maybe," she suggested, "try doing the Classics as Classics?"

She went on to stress the importance of teaching Homer, Cicero, Thucydides, Herodotus, and Demosthenes. She also declared "I am not a socialist" and "I believe in merit! I believe that the journals have articles on the basis of merit, I don't look at the color of the author."

Ms. Williams seems to have taken the ideological temperature of her surroundings, so she really ought to have seen Associate Professor Bond's retort coming. All the writers you mentioned, she objected, are "all men," and what about Sappho: "you don't think Sappho has merit?," she asked, voice dripping with disdain.

It was at this juncture that the catastrophe occurred: "You may have got your job because you're black," Ms. Williams said to Dan-el Padilla Peralta, "but I'd prefer to think you got your job because of merit."

Perhaps this was, as we said, impolitic, but was it, given the context, wrong for her to say? Was it ... (dread word) *racist*?

Everyone there excitedly said it was. The person running the Society for Classical Studies conference, like the Archangel Gabriel in Eden, banished the wretched Ms. Williams from the conference entirely. (A banishment, it is worth noting, that was reaffirmed even after the video was posted, even though it largely exonerates Ms. Williams.)

For his part, Dan-el Padilla Peralta instructed Ms. Williams that she was "going to let someone who has been historically marginalized from the production of knowledge in the Classics, *talk*."

> And here's what I have to say about the vision of classics that you've outlined: If that is in fact a vision that affirms you in your white supremacy, I want nothing to do with it. I hope the field dies, that you've outlined, and that it dies as swiftly as possible!

As we noted in our original piece, the end or death of classics is something Dan-el Padilla Peralta goes on about a lot. He seems to relish the prospect. Nevertheless, the Chairman (or, as they now say in the non-gender-specific paradise of academia, "Chair") of the Classics department at Princeton is just so pleased to have him as a colleague. On February 14, responding to an article about the episode in a publication of The National Association of Scholars, this poor man took out his bag of clichés and bleated about "promoting diversity in the study of the classics at all levels," "non-conforming sexual identities," etc., etc., assuring all and sundry that "Prof. Padilla Peralta's work challenges all of us to think hard about why the Greek and Roman past matters and powerfully articulates an intellectual perspective on that past based on personal experiences of social injustice all too common in our society, but all too rare in our discipline."

Enough. We wish these representatives of the most pampered generation in history would stop whining and get on with their work as scholars and teachers. They might start by weaning themselves from their embarrassing obsession with racism. Here's a practical suggestion. Give up talking and fantasizing about putative racism from after breakfast until luncheon. When, after a few weeks, that is mastered, extend the prohibition until tea time. Soon, they'll go for days on end without manufacturing make-believe racist climates where none exist.

That done, they might move on to distinguishing between their sex lives and their scholarly interest. Here too, bad habits will be hard to break, as a recent entry from the Council of University Classical Departments Bulletin suggests. Titled "LGBT+ Classics: Teaching, Research, and Activism," this curious document begins by announcing that "our field does not give enough visibility to the intersections between queer research, teaching, and activism." Really? It sometimes seems that one hears about little else: sexual exotica and racism, all part of today's most popular major, oppression studies. As with most academic disciplines ostensibly concerned with the humanities these days, to look into the works of classics is to peer into febrile hothouse where the announced subject is merely the pretext for juvenile and tendentious, not to say pathological, grandstanding. Even a brief acquaintance is enough to make one empathize with Macbeth when he said that he had "supped full with horrors."

March 2019

1619 & all that

We were a bit late in getting to that dog's breakfast called "The 1619 Project," *The New York Times*'s effort to "reframe"—read, "wildly distort"—the history and governing impetus of the American Founding. Readers of the satirical classic *1066 and All That* know what fun can be had if you go about your job as a storyteller serving up "all the History you can remember" and pretending that it is the truth. "Histories," we read in *1066 and All That*, "have previously been written with the object of exalting their authors. The object of this History is to console the reader."

It was to console its core readership that *The New York Times* undertook The 1619 Project in a special flood-the-zone issue of its Sunday magazine in August and then in a snazzy, graphics-heavy series of features on its website. For two years, the *Times* had invested heavily in the vaudeville entertainment called "Trump–Russia." The spectacular failure of its leading man, Special Counsel Robert Mueller, to deliver a happy ending to that fiasco underscored the essential futility of the entire enterprise.

This was something that Dean Baquet, Executive Editor of the *Times*, grasped instantly. In the summer of 2019, he huddled with his staff in a town-hall-style meeting—the proceedings of which were promptly leaked—and acknowledged a sad truth: "We built our newsroom to cover one story" (the now-debunked story that Donald Trump had "colluded" with Russia to steal the 2016 election). The story didn't pan out. "Now we have to regroup," Baquet told the assembled troops, "and shift resources and emphasis to take on a different story." What story? Henceforth, or at least "for the next two years"—the remainder of Trump's first term—the *Times* was going all in on "race, and other divisions." Robert Mueller couldn't get Trump. Maybe the *Times* could by writing about race in a "thoughtful," i.e., obsessive and one-sided, way—"something," Baquet added "we haven't done in a large way in a long time."

So there you have it. "That, to me," Baquet concluded, "is the vision for coverage. You all are going to have to help us shape that vision. But I think that's what we're going to have to do for the rest of the next two years." *Et voilà*, The 1619 Project, which the paper described in a preface as

> a major initiative from *The New York Times* observing the 400th anniversary of the beginning of American slavery. It aims to reframe the country's history, understanding 1619 as our true founding, and placing the consequences of slavery and the contributions of black Americans at the very center of the story we tell ourselves about who we are.

What followed was a stupefying race-based fantasy about the origins of the United States. The lead essay, by the black journalist Nikole Hannah-Jones, the "architect" of The 1619 Project, set the tone. "[O]ne of the primary reasons the colonists decided to declare their independence from Britain," she wrote, "was because they wanted to protect the institution of slavery." So, everything you learned about the American Revolution is wrong, or at least wrongheaded. Forget about the Stamp Act, the, Boston Tea Party, the Intolerable Acts, "No taxation without representation," etc. All that, utterly unmentioned by Ms. Hannah-Jones, was mere window dressing. The American colonists might talk about liberty. What they really cared about, according to this malignant fairy tale, was preserving and extending the institution of slavery. "[S]ome might argue," as Hannah-Jones coyly puts it, "that this nation was founded not as a democracy but as a slavocracy." Gosh. Of course, "some might argue" any number of incredible things: that the earth is flat, that the moon is made of green cheese, that *The New York Times* is still a responsible source of news and even-handed commentary. The fact that "some might argue" X does not mean that X is credible.

So it is with the preposterous idea that America was founded as a "slavocracy." Hannah-Jones asserts that "anti-black racism runs in the very DNA of this country." The claim is obviously metaphorical; countries do not possess DNA. But if one were to take the metaphor seriously, as tantamount to asserting that anti-black racism is an essential and therefore unalterable characteristic of America, then the whole 1619 Project would be pointless from the get-go. It would be like complaining about the roundness of a circle or the wetness of water.

Presumably, however, neither Hannah-Jones nor the *Times* intends for us to take the metaphor quite so seriously. For Hannah-Jones, what is wanted is an expression that simultaneously justifies the endless whining of black radicals about how victimized they are because of things that happened a few centuries ago while also stressing the perpetually renewable guilt (like the liver of Prometheus) of whites, all whites, those living today even more than those actually involved in the African slave trade in the seventeenth, eighteenth, or nineteenth centuries. For the *Times*, it fits in with what Power Line's Paul Mirengoff called its "irresistible urge to delegitimize America." That is the ultimate aim of The 1619 Project: to deliver another blow in the campaign to besmirch and diminish the political and moral achievement that is the United States of America. It is as despicable as it is mendacious.

You might say, Who cares about insane rantings in *The New York Times*? It is increasingly a niche publication for the credentialed, politically correct *nomenklatura*, totally out of touch with the main current of America and held afloat only by its unremitting attacks on anything to do with Donald Trump.

This is true. Nevertheless, the paper is not entirely without influence, even today. Indeed, more than 4,000 public school districts, including some in Chicago, have announced that they will supplement their curricula by distributing copies of The 1619 Project to students, thereby promulgating the racialist worldview expounded by that "major" "reframing" of our history. And though the copies will be paid for by the *Times* and donors, taxpayers will still be indirectly funding a version of history that is politically tendentious and wildly at odds with the facts. The Pulitzer Center (not affiliated with the famed prizes) has announced that it "is proud to be the education partner for The 1619 Project." As we write, the Center's website is full of little valentines to Hannah-Jones and her racialist, ahistorical fantasy about the founding of the United States.

We said that The 1619 Project was stupefying. What we meant was that the claims it makes are so outlandish, at once so ostentatiously at odds with historical reality while also being carefully framed in a corset of politically correct verbiage, that any critical response is at first stunned. Someone tells you that the Apollo 11 moon landing was a carefully staged hoax perpetrated by NASA or the Trilateral Commission or whatever. Your first response is a spluttering incredulity.

It is the same with the contention that 1619, the year that the first African slaves were brought to America, marked "the beginning of the system of slavery on which the country was built." But there were already slaves and various other forms of indentured labor in the Americas as there were all over the world. To say that there were slaves in America is not to say that "the country was built" on slavery. Moreover, the African slaves were not "kidnapped" by American or British slavers, as Hannah-Jones asserts, but were sold by other black Africans who were happy to profit by selling people they had enslaved to the colonists.

Fortunately, a rational, historically informed response to The 1619 Project has been building. The National Association of Scholars has inaugurated the "1620 Project," not just to commemorate the signing of the Mayflower Compact—a much more significant event in the history of the United States—but also to provide an occasion for thoughtful responses to some of the more outlandish claims made by Hannah-Jones and the other writers involved in the *Times*'s latest campaign of disinformation. (Among our favorites, the contention that double-entry bookkeeping was an innovation "whose roots twist back to slave-labor camps.")

The distinguished historian Allen C. Guelzo, writing in *City Journal*, notes that "The 1619 Project is not history: it is polemic, born in the imaginations of those whose primary target is capitalism itself and who hope to tarnish capitalism by associating it with slavery." The great irony, Guelzo writes, is that "The 1619 Project dispenses this malediction from the chair of ultimate cultural privilege in America," *The New York Times*, "because in no human society has an enslaved people suddenly found itself vaulted into positions of such privilege, and with the consent—even the approbation—of those who were once the enslavers."

We suppose it is a mark of how extreme is *The New York Times*'s latest attack on America that some of the most vigorous rejoinders appear in the World Socialist Web Site, which has run long interviews with two deans of the history of the American Founding, James McPherson and Gordon Wood, neither of whom were consulted by the *Times* for The 1619 Project. McPherson, though eminently circumspect, concludes that The 1619 Project is

> a very unbalanced, one-sided account, which lacked context and perspective on the complexity of slavery, which was clearly, obviously, not an exclusively American institution, but existed throughout history. And slavery in the United States was only a small part of a larger world process that unfolded over many centuries.

Wood concurs and notes further that the idea, propounded by The 1619 Project, that the American Revolution was fomented *in order to protect slavery* is simply ridiculous. On the contrary, "it is the northern states in 1776 that are the world's leaders in the antislavery cause.... The Revolution unleashed antislavery sentiments that led to the first abolition movements in the history of the world." The 1619 Project pretends that the British were great crusaders in the campaign against slavery. But Wood points out, first, that the "British don't get around to freeing the slaves in the West Indies until 1833," and, second, that "if the Revolution hadn't occurred," they "might never have done so then, because all of the southern colonies would have been opposed. So supposing the Americans hadn't broken away, there would have been a larger number of slaveholders in the greater British world who might have been able to prolong slavery longer than 1833."

The truth is that in 1776, the American Founders, Southerners as much as Northerners, believed that slavery was on its way out. They were wrong about the timing of that, but the fact remains, as Wood notes, that the Constitution (Article I, Section 9) set an end date on the importation of slaves and that "most Americans were confident that the despicable transatlantic slave trade was definitely going to end in 1808."

The 1619 Project represents a new nadir in the politically correct, anti-American machinations of *The New York Times*. Many sober observers would have dismissed it as beneath comment were it not that the residual prestige of the *Times* lends currency if not credibility to its illiterate and partisan contentions. Perhaps an unintended collateral benefit of this malign folly will be—finally, at last—to dissolve the vestiges of that prestige and expose the paper to the condign contempt of the public whose trust they have so extravagantly betrayed.

January 2020

III. Appreciations

The James cult

Joseph Epstein

I AM A MEMBER of a cult. Jamesians we call ourselves, less frequently Jacobites, and we are dedicated to the propagation and sanctification of the works of Henry James (1843–1916), a writer who is, to put it gently, not everybody's notion of a rollicking good time. Many are the criticisms against James, none of them entirely invalid. Some claim that in his fiction he chewed much more than he bit off; others argue that a great deal of what is at the heart of meritorious fiction—the struggle for survival, the drama of ambition, physical love—is absent from his. Those of us in the cult allow all this, though we view it as quite beside the point. Our condition is put best by James himself in "The Next Time," a story about an author named Ray Limbert who struggled to produce bestsellers but, unable to turn a silk purse into a sow's ear, could only create masterpieces. In that story, James wrote:

> We are a numerous band, partakers of the same repose, who sit together in the shade of the tree, by the plash of the fountain, with the glare of the desert all around us and no great vice that I know of but the habit perhaps of estimating people a little too much by what they think of a certain style.

That certain style, the Jamesian style, is at the crux of the cult. Either one gets it or one doesn't, and many people, even highly cultivated and well-read people, do not. It is a style in which each heavily nuanced sentence can sometimes seem a veritable barcarole. At other times the Jamesian sentence resembles a hawk, circling, circling, circling before plunging downward to strike off a penetrating observation or startling aperçu. As subordinate clause piles upon subordinate clause—especially in his late style when James took to dictating his prose to a typist—one occasionally forgets that the sentence under investigation has a subject and predicate. And yet, James's style, for all its rococo circumlocution, did exactly what he wanted it to do, which was to capture consciousness in all its complexity.

Within this elaborate syntax, there is Jamesian irony to consider. Irony is the art of obliquity, of saying one thing yet meaning another, richer, often comical thing. Entire stories of James's were written in ironic mode. Only James could have described a minor character, in his novel *The Europeans*, as "inconvenienced with intelligence." The narrator of "The Next Time," a critic, remarks of his contribution to a magazine that "I supply the most delicious irony," to which his publisher replies, "that's not in the least a public want. No one can make out what you're talking about and no one would care if he could." But when it comes to Henry James, we cultists do care, care awfully. A nineteenth-century critic in *The Nation* remarked of James's style that "the reader feels irresistibly flattered at the homage paid to his perceptive powers." This homage is part of what attracted us to the cult in the first place.

Michael Gorra, a professor of English at Smith College, a fellow Jamesian cultist, has found a new and interesting approach to writing about Henry James. In the preface to his *Portrait of a Novel: Henry James and the Making of an American Masterpiece*, Gorra declares that he has written "the tale not of a life but of a work." The work is *The Portrait of a Lady*, and Gorra's book shows how

> Henry James created Isabel Archer's portrait, and to what end: tells not only what happens in the book itself but also the story of how James came to write it and what happened to him while he was doing so; of the book's relation to the major fiction of the decades around it, and of how it was published and received and then, many years later, revised.

The Portrait of a Lady is an excellent choice for this exercise. The novel was published in 1881, then reworked in 1906 by James for the New York Edition of his collected fiction. *The Portrait of a Lady* is from James's so-called middle period; after it he wrote *The Bostonians* (1886) and *The Princess Casamassima* (1886). The novel was commercially successful, selling some five thousand copies; the two novels following it were harshly reviewed and sold poorly, plunging James into the doldrums. More important, as Gorra skillfully demonstrates, in *The Por-*

trait of a Lady Henry James greatly advanced his art, becoming the great novelist of consciousness that he remains in our time. By novelist of consciousness, Gorra means not only that "he learned to stage consciousness itself" but he was able to compose his novels so that "psychological reasons may stand as subjects in themselves, that the life within has a drama of its own . . ."

The Portrait of a Lady is the story of Isabel Archer, a young American woman taken up and swept off, first to England and thence to Italy, by a wealthy aunt, herself long expatriated and currently living in Florence. Europe introduces Isabel to a wider canvas of prospects and possibilities than America allowed. In America she had been proposed to by a well-to-do businessman named Caspar Goodwood. In England, another marriage proposal presents itself in the person of a Lord Warburton, a man of great wealth and political promise. Isabel turns down both, not wishing to run the standard track of life for women of having no greater meaning than making a conventionally good marriage.

An inheritance received at the death of Isabel's uncle is engineered by her cousin Ralph Touchett, who feels the money will set her loose to discover her grand potential. The money widens Isabel's possibilities even further and she is now free to live in any way she wishes. She wishes wrongly, and falls into a marriage with the heartless dilettante Gilbert Osmond, a man who lives for good taste and little else. The marriage had been connived with the aid of another woman, Madame Selina Merle, with whom Osmond has secretly had a child, now in her late adolescence. The novel is about Isabel's discovery of her grave error in marrying Osmond, and her reckoning of its consequences.

Henry James was thirty-eight when *The Portrait of a Lady* was published. His informal apprenticeship, during his years living in France, to Flaubert, Zola, and company—and especially to Turgenev—was over. He would soon make the decision to live permanently in England, hoping that it would be impossible for his readers to discern "whether I am, at a given moment, an American writing about England, or an Englishman writing about America." (T. S. Eliot called Henry James a European but of no known country.) During these years he had closed the books on the possibility of marriage. His failure as a playwright lay ahead as did the commercial disappointment of the New York Edition of his collected and revised fiction. But also ahead lay the advance in subtlety of the last great novels, his so-called Major Phase, including *The Wings of the Dove* (1902), *The Ambassadors* (1903), and *The Golden Bowl (1904)*.

Although an academic, Michael Gorra does not write like one. My guess is that his time spent in the literary company of Henry James has made him a more polished writer than he might otherwise have been. James has the salubrious effect of elevating many critics. Leon Edel, the towering figure among James scholars, wrote splendidly when he wrote about James. When, late in his life, Edel turned to a little book on Bloomsbury, the snobbery and the other worst aspects of his subject seemed to rub off on him. In the same way, the subtlety and sophistication of James seem to have rubbed off on Gorra.

To get further inside his subject, Gorra has traveled to the sites that supply the settings of *The Portrait of A Lady*, as well as to those in which James composed his novel. He remarks that, while living in Venice, James took his morning coffee at Florian's, which he thought one of life's "simpler pleasures," to which Gorra adds, "a phrase that will stun anyone who has ever picked up one of its checks." As someone who has, I recall thinking when my own check arrived that if I were to dine at Florian's again I should need to apply for a loan from the Small Business Administration beforehand. Visiting the Villa Castellani, where in the novel Gilbert Osmond lives with his daughter, Pansy, Gorra writes:

> Today the building is still painted an ochre-yellow. Its façade is modest, almost anonymous, and it sits directly on the street.... And on this spring morning the house was unprotected in another way: its high, brass-studded doors stood open in the sunlight, and the caretaker waved me in for a look. There was a well in one corner of its lichen-covered courtyard and a Vespa in another, while the pavement was set with the gravestones of pets—"Bubeli, 1913." I noted the names on the mailboxes of the dozen flats into which the building was divided: a German, a Scandinavian, and then a lot of Italians, including somebody called Corleone.

In 1889, remarking on the way Henry James, Sr., brought up his family, with such frequent European travel and residency as nearly to constitute expatriation, William James said his younger brother Henry was "a native of the James family, and has no other country." Gorra is excellent in chronicling this extraordinary family. Much of this ground has of course been covered earlier by F. O. Matthiessen, Leon Edel, and others, but Gorra handles it with admirable concision, integrating it smoothly into his main story, which is the creation of *The Portrait of a Lady*.

Isabel Archer supplied James with another foray into his international theme, the confrontation of Americans with the older civilization of Europe. Gorra reads the novel sensibly and, in an old-fashioned sense, passionately. He notes of the scene toward the close of the novel at the deathbed of Ralph Touchett that, "I cannot read this scene without tears." Anyone who reads Michael Gorra will come away with an enhanced sense of the power of *The Portrait of a Lady*, and wish to return to the novel straightaway.

Gorra reads the novel as a study in the loss of American innocence, even though Gilbert Osmond and Madame Merle, the two characters who deprive Isabel Archer of her innocence, are themselves Americans, though of nearly lifelong European residence. James's "account of the limits of American self-sufficiency," Gorra holds, "is what, above all, makes *The Portrait of a Lady* stand as a great American novel." Gorra deepens his reading when he demonstrates that *The Portrait of a Lady* is above all "the drama of a perceiving mind." James learned from Turgenev that great fiction begins, not in event or incident, but in character; and he extended this by broadening the meaning of character by showing how it can be affected by interior thought as much as by circumstances.

The chief lever of action in *The Portrait of a Lady* is consciousness. The novel's settings are England, Florence, and Rome. But its true stage is the mind of Isabel Archer. The subject of this novel is the growth of consciousness in Isabel as she comes to recognize how she has been used, made a convenience of, betrayed by those she trusted and thought she loved. Owing to a profound mistake in judgment, she realizes that she was trapped in a marriage to a man who despises her and whom she can no longer respect. "Between these four walls she had lived ever since; they were to surround her the rest of her life," Isabel thinks. "It was the house of darkness, the house of dumbness, the house of suffocation." As for Osmond, she now grasps that "Under all his culture, his cleverness, his amenity, under his good-nature, his facility, his knowledge of life, his egotism lay hidden like a serpent in a bank of flowers." Isabel's error is fatal. "Nothing was a pleasure to her now; how could anything be a pleasure to a woman who knew that she had thrown away her life?"

Michael Gorra observes that in his fiction Henry James's primary interest is in victims. Catherine Sloper in *Washington Square*, Hyacinth

Robinson in *Princess Casamassima*, Maisie Farange in *What Maisie Knew*, Maggie Verver in *Wings of the Dove*—these characters have been used by others, or had others wish to mold them to their own ends, or were betrayed by them in pursuit of their own desires. Victims are the people for whom James's greatest sympathies are engaged.

James sympathizes with, but does not pity them. Resignation, renunciation, in the fiction of Henry James, often enriches his characters, lending them a hard-won strength of character and sometimes even an inner radiance. Gorra notes that "James was impatient with the Anglo-American expectation that a book's last chapters should provide a grab-bag of 'husbands, wives, babies, millions;' impatient with both the reader's demand for such treats and the writer's willingness to feed it."

Not a happy-ending man, Henry James sometimes comes closer to being a no-ending man. *The Portrait of a Lady* is perhaps too vivid an example. All that we are told at the novel's conclusion is that, after returning to England to be with her cousin Ralph Touchett before he dies, Isabel has returned to Rome. But to do what? To protect her step-child Pansy from the arid chill of her father? To live out her days in a dead marriage, thus paying the full cost of her horrendous error in marrying the wrong man? We are not given the least hint. We are left to fill in what the remaining years of Isabel Archer's life will be like. If they are to be spent in the company of Gilbert Osmond—and divorce in those days in the Catholic country of Italy was well-nigh impossible—it is difficult to imagine them as anything but bleak. So bleak that, in the BBC television version of *The Portrait of a Lady*, the scriptwriter ended the story on Ralph Touchett's deathbed, with Ralph and Isabel declaring their affection for each other. Gorra calls the never quite begun love between Ralph and Isabel "one of fiction's great might-have-beens."

In the novel's final pages, Isabel is visited by her American suitor Caspar Goodwood, who, in the most openly sexual act in all of James, re-proposes to her and kisses her vehemently. In the revised edition of the novel, we read:

> His kiss was like white lightning, a flash that spread, and spread again, and stayed; and it was extraordinarily as if, while she took it, she felt each thing in his hard manhood that had least pleased her, each aggressive fact of his face, his figure, his presence, justified of its intense identity and made one with this act of possession.

But Isabel sends Goodwood away. James writes: "She looked about her; she listened a little; then she put her hand on the latch. She had not known where to turn; but she knew now. There was a very straight path."

Michael Gorra, who finds James's ending satisfactory, indeed all but inevitable, believes he knows where this path leads. He writes: "She chooses, knowing what she doesn't want, and she goes [to Rome] because at this point nothing forces her to; her choice is an active one, and she goes because she can. She goes, finally, because to stay would require her to accept an illusion. She would have to believe, with her own earlier self, that an unfallen world does indeed lie all before us." Perhaps. Yet one would have liked a more filled-out finish to the novel.

James's revisions for his New York Edition are themselves a subject of controversy among the cult of Jamesians. Max Beerbohm compared the revisions to placing patches of brown velour over gray silk. The Library of America edition of the novel is of the unrevised version. Gorra, who approves the revisions, contends that, in his 1906 revisions of *The Portrait of a Lady*, James was in better possession of his material, for between 1906 and the book's original publication in 1881, he had acquired more experience of life and was in a position to understand his heroine in greater depth.

What Gorra takes this experience to be constitutes my one serious disagreement with his excellent book. This is over the question of whether or not Henry James was homosexual. Gorra joins the majority of academic Jamesians in his certainty that James was at a minimum a strongly repressed homosexual: "while we cannot know if James ever acted upon a physical desire, nobody today doubts the shape of his erotic longings," he writes.

As it happens, there is one person who doubts it—and it turns out to be me. I have been following what I call the Henry James Homosexual Project (HJHP) for some while, and find the evidence set out for James's putative homosexuality less than thin. The project got a great boost from Colm Tóibín's novel *The Master* (2004), which Gorra calls "superb," but might be more accurately described as "suspiciously suppositious." Tóibín, who is himself homosexual, imbues James with an unrelenting eye for soldiers and servants, rough trade and smooth, and at one point has him in bed with Oliver Wendell Holmes, Jr., a connection first made in a reckless biography of Henry James written by a lawyer named Sheldon Novick. Like Claude Raines in *Casablanca*,

Gorra rounds up the usual suspects—Jocelyn Persse, Paul Zhukovsky, Hugh Walpole, all gay men with whom James kept limited company—in trying to nail down the case for the homosexuality of Henry James. He even describes James's typist Theodora Bosanquet, who wrote a charming book about her employer, as "a boyishly handsome young woman."

Like other participants in the HJHP, Gorra thinks the clinching evidence for James's barely repressed homosexuality is to be found in his relationship with a handsome young American sculptor of monstrously large nude figures named Hendrik Andersen. Gorra speaks of James's "knee-trembling love" for Andersen. James's letters to Andersen are marked by an exaggerated affection and physical metaphors of salutation, but then anyone who has read a vast quantity of James's correspondence knows of his taste for what he himself called "mere gracious twaddle." I have read the letters to Andersen, and gracious twaddle is what they chiefly are, apart from those portions in which James seriously criticizes Andersen's art. Rosella Mamoli Zorzi, the editor of the 2004 collection of James's letters to Andersen, doesn't "think these letters should be read as homosexual correspondence." She thinks instead that James viewed Andersen as a son. On this point, Andersen, while visiting James at his house at Rye, in east Sussex, described the novelist's goodness to him as "that kind of goodness that a father gives his son."

What is behind the need to turn Henry James into a severely repressed homosexual? What purpose does it serve? For some gay writers, perhaps they like the notion of having James, in the Seinfeldian phrase, "on their team." For the Freudian-minded, no one is allowed not to have sexuality at the center of his character and the motor force for his behavior—and the less evidence for this that is available, the more powerful, it is assumed, the hidden sexual element must be. For Michael Gorra, Henry James's reputed homosexuality reinforces the argument of his own book that James's "own renunciations [of his true sexual nature] and solitude allowed him to understand the renunciations of others."

All this overlooks the primary fact that Henry James was perhaps as complete an artist as the world has known. Chekhov claimed that "medicine is my lawful wife, and literature is my mistress." For James, literature was wife and mistress both. Marriage was not for him. Nor were dalliances, homo- or heterosexual. The notion of Henry James with wife and children is quite as preposterous as that of his taking on homosexual lovers. The hardest thing about being an artist, James told Desmond MacCarthy, was the loneliness. Yet this same loneliness made possible the freedom he required to practice his art, which was no less than total. James would have considered it an insult to his imagination to be told that he could only understand the power and dignity of renunciation because he had himself practiced it lifelong through hiding his own true sexual nature. Michael Gorra owes Henry James an apology.

October 2012

Froude for thought

Paul Dean

THE 1840S WERE MARKED by as distinguished an array of publications as any period of English literature can boast. In that decade alone, Dickens published *Martin Chuzzlewit* (1844) and *Dombey and Son* (1848); Thackeray, *Vanity Fair* (1848) and *Pendennis* (1849); Carlyle, *Heroes and Hero-Worship* (1841) and *Past and Present* (1843). These years also saw the appearance of Tennyson's *Poems* (1842), Disraeli's *Sybil* (1845), George Eliot's translation of Strauss's *Life of Jesus* (1846), the Brontes' *Jane Eyre* and *Wuthering Heights* (both 1847), Mrs. Gaskell's *Mary Barton* (1848), and, posthumously, Coleridge's *Lectures on Shakespeare* (1849). Yet for many, the most significant title was none of these, nor was it as pithy. *Remarks on Certain Passages in the Thirty-Nine Articles* (1841)—otherwise known as *Tract 90*—by John Henry Newman struck the Church of England with the force of a thunderbolt. Newman's book set out to show that many central Roman Catholic doctrines might be held in good conscience by Protestants, and that interpretations of the sixteenth-century Articles (to which all Anglican clergy were required to subscribe) which held that they condemned those doctrines, were erroneous. Newman was unconvinced by his own arguments, and his secession to the Catholic Church in 1845 produced another sensation. But in his heyday, according to one of his early followers, "For hundreds of young men *Credo in Newmannum* was the genuine symbol of faith."

That particular follower, James Anthony Froude (1818–1894), made his own contribution to the literature of the 1840s with a novel, *The Nemesis of Faith* (1849), which cost him his fellowship at Exeter College, Oxford, and was publicly burned by its sub-rector (vice-president). The book, which Froude later described as "a cry of pain," documented, in thinly veiled fictional disguise, his doomed attempt to embrace orthodox Anglicanism, much as Newman's novel *Loss and Gain* (1848) had done for his own case. The intellectual stars by which Froude navigated were, however, very different from Newman's, and Newman wrote from a conviction of certainty about final truths which Froude was never to attain. Newman's fame as a theologian endures, while Froude's as an historian and biographer has all but slipped into oblivion.

Until now, readers have had to depend on three works for information about Froude's life: an early and unofficial biography by Herbert Paul (1905), the authorized two-volume life by the American scholar Waldo Hilary Dunn (1961, 1963), and most recently Julia Markus's *J. Anthony Froude: The Last Undiscovered Great Victorian* (2007), a readable narrative but light on analysis of Froude's ideas. Now Ciaran Brady's magisterial "intellectual biography" (*James Anthony Froude: An Intellectual Biography of a Victorian Prophet*) gives full weight to the development of Froude's mind as it progressed through his dauntingly prolific output of publications over half a century—including a twelve-volume *History of England from the Fall of Wolsey to the Defeat of the Spanish Armada* (1856–70), estimated to run to two million words; a four-volume biography of Carlyle (1882–84); and four volumes of selected essays, *Short Studies on Great Subjects* (published between 1867 and 1890). Brady's saturation in Froude's work gives his judgements a formidable authority.

The history of Froude's biography is itself a strange story. His daughter co-operated with Dunn, giving him access to extensive manuscript materials, including an autobiographical fragment composed by Froude in the 1890s. He did not publish all of these, and they have since disappeared without a trace. It is likely that many other materials were destroyed by the family, as indeed Froude directed in his will. Accepting the shortage of primary sources, Brady addresses himself to reconstructing Froude's mental history from his published work and the surviving correspondence. Convinced that, as he puts it, Froude was "an inveterate self-writer, intensely engaged with the exploration of his own persona and its presentation before his reading public," Brady explores the variety of authorial voices and rhetorical strategies in Froude's writing, and defends him, where possible, from charges of inconsistency. Sometimes, particularly with Froude's late works on England's relationship with the colonies—which contain views that can only be called racist today—this approach is unsuccessful, but elsewhere Brady convincingly demonstrates that Froude's thought follows an inner logic.

The youngest of eight children whose father was a country clergyman, Froude was an early victim of physical and emotional bullying, recounted by Brady in chilling detail (although he is commendably suspicious of amateur psychoanalysis). His mother died when he was two. One of the few traces she has left on history is a note, written from her sickbed, imploring her eldest son Hurrell to stop torturing little Anthony in his cot. Her husband, already a cold, severe character, became frozen in grief after her death, allowing Hurrell to continue his reign of terror. Anthony was viewed as a "sawney," the family term for a weakling who must be hardened by trials. None of his achievements were praised, his slightest faults rebuked. He was frequently beaten. His three years at Westminster School, where the abuse may have become sexual, were unrelieved misery. At Oxford he took a respectable degree and became a Fellow of Exeter at the age of twenty-four. Here he was drawn into Newman's circle, in the wake of Hurrell, whose early death was seen as a devastating loss to the Tractarian movement. Having been recruited as a contributor to Newman's series of saints' lives, Froude found himself unable to believe in the historicity of the narratives themselves. Although he had taken deacon's orders, he did not feel able to proceed to the priesthood, and the agonies of conscience he underwent, as he realized that German textual criticism and scientific discovery were undermining the presumed infallibility of the Bible, were expressed in *The Nemesis of Faith*. The furor over that book, which was denounced as atheistic and immoral, compelled him to resign his fellowship. He was horrified to discover that his status as a deacon disqualified him from entering any of the regular non-clerical professions, a position which lasted until a change in the law many years later, when he was able to renounce his orders. He set out to make his living as a freelance writer. From 1861 to 1874 he was editor of the influential *Fraser's Magazine*. He undertook several controversial foreign trips: to America, where his hostility to Irish immigrants made him unpopular; to South Africa, in an unsuccessful effort to broker a peace deal between the British government and the secessionist faction in the colonies; and to Australia, where again his attitude to the indigenous population was ill-received. For the last two years of his life he was Regius Professor of Modern History at Oxford, where the heavy teaching load took a fatal strain on his health.

The abandonment of religious belief did not mean the embrace of hedonism. On the contrary, unbelief brought its own burdens. Brady defines Froude's central preoccupation as "the problem of how the blighted and utterly finite self might be made to grasp and to maintain a perception of the vast eternal realities of which it was a tiny but vital part." Nor did Froude simply cease to be concerned with questions of biblical interpretation, as can be seen from such essays as "The Book of Job" (1853) and "Criticism and the Gospel History" (1864). In the late 1840s and early 1850s, he made an intensive study of German philosophy and literature, publishing on Spinoza (twice) and Goethe, whose *Die Wahlverwandtschaften* he translated in 1854 as *Elective Affinities.* The later Spinoza essay—reprinted, along with the two just mentioned, in the first volume of *Short Studies*—was widely acclaimed, and is a key statement of Froude's unease with metaphysicians ("a class of thinkers, happily, which is rapidly diminishing"). Spinoza's idealism, his insistence that everything that exists is eternally present in the mind of God, denies the reality of time; it slights the rootedness of our moral decision-making in historical circumstance. Goethe's *Faust*, "the poem of this century," shows that the only remedy for skepticism is just such an experiential struggle against "the devil of this age of intellect" embodied in Mephistopheles. Brady finds this vision in Froude's fictions, *Shadows of the Clouds* (1847) and *The Nemesis of Faith*, about whose complex narrative structures he writes perceptively, although he does not persuade us of their permanent value.

The fact is that Froude was not a naturally imaginative writer. Given a historical character or situation to describe, he could do it wonderfully, but he could not invent. His gift was for the analytical, the discursive, the rhetorical in the good sense of the word. His style was pithy, his syntax terse, his vocabulary concrete. Invited, late in life, to contribute to a symposium, "The Art of Authorship," he recommended a plain conversational manner, simplicity and straightforwardness, and ruthless revision, commenting that in reading over his own work he habitually crossed out "every passage which had seemed, while I was writing it, to be particularly fine." Readers of Froude have no difficulty following his train of thought, so it is ironical that he fell to such an extent under the spell of Carlyle, who while being, I would maintain, a great stylist in his own way, can't be said to be economical. Brady notes the differences between Carlyle's *French Revolution* and Froude's *History*: the former thundering like some Old Testament figure, the latter cool and detached.

Carlyle's importance to Froude, however, was never as a stylistic model. He was a revelation, as Froude later wrote, "like the morning reveille," disclosing God's "actual and active presence *now* in this working world," not in dogma or abstract reasoning. Like Carlyle, Froude felt himself to be charged with a prophetic mission to his generation; also like Carlyle, he tended to see history in terms of the heroic figures whose decisions shaped its course. He had no patience with quasi-scientific or philosophical approaches to history: It taught no laws, it followed no patterns, it demonstrated no progress. It was more akin to poetry and tragedy; it was "a stage on which the drama of humanity is played out by successive actors from age to age" (he more than once invoked Shakespeare as the ideal historian). The historian's business was not with *why* things happened as they did, but with *how* they did so. Yet, contrary to what we might suppose, this did not mean Froude was content with simple, objective narrative. He did not believe in objectivity, but he did believe in the unchanging nature of moral law, whose operations could be discerned in human actions. He was severe about such writers as Gibbon, Macaulay, and above all H. T. Buckle, whose *History of Civilization in England* (1857, 1861) he criticized for its reduction of the great figures of history to "larger atoms obeying the same impulses with the rest." If the course of history followed no predetermined plan, it nonetheless had its key moments, its critical turning-points, which the historian must not ignore.

Froude's preference for the particular to the general meant that his judgments on individuals often perplexed those who wanted neat intellectual pigeonholes. Thus, in the *History of England*—remarkable for its unprecedented, extensive use of domestic and foreign archive material—he refused to conform to conventional views of the Reformation. The Catholic church was degenerate, but the integrity of Catholic martyrs gives them a degree of nobility; John Knox is admired, John Calvin condemned; the king's divorce, with its accompanying treatment of More and the dissolution of the monasteries, defended as a necessary condition of reform. Whilst not a whitewash, Froude's portrayal of Henry VIII was more positive than was then usual, and duly attacked by reviewers. Brady shows that the *History* works by accumulating multiple perspectives in the manner of Balzac or Tolstoy. Its villains are people, such as Queen Mary and Cardinal Pole, whose egotism and adherence to ideology make them unable to take that kind of complex view of the world. Those who can do so, such as Elizabeth's secretary of state William Cecil, may be censured as unprincipled opportunists, but do more good in the end. Elizabeth herself does not escape censure on account of her vacillations over foreign policy. Froude had originally intended to cover her whole reign but changed his mind and stopped with the defeat of the Armada, feeling that this was an appropriately triumphant note on which to conclude.

Froude's work on Carlyle, his next major project, is an historiographical as well as biographical achievement. At the outset of *On Heroes, Hero-Worship and the Heroic in History* (1841), to give the book its rarely used full title, Carlyle had laid down that "Universal History, the history of what man has accomplished in this world, is at bottom the history of the great men who have worked here." Froude never regarded Carlyle as less than a great man, and accepted Carlyle's trusting him to write his life as a solemn obligation. As Brady points out, the project took a distinctive shape. Carlyle's perusal of his wife's private papers after her sudden death in 1866 opened his eyes to the cruelty of his behavior towards her over the whole course of their marriage. He annotated her letters, and wrote a memoir of her, unsparing in self-reproach. In 1871 he presented Froude with these documents, saying, "They are yours to publish or not to publish as you please after I am gone." This was a poisoned chalice. If Froude published, the effect upon Carlyle's reputation was bound to be damaging; if he did not, he would be suppressing the truth about the conduct of a man who had insisted on the supremacy of moral obligation, and fidelity to the moral struggle, in each individual life. Having named Froude as his literary executor in his will, Carlyle delivered an even more extensive archive, saying "Take them and do what you can with them. All I can say to you is, 'Burn freely.'" To complicate matters further, Froude also came to believe, on good evidence from friends, that the Carlyles' marriage had never been consummated.

An intricate publication sequence was devised, whereby Carlyle's *Reminiscences*, a two-volume work including his memoir of his wife, appeared immediately after his death in 1881. Froude's biography (described in the preface as "the materials for a life") then followed in the succeeding years: *Thomas Carlyle: A History of the First Forty Years of his Life*, in 1882; *Mrs. Carlyle's Collected Letters, with Carlyle's Notes*, in 1883; and *Thomas Carlyle: A History of his Life in London*, in 1884. To read the books as they came out would be, in Brady's words, "a genuinely Carlylean way of coming to grips with Carlyle's own life," entailing "an arduous and disciplined journey of reading and reflection" with the promise of "a fully transformative experience once the obligation had been fulfilled." (There is a subtle account of how this "transformative experience" works, detailed in the chapter on Froude's *Carlyle* in Christopher Ricks's *Essays in Appreciation.*)

Froude's aims influenced his treatment of Carlyle's writings. Greatest attention is given to *The French Revolution*—Carlyle's most artistically polished work, hailed by Froude as "an Aeschylean drama"—and to the biographies of Oliver Cromwell and Frederick the Great, while *Sartor Resartus* and *Past and Present* are only glanced at. In the "revolutionary" group, Carlyle warned the English people of the conflagrations that awaited them if they did not throw off cant and delusion, repudiate political corruption, and seek higher things. Following his account of the completion of *Frederick*, Froude pens some remarkable pages on Carlyle as an historian, rating his artistic power higher than that of either Thucydides or Tacitus (Froude's own favorites). Froude insists that the ideal historian undertakes to reveal "the inner nature of the persons" whose actions are related, and that "actions" comprises not only their deeds, but their "thoughts, opinions, motives, impulses": "The actions without the motives are nothing, for they may be interpreted in many ways, and can only be understood in their causes." This passage, which Brady doesn't quote, is surely a striking anticipation of R. G. Collingwood's ideas about the historical imagination.

Froude presented Carlyle as far as possible through his own words, eschewing secondary sources. But Froude himself, as the chosen biographer, increasingly became a character in Carlyle's story, defending his own frankness and his freedom to criticize one whom he nonetheless counted among the great prophets of his generation. (Indeed, in reaction to the denunciations of his work, he wrote a further apologia, *My Relations with Carlyle*, which was posthumously published in 1903.) This was an authorial stance completely different from that of, say, John Forster in his life of Dickens. We know that Forster suppressed damaging facts about Dickens's treatment of his wife. Froude revealed all. His biography is more akin to Boswell's Johnson, which Carlyle had called the only good English biography on account of its fidelity to its subject's character. But Froude's pains were ill rewarded. Carlyle's niece and her husband made his life a misery, virtually calling him a liar for claiming Carlyle's blessing on his work. Reviews were strident in condemnation.

"What, in the name of truth, ought I to have done?" he lamented in his journal. "Ten years of worry before the book was finished, and the worry for the rest of my life."

Brady admits that Froude's post-Carlyle writings, while voluminous, are comparatively unrewarding. Two books based on his travels, *Oceania: or England and her Colonies* (1886) and *The English in the West Indies* (1888), were controversial, the latter particularly in its apparent defense of slavery. His last effort as a novelist, *The Two Chiefs of Dunboy* (1889), is conceded by Brady to be "a weak imitation of the boy's [*sic*] adventure stories of Robert Louis Stevenson." More valuably, Froude's biography of Disraeli (1890) shrewdly diagnosed the gap between Disraeli's recognition of the condition of England, as revealed in his novels, and his relative lack of success in remedying it by political activity. Despite continued publication, Froude's reputation was dwindling and was only rescued by his appointment to the Oxford professorship of Modern History, which he accepted at the age of seventy-two. There was piquancy in this situation, for not only did it constitute reparation for Froude's ignominious exit from Oxford fifty years earlier (although one should note he had been made an honorary fellow of his old college, Exeter, back in 1858), but also he was succeeding one of his fiercest critics, E. A. Freeman, whose reviews of Froude's *History* had been close to libelous.

The Regius Chair of Modern (as opposed to ancient) History had been established in 1724, with Thomas Arnold and William Stubbs notable previous holders. Recent changes in the university's statutes required the professor to give forty-two lectures during the academic year of twenty-four weeks. Two lectures a week may not sound much today, but anyone who undertakes to read Froude's lectures will realize the vast amount of preparation and composition they entailed, and the timing of the offer left him only six months. Fortunately, Froude secured exemption from this proviso, but otherwise applied himself to his duties far beyond what was necessary, holding tutorials one-to-one and, in Brady's phrase, "even marking essays"! He adapted with unexpected ease to undergraduate company and to Oriel College, of which he was a fellow *ex officio*. His inaugural lecture, in October 1892, rehearsed his well-known view of the nature of history, and announced his intention to focus on the sixteenth century, a time "where the best men were uncertain of their duties, where foresight was impossible … worst of all where none knew whom to trust." In the time left to him he gave courses on English naval explorers, the Council of Trent, and Erasmus.

As usual, Froude was interested in the checks and balances of history, the ironic tricks it plays upon those who seek to control it. The power struggle between Pope and Emperor, enacted at the Council, won a short-term victory for the Church but did long-term damage to the cause of Christendom. Erasmus's failure to support Luther was perhaps unheroic, but "heroism is not always wisdom"; Erasmus's belief that the Church could be reformed from within was sincere, albeit mistaken. Brady argues strongly that Froude's Erasmus is something of a self-portrait, issuing from an "interior monologue" (Froude was composing his autobiographical fragment around this time). Froude's extensive attention to the usually neglected treatise on free will by Erasmus revisited a topic he had addressed in his essay on Spinoza. Our freedom to act is contingent upon forces over which we have limited or no control; virtue is not innate but has to be learnt by precept, example, and experience; theological disputes over free will and predestination, or the concept of divine grace, removed the moral imperative of human beings from the everyday world where it belonged to an abstract realm which was blind to the realities of social obligation. Erasmus, for all his good intentions, turned away from the prospect of international strife and ecclesiastical civil war: History sided with Luther, who had been better able to read the signs of the times.

Froude died at his house in Salcombe, Devon, from stomach cancer just at the start of what would have been his third year as professor. He knew his days were numbered and had made a will, enjoining the destruction of all his papers and manuscripts, including "all such letters, papers, and memorials of or relating to the late Mrs. Jane Welsh Carlyle." He was buried in the parish church in a simple ceremony. He has been to some extent a victim of the historical irony which he so piercingly recognized in the lives of others. His works are out of print, with little prospect of ever being made current again (a selection of the *Short Studies*, at least, would be welcome). But Ciaran Brady concludes that Froude is unlikely to get a hearing in a world that he describes as characterized by "moral relativism, ideological sclerosis, or the self-exculpating strategies of hermeneutic suspicion." That is a rare personal note in a book which generally strives for dispassionate analysis, but after nearly five hundred absorbing pages, Brady has more than earned the right to it.

October 2013

Alexandria, Durrell & the "Quartet"

John Derbyshire

All our fashionable blather about "diversity" notwithstanding, we live in an age of ethnic disaggregation. Czechs and Slovaks, Serbs and Croats, Greek and Turkish Cypriots, Abkhazians and Ossetians and Georgians, have all separated after centuries of cohabitation. The Flemish and Walloons of Belgium look set fair to do the same. The Jews are long gone from Arabia and Persia, the Saxons have mostly decamped from Transylvania, the Nepalese are leaving Bhutan, and the Bantus want out from Somalia. The Protestants and Catholics of Northern Ireland are less mixed now than they were a hundred years ago, and, in the week of Barack Obama's inauguration, Reuters ran a report headlined "U.S. School Segregation on the Rise." Jerry Z. Muller's striking article "Us and Them: The Enduring Power of Ethnic Nationalism" in the Spring 2008 issue of *Foreign Affairs* argued that this ethnic disaggregation, far from being a historical aberration, is "propelled by some of the deepest currents of modernity."

The English writer Lawrence Durrell encountered one small instance of this trend in October 1977. Durrell had lived in the Egyptian city of Alexandria for three years during World War II. Fifteen years later he published four linked novels set in the city—the *Alexandria Quartet*. Though there were some dissenters, the overall critical reception was enthusiastic, and the *Quartet* novels, published separately from 1957 to 1960, were bestsellers. (They were republished as a set in 1961 and many times thereafter.)

Hence Durrell's presence in Alexandria in 1977. The BBC had persuaded him to visit his old haunts in Greece and Egypt for a documentary program. According to Michael Haag's 2004 book *Alexandria*,

City of Memory, a fine atmospheric survey of the city's literary life in the first half of the twentieth century, Durrell found Alexandria much changed from the city he had known thirty-odd years before:

> The city seemed to him listless and spiritless, its harbor a mere cemetery, its famous cafés no longer twinkling with music and lights. "Foreign posters and advertisements have vanished, everything is in Arabic; in our time film posters were billed in several languages with Arabic subtitles, so to speak." His favorite bookshop, Cité du Livre on the Rue Fuad, had gone, and in others he found a lamentable stock. All about him lay "Iskandariya," the uncomprehended Arabic of its inhabitants translating only into emptiness.

Even making allowances for Durrell's depressed mood—his fourth marriage was on the rocks and he was drinking heavily—he was right to think that the Alexandria he saw in 1977, a quarter-century on from Egypt's nationalist revolution, was a monochrome shadow of the city he had immortalized in the *Quartet*. Durrell's Alexandria was of the previous era, when the colorful King Farouk had reigned over an Egypt that was a British puppet state. "Never go back" is, after all, not a bad general rule.

The Alexandria of the *Quartet*, the Alexandria of that earlier era, was chaotically cosmopolitan. "Five races, five languages, a dozen creeds," says Durrell in *Justine*, the first book of the *Quartet*. If anything, that understates the case. Arabs and Jews, Greeks and Italians, French and British, Armenians and Turks jostled together. Between the mosques and synagogues could be found the churches of Copts and Maronites, Chaldeans and Melchites, and all the many varieties of Orthodox and Catholic.

There had been much linguistic churning. Arabic, still colored with some Ottoman Turkish, was the majority language of the city, while French was the commercial *lingua franca*. Greeks were the largest European nationality in residence, but as late as 1910 the traveler Douglas Sladen had been able to write that "Alexandria is an Italian city ... Italian is its staple language." Grand commercial families had their mansions, the poor had their hovels, and a multitude of traders, clerks, petty officials, and foreign bohemians occupied every kind of residence in between. Vice was rampant; the law capricious; anything could be bought.

This Alexandria was a city of a type more common then than now: busily commercial and apolitical, with a strong preference for keeping out of Great Power squabbles, the better to make money and indulge the pleasures of the senses. There have been such cities all over the world in all times. The Hong Kong I knew forty years ago was one such. In its particular colors and demography, though, Durrell's Alexandria belonged to a region, an atmosphere, whose name is not much used now: the Levant. "The eastern part of the Mediterranean, with its islands and the countries adjoining," says the *Oxford English Dictionary*. Webster's *Third* is crisper: "The countries of the Eastern Mediterranean."

(So I had thought. Nowadays, however, one does not have to guess about these things, at least so far as written usage is concerned. Google Books supplies an "Ngram Viewer" that plots the frequency of occurrence of any word or phrase you give it across the past two centuries, in all the books the company has so far scanned. The phrase "the Levant" peaked around 1820, falling off thereafter to a low about 1980, since which it has recovered slightly.)

The Levant was rather rich in these commercial, cosmopolitan cities until modern nationalisms purged them. You may not be interested in Great Power squabbles, but they are interested in you. Smyrna, on the account given by Giles Milton in his whimsically named 2008 book *Paradise Lost*, had something of the same flavor prior to its awful destruction in 1922; so did Beirut before civil war started up in the 1970s. Pre-Nasser Alexandria, though, was Queen of the twentieth-century Levant, and it was Lawrence Durrell's *Quartet* that fixed it in the minds of the fiction-reading public.

Lawrence Durrell first came to Alexandria in April 1941. He was twenty-nine years old. (Next year is his centenary.) His wife Nancy and infant daughter Penelope were with him. They were refugees in flight from Greece, where—excepting short spells in Paris and London—they had lived since 1935. When the Germans had invaded Greece and Yugoslavia on April 6, the Durrells first fled to Crete, fifteen-month-old Penelope carried in a wine basket. After six miserable weeks under constant air attack on the island, they managed to secure passage on one of the last ships out, headed for Alexandria.

Durrell was, like Kipling and Orwell before him, Indian-born. His father was a railroad engineer; his mother was the daughter of a factory accountant; both families were long-time residents of the Raj—"English *pied noir*," Durrell was wont to say, though his mother's ancestry was in fact Protestant Irish. At age eight he had been shipped to England for the traditional unhappy boarding-school education. He was a poor scholar, inattentive and disorganized; by 1930, aged eighteen, even after three years at a "crammer," Durrell failed his university entrance examinations. He had, though, discovered Europe: not so much the place as the *idea* of Europe as seen from Britain—sunshine, good food, cheap wine, easy sex, art. Durrell settled into a lifelong dislike of his ancestral country, which he called "Pudding Island." Says a character in the *Quartet*, echoing many another bohemian expatriate: "I am just a refugee from the long slow toothache of English life."

Durrell was determined on a literary career. By the time of the flight to Alexandria, he had published three novels and three slender volumes of poetry. He had also accumulated a fair literary acquaintance. It included T. S. Eliot, Dylan Thomas, and Anaïs Nin, but its brightest star (so far as Durrell was concerned) was Henry Miller, his foremost literary hero. Durrell actually gets a passing mention in George Orwell's 1940 essay on Miller, "Inside the Whale":

> Associated with Miller there are a number of writers of approximately the same tendency, Lawrence Durrell, Michael Fraenkel, and others, almost amounting to a "school."

Bohemian as he was by temperament, though, Durrell was never as thoroughly "inside the whale"—never as disengaged from worldly affairs—as the quietist Miller. Durrell was, in fact, for several years an occasional employee of the British Foreign Office: in pre-war Athens, in wartime Cairo and Alexandria, in post-war Rhodes and Belgrade, and in Cyprus during the terrorist "emergency" of the mid-1950s. Visiting him at the last of those posts in 1955, his brother Gerald (also a writer), found him installed in a palatial office with "a desk the size of a billiard table." Michael Haag's book has a 1943 photograph of Durrell in jacket and tie at an office desk not much less than billiard-table size in Alexandria, where he was a Foreign Office press attaché.

Some of this government work was from necessity: Durrell did not make a living from writing until the success of the *Quartet* in the late 1950s. Some, though, fell out naturally from that residual sense of imperial responsibility with which every Englishman of Durrell's generation and class was to some degree impregnated—even Orwell worked for the BBC during the war. You could take the boy out of the Raj, but you couldn't take the Raj out of the boy.

That was how Durrell came to settle in Alexandria for the three years between 1942–45. Arrived in the city after that desperate flight from Greece in April 1941, he was first processed as a refugee—and was actually interned for a few days—then made his way to Cairo, whither Nancy and the baby had preceded him. After some weeks of near-destitution, he was recruited by the Foreign Press Department of Britain's Cairo embassy.

In November the following year, with Rommel's army in retreat following the Second Battle of El Alamein, the embassy decided they needed a man on the spot in Alexandria (which is just sixty-six miles east of El Alamein). Durrell was the man. He settled in to Alexandria as a bachelor: his marriage had broken up earlier that year, Nancy decamping to Palestine with the baby.

There commenced the period—two years and nine months—that gave Durrell the material for the *Alexandria Quartet*. It is an odd thing that a writer can take such imaginative nourishment from quite short spans of time like this. Paul Scott's *Raj Quartet* is likewise based on only three years' acquaintance with India, the country that is its subject. It is as though a particular author, dipping a toe into the water of some particular place, were to find himself all at once soaking wet. Durrell went on to write other novels, including an entire *quintet*, but none was as well received, or is as well remembered, as the four he set in Alexandria.

Only in *Clea*, the fourth book of the *Quartet*, do we encounter the war. The first three books are set in pre-war Alexandria, which Durrell knew only by hearsay. (The irresponsible-bohemian side of Durrell's personality, speaking as the narrator of *Clea*, reacted to the war with mixed feelings: "At first it had seemed to portend the end of the so-called civilized world, but this hope soon proved vain.")

The structure of the *Quartet* is in fact based on Durrell's understanding of Einstein's Special Theory of Relativity. Or "understanding"—scoff quotes would not be out of place there. Durrell was no mathematician, and I doubt his engagement with modern physics amounted to more than having read some popularized accounts in magazines. He had, though, grasped the essential point that relativity describes the world using three dimensions of space and one of time.

That idea, by analogy, structures the *Quartet*. "A four-dimensional dance, a relativity poem," Durrell called it. The first three books are, as it were, stationary in time. They cover the same events in pre-war Alexandria from three different points of view. Only in *Clea* do we advance forward in time, into the war years. These Relativistic notions seem to have been buzzing around in Durrell's head for some time. Gordon Bowker's biography has him saying the following thing to a circle of admirers in 1939 Athens: "The problem of life is in the reconciliation of Time and Space."

Durrell was regrettably prone to metaphysical flim-flam of this sort. Here he is in 1952, though this time it seems to be Quantum Mechanics, not Relativity, that he's been browsing in some dentist's waiting-room:

> The act of thinking about something creates a field around the object observed, and in order to think about that object you must neglect the whole from which the object has been separated.... Everything is part of some greater whole. Everything is the sum of smaller parts. How, then, can we deal with the object-in-itself?

"By leaving metaphysics to the metaphysicians," would be my answer. A creative writer is entitled, however, to some self-indulgences—think of the occultist buncombe to which Yeats was susceptible—so long as they not become annoying impositions.

A weightier charge against the *Quartet* is that it is over-written. To this the author pleaded guilty in a 1959 interview for *The Paris Review*.

> INTERVIEWER: Your prose seems so highly worked. Does it just come out like that?
>
> DURRELL: It's too juicy. Perhaps I need a few money terrors and things to make it a bit clearer—less lush. I always feel I am over-writing. I am conscious of the fact that it is one of my major difficulties.

Thus in a single paragraph we get, descriptive of dusk descending on the city: "the streets turning slowly to the metallic blue of carbon paper ... the large mauve parcels of dusk moved here and there.... The great limousines soared away from the Bourse with softly crying horns, like polished flights of special geese."

You either mind this kind of thing or you don't. Probably more people mind it today, in these prosaic times, than did in 1960. And again, Durrell knows his weakness. In *Balthazar*, the second book of the *Quartet*, he commits the following sentence: "The flocks of spiring pigeons glittered like confetti as they turned their wings to the light." At once he turns and mocks himself: "(Fine writing!)" I am not much of a fan of purple prose myself, but I find it hard to mind Durrell's.

The story told, retold, and re-retold in the first three books of the *Quartet* concerns a very varied cast of characters entangled with each other in ways that become fully clear only when the three narratives have been layered on top of one another. The fourth book then jumps ahead in time to follow some of the same characters through World War II. In barest outline:

Justine is a first-person narration by Darley, a struggling Anglo-Irish writer. He takes up with Melissa, a young Greek dancer. She loves him; but Darley meets and falls in love with Justine, the Jewish wife of Nessim, a wealthy Copt. Darley and Justine have an affair. Justine's previous husband had written a novel about her; Darley reads it. Melissa suffers silently.

Balthazar, a homosexual but charismatic Jew, gives lessons in Kabbala, attended by Darley, Justine, and Nessim. Capodistria, a Jewish money-lender related somehow to Justine, also attends. We meet Pursewarden, an obnoxious but successful English writer, and Clea, a serene, virginal young painter. Scobie, an elderly transvestite retiree from the Egyptian Police, provides comic relief.

Melissa tells Nessim his wife is unfaithful. He arranges a meeting at which to interrogate her. They become lovers. Justine, Darley learns from her first husband's novel, cannot love properly because she was raped by a relative in her youth—presumably Capodistria. Pursewarden mysteriously commits suicide. Nessim arranges a duck shoot. Darley expects he will be the victim of an "accident," but it is Capodistria who is fatally wounded. Justine leaves Nessim and the city for Palestine. Melissa has Nessim's child, then dies of consumption. Darley goes to live on a Greek island with Melissa's (and Nessim's) child.

Balthazar is also narrated by Darley. He has written a novel about those events, giving it the title *Justine*. From his Greek island, he sends the manuscript to Balthazar in Alexandria. Balthazar annotates it extensively and sends it back. He knows much more than Darley about the events in *Justine*. All was not what it seemed.

From Balthazar's annotations, Darley and the reader learn much more about Nessim, his brother Narouz, and their mother Leila. Some years before, Leila, her husband old and sick, had taken as lover a young trainee British diplomat, Mountolive. He is now Ambassador. Plots and counterplots are revealed. Several characters turn out to be Intelligence operatives.

Mountolive is told in the third person. We get background on Mountolive, Nessim's family, Pursewarden, and the political shenanigans in Alexandria: Britain-Copt-Muslim-Zionist.

Clea is told first-person by Darley again. He returns to Alexandria, now at war. He renews acquaintances: Nessim, Justine (back from Palestine), Balthazar, Mountolive. He has an affair with Clea, but it is unsatisfactory. The war ends. Darley obtains a minor official post on his Greek island and decides to return. An absurd accident allows Clea to discover her soul as a painter. Darley goes to back to his island; Clea goes to France. Finis.

Thus the narrative line of the *Quartet*. Narrative, however, is not the point of the work—or not the only point. In fact there are signs of narrative sloppiness. The timeline of Mountolive's diplomatic career, for example, as given in Part II of *Mountolive*, is hard to square with his other appearances. Durrell wrote quickly, did not revise much, and hated proofreading. In the *Paris Review* interview, he gave the following writing times for the four books (in order): four months, six weeks, two months, seven weeks. In the year *Justine* came out he published a second, unrelated book, about Cyprus. Writing at that speed, it's a wonder he could keep his characters' names straight.

Durrell's own descriptions of the *Quartet* show his intent as psychological and aesthetic. In a note prefixed to *Balthazar*, he wrote that "the central topic of [the *Quartet*] is an investigation of modern love." That seems an odd thing to say about human relations in the politico-ethnic salad of a highly atypical and not actually very modern city, but one must presume a writer knows his own intentions. I think he got closer to the truth in a letter he wrote to Henry Miller after finishing *Justine*: "It's a prose poem to one of the great capitals of the heart."

I can faintly recall the fuss made by the publication of the *Quartet*. I was in my mid-teens, well-read in the kinds of books given to young people in England of the time—Mark Twain, Victorian adventure classics by the likes of R. M. Ballantyne and Sir Walter Scott, and any number of historical novels—but mainly interested in hunting down and reading every science fiction story ever written.

By the time I got to university, the *Quartet* had been well digested by educated English people. To have read it was the mark of an up-to-date literary sensibility. Also of an "advanced" outlook, at any rate among youngsters: I got the impression the *Quartet* was considerably salacious (which is not, in fact, the case). I picked up *Justine* at the time, but set it aside after a few pages as insufficiently interesting.

A few weeks ago, after a lapse of nearly half a century, I acquired by chance a neat boxed set of the four paperbacks and read them all through. I have read nothing else of Durrell's but the *Selected Poems*, which I acquired at the same time. I was quite surprised to find myself responding to the book. I disagree with Durrell's outlook on life at almost every point. I don't believe that Anglo-Saxon civilization is a disease for which Greco-Latin Europe is a cure. I think the Marquis de Sade, who supplies five of the *Quartet*'s six epigraphs, should have been strangled at birth. Formal experiments in literary form—in the case of the *Quartet*, all that Relativity stuff—more often mar than enhance a work of fiction for me. There *are* a tad too many purple passages here, and Durrell seems to have an unhealthy interest in physical disfigurement. (One character is missing a nose; another has no eyes; Narouz is hare-lipped; his mother hideously marked by smallpox …)

The *Alexandria Quartet* nevertheless sticks in the mind and with all its faults keeps one's attention and forms a rounded, satisfactory whole—creates a *world*. "You might try a four-card trick in the form of a novel," Pursewarden tells Darley in *Clea*. Lawrence Durrell did, and somehow he pulled it off.

October 2011

A Burke for our time

Charles Hill

A BURKEAN EVENT took place in New Haven not long ago when two distinguished leaders at Yale proposed to the Proprietors of the Grove Street Cemetery, before a standing-room-only crowd of townspeople, that to tear down the cemetery wall would "create an inviting and open atmosphere" for passersby.

The cemetery is the oldest municipally incorporated burial ground in the country, older than Père-Lachaise in Paris. Eli Whitney, Noah Webster, Roger Sherman, and Samuel F. B. Morse lie there along with African-American Civil War veterans. The entrance gate and wall erected in the 1840s is a unique expression of the neo-Egyptian architectural style of the time. A headstone on an empty gravesite salutes the memory of Glenn Miller, the trombonist and band leader whose plane disappeared over the English Channel during World War II; he had formed his 418th Army Air Force band at Yale.

The debate was civil and moderate in tone, but stark. It became a male versus female issue. The women of the town prevailed. Their argument was, in essence: "Who are we to do such a thing as against all those generations in the past, and those yet to be born?" It was a Burkean moment, although no one at the time seemed to recognize it as such.

For Edmund Burke, the eighteenth-century Irish statesman who served in the British House of Commons, the hallmark of a sane society is reconciliation of the present and the future to the past. We live our lives in the present, with time always progressing forward in a linear direction, so Burke's respect for the past makes him conservative. Given the modern world's appetite for change, Burke's emphasis on continuity and permanence makes him seem like a strange outsider. Furthermore, Burke's conservatism is expressed in a fierce and fiery, almost reactionary, style.

This puzzled his detractors, who were constantly suspecting Burke of some ulterior motive, of exerting some nefarious influence in the cause of some hidden agenda. The Duke of Newcastle said, "Burke's real name is O'Bourke, a wild Irishman, a Jacobite, a papist, a concealed Jesuit." At best, but equally threatening to the state, Burke was an eighteenth-century Socrates, a dangerous gadfly, challenging the settled assumptions of Britain. The portrayal of Burke in Boswell's *Life of Johnson* avoids quoting the statesman directly, and sometimes disguises the identity of the "Burkean" speaker, as if to conceal Burke from the authorities. If this was a conservative, it was a strange conservative indeed. Moreover, Burke took contrarian positions on world issues, positions his critics found difficult to reconcile: religious liberty for Ireland, independence for America, justice and respect for India's traditions, and to hell with the French Revolution.

Indeed, Burke presented a formidable challenge to friend and foe: a great intellect, a stunning orator, propelled by an intense inner energy that was hard to take. Burke seemed to concentrate all his capabilities in the immediate moment. If you found yourself conversing with Burke, it was said, you felt as if you were being "grazed by a powerful machine." Samuel Johnson, who yielded to no one in considering himself a great man, repeatedly praised Burke as a great man. If Burke should drop in at a blacksmith's shop to have his horse shod, Johnson said, the blacksmith would say, "We have had an extraordinary man here." Even to the domineering Johnson, Burke was an intimidating presence: "His stream of mind is perpetual." Once, when Johnson was feeling poorly, he said, "That fellow [Burke] calls forth all my powers. Were I to see Burke now, it would kill me."

Not since Cicero had a major political thinker been a practicing politician in the center of the arena. So it is refreshingly welcome to have Burke reassessed today by another politician, Jesse Norman, Member of Parliament for Hereford and South Herefordshire who has taught philosophy at University College London.

Edmund Burke: The First Conservative is not a standard biography. Norman has set his book in two parts. Part One, "Life," is a lively review of Burke's political career from his "outsider" origins to his entanglement in the causes of Ireland, America, India, and France. How those controversies generated his ideas is largely left to Part Two of the book, "Thought."

Norman locates Burke in many ways as an Enlightenment figure. By the same token, Burke was presciently aware that Enlightenment ideas could produce deep social pathologies as prescribed by, in Burke's words, "the perverse and paradoxical genius of Rousseau." This position enabled Burke, the author argues, to become "the hinge or pivot of political modernity," the first and greatest critic of the modern age, and the earliest postmodern political thinker. The great paradox is that "Burke the anti-radical becomes a far more radical thinker than Karl Marx himself."

Norman analyzes Burke's ideas, although they resist brief summary, through a coherent four-part framework: the social self, the political party, the individual, and human values.

First, there is the social self. Unlike Hobbes, Locke, and Rousseau, Burke does not begin with the state of nature. Rather, he takes as given the reality of human society itself, which is where most of our humanity is derived from. Norman misreads Burke in asserting that "for Burke, there can be no such thing as the state of nature"; in fact, Burke says that we *are in* the state of nature: the society we have evolved into naturally over time, with liberty as the result of a well-ordered society.

For Burke, the social order is, in the broadest sense, what constitutes a nation. The concept of nationhood as social order is one reason why Burke "is instantly able to see France as a country which has, in effect, forgotten itself." Burke's "whole philosophy stands as a reproof," Norman writes, "to the revolutionary rationalism inspired by Rousseau."

Second, Norman turns to Burke's insight that properly functioning political parties are the essence of mature governance. Through them, ideologies clash. Burke never seems to have contemplated the idea of parties as mass-membership organizations campaigning across a nation, but it is Burke who first famously defined the modern conception of a political party as "a body of men united for promoting for their joint endeavors the national interest, upon some particular principle in which they are all agreed." Parties, in Burke's view, bring stability to politics, give focus to national purpose, moderate government, give ordinary people a part to play, and provide testing grounds for political ideas. Burke stresses that the responsibility of a Member of Parliament is to exercise mature judgment, not simply carry out the wishes of his constituents. In all this, Burke developed what is, or should be, the fundamental conception of a modern representative political party.

Third, Norman focuses on the Enlightenment idea that the human individual is the basic unit of moral, political, and economic accounting.

Thus, individual freedoms are paramount. To Norman, "liberal individualism" is today pervasive across most areas of human life, including education, race, health, religion, human rights, trade, development, and migration. From a Burkean perspective, Norman says, liberal individualism has its own points of weakness. For Burke, there is little meaning in the idea of people as individuals apart from society. If individuals artificially separate themselves from society, liberty becomes license; individualism produces self-indulgence. All this, Norman says, has brought a succession of recent disasters and a kind of moral panic about Western society itself: drug use, loneliness, suicide, divorce, single motherhood and teenage pregnancy, and fears of a loss of local or national identity—all in a spreading belief that basic values of respect, hard work, and public service are being lost in celebrity worship, consumerism, and the money culture—all because of the rise of liberal individualism.

Finally, Norman finds hope in the extent to which the modern world is now rediscovering Burke's wisdom through research findings in the social sciences. In the conclusion of his book, a chapter titled "The Recovery of Value," Norman refers to recent research that supports Burke's central themes: that humans have a distinctive social nature; that emotions guide reason, which itself is limited and fallible; that allegiance and identity are grounded in institutions which are the source of human well-being; that absolute freedom or "license" is disastrous for the person and for society; and that what matters most is for humans to live together according to shared rules and norms in a moral community. Norman concludes, "It is striking how much evidence has emerged in recent years for the basically social nature of humans," as behavioral economics has, in particular, undermined the long-standing picture of man as "*homo economicus*." Equally striking are anthropological studies showing that religions, far from being viruses or parasites, as the New Atheists assert, "are likely to have had evolutionary advantages for their members."

While recognizing that Burke's persona, like Walt Whitman's, contains multitudes, Norman boldly summarizes Burke's thought for our time. Any such effort, however, is fundamentally un-Burkean. There is no catching Leviathan with a hook. Burke's writing and speaking—style and substance—are all of a piece, coming together organically. His 1790 masterpiece *Reflections on the Revolution in France* is clear, but stubbornly resistant to summation. There are no chapters or subheadings, no table of contents, no index. When the luminous intellectual historian Frank Turner edited a new edition of Burke in 2003, he was determined to produce an index. It was, Turner told me, "the damndest fool's errand I ever set myself." When he had finally completed it, he found that the first item he looked up in the index had not been included. To grasp the full force of Burke's ideas, one must read through his entire oeuvre, without assistance.

More problematic is Norman's interpretation of what it takes to bring Burke's ideas to life in our time. Each of his four main "Burkean" chapters seem to intensify some of the worst aspects of the situation today.

Burke is correct that we humans are social beings, and Norman puts stress on the larger national social order. In the United States, a distinctively American character and order was devastated by the politico-cultural degradations of the Sixties. Since then, the government has happily moved into the role of supreme social-orderer in a way that ignores or spurns the deeply traditional institutions and allegiances Burke championed. Norman's argument seems to deliver Burke bound and gagged to an overbearing state, which has eagerly moved into the vacuum left by the cultural elite's eradication of traditional American society.

Burke's advocacy for the political party may well be, as Norman argues, "the hinge of Anglo-American, and indeed the world's political modernity," with the two "big tent" political parties serving the cause of consolidating power in the United States within a political system otherwise designed by the Founders to disaggregate political sources of leverage. But this Burkean contribution, bundled inside Norman's summation, suggests that one's political party can be Burke's "little platoon," deserving deep allegiance as the foundation of social order—and this in the new twenty-first century, when the primary feature of representative government is, contrary to Burke's precept, the politician's fear of exercising mature judgment, slavishly following his constituency's shifting moods.

This reality is moving our current politics ever more toward the direct democracy that brought down Athens and which led Burke to howl that "a perfect democracy where popular authority is absolute and unrestrained is therefore the most shameless thing in the world." The same insight led the American Founders to protect their country, in its design, from the dangers of direct democracy.

In gathering Burke's thoughts, Norman sets the statesman in opposition to the modern creed of individualism. To Norman, individualism cannot but produce self-indulgence; there is no possibility for George Washington's view that a free society requires individuals capable of exercising the virtues of self-restraint, or Emerson's declaration of the importance of self-reliance. Indeed, individual liberties are an inextricable part of the American national character. That tradition, in this telling, could be interpreted as impossibly wrong from the start, and now out of control. Most bizarrely, this view could link Burke to governmental policies aimed at entrenching a collective, anti-individualistic culture.

Norman's summation of Burke's thought, useful as it is for providing some core Burkean insights in an accessible manner, is too beholden to current governmental proclivities. How, then, do we approach Burke's thought unless we go at it as did Gladstone, reading Burke's writings every day? Some have said that within the central pages of *Reflections on the Revolution in France*, there is a logic chain, but no one yet has found it. To attempt to do so is also somewhat un-Burkean; the best readers of Burke simply absorb the meanings organically. Doing so reveals that Burke *was* a man of the Enlightenment in his attempt to retell the course of human history somewhat in the manner, if not the substance, of such attempts by Hobbes, Locke, and Rousseau. These are the key points of Burke's thought:

Burke argues governance requires more than one lifetime to comprehend. This is what Immanuel Kant thought too, but Kant was thinking about history yet to come whereas Burke is referring to the past, present, and future.

Burke, like other Enlightenment thinkers, refers to human nature as basic, but unlike them, he says it is too complex for any theory, policy, or ideology. Language is at the heart of it all; and in the French Revolution, Burke sees what Thucydides saw in the course of the collapse of Athens: words losing their meaning.

Burke's most memorable passage is even more significant than its controversial fame:

> It is now sixteen or seventeen years since I saw the Queen of France, then the Dauphiness, at Versailles; and surely never lighted on this orb, which she hardly seemed to touch, a more delightful vision.

> I saw her just above the horizon, decorating and cheering the elevated sphere she had just begun to move in, glittering like the morning star full of life and splendor and joy.
>
> Oh, what a revolution! and what a heart must I have, to contemplate without emotion that elevation and that fall! Little did I dream, when she added titles of veneration to those of enthusiastic, distant, respectful love, that she should ever be obliged to carry the sharp antidote against disgrace concealed in that bosom; little did I dream that I should have lived to see such disasters fallen upon her, in a nation of gallant men, in a nation of men of honor, and of cavaliers! I thought ten thousand swords must have leaped from their scabbards, to avenge even a look that threatened her with insult.
>
> But the age of chivalry is gone; that of sophisters, economists, and calculators has succeeded, and the glory of Europe is extinguished forever. Never, never more, shall we behold that generous loyalty to rank and sex, that proud submission, that dignified obedience, that subordination of the heart, which kept alive, even in servitude itself, the spirit of an exalted freedom! The unbought grace of life, the cheap defense of nations, the nurse of manly sentiment and heroic enterprise is gone. It is gone, that sensibility of principle, that chastity of honor, which felt a stain like a wound, which inspired courage whilst it mitigated ferocity, which ennobled whatever it touched, and under which vice itself lost half its evil, by losing all its grossness.

Here, he speaks of the Queen not only as herself, but also as an "artificial person" in the Enlightenment sense. Yet, she also embodies the nation's heritage in an anti-Enlightenment way.

The key to love of country, Burke then argues, is in "the spirit" of a gentleman and in religion, in which our "passions" instruct our "reason." This calls to mind Plato's idea of the soul as a tripartite of reason, desire, and spirit. Burke is here challenging the Enlightenment's conceit that men were living in an Age of Reason.

The theater, Burke says, is "a school of moral sentiments." This echoes Adam Smith's idea of "the impartial spectator" we imagine observing and passing judgment on our doings. Here is a wholly different approach to the cult of entertainment that inundates us today. This leads to an image not unlike that in our time of "the moral—or silent—

majority." Just because "half a dozen grasshoppers under a fern make the field ring with their importunate chink, whilst thousands of great cattle, reposed beneath the shadow of the British oak, chew the cud and are silent, pray do not imagine that those who make the noise are the only inhabitants of the field." Shall we not think, here, of the media?

Burke then points to our *advantages*—that which we cherish and express in our "prejudices," a word that, for Burke, unites the best instincts, character, and conduct of the self and society—and that upon which we base our civil society.

Then come the threats we must guard against: the idea that legitimacy requires a perfect (direct) democracy and the temptation to change the state whenever we choose, making us nothing more than "the flies of a summer."

All this means that while there is no such thing as a "social contract," society now *is* a contract, a partnership of the living, the dead, and those yet to be born. When we recognize and act on this we are *in* the state of nature.

Liberty comes from this, whereas theories or declarations of rights do not. Actual circumstances, not abstract proclamations, make a people free. When Hannah Arendt, in her contemplation of the Holocaust, recognized this in Burke, an unusual bond between liberal and conservative took place.

And if Burke had appeared in New Haven that evening, he would have added that for understanding society as a partnership, "Every college should have a graveyard in its midst."

May 2013

"WE MUST BE FUNNY!!!!!!"

Robert Messenger

So wrote P. G. Wodehouse to Guy Bolton in 1952 as they planned a joint book of reminiscences of the theatrical world of the 1920s. "I think we shall have to let truth go to the wall if it interferes with entertainment. And we must sternly suppress any story that hasn't a snapper at the finish.... Even if we have to invent every line of the thing, we must have entertainment." Their book, *Bring on the Girls: The Improbable Story of Our Life in Musical Comedy, With Pictures to Prove It*, is a sprightly account of the birth of the modern musical by two men at its center. Some of the stories are somewhat exaggerated, which is a great worry to Wodehouse's biographers. The concern is more than a bit overblown, for Wodehouse and Bolton didn't overstate their own place in the music-hall world or the importance of their work. They simply shined the anecdotes up so that people might stick around for the second act.

And that's pretty much the story of Wodehouse's whole life: Make 'em laugh. Nothing was too light or serious for him not to want it to be polished and presented better: "We saw the Coronation on television," he wrote to Bolton in 1953. "I thought it needed work and should have been fixed up in New Haven. They ought to have cut at least half an hour out of it and brought on the girls in the spot where the Archbishop did the extract from the Gospel."

And just in case you think he had a republican bias: In 1961, he was asked to revise the topical lyrics in Cole Porter's "You're the Top" for a revival of the musical *Anything Goes*, which he'd worked on back in 1934. Writing to Bolton of one of the Kings of Musical Comedy, he noted, "The trouble with Cole is that he has no power of self-criticism. He just bungs down anything whether it makes sense or not just because he has thought of what he feels is a good rhyme. Can you imagine turning in stuff like 'So Mrs. Roosevelt with all her trimmins (why trimmins?) can broadcast a bed by Simmons, 'Cause Franklin knows anything goes'?"

Wodehouse even offered up new words for the title song itself:

When the courts decide, as they did latterly
We could read *Lady Chatterley*
If we chose,
Anything goes.

The desire to entertain which stood him so well at the typewriter could get him into trouble in the flesh, especially in his dealings with the press. In 1930, he went to Hollywood on a $2,000-a-week contract from MGM. He found the working habits of the studio peculiar—"The system is that A. gets the original idea, B. comes in to work with him on it, C. makes a scenario, D. does preliminary dialogue, and then they send for me to insert Class and what-not. Then E. and F., scenario writers, alter the plot and off we go again"—and easily kept up his own writing while fulfilling his studio commitments. Having agreed in May 1931 (at MGM's request) to be profiled in the *Los Angeles Times*, he made some pre-interview remarks to fill the moments as the reporter, Alma Whitaker, got settled in his living room, about how much he liked Hollywood, etc. etc., but regretted that "he had been paid such an enormous amount of money without having done anything to earn it"—"$104,000 for loafing." (Though his idea of loafing was writing "a novel and nine short stories, besides brushing up my golf, getting an attractive sun-tan and perfecting my Australian crawl in the swimming pool.")

These comments, rather than the official interview, made the front page of the paper and were picked up around the country—it was a depression after all and he found himself "a sort of Ogre to the studio now." Biographers have presented this incident in one of two lights: either as the innocent and unworldly Plum dropping a brick or as a calculated attempt to get back at his Hollywood masters. Yet he was really just employing a common type of prep-school bravado: claiming to have done no work while still achieving great success. It's an old boy's habit, and Wodehouse was the oldest of old boys—all his life he remembered his days at his boarding school, Dulwich College, as among his happiest.

He was always trying to make things a little bit easier for people. He would pre-write dialogue for radio interviews (and was not beyond cooking some up for the interviewers, too). He downplayed bad news and was almost apologetic when letting close friends know of any difficulty. There are only the tiniest asides in his letters about his being diagnosed with a brain tumor (mistakenly, as it turned out, after some anxious days) or when doctors feared he might be going blind. Wodehouse charmed by self-deprecation. Though he lived until 1975 and age ninety-three, he never lost this insouciant version of the British stiff upper lip.

It was the same story in the event that essentially blighted his life: his radio broadcasts from Nazi Germany in 1941. Wodehouse had been sure war wouldn't come and felt no need to leave his home on the French coast near Calais. The Phoney War of 1939–40 didn't make this more urgent and then he, like the British and French armies, was quite caught out by the rapid German advance in May 1940. (When he and his wife did finally try to flee it was with a plan to drive 1,300 miles to Portugal rather than take the short ferry to England as they couldn't bear the idea of their Pekinese dogs being quarantined. Their car broke down less than two miles from home.) France conquered, the Nazis ordered all male foreign nationals under the age of sixty interned. Wodehouse was fifty-eight.

He was arrested in July and imprisoned in Loos and then Belgium before being deported to an internment camp at Tost in Upper Silesia ("There was a flat dullness about the countryside which has led many a visitor to say, 'If this is Upper Silesia, what must Lower Silesia be like?,'" he later wrote). They traveled by cattle-cars "full of human excrement," and food was everywhere scarce. But he made what he could of life in Tost, which meant writing. He wrote for the camp newspaper; he kept a diary (reprinted in Frances Donaldson's 1982 biography, still the best life of Wodehouse); and he kept at his fiction (finishing *Joy in the Morning* and writing *Money in the Bank*, both masterpieces of the canon).

Settled, he was able to correspond with neutral countries and receive care packages. England was obviously busy with other concerns, but Wodehouse's American agent and friends worked to arrange his release. In December 1940, an article by the Associated Press reporter Angus Thuermer (who had found Wodehouse by accident while doing a piece on the internment camps) brought his plight to the attention of his numerous American fans. Thuermer was interested in an article Wodehouse had done on his camp experience and took excerpts back for the *Saturday Evening Post.* As ever, Wodehouse had taken the situation at hand and made it into a humorous skit. No point in complaining about what can't be fixed.

The article lead to an organized campaign to aid Wodehouse and alerted the Nazis to their guest's unexpected propaganda value. They began to treat him with careful kindness and encouraged his writing (making sure he could "rent" a typewriter, for instance) and his keeping in touch with his American fans. Wodehouse felt growing gratitude to his friends across the ocean, and a suggestion from the camp authorities in May 1941 that he might make a few broadcasts to assure his American public of his health and thank them for the support must have seemed innocuous enough. (It may not to us, but Wodehouse would have had no idea how the war was going or any sense of the evil doings of the Nazi regime.)

In June, he was released, led to believe it was because he was near sixty. Shipped to Berlin, he "ran into" two friends from his Hollywood days, and one of them brought up the idea of broadcasting again. Lonely, eager to please, and keen to thank his American fans, Wodehouse was at the typewriter that day reworking his humorous account of life at Tost—"Young men, starting out in life, have often asked me 'How can I become an Internee?' Well, there are several methods. My own was to buy a villa in Le Touquet on the coast of France and stay there till the Germans came along. This is probably the best and simplest system. You buy the villa and the Germans do the rest."

He made five recordings, which the Germans carefully rolled out over a course of weeks to give an impression of ardent support for a country at war with Wodehouse's own and stoking a furor in England. He was condemned in the House of Commons and attacked viciously in the press and by authors as varied as A.A.Milne and Sean O'Casey. Libraries banned his books. He was investigated as a collaborator by both the French and English governments and felt himself under threat of prosecution for treason for the rest of his days—a 1944 MI5 report exonerating him was kept secret until 2011. As soon as possible after the war, he moved to America and remained aloof from his native land. Wodehouse's thoughtless (in all senses) action bore repercussions for the rest of his life.

This comes through clearly in Sophie Ratcliffe's edition of his letters, *P. G. Wodehouse: A Life in Letters.* His sunny outlook was dimmed by the outrage, and he found himself at odds with all but a few close companions—Bolton and his old school chum Bill Townend being the main two. He took ever more comfort in the sole companionship of his wife, Ethel. (That her daughter, Leonora, whom Wodehouse adopted and adored, had died during the war after routine surgery bonded the two even more around their beloved Pekes.) After the war and through three more decades, his letters constantly referenced the broadcast crisis. The strain of being reviled drove him right back to the typewriter—he wrote the rollicking novels *Uncle Dynamite* and *Full Moon* while trying to get out of Germany—and the desire to hide out in his stories never passed away.

Ms. Ratcliffe believes that Wodehouse's life was more eventful than popularly perceived. Possibly. What did happen to him was mostly unpleasant—not just large tragedies like war, internment, and the early death of a daughter, but small travails, too. He was a guinea pig in the working out of international tax laws between the United States and England, for instance, and he saw the theatrical world in which he raised himself up completely vanish. How he felt about such things, we have little idea, for Wodehouse's letters and the three memoirs he put together are devoid of emotional detail—though there is a strain of anger in a few post-war letters when he was discussing writers who had attacked him for the broadcasts. Richard Usborne, author of some of the earliest commentaries of Wodehouse, noted in his *Wodehouse at Work to the End*, "It is certainly a refreshing change to find an author less fascinated by his inner self than you are. But you wish that author wasn't Wodehouse." Every event is referenced through the frame of whether his work was going poorly or well. Can you imagine another writer noting the blackouts and travel restrictions of war by being grateful for the quiet—"I don't mind very much, as I never do want to go anywhere"? Though he was worried "about how to get more typewriter ribbons."

Usborne was right that we wish to know more about Plum's inner life. He wrote the best comic novels ever penned—and not just a handful but by the bushel. He was also one of the true geniuses of the song lyric, in a class with Ira Gershwin, Lorenz Hart, Oscar Hammerstein, Yip Harburg, and Dorothy Fields. Who was this man? We have simply no idea what motivated him and pleased him. We learn in his letters that he manipulated words with astonishing ease and speed but had immense difficulty in coming up with the plots. He is always begging friends for ideas, and the letters depict his regular use of old musical plots to create his novels (and later his reuse of these reusings).

And despite Ms. Ratcliffe's assertion, it is the things that didn't happen to Wodehouse that mount up. The letters show his great closeness to his step-daughter Leonora (whose name wondrously morphs in his letters to her from Nora to S'nora to Snorky, Snorklet, and Snorkles). And there are numerous portraits of happy parenting in the Wodehouse canon. Most typical are Bingo Little's comical adventures with young Algernon Aubrey, who always pulls his father out of the soup before Mrs. Bingo can discover that her loving husband has lost his last £5 on some flutter. But there is also a charmingly sentimental account of a young marriage and its first offspring, *The Coming of Bill.* Written in the first years of the Wodehouse marriage, it suggests only the fondest feelings about fatherhood, and yet he and Ethel never had children of their own. One wonders why.

Wodehouse was only thirty-two when World War I broke out, but he took no part in the fighting and spent the years working in America. (The equally great comic writer Saki, by comparison, joined up at forty-three and was killed during the Somme.) He certainly felt some guilt, which you can hear in a 1920 letter to Townend, who had served in the army: "I'll buck you up when I get home. That's to say, if I'm not arrested and shoved in chokey for not helping to slug Honble Kaiser." Wodehouse was worried about having failed to register for the wartime draft in England. He knew numerous men killed on the Western Front, and one wonders how this affected his sense of England and self. Perhaps it made him more eager to do something during World War II and so leap at the chance to broadcast and entertain.

There are no surviving letters written by Wodehouse between June 1915 and June 1918, and it's not just his thoughts about the war that are lost but also any insight into the key moment in the artist's life. These are the years when he wrote "Extricating Young Gussie" (the first appearance of Bertie Wooster), *Something Fresh* (the first Blandings book), and the astounding one-off novels *Uneasy Money* and *Piccadilly Jim.* How did a struggling writer of school stories suddenly alight upon the mature style he would maintain for half-a-century almost unchanged?

He had married in September 1914, and the letters do indicate that Ethel brought comfort and order to his life—"When I look back and think of the rotten time I have been having all my life, compared with this, it makes me sick," he was already writing in October. He seems never to have altered that view, and it may be that the calm of having a wife to organize his social and business life freed a shy man to write at full tilt. It's as good an answer as we are likely to find.

Ethel and Leonora became his life away from the typewriter (with bits of exercise like golf, swimming, and long walks thrown in). But the marriage is again felt mostly by its absence in the letters. The Wodehouses were almost always together and had no need to write; it's only in the mid-1960s when Ethel was in the hospital that he wrote her loving letters.

The one true discovery here is that Wodehouse, who is often imagined as a naif, was well-educated, well-read, and of quite sound literary judgment. Of Anthony Trollope: "It is rather like listening to somebody who is a little long-winded telling you a story about real people. The characters live in the most extraordinary way and you feel that the whole thing is true." Of *The Naked and the Dead*: "I can't give you a better idea of how things have changed over here than by submitting that book to your notice. It's good, mind you,—in fact, I found it absorbing—but isn't it incredible that you can print in a book nowadays stuff which when we were young was found only on the walls of public lavatories."

Ms. Ratcliffe writes in her introduction that she's sought with this book to please both academic and general interest readers. It is as peculiar an idea as it is an impossible one. Wodehouse will always be tempting to scholars for the vastness of his success (he was arguably the most successful writer in the Anglophone world in the 1930s) and for the study of wartime treason. Yet to readers, he is a source of endless delight. Despite the fact that I could string together a list of good lines and anecdotes from the letters, the book is anything but a delight. It is unwieldy in size and contains numerous letters of limited interest. Almost all the letters are marred by numerous ellipses where the editor has excised material. The pages look rather like a postmodern novel. Wodehouse cries out for a lighter touch as in the previous edition of his letters (the much briefer *Yours, Plum: The Letters of P. G. Wodehouse*, edited by Donaldson along thematic lines) or the wonderful *P. G. Wodehouse, In His Own Words*, drawn by Barry Day and Tony Ring from the whole canon of his writing and which is truly a slice of Plum Pie.

What's shocking is that Ms. Ratcliffe's intensive editing actually creates gaps. If you consult the major biographies, you will find interesting passages from the letters that do not appear in her book. On February 24, 1945, Wodehouse wrote to Bill Townend from Paris discussing how he had lived in Berlin and the coming end of the war. He also noted his present reading:

> I have become very interested in Shakespeare and am reading books about him, having joined the American library here. A thing I can never understand is why all the critics seem to assume that his plays are a reflection of his personal moods and dictated by the circumstances of his private life. You know the sort of thing I mean. They say "*Timon of Athens* is a gloomy bit of work. That means that Shakespeare was having a lousy time when he wrote it." I can't see it. Do you find that your private life affects your work? I don't. I have never written funnier stuff than during these last years, when I certainly wasn't feeling exhilarated.

Interesting and amusing. The letter is included by Ms. Ratcliffe—it runs over three full pages—but this passage is lost amongst four sets of ellipses. This is simply unacceptable in a book with pretensions to scholarship and completeness. Equally irritating is that Wodehouse's 1955 letter to Richard Usborne answering a sequence of biographical questions—from "You pronounce it 'Woodhouse,' don't you?" to "Was there caning at Dulwich when you were there?"—sees at least five of the answers omitted. What is the point of a 600-page volume full of minutiae that turns out to also be sketchy?

We are legion, the Wodehouse completists—I have six volumes of translations of the sublime short story "The Great Sermon Handicap" into languages as varied as Sanskrit, Coptic, Yiddish, and Afrikaans—and the letters will find a happy place in many a library. But in the end, as with the half-dozen biographies of Wodehouse, *A Life in Letters* does little to deepen our appreciation of a comic genius. It tells me nothing of how a man could give flight to such a fancy as "Although Mr. Gedge's statement that the Vicomte de Blissac was never sober had been an exaggeration—for he was frequently sober, sometimes for hours at a time—it is undoubtedly true that he had a distinct bias toward the festive."

The English Everyman edition of the master's work that began publication in 1998 has now reached eighty-four volumes (eighty-one are already available from Overlook in the United States). Three more Everymans are due in the Spring. Having a thick tome of his letters is nothing to the prospect not too distant of Wodehouse at last collected, complete, and readily available. What ho! What ho! What ho!

February 2013

"Bovary" & le mot juste

Brooke Allen

LOOKING INSIDE the cover of Lydia Davis's eagerly awaited new translation of *Madame Bovary*, the reader is greeted with a quantity of praise for Davis's 2004 translation of Proust's *Swann's Way*, a work that not only earned her a MacArthur "genius" grant but also caused her to be named a *chevalier* of the French Order of Arts and Letters—the official Gallic seal of approval. Among the accolades Viking Penguin has included for Davis's Proust is one from Dave Eggers: "I think Davis's is definitive."

Definitive? Impossible: there is *no such thing* as a definitive translation. Not of any literary work. For translations—like art forgeries, curiously enough—are always recognizably a product of their period. They may seem neutral at first, but as the years go on, telltale features of the 1920s, say, or the 1980s, will appear. This is a problem even when the period happens to be the same as that of the original work: Victorian English has different speech patterns, different conventions, an entirely different *flavor* from the stripped-down mid-nineteenth-century French prose Flaubert labored over so painstakingly.

Davis has counted nineteen English *Madame Bovary* translations prior to her own. Some of them continue to enjoy great acclaim, like that of Eleanor Marx Aveling (daughter of Karl), for instance, written in 1886 and revised by Paul de Man in 1965, or Francis Steegmuller's 1957 version. And there is Geoffrey Wall's 1992 *Bovary*, which has long been available in the Penguin Classics edition but will soon be supplanted by Davis's. Numerous college professors are displeased by the fact that Penguin is dropping Wall's excellent *Bovary*. There is no need, they argue, for a new *Bovary*: it's simply a marketing ploy by Viking Penguin, who saw Davis as a hot property (so far as a literary translator can be a hot property!) and commissioned her to produce a new version so they could sell it all over again.

The professors may be right. The Wall version, after all, is first-rate, faithful to Flaubert's text, and admirably restrained: Wall never gave in to the temptation that has dogged so many translators, a wish to embellish and "improve" the original. His respect for the material is complete, and both his choice of vocabulary and his rendition of Flaubert's essentially inimitable rhythm is achieved with talent and stylistic discretion.

To translate Flaubert takes a confidence that amounts to audacity, for no author was ever so obsessed by style. "There are no noble subjects or ignoble subjects," the author reflected while writing *Madame Bovary*; "from the standpoint of pure Art one might almost establish the axiom that there is no such thing as subject—style in itself being an absolute manner of seeing things." How is such a style to be translated—and can it be? And what about Flaubert's identification of the best prose with poetry? "A good prose sentence," he wrote, "should be like a good line of poetry—*unchangeable*, just as rhythmic, just as sonorous. Such, at least, is my ambition." This immediately brings to mind the definition of poetry—a fine one, I think—as that which cannot be translated. Is *Madame Bovary* poetry? Can it ever, really, be adequately translated?

Let's look at one passage—an important one in that it introduces Charles and Emma Bovary's visual world. It's a world that a painter, or someone like Flaubert with a painterly eye, might find beautiful but that is, above all else, *gray*. We know that this overall grayness is vital because Flaubert has said so. "The story, the plot of a novel is of no interest to me," he claimed in a conversation with the Goncourt brothers. "When I write a novel I aim at rendering a color, a shade." In *Salammbô*, he said, that shade was a vivid purple, whereas in *Madame Bovary* "all I wanted to do was to render a gray color, the mouldy color of a wood-louse's existence. The story of the novel mattered so little to me that a few days before starting on it I still had in mind a very different Madame Bovary from the one I created."

Here is the passage, brief and spectacularly visual:

> La pluie ne tombait plus; le jour commençait à venir, et, sur les branches des pommiers sans feuilles, des oiseaux se tenaient immobiles, hérissant leurs petites plumes au vent froid du matin. La

> plate campagne s'étalait à perte de vue, et les bouquets d'arbres autour des fermes faisaient, à intervalles éloignés, des taches d'un violet noir sur cette grande surface grise, qui se perdait à l'horizon dans le ton morne du ciel.

And how have the translators rendered it? Here is the Aveling/de Man version:

> The rain had stopped, day was breaking, and on the branches of the leafless trees birds roosted motionless, their little feathers bristling in the cold morning wind. The flat country stretched as far as the eye could see, and the tufts of trees around the farms seemed, at long intervals, like dark violet stains on the vast grey surface, fading on the horizon into the gloom of the sky.

Here is the Francis Steegmuller version:

> The rain had stopped; day was breaking, and on the leafless branches of the apple trees birds were perched motionless, ruffling up their little feathers in the cold morning wind. The countryside stretched flat as far as the eye could see, and the tufts of trees clustered around the farmhouses were widely spaced dark purple stains on the vast gray surface that merged at the horizon into the dull tone of the sky.

Here is Geoffrey Wall's:

> The rain had stopped; it was getting light, and, on the leafless branches of the apple trees, birds were perching silently, ruffling up their little feathers against the chill wind of early morning. The flat landscape stretched out as far as the eye could see and the clumps of trees around the farmhouses showed up, at wide intervals, as patches of deep violet on that vast grey surface, which blurred at the horizon into the dullness of the sky.

And finally Davis's:

> The rain was no longer falling; day was beginning to dawn, and on the branches of the leafless apple trees, birds were perched

> motionless, ruffling their little feathers in the cold morning wind. The flat country spread out as far as the eye could see, and the clumps of trees around the farms formed patches of dark violet at distant intervals on that vast gray surface, which vanished, at the horizon, ino the bleak tones of the sky.

It's interesting to see that Davis's is actually the closest to the original. "The rain was no longer falling" renders the negativity of "La pluie ne tombait plus" better than does the positive verb "to stop," used by the other translators. "The leafless apple trees" is an exact translation of "les pommiers sans feuilles" whereas "the leafless branches of the apple trees" and "the branches of the leafless trees" are not. Flaubert's birds "se tenaient": Davis, with Steegmuller, has rendered this as "were perched," whereas Aveling and de Man used the more fanciful "roosted," in the active voice as well, and Wall also selected the active voice. "Bouquets d'arbres" does not have a really satisfactory English equivalent; Davis's use of "clumps," following Wall, seems more satisfactory than "tufts." Davis and Wall's "patches" is somehow less obtrusive than Aveling/de Man and Steegmuller's "stains." The French word "violet" presents the choice of two English translations, "purple" and "violet," which do not really mean the same thing; Davis has chosen "dark violet," and if readers of this article think all this sounds dull and nitpicking they should reflect on what different images are conjured up by "purple stains" and "patches of dark violet." All of our translators seem to agree on "vast gray surface," but their interpretations of the untranslatable French adjective *morne* differ wildly. Here Davis's "bleak" with Aveling/de Man's "gloom" gets closest to the text's essence, because the definition of *morne* includes sadness: Steegmuller and Wall's "dull" and "dullness" are therefore less than satisfying.

This kind of list-making might seem to reduce translation to a technique rather than an art, but in fact it is both, and it's fair to say that Flaubert would have minded enormously about each and every one of these questions: this is the man, after all, who labored for months to produce a thirty-page scene. Even a throwaway line can have tremendous importance in the greater scheme. In the introduction to his *Bovary*, Steegmuller points to the novel's penultimate sentence, in which the narrator, speaking of the pharmacist Homais (Flaubert's "life force" character), says, "Il fait une clientèle d'enfer." As Steegmuller justly observes, "a perfectly 'correct' translation of a phrase can be inadequate, in that it fails to render an essential symbolic meaning." *Il fait une clientèle d'enfer* has been variously, and not incorrectly, translated as "His practic grows like wildfire," "He is doing extremely well," and "He has a terrific practice"—but surely, as Steegmuller points out, *l'enfer* (hell) isn't in the original for nothing. How do our translators render it? Steegmuller, a little too obviously, makes it "The devil himself doesn't have a greater following than the pharmacist." Aveling/de Man: "He has more customers than there are sinners in hell." Wall, most cleverly (inserting the "hell" motif so that one hardly notices it at first) says "He is doing infernally well"—a rendition Davis echoes with "He himself has an infernally good clientele," rather stiffer and less idiomatic, though closer to Flaubert's sentence.

But then, as Paul de Man pointed out, "Flaubert himself is neither fluent nor really idiomatic (except in conversations)." This is important to remember, if the work of our translators, including Davis, sometimes appears to be less than elegantly fluid. Flaubert's method was to set a scene by the use of accretion. To quote his admirer Nabokov, Flaubert had a "fondness for what may be termed the unfolding method, the successive development of visual details, one thing after another thing, with an accumulation of this or that emotion." Let's take for an example an early visit Charles Bovary pays to the Rouault farm in Davis's translation:

> He arrived one day at about three o'clock; everyone was in the fields; he entered the kitchen but at first did not notice Emma; the shutters were closed. Through the slits in the wood, the sun cast over the flagstones long, narrow stripes that broke at the angles of the furniture and trembled on the ceiling. On the table, flies were walking up the used glasses and buzzing as they drowned at the bottom, in the dregs of cider. The daylight that came down the chimney, turning the soot on the fireback to velvet, touched with blue the cold cinders. Between the window and the hearth, Emma was sewing; she was not wearing a scarf, and one could see, on her bare shoulders, little drops of sweat.

This is vintage Flaubert: even without the clue provided by the name "Emma" one would recognize it instantly as his work, and that is to

Davis's credit. She has reinstated the serial semi-colons, a hallmark of Flaubert's style that Nabokov noticed. (While teaching *Madame Bovary* at Cornell, Nabakov saw fit to make frequent "corrections" to Aveling's translation. He would have preferred both Wall's and Davis's, I think. It is too bad he never attempted one himself.) The jarring juxtaposition of something ugly, earthy, or vulgar with something perceived to be beautiful is typical of Flaubert's technique: here, the idyllic vision of Emma sewing (like a scene from Chardin or Vermeer) is disturbed by the image of flies walking about in the cider dregs, and drops of sweat on Emma's shoulders—not "perspiration," with which Aveling and de Man softened Flaubert's original *sueur*. Nineteenth-century ladies of course did not sweat—at least they did not sweat until Flaubert made them do so—and one of the drawbacks of early translations of *Madame Bovary* was that they were too polite and circumspect for this most brutally honest of authors. Recent translators like Davis no longer labor under this handicap.

And what about dialogue—the most difficult part of any novel to translate? How can one approach the tone of the original? How idiomatic should one be? If the original is slangy, should the translation be slangy, too? And why does slanginess in a translation date so much more badly than it does in the original? Isn't that one of the factors that actually causes a translation to "date"? If one character's speech is pompous, for instance, how can the translator make his version stylistically pompous without deviating too much from the language and vocabulary of the original? Why does translated dialogue so often tend to be wooden?

Davis does well in this department, especially with the elevated, stylized language of pretentious characters like Homais, or the speechifiers at the agricultural fair. With the novel's central figures she is rather less successful—though perhaps this is because naturalistic dialogue is not really something Flaubert aspired to produce. Let's look at a speech of Rodolphe's (in Davis's translation):

> "Ah! In fact there are two moralities," he replied. "The narrow one, the conventional one, the one devised by men, that keeps changing and that bellows so loudly, makes such a commotion down here, in a perfectly pedestrian way, like that gathering of imbeciles you see out there. But the other one, the eternal one, is all around

> and above us, like the landscape that surrounds us and the blue sky that gives us light."

This is how Geoffrey Wall translated the same passage:

> —Oh, the thing is there are two moralities, he replied. The little conventional one that men have made up, one that's endless changing and that brays so fiercely, makes such a fuss down here in this world, like that mob of imbeciles you see there. But the other morality, the eternal one, is all about and above, like the fields around us and the blue sky that gives us light.

Both these versions sound unnatural. But then so does the original, for Rodolphe was, in modern parlance, a bullshit artist, wrapping banal ideas in highfalutin' language. Davis's "bellows" seems more felicitous than Wall's "brays," though the latter is closer to Flaubert's original *braille*. It's hard to imagine anyone actually making the speech as it appears in any of the three versions, but the French one seems somewhat more possible.

There is a description in the Goncourt Journals of a conversation the brothers witnessed in 1857 between Flaubert and the author Ernest Feydeau (father of the playwright):

> Flaubert and Feydeau started discussing a thousand different recipes for style and form, pompously and earnestly explaining little mechanical tricks of the trade, and expounding with childish gravity and ridiculous solemnity ways of writing and rules for producing good prose. They attached so much importance to the clothing of an idea, to its colour and material, that the idea became nothing but a peg on which to hang sound and light. We felt as if we were listening to an argument between grammarians of the Byzantine Empire.

This is precisely why the task of translating Flaubert has always been so daunting, and why it is dubious that there can ever be a definitive translation or even a wholly satisfactory one. Davis has produced a very fine one, marginally better, I think, than Wall's. Some Flaubert aficionados have been deterred by her admission that *Madame Bovary* is not actually a favorite book of hers: she has always been put off, she says, by the author's coldness and his obvious contempt for his characters and their milieu. But this alienation doesn't seem to have harmed her rendition, which displays a cool detachment not at all dissimilar to Flaubert's own.

October 2010

No flash in the pan

John Steele Gordon

If ever there was a time when I felt that "watcher-of-the-skies-when-a-new-planet" stuff, it was when I read the first Flashman.
—P. G. Wodehouse

By his own cheerful admission, Harry Flashman was "a scoundrel, a liar, a cheat, a thief, a coward—and, oh yes, a toady." He might have added that he was also a shameless womanizer, an artful seducer who was not above sexual assault. He had lost his virginity when he was only fourteen and, by his own count, he had bedded 480 women by the time he was in his mid-thirties, some of them among the most famous of their day. Although married—in a shotgun wedding, of course—he took his vows, and everyone else's, lightly at best. He prided himself on being "able to run faster with my trousers round my ankles than any man in England."

He was also, more than once, taken advantage of himself. A prisoner of the Chinese in 1860, shackled and gagged in a filthy dungeon, he was visited in his cell by "Yehonala Tzu-hsi, the Orchid, the incomparable Yi Concubine." She was the exquisitely beautiful favorite concubine of the emperor and the mother of the emperor's only son. She would soon rule China for forty-seven years as the Empress Dowager. As she settled down to work on Flashman, he wrote,"what could I do but close my eyes and think of England?"

Flashman is also one of the most entertaining, indeed fascinating, characters in all of English literature. This year is the fiftieth anniversary of the first installment of the Flashman Papers, entitled simply *Flashman*.

Through the course of twelve books Flashman finds himself, despite his best efforts, at the heart of nearly every major military disaster of the nineteenth century: the First Anglo-Afghan War, the Charge of the

Light Brigade, the Indian Mutiny, John Brown's raid on Harper's Ferry, Rorke's Drift, even Custer's Last Stand. And, thanks to luck and guile—Flashman always had plenty of both—he came up smelling like a rose every time. By the end of his life he was a brigadier general and a Knight of the Bath. He had been awarded numerous decorations for bravery, including the British Victoria Cross, the American Medal of Honor, and the French Légion d'honneur, all of them richly undeserved.

To be sure, Flashman was not without his good points. He was tall, strong, and handsome. He was an excellent horseman. His black hair and eyes allowed him to pass easily in native costume. His father was rich (at least while he was growing up), and his late mother was a Paget, the family of the Marquesses of Anglesey, and thus very well connected within the aristocracy.

And Flashman had a singular gift for learning languages. "I speak nine languages better than the natives," he wrote, "and can rub along in another dozen or so." He learned Hindi in two weeks. "My Latin and Greek had been weak at school, for I paid little attention to them," he explained, "but a tongue that you hear spoken about you is a different thing. Each language has a rhythm for me, and my ear catches and holds the sounds; I seem to know what a man is saying even when I don't understand the words, and my own tongue slips easily into any new accent."

It was only his character that was deplorable.

Flashman was the brilliant conception of the British author George MacDonald Fraser. Flashman had been a minor character in Thomas Hughes's Victorian classic *Tom Brown's School Days*—so minor he didn't even have a first name in that book. As the school bully at Rugby, Flashman had made Tom Brown's life hell until he had been expelled for drunkenness.

But Fraser took this thinly fleshed-out character and brought him to life by means of a masterly literary conceit. Had he simply written these books as third-person novels, it is unlikely they would have caught on, because Flashman was apparently devoid of the redeeming qualities that the heroes of picaresque tales always have. Consider Tom Jones, for instance, or, for that matter, Robin Hood.

Instead, Fraser wrote them in the first person, explaining that they were actually the memoirs of Harry Flashman. "The great mass of manuscript known as the Flashman Papers," he wrote, "was discovered during a sale of household furniture at Ashy, Leicestershire, in 1965.... The papers, which had apparently lain untouched for fifty years, in a tea chest ... were carefully wrapped in oilskin covers." All Fraser had to do, he explained, was edit them very lightly and supply footnotes and endnotes. As far as I know, the Flashman Papers are the only novels in the English language, perhaps besides Tolkien's, with extensive back matter, at least back matter written by the author and not an English professor determined, as they always are, to make a good book boring.

These endnotes, the product of meticulous and extensive historical research, are the source of the extraordinary verisimilitude of the Flashman Papers. Indeed they had such a feeling of verisimilitude that no fewer than ten of the twenty-eight American reviewers treated the first one as a genuine autobiography.

And the endnotes reveal another of Fraser's literary conceits. For while Harry Flashman is completely fictional, the world he lived in for so long (his dates are 1822–1915) was very real, as were many of the characters and events in the Flashman Papers. Fraser sticks to history as much as possible. Flashman wrote that he met Florence Nightingale, for instance, at Balmoral, Queen Victoria's Scottish estate, on the night of September 22, 1856, and, indeed, Nightingale was there that day, as recorded in Queen Victoria's letters.

Even when the action depicted is fictional, such as the attack on Fort Raim in central Asia in *Flashman at the Charge*, many of the major characters, such as Yakub Beg, the leader of the Tajiks in their fight against Russian imperialism, were very real. (Flashman showed considerable bravery in this episode, but only because he had been served kefir that had been surreptitiously laced with hashish.)

By casting the Flashman Papers as memoirs, Fraser is also able to show his despicable hero's few redeeming qualities.

First, Flashman is a world-class storyteller (Fraser slyly admits that Flashman "had a better sense of narrative than I have"). Certainly the Flashman Papers are as good at storytelling as novels get. They are beautiful examples of what my mother called "one-more-chapter-and-I'm-turning-out-the-light" books.

Second, he is an acute observer of his fellow humans, from Queen Victoria to Russian serfs. And he is refreshingly and delightfully candid about them. He describes Florence Nightingale, for instance, as "a waste of good womanhood; handsome face, well set up and titted out, but with that cold don't-lay-a-lecherous-limb-on-me-my-lad look in her eye . . ." He is equally candid about the human condition. The often brutal realities of the nineteenth century—from the conditions aboard a slave runner to the glitter (and often backstairs squalor) of the royal courts of Europe, Asia, and Africa—are depicted unsparingly and often amusingly.

Third is Flashman's long and, in his own way, loving relationship with his wife, Elspeth. Though he was flagrantly unfaithful to her (and he strongly suspected but never proved that she often returned the favor), she was always his favorite and her supposed infidelities caused him to be jealous. Though the marriage had been forced, they turned out to be a very compatible couple, always linked by a strong mutual sexual attraction. Flashman thought her utterly brainless, not that that bothered him in the least. Most important, he thought her one of the three most beautiful women he had ever met:

> Elspeth clothed could stop a monk in his tracks; naked and pouting expectantly over a handful of red feathers, she'd have made the Grand Inquisitor burn his books.

After his often long absences, Harry Flashman was always glad to get home to his Elspeth and this does much to humanize him.

Finally and most importantly, Flashman is absolutely honest and forthright about his manifold deficiencies as a human being. Memoirs are not exactly famous for their warts-and-all qualities, but the Flashman Papers are most definitely warts and all and then some. Flashman knew exactly what a rotter he had been all his life and had no trouble with it.

When he and a native, Muhammed Iqbal, who had taught him Pashto, the most common language in Afghanistan, were attacked by four horsemen, Iqbal turned to confront them. Flashman headed for cover and hid behind a tree. Iqbal got three of the attackers but was mortally wounded, while Flashman got one, but only when he saw it was safe to do so. He bent over the dying Iqbal, who

> groaned and fell back, but as I knelt over him his eyes opened for a moment, and he gave a little moan and spat in my face, as best he could. So he died, calling me "son of a swine" in Hindi, which is the Muslim's crowning insult. I saw his point of view, of course.

With the reader, like Diogenes, having found an honest man, it is impossible not to like him, although you probably wouldn't want to introduce him to your daughter.

George MacDonald Fraser was born in 1925 in Carlisle, in the north of England, but was of Scottish descent, a fact of which he was proud. He served in the Border Regiment in India and later as an officer in the Gordon Highlanders in Africa and the Middle East. After leaving the army, he became a journalist, working for several papers in Britain and Canada and then, for some years, with the *Glasgow Herald*, where he served as deputy editor and, briefly, as editor. In 1969, he published his first book, *Flashman*, which was an immediate critical and commercial success.

The success of the book allowed Fraser to become a full-time writer, and he had a prolific career until his death at eighty-two in 2008, writing not only the twelve Flashman books but three volumes of short stories, two volumes of memoirs, six other novels (in one of which, *Mr. American*, an elderly Flashman appears as a minor character), and eight screenplays (including the James Bond movie *Octopussy*, and the 1973 version of *The Three Musketeers*).

Fraser had a remarkable ability to delineate a character, even a minor one, in only a few words. Consider, for instance, the scene where Flashman, still half-drunk, is hauled before Thomas Arnold, the legendary headmaster of Rugby School, to be expelled. (For those who did not go to a boarding school, which in England are called public schools, be advised that a prep school headmaster is the nearest thing there is to a god who walks the earth. All-powerful in his academic domain, he is held in awe by students and faculty alike. To be summoned to the headmaster's office, even if your conscience is clear, produces an immediate reaction in the pit of your stomach. And Flashman's conscience—if he actually had one—was, as usual, anything but clear.)

> He was standing before the fireplace, with his hands behind looping up his coat-tails, and a face like a Turk at a christening. He had eyes like sabre-points, and his face was pale and carried that disgusted look that he kept for these occasions. Even with the liquor still working on me a little I was scared in that minute as I've never

> been in my life—and when you have ridden into a Russian battery at Balaclava and been chained in an Afghan dungeon waiting for the torturers, as I have, you know what fear means. I still feel uneasy when I think of him, and he's been dead for sixty years.

Fraser is equally adept at scene-setting. The second half of *Flashman at the Charge* is not set in Crimea at all, where Flashman had been an unwilling participant in the Charge of the Light Brigade (just recovering from a bad case of dysentery, his flatulence had spooked his horse). Indeed, after Flashman is captured, he is sent to an estate deep in the Russian steppes to be held, comfortably, as a prisoner until exchanged or the war ends. He is appalled at the serfs he sees along the way:

> So as we lumbered along, the courier in state in the first *telegue* [a type of wagon used by Russian officials], and Flashy with his escort in the second, there were always peasants standing by the roadside, men and women, in their belted smocks and ragged puttees, silent, unmoving, staring as we rolled by. This dull brooding watchfulness got on my nerves, especially at the post stations, where they used to assemble in silent groups to stare at us—they were so different from the Crim[ean] Tartars I had seen, who are lively, tall, well-made men, even if their women are seedy. The steppe Russians were much smaller, and ape-like by comparison.

Part of the reason for this was that the Russian serfs had no rights whatever; they were effectively slaves at the mercy of their often brutal landlords. But it was also, thought Flashman, because of the land itself:

> The land we traveled through was a fit place for such people—indeed, you have to see it to understand why they are what they are. I've seen big countries before—the American plains on the old wagon-trails west of St. Louis, with the whispering grasses waving away and away to the very edge of the world, or the Saskatchewan prairies in grasshopper time, dun and empty under the biggest sky on earth. But Russia is bigger: there is no sky, only empty space overhead, and no horizon, only a distant haze, and endless miles of sun-scorched rank grass and emptiness. The few miserable hamlets, each with its rickety church, only seemed to emphasize the loneliness of that huge plain, imprisoning by its

very emptiness—there are no hills for a man to climb into or to catch his imagination, nowhere to go: no wonder it binds its people to it.

Not all of Flashman's adventures take place in the back of beyond like central Asia, Ethiopia, and the Little Bighorn River. One took place in 1890 in the abiding comforts of an English country house, Tranby Croft. There one of the greatest scandals of the nineteenth century erupted over a game of baccarat. It's a perfect example of how Fraser skillfully inserts the fictional Flashman into real history.

Because it involved the Prince of Wales, later King Edward VII, the scandal, which played out over several months, was reported all over the English-speaking world, to the intense embarrassment of the prince, and to the equally intense disapproval of his mother, Queen Victoria. Already saddled with a well-deserved reputation for gambling, high life, and womanizing, the prince was savaged in the newspapers for being involved in the affair at all, and his reputation, never good during his long years as Prince of Wales, sank to its lowest point.

Among the Victorian aristocracy, nothing ruined a man's reputation more utterly than being credibly accused of cheating at cards. And that was exactly what Sir William Gordon-Cumming was accused of at Tranby Croft. Needless to say, he vehemently denied it and, indeed, it is hard to see why he would cheat. The stakes were modest, at least by the standards of wealthy Victorians, and Gordon-Cumming was very rich. Why would he take such a fearful social risk for so trivial a gain?

After the accusation was made, the Prince of Wales summoned Flashman, who was a member of the house party along with his wife. The other characters in this story, "The Subtleties of Baccarat," are all historical figures. The prince's one concern, of course, was to make the scandal go away for the sake of his own reputation. "See here, Flashman," he wailed, "you must get me out o' this. God knows what Mother would say."

Flashman doubted the truth of the accusations, and tried his best, but it was decided that Gordon Cumming was guilty, and the prince asked, "how is it to be hushed up?"

> They stood mum, so I put my oar in again. "'Fraid it can't be, sir … unless you and Williams [an army officer and one of the

guests at Tranby Croft; the prince was a field marshal] are prepared to risk a court martial."

If I'd said "are prepared to steal the Crown Jewels and make a run for Paraguay," I couldn't have provoked a finer display of consternation …

Before the prince could erupt, it was decided to make Gordon-Cumming sign a paper swearing never to play cards again while everyone else swore to keep the matter a secret, and Gordon-Cumming, seeing no alternative, signed. Naturally the story leaked (as Benjamin Franklin wrote in *Poor Richard's Almanac*, "Three may keep a secret, if two of them are dead"), and Gordon-Cumming sued. The trial was a sensation, especially as the prince had no way to avoid testifying, but Gordon-Cumming lost the suit and was ruined, dismissed from the army, cut dead by his friends, and forced to resign from his clubs.

The story has lived on—the latest book on the Tranby Croft affair came out in 2017. And it has lived on just as the Lizzie Borden and Jack the Ripper cases of the same era have lived on and for precisely the same reason: the truth will almost certainly never be known for sure. Except, of course, Flashman learned the truth and obligingly tells his readers what really happened.

Some of the finer literary touches in the Flashman Papers are the offhand remarks by Flashman and other characters that catch the reader by surprise and make him roar with laughter.

Major-General William Elphinstone, for instance, was the hopelessly incompetent commander of the British army in the First Anglo-Afghan War (the British army was utterly destroyed—except, of course, for Flashman). He was loathed by his staff for his endless dithering. Before one staff meeting, Elphinstone's servant dropped a pistol he had been loading, and it discharged, hitting the chair Elphinstone was sitting in and grazing his buttocks.

His second in command, hearing about the incident, said,

> "The Afghans murder our people, try to make off with our wives, order us out of the country, and what does our commander do? Shoots himself in the arse—doubtless in an attempt to blow his brains out. He can't have missed by much."

When Flashman is being held a prisoner of war after his capture in Crimea, he is comfortably billeted with Count Pencherjevsky, and one day the local priest and an agitator named Blank (Fraser points out in the endnotes that Blank was the name of one of Vladimir Lenin's ancestors, but thinks it a coincidence) come to see the count, hoping he will pay a tax that is due but which a widower with two sons can't afford. After a fierce argument, the count sends them packing and orders one of his Cossacks to go after them and teach Blank a lesson. When the Cossack returns, however, the count learns to his horror that Blank had escaped but the Cossack had flogged the priest to death:

> "My God! . . . What will this mean?" says East [a fellow prisoner and former classmate at Rugby].
>
> "Search me," I said. "They butcher each other so easily in this place—I don't know. I'd think that flogging a priest to death is a trifle over the score, though—even for Russia. Old man Pencherjevsky'll have some explaining to do, I'd say—shouldn't wonder if they kick him out of the Moscow Carlton Club."

Each of the twelve Flashman books stands alone and can be read independently in any order. They were certainly not written in chronological order. But if you are new to Flashman, I'd advise reading them in chronological sequence, though not one right after another. Like a rich and delicious dessert, the Flashman Papers should be consumed one portion at a time.

Note that *Flashman and the Redskins* is in two parts, widely separated in time. *Flashman and the Tiger* is in three, each a self-contained short story. *Royal Flash* has two episodes separated in time, but they are one story.

And one final note of caution: these wonderful books are best read either alone or in the bosom of the family. For if you read them in a public place such as a suburban commuter train or a doctor's waiting room, you will, from time to time, burst out in helpless laughter and everyone will turn around and look at you.

You have been warned.

February 2020

Gertrude Himmelfarb & the Enlightenment

Keith Windschuttle

> The beasts of modernism have mutated into the beasts of postmodernism—relativism into nihilism, amorality into immorality, irrationality into insanity, sexual deviancy into polymorphous perversity. And since then, generations of intelligent students under the guidance of their enlightened professors have looked into the abyss, have contemplated those beasts, and have said, "How interesting, how exciting."
>
> —Gertrude Himmelfarb, *On Looking into the Abyss* (1994)

When Gertrude Himmelfarb wrote about the abyss that was consuming the intellectual and moral traditions of her own time, she was one of the first to recognize how seductive was its appeal and how depraved its outcome. In her book *On Looking into the Abyss*, she attributed the original insight to the critic Lionel Trilling, who detected it in the early 1960s in the underbelly of the modernist movement that had dominated literature and the arts since the early twentieth century. Himmelfarb, however, came to her own recognition from another direction entirely, partly from her study of the history of ideas in Britain's Victorian era, but also from the apparently unlikely field of the history of social policy and of the ideas that led the Victorians to define poverty as a social problem. As she produced insightful books and essays, almost until her death on December 30 last year, aged ninety-seven, those who knew her work came to regard her as not only one of the great American historians of her time, but also one of this nation's most compelling moral critics.

Modernists, from their earliest public manifestations in London's

Bloomsbury, had regarded the Christian morality of the English-speaking world as the greatest obstacle to the "free thought" and "free love" they craved. They cleverly redefined the prevailing moral environment as "Victorian," which, after the death of the Queen in 1901, they declared out of date and out of place in the new, modern twentieth century. By the time Himmelfarb began postgraduate studies in the 1940s, this was the assumption of almost all who saw themselves as progressives, not only in universities but also in newspapers, literature, the arts, and the entertainment industries. It largely remained so until she contested the ground on which it stood with a series of essays and books from the 1970s to the 1990s that urged reconsideration of the modernist vision and its postmodern descendants.

In 1983, Himmelfarb published *The Idea of Poverty: England in the Early Industrial Age*, and in 1991 the sequel *Poverty and Compassion: The Moral Imagination of the Late Victorians*, arguing that, instead of imposing unregulated Dickensian institutions and dark satanic mills on the lower orders, the Victorians had redefined poverty as a moral issue that demanded both compassion from society at large and a sense of responsibility from the poor themselves. In describing the latter, she made an important intervention in the language of morality. She did not use the term "Victorian values," as almost every historian of the subject did at the time. The Victorians themselves, she pointed out, did not use the word "values." This anachronism only arose in the mid-twentieth century as a way to relativize morality. It implied that anyone's values were the moral equivalent of anyone else's. Some values could not be better than others, only different. Instead, she insisted on using the term "virtues." In a much-quoted passage Himmelfarb wrote:

> Hard work, sobriety, frugality, foresight—these were modest, mundane virtues, even lowly ones. But they were virtues within the capacity of everyone; they did not assume any special breeding, or status, or talent, or valor, or grace—or even money. They were common virtues within the reach of common people.

To the Victorians, she argued, virtues were fixed and certain, not to govern the actual behavior of all people all the time, but to serve as standards against which behavior could be judged. When conduct fell short of those standards, it was deemed to be bad, wrong, or immoral, she said, not merely misguided, undesirable, or, that weasel-word, "inappropriate." From the historical record, she could point to the consequences of today's misuse of moral principles:

> In recent times, we have so completely rejected any kind of moral principle that we have divorced poor relief from moral sanctions and incentives. This reflects in part the theory that society is responsible for all social problems and should therefore assume the task of solving them; and in part the prevailing spirit of relativism, which makes it difficult to pass any moral judgments or impose any moral conditions upon the recipients of relief. In retrospect, we can see that the social pathology—"moral pathology," I would call it—of crime, violence, illegitimacy, welfare dependency, and drug addiction is intimately related to the "counterculture" of the 1960s that promised to liberate us from the stultifying influence of "bourgeois values."

As well as detecting profound consequences from small manipulations of language, Himmelfarb's historical eye also allowed her to understand the broad intellectual contours of the periods she studied better than almost any of her peers. She went on to use that understanding to illuminate the basis of ideological divisions with her own time. This was best demonstrated in her daring but highly successful history of the Enlightenment in Britain, France, and the United States.

In 2005, she published *The Roads to Modernity: The British, French, and American Enlightenments.* It is a provocative revision of the typical story of the intellectual era of the late eighteenth century that made the modern world. In particular, it explains the source of the fundamental division that still doggedly grips Western political life: that between Left and Right, or progressives and conservatives. From the outset, each side had its own philosophical assumptions and its own view of the human condition. *Roads to Modernity* shows why one of these sides has generated a steady progeny of historical successes while its rival has consistently lurched from one disaster to the next.

By the time she wrote, a number of historians had accepted that the Enlightenment, once characterized as the "Age of Reason," came in two versions, the radical and the skeptical. The former was identified with France, the latter with Scotland. Historians of the period also acknowledged that the anti-clericalism that obsessed the French *philosophes* was not reciprocated in Britain or America. Indeed, in both the latter countries many Enlightenment concepts—human rights, liberty, equality, tolerance, science, progress—complemented rather than opposed church thinking.

Himmelfarb joined this revisionist process and accelerated its pace dramatically. She argued that, central though many Scots were to the movement, there were also so many original English contributors that a more accurate name than the "Scottish Enlightenment" would be the "British Enlightenment."

Moreover, unlike the French who elevated reason to a primary role in human affairs, British thinkers gave reason a secondary, instrumental role. In Britain it was virtue that trumped all other qualities. This was not personal virtue but the "social virtues"—compassion, benevolence, sympathy—which British philosophers believed naturally, instinctively, and habitually bound people to one another. This amounted to a moral reformation.

In making her case, Himmelfarb included people in the British Enlightenment who until then had been assumed to be part of the Counter-Enlightenment, especially John Wesley and Edmund Burke. She assigned prominent roles to the social movements of Methodism and Evangelical philanthropy. Despite the fact that the American colonists rebelled from Britain to found a republic, Himmelfarb demonstrated how very close they were to the British Enlightenment and how distant from French republicans.

In France, the ideology of reason challenged not only religion and the church, but also all the institutions dependent upon them. Reason was inherently subversive. But British moral philosophy was reformist rather than radical, respectful of both the past and present, even while looking forward to a more enlightened future. It was optimistic and had no quarrel with religion, which was why in both Britain and the United States, the church itself could become a principal source for the spread of enlightened ideas.

In Britain, the elevation of the social virtues derived from both academic philosophy and religious practice. In the eighteenth century, Adam Smith, the professor of moral philosophy at Glasgow University, was more celebrated for his *Theory of Moral Sentiments* (1759) than for his later thesis about the wealth of nations. He argued that sympathy and benevolence were moral virtues that sprang directly from the human condition. In being virtuous, especially towards those who could not help themselves, man rewarded himself by fulfilling his human nature.

Edmund Burke began public life as a disciple of Smith. He wrote an early pamphlet on scarcity which endorsed Smith's *laissez-faire* approach as the best way to serve not only economic activity in general but the lower orders in particular. His Counter-Enlightenment status is usually assigned for his critique of the French Revolution, but Burke was at the same time a supporter of American independence. While his own government was pursuing its military campaign in America, Burke was urging it to respect the liberty of both Americans and Englishmen.

Some historians have been led by this apparent paradox to claim that at different stages of his life there were two different Edmund Burkes, one liberal and the other conservative. Himmelfarb disagreed. She argued that his views were always consistent with the ideas about moral virtue that permeated the whole of the British Enlightenment. Indeed, Burke took this philosophy a step further by making the "sentiments, manners, and moral opinion" of the people the basis not only of social relations but also of politics.

Apart from the different philosophical status they assigned to reason and virtue, the one issue where the contrast between the British and French Enlightenments was sharpest was in their attitudes to the lower orders. This is a distinction that has reverberated through politics ever since. The radical heirs of the Jacobin tradition have always insisted that it is *they* who speak for the wretched of the earth. In eighteenth-century France, they claimed to speak for the people and the general will. In the nineteenth century, they said they represented the working classes against their capitalist exploiters. In our own time, they have claimed to be on the side of blacks, women, gays, indigenes, refugees, and anyone else they define as the victims of discrimination and oppression. Himmelfarb's study demonstrates what a façade these claims actually are.

The French philosophes thought the social classes were divided by the chasm not only of poverty but, more crucially, of superstition and ignorance. They despised the lower orders because they were in thrall to Christianity. The editor of the *Encyclopédie*, Denis Diderot, declared that the common people had no role in the Age of Reason: "The general mass of men are not so made that they can either promote or understand this forward march of the human spirit." Indeed, "the common people are incredibly stupid," he said, and were little more than animals: "too idiotic—bestial—too miserable, and too busy" to enlighten themselves. Voltaire agreed. The lower orders lacked the intellect required to reason and so must be left to wallow in superstition. They could be controlled and pacified only by the sanctions and strictures of religion which, Voltaire proclaimed, "must be destroyed among respectable people and left to the *canaille* large and small, for whom it was made."

In Britain and America, by contrast, the chasm between rich and poor was bridged by the moral sense and common sense the Enlightenment attributed to all individuals. Everyone, including the members of the lower orders, had a common humanity and a common fund of moral and social obligations. It was this social ethos, Himmelfarb argued, that in the English-speaking world was the common denominator between Adam Smith, Edmund Burke, secular philosophers, religious enthusiasts, Church of England bishops, and Wesleyan preachers.

"Man is by constitution a religious animal," Edmund Burke famously wrote in his *Reflections on the Revolution in France*. For Burke, religion itself, and religious dissent in particular, was the very basis of liberty. The Methodists went one step further and also made it the basis of social reform.

John Wesley's great mission was to foster not only the spiritual salvation of the poor, but also their intellectual and moral edification. There was no conflict between reason and religion. "It is a fundamental principle with us," Wesley argued, "that to renounce reason is to renounce religion, that religion and reason go hand in hand, and that all irrational religion is false religion." It was only by "religion and reason joined" that "passion and prejudice" and "wickedness and bigotry" could be overcome.

In pursuit of their mission, the Methodists produced a huge volume of literature not just on Christianity, but also on grammar, medicine, electricity, natural history, Shakespeare, Milton, Spenser, Locke, and other classics. Himmelfarb observed: "The whole of this quite extraordinary publication industry, comprising books, pamphlets, and tracts on a variety of subjects and directed to different levels of literacy and interest, constituted something like an Enlightenment for the common man."

In the American colonies, the First Great Awakening—the religious revival of the 1730s and early 1740s—paralleled the Methodist revival in

Britain. The contrast with France was dramatic. In seeking respite from the religious passions of the Old World, Himmelfarb wrote, the Americans did not, like the French, turn against religion itself. Instead, they incorporated religion into the mores of society. They "moralized" and "socialized" religion, turning its energies into movements for voluntary association, local organization, and, ultimately, the politics of liberty.

In Britain and America, the Enlightenment was both a theoretical and a practical expression of this outlook. Religion, moral philosophy, and their egalitarian assumptions shaped the era. They worked together for the common cause: the material as well as the "moral reformation" of the people. In *Roads to Modernity*, Himmelfarb revealed more clearly than in any other book on the subject the environment in which these ideas and practices were born. At the same time, however, her vision into the abyss continues to warn us all what we have to lose if we persist in feeding the theoretical beasts that lurk there and are now clawing their way onto our once-solid ground.

February 2020

A schoolboy's guide to war

Andrew Stuttaford

ON AUGUST 3, 1914, twenty-two of England's best public school cricketers gathered for the annual schools' representative match. The game ended the following evening. Britain's ultimatum to Germany expired a few hours later. Seven of those twenty-two would be dead before the war was over. Anthony Seldon and David Walsh's fine new history of the public schools and the First World War (*Public Schools and the Great War*) bears the subtitle "The Generation Lost" for good reason.

Britain neither wanted nor was prepared for a continental war. Its armed forces were mainly naval or colonial. The regular army that underwrote that ultimatum was, in the words of Niall Ferguson, "a dwarf force" with "just seven divisions (including one of cavalry), compared with Germany's ninety-eight and a half."

Britain's more liberal political traditions, so distinct then—and now—from those of its European neighbors, had rendered peacetime conscription out of the question, but manpower shortages during the Boer War and growing anxiety over the vulnerability of the mother country itself led to a series of military reforms designed to toughen up domestic defenses. These included the consolidation of ancient yeomanry and militias into a Territorial Force and Special Reserve. The old public-school "rifle corps," meanwhile, were absorbed into an Officers' Training Corps and put under direct War Office control.

Most public schools signed up for this, and by 1914 most had made "the corps" compulsory. Some took it seriously. Quite a few did not. Stuart Mais, the author of *A Public School in Wartime* (1916), wrote that Sherborne's pre-war OTC was seen as "a piffling waste of time … playing at soldiers" that got in the way of cricket. Two decades later, Adolf

Hitler cited the OTC to a surprised Anthony Eden (then Britain's foreign secretary) as evidence of the militarization of Britain's youth. It "hardly deserved such renown," drily recalled Eden (in his unexpectedly evocative *Another World 1897–1917*), "even though the light grey uniforms with their pale blue facings did give our school contingent a superficially Germanic look."

And yet this not-very-military nation saw an astonishing response to the call for volunteers to join the fight. By the end of September 1914 over 750,000 men had enlisted. But where were the officers to come from? A number of retired officers returned to the colors, and the Territorials boasted some men with useful experience, but these were not going to be close to sufficient numbers. The army turned to public-school alumni to fill the gap. In theory, this was because these men had enjoyed the benefit of some degree of military training, however inadequate, with the OTC, but in truth it was based on the belief of those in charge, themselves almost always former public schoolboys, that these chaps would know what to do. Looked at one way, this was nothing more than crude class prejudice; looked at another, it made a great deal of sense. In the later years of the war, many officers ("temporary gentlemen" in the condescending expression of the day) of humbler origins rose through the ranks, but in its earlier stages the conflict was too young to have taught the army how best to judge who would lead well. In the meantime, Old Harrovians, Old Etonians, and all those other Olds would have to do.

To agree that this was not unreasonable implies a level of acceptance of the public school system at its zenith utterly at odds with some of the deepest prejudices festering in Britain today. British politics remain obsessed with class in a manner that owes more to ancient resentments than any contemporary reality. A recent incident, in which a columnist for the far left *Socialist Worker* made fun of the fatal mauling of an Eton schoolboy by a polar bear ("another reason to save the polar bears"), is an outlier in its cruelty, but it's a rare week that goes by in which a public school education is not used to whip a Tory cur, as David Cameron (Eton) knows only too well.

Under the circumstances it takes courage to combine, as Seldon and Walsh do, a not-unfriendly portrait of the early twentieth-century public schools (it should be noted that both men are, or have been, public schoolmasters) with a broader analysis that implies little sympathy for the sentimental clichés that dominate current British feeling—and it is *felt*, deeply so—about the Great War: Wilfred Owen and all that. It is not necessary to be an admirer of the decision to enter the war or indeed of how it was fought (I am neither) to regret how Britain's understanding of those four terrible years has been so severely distorted over the past decades. Brilliantly deceptive leftist agitprop intended to influence modern political debate has come to be confused with history.

Oh! What a Lovely War smeared the British establishment of the 1960s with the filth of Passchendaele and the Somme. Similarly, the caricature of the war contained in television productions such as *Blackadder Goes Forth* (1989) and *The Monocled Mutineer* (1986) can at least partly be read as an angry response to Mrs. Thatcher's long ascendancy. Coincidentally or not, the late 1980s also saw the appearance of *The Old Lie: The Great War and the Public-School Ethos* by Peter Parker. For a caustic, literary, and intriguing—if slanted—dissection of these schools' darker sides, Parker's book is the place to go.

Seldon and Walsh offer a more detailed and distinctly more nuanced description of how these schools operated, handily knocking down a few clichés on the way: There were flannelled fools aplenty, but there was also the badly wounded Harold Macmillan (Eton), "intermittently" reading Aeschylus (in Greek) as he lay for days awaiting rescue in a shell hole. Aeschylus was not for all, but a glance at the letters officers wrote from the front is usually enough to shatter the myth of the ubiquitous philistine oaf. There was much more to the public schools than, to quote Harrow's most famous song, "the tramp of the twenty-two men."

But however harsh a critic he may be ("that men died for an ethos does not mean that the ethos was worth dying for"), Parker is too honest a writer not to acknowledge the good, sometimes heroic, qualities of these hopelessly ill-trained young officers and the bond they regularly forged across an often immense class divide with the troops that they led. "I got to know the men," wrote my maternal grandfather Richard Ropner (Harrow, Machine Gun Corps) in an unpublished memoir half a century later, "I hope they got to know me." In many such cases they did. It is tempting to speculate that such bonds (easier to claim, perhaps, *de haut* than *en bas*) may have been more real in the eyes of the commanders than of the commanded, but there is strong evidence to suggest that there was nothing imaginary about them. Men died for their officers. Officers died for their men.

My grandfather owned a set of memorial volumes published by Harrow in 1919. Each of the school's war dead is commemorated with a photograph and an obituary. It is striking to see how frequently the affection with which these officers—and they almost all were officers—were held by their men is cited. Writing about Lieutenant Robert Boyd (killed at the Somme, July 14, 1916, aged twenty-three), his company commander wrote that Boyd's "men both loved him and knew he was a good officer—two entirely different things." This subtle point reflects the way that the public school ethos both fitted in with and smoothed the tough paternalism of the regular army into something more suited to a citizen army that now included recruits socially, temperamentally, and intellectually very different from that rough caste apart, Kipling's "single men in barricks."

The public schools relied heavily on older boys to maintain a regime that had come a long way from Tom Brown's bleak start. This taught them both command and, in theory (Flashman had his successors), the obligations that came with it. That officers were expected both to lead and care for their men was a role for which they had thus already been prepared by an education designed, however haphazardly, to mold future generations of the ruling class. Contrary to what Parker might argue, these schools had not set out to groom their pupils for war. But the qualities these institutions taught—pluck, dutifulness, patriotism, athleticism (both as a good in itself and as a shaper of character), conformism, stoicism, group loyalty, and a curious mix of self-assurance and self-effacement—were to prove invaluable in the trenches as was familiarity with a disciplined, austere, all-male lifestyle.

There was something else: The fact that many of these men had boarded away from home, often from the age of eight, and sometimes even earlier, meant that they had learned how to put on a performance for the benefit of those who watched them. A display of weakness risked transforming boarding school life into one's own version of *Lord of the Flies*. That particular training stayed with them on the Western Front: "I do not hold life cheap at all," wrote Edward Brittain (Uppingham), "and it is hard to be sufficiently brave, yet I have hardly ever felt really afraid. One has to keep up appearances at all costs even if one is." It was all, as Macmillan put it, part of "the show."

There are countless examples of how stiff that upper lip could be, but when Seldon and Walsh cite the example of Captain Francis Townend

(Dulwich), even those accustomed to such stories have to pause to ask, who *were* these men?: "Both legs blown off by a shell and balancing himself on his stumps, [Townend] told his rescuer to tend to the men first and said that he would be all right, though he might have to give up rugby next year. He then died."

Pastoral care was all very well, but the soldiers also knew that, unlike the much-resented staff officers, *their* officers took the same, or greater, risks that they did. This was primarily due to the army's traditional suspicion that the lower orders—not to speak of the raw, half-trained recruits who appeared in the trenches after 1914—could not be trusted with anything resembling responsibility, but it also reflected the officers' own view of what their job should be. And so, subalterns (a British army term for officers below the rank of captain), captains, majors, and even colonels led from the front, often fulfilling, particularly in the case of subalterns, a role that in other armies would be delegated to NCOs. The consequences were lethal. Making matters worse, the inequality between the classes was such that officers were on average five inches taller than their men, and, until the rules were changed in 1916, they always wore different uniforms too. The Germans knew who to shoot. The longer-term implications of this cull of the nation's elite may have been exaggerated by Britons anxious to explain away their country's subsequent decline, but the numbers have not: some 35,000 former public schoolboys died in the war, a large slice of a small stratum of society.

Roughly 11 percent of those who fought in the British army were killed, but, as Seldon and Walsh show, the death rate among former public schoolboys (most of whom were officers) ran at some 18 percent. For those who left school in the years leading up to 1914 (and were thus the most likely to have served as junior officers) the toll was higher still. Nearly 40 percent of the Harrow intake of the summer of 1910 (my grandfather arrived at the school the following year) were not to survive the war. *Six Weeks: The Short and Gallant Life of the British Officer in the First World War* (2010) by John Lewis-Stempel is an elegiac, moving, and vivid account of what awaited them. Lewis-Stempel explains his title thus: "The average time a British Army junior officer survived during the Western Front's bloodiest phases was six weeks."

To Lewis-Stempel, a fierce critic of those who see the war as a pointless tragedy, the bravery and determination of these young officers made them "the single most important factor in Britain's victory on the Western Front," a stretch, but not an altogether unreasonable one, and he is not alone in thinking this way. The British army weathered the conflict far better—and far more cohesively—than did those of the other original combatants, and effective officering played no small part in that.

Lewis-Stempel attributes much of that achievement to the "martial and patriotic spirit" of the public schools, a view of those establishments with which Parker would, ironically, agree, but that is to muddle consequence with cause. Patriotic, yes, the schools were that, as was the nation—being top dog will have that effect. But, like the rest of the country, they were considerably less "martial" than Britain's mastery of so much of the globe would suggest. A public school education may have provided a good preparation for the trenches, but it did not pave the way to them. That so many alumni came to the defense of their country in what was seen as its hour of need ought not to form any part of any serious indictment against the schools from which they came. That they sometimes did so with insouciance and enthusiasm that seems remarkable today was a sign not of misplaced jingoism, but of a lack of awareness that, a savage century later, it's difficult not to envy.

And when that awareness came, they still stuck it out, determined to see the job done. Seldon and Walsh write that "It was the ability . . . to endure which underpinned the former public schoolboys' leadership of the army and the nation." Perhaps it would have been better if they had had been less willing to endure and more willing to question, but that's a different debate. To be sure, there was plenty of talk of the nobility of sacrifice—and of combat—but, for the most part, that was evidence not of a death wish or any sort of bloodlust, but of the all too human need to put what they were doing, and what they had lost, into finer words and grander context.

And that they clung so closely to memories of the old school—to an extent that seems extraordinary today—should come as no surprise. These were often very young men, some, even, still in their teens. School, especially for those who had boarded, had been a major part of their lives, psychologically as well as chronologically. "School," wrote Robert Graves (Charterhouse), "became the reality, and home life the illusion." And now its memory became something to cherish amid the mad landscape of war.

They wrote to their schoolmasters and their schoolmasters wrote to them. They returned to school on leave and they devoured their school magazines. They fought alongside those who had been to the same schools and they gave their billets familiar school names. They met up for sometimes astoundingly lavish old boys' dinners behind the lines, including one attended by seventy Wykehamists to discuss the proposed Winchester war memorial. The names of three of the subalterns present would, Seldon and Walsh note, eventually be recorded on it.

So far as is possible given what they are describing, these two authors tell this story dispassionately. Theirs is a calm, thoroughly researched work, lacking the emotional excesses that are such a recurring feature of the continuing British argument over the Great War. That said, this book's largely uninterrupted sequence of understandably admiring tales could have done with just a bit more counterbalance. For that try reading the recently published diaries written in a Casualty Clearing Station by the Earl of Crawford (*Private Lord Crawford's Great War Diaries: From Medical Orderly to Cabinet Minister*) with its grumbling about "ignorant and childish" young officers arousing "panic among the men [with] their wild and dangerous notions."

Doubtless the decision by Captain Billy Neville (Dover College) to arrange for his platoons to go over the top on the first day of the Somme kicking soccer balls is something that Crawford would have included amongst the "puerile and fantastic nonsense" he associated with such officers. Seldon and Walsh, by contrast, see this—and plausibly so—not as an example of Henry Newbolt's instruction to "Play up! play up! and play the game!" being followed to a lunatic degree, but rather as an astute attempt by Neville to give his soldiers some psychological support. "His aim was to make his men, who he knew would be afraid, more comfortable." Better to think of those soccer balls than the enemy machine guns waiting just ahead. Nineteen thousand British troops were killed that day, including Neville. He was twenty-one.

Crawford was a hard-headed, acerbic, and clever Conservative, but occasionally his inner curmudgeon overwhelmed subtler understanding, as, maybe, did his location behind the lines, fifteen miles from where these officers shone. Nevertheless, one running theme of his diaries, the luxuries that some of them allowed themselves ("yesterday a smart young officer in a lofty dogcart drove a spanking pair of polo ponies tandem past our gate") touches on a broader topic—the stark difference in the ways that officers and men were treated—that deserves more attention than it gets in *Public Schools and the Great War*. Even the most junior officers were allocated a "batman" (a servant). They were given more leave, were paid a great deal more generously, and, when possible, were fed far better and housed much more comfortably than their men. Even in a more deferential age, this must have rankled. Perhaps unsurprisingly, Parker dwells on this issue in more detail than Seldon and Walsh, but, fair-minded again, agrees that what truly counted with the troops was the fact that "when it came to battle [the young officers'] circumstances were very much the same as their own."

They died together. And they are buried together, too, not far from where they fell. As the founder of the Imperial War Graves Commission explained, "in ninety-nine cases out of a hundred, the officers will tell you that, if they are killed, they would wish to be among their men."

A century later, that's where they still are.

October 2014

Mining the ash heap

Alexandra Mullen

Be no longer a chaos, but a world, or even worldkin. Produce! Produce! Were it but the pitifullest infinitesimal fraction of a product, produce it in God's name! 'Tis the utmost thou hast in thee: out with it, then.
—THOMAS CARLYLE, *Sartor Resartus* (1834)

Get leave to work
In this world,—'tis the best you get at all;
For God, in cursing, gives us better gifts
Than men in benediction.
—ELIZABETH BARRETT BROWNING, *Aurora Leigh* (1856)

There is a cant abroad at the present day, that there is a special pleasure in industry, and hence we are taught to regard all those who object to work as appertaining to the class of natural vagabonds; but where is the man among us that loves labour?
—HENRY MAYHEW, *London Labour and the London Poor* (1861–62)

IN 1851 QUEEN VICTORIA opened the Great Exhibition of the Works of Industry of All Nations. The Crystal Palace (as it came to be dubbed) housed 13,000 exhibitors—an amazing collection of human labor and ingenuity. But readers of a local London paper already had a good sense of the extraordinary variety of human labor right in their own backyard. Beginning in 1849, the *Morning Chronicle* published two or three installments a week from their metropolitan correspondent Henry Mayhew in which he presented his reports on "the industry, the want, and the vice of the great Metropolis," "from the lips of the people themselves," "in their own 'unvarnished' language." Mayhew walked among the London streetfolk, interviewing them, at least initially, with a kind of questionnaire and a shorthand reporter. Occasionally a photographer accompanied him; the daguerreotypes were turned into woodcuts that accompanied the articles. Throughout 1851 and 1852 Mayhew published further weekly installments on his own. When he finally collected them, they made up four fat, closely printed, double-columned volumes.

Almost as remarkable as Mayhew's labor in collecting and writing *London Labour and the London Poor* is the pleasure his contemporaries had in reading it. Everybody seemed to follow his columns, even the street people he depicted. A gingerbread seller told Mayhew that he recognized a description of his old partner from twenty years back when they'd sold mincemeat pastries in the shape of pigs with currant eyes. But Mayhew particularly fascinated the novelists. Thackeray commented that he drew "a picture of human life so wonderful, so awful, so piteous and pathetic, so exciting and terrible, that readers of romances own they never read anything like it." And as for Mayhew's exact contemporary and friend Charles Dickens—well, as John D. Rosenberg notes, "To pass from Mayhew's case-histories to Dickens's inventions is merely to cross sides of the same street."

It's hard to resist the voices we hear so directly through Mayhew. Take the man I mentioned above who has been making and selling gingerbread "nuts" after a financial misadventure:

> Other great houses in the City were found that way, *they* made it all right; paid something, as I've heard, and sacked the profits. Well; when *I* was called on, it wasn't, I assure you, sir—ha, ha, ha!—at all convenient for a servant—and I was only that—to pay the fifteen hundred and odd; so I served 12 months and 2 days in prison for it. I'd saved a little money, and wasn't so uncomfortable in prison. I could get a dinner, and give a dinner. When I came out, I took to the nuts. It was lucky for me that I had a trade to turn to; for, even if I could have shown I wasn't at all to blame about the Exchequer, I could never have got another situation—never. So the streets saved me: my nuts was my bread.

A seller of a newish treat, ice cream:

> I don't think they'll ever take greatly in the streets, but there's no saying. Lord! how I've seen the people splutter when they've tasted them for the first time.... I knew one smart servant maid, treated to an ice by her young man—they seemed as if they was keeping company—and he soon was stamping, with the ice among his teeth, but she knew how to take them, put the spoon right into the middle of her mouth, and when she'd had a clean swallow she says: "O, Joseph, why didn't you ask *me* to tell you how to eat your ice?" The conceit of sarvant gals is ridiculous.

A ham sandwich-seller:

> Once, a gent kicked my basket into the dirt, and he was going off—for it was late but some people by began to make remarks about using a poor fellow that way, so he paid for all, after he had them counted. I am *so* sick of this life, sir. I *do* dread the winter so. I've stood up to the ankles in snow till after midnight, and till I've wished I was snow myself, and could melt like and have an end.... Time's very heavy on my hands, sometimes, and that's where you feel it. I read a bit if I can get anything to read, for I was at St Clement's school; or I walk out to look for a job. On summer-days I sell a trotter or two. But mine's a wretched life, and so is most ham sandwich-men. I've no enjoyment of my youth and no comfort.

These snippets are taken from what Mayhew, taking himself out of the conversation, presents as long monologues; shorter vignettes are equally powerful, such as the blind hurdy-gurdy woman Sarah riding in a cab for the first time. Mayhew's got a great eye for the odd detail, such as a candy-seller who wraps his sweeties in old Acts of Parliament. He grabs onto peculiar facts, like the profit to be made from different parts of a dead horse, which include not just hooves for combs or tendons for glue, but also blood for sugar refiners and the maggots for giving a "'high' flavor to pheasants." The facts he learns are often so bizarre that he is led into imaginative speculation. When he learns that some people make money by picking up cigar-ends (by his reckoning "nearly a ton of refuse tobacco collected annually"), he wonders, Who *buys* old cigar-ends anyway? "It is supposed that they are resold to some of the large manufacturers of cigars, and go to form the component part of a new stock of the 'best Havannahs'; or, in other words, they are worked up again to be again cast away, and again collected by the finders, and so on perhaps, till the millennium comes."

Mayhew's keen sympathy for the travails of the poor perhaps came naturally to him, for although he had talent and he could work hard, he found it difficult to settle on any single enterprise.

> We are all innately erratic—prone to wander both in thought and action; and it is only by vigourous effort . . . that we can keep ourselves to the steady prosecution of the object, to the repeated performance of the same acts, or even to continuous attention to the same subject.

Mayhew was born in 1812, the fourth of seven sons (there were also ten daughters) of a respectable solicitor in London. Their father was strict: "While living at home, if any son returned home after midnight, he would find the house locked. His father would toss a shilling from an upper window, telling the offender to 'go and get yourself a bed somewhere else.'" Mayhew attended the historically prestigious Westminster School, but he ran away from school at fifteen "under some sense of ill-usage"—he'd been caught reading his Greek grammar during chapel and refused to face the punishment of flogging. He served for a year or so as a midshipman on an India run. On his return, he proved an incompetent assistant in his father's legal practice. Michael Faraday was a friend of the family, and during the 1830s young Henry thought he too might become a chemist—he did, at any rate, conduct a number of experiments including one trying to make artificial diamonds that nearly blew up his brother's house.

As an adult, Mayhew was in and out of debt and even declared bankruptcy; he was apparently unable or uninterested in holding a job for more than a year or two. Contemporaries commented upon his indolence, his bursts of energy, his charm. Whatever his experience, though, he was quick to turn it into sellable literary material whether in fugitive journalism for Fleet Street or in comic novels and plays co-written with a brother. Out of the miscellany of writing jobs to which he turned his hand, he emerged in 1841 as one of the founders of *Punch*, only to be kicked out of his position as editor after less than a year. Such was his life until his mid-thirties. But then, what had looked to be a makeshift, if jovial, life turned out to be an apprenticeship that perfectly fitted him to be the author of *London Labour and the London Poor*. King Cholera was the catalyst.

Asiatic Cholera first arrived at the port of London in 1831 where it found a perfect environment. The population of London had almost doubled since the beginning of the century and the problem worsened more sharply beginning in 1845 when huge numbers of Irish displaced by the potato famine came to London. The Thames had become an open sewer, and, still unbeknownst to the inhabitants, cholera is a water-borne bacteria found in feces. In three months during the summer of 1849, 13,000 Londoners died, 432 of them on just one day in early September. The Whiggish and evangelical *Morning Chronicle* asked Mayhew to report. And Mayhew, based in the capital of what was arguably the most advanced country in the world, went to "the very capital of cholera . . . the Venice of drains." This was Jacob's Island, the squalid London neighborhood where Bill Sikes goes to earth after murdering Nancy in *Oliver Twist* (1838).

After this assignment, Mayhew was newly impassioned. With the same energy as those other fearlessly energetic Victorian tabulators, engineers, and reformers, Mayhew set out to bring his sharp attention to Work—as his subtitle declares, "those that *will* work, those that *cannot* work, and those that *will not* work." (By Volume IV he adds another class: "those that need not work." But this is merely a logical afterthought—he's not really interested in them, and as far as I know he never interviewed any landlords, shareholders, pensioners, sinecurists, sleeping partners, or protégés.) He rolled up his sleeves and tried to get organized.

> Those who obtain their living in the streets of the metropolis are a very large and varied class; indeed the means resorted to in order to "pick up a crust," as the people call it, in the public thoroughfares (and such in many instances it *literally* is,) are so multifarious that the mind is long baffled in its attempts to reduce them to scientific order or classification.

Mayhew began with the largest—or at any rate the most visible—of London laborers, the costermongers, that is, the people who you'd see hawking their wares on respectable streets. So he categorizes them by what they sell: fish, fruit and vegetables, game, poultry, rabbits, butter, cheese, eggs, trees, shrubs, flowers, roots, seeds, branches, green stuff, eatables and drinkables, literature and the fine arts, and manufactured articles. But wait—some street sellers remained stationary, at a designated location every day, and some moved about. Would that be a better way to classify them? Some were women, some were children, or Irish … Mayhew regrouped, came up with more categories, and went out to collect more stories and data. By the beginning of Volume IV, despising the government's mingy categories of labor, he has devised his own Classification of the Workers and Non-Workers of Great Britain that includes both himself (reporters are I.B.3.p) and the Sovereign (IV.B.1.a). It is sixteen pages long and so comprehensive that on one occasion his growing subheads require him to draw on the Greek alphabet (II.B.5.b.α includes Cabmen, Donkey-boys, Goat-carriage boys, Sedan and Bath Chair Men, and Guides).

Mayhew was faced with people who sold eels or second-hand nutmeg-graters or engravings displayed inside umbrellas (pictures of kittens sold particularly well) or conundrums or views through a microscope or themselves. Is Mayhew just running around in circles when he divides "cheap workmen" into these three classes?

1. The unskillful.
2. The untrustworthy.
3. The inexpensive.

But no matter how idiosyncratic or super-specific the lines he drew, "Many classes of labour are necessarily uncertain or fitful in their character" due to seasonal work or industrial innovation or economic fluctuations. People might perform several different kinds of labor. The legless nutmeg-grinder vendor sells any other items he can; the street microscope exhibitor has a weekday job; one informant has been a cottonspinner, a navvy, a soldier, and a prisoner, before falling out of the world of work altogether to become a vagrant. (More about vagrants in a bit.) By the time Mayhew gets around to his third volume, he's throwing his hands in the air:

> I would rather have pursued some more systematic plan in my inquiries; but in the present state of ignorance as to the general occupation of the poor, system is impossible. I am unable to generalize, not being acquainted with the particulars; for each day's

> investigation brings me incidentally into contact with a means of living utterly unknown among the well-fed portion of society.

Ah, the "well-fed portion of society." A large part of Mayhew's problem is that work seems to be everywhere he looks no matter how small the task, like a man who makes the eyes of dolls. But as he works his way down the scale to, say, homeless children, another problem comes in identifying work that might not look like work to middle-class eyes at all. What at first glance looks likes kids larking about on the banks of the Thames turns out on closer inspection to be "mudlarks"—mostly little boys and girls and old women—scavenging knee-deep in the slime at low tide for junk to resell: "coal, bits of old-iron, rope, bones, and copper nails that drop from ships." Mayhew identifies a number of similar occupations: people who gather and sell rags, bottles, glass, waste paper, used tea leaves, dogs' dung.

Mayhew spends a lot of energy getting his largely well-fed audience to understand the value of these incremental pieces of work. Take, for example, the people who trade in waste paper. He converts the waste paper to a unit middle-class readers are likely to understand—½ oz letters: "It would supply material, as respects weight, for *forty-four millions, seven hundred and twenty-eight thousand, four hundred and thirty* letters on business, love, or friendship." He reckons, "The gross total ... we may firmly put ... at a million and a half of pound sterling!" That's a lot of business, love, and friendship. With indignant italics, Mayhew points out that these workers on the margins, in gutters, sewers, alleys, chimneys, and garbage heaps, contribute their mite to the British economy: "They are classed as unauthorized or illegal and intrusive traders, though they *'turn over' millions in a year.*"

Part of Mayhew's purpose in making this "defense of the poor" is to persuade the "well-fed portions of society" that the streetfolk provide economic value; often (although he eschews the "sheer sentimentality" of allowing feelings rather than judgment to form opinions) he pleads for them on the high ground of human sympathy; sometimes, as he addresses the well-fed, he aims lower: "if we knew but the whole of the facts concerning them, and their suffering and feelings, our very fears alone for the safety of the state would be sufficient to make us do something in their behalf." The threat of the mob is not an idle appeal just a few years after the political convulsions of 1848.

By the end of the third volume, Mayhew would seem at long last to be approaching closure, the bottom class of those who *will not* work and who slide into the criminal classes: vagrants. The class of vagrant raises a new moral dimension. Mayhew fears vagrants are such both by "disposition and principle"—and thus their degraded condition is a function of both nature *and* will.

Here is Mayhew's stab at defining "vagrant."

> A vagrant . . . is an individual applying himself continuously to no one thing, nor pursuing any one aim for any length of time, but wandering from this subject to that, as well as from one place to another, because in him no industrial habits have been formed, nor any principle or purpose impressed upon his nature.

This is raw, unconstructed, unredeemed human nature, and it's not a pretty sight. But how to distinguish a parasitic vagrant from an honest working man who is traveling to seek new employment? In this matter, classification can have serious real-world consequences. As Mayhew points out, "To refuse asylum to the vagrant is to shut out the traveller; so hard is it to tell the one from the other." For although they might look identical, vagrants "are the very opposite to the industrious classes, with whom they are too often confounded." But their misleading appearance is not the worst problem; even this theoretic dividing line between traveler and vagrant can become blurred or, worse, erased completely if the acquired habits of work slip away: "Another class of vagrants consists of those who having been thrown out of employment, have travelled through the country, seeking work without avail. . . . The industrious workman has become changed into the habitual beggar." Culture can too easily fall back into nature.

Mayhew declares himself "anxious" that his well-fed audience "should see that the working class is as respectable and worthy as the vagrants are degraded and vicious." But he seems anxious on his own account as well.

What did Mayhew's work look like to other people? He worked on the streets of London gathering odd nuggets of information just as the mudlarks or purefinders gather lumps of coal or dung. Few people were as aware as he just how little such scavenging, piecemeal work, however incrementally useful, was valued or even recognized. There had been a number of philanthropic do-gooders and parliamentary fact-gatherers interviewing the poor, but there was really no precedent for the occupation of going around asking questions for the advancement of some kind of not very clear knowledge. Was Mayhew an intellectual vagrant?

One of the more than peripheral interests in reading *London Labour and the London Poor* is watching Mayhew searching for a model for what he was doing, trying to fit his own work into respectably preset categories. To start with, he compares himself to an explorer like James Bruce tracing the source of the Nile, a "traveller in the undiscovered country of the poor." Only one page later, he compares himself to the early ethnologist James Prichard, the author of *The Natural History of Man* (1843)—after all, they both studied "the wanderers and the settlers—the vagabond and the citizen—the nomadic and the civilized tribes." Sometimes he is eager to impress others with his rigor: "I made up my mind to deal with human nature as a natural philosopher or a chemist deals with any material object." (At such times, he might briefly adopt technical-sounding language, alluding to "the physics and economy of vice," or defining the "allobiism" of the streetfolk, dividing them into the "energetic" and the "an-ergetic.")

It certainly looks like he's flailing about for a respectable category in which to place his own work. But in a speech he gave to about fifty ticket-of-leave men (basically parolees) that he later included in Volume III of *London Labour and the London Poor*, on what would be page 1,427, he reaches a conclusion about his role.

> When I first went among you, it was not very easy for me to make you comprehend the purpose I had in view. You at first fancied that I was a Government spy, or a person in some way connected with the police. I am none of these, nor am I a clergyman wishing to convert you to his particular creed, nor a teetotaler anxious to prove the source of all evil to be overindulgence in intoxicating drink; but I am simply a literary man, desirous of letting the rich know something more about the poor. (Applause.) Some persons study the stars, others study the animal kingdom, others again direct their researches into the properties of stones, devoting their whole lives to these particular vocations. I am the first who has endeavored to study a class of my fellow-creatures whom Providence has not placed in so fortunate a position as myself, my

> desire being to bring the extremes of society together—the poor to the rich, and the rich to the poor. (Applause.)

Mayhew has earned the honest applause of ex-convicts looking for work, not least because he'd persuaded the police to stay away from the meeting.

In an age that genuflected to the idea of work—and there are worse gods—Mayhew graphically showed that work can be irksome, humiliating, painful, dangerous, coarsening, soul-destroying drudgery. And he could do it with some authority because his readers can see him struggling as hard and sometimes as fruitlessly as the workers he labored to describe. Free from cant, *London Labour and the London Poor* was, in great part, a remarkable labor of love.

Mayhew's early habits of losing interest in one project and moving on to another continued. The scholar James Bennett points out Mayhew "abandoned some works unfinished—*Low Wages* in mid-sentence, *Criminal Prisons* on page 498." He wrote and wrote and wrote, including biographies of famous figures as young men (Davy, Franklin, and Luther), and, after trips to Germany, *The Upper Rhine and its Picturesque Scenery* and *German Life and Manners as Seen in Saxony at the Present Day*; he acted with Dickens and wrote a flop with his son. As Mayhew later said of himself: "I had been everywhere—seen everything which maybe a gentleman should not." He died in 1887, not much regarded. When Dover first reprinted all four volumes in the interesting year 1968, W. H. Auden, a writer not much given to exaggeration, wrote in his review, "I am inclined to think that, if I had to write down the names of the ten greatest Victorian Englishmen, Henry Mayhew would head the list."

One quality *London Labour and the London Poor* shares with the novels of his contemporaries is being very long. As Christopher Herbert notes, "The salient stylistic features of *London Labour* are its mind-boggling profusion and density of ethnographic detail and its resultant sense of uncontrollable expansiveness, features which both give this text its gigantic power and at the same time, paradoxically, render it next to unreadable." A very readable selection with a wide-ranging and deeply knowledgeable introduction by Robert Douglas-Fairhurst has recently been published. But is being "readable" really true to the experience of reading Mayhew? Troubling to our consciences might be John D. Rosenberg's observation in his introduction to the Dover edition that portions of it might "provide the reader with a gallery of picturesque portraits but tear from the fabric of the work the larger social background that gives it coherence and authority." The new Oxford edition is only about one-tenth of the original. Thus we risk becoming mere touristic vagrants, gawking at one curiosity before moving on to the next. But Mayhew's willingness to risk being thought a vagrant turned out to be the quality that revealed his genius. We could do worse as we dip into it than take the ever curious, ever earnest, and ever distractible Mayhew himself as our model, observing and analyzing, marveling and doubting, connecting dots and making wild surmises.

November 2012

The student of political behavior

Donald Kagan

THE STUDY OF Thucydides and his famous *History of the Peloponnesian War* has never been so intense, so widespread or influential, as in our time. Thucydides claimed that his work is "a possession forever" meant to be useful to "such men as might wish to see clearly what has happened and what will happen again, in all human probability, in the same or a similar way." More than twenty-four-hundred years later, political leaders and students of politics treat it in just that way.

In the ancient world, Thucydides' focus on politics routed the broader but shallower purview of his predecessors. Herodotus, with his meandering style full of discursive side trips into the customs and habits of various peoples and his serious consideration of the causal role of the gods in human affairs, did not become the model for what was thought to be the best historical writing in antiquity. Polybius and the Romans Sallust, Livy, Tacitus, and Ammianus Marcellinus were the great classical historians, and they wrote chiefly about their own times, their own nations, and, especially, about war and politics.

During the Renaissance and the early modern period of European history, Polybius, whose history of Rome's conquest of the Mediterranean world followed the Thucydidean model, and Tacitus, who focused on politics in Rome, were the favorites. In the seventeenth century, Thomas Hobbes published the first complete English translation of Thucydides' *History* directly from the Greek original. "Thucydides," he said, "is one, who, though he never digress to read a lecture, moral or political, upon his own text, nor enter into men's hearts further than the acts themselves evidently guide him, is yet accounted the most politic historiographer that ever writ." That is, he provides both an instructive account and guidance to an understanding of the subjects included in the category "politics": the internal political competition within a city-state or nation and interstate relations in time of peace and war.

The writers of the eighteenth century, with their interest in the manners and civilization of earlier periods and of the entire world, rediscovered Herodotus, although as philosophical historians themselves they also admired Thucydides' search for a useful history that sought the causes of events in the lasting elements in human nature and the human condition. The nineteenth century, however, especially in Germany, saw the triumph of political history and the eclipse of Herodotus by Thucydides.

Another great wave of interest arose with the coming of the Cold War. People saw the long struggle between Athens and Sparta as strikingly similar to the contest between the United States and its NATO allies and the Soviet Union and its Warsaw Pact satellites. In 1947, the American Secretary of State George C. Marshall said, "I doubt seriously whether a man can think with full wisdom and with deep convictions regarding certain of the basic international issues today who has not at least reviewed in his mind the period of the Peloponnesian War and the Fall of Athens." Devotees of the "realist" or "neo-realist" schools of international relations regard Thucydides as their founder.

In fact, the Thucydidean approach so dominated historical studies that it was necessary to remind ourselves that historiography must combine the story of politics, diplomacy, and war with that of society, culture, and civilization, and a movement away from Thucydidean political history grew stronger. But now the world of historical writing has changed so much as to make these remarks seem dated. In much of the American academy, "extra-political history" has all but pushed political history out the door. The most famous and influential of the social historians, Fernand Braudel, dismissed the elements of politics, diplomacy, and war as mere *évènements*, transient and trivial in comparison with the greater and longer-lasting issues posed by geography, demography, and social and economic developments over long periods of time. In his best-known work, *The Mediterranean and the Mediterranean World in the Age of Philip II*, the political decisions, events, and developments are of small moment compared to the inanimate and impersonal forces that shape societies over the very long run.

It is clear enough that such forces exist and that they have considerable impact on politics, war, and diplomacy, chiefly in establishing the limits of what is possible. Within those limits, however, individuals and groups of human beings make decisions that are of vital importance, and those decisions that are military, diplomatic, and political influence ever larger groups of people in ways that can affect the very existence of peoples, nations, and the human race. It is important that we understand the underlying conditions and forces that help to frame and influence the choices that people make in these decisive realms, but the historian must connect this knowledge to the specific facts, decisions, and events made in the public arena, that is, in the world of politics. "Extra-political" historians have not made those connections, preferring to leave unasked the great political questions that have always been the spark that ignited interest in history from the first and still inspire it among non-professionals today.

What Thucydides called "the war between the Peloponnesians and the Athenians" and we call the Peloponnesian War broke out in 431 B.C. One of the principal antagonists, the Spartans, had been the head of the Peloponnesian League, a Greek coalition that resisted the Persian invasion of 480–79, and the leading power in Greece. Just before that invasion, the Athenians had built a great new fleet, which proved to be the core and backbone of the Greek navy that crushed the Persians at the battles of Salamis and at Mycale. These victories raised Athens to a level of prestige that challenged Sparta's position even after the Spartans led the Greeks to victory in the concurrent decisive land battle at Plataea.

The power and prosperity of the Athenian democracy grew to depend on its command of its great maritime empire. It began as "the Athenians and their allies" (modern scholars call it the Delian League), a voluntary alliance of Greek states who invited Athens to take the lead in continuing the war of liberation and vengeance against Persia. It gradually became an empire under Athenian command functioning chiefly for the advantage of Athens.

As the Delian League grew more powerful, some Spartans became jealous, suspicious, and fearful of the Athenian challenge to their supremacy. Quarrels in the 460s led to the First Peloponnesian War that started about 460 and lasted, on and off, until 445. It came to an end with the Thirty Years' Peace in which each side recognized the hegemony of the other in its own sphere, and each side agreed to submit any future disagreements to binding arbitration. The peace lasted for well over a decade, but a series of conflicts between Athens, on the one hand, and

Sparta and several of its allies, on the other, led to the great war. In the winter of 432–31, Sparta's ally Thebes attacked Athens's ally Plataea and sparked off the ten years' war the ancients called the Archidamian War, after the Spartan king who led the first invasions.

The leading man of Athens at the outbreak of the war was Pericles. His strategy was to avoid land battles, launch commando raids around the Peloponnesus, and wait until the Spartans realized that they had no winning strategy—within a year or two or three, he thought. In 430, however, the terrible plague broke out, causing fearful physical, social, and psychological disasters. Pericles' political opponents convinced the Athenians to ask the Spartans for peace, removed Pericles from office, and punished him with a heavy fine. But the enemy refused any acceptable terms, and the war went on. With peace no longer an option, the Athenians reelected Pericles and resumed his policy. He himself contracted the plague and, in the fall of 429, died.

After Pericles' death, no dominant leader emerged to hold the Athenians to a consistent policy. Two factions vied for influence: one, led by Nicias, wanted to continue the defensive policy, and the other, led by Cleon, preferred a more aggressive strategy. In 425, the aggressive faction was able to win a significant victory: four hundred Spartans surrendered and Sparta offered peace at once to get them back. The Athenians, however, wanted to continue, for the Spartan peace offer gave no adequate guarantee of Athenian security.

In 424, the Athenians undertook a more aggressive policy, which failed, leading to a truce in 423. Meanwhile, Sparta's ablest general Brasidas captured Amphipolis, the most important Athenian colony in Thrace. Thucydides was in charge of the Athenian fleet in those waters and was held responsible for the city's loss. In 422, the deaths of the aggressive Cleon and Brasidas paved the way for the Peace of Nicias, which was concluded in the spring of 421.

The peace, officially supposed to last fifty years and, with a few exceptions, guarantee the status quo, was, in fact, fragile. Neither side carried out all its commitments, and several of Sparta's allies refused ratification. In 415, Alcibiades persuaded the Athenians to attack Sicily to bring it under Athenian control. This ambitious and unnecessary undertaking ended in disaster in 413 when the entire expedition was destroyed. It shook Athens's prestige, reduced its power, provoked rebellions, and brought the wealth and power of Persia into the war on Sparta's side. It is remarkable that the Athenians could continue fighting despite the disaster.

They won several important victories at sea as the war shifted to the Aegean. Their allies rebelled, however, and Persia paid for fleets to sustain the insurrection. Athenian financial resources shrank and finally disappeared. When its fleet was caught napping and was destroyed at Aegospotami in 405, Athens could not build another. The Spartans, under Lysander, cut off the food supply through the Hellespont and starved the Athenians into submission. In 404, they surrendered unconditionally; they dismantled the city walls, gave up their fleet, and lost their empire. Thucydides never finished his *History*.

Who was this Thucydides, and what was the nature of his work that continues to interest and influence us today? He was an Athenian aristocrat of one of the noblest families and considerable wealth who came of age at the height of the greatness of Periclean Athens. Born between 460 and 455, he was still in his twenties when the Peloponnesian War broke out, and he died not many years after the end of the war, his great work unfinished. He is careful to let us know that he was old enough to understand events from the beginning: "I lived through the whole war, being of an age to understand the events, and I applied my mind to them so as to see them accurately." His father, Olorus, bore not an Athenian but a Thracian name. It was the same name as the grandfather of Cimon, the great general and statesman who dominated Athenian public life in the two decades following the Persian invasion. Thucydides was almost surely related to Cimon and also to another Thucydides, the son of Melesias, who was the most dangerous political opponent of Pericles in the 440s. As one scholar has put it, "born in the anti-Pericles opposition, he followed Pericles with a convert's zeal."

He was in Athens from the start of the war until 424, during which time he caught the great plague that struck Athens between 430 and 427. He was lucky to survive because the contagion killed about a third of the population. In 424, he was elected general, one of ten men who were the leading military and political leaders in Athens. He commanded the naval force in the Thracian area whose chief city was the Athenian colony of Amphipolis, a place of great economic and strategic importance. He may have gained that assignment because of his influence in the area. He tells us that he controlled gold mines there and "had great influence among the leading men" of the region. When the brilliant Spartan general Brasidas took the city by surprise, the Athenians held

Thucydides responsible and convicted him of treason. They sent him off to exile for the twenty years that remained in the war. This great misfortune had its advantages, especially for us, his readers, because it allowed him "to know what was being done on both sides, especially the Peloponnesian ... and this leisure permitted me to get a better understanding of the course of events."

Thucydides was not the first to write history. The Greeks believed that Homer's epic poems, the *Iliad* and *Odyssey*, though composed in poetic meter and filled with divine and mythological characters, nevertheless reported on real events and people of the distant past. Even the hardheaded Thucydides used them as evidence for the early history of the Greeks. In the sixth century, however, a new way of thinking arose among the Greek cities of Ionia on the western coast of Asia Minor and especially Miletus. It is not too much to say that the new approach substituted rational, even scientific, thought for myth as a means of understanding and explaining the world and the universe.

This intellectual revolution took place at some time between the poet Hesiod who described much of Greek mythology about 700, and Hecataeus of Miletus, who lived about two centuries later. Hecataeus, unlike earlier Milesian inquirers who speculated about philosophical-scientific questions like the nature and composition of the universe, concerned himself with more tangible matters. He produced the first map of which we know, a "description of the earth." He also investigated the past experience of human beings in the form of *Genealogies*, in which he brought reason to bear on the heroic myths of the past. He applied critical judgment to the stories of noble families who claimed descent from the gods. He began his *Genealogies* with a challenge to tradition: "I Hecataeus will say what I think to be the truth; the stories of the Greeks are many and ridiculous." That did not lead him either to make up whatever story he liked or to despair of finding the truth. It led him to questioning and research and the reasoned quest for accurate knowledge and understanding—that is, toward history.

It is not Hecataeus, however, whom we call the father of history but Herodotus, born in Halicarnassus, a Greek city on the same Aegean shore of Asia Minor, in 484. He died about 425, several years after the start of the Peloponnesian War. He did not write about his own times like Thucydides but relied chiefly on what he was told about earlier times. Hecataeus appears to have confined himself to the comparison and reasoned criticism of what was thought to be known. Herodotus undertook new inquiries, even traveling to foreign countries to gather new evidence. He sought not merely to preserve traditions but also to discover new facts. Both men demanded a new method that required not only the rational weighing of likelihoods but also the evaluation of the reliability of evidence.

Herodotus, nevertheless, did not enjoy a reputation for accuracy, truthfulness, and objectivity among ancient writers. They pointed to his factual inaccuracies, many called him a liar outright, and Plutarch wrote an essay on his "malignity," charging him with a lack of patriotism and a prejudice in favor of Athens. The "Father of History," in fact, is said to have read his work in public performances, like epic poetry, for the delight of his audiences. It was Thucydides, a younger contemporary of Herodotus, who reinvented history by approaching it in a thoroughly different way. He criticized Herodotus without directly naming him and corrected some of his factual errors, dismissing the historian of the Persian Wars as one who wrote "a prize-essay to be heard for the moment" compared to his own more serious effort.

Grasping the ideas of Thucydides is not easy. He did not write a philosophical or political treatise in which he presented his views and the arguments for them. He wrote a history, aiming at the highest possible objectivity, clinging relentlessly to the subject of the Peloponnesian War and avoiding tangents almost entirely. He makes important direct statements of his opinion, and these form the soundest basis for understanding his thought. Some of them deal with his method of inquiry, and others with his view of the general processes of political life.

In considering the ideas embodied in the *History*, it is useful and interesting to compare Thucydides with his great predecessor Herodotus. Thucydides seems to have taken a spectacular leap into modernity. He neither accepted nor rationalized myths but ignored or analyzed them with a cold eye. He did not seek explanations for human behavior in the will of the gods or, sometimes, not even in the will of individuals but in a general analysis of the behavior of men in society. Thucydides, however, was not a sort, who miraculously and inexplicably appeared on the scene. He reflected the growth of intellectual forces in the fifth century that came to exert an important influence on Greek life and which together are sometimes called "the Greek enlightenment."

Two elements of that movement seem to have affected the thought of Thucydides with great force: the Sophistic movement and the school of medical writers surrounding Hippocrates of Cos. In their different ways, each of these was a branch of the tree of rational investigation of the universe that took root in the Greek cities of Asia Minor in the sixth century. Thales, Anaximander, Anaximenes, and their successors differed from previous speculators on the nature of the world and its origin in that their guesses were entirely naturalistic. Thales, for instance, proposed a theory of the origins of the earth in which everything developed naturally, without divine intervention, out of primeval water in a process like the silting up of the Nile.

This tradition of naturalistic theorizing gave birth to both science and philosophy, which were undistinguishable in the early speculations about the physical world. By the fifth century, speculation in physics seemed to have come as far as it could, and what remained alive and potent was the spirit of inquiry in the naturalistic vein. The sense of the new age was that the proper study of man was man. The Sophists took a deep interest in the role of man in society; the Hippocratic school of medicine concerned itself with the investigation of the physical well-being of men. Both continued to avoid non-rational or supernatural explanations and to seek an understanding of man with reference only to his own nature.

The field of Thucydides' investigations was not the nature of the physical universe nor the physical nature of man, but the society of man living in the polis. Politics in the largest sense, the search for an understanding of the behavior of man in society, was his surpassing interest. In this he differed from physical theorists, Sophists, and Hippocratics, but their ideas influenced and helped shape his mind. Like all of them, he began with the observation of phenomena and proceeded to discern and describe the rational pattern that emerged. His data were the historical actions of men in the past, remote or very recent. When sufficiently multiplied and properly grasped, these gave rise to general rules of human behavior that might prove useful to men in the future. The student of social behavior—that is, the historian—has a dual responsibility: first to seek out with diligence and accuracy the truth of what has taken place and, then, to interpret the events with wisdom and understanding, in this way making a permanent contribution. To establish the facts (*ta erga*) was of vital importance but was subordinate to the formulation of interpretations (*logoi*) that emerged from them.

Thucydides was both less and more than a scientist of any kind, but no one reading the historian's account of the great plague in Athens can fail to see Thucydides' debt to the Hippocratics in his account of that disease, with which he himself was infected. He gives a detailed and precise description of its symptoms and progress so that "perhaps it may be recognized by the student, if it should break out again." The clear implication is that an accurate account of what occurred may be used in the future to help arrest the progress of the disease or, at least, to prepare to deal with its symptoms.

But Thucydides is a student of society and his description of the plague includes more than its physical consequences. The effect of so great a shock on the morale of a society was of greater interest. As death and desperation weakened the moral fiber of the community, the normal religious and legal restraints on men's actions ceased to operate, and the Athenians yielded to a lawless hedonism which may have been as damaging to the Athenian cause as the physical suffering. The description of the plague is not merely a useful and humane digression but a necessary component of the *erga* that will help account for the outcome of the war.

But the careful description and analysis of the plague does not illuminate only the future course of the Peloponnesian War. A proper understanding of events can assist a better comprehension of all human history. The revolutions that disturbed Greece during the war, as in Corcyra for instance, brought with them terrible calamities, "such as have occurred and always will occur, as long as the nature of mankind remains the same; though in a severer or milder form, and varying in their symptoms, according to the variety of the particular cases."

To this examination of the description and analysis of politics that he had invented, Thucydides brought the tools supplied by the Sophists as well as those of the Hippocratics. One of the characteristic ideas of the Sophistic movement was the distinction drawn between two elements that determine man's behavior in society: *physis* (nature) and *nomos* (custom or law). In the Sophists' view *physis* represents the innate inclination of man to satisfy his wants, while *nomos* is the artificial device by which society protects itself against the antisocial drives of man's *physis*. Greek society rested on the common acceptance of *nomos* as sacred, and the radicalism of the Sophists lay in large measure in their skeptical attitude towards it. Thucydides did not accept the extreme iconoclasm of some Sophists, but he did find the distinction between *physis* and *nomos* a useful tool in his political analysis. How are we to understand the fearful atrocities that men commit in time of civil war? How can we explain the transformation of normally law-abiding citizens into ravening beasts carried away by uncontrollable passion? "In the confusion into which life was now thrown in the cities, human nature (*hê anthropeia physis*), always rebelling against the law and now its master, gladly showed itself ungoverned in passion, above respect for justice, and the enemy of all superiority."

This passage is a splendid example of Thucydides' method. It assumes the essentially uniform nature of man, in this instance, his jealousy and suspicion of all distinction and superiority. Under normal conditions, custom and law control it, but when circumstances—in this case protracted warfare—permit, these artificial bonds dissolve and men revert to their natural state. Proper analytical diagnosis can foresee their emergence and development in the same way that a physician acquainted with the symptoms of his patient can predict with great likelihood the progress of the disease, since he knows its general character and natural course.

Such austerity, such a close approximation to the methods of the natural sciences, might seem to lay Thucydides open to the charge that he is too scientific and thus anti-historical. It is, however, wrong to suggest that Thucydides cared little for events; his very closeness to the Hippocratic idea requires a careful concern for the specific events that make up the whole subject of his study. No one, moreover, who reads Thucydides' brilliant and touching account of the Sicilian campaign, from its buoyant planning stage to its tragic ending, can doubt his narrative genius or his historian's love for the events themselves. It is wrong, furthermore, to chide Thucydides for seeking patterns in history: it is misleading to view Thucydides' attempt to establish a rigorous empirical study of politics as a search for "some unchanging and eternal truth." He sought only the degree of certainty and consistency possible in the study of events in human society, not of elements in nature.

Thucydides' own statements make it clear that his understanding of human events has nothing to do with laws like those of physics or the "absolute" truths of the philosophic sort. The Thucydidean view of political analysis contains no adamantine chain of determinism and in fact takes real cognizance of the unaccountable. At several crucial points in his *History* he explains important events by reference to *tychê* (chance), though these cases are not evidence of the historian's belief in the essential irrationality of the world. On the contrary, he believed the world to be subject to reasoned analysis, just not to absolute or scientific certainty. Intelligent people with unusual gifts could, by careful and systematic study of human behavior, make useful estimates of the likely reaction of people, especially *en masse.*

In a still more basic way Thucydides' conception of the study of political behavior differs from the determinism that has been held to underlie the physical sciences. He lays great emphasis on the role of the individual in history and on his ability to change its course. The didactic aspect of his work, the attempt to discern underlying patterns, is intended to supply perceptive individuals with the insight (*gnômê*) with which to see the course of political events and to control them. And there were such perceptive political leaders. Themistocles, for instance, "was the best judge of what was about to happen and the wisest in foreseeing what would happen in the distant future" and could "excellently foresee what was better or worse that was hidden in the unseen future." As a consequence, "he surpassed all others in the faculty of intuitively meeting an emergency." Even clearer is Thucydides' conviction that the special talents of Pericles affected the course of the war. He possessed the qualities of foresight, patriotism, and incorruptibility: "For so long a time as he was at the head of the state during the peace, he pursued a moderate and conservative policy and in his time its greatness was at its height," but he was succeeded by men who lacked his talents and deviated from his wise policies. "And yet," says Thucydides,

> they still held out for ten years against their original enemies ... and against their own allies ... and against Cyrus, son of the King of Persia.... And they did not give in until they had destroyed themselves by their own internal conflicts. So immensely great were the resources that Pericles counted on at the time through which he foresaw an easy victory for Athens over the Peloponnesians alone.

There can be no clearer endorsement of the idea that wise men can make accurate and well-founded plans for the future.

It is precisely this expectation that such men will find his account useful in the future that explains his extraordinary emphasis on accuracy in the work of the historian. Apart from the rare direct statements, the historian's own opinions may be sought in the speeches he puts into the mouth of his characters. Thucydides tells us about his treatment of the speeches:

> It was in all cases difficult to carry them word for word in one's memory, so my habit has been to make the speakers say what was in my opinion demanded of them by the various occasions, of course adhering as closely as possible to the general sense of what they really said.

That is a claim to report speeches that were really spoken, not invented by the historian, and to the attempt to report them as accurately as possible. If Thucydides did something else, if he invented speeches or inserted his own ideas rather than trying to retain the topics addressed by the speaker in the manner he used, then he has lied to his readers. The assumption here is that Thucydides meant precisely what he most obviously said: those speeches which he is likely to have heard himself should be taken as reasonably accurate accounts of the speaker's ideas. Speeches he could not possibly have heard or about which he is not even likely to have received a reliable report, if there are any, may be taken to be expressions of the ideas of Thucydides.

After explaining his method of depicting the speeches, Thucydides tells the reader of the great pains he took to ascertain the course of events:

> But as to the facts of the events of the war, I have thought it right to write them down, not just as they happened to come my way, nor according to my own predispositions, but only after investigating each one with the greatest possible accuracy, concerning both the events at which I myself was present and of those about which I was informed by others. And the effort to discover the truth about these facts was very hard work, because those who were eye-witnesses of the events did not give the same reports about the same things, but each report differed because of partiality for one side or the other or because of faulty memory.
>
> And, perhaps, my account will seem less pleasing to those who hear it because of its lack of fabulous tales, but if it be judged useful by those who seek an exact knowledge of the past as an aid to the interpretation of the future, which in the course of human things must resemble if it does not reflect it, I shall be satisfied.

Donald Kagan

Few have sufficiently noticed that the last paragraph is closely tied to what comes before and is its necessary complement. It explains *why* Thucydides has taken such great pains to present the facts of his history as accurately as possible. Only then can it serve his purpose as the material from which wise men of the future can study the pattern of human behavior, especially in such strained circumstances as war, learn from it, and thereby make better decisions. If the facts of his account are wrong, so will his interpretations be wrong, and neither will serve to foster political wisdom.

Thucydides' magnificent *History* addresses issues that remain ever vital in the critically important areas that are his subject: politics, international relations, and war. They continue to be inescapably crucial and central in the understanding and conduct of human affairs, regardless of the intellectual fashions of our time. Thucydides was the first to take up such questions of permanent significance by using reason and the most arduous and careful examination of the history of his time as a way to shed light on them.

September 2009

The Vatican's Latinist

John Byron Kuhner

IN 1970, the Procurator General of the Discalced Carmelite Order, Finian Monahan, was summoned to the Vatican for a meeting. The subject of the meeting was a promising young American priest by the name of Reginald Foster. The head Latinist of the Vatican's State Department had tapped Foster to write papal correspondence, which was at the time composed entirely in Latin. Foster wanted the job but was bound by a vow of obedience, and the decision would be made by his superiors. Monahan intended to resist. Foster, thirty years of age, had proven himself to be both supremely intellectually gifted and utterly reliable—a precious thing at a time when the Catholic Church's religious orders were hemorrhaging priests. Monahan thought Latin was a dead end. He didn't want to lose one of his best to a Vatican department that would only get less and less important every year. He said Foster would go to the Vatican "over my dead body."

Foster remembers the meeting vividly. "So we arrive there, and we're ushered into this office, and who do we find there but Ioannes Benelli," Foster says, using Benelli's Latin name, as was customary at the Vatican at that time. He continues:

> Benelli was Paul VI's hatchet man—whenever he wanted something to get done, he called on Benelli. He was very energetic—got things done, and no nonsense. Everyone was terrified of him. I was too, and now here we were in the room with him, and he turns to Monahan and says, "This is Foster?" The General said yes. Then Benelli said, "Thank you very much, we won't be needing you anymore." And he took me by the hand and brought me down to the State Department and that was the end of that. Monahan didn't say a word. I was now working for the Pope, and it was like

> I was more or less out of the Carmelite Order. A lot of the time the Order didn't even really know what I was doing.

Foster would spend the next forty years at the Vatican, part of a small team of scribes who composed the pope's correspondence, translated his encyclicals, and wrote copy for internal church documents. His somewhat unique position between the Carmelite Order and the Vatican bureaucracy meant that in fact he had a great deal of freedom for a priest. Later in his career his loose tongue—some in the church called it a loose cannon—would attract the notice of journalists looking for interesting copy. "Sacred language?" he said when asked about Latin as the "sacred language" of the church. "In the first century every prostitute in Rome spoke it fluently—and much better than most people in the Roman Curia." The Minnesota *Star Tribune* quoted him as saying "I like to say mass in the nude," which caused a small Curial kerfuffle (Foster claims he was misquoted). He appeared in Bill Maher's movie *Religulous*, which featured him agreeing with the proposition that the Vatican itself was at odds with the message of Jesus, that the pope should not be living in a palace, and that hell and "that Old Catholic stuff" was "finished" and "gone." Foster says the pope received complaints from bishops and cardinals about his appearance. "They said 'Who is this Latinist of yours and what the hell is he doing?' They would have fired me for sure. But by the time the film came out I was sick and a few months away from retirement anyway. So they just waited it out and let me go quietly." He had already been fired from his post at the pontifical Gregorian University for allowing dozens of students to take his classes without paying for them.

Besides being the Pope's Latinist and "one of the Vatican's most colorful characters" (as the Catholic News Service called him), Foster has been a tireless champion of Latin in the classroom. Indeed, Foster's greatest legacy may be as a teacher. "The most influential Latin teacher in the last half-century is Reggie Foster," says Dr. Nancy Llewellyn, professor of Latin at Wyoming Catholic College. "That's not just my opinion—that's a fact. For decades, he had the power to change lives like no other teacher in our field. I saw him for an hour in Rome in 1985 and that one hour completely changed my life. His approach was completely different from every other Latin teacher out there, and it was totally transformative."

A humanist par excellence, Latin for Foster was not something to be dissected by linguistic analysis or serve as the raw data for a theory of gender or poetics: it was a language, a medium of human connection. I first met Foster in 1995, at his summer school, and couldn't get enough: I returned seven times. No one on Earth was reading as much Latin as he and his students were, but he was more like an old-school newspaper editor than an academic: he wanted the *story*. But for that you actually had to know Latin, and know it well. Foster was ruthless about ignorance, and equally ruthless about anything that to him looked like mere academic posturing. "I don't care about your garbage literary theory!" he barked at his students one day. "I can tell in about ten seconds if you know the Latin or if you are making it all up." "Latin is the best thing that ever happened to humanity. It leaves you zero room for nonsense. You don't have to be a genius. But it requires laser-sharp concentration and total maturity. If you don't know what time of day it is, or what your name is, or where you are, don't try Latin because it will smear you on the wall like an oil spot." The number of Foster's students runs into the thousands, and many of them are now themselves some of the most dedicated teachers in the field. "When I was in college I asked people, 'Hey, we all know Latin is a language. Does anybody actually speak it anymore?' And they told me there was one guy, some guy at the Vatican, who still spoke the language, and that was Fr. Foster," says Dr. Michael Fontaine, a professor of Classics at Cornell University. "I said to myself, 'I have to study with this guy.' And that changed everything for me." Dr. Paul Gwynne, professor of Medieval and Renaissance Studies at the American University of Rome, said of Foster, "He is not just the best Latin teacher I've ever seen, he's simply the best teacher I've ever seen. Studying Latin with the Pope's apostolic secretary, for whom the language is alive, using the city of Rome as a classroom ... it changed my whole outlook on life, really."

Time seems to bend around Foster, and past and present intertwine. When I wrote to Fr. Antonio Salvi, the current head of the Vatican's Latin department, for comment about Foster, he responded entirely in Latin, beginning with four words that sounded like an old soldier praising Cato—"Probus vir, parvo contentus." An upright man. Content with little. And in many ways Foster's resembles the life of a medieval saint: at the age of six, he would play priest, ripping up old sheets as vestments. He entered seminary at thirteen. He said he wanted only three things in life: to be a priest, to be a Carmelite, and to do Latin. He has spent his entire life in great personal poverty. His cell had no mattress:

he slept on the tile floor with a thin blanket. His clothes were notorious in Rome: believing that the religious habit no longer reflected the simple garb of the people as it once had, he gave up his cassock and bought his clothes at Sears: blue pants and a blue shirt, with brandless black sneakers. When it was cold he added a zip-up blue polyester jacket. The Vatican's Swiss guards called him "il benzinaio," the gas-station attendant. Reporting for work at the Vatican, he looked like someone called to fix one of the washing-machines in the laundry room. His outfit was more like something his own father, a plumber in Milwaukee, would have worn. When people would give him gifts, he would give them to the poor. He owned almost nothing, and his Vatican office was legendarily spare: a typewriter, pens and paper, one chair, one desk, and a Latin dictionary. Nothing mattered to him except Latin.

But through the Latin language and his work, Foster might just as well have been living during the Italian Renaissance. He made two exceptions to his no-gifts policy: books, because he loved them, and music, because he could not resist. He covered all his books in brown packing paper, and treated them as precious relics. The solitary pleasures of his cell were the words of Cicero and Leo Magnus, and the music of Handel and Haydn. And outside his cell he reveled in the artistic treasures of Rome. He would show visitors around the Vatican with evident pride, to Raphael's loggia, a private balcony overlooking Bernini's colonnade, or the Pauline Chapel (like the Sistine Chapel painted by Michelangelo, but closed to the public and reserved only for Vatican employees).

The papal Latin secretaries have a storied history: the first to hold the office was St. Jerome, Latin secretary to Pope Damasus. During the Renaissance such Humanist luminaries as Lorenzo Valla and Poggio Bracciolini held the post. Foster was the first American so honored. "When I first started, there were two people in the Latin office," Foster explained to me when I interviewed him for this profile. "They had traditional names, which they got rid of after Vatican II. One was the *Secretarius Brevium ad Principes*, the Secretary of Briefs to Princes. That was all the diplomatic correspondence. That was Monsignor Amleto Tondini, and it was his death that opened up a position for me. The other was the *Secretarius Ab Epistolis Latinis*, the secretary for the pope's letters. That was Carlo Egger. It was Egger who was my teacher in Rome, and he was the one who wanted me to work with him. I remember the day like it was yesterday. He came into the classroom where I was studying and said 'Foster, would you like to be the pope's Latinist?' and I said '*Certissime.*'"

Foster's Latin abilities turned out to be truly extraordinary. Fr. Salvi wrote to me: "He was at the Vatican for forty years. In that time he developed a reputation for being one of the greatest masters of the Latin language since the Renaissance." He was a master of both types of tasks assigned the pope's Latin secretaries: free composition and faithful translation. The papal correspondence is mostly freely composed, in a particular style known as the Curial style. Highly formulaic and traditional, it is laden with scriptural metaphors and classical flourishes. "He had such an incredible command of the language that he could work quickly and flawlessly," says Monsignor Daniel Gallagher, who worked in the Latin office of the Vatican after Foster. "Whenever there was an urgent document that needed to be composed within minutes, everyone would turn to him." Foster drafted acceptance speeches for three popes, each with an immediate deadline. The other part of the work consisted of official papal pronouncements, such as encyclicals. These are accepted as authoritative and translations into Latin must be extremely faithful and precise. "That's the hard part," Foster concedes. "Paul VI's writing was very concrete, and avoided jargon. John Paul II—not so much. So how are we going to say 'the economic consequences of globalization' in Latin? That stuff doesn't mean anything in Latin. You need to think."

While Foster was adapting the Latin language to modern concepts, the general decline of the language his superior Monahan had foreseen picked up speed. Foster had first arrived in Rome in 1962, the year the Second Vatican Council opened. The entire Council was conducted in Latin: speeches, debates, drafting and editing and finalizing documents, everything was in Latin. "In those days they would play games where one bishop would recite a line of Vergil and the next guy had to give the next line and on they would go, until someone couldn't remember a line. That's all gone now." The destruction of the Church's Latin culture would remain the abiding sorrow of Foster's life. But it was also an opportunity. By 1974 Foster was asked to start teaching a remedial Latin course. In 1977 he started teaching at the Pontifical Gregorian University, where he would teach for the next thirty years.

During that time he may well have undertaken the most strenuous teaching schedule ever attempted by a university professor. Rising every day at 3:58 A.M., he said mass in Latin, graded papers, and then headed to his full-time job as papal Latin secretary. By 2:00 P.M. he would complete his day's work at the Vatican and be ready to teach. Every year he taught ten semester-long courses at the Gregorian, from Latin rudiments to the most difficult authors. Beginning in 1985 he began a summer school, at the request of some students, to fill up his time in between semesters. Here, unconstrained by university policies and scheduling, he could teach as he desired: he hired space at his own expense, and taught six to eight hours every day, seven days a week for eight consecutive weeks. Sundays were not off days but day-long excursions into the countryside with twenty-page packets of Latin texts: to Cicero's birthplace, Tiberius's cave at Sperlonga, Horace's villa in the Sabine mountains, and many other locations. The course was free and no one received any official credit for taking it—Foster wanted only people who loved Latin for its own sake. "Summer school" became a kind of legend in Rome, particularly within the American expatriate community (it was taught in English and attracted mostly Americans). By the late 1990s a hundred people were passing through every summer. He also tutored, kept up a vast correspondence, recorded a weekly radio program for Vatican Radio called "The Latin Lover," did any interviews he could, and kept up his priestly duties, saying mass and hearing confessions. All this while serving as the pope's Latin secretary.

This Herculean effort led to Alexander Stille calling him "a one-man Audubon Society for the Latin language, determined to save it from extinction." Stille, a journalism professor at Columbia University, wrote a lengthy profile of Foster—still the best in print—which appeared in *The American Scholar* in 1994 and was later gathered into his book *The Future of the Past*. Stille had doubts as to how much success Foster would have with his attempts to save Latin—he found his work "quixotic but compelling."

Foster is now approaching his eighties but is still teaching, now in the basement of the Milwaukee nursing home where he lives. Physically reduced—he can no longer walk—but still mentally fit, Foster has reduced his teaching load to six hours a week to work on consolidating his legacy. During his last years in Rome the signs of wear were evident—he would sometimes teach with a beer in hand, or lapse into angry tirades embarrassing to students and visitors. In 2008 he collapsed while teaching and nearly died in the hospital. Since his move to Milwaukee, he has grown healthier and more productive. October 2016 saw the publication of his first book, *The Mere Bones of Latin* (*Ossa Latinitatis Sola*), from The Catholic University of America Press. A second volume is nearly ready to go to press, though Foster, ever intent on doing things his own way, has been squabbling about fonts and covers.

In the meantime, Foster's students have become the teachers, and the decades he spent dedicated to his students are now showing signs of paying off. "You have to understand that many if not most of the people who went through Foster's classes were Latin teachers when they got there, or became Latin teachers later," says Matthew McGowan, professor of Classics at Fordham. "That has had a ripple effect through the entire discipline. People know that there's a way to do Latin the way Foster did it—with passion and pleasure. And with real human connection. And it's starting to take off."

Second-generation efforts by Foster's students—known as "Reginaldians"—are becoming respectable enterprises in their own right. Anthony Grafton, professor of history at Princeton, wrote a piece in *The Nation* in 2015 where he confessed that the single most dramatic change during his forty years in academia had occurred in the past four or five years, when suddenly he began seeing "an infestation of undergraduate genius" and "an outbreak of inspired work," which he traced back to a cadre of Foster's students. In 2008 Foster was too sick to finish his summer school; in 2009 none was held. But by 2010 a pair of Reginaldians, Jason Pedicone and Eric Hewett, reconceived Foster's school as their "Living Latin in Rome" program for college students, and started a not-for-profit called the Paideia Institute to keep it going. Since its founding, Paideia has moved from success to success, growing as quickly as a Humanities start-up possibly could, now running Latin programs in Rome, Paris, Provence, and New York, a Greek program in Greece, an online Classics journal called *Eidolon*, as well as elementary-school Classics enrichment programs at fifteen different sites throughout the United States. Last summer Paideia had more than a hundred people involved in its programs in Rome alone. In 2016, Paideia's founders were presented with the President's Award from the Society for Classical Studies, the highest honor in the field of Classics, a kind of capture-the-castle moment for Foster alumni. In Grafton's glowing panegyric for the Institute he writes:

> Reginaldus's method remains the groundwork of their teaching, and he himself is present in the conversation every day, as the ruling spirit. They celebrate him with inspiring loyalty. But they have also found ways to build an infrastructure—something Reginaldus's courses lacked.... Paideia has five universities as institutional members—Brown, Cornell, Dartmouth, Harvard and Princeton. They support Paideia by sending students to study and faculty members to teach in its programs.

That was in 2015. By the end of 2016, Paideia counted nineteen universities among its institutional members.

Paideia isn't even the only not-for-profit inspired by Foster. In 1997, Nancy Llewellyn founded the Septentrionale Americanum Latinitatis Vivae Institutum, the North American Institute of Living Latin Studies, or SALVI for short. SALVI promotes the use of active-language pedagogy in the teaching of Latin—the kind of speaking and hearing that Llewellyn first saw when she met Foster. More than two hundred people are expected to pass through SALVI's programs in 2017, which will take place not only in New York and California, but also West Virginia and South Africa.

What is most exciting about these developments is these programs are generating the same kind of enthusiasm as the Foster classes that inspired them: "I've not looked at Latin the same way since." "An initiation." "Without a doubt the most valuable course I have ever attended in my academic career." "Transformative." "Mindbending." "All people that want the classical languages to survive should really be doing these courses." Foster's model has proven to be imitable (though his energy and expertise is not—Paideia last year used six teachers to cover what Reginaldus would do alone).

And Foster taught innumerable other teachers, who have been at work in schools from Santa Monica High School to Harvard University. And the fact that the Catholic Church sends its most promising young priests to Rome means that Foster ended up teaching an entire generation of church leaders. "His alumni are filling ecclesiastical offices, tribunals, and episcopal cathedrae throughout the world right now," says Fr. Daniel Gallagher from his Vatican office. "And because of that, things are much better off for Church Latin than they were forty years ago." Foster confirms this: "I don't keep up on what's going on all over the world, but I can go through almost every episcopal see in the Midwest and the bishop now is a former student of mine."

What was it that was so revolutionary in Foster's approach? Some sense of what the experience was like can be found in his new book, the *Ossa Latinitatis*. The book is divided not into chapters or lessons but "experiences" and "encounters." The language is significant. Foster's method was primarily to be present in the room when exposing students to real Latin. He would settle on one particular thing he wanted students to look for, cold-call, and then correct mistakes publicly. About this method he said, "You don't need a hydrology course to learn to swim. You don't point at the water and say, 'This is water, this is how water works.' you just throw the babies in."

As with throwing babies into swimming pools, the method depends on the presence of a teacher, and is not for autodidacts. But as a template for trained teachers, the book is priceless. And a glance at the readings shows what kind of intellectual experience Foster's students got. The book is more or less a transcript of Foster's 2010–11 Latin classes in Milwaukee. The vast majority of students who study Latin study five or fewer authors (Caesar, Cicero, Vergil, Ovid, and Catullus), and take four or more years to see even those five. A select percentage of students may read as many as half a dozen more. But students who studied with Foster in 2011 read what can be found in *Ossa*: all of those five authors, plus Roger Bacon's *Compendium of Philosophy*, Lucretius's *On the Nature of Things*, the correspondence of Marcus Aurelius with his teacher Fronto, Seneca's *Consolation to Helvia*, Raphael's epitaph, the personal letters of Anselm of Canterbury, the dedicatory plaque of the cathedral of Milwaukee, Boccaccio's *On Famous Women*, Tacitus on the Germans, Clement XIV on the suppression of the Jesuits, Kepler's *Commentary on Galileo's Starry Messenger*, Walter of Chatillon's twelfth-century *Satire Against the Curia*, Antonius Galateus's *Hermit*, Giovanni Pietro Maffei's sixteenth-century description of China, documents from the Councils of Constance, Trent, Vatican I and II, and dozens more texts by dozens more authors: Livy, Raymond Lull, Ambrose, Bede, John Paul II, Thomas More, Tibullus, Plautus. Foster's method put back together what language courses generally separate: the experience of learning a language and the cultural value of knowing it.

What the book cannot give, of course, is the experience of not only reading these texts with Foster but strolling through the streets of Rome with him. For that we will need his like—or to wait for the Reginaldians to start writing memoirs. Alexander Stille writes of him:

> Seeing Rome with Reginald Foster is somewhat like hearing music for the first time. The city is threaded with a vast web of Latin inscriptions. They line the cornices of buildings, the base of statues and monuments, the tops of fountains and gates. The biographies of tens of thousands of dead souls are carved onto tombs and sarcofagi. They provide a running commentary on all you see, although virtually all of Rome's three million inhabitants walk by without noticing them. To see Rome without having access to this Latin subtext is like going to the opera without a libretto—you can love the music, the singing, and the spectacle but you miss a lot of the drama.

Foster has lived his life immersed in the river of recorded human experience that is the Latin language. "It's as if the whole Latin tradition—Classical, Medieval, Renaissance—came down to just one man," Michael Fontaine says. "He was like the funnel-point for all that culture. And he worked tirelessly to bring it to people—hundreds, thousands of people. And now it comes down to the rest of us to carry it on."

March 2017

* Born in 1939, Reginald Foster died on Christmas Day 2020, three years after the original publication of this essay in *The New Criterion*.

Homer in the tropics

Alexander Suebsaeng

I WAS STILL in the sixth form when I first heard of Kamuzu Academy. My Greek teacher had read about a school in the African bush where pupils in boaters and Eton collars sweated over Homer and Virgil in the glare of the tropical sun. The school, he told us, was the obsession of Malawi's dictator, Dr. Hastings Kamuzu Banda. Banda wanted his country's most gifted children to learn Latin and Greek as a preparation for political leadership. Equipped with the lessons and ideals of antiquity, they would one day govern with wisdom and moderation. Plato's ideal Republic would be reborn in central Africa.

The idea appealed to me, but I did not think of it again until many years later. I had just finished my Classics degree and the cold appetency of London was jarring after the languid delights of Oxford. I began looking for work in Africa, and one day a vacancy at Kamuzu Academy came up.

In all directions, vast, featureless plains extend to the horizon. For the length of the journey from the capital there are only small holdings of maize and cassava, a few tobacco plantations, the odd derelict trading-center, and scrub. The thatch roofs of mud-brick houses are reinforced, here and there, by scraps of plastic bag weighed down with stones. After many hours, you arrive at a dismal town with an empty shop, a bar/brothel, a defunct post office, and a "butchery," outside of which a fly-blown carcass twists slowly on a rope. But the tarmac continues. One mile further and you reach a gatehouse with a large illuminated sign: *Kamuzu Academy—Honor Deo et Patriae.*

A retired engineer told me how the site was chosen. Banda wanted the academy built beside the same *kachere* tree under which he had received his first lessons as a boy. And so he assembled a party of surveyors and architects and men with panga knives and led them into the bush. After three days of grubbing about, the tree was identified. The Foundation Myth was secure and work could begin. Bush was cleared, a dam was built, the school went up. At the opening ceremony in 1981, Banda arrived by helicopter in a three-piece Savile Row suit and Homburg hat. He knelt to drink from a brackish pool remembered from his childhood and then mounted a podium to address the expectant crowds. While he spoke in English, his strongman JZU Tembo translated into Chichewa. And as he proceeded to declaim page after page of Caesar's *De Bello Gallico* in Latin, Tembo remained unfazed: *mwamva zimene amene Kamuzu!* "You heard what Kamuzu said!" The crowds roared, an honor guard stood to attention, and throngs of dancing girls wailed and cavorted in adulation.

At its height, the academy consumed a third of the country's whole education budget. It was modeled on Eton and was to lack nothing. There was a Greek theater, a replica of the Library of Congress, a clock tower beside a lake arrayed with lilies, ornamental waterfowl, and monitor lizards. There were music rooms, a model farm, a golf course, and a cavernous refectory where grace would be said in Latin. The grounds encompassed lawns, gardens, sports fields, and parkland.

Nothing local—save the monitor lizards—was allowed to spoil the vision. Everything was imported—even the trees. The curriculum was strict: "anyone who does not want to learn Latin and Greek has no place at Kamuzu Academy." Both were compulsory to A-level. But most controversial was the staff: Banda was adamant that no black teacher would ever work at his school. Everyone had to know Latin, and everyone had to be white. Of course, staff meeting those criteria could be obtained only on an expatriate salary.

For several years, things functioned well. But the arrangement could last only as long as Banda's practically unlimited budget. When I arrived, over a decade had passed since the collapse of his regime. The school had survived, but as a shadow of its former self.

The masonry is cracked and the roofs leak water. The clocks have stopped and the school bells are broken. Through holes in the perimeter fence, the bush is encroaching. Hyenas bay and prowl in the gardens after dark.

And the humbler employees forage and hunt for swamp rats in the woods by the boarding houses.

In the Classics department, Latin and Greek texts and grammars, primers and dictionaries are casually heaped on the floor in extraordinary numbers. Library issue stamps and academy bookplates, inscribed with African names, record a succession of readers brought abruptly to an end. Dusty shelves teeter with neglected humanist bric-à-brac: masks for a Greek play, tattered journals, slides of archeological sites, and souvenir guides to museums in Europe.

Without government money, the academy now employs local staff and depends on fee-paying pupils. These are of the elite, their fathers Big Men: *wa-Benzi* (members of the new ruling class) from the capital, government officials, senior bureaucrats, local managers of wealthy NGOs. Flaunting their status is more important than academic achievement. And the humble new teaching staff pander to them cravenly.

A small cohort of new government scholars was reintroduced by one of Banda's successors in the presidency. Like the school's original pupils, they come mostly from the villages and conditions of often desperate poverty. They are keen and able, but few and exceedingly timid. Unfortunately, their integration with the fee-paying pupils is not always happy.

Each school house has an annual celebratory dinner to which pupils wear their own clothes. The fee-paying pupils arrive bathed in cologne and immodestly attired. The girls are over-painted and under-dressed. The boys exhibit the "gangster rap" style: oversized basketball shirts and sagging pants, fake gold chains and designer sunglasses, and loping gaits copied from MTV. The government scholars enter behind them, carefully dressed in shabby costumes put together from their village clothes. The girls are often in a monochrome Sunday-best dress obviously sewn by amateur hands. A few boys wear their school uniform for want of anything smarter. And all of them huddle out of the limelight in which their wealthier peers disport themselves triumphantly.

It is the fee-paying pupils' style of dress, with its associated music, idiolect, and culture, to which pupils (but also teachers, Big Men, even wealthier peasants) aspire after the slightest contact. This aesthetic glitters from satellite TV and the internet. Its sounds thunder from car stereos and grate from the tinny speakers of cellphones. Its costume can be bought off the back of a truck bringing cheap Chinese imports from Dar or Durban. It is a vision of idleness amid plenty that has nothing to do with the White Man. For them it is the new black American Dream.

It excites an enthusiasm that entirely eclipses anything local, which lacks status in comparison. The music is supposed to have its roots in Africa. True or not, the local culture withers in its wake.

Of course this lifestyle is far too remote to be attained by labor or ability. But a lucky few might be elevated to it by Fortune: the favor of a philanthropic singer-celebrity, selection by a passing football talent scout, perhaps even political office by the lottery of election. For the rest, though, the dream can only be played at.

The psychedelic quality of academy life is most powerful on Founder's Day. Depending on the identity and status of the guest of honor, there may be a welcoming party comprised of uniformed police and soldiery; regiments of women, swaying and ululating, dressed in *chitenjes* printed with the face of the Big Man; corpulent dark-suited ministers; Lords Spiritual, cassocked, surpliced, and tippeted in crimson and mauve; Paramount Chiefs in gay apparel; Traditional Authorities, High Commissioners, Chief Justices, Right Honourables, and Excellencies. The whole academy meanwhile assembles in spectacular array: straw boaters and buttons glimmer in the brilliant morning sunlight; the outlandish hoods and gowns, caps and tassels of diverse African universities compete with lurid creations run up in neon cloth by the academy tailor for those without degrees. You can even descry the purple and scarlet doctoral robes of Oxford. This procession marches through the grounds to the clock-tower. But formation is broken as the column reaches the bottleneck into the auditorium so that pupils and masters, bishops and dancing girls, sergeants and servants of state and doctors of philosophy are jumbled pell-mell as the cavalcade of black Mercedes rolls up at the porte-cochère to deliver the Big Man.

Waiting is an important part of the occasion: the higher the status of the guest, the longer everyone expects to wait. When the Big Man's second wife came, it was only after many hours that the stream of limousines began to pour through the gates. For the Big Man's own visit, the day was nearly at an end and his entourage had long since arrived, when the fire engine (taken from the international airport) and its police escort screamed in just ahead of two presidential helicopters. His entry into the vestibule prompted a deafening crash of amplified percussion as the director of music—clad in a golden suit—started the choir in his own arrangement of the "Hallelujah Chorus" for voices, electric guitar, drums, and a trombone. The Big Man approved and called for an encore. Later, the Chaplain was heard to remark on the great honor shown the academy by the obvious extravagance of the visit.

The visit of the Chinese ambassador was memorable. He cut a handsome figure in smart gray pinstripe with an improbable spray of violets in his buttonhole. He spoke at length, and at first the pupils grew restless. But his delivery was deliberate, charismatic, even portentous, and it was remarkable to watch his audience slowly captured: "China is both big and small; she is young and old, modern and ancient; she is rich and she is poor; China is . . ." After half an hour he rewarded their attention richly. At his signal the doors were flung open and a train of native bearers staggered in with crates of laptops and stereos, rackets and trainers, keyboards and plastic recorders, illustrated histories and Chinese textbooks. The head boy and head girl stood beside him as, crate by crate, the treasure was emptied out at his feet. The crowd's frenzy only died down as the ambassador called for silence to announce his final offering: a pair of Mandarin teachers and an annual university scholarship to the PRC.

How different the visit of Britain's High Commissioner: an unprepossessing figure in a crumpled suit who—it was well noted—arrived in a solitary Japanese pick-up. He lost his audience after twenty minutes of meekly reminding them of Britain's commitment to aid, to righting the wrongs of the past. He even solemnly disclaimed colonialism, but his audience seemed to have little idea what he was talking about and began muttering impatiently. (A few months later, he was expelled from the country for his [leaked] observation that the president was becoming intolerant of criticism.)

The more typical guest speaker, however, makes for an anticlimactic afternoon. Ludicrous preambles are followed by speeches of irremediable tedium: a histrionic sermon, an eccentric ministerial discourse on the price of cement, or perhaps only a few mumbled words of unfathomable import. Even so, if the speaker is important enough, the most platitudinous or even inaudible statements are enough to whip up the crowd. The din is appalling. The novelty wears off, and the heat and the sweat and the giddy surrealism make you queasy.

The only antidote, a friend explained to me, is the village-life to be found immediately outside the academy's fraying chain-link fence. We slip out during "I vow to thee, my country," and are presently at his maize farm. The site is beautiful and affords an enormous view of fields thick with flourishing crops, a patch of sunken marshy wood, and mountains in the distant haze.

We stroll to a cluster of tiny dwellings where the tenants live and the ageless activities of village life go on: sowing, tending, and harvesting of crops; hewing of wood; drawing of water. The huts are well wrought, with tidy thatch and a clean *khonde* for sitting out. And they are set in a clearing, meticulously swept, and bordered with fruit trees. Here we are entertained, amid long shadows, by a trio of musicians who play finely on guitars fashioned from refuse. The moon is already risen as the sun plunges, red and huge, over the distant hills.

It is idyllic, but it is also a world of great and obvious insecurity. The harvest may or may not be sufficient unto the year ahead. And there is a broader context of land shortage, dependency on (subsidized) fertilizer, and a population predicted to double again in the next twenty years. For the boys in the village there is often nothing to do except help a little with the fields—but with so many hands and so little land, there is a lot of what is descriptively termed "just staying." The girls are preoccupied from an early age with the bearing and mothering of children. For villagers there is so little access to any cash economy that calculation of GDP *per capita* is academic.

It is to this world of beauty and hardship that the government scholars return at the end of each term—and then for good after taking their A-levels. Even for those who do well, opportunities are scarce. A few jobs exist in government and the banks, but it would be naive to imagine that these are won by merit. Private enterprise is almost non-existent. The NGOs support a tiny, artificial middle class that depends on foreign donation. Most return to the land.

One morning in the last few weeks of term, "Nearer, my God, to thee" is sung at assembly. This is the signal to everyone that the senior staff are about to leave and that anyone with means should quickly do the same. The fee-paying pupils are collected in clusters by chauffeurs sent up from the capital in a flurry of social anxiety—the higher the status of the parents, the earlier before the end of term their children should depart.

The electricity and water supply become more than usually intermittent; the kitchens stop attempting to serve anything besides maize porridge; paper, pencils, and chalk run out; and the ancillary workers vanish.

The last claims to authority over the boarding houses are surrendered. Handfuls of pupils wander aimlessly through the grounds; a few others are paddling in a half-drained swimming pool. The sound of a single lesson in an almost deserted classroom echoes round the courtyard.

Of course, the government scholars are still there, bivouacking in the dormitories. They are the last to leave, in faltering buses hired to convey them up and down the length of the country and deposit them along the tarmac at the point closest to their homes.

Amongst them is Kondwani—probably my best pupil. Before he goes, I hand him a lexicon and a Greek anthology. There is always some uncertainty as to whether the government will in fact support its scholars through the following year—but we do not touch on this. Instead, I urge him to find time for reading over the holiday and to keep up Greek prose composition next year. Then I bid him farewell. His lexicon balanced on his head, he walks towards the bus that will take him back to the torrid sugar plantations of the south and his widowed mother.

I went home to begin a different life in England. But Kondwani, I learn, did indeed return to the academy and is currently reading *Iliad* XXIV for A-level with a colleague of mine. "What is the point in studying Classics?" In England, the question is often sarcastic. But of an African context, it is usually asked conscientiously. To be sure, an answer is difficult. There are a few practical benefits, but real engagement with the subject is rare. Indeed for most, total incomprehension is the standard.

Mandarin is the new prestige subject at the academy. It will be interesting to follow the consequences of this experiment. So far teaching Chinese characters looks to be even more futile than the "baleful signs" of Greek and Latin. But perhaps with time, something will be achieved. But then perhaps with time Banda's vision might have succeeded.

Things fall apart in Africa, it has been observed, faster or at least more obviously than elsewhere. The result is the chaos of change, decay, and novelty with which the continent is famously—even proverbially—associated. Paradoxically, this evokes a powerful sense of changelessness: against what is constant—even and especially constant change—all human activity appears feeble, all ambition futile. And from this comes a feeling of liberation from utilitarian concerns, from the prejudices of profit and loss that trouble one elsewhere. There is no justification—but there is also no need of justification. In such a place, you grow accustomed to the bizarre and accept it as you accept the terrible and the wonderful.

In that huge uncluttered landscape, in its limpid air, perhaps even under a *kachere* tree, you see a small boy reading of Priam's embassy to Achilles—and only rejoice in it.

March 2015

IV. Discriminations

Piero della Francesca: the world knew him not

Marco Grassi

In one of his famous letters, the Roman official Pliny the Younger—who surely knew his way around the empire—wrote to a friend describing the upper Tiber Valley: "You will experience great pleasure when observing this region from the heights of its surrounding hills: rather than a territory, you will think, in fact, that you are gazing at a painting executed with incredible skill—such is its rich variety and felicitous arrangement [of features]—that your eyes will be satisfied wherever they dwell." It would be another thirteen centuries before Piero della Francesca, a native of that valley, painted the picture that Pliny imagined. He was born about 1412 in Sansepolcro, a small, reasonably prosperous provincial town, often a pawn in the shifting alliances of Central Italy's larger seigniorial city-states. Although Piero visited Florence, Ferrara, and possibly Venice—he also received a number of important commissions from the churches and courts of Arezzo, Urbino, Rimini, and even Rome—the topography of Sansepolcro and its surroundings always remained the informing locus of his art. It appears, somewhat timidly, in what may be the artist's very first surviving work (the *Madonna and Child*, Alana Collection) and positively dominates his last (*The Nativity*, National Gallery, London).

Piero's affection for his hometown is not surprising; his large, well-to-do family was firmly rooted there, and Sansepolcro awarded him early, important commissions (*The Resurrection* and the *Misericordia* polyptych). But despite having been occasionally described as a "provincial," he was anything but. Like Lorenzo Lotto about a century later, Piero traveled almost continually. Although both artists have been identified by their regional origins, they were never particularly active in those local contexts. Piero is no more "Florentine" than Lotto is "Venetian." Each derived from their travel experiences a diverse mix of influences that were then transformed into very personal, almost idiosyncratic, visual idioms. Similarly, neither served long apprenticeships with established masters nor, becoming masters themselves, formed lasting relationships with pupils.

This outsider status unfortunately did not serve Piero well in his posthumous standing among early Renaissance artists. Vasari, that ultimate insider and committed celebrant of all things Florentine, was reasonably even-handed in his judgment, but, of course, he was from Arezzo, only an afternoon's ride from Sansepolcro, and home to Piero's supreme masterwork, the frescoed apse of the church of Saint Francis, known as the Bacci Chapel (*The Legend of the True Cross*). Nonetheless, from Vasari's perspective, Piero appeared hopelessly old-fashioned in comparison to Raphael and Michelangelo. A scant sixty years after Piero executed one, possibly two, frescoes in the papal "Stanze" of the Vatican, Pope Julius II ordered them destroyed and replaced by Raphael—an act of either reckless desecration or insuperable self-assurance and chutzpah.

Things only got worse for Piero's legacy. By the mid-eighteenth century, *The Resurrection* fresco in Sansepolcro's city hall (the town's very symbol as "Holy Sepulchre") had been whitewashed and, within sixty years, the giant *Sant'Agostino* polyptych was cut up and dispersed. These actions came on the heels of the migrations abroad (to London) of two other capital works from Sansepolcro, *The Nativity* and *The Baptism of Christ*. As late as 1896, the Florentine art dealer Elia Volpi was negotiating with the owners of Piero's former house for the purchase of the *Hercules* fresco. The deal was quickly done and, as a result, the artist's only surviving treatment of a classical subject found its way to Boston.

The two painstakingly reasoned and illustrated treatises on perspective and geometry to which Piero devoted himself later in life fared little better. The first was overshadowed by its prototype, published by Leon Battista Alberti some twenty years earlier; the second was mostly cribbed in the early sixteenth century by the more famous Luca Pacioli. Once rediscovered in the wake of renewed interest in Piero's art in the later nineteenth century, these remarkable manuscript texts revealed the full range and extent of the artist's intellectual engagement in the creative process as well as the novelty of some of his insights. Piero suddenly emerged from obscurity and was recognized as a worthy predecessor to Leonardo and Vasari, the two emblematic figures identified with the

Renaissance transformation of the humble painter/craftsman into the modern artist/philosopher.

Despite Karel van Mander's failure to mention Piero in his monumental 1604 compilation of European painters, a smattering of references to the artist began to appear at the beginning of the nineteenth century. Notable is Luigi Lanzi's favorable judgment, although still ranking Piero below Masaccio, Perugino, and, of course, Raphael. As the diaspora of Piero's works suggests, the English were the first to become aware that, somehow, a great Italian painter of the Early Renaissance had gotten lost in the historical shuffle. The sense of excitement and discovery was enhanced by the fact that eighteenth-century Grand Tourists had, by and large, bypassed the Tiber Valley and the Adriatic provinces in their travels; they were areas not particularly rich in the classical antiquities so dear to those "enlightened" dilettanti.

One young Englishman who did take notice was Charles Lock Eastlake, a painter of middling talent who arrived in Rome in 1816 and stayed until 1830. It's not known where or when, in the course of his extensive Italian travels, Eastlake crossed paths with Piero, but he holds the distinction of having made the first mention of the artist in a published English text. By then, Eastlake had returned home and was no longer painting; he was well on his way to becoming not only the National Gallery's first Director (as "Sir Charles") but also a formidable influence on the developing taste for "early" painting. It is to Eastlake's insistence and perception that the National Gallery owes its two Piero masterworks (*The Baptism of Christ* and *The Nativity*). Not only did the aesthetics and perceived spirituality of the pre-Renaissance appeal to these Victorians; there was also, with Piero, a beguiling sense of mystery about a great artist whose memory and very identity appeared to be on the verge of extinction.

With Piero della Francesca almost everything had to be learned; the date of his birth, what his early training and working methods might have been, how and when he received his court and church commissions, and, finally, the identity of his pupils, had they actually existed. Some anecdotal details, such as his blindness in old age, survived in local lore but eventually proved elusive to verify. Essentially, Piero emerged from the past as that rarest of paradoxes, an artist of compellingly singular vision—rigorously coherent and consistent in the components of his imagery and therefore immediately recognizable in his relatively large body of surviving works—yet free of any readily identifiable geographic or stylistic attributes. Other than the recurring tropes—rural vistas to the Tiber Valley and the robust presence of its rustic but noble inhabitants—Piero's vision existed as if suspended in a cultural vacuum. Sansepolcro and, for that matter, not even Arezzo and the other centers where Piero is known to have worked, could claim well-defined local artistic "schools" or traditions. As a result, over the last century, there has been endless spirited art-historical debate as to how much is "Florentine," "Venetian," or even "Sienese" in Piero's art.

Ultimately, philology and iconography, those specifically art-historical disciplines, have yielded ever-diminishing returns in analyzing Piero della Francesca's art. Even the river of ink spilled in dissecting *The Flagellation*, that most enigmatic of Piero's images, has failed to shed much light on the unique phenomenon of this Early Renaissance masterpiece and the genius of its creator. The measured, indeed mathematical, construction and disposition of elements; the reasoned, perspectival clarity of fictive space; the unerring apportioning of light and shadow; all these allow instant *perception*, if not instant *understanding*. "Classic" is how such a forthright, yet idealized, representation of reality has often been described. Piero was classic (as opposed to classical) in the accuracy with which he analyzed the physical world and the rigor he exercised in transforming essential components of that world into two-dimensional images. These components never serve simply as anecdotal appearances, but were carefully selected to the exclusion of a potentially infinite range of options. It was a distinctly cerebral (as opposed to intuitive) process without which a knowledge of Euclidian geometry would have been impossible.

And what about those austere and flinty giants that inhabit Piero's world? The art historian Bernard Berenson called them "impersonal" and "impassable," untouched by human emotion; a quality that, he claimed, the figures share with those of the Parthenon pediments. The fact that they owe much of their potent *gravitas* to Masaccio has always been noted. Confirmation of this came in the mid-nineteenth century with the identification of a rare documentary entry mentioning the artist's name and establishing his presence in Florence in 1439. A recent further archival discovery tells us that by that date, however, Piero was already twenty-seven years old, well beyond his apprenticeship, only deepening the mystery of the artist's early formation. It's as if the majestic, silent, and self-aware creatures that appear in Piero's paintings alighted fully formed from another planet. They really look nothing like their Florentine elder cousins—nor much else in Central Italian art for that matter. In the end, the visual record of the works themselves and the studies he penned in his own hand have served to reveal the man and the artist far better than stylistic comparison or archival documentation.

Despite this—or perhaps because of it—over the last century, Piero's imagery and his texts have attracted the attention of art history's most formidable intellects, resulting in a steady stream of critical insights and opinions that have consecrated the artist as a central, albeit isolated, figure of the Italian Early Renaissance. The "Piero Itinerary" (Sansepolcro–Arezzo–Monterchi–Urbino) has become a well-established ritual for enthusiasts since long before the Second World War. The search for connections between the "proto-modern" Piero and Post-Impressionism has continued ever since Roger Fry pointed out the little-noticed fact that full-sized painted copies of two scenes from the Arezzo fresco cycle had hung in the École des Beaux-Arts since the early 1870s. The connection with Puvis de Chavannes was all too obvious. This, in turn, led to Seurat, reaching to Cézanne and eventually Picasso. In 1929, André Lhote went so far as to salute Piero as "the first Cubist"! Roberto Longhi, who contributed probably more than any other twentieth-century scholar to an understanding of Piero della Francesca, wholeheartedly subscribed to the "French connection" but also developed his own grand theory about the artist's far-reaching influences on later European painting—through the Venetians Giovanni Bellini and Antonello da Messina. While this view has not found universal acceptance, Longhi also rightly emphasized the significance of those reciprocal contacts with the art of Flanders probably initiated during Piero's visit to Ferrara between 1448 and 1450. These, and possibly even earlier experiences with Flemish painting, were to condition *the way* Piero painted for the rest of his long career.

By the mid-fifteenth century, the use of linseed oil as a painting medium—already the preferred technique in Northern Europe—was beginning to filter into Italy not only via Milan and Venice but through Angevin Naples as well. Piero, not having experienced a long shop apprenticeship in the prevailing Italian tempera tradition, must have realized the potentials of the new material, especially the possibility of creating finely detailed forms of solid, polished color and smooth, uninterrupted passages of transparent shadow. He took to the new technique at once, realizing that the resulting surfaces acquired a rich and saturated glow not obtainable with water-based tempera. There were, however, some problems. Faulty medium/pigment ratios often produced disfiguring cracks as the oil dried. Oil-based surfaces were also significantly more delicate, and certain pigments eventually became chemically unstable when mixed in oil. Moreover, Piero's experiments when working in fresco, particularly the use of a mixed "wet/dry" technique, proved to be a dangerous departure from the traditional Florentine *buon fresco.*

Unfortunately, time has taken its toll on many of the artist's works. The *Legend of the True Cross* frescoes were plagued almost from the beginning with cracks due to the unsteady walls of the Bacci Chapel. These, in turn, led to frightful infiltrations of humidity and the consequent formation of corrosive saltpeter deposits on the pictorial surfaces. Many of the panel paintings fared no better, few escaping brutal "cleanings" during the eighteenth and nineteenth centuries. More often than not these procedures were left in the hands of local artisans or, worse, churchwardens whose preferred "solvent" was caustic soda. One need only to stand in front of the majestic *Nativity* in London to realize how tragically it was abused; even the nearby and much-abraded *Baptism of Christ* has, by comparison, retained a reasonably strong pulse. The twentieth century did not spare further punishment of some of Piero's capital works with injuries now inflicted in aberrant exploits of modern "scientific conservation." A particularly melancholy result of such zeal is the *Madonna del Parto*, to which generations of "Piero pilgrims" paid homage in the tiny cemetery chapel at the gates of Monterchi, near Sansepolcro. The fresco, though detached from the wall in 1911, was soon wisely replaced in its original context. Definitively removed about twenty years ago, it has since resided as a forlorn exile in an antiseptic and nondescript "museum" environment in the village (closer, of course, to the restaurants and souvenir shops).

Less than a year after the Frick Collection's ambitious undertaking "Piero della Francesca in America" (see my exhibition note in *The New Criterion* of April 2013), the artist returns to New York with a selection of four works exhibited at the Metropolitan Museum in "Piero della Francesca: Personal Encounters." The equilibrium between the two

Fifth Avenue institutions is a bit lopsided when one considers that, of the seven works on view last year at the Frick, four actually belonged to that collection. Unfortunately, Piero seems to have eluded the Metropolitan's grasp despite the fact that Roger Fry, one of the artist's early champions, served briefly (starting in 1909) as that museum's Curator of European Paintings—and this at a time when several examples of the master's work were still on the market. And so, Fry's current successor as curator, Keith Christiansen, eagerly jumped at the chance of welcoming Piero, at least temporarily, to the Metropolitan when Italy's Ministry of Culture suggested the idea as part of a yearlong program of international events.

The tiny gathering of works, shown in splendid isolation in a separate gallery, surround one of Piero's supreme achievements; the so-called *Madonna of Senigallia* whose permanent home is now in Urbino. The modestly sized panel was probably executed as a commission for the ducal court of Urbino in the early 1470s. It may, therefore, be one of the artist's last works before he abandoned the practice of painting altogether, devoting the rest of his almost twenty years of life to theoretical writing and speculation. It is also one of the very few paintings by his hand (the other is the so-called "Montefeltro Altarpiece" now at the Brera in Milan) to have survived in exemplary condition. In the context of this mini-show, the *Madonna of Senigallia* serves as a very appropriate contrast and bookend to the *Madonna and Child*, which may very well be the earliest surviving work by the master and is now in a private New York collection. The painting has not been seen publicly for almost sixty years and has recently benefitted from a careful conservation campaign. We can now, despite its ruined state, assess a variety of fascinating references to what was happening in Florence in the 1430s when Piero visited the city. Particularly intriguing is a perspectival rendering of a facetted bowl at the rear of the panel that instantly calls to mind not only the famous drawings of Paolo Uccello but, more specifically, the *trompe l'oeil* intarsia shutters by Antonio Manetti in the north sacristy of the Florence Cathedral. The odd, almost accidental, presence of Piero's study on the panel attests to his early—and proficient—grasp of visual perception theories being formulated in the early Renaissance.

The other two paintings, also small works intended for private devotion, both feature Saint Jerome, although in conspicuously different attitudes. The earlier of the two is signed and dated 1450 and shows the ascetic Doctor of the Church in a verdant Tiber Valley landscape, not quite the "wilderness" of familiar tradition. Much reduced in effectiveness by brutal abrasion, the panel still suggests a sense of spatial depth conveyed by the careful placement of trees and receding clouds as perspectival "markers." The other rendering of the saint, although only slightly larger in size, represents a huge leap forward in terms of compositional sophistication. Saint Jerome is no longer the solitary hermit, but a biblical scholar in intense dialogue with a supplicant/pupil who kneels in profile before him. They are in an open landscape just outside the walled town of Sansepolcro, with the receding Apennine range behind them; it is the very picture of a calm, reasoned discourse between two humanists. Two small details, once noticed, almost shock for their verisimilitude: the cast shadows of the saint's crossed legs and the astonishing foreshortening of his proper right hand as it turns a page. It is difficult to imagine that such pitch-perfect imagery could spring to life without a single preparatory drawing, though none has ever been identified. Research has shown that, at most, Piero may have transferred only some elements of his larger compositions by means of pricked cartoons, and always with virtually no revision or re-working. It is simply one of the many conundrums that still surround the life and work of this genius and contribute to the powerful spell he casts on our imagination.

Meanwhile, the exegeses on every aspect of the man and the artist continue. The latest addition to the long list is *Piero's Light: In Search of Piero della Francesca: A Renaissance Painter and the Revolution in Art, Science, and Religion* by Larry Witham. The author grapples with a sweeping retelling of the known story, not only in the context of Italian early Renaissance culture but also in terms of how that story was interpreted in nineteenth- and twentieth-century criticism. It is in this latter perspective that Witham's contribution is most illuminating, particularly the chapter entitled "Piero and Modernity." While most informed readers may enjoy hearing again about the sensation caused by the Byzantine Emperor and his court at the Council of Florence in 1439, or of how neo-Platonism informed Florentine humanism, many will learn for the first time about the Marxist, Freudian, and even Lacanian interpretations with which, over the past century, scholars have gone after Piero. Witham, not himself an art historian, is careful to avoid judging the validity of such speculations, whereas the late and eminent John Pope-Hennessy, knowing all too well of what he spoke, called one of these—Carlo Ginzburg's fanciful *Enigma of Piero*—"a tissue of tendentious nonsense." The accretion of such conjectures and assumptions has adhered to Piero's legacy like barnacles, obdurate and perverse.

With a good percentage of the artist's known work exhibited in the span of a few blocks on Fifth Avenue, New Yorkers have been given a rare opportunity to discover and explore for themselves Piero's realm of magical reality guided only by their eyes and imagination.

March 2014

Raphael, interrupted

James Hankins

Poor Raphael! This year, the five-hundredth anniversary of his death, was to have been his year of glory. After major exhibitions of Michelangelo in 2018 and Leonardo da Vinci in 2019, the museum world was in the midst of celebrating the third member of the glorious trinity of High Renaissance art. Then fear of a new coronavirus forced museums everywhere to take down their banners, chase away visitors, and close their doors. Lectures and conferences, canceled! "Raphael and His Circle" at the National Gallery in Washington, closed! "Raphael: The Teacher and His Pupils" at the Musée Condé outside of Paris, closed! Will they reopen once the panic has passed? Nobody knows. At least the currently shuttered "Raffaello" at the Scuderie del Quirinale in Rome has now announced plans to reopen on June 2. The last has been billed as the largest show ever dedicated to Raphael, with over two hundred masterpieces, including one hundred paintings and drawings by Raphael himself, lent by the Uffizi, the Louvre, the Prado, and London's National Gallery, among others. And there is hope that reason will return to its throne in time for London's National Gallery to open its doors in October for what will be the second-largest exhibition of the year.

It's a kind of tragic coincidence, or perhaps poetic injustice, that celebrations of Raphael's achievement were interrupted by a deadly virus. It was a viral pneumonia ripping through the papal court that killed Raphael himself, aged thirty-seven, on April 6, 1520. The overworked and exhausted artist was carried off, biographers tell us, by a *grandissima febbre*. His greatest patron, the Medici pope Leo X, died suddenly of pneumonia a year and a half later, aged forty-six. The most fruitful partnership between artist and patron in High Renaissance Rome had lasted just over seven years. Among the casualties was Raphael's career as an architect, cut off just as it was beginning to blossom.

Raphael, interrupted

Earlier in his artistic life, Raphael was chiefly known as a highly accomplished painter, a maker of tender religious scenes in oil as well as the breathtaking visions of ancient philosophy, theology, and the arts frescoed onto the walls of the *Stanze*, the pope's apartments in the Vatican palace. In 1514, however, Pope Leo pushed the young artist's career in a new direction when he chose him to be chief architect of New St. Peter's Basilica, following the death of its first architect, Bramante. Raphael had long had an interest in architecture and had dabbled in a few projects before 1514, but the new appointment made him, in effect, the leading architect in Christendom.

There was no greater symbol of the cultural confidence of High Renaissance Rome than New St. Peter's. Pope Julius II's decision to build an enormous new church of classical design in the capital of Christianity had been nothing short of audacious. Its construction required the pontiff to tear down the most venerable church in Christendom, Old St. Peter's Basilica, built by the emperor Constantine in the fourth century on the ruins of Nero's circus. According to one tradition, the basilica commemorated not only St. Peter's place of burial but also the place where he had been martyred. The old church was filled with relics of the saints, tombs of popes and martyrs, and famous works of art, including beautiful ancient mosaics and fourteenth-century frescoes by Giotto. All this had to be torn down for the new church, a monument (said many) to the vanity of Pope Julius. Certainly no one could accuse that pope of an excess of humility. Under the central crossing of the new basilica and over the tomb of St. Peter, where the *baldacchino* and high altar now stand, Julius's chief architect, Bramante, planned to erect a three-story sculptural installation with over forty sculptures, all created by Michelangelo, as a tomb for—who else?—Pope Julius himself.

Although that part of the project, thankfully, was in the end set aside, Leo X and subsequent popes continued to pour vast resources into building the basilica. It remained the centerpiece of papal patronage of the arts for 150 years. So why did Pope Leo, the age's most intelligent patron, appoint young Raphael as its architect, a man with little experience in building design? Readers of Giorgio Vasari, Raphael's principal biographer, could be excused for asking that question. Vasari praises Raphael's painting to the skies but barely mentions his involvement with architecture. Many modern scholars have dismissed Raphael the architect as a mere epigone of Bramante, a master builder *manqué* who completed no major monuments. Most connoisseurs of art, if they think of

Raphael's buildings at all, think of the architectural backgrounds in paintings like the *School of Athens* (1509–11), where ancient philosophers teach and debate on the steps outside a breathtakingly large, centrally planned church, strongly reminiscent of Bramante's designs for New St. Peter's.

Raphael's contemporaries, though, did not think of him as a failed or derivative architect. For them he was a man just hitting his stride in a new art when death brought an end to his many projects. Only a few petty detractors thought Leo had made a mistake. A line in the inscription on Raphael's tomb in the Pantheon extols him for "enhancing the glory of Popes Julius and Leo with his works in painting *and architecture*" [italics mine]. The humanist literati who composed dozens of poetic epitaphs for him after his death mourned the interruption of his great project to reconstruct the built environment of ancient Rome. The humanist Celio Calcagnini, writing to a friend just before Raphael's death, described him not only as the "prince of all painters" but also as "such an assiduous architect that he discovers and perfects those things that the cleverest talents considered impossible." Raphael, he noted, even comments on the text of Vitruvius—the great Roman authority on architecture—with a charm that excuses his shrewd criticisms of that author's limitations.

The greatest modern authority on Raphael, John Shearman, believed that the eclipse of Raphael's fame as an architect was more than undeserved: it was a tragic injustice that architectural historians should do their best to rectify. The task is by no means easy, since so many of Raphael's architectural projects were destroyed or left unfinished, to be completed by other hands. Reconstructing his ideas from drawings, early engravings, documents, literary testimony, and the surviving physical evidence is a delicate and daunting scholarly task which few today are qualified to undertake.

Nevertheless, when one considers that Raphael only began to erect buildings to his own designs in 1512, aged twenty-seven, it is remarkable how many projects he did undertake, all the while maintaining his extraordinary productivity as a painter. He built two large palaces in the Borgo, both of which were torn down, one to make room for Bernini's colonnade in the seventeenth century, the other when the Via della Conciliazione was laid out in 1937. He left plans for at least two more palaces that were modified and built by other architects. He began construction on two villas, the grand Villa Madama in a park north of the Vatican, now the resort of Italian diplomats, and an exquisite *gioello*, the Villa Lante, on the Gianicolo. The Villa Madama project was carried forward after Raphael's death by his most accomplished disciple, Giulio Romano, who also finished the Villa Lante in 1523–24. In both cases he made major alterations to Raphael's original design. The huge, elegant stables Raphael built for the banker Agostino Chigi at his *villa suburbana* were torn down in 1808. The small church of San Eligio degli Orefici, his earliest church design, was radically altered and finished by his collaborators Baldassare Peruzzi and Bastiano da San Gallo. He left competition designs for San Giovanni de'Fiorentini in Rome and for the façade of San Lorenzo, the Medici church in Florence; neither were built.

Of all his work, only the chapel he built for the Chigi family in Santa Maria del Popolo gives us a real sense of what might have been. Inspired in its main lines by the Pantheon, the space was designed as a harmonious classical armature on which to display the arts of painting, sculpture, *pietra dura*, and (originally) mosaic. It would thus commemorate Agostino Chigi's unmatched career as a patron of the arts. It makes brilliant use of colored marbles and elegant ornamentation creatively adapted from the antique. Its craftsmanship is exquisite. But even this chapel had to be completed by other hands. It was not finished before the middle of the seventeenth century.

What of New St. Peter's, Raphael's chief responsibility as an architect? Raphael had nowhere near the impact on the final state of the building that Michelangelo was to have in his eighteen years as chief architect. Raphael left just a few drawings, tomb designs, and a new floor plan. But that floor plan turned out to be of immense significance for the building's future. Bramante had conceived of a centrally planned church inspired ultimately by the Pantheon—the most fully preserved classical temple in Renaissance Rome. Circular or centrally planned churches, reflecting Platonic principles, had been the ideal for Christian classical architecture from the time of Brunelleschi and Alberti in the quattrocento down to Leonardo da Vinci and Bramante in the High Renaissance. Raphael's design, by contrast, called for extending one of the four wings of the church into a nave, thus forming a Roman cross, to be entered through a monumental colonnaded porch. In other words, he took the key step that began the church's evolution into the basilican form we see today.

Raphael's boldness in modifying Bramante's designs was not some dilettantish flight of fancy but, like all his mature work, the result of careful, disciplined study of the antique. Humanists since Petrarch had mourned the destruction of Rome's ancient fabric and dreamt of restoring the city's physical grandeur. Earlier pontiffs such as the humanist pope Nicholas V had begun to rebuild Rome in a more classical style. But it was Raphael, supported by Pope Leo and his humanist advisers, especially Baldesar Castiglione and Angelo Colocci, who undertook the serious work of surveying the ruins of Rome and attempting to reconstruct the appearance of the ancient city district by district, building by building. It was this quasi-philological project that fired the imaginations of Renaissance literati and led them to praise Raphael as the greatest architect of the age.

Yet Raphael's *Plan of Rome*, with its reconstructions of major monuments—temples, baths, theaters, palaces, fora, and public buildings—was not simply a learned contribution to antiquarian studies. It was a practical project, designed to serve architects and patrons interested in building in the modern classical style, the Renaissance style. In his work as a painter Raphael was famous for collecting the designs of other artists throughout Italy and making their inventions and techniques his own. Michelangelo and his coterie sneered at him, with appalling injustice, as a mere magpie, stealing his best ideas from other artists. As an architect Raphael practiced the same kind of recombinant classicism, choosing elements from innumerable antique structures but reassembling them in harmonious, creative ways. He understood, as modern educational theory does not, that creativity is the child of knowledge.

In his *Plan of Rome*, Raphael's goal was to go beyond the basic grammar of the classical orders he had reconstructed from Vitruvius, and to populate a vast memory palace with classical forms and ornaments. In this way, like Socrates, he would stand as midwife to the genius of architects and *disegnatori* of every kind. Had it been completed, it would have become the greatest treasure-trove of classical style ever assembled. But this visionary project, too, was still in its early stages when Raphael's life was cut short. It, too, would be carried out later by less skilled hands—by scholar-architects like Pirro Ligorio and antiquarians like Jean-Jacques Boissard. Raphael was, as John Shearman concluded in a classic study, "the unluckiest of all the great Renaissance architects."

June 2020

Unmaking the Met

James Panero

The Metropolitan Museum of Art reopened to the public in late August. Those of us who lined up outside early shared a special sense of relief at its return. As goes the Met, so goes the metropolis. Since its founding in 1870 all the way up to March 2020, the museum had closed for at most only three consecutive days. The COVID-19 pandemic kept it shuttered for six months. As spring turned to summer, the effects of this closure became palpable. The lockdown combined with social unrest to rock the foundations of our institutions. The Met's reopening therefore seemed to signal a restoration. It was a sign of resilience against a backdrop of unease.

Since the reopening, I am not the only one who has been unable to stay away. Time at the museum can do wonders for an otherwise crumbling sense of loss and dislocation. Each visit builds on the next. New discoveries add to familiar friends. I move from one room to the other across the landscape of time and space without any particular path or destination. Greek terracotta leads to the art of the Sahel, which deposits me with French portrait busts. German metal appears next to British glass. Italian armor opens up onto American nude sculpture. Head up and make a right at Robert Joyce's tall clock and land in the art of Kyoto. "What's the best way to get back to Egypt?" I ask a guard. "Go through Asia," she helpfully replies. Somewhere among Archaic art from Cyprus, I realize I have lost my bearings. At such a point, I consider my visit a success. I am exactly where I want to be.

Unlike any other institution, the Metropolitan is the museum of the metropolis. It is a city in the city, a cosmos for the cosmopolitan, expansive and uncontainable, a home for culture owned by no one person and belonging to all. "It feels like New York," my young son tells me after a recent visit. "It feels like we are back home." Not named for a single patron, or place, or style, the Met has achieved, beyond all expectation, the Enlightenment idea of the encyclopedic museum. It is about as close as you can get to that "ideal museum," as the founding trustee George Fisk Comfort described it in 1870, one that is "cosmopolitan in its character" presenting the "whole stream of art-history in all nations and ages." The Met set out to be "worthy of this great metropolis and of the wide empire of which New York is the commercial center," the civic leader William Cullen Bryant declared at its inception. Through a history of dedicated leadership, dutiful scholarship, and astonishing private beneficence, such ambitions have been more than realized.

Five years ago, I spent a day traversing every room at the museum, checking off each room number as I went. It took seven hours and twenty thousand steps, or about ten miles of walking to visit all four-hundred-odd rooms. The experience took me to corners of the collection I would not otherwise think to see. I ended up gravitating to a hidden corridor with Egyptian Middle Kingdom objects from Lisht and Thebes. Far off in another room, I lingered in the Chinese Treasury with intimate works of the late Ming and Qing dynasties, including a wall of snuff bottles. In my mind, bits of Roman glass started to melt into the colorful assembly of American glassmaking in the visible storage at the other corner of the museum. With amazingly varied results, across its two million square feet of space, the Met puts on display a particular cultural equation. The nineteenth-century Viennese art historian Alois Riegl called it the *Kunstwollen*—a "will to art." What we find at the Met is a sum of humanity's creative urges.

Today I seek out this urge with a greater sense of urgency. If 2020 has revealed anything, it is the contingent nature of seemingly permanent things. The Met is an ocean liner of culture, one that conveys the world to America's port. Over its history, the institution has more than proven its seaworthiness as a vessel that mostly stays true to course, not easily affected by prevailing winds or swamped by rogue waves. But even our mightiest institutions can take on water and list. Our institutions can also be easily scuttled from within, perhaps under the mistaken impression that they ride too high in the water, or simply that the ocean would be better off with a new addition to the sea floor.

The year 2020 was meant to be the Met's jubilee. With a season of planned festivities celebrating 150 years in existence, museum attendance might easily have exceeded the seven million visitors that pressed through its doors in 2019. An anniversary exhibition called "Making The Met, 1870–2020" was even set to open on March 30; its scholarly catalogue was already printed and in circulation by spring. Instead, the pandemic closures hit just days before this exhibition's gala preview. As weeks turned to months and riots hit the streets, there were moments when one wondered if our institutions would make it to 2021. The museum projected an annual shortfall of $150 million as it laid off 20 percent of its staff.

Now, just because the Metropolitan has reopened, this does not mean its operations have returned to normal. Visiting hours are more limited. Curators and employees are still largely forbidden from returning to their offices. Thanks to timed tickets and the requirements of social distancing, the museum's galleries are often now mercifully unpopulated when open. At the same time, with the spigot of foreign tourism clamped shut, the turnstile revenue on which the Met has grown ever more dependent may not return for some time.

But beyond the economic losses and the interruptions of the pandemic, a cloud of doubt now hangs over the institution. There has never been a moment of lower confidence in American museums than now. Against a backdrop of alarming cultural convulsions, the Met has not shown itself immune to political upheavals. In recent years our great public treasure house has presented its abundance as an embarrassment of riches. Now its hand-wringing, false confessions, and aesthetic effacements have begun to cast a pall over the very idea of its encyclopedic mission.

The question now is whether the obsessions of the moment will continue to undermine the institution. Or will present realities inspire a reaffirmation of the museum's resolve as a solid foundation in shifting sands? The anniversary season and its anniversary exhibition, now finally available to view, should encourage us to take stock of the museum's historical achievements in even sharper relief. We should also consider whether this fraught year represents a temporary bump in the museum's history or an inflection point in its upward trajectory.

On its anniversary, what is most remarkable about the Met is not its old age but its relative youth. At a mere one hundred and fifty years old, the museum is a surprisingly modern creation. Because it presents the full history of art across a complex of buildings designed in a wide range of architectural styles, the museum can feel many millennia older. That it was all created not by the actions of church or state but through private contributions is an even more unusual achievement in the history of culture.

With 250 works from the collection presented in a rather overworked display, "Making The Met" requires repeated viewing. The extensive exhibition catalogue ably complements its representative objects and helps to fill out the storyline. Of course, the history of the Metropolitan is best told in full, across its sprawling Fifth Avenue campus as well as its ethereal Cloisters in northern Manhattan, with its collection of Medieval art and architecture. The anniversary show, organized by Andrea Bayer and Laura D. Corey, nevertheless does well to feature the leaders, architects, and especially the benefactors who, indeed, "made the Met." The exhibition leads us to look at the permanent collection in a new light. One place to start is the bequest name and accession date for each work on view. After all, not one of the 1.5 million objects now in the museum originated in its permanent collection. Nor was that grand Fifth Avenue edifice a foregone conclusion when civic-minded men called out for a new museum in the efflorescence of American spirit that followed the conclusion of the Civil War. They made it all out of nothing, and they gave it to us.

The immediate post-war period saw the founding of encyclopedic museums in Boston, Philadelphia, and Chicago in rapid succession. New York's iteration began at a Fourth of July party at Le Pré Catelan in Paris celebrating the ninetieth anniversary of the signing of the Declaration of Independence. "It was time for the American people to lay the foundation of a National Institution and Gallery of Art," the New York attorney John Jay, the grandson of the first Chief Justice of the United States, urged his assembled countrymen in 1866. They formed a group on the spot to do just that. Back in New York in 1869 at the Union League Club, where Jay was president, he tasked its Art Committee to rally the city's other civic associations to the cause of forming an "amply endowed, thoroughly constructed art institution, free alike from bungling government officials and from the control of a single individual."

It helped that an eastern quadrant of Central Park, hemmed in by two reservoirs and two crosstown transverses and originally intended as a parade ground, had recently been set aside for a museum in Frederick Law Olmsted and Calvert Vaux's "Greensward Plan" of 1857. As the

Met was granted this parcel of park land for its new private museum in the public trust, Vaux and a third park designer, Jacob Wrey Mould, planned the museum's first building in the very center of this location.

From the start, the museum's facilities proved to be insufficient for its ambitions. The Gothic Revival design of the original wing, later called "Building A" and now the Medieval Court, was deemed outmoded even by the time of its opening in 1880 under the Met's first director, Luigi Palma di Cesnola, a colonel in the Civil War and a former American consul to Cyprus. The many subsequent expansions of the Met then grew out of this central core building, just as the arrondissements of Paris spiraled out, nautilus-shaped, from the premier of the Louvre, eventually surrounding it. In 1888 Theodore Weston covered Building A's southern face with a classical addition. In 1902 Richard Morris Hunt added his grand Beaux-Arts entrance to the east, facing Fifth Avenue; over the following fifteen years McKim, Mead & White extended Hunt's street line to the northern and southern extent of the plot's original designation. Since 1908, a century of infill has completed McKim's master plan, in scope if not in style. Initiated by the board president C. Douglas Dillon and the director Thomas Hoving, a 1970 revision by Kevin Roche, John Dinkeloo and Associates eventually sealed the museum envelope to the north, west, and south in a rectangle of concrete and glass. As the museum has reached the limits of its footprint granted by the city, all new amendments are now made within this existing portfolio.

Rather than the unity we see in John Russell Pope's National Gallery of Art, the result at the Met has been a conglomeration of various architectural styles and meandering pathways that well reflects the confederation of departments making up the museum's durable curatorial foundations. Recent efforts have further revealed the evolution of the Met's design, such as the reuse of Weston's south façade for the interior wall of the Carroll and Milton Petrie European Sculpture Court of 1990 and the restoration of one of the original 1880 Victorian staircases in 1995. More evidence of the museum's own history appears in Vaux and Mould's pointed stone archways, which pop out of a wall in a second floor hallway and also lead on to the 1975 Lehman Wing. In 2008 the museum even repurposed the foundations of Hunt's 1902 grand staircase into a new crypt for Byzantine art.

As with this combination of styles, a constellation of benefactors, working with the museum's directors, has underwritten the Met's making and helped fulfill its encyclopedic ambitions. J. Pierpont Morgan was undoubtedly its brightest star when he became the museum president in 1904. His largesse funded the museum's Fifth Avenue expansions and added thousands of works to its treasury. He also underwrote, anonymously, its first archaeological excavations, which led to one of the most significant collections of Egyptian art in the world. In 1911 a cartoon in *Puck* magazine illustrated one aspect of Morgan's powers of attraction. In the depiction, Morgan can be seen straddling the globe above New York. As he holds up a magnet in the shape of a dollar sign, the world's treasures are conveyed across the ocean.

A more charitable understanding would be to see this as an example of the great beneficence of capital in the service of culture, unlike those European collections created through the church, the state, or force of arms. "He was as unselfish with his treasures of art as he was with his fortune," stated the museum's memorial tribute to Morgan in 1913. "He believed that the happiness of a whole people can be increased through the cultivation of taste, and he strongly desired to contribute to that end among his own countrymen." Beyond attracting the "best of historical European culture" to his American museum, Morgan's charitable magnetism attracted more donors and dollars to the growing institution. "That a man known universally for his acumen in finance should devote both time and talent to the active administration of a museum of art placed such institutions on a new footing," Winifred Howe wrote in her 1946 history of the museum. "Other men of affairs decided that art was worthy of their attention, even their collecting, and the Museum deserving of their support."

"Making The Met" features some of these other supporters who made significant contributions to the history of the museum. The Met's board president Robert de Forest, along with his wife Emily, spearheaded the creation of the American Wing, which opened in 1924, with their own collection and funds, the first such expansion underwritten by donor initiative. The Rockefeller family has contributed over generations. John D. Rockefeller, Jr., created and gifted the Cloisters in 1938—a history of its own that deserves more attention in the anniversary survey. His son Nelson seeded the Met's collection of art from Africa, Oceania, and the Americas with a gift of three thousand works in 1969 and underwrote a new wing named in honor of his son Michael, who died while researching the art of the Asmat people of Indonesia. Jacob S. Rogers was a steam locomotive manufacturer who left his estate to the museum in 1901 for the creation of an acquisitions fund. With his $5 million endowment, the Rogers Fund has supported the acquisition of many of the museum's greatest treasures. The Hearn Fund, the gift of George A. Hearn established in 1909 to purchase recent art for the museum, was likewise used to acquire John Singer Sargent's *Madame X* (1883–84) in 1916.

More times than not, from J. P. Morgan to Jayne Wrightsman, Benjamin Altman to Robert Lehman, the art at the Metropolitan has come through bequests from private collections. Henry (Harry) Osborne and Louisine Havemeyer were two such pioneers, collecting French modernism at a time when institutions like the Met showed little interest in it. Fortunately for the museum, Louisine bequeathed 1,967 objects from her family's farsighted collection in 1929. The collection included 112 works by Degas from the 1860s through the 1890s, as well as significant paintings by Rembrandt, Lucas Cranach, Veronese, and Bronzino. The Met's first painting by Pissarro came from them along with its first Cézanne and second Renoir. Examples of Roman glass and Islamic pottery also entered the collection, as well as Asian works in all media outnumbering any other category in the bequest.

For all of these successes, there were a handful of significant missteps. The case of Gertrude Vanderbilt Whitney was the most infamous example. In 1929 the museum rejected her collection of 500 works of American modernism along with the funds to house them. In 1931 she founded the Whitney Museum of American Art instead. Through the 1940s the Met continued to come up short with Whitney as the two museums attempted, and failed, to merge. Throughout the time of this planned agreement, the Metropolitan ceded the collecting of American modern art to its supposed partner institution. Similarly, one-time exchange agreements with the Museum of Modern Art and the American Museum of Natural History prevented the Metropolitan from pursuing collections of modernism as well as prehistoric and "primitive" art through its formative years.

Over time, the history of collecting at this encyclopedic museum has been determined by an ever-expanding definition of art worthy of the metropolis. Each revision might add a new volume to the book, new work for the collection, a new wing for the building, and a new department for curation. There was a time when even American painting was overlooked at this most American of museums. Modern art, photography, musical instruments, the decorative arts, Asian art, and the other non-Western arts have all become concerted later additions to the big book. Up through the three-decade tenure of Philippe de Montebello, who retired in 2008, the leaders of the museum have largely balanced this expansion with discernment and a respect for the vast collection and the benefaction put in their trust.

Today that balance is in question. The year 2020 has challenged the American museum as never before. Under cover of the pandemic, activists have used the energy of civil unrest to take aim at the Enlightenment ideal of the encyclopedic institution and the legitimacy of private museums in the public trust. Over the summer, wide-ranging petitions of social grievance were issued against the Detroit Institute of the Arts, the Virginia Museum of Fine Arts, the New Orleans Museum of Art, the Getty, SFMOMA, and the National Gallery of Art, among many other institutions, including the Metropolitan.

A survey of these episodes provides a background for the Metropolitan's own contemporary travails. In Detroit, activists denounced the 2019 exhibition of a painting by Paul Gauguin for not including sufficient trigger warnings and shieldings for schoolchildren. At the National Gallery, a petition castigated the museum as being the "last plantation on the National Mall" for its "exploitation and unfair treatment of employees identifying as BIPOC, LGBTQ, or womxn." At the Getty, an open letter blasted the museum, trust, and research institute for "frequent microaggressions experienced by staff and visitors of color to collecting practices and exhibition programs that glorify the work of white heterosexual cisgender male artists to the exclusion of others." At the Virginia Museum of Fine Arts, a petition demanded more exhibition labels addressing the "impact of oppressive systems" as well as the "territorial acknowledgment of Indigenous land occupied by VMFA buildings." At SFMOMA, staffers called out the seventy-five museum trustees as "culpable" for the "ongoing violent treatment of BIPOC, disabled, queer and trans employees and the continued development of a white supremacist exhibition and collecting program"; they also singled out the former board chairman Charles Schwab, the financier, for creating an "unsafe space for many employees and visitors" due to his support of President Donald Trump.

An inspiration for many of these petitions was an open letter signed in July by over a hundred past and present associates of the Metropolitan called "#fortheculture." This document accused New York's top cultural institutions of "covert and overt white supremacy" and "egregious acts of white violence toward Black/Brown employees." The signatories called for the installation of diversity personnel at all levels of governance and for museums to "support the movement to defund the police."

The specter of widespread staff revolt sent many museums' communications departments into overdrive. "Today we make clear our solidarity with Black Lives Matter and the protestors who are effecting change," responded the National Academy of Design, America's oldest honorary society for artists and architects, pledging to donate to "70+ bail funds, mutual aid funds, and activist organizations across the U.S." "The Frick Collection stands with all the individuals and organizations that seek justice, demand equality for all, and strive to end incidents of police brutality and systemic discrimination," responded the keepers of Henry Clay Frick's picture gallery, in a message that included links to Color of Change and Black Lives Matter "as resources for activism and involvement." To these responses the Metropolitan added its own statement: "Many of you have raised your voices on the streets and on social media, rightly demanding justice," wrote the current museum president and CEO, Daniel H. Weiss, and the director, Max Hollein, in an open letter to staff. "There is much that The Met needs to do, and we are dedicated to doing it. Black Lives Matter"—a response that was deemed insufficient by museum critics.

After a season of rhetorical gambits, recent actions have only fractured the fault lines of our collecting institutions more spectacularly in full public view. In September, four major museums chose to postpone a retrospective of the paintings of Philip Guston to 2024 due to perceived sensitivities around his imagery of Ku Klux Klansmen. The directors of Washington's National Gallery of Art, the Museum of Fine Arts, Houston, The Tate Modern in London, and the Museum of Fine Arts, Boston, announced the delay "until a time at which we think that the powerful message of social and racial justice that is at the center of Philip Guston's work can be more clearly interpreted." As the exhibition was presumably torpedoed by such cultural leaders as Darren Walker, the powerful activist president of the Ford Foundation and a new National Gallery trustee, who called the proposed exhibition "tone deaf," the directors demanded "additional perspectives and voices" due to the racial makeup of the exhibition's curators.

Artists and curators rallied against the postponement, potentially reducing the delay. Mark Godfrey, the senior Tate curator and co-organizer of the exhibition, led the charge for reinstatement by responding that it was "extremely patronising to viewers" for museums to be "scared of displaying and recontextualizing the work they had committed to for their programs." As a result of his outspokenness, he was suspended from his position at the museum in a chilling institutional response.

Fifty years ago, Hilton Kramer famously criticized Guston in *The New York Times* for his shift from abstraction to a faux-naif style, calling him "A Mandarin Pretending To Be A Stumblebum." Now for his anti-racist commentaries, Guston is banned by cultural mandarins who seek to undermine the encyclopedic museum by finding any cause to redact the entries available for display.

At the Baltimore Museum of Art, these mandarins have taken aim at their encyclopedic charge by subjecting their permanent collections to nothing less than racialized struggle sessions. Since his appointment in 2016, the BMA's white, British-born director, Christopher Bedford, has used critical race theory to guide his stewardship of the collection. For some white leaders, identity politics have turned into an engine and cover for their own advancement and protection at the expense of the public trust. "I'd rather make a mistake going a million miles an hour than do nothing," he said of his appointment. As he set about "re-correcting the canon," two years ago he made a diversity audit of his permanent collection and began pulling out the work of white artists to be exchanged for non-white ones. The practice of selling or "deaccessioning" duplicative works from a permanent collection to fund new acquisitions has long been accepted industry policy. Some of Bedford's new acquisitions at the BMA were indeed welcome additions to the collection. Nevertheless, using the race or gender of the artists as your determining criteria—depriving the museum and the people of Baltimore of works by Andy Warhol, Franz Kline, Kenneth Noland, and Jules Olitski—pushed the envelope of this understanding in a way that only accelerated Bedford's speeding ambitions.

For years progressive museum directors have been angling to monetize the vast resources of capital stored in the art in their trust. Fifty years ago, Thomas Hoving's horse-trading of the bequeathed art of Adelaide Milton de Groot so rattled the museum world that it attracted the attention of the New York attorney general and forever tightened deaccessioning standards—up until the current pandemic. This spring, the American Association of Art Museum Directors loosened its deaccessioning standards, temporarily, in the wake of COVID-19. The Brooklyn Museum and the Baltimore Museum both used the emergency measures as a pretext for a firesale of the permanent collection. This time at the BMA, the works on offer—by Andy Warhol, Brice Marden, and Clyfford Still—were canonical paintings singularly selected for the cash they would render at auction and public sale. This time the funds would not go to acquisitions but rather, in part, to "DAEI (diversity, accessibility, equity and inclusion) programs to restructure the museum's staffing" and "salary equity across the institution." Bedford suggested that criticism of his sales "is itself an investment in a system of operating institutions that is very deeply centered in white power and white privilege." "We are not seeking any longer the trust of the privileged white few that has enjoyed museums like the BMA historically," Bedford concluded. His wish for an erosion of trust came true at a million miles an hour.

Two weeks before the proposed Sotheby's sale, eleven former BMA board members submitted a letter to Maryland's secretary of state and its attorney general with concerns about the sales' potential conflicts of interest and other irregularities. Current and former BMA board members also publicly objected. The artists Adam Pendleton and Amy Sherald resigned from the board, seemingly in protest of the sale. Two former board chairs rescinded planned gifts totaling $50 million. On the morning of the scheduled auction, fourteen former presidents of the AAMD affirmed that long-term museum funding must not come from the sale of art and urged that the liquidation be reconsidered. The auction was reported to be off, then back on. As of press time, the museum announced it "must pause our plans to have further, necessary conversations"—even as it affirmed "our vision and our goals have not changed . . . we will do so through all means at our disposal."

In style if not yet in substance, the Metropolitan Museum of Art has embraced this new revisionism. There was a time when the Met served as a counterweight to the more buoyant excesses of its peer institutions. Since his appointment in 2018, the director Max Hollein has instead turned the opprobrium of the encyclopedic museum into his own core theme while staying silent on the national erosion of museum standards. Often he solicits contemporary artists to do his complaining. The son of a postmodern Viennese architect, Hollein's stock-in-trade is the unwanted contemporary intervention inserted into the historical fabric. When he was the young director of the Schirn Kunsthalle in Frankfurt, for example, he mounted an exhibition called "Shopping" and covered the façade of a department store with a mural by Barbara Kruger that criticized the commerce within.

It hasn't helped that Hollein, according to *The New York Times*, "learned at the knee of Thomas Krens," the discredited franchiser of the Guggenheim museums who mounted exhibitions of Giorgio Armani and Harley-Davidson. At the Met, the new director has spent his inaugural years dragooning contemporary art "to lay bare the inadequacies of the encyclopedic museum and its outdated reliance on taxonomies of schools, regions, and media," as he writes in his own final essay for "Making The Met." Here he laments the "nationalist overtones and inherent noblesse oblige of the founders' ambitions" and claims the museum is "progressively coming to terms with its own role in perpetuating inequalities." Likewise, seemingly late-stage interventions into the anniversary exhibition are the labels informing us that the "Havemeyer fortune derived from control of the sugar refining industry, which was known for its harsh labor conditions" and (regarding J. P. Morgan) that "a legacy of cultural beneficence cannot overturn widespread social injustice."

The "bold interventions" promised by Hollein has included two 24-by-26-foot banners for the façade commissioned from Yoko Ono that read DREAM TOGETHER. He also tapped the Kenyan-American artist Wangechi Mutu to cast four new bronze sculptures to fill Hunt's empty Beaux-Arts niches. Based on African figuration, the works with resplendent crowns and ill-crafted bodies well advertise this director's ambitions to "bring together past and present and solicit community interaction."

Yet if there is any question that such interventions are ultimately meant to impugn the art within and castigate the institution that contains them, two twenty-six-foot-long murals now just inside Hunt's Great Hall should remove any doubt. Entailing two paintings called *Welcoming the Newcomers* (2019) and *Resurgence of the People* (2019), the diptych recasts Met masterpieces such as Emanuel Leutze's *Washington Crossing the Delaware* (1851) and John Singleton Copley's study for *Watson and the Shark* (*ca.* 1778) as ghastly racialized agitprop. In one, indigenous figures can be seen rescuing stranded white settlers, while in the other, white figures are presented as soldiers and policemen displaying racist symbols at a boat of non-white refugees. The artist,

Kent Monkman, even inserts himself front and center into both scenes as "Miss Chief Eagle Testickle," his gender-fluid alter ego.

In October, Hollein purchased this supposedly temporary commission for the museum's permanent collection. "There is no doubt that the Met and its development is also connected with a logic of what is defined as white supremacy," he suggested in June. The viewpoint is now reflected at the very top of the museum, as Candace K. Beinecke, the board member who led the search committee that hired Hollein, has just been named Met co-chair. Yet such castigating commissions and false confessions do a disservice to the truly anti-racist history of the institution. The Met was founded out of victory in the Civil War and first helmed by a veteran of that bloody conflict to end slavery. Since then, the museum has dedicated entire wings and hundreds of millions of dollars to present the art of Western and non-Western peoples on equal footing. This history is real, but it presents an inconvenience to contemporary progressive narratives, one that seeks to undermine the encyclopedic collecting institution just when it is needed most.

One final episode well illustrates this danger. In June, Keith Christiansen, the museum's chairman of European paintings, posted to his personal Instagram feed a print featuring Alexandre Lenoir, a figure who tried to save monuments during the French Revolution. "Alexandre Lenoir battling the revolutionary zealots bent on destroying the royal tombs in Saint Denis," Christiansen wrote. "How many great works of art have been lost to the desire to rid ourselves of a past of which we don't approve?"

The post came at a moment of national riots that had quickly moved beyond the dismantling of Confederate monuments to the indiscriminate destruction of any and all public works. "And how grateful we are to people like Lenoir," Christiansen continued, "who realized that their value—both artistic and historical—extended beyond a defining moment of social and political upheaval and change."

A member of the Metropolitan staff since 1977, Christiansen well understood that the encyclopedic museum, including his own, is the direct descendant of Lenoir. From the French Revolution, coming out of the American Civil War, on through the Monuments Men of the Second World War, collecting institutions have saved culture from the forces of destruction. "The losses that occur" when major works of art are destroyed by "war, iconoclasm, revolution, and intolerance," as he explained, are the enemies of art history, diminishing our "fuller understanding of a complicated and sometimes ugly past."

Christiansen was denounced for daring to compare Jacobin-like terror to the Jacobin Terror. This fall, he was among the 20 percent of Met staff to announce their retirement, to resign, or to be pushed out. One of his final acts at the museum has been the restoration of the second-floor skylights for its collection of European paintings. It took one hundred and fifty years for that light to make the Met what we see today. It might take far fewer for the museum's future to dim into its unmaking.

December 2020

Lois Dodd in Portland

Karen Wilkin

"Lois Dodd: Catching the Light," on view at the Portland Museum of Art, Maine, is a disarming show. The seemingly modest, straightforward paintings in this thoughtful survey (organized by the Kemper Museum of Contemporary Art, Kansas City, Missouri, and largely chosen by the artist herself) draw us to them initially because of their comforting sense of familiarity. Dodd, like a musician with perfect pitch, never gets a tone wrong. Apparently without effort, she builds her pictures out of hues and values that conjure up particular seasons, times of day, and vagaries of weather. We recognize the mood and temperature of a crisp winter day, a voluptuous summer night, an equivocal morning in early spring, a sun-drenched autumn afternoon. If we know New England, Dodd's austere clapboard houses and weathered barns (buildings in rural Maine, where she has spent summers for decades) have special resonance, but like her seemingly dispassionate accounts of northeastern landscapes, backyards, laundry lines, flowering trees, and garden close-ups, her Down East images also read as classic Americana that transcends geography. In the same way, while Dodd's paintings of the interiors of her Lower East Side studio and the urban views from its windows may trigger instant recognition from her fellow New Yorkers, they require no particular knowledge of her sources to demand and hold our attention.

Such specificity—of place, of quality of light, of temporal details—is a major part of what Dodd's paintings are about. She has long been dedicated to working from direct perception. Often this translates into classic *plein air* practice: a trek to the motif with a folding French easel and paint box, a struggle with wind and weather, and all the rest of it, including fastening canvases to trees and covering them with plastic between campaigns. (A delightful photograph in the exhibition catalogue shows the intrepid artist, folded easel in hand and a canvas stool slung over her shoulder, ready for all contingencies in a broad brimmed hat and a rain poncho.) In discussing particular paintings, Dodd will pragmatically note that the location was convenient to where she lives or reminisce gratefully about a day when the temperature was right and annoying insects were absent: Asked about the history of a luminous snow-filled landscape with dramatic shadows, she says, "It was very sunny and I was standing against the wall of a building, warm from the sun, so the paint wasn't affected by the cold. Winter's great—no bugs." The selection of works in "Catching the Light" is notably wide-ranging—one or two pictures of a particular motif can stand for whole families of images—but we soon realize that the territory Dodd explores is circumscribed. If we spend enough time with her work, we begin to recognize a lexicon of places: her Lower East Side loft and its environs, her Cushing, Maine, house and yard, her own outbuildings or those on the adjoining property, a house down the road, a close friend and neighbor's garden, woods and fields a short walk away, the hilly landscape of New Jersey, near the Delaware Water Gap. Most intimate, perhaps, are the interiors and the views out (or into) the window. Dodd seems to know her chosen scenes thoroughly, to have studied them all over a long time and to have found new ways of thinking about them or even of seeing them, in part because of long scrutiny. Each painting, however easily we recognize its starting point or whatever clues Dodd provides in her titles, seems freshly conceived. "When I first came to Maine," she says, "I thought I'd stay here a while, until I'd exhausted what there was to paint, and then I'd have to move on. But things change all the time. Trees grow or they fall down. It's never the same."

Whatever their nominal subjects or their place of origin, all of the works in "Catching the Light" have their basis in a direct confrontation with the motif, *in situ*. Even the largest, done of necessity indoors, begin with more modestly sized versions made on the spot; what's impressive is that the larger canvases somehow magically preserve the immediacy of the first, smaller works done entirely *en plein air*. It's a time-honored way of working, dating back at least until the late-eighteenth century, even though it took more than fifty years, until the mid-nineteenth century, for directly observed paintings to be seen as complete works of art in their own right, not merely as helpful studies for more ambitious efforts. (See Jean-Baptiste-Camille Corot, the Barbizon School, and the Impressionists.) But also since the mid-nineteenth century, the tacit, "stop time" message of works of this type—"this is what this place looked like, at this moment, under these conditions"—has been increasingly associated with photography, despite the obvious fact that photographs are not necessarily truthful. The message of Dodd's paintings is more personal. She bears witness but in wholly pictorial terms: "I was there, at that moment, under those conditions, and this is how I responded to that very specific experience in the language of paint."

Dodd has been working this way since she first started going to Maine, in the early 1950s, as an eager young painter—she was born in April 1927—with a group of her New York artist friends and colleagues. "Alex Katz was painting outside," she recalls, "so I thought I would, too." Before that, she would draw from the subject and use the drawing as the basis of a studio painting. Of the works included in "Catching the Light," Dodd says, only the very earliest—a few loose-limbed landscapes, including one with cows and one with clam diggers, made between 1955 and 1961—could be described this way. "But," she points out, "I worked on them much longer than the paintings done outdoors." The fluent, cursive drawing that threads though these early paintings, loosely defining soft-edged shapes and establishing sinuous rhythms, reflects her awareness of Abstract Expressionism, particularly the paintings of Willem de Kooning, whom Dodd knew and whose work set a standard for much of her generation. But conspicuously absent from her early paintings is the sense of contingency and mutability, typically embodied by wet-into-wet, dragged paint handling, that was both characteristic of de Kooning's work and a hallmark of the aspiring younger New York painters in the 1950s who admired him. That approach was so common that Clement Greenberg coined a dismissive term for it: "the Tenth Street touch." Dodd's early work, by contrast, is clearheaded and firm, predicting, it seems, the lucidity and directness, the sense of a particular moment, and, above all, the Yankee plain-spokenness that would characterize her mature paintings (and the artist herself).

Clarity, a sense of specificity, and a powerful evocation of place, time, and season are what first attract us to Dodd's work, but she is anything but a literal or anecdotal painter. Her paint handling is broad and assured, her imagery economically simplified, her approach to scale often uninhibited, her palette always inventive. She evokes the hues of, say, a spring landscape under particular conditions of light, but she plainly doesn't feel constrained by "local color"—the naturalistic hues "given" by any selected subject—nor does she resort to seemingly irrational, arbitrarily "different" chroma in order to escape from local color. Dodd transubstantiates her perceptions into paint very freely, intensifying some colors, reinventing others, and subtly shifting still others into new territory by heating them up or cooling them down. Yet while deploying this inventive palette, she manages to remain completely faithful to the spirit and feeling of her chosen subject, so much so that we are completely convinced by the apparent accuracy of her observations.

We're convinced, too, by the compelling quality of immediacy and the deceptive casualness of Dodd's paintings, which we interpret as by-products of their being provoked by what she sees. We feel, not without reason, that we're being made privy to something she has just noticed, something ordinary, made significant by her awareness: her shadow on the grass, a shaft of light creating a clear reflection, a newly opened wealth of blossoms. "I'm not interested in still lifes," Dodd says, "because I don't like the idea of arranging things. I like to discover what's already there." Part of what she discovers is the inherent geometry of her surroundings; she seems to follow, without insisting on it too much, Paul Cézanne's recommendation "to seek the cone, the cylinder, and the sphere," ideal forms that underlie irregularities and imperfections. Unremarkable elements somehow reveal their perfect Platonic underpinnings, without losing their everyday functions: the rectangles of windows, the horizontals of clapboard, the right-angle oppositions of mullions, the unembellished shapes of New England architecture. In paintings of the natural world, tree trunks and branches, along with flower stalks and the shapes of petals and leaves, seen close up, function as less rigid versions of the "purer" man-made shapes that populate Dodd's "architectural" paintings. In works of both types, a potent sense of logic derives from the trued-and-faired relationship of the elements of "discovered" subject matter to the shape and proportion of the support. At the same time, this subtle evidence of discipline creates energizing tension with the unstudied, unlooked-for quality of her choice of motifs.

"If I don't have the geometry," Dodd says, "I can't go on." Some of the most arresting paintings in "Catching the Light" seem to have been pared down to their geometric bones, although the geometry does not always seem Euclidian. A small 1983 painting floats a pair of stiff, angular, orange-red curtains on a clothesline against an expanse of snow, with the dark, flat rectangle of a building filling one corner. There's a lot of white, but the building, its door, its shadow, and a bit of sky together present a range of murky mauve-browns, lavenders, and off-blacks. We briefly wonder if the brittle shapes of the flying curtains mean that they are frozen—all that snow, after all—but the thought doesn't preoccupy us long. However truthfully Dodd responded to the generating event—and however much we recognize that starting point—the potency of the little painting, like that of many other equally stripped-down works in the show, depends not on the accuracy of the artist's observation, but on its abstract structure—the structure "discovered" by Dodd's probing eye. Yet what she discovers can often be visually extraordinarily complex, as if she were fascinated by the multivalence of perception itself. A noteworthy number of works in "Catching the Light" deal with windows. Dodd is evidently fond of how they "select" and isolate a motif and how they offer passage into another space, but she seems even fonder of their power to reflect, both perfectly and imperfectly, disrupting spatial coherence and justifying a wide variety of touches and hues to evoke those reflections. She also occasionally includes mirrors in her interiors, playing fictive images against "real" views. In *Self-Portrait in Green Window* (1971, Portland Museum of Art), for example, we slowly decipher a minimally indicated allusion to the slender artist, wearing a striped shirt and big hat. The figure is dematerialized by strong sunshine, nearly conflated with the window mullion, and almost subsumed by reflected trees; a stalk of goldenrod, as narrow as Dodd herself, indicated both outside the window and reflected, further intensifies way space lurches and scales shift in this complicated image. Everything is held in check by the reiterated horizontals and verticals of the window frame and sill, the mullions, and the clapboard siding, which create a discontinuous grid controlling the uneasily related visual phenomena in the reflection; in counterpoint, Dodd's palette—a range of greens from acidic to murky, with notes of lavender, plus yellows from lemon to ochre—sets up new activity that further enlivens the symmetrical composition.

Other paintings explore the destabilizing effect of seeing into the layered, defined spaces of a sequence of rooms or allow us the guilty pleasure of peering into illuminated windows. In *View Through Elliot's Shack Looking South* (1971, the artist and Alexandre Gallery, New York), the pale window frame is made congruent with the edge of the canvas, so that the events contained by the depicted panes start to read as a painting within a painting. At first, the loose suggestion of foliage and the triangle of a rooftop on the expanse of glass reads as a comprehensible reflection of a house among tall Maine evergreens, but that interpretation is stopped by a floating rectangle of brightly illuminated, crisply indicated tree trunks and sky. We are momentarily unable to decide what is where, and settle for enjoying the contrast of pictorial languages and touches, and the orchestration of heightened and softened colors, trapped by the rectangle of the window. Then, with concentration, attention to the broadly indicated shadows on the window surround, and a little help from the title, we work out that we are *outside* a building, looking through its dark interior to the sun-lit world beyond, visible through a window on the opposite site. Once we've cracked the code, we return to enjoying the sturdy geometric scaffolding of the composition and the free-wheeling paint handling within that framework. And then Dodd's spatial conceit reasserts itself.

A couple of New York city interiors, day and night, investigate similar clashes of logic, pitting the view from Dodd's loft against disjunctive, fragmented images captured by mirrors propped against the furniture. "What I was really interested in," she says, "was the big oval and the rectangle against the shape of the window." Important as their clear geometry is to the pictures, it's the irrational relationship of what the mirrors capture, the interrupted view of the studio, and the exterior view that holds our attention; the geometry serves as a stabilizing influence, something to hold on to and orient us, as we navigate the abrupt shifts of the paintings. In Portland, the most eye-testing of these paintings is a Maine interior, *The Painted Room* (1982, Farnsworth Art Museum, Rockland, Maine). An open window, with yellow curtains framing a leafy view, seems to hang, Magritte-like, against a broadly suggested forest of slim tree trunks that spring from a rosy ground plane. Then we notice a narrow suggestion of ceiling at the top of the picture and a light bulb that projects to create a fictional space in front of the window. Suddenly everything makes sense. The window takes its place in a wall on which a forest landscape is painted. The vertical folds of the curtain enter into a conversation with the repeated verticals of the trunks, and the staccato horizontals of the branches start a dialogue with the window frame and sill; the yellow of the curtains, a little warmer than lemon, challenges the dull rose, Pompeian red, and dusty neutrals of the eponymous "painted room." Once again, Dodd claims our attention by appealing to perception and then seduces us with solid pictorial invention, laced with a liberal shot of wit.

If this sounds as if Dodd's paintings of this type are elaborate visual games designed to perplex the unwary viewer, think again. For all their spatial pulse, her paintings of windows, reflections, and what we might call "multiple spaces" are as uncompromising and clean as her most elemental landscapes or views of bare-bones Maine buildings. She notices and points out to us things we might miss on our own, underscoring the likeness and unlikeness among disparate elements to create a "continuo" of geometric order that supports her painterly inventions. In *Red Vine and Blanket* (1979, Private collection), Dodd rhymes the neat, repeated squares of a coverlet—that backyard clothesline, again—with the blocky, undisciplined patches of a scarlet autumnal vine, enriching the confrontation by twinning a multi-paned window and a checked shirt hung nearby, then contradicting these crisp grids by swelling the laundry with a stiff wind.

Just when we think we have Dodd figured out, however, she surprises us. Nothing is ever quite what it seems. She may be a painter who works from the motif and strives to be faithful to perception, but echoes of her knowledge of the history of art resonate in even the most apparently straightforward of her pictures. J. M. W. Turner's views of the blazing Houses of Parliament haunt a lively painting of a burning building near her Maine house—a training exercise for the local volunteer firemen, Dodd reassures us. A confrontational view of a pale lavender staircase through an open door hints at Charles Willson Peale's full-length portrait of his sons on a similar stair. A series of exuberant female nudes in sunny gardens seems to pay homage to Cézanne, Henri Matisse, and perhaps Pablo Picasso, with economically modeled forms, fluid proportions, and expressive silhouettes, but, unlike her distinguished male ancestors, Dodd is not reimagining Arcadia. Her unclothed women are not languorous nymphs waiting for shepherds to offer love poetry. They are active, self sufficient, and purposeful. In *Four Nudes and Woodpile* (2001–02, Coldbeck Gallery, Maine), they saw, carry, and stack wood in brilliant sunlight. Dodd's forthright garden paintings similarly challenge tradition, in part through their scale. "I didn't want to be another woman painting flowers," she says, "so I made them big." And instead of treating flowers as still life components, decorously arranged in a vase, Dodd "discovers" her botanical subjects where they grow and presents them with large sweeps of her brush, uncut, alive and kicking, as vigorous specimens with generous leaves, large, distinctively shaped petals, and sturdy stalks.

Note to visitors of "Catching the Light": The Portland installation adds a group of Dodd's most direct, intimate studies, done on small aluminum panels between 2009 and 2012. Together, they offer a highly distilled crash course in Lois Dodd in miniature—everything from cloud patterns and night scenes to cast shadows, blooming trees, and a bonfire, evoked with stunning economy and specificity. Hung in a narrow space near the exit, they could be overlooked. Don't miss them.

March 2013

A better London

Benjamin Riley

ONE OF THE DANGERS in writing about Ian Nairn, the architectural critic who died in 1983, is his quotability. No page goes by in *Nairn's London* without a veritable zinger, the sort of quip that should be reproduced endlessly in anthologies of quotations. A piece on Nairn could easily degenerate into an infinite list of Nairn's best lines, of which there are naturally too many to relate in a single space. But even with this word of warning stated, one must quote Nairn liberally to give a sense of his gift: a clear-eyed, often withering wit.

His biographical credit, almost certainly written by himself, states that Nairn "was brought up in a part of Surrey that produced a deep hatred of characterless buildings and places … he [took] a bad degree in mathematics and [was] a pilot in the RAF." These are the rough outlines of a man whom an architectural historian friend of mine (and fellow Nairn devotee) is fond of calling, in a paraphrase of Jonathan Meades, "almost defiantly red-brick." Indeed, there is a touch of the Angry Young Man about Nairn, a point the Nairn acolyte Gavin Stamp makes in his afterword to the reissued 2014 edition of *Nairn's London*. Nairn was disgusted by the pretension of most modern architecture, which presumed to tell people in what kind of buildings they should want to live, work, and worship. A 1966 polemic entitled "Stop the Architects Now," written for the *Observer*, disparaged modern architecture as "just not good enough … beneath the buildings of quality there is a soggy, shoddy mass of half-digested clichés, half-peeling façades, half-comfortable rooms, untested preconceptions about what people want." In a sense Nairn was a forerunner of the "New Urbanism" movement, which sought to create sensible developments based on traditional principles. But Nairn can't be pigeonholed so easily—his tastes were admittedly subjective, and he never approached architecture with a moralizing framework in the way that Jane Jacobs did. He merely wanted to see the decent, old buildings of England left alone, and not be subsumed into an indistinct mass, endlessly repeatable but never memorable.

His *London*, then, is a sort of bleary-eyed love letter to the buildings that define the city. When the book was published in 1966 Nairn had only lived in London for ten years, and yet he had perceived something essential about the place, namely that it was the quirks that made it grand.

Any discussion of Nairn, and architecture in England generally, must at some point make reference to the late Sir Nikolaus Pevsner, whose guides to the buildings of England remain the principal reference works in any architectural historian's library. Including all of England's counties, with six books on London alone, the Pevsner guides achieve a remarkable comprehensiveness and seem to strive towards objectivity, both in content and tone (though aesthetic judgments are buried in the histories). In this way, they stand as the apparent opposite of Nairn's work—ice-cold, assured, and unequivocal, they have no taste for the giddy metaphors that pepper Nairn's accounts. To wit, Pevsner on Soane's Chelsea Hospital stables: "its stock brick front the most elegant of minimal designs, just three concentric arches." And Nairn: "a clear, Euclidian proof of the argument of this book, that 2 + 2 = 5." But this easy contrast obscures the muddled truth of the matter. For one thing, Nairn was a great admirer of Pevsner, saying that "for architectural information there is nothing to beat *The Buildings of England*." Nairn got his own chance to contribute to the Pevsner guides with the 1962 edition for his home county of Surrey. The working relationship between Pevsner and Nairn seems to have functioned well enough, though it must have been slightly uneasy, with Nairn working on half of *Sussex* before declining to continue the partnership, citing the necessity of providing detailed descriptions as too taxing. Nonetheless, a level of mutual respect existed between the two, with Pevsner freely admitting that Nairn "writes better than I could ever hope to write."

Perhaps the foremost joy to be had in reading Nairn is to survey his comments on one's own London area of operations. On Belgravia, the area directly north of my flat: "some of the richest, the wickedest, the oddest of London is to be found in the square mile between Knightsbridge and Victoria." He singles out a favorite pub of mine, the Grenadier, on the site of an old Guards' Mess: "untouched by half timber, leaded light, chromium plate, or Festival of Britain lettering. It is the old servants' pub that has short-circuited to become a local for the rich mews-dwellers, rich enough to appreciate the shabbiness and leave it alone." Nairn had a keen social eye, and he continues his description with an obscure, but percipient truth: "The English *ancien régime* had and still has a lot of faults; but one of its great virtues was that it was really prepared to tolerate eccentricity." This was made clear to me one night when, in another pub at the nexus of Chelsea, Belgravia, and Pimlico, a man dressed in full shooting attire—plus-fours and matching tweed jacket—walked in. No one blinked.

But there are treats to be had farther afield, too. Nairn is particularly good on churches. St Paul, Wilton Place is "one more lean nineteenth-century church, religion on the cheap"; St James, Piccadilly is "Wren's favourite church and no wonder. This is as far as the Wren virtues can take you, as good of its kind as it could be ... a parallel to Inigo Jones's idea of plain exteriors and rich interiors" with a superb Grinling Gibbons reredos: "like a Chardin still-life, this fruit is more fruity than the real thing." Of Jones's own ecclesiastical work at St Paul, Covent Garden—and to my eye, his best—"a box with a lid on it; but 'box' and 'lid' never mean quite the same again." Moving on to the City, Nairn reserves his highest praise for Hawksmoor's endearingly odd St Mary Woolnoth, immortalized (as if it needed it) in Eliot's *Waste Land*—"A crowd flowed over London Bridge/ ... Flowed up the hill and down King William Street,/ to where Saint Mary Woolnoth kept the hours/ With a dead sound on the final stroke of nine." For Nairn, St Mary Woolnoth is "the one City church you must go in. By comparison almost all Baroque churches on the Continent seem overloaded and hysterical.... It feels like being on the hot end of a burning glass ... for the price of a bus ticket to the City, the super-reality of the mystics of mescalin." Westminster RC Cathedral, where I occasionally take in an organ concert for its acoustics, comes in for a bag of critique: "almost accidentally, a superb religious warehouse" where "the great domed bays, built of yellow bricks which have gone almost black [now, totally so], are a true nineteenth-century equivalent to the austerity of the Cistercians." The original plan was to face the brick in marble and Nairn lamented the ongoing process, while allowing that "in the face of such devotion, how can I say that it is misplaced?" He would be gratified to know that, fifty years on, the marbleizing has not gotten very far. Despite his apparent lack of religion, Nairn had a great feeling for churches, not in Larkin's "Church

Going" sense, but for their architectural possibilities. The greatest summation of London's ecclesiastical patrimony is reserved for its grandest—Westminster Abbey. Nairn calls it "the perfect governmental report on the French Gothic; prepared, as it were, to see if the European style was suited to the English practice. Level-headed, solving all of its problems, translating them correctly into meticulous English."

But what really delighted Nairn were the seedier bits of London, those particular joys of urban living. Soho was "the free port that every city must have.... If you want the wickedest place in Britain, you can find it; if you want a cosmopolitan village in the city, with village shops and pubs, it is there also." This potent admixture, with both the *haut* and *bas* elements set into higher relief by the contrast, is Soho's charm, and Nairn's affection for the scene is clear, if tinged with wist: "The tarts are off the streets now. Instead there are traffic wardens, taking up the same kind of stance but not looking nearly so inviting. If you want a lady, ring on doorbells marked Marie or Sabrina; and good luck." He saw London as it is: a city of villages, each with its own high street and own specific flavor. Shepherd Market, situated enviably in W1 behind Piccadilly and before Mayfair, was "Mayfair's original village"—according to the recent signage appearing there—and to Nairn its "most determined and unexpected.... [Shepherd Market] is still rough; or rather, rough and very smooth at the same time. The two seem to get on." In Shepherd Market, where still today a Polish-Mexican restaurant trades across from one of London's most exclusive members clubs, "The whole pack of humanity is dealt to you, knaves and jokers included. Anything can happen to you, but it is your own choice." Nairn saw and relished the unlimited potential of the organic city, which always was at its highest in the liminal spaces. There is no reason Shepherd Market should continue to exist—it is surrounded by the most expensive real estate in London, where houses run into the tens of millions of pounds. And yet it does still, illogical as always, a stubborn hold-out against development, an always buoying warren of streets where the squalid and high society not only coexist but feed off each other.

Nairn did, however, anticipate the way most of London would become too dear for the average citizen, with the finest buildings often turned into embassies. Of Kensington Palace Gardens: "A Victorian Millionaire's Row ... a motorist's shortcut from Notting Hill to Kensington High Street—if you can outface the formidable guardians at either end. Yesterday's money-power has given way to today's much more sinister political power. . . . It is quite a relief to go downhill to Kensington Palace where normal people like Princess Margaret live." But even he could not foresee the towering ascent of London's property market. In 1966 he could still write that Belgravia was "the equivalent of pre-war Mayfair." But no one gives dances in Eaton Square anymore, and many of the leases in SW1X are taken by hedge funds and other more insidious businesses. The lights tend to be dark at night, and in February a group of anarchist squatters commandeered an unoccupied terrace house for a few days before the police dispatched them; throughout the saga, the absentee Russian oligarch owner could not be reached for comment.

My sympathy for Nairn may be instinctual; he lived, as I do now, in what Anthony Powell called "a vast, desolate region of stucco streets and squares upon which a doom seemed to have fallen." Pimlico, our little corner of Stuccovia, is no longer so gloomy—like the rest of London it's been smartened up—and the shabbily genteel (and often plain-shabby) early Victorian terrace houses of Nairn's day have been scrubbed and refitted. The pub where Nairn drank himself to death is now—like many old London boozers—genericized, and owned by a group with nearly eighty pubs to their name, all simulacra of authentically "ye olde" British public houses. Time moves on without concern for the minor figures populating its sweep; the planners—or, as Betjeman called them, the "plansters"—have won. In another twenty years' time, London may be unrecognizable. As I write this the cranes have descended on "Nine Elms," a fake neighborhood sitting on the remains of Battersea Power Station where the American Embassy will move next year. Those who keep an eye on such things have noticed London is becoming more like New York—tall buildings for tallness's sake, with a wanton disregard for history. In the introduction to his guide, Nairn, with characteristic self-effacement, wonders "whether this grandiose programme has achieved anything more than a collection of subjective maunderings." I fear he may be right. Preservation remains a tenuous goal, forever pushed aside by perfectly legitimate yet callously ugly and unfeeling projects. Some of the buildings Nairn wrote about are now gone, more will follow in turn. As long as *Nairn's London* stays in print, however, a better London can, at the very least, be evoked.

May 2017

Albert Pinkham Ryder: isolato of the brush

Andrew L. Shea

In one of his only published comments on art, a 1905 treatise titled "Paragraphs from the Studio of a Recluse," the American painter Albert Pinkham Ryder (1847–1917) wrote that "the artist needs but a roof, a crust of bread, and his easel, and all the rest God gives him in abundance." Ryder continued: "He must live to paint and not paint to live. He cannot be a good fellow; he is rarely a wealthy man, and upon the potboiler is inscribed the epitaph of his art." A quarter-century later, Virginia Woolf struck a similar note when she famously argued that a woman wanting to write fiction requires just two things: enough money to get by on, and a "room of one's own." In context, the two essays aren't at all alike: Woolf's broader argument is about making space for women in the literary tradition, whereas Ryder offers a personal defense of thrift and simplicity. Shared by both, however, is the understanding that isolation is a positive and essential—perhaps *the* essential—condition for artistic creation. A room "of *one's own*," that is—the studio of a *recluse*.

The sentiment isn't widely accepted today, to say the least. Within the art world, the rise of Masters in Fine Arts programs whose symbolic center is "the group critique"—a communal evaluation of how an artist's work fits within the shared "theoretical discourse"—has helped to spur a dramatic change in the way artists view themselves in relation to society. As Gary Alan Fine writes in his 2018 ethnographic study of these programs, *Talking Art: The Culture of Practice and the Practice of Culture in MFA Education*,

> Today artists increasingly create for each other, hoping for approval from those within the guild, and they must explain what they

> intend. Once artists were mute; today they talk and write as well as create. The art world is an occupational community, like sociology, medicine, or law. Now embedded within universities and art schools, art increasingly constitutes an academic discipline.

The romantic image of the lonely visionary toiling away in a bedraggled studio is consistently disparaged as foolish myth. Fine records a professor admonishing a student with the help of John Donne: "The biggest weakness is that you are thinking of yourself as a single artist. No one is an island in themselves." At another school, a student proclaims that "the individual artist is not something I believe in"—to which his professor fires back, "does anyone? … There's nobody who thinks of an artist like that anymore."

In a sense, these academicians have a point. The idea that people are out there making good art in a vacuum rarely holds up upon close inspection, if ever. Even so-called "outsider artists" usually turn out to have had more training and more knowledge of other art and artists than is usually acknowledged. Society's role in fostering artistic achievement can hardly be overstated. Like any human community, artists share ideas and build off one another to reach otherwise unthinkable heights. Competitive drive plays perhaps an even more crucial role, and goes back, at the very least, to the origins of art history: see Pliny the Elder's famous account of the ancient Greek artists Zeuxis and Parrhasius battling it out in a *trompe l'oeil* tournament for the title of greatest living painter. In Renaissance Italy and elsewhere, architects, sculptors, and painters strove passionately against one another to win the largest and most glorifying commissions. Michelangelo and Raphael, Borromini and Bernini, Ingres and Delacroix, Turner and Constable, Matisse and Picasso—rivalries have inspired not only legendary historical anecdotes, but also immortal artistic achievements.

Nevertheless, the over-socialization of art presents a chronic risk. Schools designed to teach foundational skills can end up enforcing sterile academicism. A robust patron class might breed commercial decadence. Rabid one-upmanship will often beget mere spectacle. In the mainstream of today's art world these all are real and present afflictions. But they're also not new. Were those pictures by Zeuxis and Parrhasius actually *good paintings*, in addition to being immaculate demonstrations of mimetic technique? The latter, after all, doesn't imply the former.

Thus, throughout history there have been those who call for the return of a more private, individual, "authentic" aesthetic, one uncorrupted by social influences. In a first century A.D. text titled *On the Sublime*, the author known as "Longinus" deplores the decay of rhetoric in his day. Begging for a return to a poetic mode of greater simplicity, Longinus argues that the writer hoping to elevate his craft must look inward: "a writer can only learn from art when he is to abandon himself to the direction of his genius." Fast forward seventeen centuries and Jean-Jacques Rousseau was similarly arguing that artists were better off working alone, beyond the constricting reach of civilization: "so long as they undertook only what a single person could accomplish and confined themselves to such arts as did not require the joint labor of several hands, they lived free, healthy, honest, and happy lives."

Closer to our own time, the image of the artist in isolation finds perhaps its most vital expression in the more romanticist strains of modern literature: the ostracism of Frankenstein's monster, Thoreau's pond-side solitude, the spiritual exile of Stephen Dedalus, the emotional paralysis of J. Alfred Prufrock, the invisibility of Ellison's narrator. Isolation and loneliness, in their manifold varieties, became productive, advantageous states of mind, enabling the artist to level his denunciation of an increasingly Enlightened, idealist, and industrial modernity. Even Melville's crew, working and living together in close proximity aboard the cramped and oil-grimed *Pequod*, were souls apart, refuting both Donne and that unnamed art prof: "They were nearly all Islanders in the Pequod, Isolatoes too, I call such, not acknowledging the common continent of men, but each Isolato living on a separate continent of his own."

But it is just this modernist belief in the creative powers of the individual soul that has come under fierce attack in our own more nihilistic and totalizing times. It is thus both surprising and encouraging to learn that painters like Albert Pinkham Ryder are garnering new attention from historians and artists alike. This summer, a major monograph on the painter, the first in more than three decades, was published by Rizzoli. It was intended to coincide with a significant retrospective exhibition, also the first of its kind since 1990, at the New Bedford Whaling Museum, though unfortunately this was postponed until June 2021 due to the COVID-19 outbreak. With color illustrations as well as insightful essays by Christina Connett Brophy, Elizabeth Broun, and William C. Agee that analyze, respectively, Ryder's historical context, his elusive painterly ideas, and his outsize influence on generations of artists, *A Wild Note of Longing: Albert Pinkham Ryder and a Century of American Art* offers us the exceedingly welcome chance to reflect on this austere, stirring, and wholeheartedly strange painter.

It has often been said that Ryder was both America's last great romanticist and her first prophet of modernism. Born in New Bedford in 1847—just four years before the publication of *Moby-Dick*, whose early chapters take place in the southeastern Massachusetts whaling town—the artist moved with his family to New York City's Greenwich Village in 1868, where he lived and worked in various small apartments for the rest of his life. By the time he died in 1917, Ryder was the subject of intense veneration among a coterie of early American modernists such as Marsden Hartley, Milton Avery, and Arthur Dove. These three and others looked up to Ryder as a spiritual and aesthetic forefather, and saw him as the fountainhead of a specifically American stream into modern painting. As Hartley recalled first encountering a Ryder in 1909, "when I learned he was from New England the same feeling came over me in the given degree as came out of Emerson's *Essays* when they were first given to me—I felt I had read a page of the Bible.... The picture has done its work and I was a convert to the field of imagination into which I was born."

In his own 1905 "Paragraphs," Ryder assumes a deliberately antisocial and anti-commercial posture, suggesting that, for him, independence of mind and body was a matter of artistic authenticity. Elsewhere in the short essay, which is reproduced in full in the opening pages of the present volume, his obsession with artistic self-reliance verges on the Emersonian:

> The artist should not sacrifice his ideals to a landlord and a costly studio.... [He] should once and forever emancipate himself from the bondage of appearances and the unpardonable sin of expending on ignoble aims the precious ointment that should serve only to nourish the lamp burning before the tabernacle of the muse.

That Ryder seemed to live by this code, too, undoubtedly contributed to his late-in-life celebrity among the young bohemians of New York's avant-garde. Certainly, the self-titled "recluse" was eccentric. He never married and became a notorious slob. Sometime in the mid-1890s he stopped throwing things out of his cramped room in Greenwich Village. One friend recounted that it "was a mass of papers, pasteboard boxes, some with food, others, empty, piled high.... He slept on a cot, but not being able to keep it clean he abandoned it and slept on the floor."

At around the same time he started to hoard his paintings as well, endlessly adjusting, re-touching, re-glazing, and re-varnishing old pictures in lieu of beginning new ones. This was bad for business, to say the least. Many would-be buyers recalled eagerly purchasing a painting still on the easel, only to wait years before Ryder would let the thing out of his studio. One exasperated collector demanded that Ryder hand over a "finished" work; the artist responded by raking a hot comb across the picture's surface, bringing all parties involved back to square one. Another was more resigned to the interminable process, informing Ryder that he left directions in his will to have the funeral procession stop by the studio to pick up the long-awaited work. Even then, "Not unless 'twas done" was Ryder's reply.

Nevertheless, the image of Ryder as a world-renouncing "outsider" has been greatly exaggerated. Contrary to claims that he was a self-taught naif, the artist had been trained in academic draughtsmanship, was knowledgeable of art history, and kept close ties with fellow painters. His turn towards extreme seclusion happened only late in life. In addition to the pastoral landscapes and maritime nocturnes for which he's best known, Ryder painted allegorical scenes from the Bible, Greek mythology, history, Shakespeare, Wagner, and more. He read the Romantics—Byron, Coleridge, Keats, Poe—and wrote poetry himself. (The title of the book, "A Wild Note of Longing," comes from a line of Ryder's own verse.) And though he never became rich, Pinky (as he was known to friends—"The Reverend" was another moniker) had loyal dealers through most of his working life, as well as a small but energetic group of collectors that sustained his painterly ambitions and tolerated his vexing habits.

But putting aside such extraneous biographical niceties, it is Ryder's formal solitude, the intensely lonely nature of the paintings themselves, that remains crucial to us today. Indeed, Ryder's private visions, fired in the kiln of imagination and memory, could not have been more inimical to the prevailing taste of his own time. One of the only works by the painter on regular public view in New York (much of his oeuvre can be found in Washington, D.C., at either the Phillips Collection or the Smithsonian American Art Museum) is the Metropolitan Museum's

Toilers of the Sea (*ca.* 1880–85), a nighttime maritime scene in which a lone small boat crests a wave before a silent horizon in the distance. Tucked away in a corner of the Met's American Wing, the tiny painting—just about a foot tall and wide—is accessible only by passing the expansive and expansionist landscapes of Hudson River School painters like Thomas Cole, Albert Bierstadt, Frederic Edwin Church, and William Bradford. As Brophy notes in her introductory essay, these latter painters' works, glistening with gold and filled with flawlessly rendered detail, traveled the country as public spectacles, viewers dropping coins to have curtains drawn back in a flourish, revealing the images for short periods of privileged gazing.

It's hard to believe that anyone would pay for such an encounter with Ryder's *Toilers*. On first glance, the painting seems modest and mute, even clumsy. In his endless quest to transform paint into something utterly new ("less painty-looking than any man before me," he once said), Ryder was prone to brazenly mixing and matching his paints with wildly different mediums—introducing such alien materials as dirt, tar, wax, and even tobacco juice—as he built up his surfaces over the months and years. This kind of maniacal studio experimentation has caused many of his pictures to disfigure irreparably, almost before our very eyes, as fast-drying outer surfaces harden over under-layers that remain viscous and wet, flowing like lava and crackling the image into islands of slowly sagging pigment.

Though not quite as mangled as some of the grisliest examples, *Toilers* has cracked and deteriorated to a degree, its surface acting almost like a barrier to entry, the strange and knobby textures of time pulling the eye from the image within. Only by sustained contemplation can you hope to unlock the door onto Ryder's private world. Spend enough time with it, though, and secrets do unfold. Despite its discoloration you begin to notice extremely subtle variations in tone, and gem-like hues—orange, red, green, blue—begin to glow underneath the pale yellows and blacks of its monochromatic drawing. As you trace the wavering contours of its interlocking forms you begin to feel its compact rhythms, its contrapuntal masses taking on a shifting and palpable weight, whether boat or moon or wave or cloud. Lost in the picture's internal movements, you've now closed the door behind you, shut off from the outside world. This small and strange panel is yours, and yours alone.

In pictures such as the Phillips Collection's *Moonlit Cove* (*ca.* 1880–90), Ryder goes further, simplifying to the extreme, restricting himself to only a handful of ostensibly flat forms, the largest a monumental, black, glob-like mass within which are the impossibly faint suggestions of a cove, a boat, and their shadows. Almost entirely devoid of discernible subjects, such paintings thrilled and inspired Ryder's avant-garde champions in the early twentieth century, earning him pride of place at the center of their landmark Armory Show of 1913. Indeed, the sixty-six-year-old painter was the lone American to be included in that exhibition's section of "Old Masters." But to regard Ryder as an almost-abstractionist, someone who would have dropped content completely if only he had been born a few decades later, is to miss the essential figurative nature of his vision. Indeed, with *Moonlit Cove*, despite the sturdy decoration of its arabesque contours, it is precisely the more numinous qualities of atmosphere, space, and absorptive moonlight that give the picture its enduring energies.

Jonah (*ca.* 1885–95, Smithsonian American Art Museum), perhaps Ryder's greatest masterpiece, kicks these energies into maximalist overdrive. Amid a whorling maelstrom of crashing waves and devouring black depths, we find the Hebrew prophet cast overboard, abandoned by his shipmates, flailing and gasping for air. The treacherous black whale eyes Jonah hungrily from the shadows to the right, while above, emerging through the amber light of parting clouds, is the divine image of God in benediction, a force of celestial calm amid the general confusion. The picture lands somewhere between Turner's *Slave Ship* (1840) and William Blake's mystical monotypes, but its painterly language is wholly Ryder's own. None of it looks sensibly "real" in the way that a Bierstadt or Bradford wows us with impeccable detail and crystal-clear naturalism, yet somehow the chaos feels frighteningly plausible. As Ryder himself once said, "What avails a storm cloud accurate in form and color if the storm is not therein?"

Given the cetaceous subject matter, another glance towards Melville and his own great whale is inevitable. Struggling to make sense of the tempestuous painting, with its churning gestures and inscrutable textures that are saturated with the mystery of ten years of overpainting, one might even think of that "boggy, soggy, squitchy picture truly, enough to drive a nervous man distracted" that utterly bewitches Ishmael in the dark hallways of New Bedford's Spouter Inn. But the resemblances run deeper even than subject and style. "Ryder, like Melville, was concerned with the depths, the parts of experience that elude statement, that must be hinted at, approached obliquely, rendered in parables," Lewis Mumford brilliantly observed back in 1931: "When he chose to portray the loneliness of the soul, he might convey the meaning through a little boat with a torn sail, swallowed by the ocean."

Is it possible that artists still busy themselves with pursuing such depths, with digging into those "parts of experience that elude statement, that must be hinted at, approached obliquely, rendered in parables"? In his essay on Ryder's enduring legacy, which concludes the monograph, William C. Agee makes the case that they do—in increasing numbers, and with growing enthusiasm. In this "postmodern" age, anesthetized by technology and obsessed only with style and easy superficialities, Agee's argument for the painter and his followers reads something like a voice crying out in the wilderness:

> For years, much art writing was in the stifling grip of conceptual and theoretical speculation, much of it incomprehensible. That is changing, for art, like life, is real, and must be experienced to be known. A younger generation of artists wholeheartedly embrace such things and speak openly and with passion about Ryder.

There are the well-documented acolytes such as Marsden Hartley, Arthur Dove, Milton Avery, Jackson Pollock, and Mark Rothko, but also less obvious offshoots such as Robert Rauschenberg and even Donald Judd. Moving to the contemporary period we find, among others, Albert York (who died in 2009), Wolf Kahn (who died this March), and diverse living veterans such as Lois Dodd, Katherine Bradford, Sanford Wurmfeld, and John Walker. Younger painters include Alan Prazniak, Peter Shear, and Emily Auchincloss. Against Frank Stella's claim that "what you see is what you see"—the "God is Dead" moment of romantic painting—these painters look with Ryder for "the reality of forces below the surface," as perhaps his most vocal champion, the contemporary painter Bill Jensen, has written.

Are there others? I was surprised not to find mention of Jake Berthot, whose dark-toned and closely valued late paintings (he died in 2014) of trees and mountains, with their intriguing surfaces and mysterious translucencies, owe much to Ryder. Enrique Martinez Celaya's inexplicable and mystical landscape narratives, infused with a Kierkegaardian sense of doubt and foreboding, also relate to Ryder's poetic sense of solitude. Two exhibitions in New York last month—of Tom Uttech's dream-like pictures of imagined Northwest woods at Alexandre Gallery, and, at DC Moore, of Eric Aho's alchemical abstractions based on the hinterland wilderness of northern New England—were yet more evidence that artists are charting interesting, new ground by turning the eye inward.

It's a bitter irony that a pandemic which has forced entire populations into various positions of physical isolation has also prevented us (for now) from experiencing Ryder's lonely art in full, and in person—which, of course, it utterly demands. Thankfully, art is long, and just as the artist "must buckle himself with infinite patience," as Ryder wrote 115 years ago, so must we bide our time in anticipation of the chance to do so.

December 2020

Le Sacre turns 100

Laura Jacobs

It was in two scenes, but had no real plot, the action representing merely a series of primitive rites. With one exception there were no individual dances, but only big ensembles. Stravinsky's music was quite unsuitable for dancing; but this troubled neither Diaghilev nor Nijinsky, whose aim was to present only a succession of rhythmically moving groups.

—S. L. Grigoriev, *The Diaghilev Ballet 1909–1929*

Serge Leonidovich Grigoriev was the *régisseur* of Serge Diaghilev's Ballets Russes, and his firsthand account of *Le Sacre du printemps*—its creation and reception—possesses an eye-of-the-storm quiet, as if he's still under the spell of Diaghilev's directive on the night of the premiere: Keep calm and carry on. "Whatever happens," Diaghilev said, "the ballet must be performed to the end."

Diaghilev knew he was presenting Paris with something it wasn't prepared for. Igor Stravinsky's score was symphonic, but it was without the symmetrical structures or architecturally reinforced melodies that are the body and soul of a symphony. Indeed, he meant his score to be soulless. Vaslav Nijinsky's dance was called a ballet, but it did not attempt to dispel or transcend gravity as classical ballets were expected to do; instead, his dancers bowed down under a cosmic weight, burdened by it and in awe of it. The third collaborator, the artist, anthropologist, and mystic Nicholas Roerich, provided the least jarring elements of the ballet: ethnographically correct costumes of pagan Russian folk dress and painted backdrops that suggest the earth of an earlier age. He also helped devise the ballet's thirteen-movement scenario and provided the Lithuanian folk tunes that Stravinsky absorbed into his score.

Three Russians, three unique geniuses, and despite the accounts of push-pull during the collaboration all three reaching simultaneously forward by going backward, making a ballet that was not a ballet at all, but something clean and raw and new and hungry. In a letter to Roerich, Stravinsky referred to the work that would become *Le Sacre* as "our child."

By ballet standards, it was a long gestation, dating from a vision Stravinsky had in 1910 while finishing *The Firebird*. He saw "a solemn pagan rite: sage elders, seated in a circle, watch[ing] a young girl dance herself to death. They were sacrificing her to propitiate the god of spring." Roerich had come up with a similar "Stone Age" scenario in 1909. So the two were on parallel tracks. *The Great Sacrifice* and *Holy Spring* were Stravinsky's early working titles; *Supreme Sacrifice* was Roerich's. "Who else knows the secret of our ancestors' close feeling to the earth?," Stravinsky wondered before he teamed up with Roerich. A secret worth discovering, this primitive closeness to the earth. Here was a circling back, a beginning over. The subject opened up powerful associations: ignorance-imagination, primal-amoral, death-life, destruction-creation. Part I of the ballet, Adoration of the Earth, has young men and maidens, a fortune teller and a sage performing formal and boisterous spring rituals. Part II, The Sacrifice, presented inscrutable nighttime games, the selection and glorification of a chosen maiden, and her solo—the *Danse Sacrale*—a climactic dance of fear, flight, and finality.

Diaghilev, who was not initially involved in the developing idea—an exclusion he didn't like—embraced the project anyway. His instinct for salable controversy was as keen as his instinct for innovation, and here were both. Although Michel Fokine was the company's house choreographer, Diaghilev saw to it that Nijinsky replaced Fokine, even though Nijinsky was still unformed as a choreographer and the score before him was monstrously complex. Diaghilev knew that if anyone had a "close feeling to the earth" it was Nijinsky. ("I am a man and not a beast," the dancer would one day write in his diary, "I am a man and not God . . . I am the earth.") At great expense Diaghilev made possible an unheard of 100 rehearsals.

Approaching thirty when he was at work on *Le Sacre*, "Stravinsky was brimming with self-assurance, even hubris," writes Charles M. Joseph in *Stravinsky's Ballets*. "Moreover, he knew exactly what he was provoking, and he relished the apostasy of which others accused him." The agenda for Stravinsky, and for Nijinsky as well, was rupture and rebirth—revolution, if you will—a throwing off of the tried and true, or rather, the true that had become decorative, formulaic, *untrue*. Diaghilev's agenda—"The ballet must be performed to the end"—was framed differently. Unfinished works do not make history and making history is what Diaghilev was all about. It is doubtful he knew that this work of art would become the most symbolic of the twentieth century. What he did know was that *Le Sacre* had taken on a life of its own. It had to be born.

The accounts of the premiere that took place on May 29, 1913—it was actually the second performance; the first, an open dress rehearsal on the 28th, passed without problems—are contradictory in particulars but generally in accord. Count Harry Kessler, a patron of the arts and of the Ballets Russes, reports in his diary that the audience, "the most elegant house I have ever seen in Paris—aristocracy, diplomats, the demimonde—was from the beginning restless, laughing, whistling, making jokes." In *Stravinsky: A Creative Spring*, Stephen Walsh writes, "Word had got about after the final rehearsals that the new ballet was difficult, violent, incomprehensible; what better response to these disturbing qualities than laughter and ridicule?" Defenders shouted at detractors. Commotion grew. "And above this crazy din," Kessler continues, "the music raged and on the stage the dancers, without flinching, danced fervently in a prehistoric fashion." The conductor Pierre Monteux, also unflinching, spurred the orchestra through to the end, deaf to the storm around him. Stravinsky and Nijinsky were beside themselves. Five minutes into the ballet Stravinsky left his seat in the audience and raced backstage, where he says he found Nijinsky on a chair shouting counts at the dancers, who couldn't hear the music over the din. Grigoriev, however, remembers Nijinsky standing "silent in the wings," stunned.

Some accounts blame Stravinsky's music for the uproar—the savage dissonance, the screaming brass, the ferocious momentum and mad-seeming rhythms. Nijinsky thought this was so. Others pointed to Nijinsky's "ugly" choreography, the turned-in, pigeon-toed, note-for-note stamping and trembling of the dancers—"a crime against grace." Was one more inflammatory than the other, or was it the combination of the two? Kessler, clear-eyed, wrote of *Le Sacre*, "A thoroughly new vision, something never before seen, enthralling, persuasive, is suddenly there, a new kind of wildness, both un-art and art at the same time."

In the 1959 book, *Memories and Commentaries*, Robert Craft asked Stravinsky, What did you love most in Russia? Stravinsky answered, "The violent Russian spring that seemed to begin in an hour and was like the whole earth cracking. That was the most wonderful event of every year of my childhood."

There's no question that the first two ballets Stravinsky wrote for Diaghilev, *The Firebird* (1910) and *Petrushka* (1911), made big impressions among musicians and audiences. *The Firebird* was precocious, but tonally derivative. *Petrushka* was audacious, freer of form; it ruffled peers, inspiring envy and resentment. With *Le Sacre*, Stravinsky tapped into the springs of his childhood, but without a glint of sentiment, as heartless as a plant or a mantid, and matured overnight. "It seems," he would write, "that twenty years, not two, have passed since *The Firebird*." The first movement of *Le Sacre*, an Introduction about three minutes in length, recreates "the violent Russian spring that seemed to begin in an hour." It opens with a solo bassoon at high register, articulating an ancient melodic line that curves and drops like a creeping vine, quickly joined by other woodwinds that creep and climb, greenery quickening in the reeds, buds swelling, birdsong trilling in branches, calls mournful and raucous, while almost imperceptibly a beat—the pulsing earth—rises into these boughs of sound. The lyricism is sharp and impersonal, yet not without precedent for ballet-goers. The slow opening notes of Tchaikovsky's *Swan Lake*, premiered in 1877, are dominated by a lone oboe. And Claude Debussy's *L'Après-midi d'un faune*, composed in 1894 and made into a ballet by Nijinsky that premiered in 1912, opens with a solo flute. *Le Sacre*'s introduction, even in 1913, resides in the realm of art.

It is the transition into the second movement, "Augurs of Spring," that summons what Kessler called "un-art." Immediately the famously stressed ostinato chords of horns and strings sound out—juttingly percussive strokes that are like the burnt-black ties of a railroad track. In an interview just before the premiere, Stravinsky spoke of *Le Sacre*'s melody developing "along a horizontal line which swells or contracts only according to the volume of instruments—the intense dynamism of the orchestra rather than the melodic line itself." And in 1964, critiquing a recording of the score conducted by Herbert von Karajan, he wrote, "I doubt whether *The Rite* can be satisfactorily performed in terms of Herr von Karajan's traditions. I do not mean to imply that he is out of his depths, but rather that he is in my shallows.... There are simply no regions for soul-searching in *The Rite of Spring*." The swelling, thinning, hurtling locomotion of *Le Sacre* is one of its terrors, the linear drive of a behemoth on horizontal rails, compelled forward, unable to turn right or left or stop. In the sixth movement, "Procession of the Sage," the ostinato chords—louder, slower, scarier—have such leaden heaviness and drag it's hard not to think of an engine pulling out of a station.

During the planning and composition of *Le Sacre*, Stravinsky was bedeviled by trains. In July of 1911, having traveled to Talashkino to work on the scenario with Roerich, the composer "discovered that I would have to wait two days for the next train to Smolensk. I therefore bribed the conductor of a freight train to let me ride in a cattle car, though I was all alone in it with a bull! The bull was leashed by a single not-very-reassuring rope, and as he glowered and slavered I began to barricade myself behind one small suitcase." And Stephen Walsh tells us that three months later in Clarens, grappling with the first part of *Le Sacre*, Stravinsky was interrupted every morning "by a train [which] he used to anticipate ... with hatred and baited nerves." Freight and hatred. Horns and nerves. A cattle car. In his cultural history *Rites of Spring*, Modris Eksteins calls *Le Sacre* "perhaps the emblematic *oeuvre* of a twentieth-century world that, in the pursuit of life, has killed off millions of its best human beings." Another commentator ventured, "The composer has written a score that we shall not be ready for until 1940." There is no question that the symbolic half-life of Stravinsky's score, its frightening modernism, owes much to this machinery.

And its symbolisms proliferate. *Le Sacre*'s overlapping linearities are like shifting tectonic plates, an epochal realignment; its extravagant syncopations like nineteenth-century musical meter cracked open, a freshly aggressive energy unleashed. The work is uncanny in its foreshadowing of World War I, which commenced a year later and was the first war to use armored tanks. In a different vein, the critic Jacques Rivière called *Le Sacre* "a biological ballet ... spring seen from the inside, with its violence, its spasms and its fissions," which makes one think first of Darwinism and then of Richard Dawkins and his more recent theories in *The Selfish Gene*. The fact that Nijinsky's sister Bronislava was supposed to dance the Chosen Maiden, but couldn't because she became pregnant, brings a metaphor of fertility, birth, to the foreground. And Martha Graham's dancing of the role in 1920, when Léonid Massine re-choreographed the ballet, suggests that the singular women of modern dance, each creating her own movement language in the twentieth century, are a generation of self-invented "chosen maidens." In teaching the role to Bronislava's replacement, Maria Piltz, Nijinsky himself danced it a number of times. "His ecstatic performance," his assistant Marie Rambert recalled, "was the greatest tragic dance I have ever seen." In 1919 Nijinsky was diagnosed as schizophrenic.

New commentary on Stravinsky and bar-by-bar analysis of his *Le Sacre* are being published to this day. But Nijinsky's ballet—which received a mere handful of performances in Paris and even fewer in London—was all but lost by 1920, when Diaghilev asked Massine for new choreography. In the decades that followed, Nijinsky's choreography existed only in written descriptions, illustrations, old photos, and the memories of those who had taken some part in the eight performances. In 1987, however, the Joffrey Ballet presented a reconstruction of *Le Sacre du printemps* that was the fruit of sixteen years of research by the choreographer and dance historian Millicent Hodson. Working with every scrap of choreographic evidence and recollection she could find, plus the original prompt books and sketches, she pieced together a stage-worthy version of Nijinsky's "succession of rhythmically moving groups." Roerich's sets and costumes were reconstructed by Kenneth Archer.

The Hodson–Archer *Le Sacre* was controversial, as just about every reconstruction of a late-nineteenth-century or early twentieth-century dance has been. There is no way to measure the authenticity of the final product and this makes critics, who don't want to be wrong, uncomfortable. Obviously, reconstructions are imperfect. Even when every step, pose, and posture is pulled from a trusted notation, there will be flaws of accent, dynamics, atmosphere, tone. In the end it comes down to whether or not there is enough to believe in, to embrace. A film of the Joffrey reconstruction taped in 1989 is now available on YouTube in three parts—a few computer clicks away. It is gripping, it is gorgeous, and, to this eye, it is persuasive.

Stravinsky was well-pleased with the ballet of 1913—"Nijinsky's choreography was incomparable," he would write—but with the decades he began to distance himself from Nijinsky's contribution, preferring to see his *Le Sacre* as complete in itself, cut free of its roots in narrative. The compositional gambit Stravinsky complained of in the Thirties—Nijinsky's belief "that the choreography should re-emphasize the musical beat and pattern through constant co-ordination"—is vividly present in the reconstruction. It is a strength, not simplistic at all, but animating. The stylization of dancers in circles, in rows, in profile, like shallow etchings in relief, set against muscular hops and jumps on a repeating beat, reinforces the horizontal flow of Stravinsky's music, its sense of the inevitable. The percussive arm gestures have an iconic heft and the light-footed skittering a velocity that is exciting. It's as if every pore is open to the sounds of Stravinsky, and every life is moving a little too fast.

Part I is colorful; perhaps too colorful for those grown used to the black-and-white photos of *Le Sacre*'s original dancers. Part II is moonlit, mysterious, and its first movement, Mystic Circles of the Young Girls, is spellbinding, hushed yet structurally masterful. The maidens in their white shifts—soft and complicit, lambent and ruthless—seem to carry the secret Stravinsky sought to know. It is from within these woven patterns, with their strange glides and stops, that the chosen maiden tumbles forward. She is danced by Beatriz Rodriguez, and the performance is one of ice and fire. Analyzing the *Danse Sacrale*, which is the only solo in the ballet, the musicologist Peter Hill has described how it is set off from the rest of the work: "The music suddenly becomes taut, expectant, purposeful—'vertical,' not linear." Hearing Stravinsky profoundly, Nijinsky sends the maiden rocketing upward, reaching into the sky for escape. She whirls, trembles, buckles, makes a break but is hemmed in, shoots upward once more. She jumps frantically, as if skipping the rope of a giant. The choreography is in every way equal to the music because it is direct, un-decorative, and deeply childlike. Un-art and art at the same time, at every turn.

May 2013

Teaching modern poetry

Denis Donoghue

When I was appointed to the Henry James Chair of English and American Letters at New York University, I asked the chairman of the department, the late James W. Tuttleton, if I might be treated as a generalist—one who might be allowed to teach any courses in the Department that he regarded himself as competent to teach, without having to confine himself to a particular "area" or "field." Professor Tuttleton had no problem with that request. Years later, when NYU elevated me to a University Professorship, the then-president, L. Jay Oliva, told me to discuss my teaching duties with the Chair. I saw no reason to do that; I was quite content with my conditions, specifically with my unquestioned movement among the literatures of England, Ireland, and the United States.

Over the years at NYU, I have taught lecture courses in the history of English poetry from *Beowulf* to *Paradise Lost*, Shakespeare—the sonnets and about ten plays—the seventeenth-century metaphysical poets, and "Yeats and Modern Irish Poetry." (When I taught this Yeats-and-after course, I included Austin Clarke, Louis MacNeice—not the expected Patrick Kavanagh, whose poems I don't warm to—Beckett, Kinsella, Longley, Heaney, Muldoon, and Mahon: I should have included Montague and MacGreevy, too.) I have also taught graduate seminars in Jane Austen, Henry James, Virginia Woolf, and Joyce. I recall with some affection one graduate seminar I taught in "The Language of Literary Criticism," in which for each class I chose one word, offered a list of readings in it, and suggested how it might validly be used in literary criticism. The words included: form, action, meaning, structure, plot, poem, fiction, metaphor, voice, tone, and a few others that I have forgotten. Normally I would teach such a course and then set it aside for a year or two. But there was one course I got into the way of offering year after year, "Modern British and American Poetry," a graduate seminar, to begin with, though I was happy to see some interested undergraduates join up. "British" was deemed to include "Irish" without any political to-do being made about the inclusion. The class was supposedly a seminar, but I must report that my voice appeared to reduce other voices to a whisper and then to silence. Students, normally voluble, seemed to think they should withhold themselves in my favor.

For some years, I taught the course in two parts. The first part started with Whitman's *Leaves of Grass* (1855), went on to Dickinson, Hopkins, Hardy, Yeats, sometimes E. A. Robinson, always Frost, Stevens, sometimes William Carlos Williams, sometimes D. H. Lawrence, then Pound, and the early Eliot, culminating with *The Waste Land* (1922). The second part started with Hart Crane, and went on through Beckett, Empson, Auden, Roethke, and Olson, to Elizabeth Bishop, John Berryman, Robert Lowell, Richard Wilbur, Philip Larkin, and Geoffrey Hill. The students found part two of the course to be either difficult or otherwise tiresome. Gradually, I lapsed into teaching only part one, as in the Fall of 2011.

The first problem we met was how to understand the word "modern" in the title of the course. I indicated that many of the most alert writers of that period thought of themselves as living at a time of cultural crisis, but I confessed that it was not clear to me what the crisis was. I referred to three such writers, not in chronological order. The first was Yeats and I quoted one of his cryptic poems, "Three Movements," a mere three lines:

> Shakespearean fish swam the sea, far away from land;
> Romantic fish swam in nets coming to the hand;
> What are all those fish that lie gasping on the strand?

I did the little I could with that poem: noted the three lines, the monosyllabic masculine rhyme at the end of each line, the first two lines being indicatives, set off against the third, a rhetorical question, one of Yeats's favorite devices when he was being grand or apocalyptic. Then I anticipated a student's asking me: "Yes, but what precisely was troubling him?" I remarked that Yeats wrote a prose version of the poem in which he said, "passion in Shakespeare was a great fish in the sea, but from Goethe to the end of the Romantic movement the fish was in the net. It will soon be dead upon the shore." And in his essay on Bishop Berkeley, reprinted in *Essays and Introductions*, Yeats started with a large sweep:

> Imagination, whether in literature, painting, or sculpture, sank after the death of Shakespeare; supreme intensity had passed to another faculty; it was as though Shakespeare, Dante, Michelangelo, had been reborn with all their old sublimity, their old vastness of conception, but speaking a harsh, almost unintelligible, language. Two or three generations hence, when men accept the inventions of science as a commonplace and understand that it is limited by its method to appearance, no educated man will doubt that the movement of philosophy from Spinoza to Hegel is the greatest of all works of intellect.

There was no point in pursuing that immense assertion. None of us knew enough philosophy—nor did Yeats—to engage usefully in a debate; and besides, Yeats offered no explanation for the decline of literature after Shakespeare except to say that "supreme intensity had passed" from literature to philosophy. Why had it passed? I moved on to another distressed artist.

In a preface to the 1853 edition of his poems, Matthew Arnold explained why he had not included in his new book the poem "Empedocles upon Etna":

> I intended to delineate the feelings of one of the last of the Greek religious philosophers, one of the family of Orpheus and Musaeus, having survived his fellows, living on into a time when the habits of Greek thought and feeling had begun fast to change, character to dwindle, the influence of the Sophists to prevail. Into the feelings of a man so situated there entered much that we are accustomed to consider as exclusively modern; how much, the fragments of Empedocles himself which remain to us are sufficient at least to indicate. What those who are familiar only with the great monuments of early Greek genius suppose to be its exclusive characteristics, have disappeared; the calm, the cheerfulness, the disinterested objectivity have disappeared: the dialogue of the mind with itself has commenced; modern problems have presented themselves; we hear already the doubts, we witness the discouragement, of Hamlet and of Faust.

Arnold persuaded himself that he was morally bound "to inspirit and rejoice the reader." He was not justified in presenting circumstances "in which the suffering finds no vent in action; in which a continuous state of mental distress is prolonged, unrelieved by incident, hope, or resistance; in which there is everything to be endured, nothing to be done.... In such situations, there is inevitably something morbid, in the description of them something monotonous."

When he gave his inaugural lecture as Professor of Poetry at Oxford, Arnold chose the title "On the Modern Element in Literature." He planned to give a full course of lectures on the topic, but he found that he didn't know enough about several of the issues that would inevitably arise, so he broke off the course and published only the inaugural. His main idea was that those eras that think of themselves as modern are those that demand "an intellectual deliverance":

> The demand arises, because our present age has around it a copious and complex present, and behind it a copious and complex past; it arises, because the present age exhibits to the individual man who contemplates it the spectacle of a vast multitude of facts awaiting and inviting his comprehension. The deliverance consists in man's comprehension of this present and past. It begins when our mind begins to enter into possession of the general ideas which are the law of this vast multitude of facts. It is perfect when we have acquired that harmonious acquiescence of mind which we feel in contemplating a grand spectacle that is intelligible to us; when we have lost that impatient irritation of mind which we feel in presence of an immense, moving, confused spectacle which, while it perpetually excites our curiosity, perpetually baffles our comprehension.

In class, I cut short the quotation at that point because I didn't share Arnold's faith in the calmative power of an idea. I was under the sharper sway of T. S. Eliot who thought that England had become infested with ideas "in about the space of time within which Australia has been overrun by rabbits." Eliot wrote of Henry James that his "critical genius comes out most tellingly in his mastery over, his baffling escape from, Ideas; a mastery and an escape which are perhaps the last test of a superior intelligence." James "had a mind so fine that no idea could violate it."

The third and last piece of documentation I put before the students was impossible to choose. I had read Georg Simmel's *The Philosophy of Money* (1900) for some purpose of my own. I found the first part of the book to be heavy lifting, but the second part was endlessly suggestive, alive with perceptions about social class, public and private life, money of course, but also on the conditions of modern life, insights that any reader of modern poetry should be ready to receive. But the book is too long, too gritty, too slow: it was naive to think that young people, who have a hundred more attractive things to do with their time, would read a heavy book by Georg Simmel. In class I merely gave the bibliographical reference, a summary account of the book, and moved on to other things.

To Whitman, at last. But again there was something to read, or so I thought, before getting to *Leaves of Grass.* The late Quentin Anderson, a friend of mine for many years, held a contentious judgment of Whitman. Far from thinking him the great poet of Democracy, he regarded him as an autocrat. While Whitman seemed to be saying to readers, "Feel free, feel whatever you like," Anderson heard him saying, "You will feel what I feel, exactly and only what I feel, dammit, because mine are the true feelings." Anderson maintained that if you were to read, say, "Crossing Brooklyn Ferry" with your mind and your ears wide open, you would hear an autocrat telling you to take your bearings from him.

So I set the class to read that poem aloud and to pay attention to Whitman's sensibility, so far as they could discern it from that evidence. Maybe my way of presenting the question was blunt: democrat or autocrat—which? Some hands were raised for the first, some for the second, no further comments being offered. I didn't bother to count hands, the choice didn't seem worth making. But in the end and with considerable expenditure of patience on my part, I elicited a few good questions: Why does Whitman invoke something, only to say nothing about it—"The flags of all nations, the falling of them at sunset"? Why do so many lines consist of two or three loosely linked phrases—"The sea-gulls oscillating their bodies, the hay-boat in the twilight, and the belated lighter?"—rather than a couple of clauses legally joined in a sentence? In fact, why is Whitman's unit of expression the phrase rather than the clause? Had he some objection to complex sentences? I interrupted to mention that the poet and scholar Josephine Miles bruited the question about phrase and clause many years ago: more bibliographical references followed.

At worst we were on our way, and went on to read "Of the Terrible

Doubt of Appearances," "Out of the Cradle Endlessly Rocking," "As I Ebb'd with the Ocean of Life," "From Paumanok Starting," "Lo, Victress on the Peaks," "When Lilacs Last in the Dooryard Bloom'd," "There Was a Child Went Forth," "The Sleepers," and—for prose—"A Backward Glance o'er Travel'd Roads." I kept the best for the last: "Song of Myself." Berryman said that it was the best poem ever written by an American poet. By the time we came to the spotted hawk in the last section of the poem, I felt that some members of the class were converted to Whitman's audacities. Their lives would never be quite the same again:

> The last scud of day holds back for me,
> It flings my likeness after the rest and true as any on
> the shadow'd wilds,
> It coaxes me to the vapor and the dusk.

When I read those lines aloud, there seemed no point in discussion. It was a time for intelligent appreciation, for coming into the presence of the poetry.

The course proceeded happily enough. There were a few high points. When we read Dickinson's "I heard a Fly buzz—when I died—" and came to the last line, "I could not see to see," I wondered aloud how it differed from "I could not see." That, as I recall, held us for the rest of the class. Why were the first lines of Frost's "Never Again Would Birds' Song Be the Same" so good?

> He would declare and could himself believe
> That the birds there in all the garden round
> From having heard the daylong voice of Eve
> Had added to their own an oversound,
> Her tone of meaning but without the words.

We asked one another why the declaration came before the belief, but mainly we remarked that the unit of sense, in five lines, played off powerfully against the unit of sound, in four; and that the unit of sense was variously five lines, and three, and one in the rest of the sonnet. I mentioned that Frost fulfilled a suggestion well-established that the best rhymes rhyme different parts of speech—verb and noun, *believe* and *Eve*, and later in the couplet, substitute-noun and verb, *same* and *came*. Frost disobeyed the rule, in this poem, only with *words* and *birds*. What is the difference, in Stevens's "The Snow Man," between "regard" and "behold," and how would you establish a difference? In the same poem, we tried to indicate the difference, in the unforgettable ending, between "Nothing that is not there" and "the nothing that is." I made much of the much that is there already in the word "indignant" in Yeats's "The Second Coming"—

> somewhere in sands of the desert
> A shape with lion body and the head of a man,
> A gaze blank and pitiless as the sun,
> Is moving its slow thighs, while all about it
> Reel shadows of the indignant desert birds.

—and said that it is the word in Yeats's poetry that most decisively shows the force of his imagination. Nobody disputed that claim. One of the students was inspired by Pound's "The River-Merchant's Wife: A Letter" to write a term paper consonant with the line "At fourteen I married My Lord you." I celebrated the last class by playing a recording of *The Waste Land* as spoken by Alec Guinness. There were a few responses, but I felt unable to go far into them.

I would have needed another semester to examine a claim made by I. A. Richards in *Principles of Literary Criticism* (1924):

> There are those who think that [Eliot] merely takes his readers into *The Waste Land* and leaves them there, that in [*The Waste Land*] he confesses his impotence to release the healing waters. The reply is that some readers find in his poetry not only a clearer, fuller realization of their plight, the plight of a whole generation, than they find elsewhere, but also through the very energies set free in that realization a return of the saving passion.

So we brought the course to a quiet end.

Can I draw any worthwhile conclusions? The students seemed not at all beset by the motif of crisis with which I began. I tried to bring them into intelligent relation to some notable achievements in modern poetry. Perhaps I succeeded to some extent. The students were not much interested in judgments of comparative value: Is this poem better than that? They were more interested in another question: Why poetry? I told them that Edmund Wilson wrote an essay called "Is Verse a Dying Technique?" and that he came close to answering "yes." He thought that prose, after Stendhal and Flaubert—and presumably after Jane Austen, George Eliot, Henry James, Conrad, D. H. Lawrence, Joyce, and Virginia Woolf—could do anything that verse can do. But I doubted Wilson's claim. No novel or short story, not even Woolf's *The Waves*, could accommodate this sentence: "A woman drew her long black hair out tight and fiddled whisper music on those strings." But two of the most productive lines in *The Waste Land* read:

> A woman drew her long black hair out tight
> And fiddled whisper music on those strings

I don't think prose, even Joyce's, could do what Hardy does in the last stanza of "The Voice":

> Thus I; faltering forward,
> Leaves around me falling,
> Wind oozing thin through the thorn from norward,
> And the woman calling.

Another poem of Hardy's is "If It's Ever Spring Again." I quote the first half, and the second is just as good:

> If it's ever spring again,
>   Spring again,
> I shall go where went I when
> Down the moor-cock splashed, and hen,
> Seeing me not, amid their flounder,
> Standing with my arm around her;
> If it's ever spring again,
>   Spring again,
> I shall go where went I then.

Denis Donoghue

William H. Gass recovered this poem from Hardy's *Late Lyrics and Earlier* (1922) and liked it so well that he quoted it entire in two books, *Reading Rilke* (1999) and *Life Sentences* (2012). I wish I had more emphasized, in class, the pleasure of living among such vivacities.

April 2012

Puttin' on the style

Dominic Green

I HAVE BEEN READING books on writing style. My teachers at Beechwood Park Preparatory School for Boys taught me to avoid writing in the first person whenever possible, so up with that opener one shall not put, though of course, nowadays only the Queen uses the Nob's Pronoun. Begin again.

This reader has been reading books on writing style. But that is a tautology: all readers read, and all writing has style, good or bad. Worse, I have blundered into the bog of *elegant variation*. Henry Fowler, coining *elegant variation* in *The King's English* (1906), filed it under "Airs and Graces," as a kind of unmanly vice. Beechwood Park Preparatory School for Boys was a hotbed of unmanly vices, but inelegant variation was not one of them. I was taught that elegant variety was a mark of learning and taste, and a necessary technique for avoiding confusion. Begin again, again.

This reader has been perusing books on writing style. But *This reader* is now archaic. And *perusing* is mock-archaic, used by the sort of wag who prefers *quaffing ale* to *drinking beer*. Anyway, what do I mean by *perusing*? Even the most attentive critic rarely *peruses* books in the etymological sense, for the medieval Latin *perusitare* means *to use up* or *to wear out*. Am I confessing to *perusing* in the current sense of casual inspection or skimming, a usage that we all recognize, but which is proscribed by the Oxford American Dictionary? Or am I that conscientious critic who *peruses* in the Victorian sense of close inspection, as in *Jane Eyre*: "I examined her figure; I perused her features"?

Perhaps I am *perusing* somewhere in the middle, in the general sense of *reading*, a synonym in use since the sixteenth century. In which case, the substitution of *perusing* for *reading* adds nothing to the meaning. Instead, just as Fowler warned, it creates the confusion that it hoped to avoid. It also introduces all kinds of unhelpful and unpleasant associations with ale quaffers, Tudor beams on suburban garages, and the kind of person who *repairs to a hostelry* when he *goes to the pub*, and who, when he gets there, addresses the landlord as *Mine host.*

Before I scan the history of *peruse*, I really should peruse the history of *scan*. A *scan* can be a quick summary, as in *scanning the headlines.* A *scan* is also a detailed scrutiny, as in the digital image assembled by a photoelectric *scanner*. While the etymology of *peruse* is no use to anyone, only the etymology of *scan* can explain these variant meanings. The Middle English *scan* derives from a scholarly secondary sense of the Latin *scandere*, to climb. As the monk memorized a text, his foot kept the beat, as though climbing a heavenly staircase. The rhythm is the summary that contains the details. When later scholars looked for the *scansion*, they scoured the details in order to locate the summary. This habit produced an emphasis on the details over the summary. That emphasis was intensified by the advent of mechanical *scanning*.

All this suggests that etymology is worthless, except when it is essential; that principles of good style are arbitrary, except when they are not; that usage is flexible as well as historical; that the more you know about language, the harder it gets to write anything with conviction or accuracy; and that Aldus Manutius should be the patron saint of grammarians, as the inventor of the semicolon.

English is in an age of decline; English is in an age of vigor. No language, not even Latin when it was *lingua franca*, has attained the full-spectrum dominance of Global English. Meanwhile in the home territories, the quality of written English has declined as its quantity has increased. In expression, the hierarchies of formality are flattened rather than reinforced. Grammar, once a benchmark of basic literacy, is now a luxury. In spelling, the prizes go to texted acronyms. *KWIM?*

If the English teachers of Beechwood Park were able to work around the background checks and gain admittance to the liberal arts colleges where I've been teaching, they would run screaming into the ornamental lake. Many of my students cannot write a legible, joined-up hand. Many struggle to assemble a two-clause sentence without fumbling the grammar. They have trouble spelling "i before e except after c." They know that there are differences between formal and informal communication, but why should they care? The last president of the United States to write his own speeches was Woodrow Wilson. If you are a freshman in 2018, you will never have known a president who could deliver a speech without the aid of a teleprompter.

Here are some of my souvenirs from a famous and very expensive liberal arts college near Boston:

> History repeats itself over and over again from time to time.

> In the Middle Ages was when in Greece and Rome there was a rise in the interest of the science field of study.

> America was doing nothing to even try to stop any one of these countries from gaining too much power and it eventually bit them in the butt when June 7, 1941 came around.

> [In *Dangerous Liaisons*,] Valmont makes a good job of being what we today would call an asshole.

> It is often argued that had the inelegance agencies and department of defiance not failed to share the information [about the impending attack on Pearl Harbor] more could have been done to prevent this epic tragedy but should that have been the case no doubt the face of history would have been greatly altered.

> [On the Holocaust] The Nazi's did this through their work and concentration camps in which millions of people were murdered in gas tanks.

> During the war years, the comfort women weren't even treated as people; the Japanese considered them second-rate sex machines.

I cling to the last example's correct use of the semicolon as a monk might have clung to his copy of Bede's *Ecclesiastical History* when the Vikings sacked the abbey. I tell myself that malapropisms like "the inelegance agencies and the department of defiance" are proofs of life, and that language can fructify itself even in a devastated mind. But the infallibly high correlation between ignorance of the facts and failure of expression tends towards immorality. The grammatical confusion over whose butt was bitten by whom in 1941 leads inexorably to the misdating of the month in which the biting occurred. The needless apostrophe in "Nazi's" is like an air-raid siren, warning that the author is about to launch a brutal assault on historical fact, like confusing gas chambers with gas tanks. Henry Higgins called Eliza Doolittle's speech "the cold-blooded murder of the English tongue." He never had to mark her papers.

Written English is at what the euphemists would call an *inflection point*. The nineteenth-century ideal of a democratic mass culture is a bizarre historical dream. The twentieth-century empire of "Mid-Cult" is gone. The departments of English got the theoretical barbarians for whom they were waiting. Standards of literacy are declining, even though the tests are getting easier. Knowledge of a foreign language, even Spanish, is rare among those without immigrant parents. Young Americans, like Romans among the British tribes, struggle to understand the language of their servants.

Digital communication has inflected written English in the way that the guillotine inflected Marie Antoinette's neck. It is not enough that the lawmakers of the old order lose their heads: the symbols of the age of linguistic chivalry must go, too. For when quantity is all, quality is the enemy. That is why one of the aristocrats of the English language, a frequently superfluous but usually elegant construction we could live without but prefer not to on stylistic grounds, is arraigned in the title of Emmy J. Favilla's *A World Without "Whom."*

Favilla is the Global Copy Chief for BuzzFeed. As a compound noun, *BuzzFeed* resembles an Old Norse kenning, one of those fused, frozen images of the northworld at the roots of English poetry. As a fused image of the fictive digital world, BuzzFeed promises to impart information in the way that a foie gras producer imparts grain to a goose. It is hard to tell if Favilla is a mock-apologetic *humble-bragger*, or genuinely ashamed of her part in feeding us the buzzy slops of language:

> I am constantly looking up words for fear of using them incorrectly and everyone in my office and my life discovering that I am a fraud. I was a journalism student (and a FASHION journalism graduate student, lol—cut me some slack, I wanted to live in London) with minors in creative writing and Italian studies.

Favilla claims to be more of a "feelings-about-language expert" than a "straight-up language expert," and to have "neither the fortitude nor the brain capacity" for diagramming sentences. She claims that there is no such thing as "correct style," and that "sometimes there's no such thing as correct spelling." But she also assumes some entirely traditional positions, including the last of Orwell's six rules, that all rules should be broken: "It's fine to flout 'the rules' when you have a solid understanding of what the rules are and a calculated reason for doing so—for tone, for humor, for readability."

Favilla goes on to say:

> You should know your *imminents* from your *eminents* from your *immanents*, because, really, how am I to have faith that the guy who can't be bothered to get his *stationery* and *stationary* straight got the reported facts correct in a story about a missile strike.

In "On Difficulty" (1978), George Steiner, who is not a BuzzFeed guy, identified three types of difficulty in writing. Firstly, "Contingent difficulties arise from the obvious plurality and individuation which characterize world and word." Emerging from the text, they can be suppressed or managed textually, by consulting a dictionary or encyclopedia. Secondly, modal difficulties "lie with the beholder." They arise from the historical and moral fissures between an author's perceptions and ours, and "challenge the inevitable parochialism of honest empathy." Thirdly, tactical difficulties are created by writers to "deepen our apprehension by dislocating and goading to new life the supine energies of word and grammar."

Digital communication has changed all three of these difficulties. When the image dominates the text, world and word cannot individuate in the same way as they do from a text alone. A "text" is not an authorless object to be probed by French theorists, but a highly personalized message. The digital environment is so comprehensive that our parochialism becomes inescapable, and the past incomprehensible. As for tactical difficulties, texting instantly dislocates the generations and goads the parents. The problem is not the quantity of "new life" that this generates, but the quality of life.

Difficulty is the quality that opposes quantity. Variety slows the production line. "Easy solution?," Favilla advises. "Avoid *whom* altogether, for as long as you shall live!" Semicolons are "a little stodgy," but comma splices, the diarrhea of written expression, are a "radical grammatical move." Anyway, a peer-reviewed Public Library of Science study proves that "people who are obsessed with grammar aren't as nice as their don't-give-a-crap-about-grammar counterparts." Take that, Aldus Manutius.

The truth is that Favilla does care about grammar and rules. She just has a "calculated reason" for throwing in her lot with the digital rule-changers. If there is to be a new order, it is better to be a legislator than a conscript. But the analog history of revolutions still applies. She cannot stay ahead of the tumbrils forever. Soon, she will be consumed by the revolution. There may be a "suuuuuuper easy way" to avoid the gender equality "he or she" problem by using "they." There is no "suuuuuuper easy way" of avoiding digital superannuation. Everything Favilla writes is of historical interest, because none of it has a future.

To whom shall we turn as we digitate into a new Dark Age? *Whom* knows?

"I can write from authority," Steven Pinker promises in *The Sense of Style*. Strunk and White, he reminds us, lived "before the advent of modern linguistics and cognitive science, before the wave of informalization that swept the world in the second half of the twentieth century." Today's writers are "infused by the spirit of scientific skepticism and the ethos of questioning authority." They expect "reasons," not "superstitions, fetishes, shibboleths, and initiation ordeals." They need "a writing guide for the twenty-first century." *Yay!*

Pinker calls himself "a descriptive linguist," writing an "avowedly prescriptive book." His descriptions are mostly accurate and useful. The "main problem" in writing is the "Curse of Knowledge," the "difficulty of imagining what it is like for someone else not to know something that you know." One solution is to remember the old adage about "the reader over your shoulder." A "better way" is to avoid "jargon, abbreviations, and technical vocabulary," just as Robert Graves and Alan Hodge advise in *The Reader Over Your Shoulder* (1943). If you must be technical, add "a few words of explanation." Pinker does that in his next chapter, a lucid and detailed description of the mechanics and value of syntax. In descriptive terms, style emerges here as the clarifier of communication. Perfect style is the enemy of "good" writing.

The trouble starts when it comes to the prescriptions. Pinker identifies a hundred "usage issues," and resolves them by the "thoroughly conventional" method of combining "data" from various dictionaries and experts. When they disagree, or when "the examples are all over the map," he offers his own "best judgment." This sounds logical but, as historians know too well, data is only the plural of anecdote. Language is social, and people are all over the map. While "good" writing is elevated by following the rules, better writing deviates from the blandness of perfection. We recognize the best writing as Kenneth Clark recognized civilization: "I think I can recognize it when I see it." That method might be empirical, but it is not scientific; hence the varieties of taste. As usage changes, Pinker keeps having to use his best judgment. When he does, he gets angry.

Arguments, Pinker writes, should be "based on reasons, not people." You do not win by "slinging around insults" or impugning people's motives to "show you are smarter or nobler than your target." But linguistic rules are social artifacts, and ordinary users *decimate* and *delapidate* reasonable meanings whenever they feel like it. Such insults to reason enrage Pinker. The taboo against split infinitives is a "thick-witted" Latinate "superstition," persisting "only among know-it-alls who have never opened a dictionary or style manual to check." Prescriptivists are accused of "misanthropy," "misplaced emotion," and "purist rants." The "vitriol" and "bile" of the "vilifiers" is "full of baloney." *Enraged much?*

English has no gender, but Pinker seems keen to gender good and bad practice. Like Fowler, he derogates as unmanly the usages of which he disapproves. The use of *whom* should be calibrated to "the complexity of the construction and the degree of formality" desired, but even in formal prose you may prefer to be "lean and direct," and use *who*, like the always lean and direct Hemingway did when, improving on Donne, he titled a novel *For Who the Bell Tolls*. The predicative nominative, which would have Ophelia crying "Woe is I," is a "schoolmarm rule." Prescriptivists are "usage nannies." Good writers must eschew "trendy terms which tart up a banal meaning," like Anthony Blanche with his eyeliner. More interested in colons than semicolons, Pinker calls objections to the *verbing* of nouns "anal retentive." Bizarrely, anality is personified as a straw woman named "Ms. Retentive." *ROFL—not! ;-)*

Pinker rightly argues that there is "no dichotomy between describing how people use language and prescribing how they might use it more effectively." But that does not make him an authoritative prescriber. "In considering questions of usage," Pinker writes, "a writer must critically evaluate claims of correctness, discount the dubious ones, and make choices which inevitably trade off conflicting values."

This sounds authoritative, but it is pure fudge. Unless a writer is meant to evaluate truth-claims emotionally, the "critically" is superfluous. Does "discount" mean *dismiss* the claims entirely, or *reduce the value* of the claims? Are "dubious" claims only *uncertain*, and deserving of further investigation; or are they false coinages of *suspect* origin? Do linguistic choices "inevitably" involve a "conflict of values"? When values are in conflict, can they always be "traded off"? A "trade-off" is a compromise between two desirable but incompatible features of roughly equal value. Are all claims about usage of roughly equal value?

Pinker, see me after class.

"He that has once studiously formed a style," Johnson observed of Pope, "rarely writes afterwards with complete ease." It is hard to write with ease, harder still to declare for a style. The Language Wars between Prescriptivists and Descriptivists are a shadow play of the Culture Wars. "Puttin' On The Style," Lonnie Donegan sang in his mildly rebellious Skiffle hit of 1957, means "Puttin' on the agony," and taking on the *agon*. The conflict between the speech of the living and the grammars of the dead is only one of the struggles over hereditary rights and the hierarchies that they create. As I learned at Beechwood Park, rights and hierarchies, and the style that they teach, are forms of class war. *QED*, to use the right sort of acronym.

Pinker writes for his class. Not for the public, but for "the smaller virtual community of literate speakers" who write "in public forums such as government, journalism, literature, business, and academia." Reading Pinker, it is surprising how little has changed since Graves and Hodge looked over that class's shoulder in 1943: the same warnings against vagueness and bureaucratic pomp, the same pleas for the semicolon and the comma. Reading Emmy Favilla, it is terrifying how rapidly the linguistic floor has caved in. Linguistically, as socially and economically, the middle class is falling away, while the upper echelons fight over their formal usage. *SMH*.

English, unlike French, has no academy to protect its virtue. Market forces have done the job instead. The concentrations of class and power they create now threaten to undo the language. Meanwhile, the real language war goes on. This, as Kingsley Amis observed in his own *King's English* (1997), is not between academic Prescriptivists and Descriptivists, but between guerrilla outfits of Berks and Wankers.

> *Berks* are careless, coarse, crass, gross, and of what anybody would agree is a lower social class than one's own. They speak in a slipshod way with dropped *H*s, intruded glottal stops, and many mistakes in grammar. Left to them the English language would die of impurity, like late Latin.
>
> *Wankers* are prissy, fussy, priggish, prim, and of what they would probably misrepresent as a higher social class than one's own. They speak in an over-precise way with much pedantic insistence on letters not generally sounded, especially *H*s. Left to them the language would die of purity, like medieval Latin.

Professional writers are mercenaries in this battle. Sometimes you defend beauty from the Berkish horde. At other times only Berkish vigor can revive the Wankers' languor. In this, Pinker's "professional" writers are closer than they realize to the real professionals, the freelance writers for whom valor is also the better part of discretion, and who always write with a reward in mind.

Sam Leith's *Write to the Point* calls for a ceasefire in the war of Berks and Wankers, and a "Christmas kick-about for the troops in no-man's land." Leith, the literary editor of *The Spectator*, advises pragmatism, and persuasion over prescription. It is a sociological fact that many speakers of Standard English "place a high value on getting it right." If you know the battlefield, you are less likely to fall into a shell hole and "break your silly neck." So learn the rules of English warfare. Fight the English way, with courtesy, common sense, and a touch of cold steel.

The hierarchy of language reflects social hierarchy. On the first recording of "Puttin' On The Style," from 1925, the trained tenor Vernon Dalhart pretends to be a hick. Two years later, Irving Berlin's "Puttin' On The Ritz" in its original verse satirizes the upwardly aspirational style of black Harlemites. Today, BuzzFeed's inversion of value reflects the inversion of the Romantic cult of youth into commercial youth culture.

Change is inevitable: some of the stylistic proscriptions in the first edition of Fowler's *King's English* are now prescriptions of good style. The issue is whether we accelerate or manage the process. The digitization of manners is separating the written *langue* from the spoken *parole*. This is bad for literature, and worse for social mobility and democracy.

It is in the writer's interest, Leith argues, to bridge Steiner's "modal difficulties" and show empathy for the reader. The person who believes that infinitives must not be split is "technically, quite wrong." So is the person who, like Steven Pinker, believes in the "folklore" that the split infinitive rule derived from analogy with Latin. But rhetoric is about persuasion, not proving people wrong, and language is common property. "If that's the sort of person you're writing to, *or even if there's a decent chance such a person will be in your audience*, leave that infinitive unsplit with a good grace and an inward smile."

Persuasion also requires the striking of the correct "register." You can use "It's me" or "It is I," but the latter strikes a more formal register. The same goes for double negatives whose spoken sense is obvious, but which provoke the pedants and confuse the readers. And though *whom* is "going the way of the rest of the inflectional system," show some consideration for those who may mourn its passing. Even a BuzzFeeder does not wear flip-flops to a funeral.

Leith fixes bayonets for the combats on whose outcomes the fate of written English depends. There is, he writes, "a special place on the end of the Devil's toasting fork" for the comma splicers. And semicolons are not, as Kurt Vonnegut said in another of those macho outbursts that grammar seems to inspire, "transvestite hermaphrodites representing absolutely nothing." Semicolons, like language itself, are flexible enough to accommodate development, but rigid enough to contain ideas and sustain their expansion. A well-turned semicolon, like a twist of the painter's brush or a turn of a dancer's body, is formed after the natural object it describes.

Style is the silent art. Leith quotes the poet-etymologist-doctor Lewis Thomas's *The Medusa and the Snail* (1979):

> The thing I like best in T. S. Eliot's poetry, especially in the Four Quartets, are the semicolons. You cannot hear them, but they are there, laying out the connections between the images and the ideas. Sometimes you get a glimpse of a semicolon coming, a few lines farther on, and it is like climbing a steep path through woods and seeing a wooden bench just at a bend in the road ahead, a place where you can expect to sit for a moment, catching your breath.

February 2018

T. S. Eliot's animus

Adam Kirsch

When I was beginning my career as a writer in the late 1990s, I met an older literary critic who talked about "crushing" people with his negative reviews. He said it ironically, but still with a certain infectious glee—knowing it was exactly the kind of thing that creative writers accuse critics of thinking in secret. For a critic to take pleasure in crushing a writer or a book suggests that he is governed by aggression and envy thinly disguised as impartial judgment. The English critic Cyril Connolly seemed to substantiate this idea when he wrote that the function of the critic is to stand at the gates of Parnassus, where writers line up for admission to immortality, and as each one steps forward to bash him over the head with a club.

But mere spite could never motivate anyone to write lasting or truly interesting criticism—all it can produce is hatchet jobs, designed to demolish rather than to convince. (Indeed, who reads Connolly's reviews now?) If I kindled, as a young writer, to the idea of crushing bad writing, it was more in the spirit of Voltaire's battle cry against the Church, *écrasez l'infame*—a kind of principled fury at the violation of literature. This idea notoriously appeals to young critics more than older ones, who almost always mellow into appreciation, for the same reason that all kinds of aggressive idealism appeal primarily to the young. They don't yet know that mediocrity is not an aberration but the way of the world, nor do they have a sufficiently developed power of empathy to want to avoid hurting real individuals in the name of an abstract ideal.

Still, I continue to believe that any critic who wants to write something lasting—who believes that criticism can be a species of literature—must write partly out of aggression. Or perhaps a better word is animus, in the sense of a fixed intention, a partiality. Literary journalism describes and explains literature and ideas as they are—the way Edmund Wilson, a master journalist, explained modernism in *Axel's Castle* and Marxism in *To the Finland Station*. Criticism tries to move literature and ideas in the direction of what should be.

Few critics in history have been more successful in that endeavor than T. S. Eliot, whose poetry and criticism worked in tandem to redefine the way the twentieth century thought about literature. He was the rare writer whose best essays were as significant and influential as his best poems. In the years following World War I, he produced a clutch of masterpieces in both genres: poems like "Gerontion" (1919) and *The Waste Land* (1922) alternated with essays like "Tradition and the Individual Talent" (1919) and "The Metaphysical Poets" (1921). In his 1932 Norton Lectures at Harvard, Eliot took as his subject "The Use of Poetry and the Use of Criticism," and the writers he focused on were almost all poet-critics, from John Dryden in the seventeenth century to Matthew Arnold in the nineteenth. That he himself was the latest, and perhaps greatest, member of this lineage was left implied, but by then it didn't need to be stated outright.

The poet-critic has been an institution in English literature because usually only an artist has the stubborn animus, the conviction that art should be one way rather than another, that makes for interesting criticism. To write something new is to imply that the writing which already exists is insufficient. Of course, this can never be demonstrably true: there is always already more than enough literature to occupy any reader for a lifetime. Only an artist's egotism, his certainty that he has something new to offer that the world should not be without, gives him the fruitfully skewed perspective on literature required to see it as deficient. Harold Bloom's theory of "the anxiety of influence" gave formal statement to this agonistic element in all artistic ambition. "To imagine is to misinterpret," Bloom writes, which means, among other things, to misinterpret all existing poetry to its own detriment in order to make room for something new.

Bloom's own antagonism to Eliot has various literary and ideological sources, but the most important is just this expressive antagonism of the "descendant" for the "precursor." For it was Eliot who first formulated this dialectic in his essay "Tradition and the Individual Talent." Characteristically, however, where Bloom describes the relationship between past and present in terms of anxiety and rivalry, Eliot emphasizes the mutual adjustment that brings both sides into harmony, or as he says, "conformity":

> The existing order is complete before the new work arrives; for order to persist after the supervention of novelty, the *whole* existing order must be, if ever so slightly, altered; and so the relations, proportions, values of each work of art toward the whole are readjusted; and this is conformity between the old and the new.

For Eliot, criticism is one of the means of effecting that adjustment. "The poetic critic is criticizing poetry in order to create poetry," he writes, and it is certainly true that Eliot the critic helped to create the taste by which Eliot the poet was enjoyed, even though—or, better, precisely because—his work in the two genres was so different in tone and approach. *The Waste Land* famously baffled many of its first readers with its fragmented, allusive, chaotic voices; one critic (the father of the novelist Evelyn Waugh) called it the work of a "drunken helot." It's easy to condescend to such a reaction now, but it would be a mistake to discount the provocative, disruptive force that Eliot deliberately brought to bear in *The Waste Land*. The leading English poets of the period were the so-called Georgians, who favored plain-spoken language and country settings—as, for instance, in Gordon Bottomley's "The Ploughman":

> The seasons change, and then return;
> Yet still, in blind unsparing ways,
> However I may shrink or yearn,
> The ploughman measures out my days.
> His acre brought forth roots last year;
> This year it bears the gleamy grain;
> Next spring shall seedling grass appear:
> Then roots and corn and grass again.

A reader schooled on verse like this—spoken straightforwardly by a single lyric voice, using ideas and imagery that would have been familiar to the Greek and Latin poets—could only have been discomfited to open *The Waste Land* and find lines like these:

> I remember
> Those are pearls that were his eyes.
> "Are you alive, or not? Is there nothing in your head?"

But

O O O O that Shakespeherian Rag—
It's so elegant
So intelligent

At first sight, the disorganization here—the cross-cutting voices and mixed-up allusions spanning centuries—could well sound like a direct transcript of a disorganized mind. But the magisterial tone of Eliot's criticism instantly dispels that possibility. Clearly, the writer of the essays is a person of intelligence and judgment, a writer who knows exactly what he is doing. It follows that what looks like chaos in his poetry must actually be a deliberately chosen difficulty whose function it is up to the reader to figure out.

In fact, Eliot argues in his criticism that difficulty is the only possible approach for a truly modern poet to take. In his essay "The Metaphysical Poets," he made the case for the rehabilitation of that school of seventeenth-century English poets, such as John Donne and Andrew Marvell, who had long been critically disdained for being artificial and over-intellectual. The subsequent course of English poetry had left their kind of writing behind, cultivating instead the sonorous rhetoric of Milton, the urbane balance of Pope, the rich fantasy of Keats and Shelley. It was Samuel Johnson who named this school "the metaphysical poets," and he didn't intend it as a compliment. "Their amplification had no limits; they left not only reason but fancy behind them, and produced combinations of confused magnificence that not only could not be credited, but could not be imagined," Johnson wrote in his *Lives of the Poets* in 1779.

Almost a hundred and fifty years later, Eliot insists that the standard Johnsonian view of poetic history has things backwards. The metaphysicals were not a dead end, but instead the embodiment of an intellectual vitality that poetry needs to rediscover. If they appear strange and artificial, that is only because English readers have lost the expectation that a poet should appeal to the mind as well as the ear and the heart. Eliot's essay concludes by drawing a direct line from the seventeenth century to the twentieth:

> Poets in our civilization, as it exists at present, must be *difficult*. Our civilization comprehends great variety and complexity, and this variety and complexity, playing upon a refined sensibility, must

> produce various and complex results. The poet must become more and more comprehensive, more allusive, more indirect, in order to force, to dislocate if necessary, language into his meaning.

Clearly, this is a defense of the poetics of *The Waste Land*, which Eliot would publish the following year. Eliot here proposes what the American critic Yvor Winters later attacked as "the fallacy of imitative form"—the idea that expressing chaotic inner experience requires a chaotic arrangement of language. But it's characteristic of Eliot that he finds an impeccably traditional warrant for the difficulty and complexity that, in his own verse, sounds so revolutionary. The drunken helot turns out to know much more about the history of poetry, and about the hidden resources of that history, than his opponents do.

Eliot wrestled, however, with the question that he imagined a reader would ask: why should someone capable of writing great poems choose to spend his time writing critical prose? Eliot wrote an enormous amount of criticism—his prose output exceeds his verse by at least ten to one—but he was never able to arrive at a satisfactory formulation of his motives. Certainly he is unwilling to argue that criticism can be written, like poetry, for its own sake—that it is, in his philosophical term, "autotelic," an end in itself. His very reverence for poetry compelled him to see criticism as a lower form of writing, an adjunct to literature rather than literature itself. In this Eliot agreed with most literary opinion throughout history. No one has ever said of criticism what Keats said of poetry, that it should come as naturally as leaves to a tree. Criticism seems incapable of immediacy because it is always necessarily about something—about literature, whose direct relationship to life and language it can only envy.

Fifty years before Eliot wrestled with this problem, it had also troubled Matthew Arnold, a poet-critic who was in many ways Eliot's role model and, also, for that very reason, the frequent target of his sarcasm. When Eliot set himself to think about the purpose of criticism in a major early essay, "The Perfect Critic," from 1920, he did so in dialogue with Arnold's 1864 essay "The Function of Criticism at the Present Time."

Arnold, like Eliot, worked at a demanding job—the nineteenth century poet was a school inspector, the twentieth-century poet a bank clerk and publisher—and both produced comparatively little poetry. Yet they devoted much of their writing, especially as they grew older, to critical essays about literature, religion, and politics. When Arnold writes about the function of criticism, there is a certain note of apology. It's all very well to suggest that a writer is better off focusing on creation than criticism, Arnold says, but what if one simply has a greater talent for criticism? "It is almost too much to expect of poor human nature, that a man capable of producing some effect in one line of literature, should, for the greater good of society, voluntarily doom himself to impotence and obscurity in another," he writes, with barely concealed reference to himself.

While Arnold readily grants that "the critical power is of lower rank than the creative," he goes on to mount a defense of the critic, especially in the context of nineteenth-century English literature. It is not open to writers in every age, he argues, to create works of genius. To reach the heights of Greek tragedy or Elizabethan drama a writer needs a healthy culture to provide him with the "elements" and "materials" of his work—above all, with vital and credible ideas. And this is where the critic comes in: it is up to the critic to "make an intellectual situation of which the creative power can profitably avail itself" by distinguishing between what is genuine and what is inferior in the art and thought of his age.

In Victorian England, which Arnold saw as philistine and intellectually provincial, there was a wide field of activity for such a critic—not just in the sphere of literature, but in politics and society as well. "Life and the world being in modern times very complex things, the creation of a modern poet, to be worth much, implies a great critical effort behind it," Arnold says. The implication is that, while he himself was born at the wrong time to become a great poet, he can at least contribute to the future flowering of poetry through his critical work. He concludes by comparing himself, with no little pathos, to Moses on Mount Nebo:

> That promised land it will not be ours to enter, and we shall die in the wilderness: but to have desired to enter it, to have saluted it from afar, is already, perhaps, the best distinction among contemporaries; it will certainly be the best title to esteem with posterity.

Eliot's early essay "The Perfect Critic" offers a rather different defense of criticism, arguing that it is only the creative writer who can be an adequate literary critic. He makes this point by attacking two critics to whom he was, in fact, deeply indebted: Arnold, whom he dismisses in the essay's first paragraph as "rather a propagandist for criticism than a critic," and the British man of letters Arthur Symons. It was Symons whose book on French Symbolist poetry had first introduced Eliot the undergraduate to writers like Jules Laforgue and Tristan Corbière, who proved to be the keys that allowed him unlock the sound of modernism in his own work.

Eliot does pay tribute to that book, calling it an "introduction to wholly new feelings" and a "revelation." But it served that purpose, Eliot says, only because he was not yet familiar with the poetry Symons was writing about. When it comes to more familiar material—for instance, Symons's book on Shakespeare's plays that Eliot is reviewing—the defects of his criticism become plain. These are the defects of what Eliot calls "impressionistic" criticism, an approach which ostensibly offers "the faithful record of the impressions, more numerous or more refined than our own, upon a mind more sensitive than our own."

Though Eliot does not name him, it was Oscar Wilde who offered the classic formulation of this approach to criticism, in his 1890 essay "The Critic as Artist." Here Wilde takes a paradoxical pleasure in overturning the conventional hierarchy that places creative writing above criticism. Wilde says that "the highest Criticism, being the purest form of personal impression, is in its way more creative than creation." The critic makes art out of his experiences of art; criticism is "the record of one's own soul" as it encounters great poems, paintings, or music. And since the purpose of art is nothing else than to provoke such impressions in its audience, one can say that the goal of art is to inspire criticism—a direct reversal of the usual belief that the goal of criticism is to increase our appreciation of art.

In taking issue with this idea, Eliot strikes at the weak point of impressionistic criticism, which is that the "art" it creates—the verbal record of an aesthetic experience—is never as good as the art that inspired that experience. In fact, Eliot argues, the more directly a critic attempts to turn his criticism into a work of art—to compete with the poem, play, or painting he is writing about—the more clearly he reveals that he is not capable of free artistic creation. With a critic like Symons, Eliot writes, "reading sometimes fecundates his emotions to produce something new which is not criticism, but is not the expulsion, the ejection, the birth of creativeness." Impressionistic, aesthetic criticism, this metaphor suggests, is abortive, a miscarriage of the imagination; in such critics, there is "a defect of vitality or an obscure obstruction which prevents nature from taking its course."

This metaphor suggests an explanation for why poets make the best critics of poetry: they are not trying to use prose for the aesthetic purposes that only poetry can achieve. The criticism of an artist "will be criticism, and not the satisfaction of a suppressed creative wish," Eliot writes. He contrasts Symons with the poet Algernon Swinburne, whose poetry is hypnotically musical, but whose prose is clear and logical. Symons's prose, Eliot notes, does not resemble Swinburne's prose, but his verse, which leaves it betwixt and between—neither true poetry nor true criticism.

What true criticism sounds like, instead, Eliot shows by example. It is not woozily impressionistic but logical and argumentative, concerned above all with clear definitions. The epigraph to "The Perfect Critic" is taken from the French critic Remy de Gourmont, whom Eliot and Pound both admired: "Eriger en lois ses impressions personnelles, c'est le grand effort d'un homme s'il est sincère." The goal of a "sincere" man is "to erect his personal impressions into laws"—a formulation Eliot returns to in the body of the essay. "The moment you try to put [aesthetic] impressions into words, you either begin to analyse and construct, to '*ériger en lois*,' or you begin to create something else," he writes.

Yet as the essay develops, it becomes clear that Eliot does not believe the critic should literally issue laws about how poetry should be written—the way the neoclassical critics of the seventeenth century did when they decreed that all dramas must observe the Aristotelian unities of time, place, and action. "The dogmatic critic, who lays down a rule, who affirms a value, has left his labour incomplete," Eliot writes; "a precept . . . is merely an unfinished analysis." Issuing a blanket rule or prohibition incites defiance in the thoughtful reader. When a critic does his job properly, this defiance is outwitted; the critic's insight into a particular work or author is so convincing that the reader "will form the correct judgment for himself."

Of course, there is no objectively correct standard of judgment in literature; the act of judgment is a process that takes place in an individual human mind, rather than a permanent decree or canon declaring that one poet is better than another. What Eliot means by the "correct" judgment, then, is really the judgment that the critic wants the reader to adopt. The goal of the critic is to impose his way of reading on his audience, to make it seem so natural and inarguable that one has no choice but to follow it. This sounds authoritarian, and indeed Eliot's critical voice is extremely commanding, issuing pronouncements as if they were self-evident and banishing dissent with sharp sarcasm.

But a way of reading is finally a way of thinking and experiencing. Poetry is a means of giving the reader access to the poet's thoughts and experiences, but when a poet does this, we call it a gift: the poem is an offering of one mind to another, a way of breaching the individual's usual painful isolation. When a critic does the same thing, his communication of consciousness tends to be called an imposition, even an act of arrogance, as though the critic wanted to commandeer the reader's mind.

Eliot concludes "The Perfect Critic" by attacking "the torpid superstition that appreciation is one thing, and 'intellectual' criticism something else." After all, the attempt to "analyze and construct," to *ériger en lois*, stems from the same root as the impulse to create a poem: both should be understood as responses to inner experience and attempts to share that experience. "The two directions of sensibility are complementary," Eliot writes. Their difference stems from a difference in form: the form of criticism is necessarily argumentative and forensic, seeking to control and define rather than to give and express.

But giving and controlling, Eliot suggests in *The Waste Land*, have the same root. In the last section of the poem, "What the Thunder Said," the single syllable "DA" is interpreted as the beginning of different Sanskrit words: "datta" means "give" while "damyatta" means "control." When I first read Eliot's criticism, it was the desire for control—to reshape the world of literature according to the dictates of his own particular animus—that most impressed me and appealed to me. The young critic—and Eliot was at the beginning of his literary career when he wrote his most important essays—needs to express that animus as much as the poet needs to express his visions.

But control, in literature as in life, never lasts very long. Eliot's lasted longer than most, two or three decades, but today it has vanished and may even work to his disadvantage as our more democratic republic of letters strongly resists the type of authority that he incarnated. What remains is what his criticism tries to give—a particular way of experiencing poetry that is, ultimately, inseparable from his own deepest needs and desires.

Eliot's affinity for complexity and difficulty, combined with his longing for order and discipline; his need for clear distinctions that allow each thing to be what it is and not something else; his love of the past and desire to be absorbed into it, so as to deflect the existential risk and terror of the present—all these qualities shine out from Eliot's criticism as much as from his poetry, his thought about religion and politics, or indeed his biography. And it is this unity, this ability to impress his way of being on every form he touched, that marks Eliot as a great artist.

April 2020

The unbearable rightness of criticism

William Logan

When critics play parlor games, they imagine how they would have reviewed the controversial books of the past. Critics are later judged, not by the book they failed to pan, but by the book they failed to praise. Most are certain that, given the chance, they would have recognized the genius of *Lyrical Ballads*, or *Leaves of Grass*, or *The Waste Land*. We pour bile on the heads of the dolts of 1798 and 1855 and 1922 who didn't realize what was on the desk before them.

When you look at those wrongheaded, purblind reviews now long forgotten, however, it's surprising how shrewd they are, even the most notorious ones. The critics (like the poets themselves) were creatures of their day, and subject to the prejudices of the day. The reviewer is most vulnerable facing a poetry that threatens convention—violations of form and formality tend to provoke the most ill-considered judgments. Yet even there, after you have adjusted for bias, the critic can be uncannily canny about the poetry itself. Such contemporary insight is important not just for its punctuality. The reviews expose how the poets failed the time—or how their time failed the poets. Only by knowing how critics resisted the work can we see what the poetry put in danger.

The first review of *Leaves of Grass* was written by Charles A. Dana, editor of the *New York Daily Tribune*.

> From the unique effigies of the anonymous author of this volume which graces the frontispiece, we may infer that he belongs to the exemplary class of society sometimes irreverently styled "loafers." He is therein represented in a garb, half sailor's, half workman's, with no superfluous appendage of coat or waistcoat, a "wide-

> awake" perched jauntily on his head, one hand in his pocket and the other on his hip, with a certain air of mild defiance.

The book's frontispiece, a stipple engraving after a lost daguerreotype of the author, displayed a New York rough with his loose clothing and workman's hat—a sailor's open-collared blouse, the moleskin pants of a carpenter, and a slightly crushed soft-crowned hat, called a "wide-awake" supposedly because it lacked the felt "nap." Here was the perfect democrat, a man showing where he stood by wearing neither coat nor waistcoat, while he slouched, hip cocked, staring out boldly at the reader.

Whitman's extraordinary loose-limbed preface to *Leaves of Grass* made grand claims:

> There will soon be no more priests.... Through the divinity of themselves shall the kosmos and the new breed of poets be interpreters of men and women and of all events and things.

Dana distilled Whitman's vision of the poet as a democratic bard:

> His language is too frequently reckless and indecent.... His words might have passed between Adam and Eve in Paradise, before the want of fig-leaves brought no shame; but they are quite out of place amid the decorum of modern society, and will justly prevent his volume from free circulation in scrupulous circles.... *The Leaves of Grass* ... are full of bold, stirring thoughts ... but so disfigured with eccentric fancies as to prevent a consecutive perusal without offense.

The idea that poetry has a proper language had been invoked against *Lyrical Ballads* half a century before and would be repeated against *Howl* a century after. However irritated Whitman made the critic, Dana detected something in this "odd genius." What fair-minded reader now would claim that Whitman's verse is not "disfigured with eccentric fancies," even if we can't quite believe that his language would have served "Adam and Eve in Paradise, before the want of fig-leaves"? (Surely Dana meant "brought shame," not "brought no shame.") If we are no longer offended, the critic has merely registered the local propriety, as Emily Dickinson did when she wrote Thomas Higginson: "You speak of Mr Whitman—I never read his Book—but was told that he was disgraceful."

The young Charles Eliot Norton, later editor of the *North American Review*, discovered, in a roundup of books,

> a curious and lawless collection of poems, called *Leaves of Grass*, and issued in a thin quarto without the name of publisher or author. The poems, twelve in number, are neither in rhyme nor blank verse, but in a sort of excited prose broken into lines without any attempt at measure or regularity, and, as many readers will perhaps think, without any idea of sense or reason. The writer's scorn for the wonted usages of good writing, extends to the vocabulary he adopts; words usually banished from polite society are here employed without reserve and with perfect indifference to their effect on the reader's mind; ... the introduction of terms, never before heard or seen, and of slang expressions, often renders an otherwise striking passage altogether laughable.

The word "lawless" now reads more like a compliment—the laws Norton had in mind have come to seem antiquated, remote, even charmingly naive (and so were not laws but practicalities).

The diction of English poetry has gone through many cycles of contraction and release, when the fashion of one day has hardened into the law of the next—just as certain styles of clothing have fossilized into custom, like the vestments of Catholic priests, some of them more than a millennium old. More telling are periods when taste reversed direction, so that fifty years after his death Shakespeare was rewritten for the delicate tongue, and more than a century after that bowdlerized for the delicate ear.

Norton observed the violence in Whitman's violations—the "excited prose," the rejection of the authority of taste, the speech without reserve. It isn't known to what obscenities the Manhattan Island ear was exposed in the "blab of the pave," but Norton was objecting to Whitman's embrace of American slang. Who now could dislike a poet who vilified government, as Whitman did in his preface, for its "swarms of cringers, suckers, doughfaces, lice of politics.... It is better to be a bound booby and rogue in office at a high salary than the poorest free mechanic or farmer"?

Norton was embarrassed by Whitman's lack of embarrassment. The judgment is a matter for social history and psychology; even if our ancestors never stitched skirts around piano legs, there was a nicety to language we should now think absurd. We moderns are not yet above such arguments, with the insistent self-censorship of television, newspapers, and magazines (even the *New Yorker* long maintained a list of banned words). Television's casual murders, blood sports, and vulgar humor bother few—though its adolescent carnality and cable porn might have jaded even Lord Rochester. Whitman's critics were disturbed by the indecency of passages like:

> Limitless limpid jets of love hot and enormous .... quivering
> jelly of love ...
> white-blow and delirious juice,
> Bridegroom-night of love working surely and softly into
> the prostrate dawn,
> Undulating into the willing and yielding day,
> Lost in the cleave of the clasping and sweetfleshed day.

Norton saw the barbarians at the gates in Whitman's "mixture of Yankee transcendentalism and New York rowdyism" (married, he was surprised to see, in the "most perfect harmony"); yet, despite his bluestocking sensibility, he found himself drawn to "this gross yet elevated, this superficial yet profound, this preposterous yet somehow fascinating book." (Whitman's contradictions have perhaps never been better sketched.) The critic's prejudices were largely social, but he understood the poet's means and ambition. Though Norton was prepared to believe that Whitman was what he claimed to be—an American rough—he had his doubts whether the poet was a kosmos. Honest critics doubt that still.

Once we discount Norton's reflexive resistance, his insights seem largely acute, the better for his occasional wit—he wrote his friend James Russell Lowell that the poet "combines the characteristics of a Concord philosopher with those of a New York fireman," continuing, however,

> there are some passages of most vigorous and vivid writing, some superbly graphic descriptions, great stretches of imagination,—and then, passages of intolerable coarseness,—not gross and licentious but simply disgustingly coarse. The book is such indeed that one cannot leave it about for chance readers, and would be sorry

> to know that any woman has looked into it past the title page. I have got a copy for you.

The British, who took to Whitman more eagerly than the Americans, were not immune to exaggerated complaint. The reviewer in the *Critic* thundered that the poems could be compared to "nothing so much as the war-cry of the Red Indians," while the poet was "as unacquainted with art, as a hog is with mathematics" (the critic had forgotten Toby the Sapient Pig, who had made his debut on the London stage in 1817):

> We had ceased, we imagined, to be surprised at anything that America could produce. We had become stoically indifferent to her Woolly Horses, her Mermaids, her Sea Serpents, her Barnums, and her Fanny Ferns; but the last monstrous importation from Brooklyn, New York, has scattered our indifference to the winds.

The Woolly Horse was one of Barnum's "humbugs," though a real genetic mutation. The Fejee Mermaid was another humbug, but a fake. Fanny Fern was the first woman newspaper columnist (and therefore as freakish as the woolly horse or Fejee mermaid), and later a defender of Whitman. The comparisons tell us something of the British view of America in the decades following *Martin Chuzzlewit* and Mrs. Trollope's *Domestic Manners of the Americans.*

Few now recall Martin Farquhar Tupper, the author of *Proverbial Philosophy* (1838), a volume of poetic fustian composed in long prosy lines, which sold more than a million copies. A review in the London *Examiner* called Whitman a "wild Tupper of the West."

> Suppose that Mr. Tupper had been brought up to the business of an auctioneer, then banished to the backwoods, compelled to live for a long time as a backwoodsman, and thus contracting a passion for the reading of Emerson and Carlyle; suppose him maddened by this course of reading, and fancying himself not only an Emerson but a Carlyle and an American Shakespeare to boot, when the fits come on, and putting forth his notion of that combination in his own self-satisfied way, and in his own wonderful cadences? In that state he would write a book exactly like Walt Whitman's *Leaves of Grass.*

The Brooklyn poet may indeed have borrowed some notion of the poetic line from Tupper, or from others who wrote in quasi-Biblical cadences—Whitman's free verse was not without precedent. Yet the reviewer saw beyond the defects:

> He asserts man's right to express his delight in animal enjoyment, and the harmony in which he should stand, body and soul, with fellow-men and the whole universe. To express this, and to declare that the poet is the highest manifestation of this, generally also to suppress shame, is the purport of these *Leaves of Grass.* Perhaps it might have been done as well, however, without being always so purposely obscene, and intentionally foul-mouthed.

Filter out the qualms about language, the language not meant for poetry, and the remarks are cunning even while cutting. However scathing the criticism, however it looked down its nose at the upstart American, the droll mingling of Emerson, Carlyle, and Shakespeare was insightful, and the backhanded remarks hilarious—what do we have in *Leaves of Grass* but pages and pages of a man of some culture, playacting the rough? Only the Whitman Whitman wished to be had sheltered a runaway slave or seen the marriage of a trapper and a "red girl." (When Bronson Alcott visited Brooklyn, Whitman claimed to be a house-builder—but Whitman's mother confessed that the poet's brother was the builder and that Walt "had no business but going out and coming in.")

The anonymous reviewer then wrote a burlesque of this backwoodsman, as if his leaves had been torn from an auction catalogue:

> Surely the house of a poet is a poem, and behold a poet in
>   the auctioneer who tells you the whole lot of it—
> The bath stone, compass front, open border, fender, shovel,
>   tongs, and poker,
> The blue moreen festoon window-curtain, the mahogany dining-
>   table on the floor,
> The six ditto hollow seat chairs covered with blue moreen,
> Covered with blue moreen and finished with a double row of
>   brass nails and check cases,
> The Wilton carpet, sun shade, line and pulleys, the deal side
>   board stained, . . .
> The Tragic Muse in a gold frame.

No matter how trivial Whitman sometimes seems, he is never as trivial as this—and never as giddy (Whitman lacked few things, but among them was a sense of humor). Yet here, here too, what was misguided was not unfair. The untidy Whitman is easy to love—the reviewer simply had not learned how.

The most difficult book to review is, like a Fejee Mermaid, unlike anything seen before—or one that, despite superficial similarities to the literature of the day, is radically different. Often the author knows he is presenting a work strange and difficult. When Whitman published *Leaves of Grass* anonymously, adding his self-justifying preface, he had done no more than the authors of *Lyrical Ballads* before him. Whitman went one better by also sending his freshly printed book to the most famous literary man of the day, who in 1844 had called for an American poetry in his essay "The Poet":

> Our logrolling, our stumps and their politics, our fisheries, our Negroes, and Indians, our boa[s]ts, and our repudiations, the wrath of rogues, and the pusillanimity of honest men, the northern trade, the southern planting, the western clearing, Oregon, and Texas, are yet unsung. Yet America is a poem in our eyes.

Emerson could not have imagined that the young author would print the sage's effusive reply in the second edition, issued months later, with an excerpt stamped in gold on the spine—"I greet you at the beginning of a great career." (This is perhaps the earliest example of the purloined blurb.) However shy and gentle Whitman was in his codgery years, when he published *Leaves of Grass* he was a bustling, go-ahead young man—restless as a hyena, in the argot of the day, and sharp-practiced enough to write no fewer than three reviews of the book himself.

The "advertisement" to *Lyrical Ballads*, probably written by Wordsworth, was a canny defense of a revolution in poetic diction.

> The majority of the following poems are to be considered as experiments. They were written chiefly with a view to ascertain how far the language of conversation in the middle and lower classes of society is adapted to the purposes of poetic pleasure. Readers accustomed to the gaudiness and inane phraseology of

> many modern writers ... will perhaps frequently have to struggle with feelings of strangeness and aukwardness: they will look round for poetry.

By "experiments," Wordsworth was referring to those of the scientist. This was not the first time poetry had been called experimental. Henry Pemberton, in *Observations on Poetry* (1738), remarked that epic and dramatic poetry show the "natural effects of different tempers and passions under feigned actions" and "may very justly be compared with the experimental part of natural philosophy" (the term for what we now call science). If experimental poetry still aims to upend convention, the scientific overtone has been lost—perhaps unfortunately, for experiments in literature succeed far less frequently than those in the lab, which rarely succeed at all.

The poems Wordsworth and Coleridge wrote before *Lyrical Ballads* were typical of their late Augustan day. They gave little hint of such a departure in style and ambition—and the mask of anonymity protected the small reputations they had already gained. With England at war against France, the French Revolution still in progress (Louis XVI had been executed only five years before), and growing fears at home about the discontent among laborers and the poor, the notion of overthrowing the high-flown, regal diction of Pope in favor of the humble language of cottage and field might have been called seditious, had people feared poetry more.

It was on the problem of diction that many of the reviews concentrated their wrath. Charles Burney remarked in the *Monthly Review*,

> Though we have been extremely entertained with the fancy, the facility, and (in general) the sentiments, of these pieces, we cannot regard them as poetry, of a class to be cultivated at the expence of a higher species of versification, unknown in our language at the time when our elder writers, whom this author condescends to imitate, wrote their ballads.

This argument over the identity of poetry—that the poems, whatever their virtues, were not poems—has often been at the center of the attack on the "experimental."

We have become so inured to Wordsworth's and Coleridge's title, it's easy to forget that to the readers of 1798 it meant some scraps that had fallen out of Bishop Percy's *Reliques of Ancient English Poetry* (1765). *Lyrical Ballads* offered, not a march forward, but a leap backward to the poetry of centuries before—it was peddling the faux antique only a generation after the Ossian hoax, and just eleven years after the publication of Chatterton's fake Rowley poems. The difference was that the poems in *Lyrical Ballads* were, at worst, self-conscious imitations of antique style. (Burney overplayed the point—they don't seem *that* antique). It was easy to dismiss imitation while ignoring the means provided for a change more radical—the use, not just of common diction, but of the lives of the poor, of sailors, of shepherds, of the dispossessed. In the end, poetry always ends up republican.

The reaction was akin to what might be expected if Sotheby's started to auction Ethan Allen furniture. Burney continued:

> Would it not be degrading poetry, as well as the English language, to go back to the barbarous and uncouth numbers of Chaucer? Suppose, instead of modernizing the old bard, that the sweet and polished measures, on lofty subjects, of Dryden, Pope, and Gray, were to be transmuted into the dialect and versification of the xivth century? Should we be gainers by the retrogradation? *Rust* is a necessary quality to a counterfeit old medal: but, to give artificial rust to modern poetry ... can have no better title to merit and admiration than may be claimed by any ingenious forgery.

Ingenious forgery. There is the taint left by Chatterton and Macpherson. Recall that "The Foster-Mother's Tale" would have seemed an allusion to *The Canterbury Tales*—Chaucer had gained a reputation for barbarousness largely because people had forgotten how to pronounce Middle English (Shakespeare's and Donne's "numbers" were also uncouth, compared to the smooth lack of anapestic variation in Pope). This is always the problem with Whiggish criticism—the present has evolved from a savage past, and civilization can be defended only by barring the uncivilized. The sacrifice of the broader subjects available in freer diction is not admitted. The source of *retrogradation*, however, lay in the retrograde motion of planets, which at times move backward across the sky—a mystery until Copernicus. Burney should have known that the apparent drift backward concealed nothing but forward progress.

Despite all this fuss about the upstart poets, marching toward the ill-numbered past, when Burney finally came to the poems he was remarkably reasonable.

> When we confess that our author has had the art of pleasing and interesting in no common way by his natural delineation of human passions, human characters, and human incidents, we must add that these effects were not produced by the *poetry*:—we have been as much affected by pictures of misery and unmerited distress, in *prose*. The elevation of soul, when it is lifted into the higher regions of imagination, affords us a delight of a different kind from the sensation which is produced by the detail of common incidents.

This was the point of rupture with the poetic diction of the time. If for nothing else, we can be grateful that the doctor's crack about prose probably fired Wordsworth to compose the longer preface to the 1800 edition of *Lyrical Ballads*, in which he defended poems written in the "real language of men."

At every point where Burney might have glimpsed the book's virtues, he was prevented by a hidebound view of what poetry is; yet he sensed, in the darkened mirror of taste, something he could not quite put a name to.

> The author's first piece, the Rime of the ancyent marinere, in imitation of the style as well as of the spirit of the elder poets, is the strangest story of a cock and a bull that we ever saw on paper: yet, though it seems a rhapsody of unintelligible wildness and incoherence, … there are in it poetical touches of an exquisite kind.

There *is* a kind of unintelligible wildness in Coleridge's youthful work (as well as an intelligible wildness)—that is part of its importance, and much of its charm. The critic was right in perhaps every way except the one that matters—he did not understand that the earth had shifted. Just such a quake occurs symbolically in "The Foster-Mother's Tale." *Lyrical*

Ballads failed to fit the definition of poetry because the definition of poetry was suddenly out of date.

Burney went through the book at length, praising where he could, hurling the critic's darts everywhere else ("All our author's pictures, in colouring, are dark as those of Rembrandt," "Here candour and tenderness for criminals seem pushed to excess," "Another tale of woe!"). He was bemused when he sensed political radicalism ("if all the poor are to ... supply their wants from the possessions of their neighbours, what imaginary wants and real anarchy would it not create?"). Burney was a bit too worried by the poets' fondness for criminals and the poems' criticism of the army.

The good doctor certainly missed the point at times, claiming of "The Foster-Mother's Tale" that it "seems meant to throw disgrace on the savage liberty preached by some modern *philosophes*." It's true that the boy in the poem is brought to "heretical and lawless talk" by too much reading, but Coleridge hardly intended a sermon on the danger of books. Yet Burney praised numerous poems, including "The Nightingale" ("Miltonic, yet original"), "Simon Lee," and "The Idiot Boy." And it takes a hard heart not to admit that "We Are Seven" is "infantine prattle."

Burney may have been right that Wordsworth strained logic here and there. The doctor suggested that in "The Last of the Flock" the Job-like shepherd "had, indeed, ten children: but so have many cottagers; and ere the tenth child is born, the eldest begin to work, and help, at least, to maintain themselves." Perhaps—but Burney overlooked the crushing truth beneath, that in straitened times the shepherd might have to sell all he had to keep his children from starving. The weepy melodrama hides an uncomfortable truth. Whatever his animadversions, and however narrow the needle through which he was forced to view the poems, Burney frequently succumbed to grouchy praise:

> The style and versification are those of our antient ditties: but much polished, and more constantly excellent. In old songs, we have only a fine line or stanza now and then; here we meet with few that are feeble:—but it is *poesie larmoiante*. The author is more plaintive than Gray himself.

Poesie larmoiante—sob-story poetry. (The remark that Wordsworth had out-Grayed Gray would have stung—Wordsworth detested Gray.) There's an uncommon amount of tear-jerking in *Lyrical Ballads*, far more than in the border ballads from which they distantly descended—so many are the tears described or evoked that the cock-and-a-bull story of "The Ancient Mariner" serves almost as comic relief. It's hard not to agree that "Tintern Abbey," though the "reflections of no common mind; poetical, beautiful, and philosophical," is also "tinctured with gloomy, narrow, and unsociable ideas of seclusion." *Lyrical Ballads* is an uncomfortably dark book—when the city looks at the country, it rarely sees how poor and hardscrabble it is. (Poets of eclogue and pastoral often seem willfully obtuse.)

The Waste Land, another gloomy poem, famously confounded early reviewers. Some insisted on reading it through the lens of the author's earlier work (a strategy that would have produced poor results for *Lyrical Ballads* and *Leaves of Grass*, had they not been published anonymously). Some spent a long time talking about anything but the poem: F. L. Lucas offered a long digression on Alexandria, Clive Bell a pointless anecdote about plumping for Eliot by reading "Prufrock" at a country-house weekend in 1916—or was it 1917? Some listed the allusions, at length, or quoted, at greater length. Some, like J. C. Squire, gave the whole thing up as a bad job ("I am still unable to make head or tail of it"). It occurred to few that a poem weighed down by allusion was also a man weighed down by allusion, which in the dreary wasteland of post-war London might have suggested that culture had reached a saturation, where little could be said that had not been said before. And almost no one saw that the real wastes that haunted the speaker (as opposed to the interior desert of a man at the end of his tether) might have been the torn-up battlefields across the Channel. If reviewers resist actually reviewing the book, it tells us something about reviewers, but much more about the book.

When critics tried to come to grips with the poem, however much they disliked it, the results were more telling. Louis Untermeyer was a bad poet and a worse critic, but he struggled resolutely with a poem he had every reason to dislike (later he included it, perhaps a little grudgingly, in his endless string of anthologies). He had a stronger sense than most critics, however, of the inner relation between *The Waste Land* and Eliot's previous work—the traits of Eliot's earliest poems ("an elaborate irony, a twitching disillusion, a persistent though muffled hyperaesthesia") had been merged with the "harder and more crackling tone of voice" of the later, which reveled "in virtuosity for its own sake, in epigrammatic velleities, in an incongruously mordant and disillusioned *vers de société*." The characterizations were not unfair—they were merely misdirected. *The Waste Land*, Untermeyer concluded,

> is a pompous parade of erudition, a lengthy extension of the earlier disillusion, a kaleidoscopic movement in which the bright-coloured pieces fail to atone for the absence of an integrated design. As an echo of contemporary despair, as a picture of dissolution of the breaking-down of the very structures on which life has modelled itself, "The Waste Land" has a definite authenticity. But an artist is, by the very nature of creation, pledged to give form to formlessness; even the process of disintegration must be held within a pattern.

Untermeyer sought pattern, and was disturbed when he could not find it (pattern was there, but not in the place he looked): "This pattern is distorted and broken by Mr. Eliot's jumble of narratives, nursery-rhymes, criticism, jazz-rhythms, 'Dictionary of Favourite Phrases' and a few lyrical moments." Exactly, but to the critic this was not poetry:

> Possibly the disruption of our ideals may be reproduced through such a *mélange*, but it is doubtful whether it is crystallized or even clarified by a series of severed narratives—tales from which the connecting tissue has been carefully cut—and familiar quotations with their necks twisted, all imbedded in that formless plasma which Mr. Ezra Pound likes to call a Sordello-form.

The critic committed the common sin of projecting an obligation, here the artist's promise "to give form to formlessness"—in *The Waste Land*, the breaking of this promise is the point. Untermeyer understood the poem's defects but not that they were the medium for something more interesting. It was exactly the lack of integration that told the tale, or the tales. Yet more favorable critics might not have been stringent enough to characterize Eliot "as an analyst of desiccated sensations, as a recorder of the nostalgia of this age," and *The Waste Land* as a poem "whose value is, at least, documentary." (Eliot is one of the great poets of city life, and urban manners.) The truths of the bad reviewer are often more troubling than the emollient praise of critics without an axe to grind.

The sins of the critic are almost all sins of damaged expectation. A reviewer like the anonymous J. M. in the *Double Dealer* may have believed that *The Waste Land* was the "agonized outcry of a sensitive romanticist drowning in a sea of jazz," nothing more than a "medley of catch-phrases, allusions, innuendos, paraphrase and quotation [that] gives unmistakable evidence of rare poetic genius," and that the poem would have been perfectly clear to Eliot, "for whom every quotation has an emotional and intellectual connotation of intense significance." To everyone else, however, "it must remain a hodge-podge of grandeur and jargon." Of course *The Waste Land* is that—it was everything J. M. said. The poem merely required readers who could believe that such a work was no bad thing.

The decades after such reviews would prove that *Leaves of Grass*, *Lyrical Ballads*, and *The Waste Land* offered poetry a way out of the past—it's always hard for critics to recognize opportunities before some poet has taken advantage of them, and hard even then to admit that they *were* opportunities. The problem was never that the critics did not see, but that they did not know how to value what they saw. That would take no more than time—or other critics.

Once the genius of Shakespeare, or Coleridge and Wordsworth, or Whitman, or Eliot is generally agreed, the critics who backed the wrong horse are generally written out of literary history, or held up to ridicule. Yet those critics of whom time makes fools—John Wilson Croker on *Endymion* ("We almost doubt that any man in his senses would put his real name to such a rhapsody"), Francis Jeffrey on *The Excursion* ("This will never do"), and many another—are often more worth reading than the critics of the day who got it right. We know what the latter critics will say—their taste is what our ears have been filled with; but, unless we read the other critics with attention, we can forget what an uncertain thing a poet's reputation was at the start, forget what withering glances the poems themselves had to overcome, forget that, if the naysayers had had their way, literary history might have been different. Reading the reviews that mistook genius is not simply cold comfort for critics whom taste passed by, or an exercise in antiquarian taste. The critics who got it wrong remind us that poets in whom we now see only virtues once seemed full of vices, and that, though we may value those vices differently, sometimes it is their presence that makes the virtues virtues.

April 2012

Sound & sensibility

David Yezzi

[By audible reading,] I mean to indicate something more than the reading of poetry aloud. I mean to indicate the reading of poetry not merely for the sensual ear, but for the mind's ear as well; yet the mind's ear can be trained only by way of the other, and the matter, practically considered, comes inescapably back to the reading of poetry aloud.
—YVOR WINTERS, "The Audible Reading of Poetry"

Writing is not an exercise in excision, it's a journey into sound. How about "Tomorrow and tomorrow and tomorrow"? One tomorrow would suffice, but it's the other two that have made the thing immortal.
—E. B. WHITE

POETRY READINGS are like mice, largely unnoticed, though once you've become aware of them you begin to see them everywhere. Slams, spoken word, open mics, national recitation competitions—there are more modes and venues for live poetry than ever before. Then come the universities and bookstores and what W. H. Auden referred to ruefully as being "On the Circuit," by which he meant singing for one's supper as a famous poet on the reading or lecture circuit: "Since Merit but a dunghill is,/ I mount the rostrum unafraid:/ Indeed, 'twere damnable to ask/ If I am overpaid."

For the most part, the proliferation of poetry readings bodes no ill and goes a long way toward restoring poetry's ancient and fundamental connection to the human voice. The page has much to offer: it provides an object for study. It performs vital work both in visual terms and in the preservation and dissemination of poetry (though the Internet now does a better job in these respects), but, for my money, the poem exists primarily for the ear. "The ear is the only true writer and the only true reader," wrote Robert Frost. As critics and poets from Whitman and Dickinson to I. A. Richards and Paul Fussell have noted, poetry is a corporeal sensation, akin to dancing or singing; meter exists not on the page but in the bodies of the reciter and listener. As the prosodist Thomas Cable reminded me recently, *The Oxford English Dictionary* ties the metrical "foot" directly to "the movement of the foot in beating time." As Fussell points out in *Poetic Meter and Poetic Form*: "The 'body swayed to music' of Yeats's 'Among School Children' is a sort of emblem of the reader responding to silent metrical effects. A kind of motionless, silent dancing is what the reader seems to be doing when he is responding metrically—as he must—to his own silent reading of a poem." As Yvor Winters argues, the only tutor for this kind of silent reading is audible reading.

Hearing an author read his work aloud, I frequently feel that I have understood it for the first time. Aspects of the work that I'd missed in silent reading come clear. I never realized how funny *Middlemarch* was until my wife and I took turns reading it to each other on a cross-country car trip. A friend told me recently that the same thing happened to him with the Anna Livia Plurabelle section of *Finnegans Wake* at a Bloomsday celebration in New York. I recently spent an afternoon with the British poet laureate Andrew Motion, who said that, as he saw it, the notion of a poet finding his or her "voice" is directly connected to the poet's own speaking voice; his examples included the BBC English of Philip Larkin and the mandarin mid-Atlantic melodies of Anthony Hecht. One might add the sonorous barking of Geoffrey Hill (one of our greatest readers of poetry), along with Larkin and Ted Hughes, as described in Seamus Heaney's splendid essay "Englands of the Mind." Motion added that, when he was writing his biography of Larkin, he dictated a draft of the entire book into a tape recorder so that he could test each sentence on the voice and revise accordingly. This is partly what Michael Elbow is referring to in *Vernacular Eloquence: What Speech Can Bring to Writing*, when he describes "speaking onto the page."

If auditory reading is essential to the life of poetry, why is it that I typically equate the idea of attending a poetry reading with a trip to the dentist? Strike that. I have a wonderful dentist, who is genial and completely pain-free, nothing like most poetry readings. After the best performances of poetry, one feels enlivened and elevated, much as one does after hearing Placido Domingo (now singing baritone roles) or viewing an exhibition of Poussin landscapes. A transporting and memorable communication takes place, and it is worth remembering in this context that "aesthetic" refers at its root to sensation. That is why it is particularly dispiriting to hear poets who give no thought to the vocal presentation of their poems, as if Domingo never practiced his scales or Poussin never studied perspective. Instead, these desultory readers adopt, either by default or instinct, a repetitive rising inflection, which repels the ear and bears no relation to sense. It's what G. Burns Cooper, in *Mysterious Music: Rhythm and Free Verse*, calls the Generic American Poetry Contour: "a slight but sustained rise at the end of each line or intonation phrase." Here is the example Cooper provides (with my thanks to the critic Natalie Gerber):

> I never met a purple cowww,
> I never hope to see onnne,
> But I can tell youu
> here and nowww
> I'd rather seee
> than bee onne.
> Thank you very much. [bow]

One of the reasons people fall into this odd singsong may be, as Cooper suggests, that "it serves to mark the language as poetic" and is therefore "pragmatically very effective" in that regard. He hastens to add that this imposed melody "is often not aesthetically effective." Copper's thoughtful generosity, his benefit of the doubt, nettles me a bit. Shouldn't a poem's language by definition be poetic and deeply so, without any imposed vocal indicators? The cases in which that would be aesthetically effective would have to be relative outliers, if one accepts Auden's sense of poetry as "memorable speech." It can be common speech or hieratic speech, comic or scathing, but the truth is people don't talk in droning rising inflections! And there's a good reason why: sense makes a particular sound. One can promote the musical aspects of a vocal performance, but not at the cost of the "sound of sense."

This phrase—as well as "sentence sounds"—comes, of course, from

Robert Frost. For Frost, thought and meaning in a poem were coterminous with the human voice: "The brute tones of our human throat that may once have been all our meaning. I suppose there is one for every feeling we shall ever feel, yes and for every thought we shall ever think. Such is the limitation of our thought." A sentence makes two kinds of sounds. First there is the music of "meaning conveyed by word and syntax." Sound conveys to the hearer the main elements of the sentence along with a host of subordinate phrases and clauses—all with the voice, heard either silently or aloud. As proof of this, listen to any great Shakespearean actor. Paul Scofield, for example, could organize and clarify with the pitch of his voice elaborate periods, which run over a dozen or more lines. Where he means to continue at the end of a phrase or clause, his voice rises. Where he means to conclude his thought (or Hamlet's or Malvolio's thought), his music lowers toward a full stop. In between, his vocal pitch stair-steps through a host of lists and contrastive stresses, keeping each in its place and in perfect relation to the whole. As a further example of Scofield's skill, listen to the Naxos recording of Scofield's *King Lear* (2001), with a full cast, including Kenneth Branagh as a hugely affecting and musical Fool. Scofield's Lear has been voted by the RSC as the greatest Shakespeare performance in living memory, and this late recording by him is the finest by far that I have ever heard. At play's end, his vocal instrument keens and rages, slowly, painfully, through "Howl, howl, howl, howl! O you are men of stones," encompassing in this single pentameter most of the five stages of grieving. This sense of pure sound must be what Frost is referring to when he says, "The best place to get the abstract sound of sense is from voices behind a door that cuts off the words." Of course, we all make this music of sense instinctively when we speak to one another, but then we foolishly eject it for some reason when we get up to read poetry aloud.

The second sound of sense tends toward the mystical. "I shall show the sentence sound saying all that the sentence conveys with little or no help from the meaning of the words. I shall show the sentence sound opposing the sense of the words as in irony. And so till I establish a distinction between the grammatical sentence and the vital sentence." The work of the vital sentence, as opposed to the grammatical one, has to do with the communication of thought and emotion through "music," which in poetic terms is rhythm broadly construed, e.g. meter, a range of sonic effects, diction, syntax, and even imagery and thematic tissue. In "The Use of Poetry and the Use of Criticism," T.S. Eliot speaks of "meaning" as separate from (and, he is tempted to add, extraneous to) the real work of the poem:

> The chief use of the "meaning" of a poem, in the ordinary sense, may be (for here again I am speaking of some kinds of poetry and not all) to satisfy one habit of the reader, to keep his mind diverted and quiet, while the poem does its work upon him: much as the imaginary burglar is always provided with a nice piece of meat for the house-dog.

This is E.B. White's point about "Tomorrow and tomorrow and tomorrow": one tomorrow conveys the meaning but the other two cast a rhythmic spell that is the line's real work, a specific emotion conveyed by the music of the words. Of course, no writer is more generous than Shakespeare in this regard: "Once you find the heart beat and the speed of it, it really does play you," the brilliant English Shakespearean Rory Kinnear said recently, during his stint as Hamlet at the National. Beyond denotation, sound conveys the connotations of words, which Yvor Winters understood as constituting the emotional charge of language. Sound carries the emotion and is, in this way, itself the meaning.

The reason why poets fuss over every word has as much to do with sound as anything. A word may mean the correct thing but fail to express the precise feeling because of a deficit on the level of music or rhythm. As quoted by Walter Kerr in *How Not to Write a Play*, W.H. Auden puts it this way:

> A poet writes "The chestnut's comfortable root" and then changes this to "The chestnut's customary root." In this alteration there is no question of replacing one emotion with another, or of strengthening an emotion, but of discovering what the emotion is. The emotion is unchanged, but waiting to be identified like a telephone number one cannot remember. "8357. No, that's not it. 8557. 8457, no it's on the tip of my tongue, wait a minute, I've got it, 8657. That's it."

The discovery of the emotion, I want to suggest, inheres as much in the sound, as in the denotative meaning of the words. For Frost, this sound of sense "is the abstract vitality of our speech. It is pure sound—pure form. One who concerns himself with it more than the subject is an artist." Without question, Frost was a great artist in exactly these terms. No other American poet has made sound mean as much, or to put it another way sound and sense are so seamlessly wedded as to form a unified expression, sound as pure form.

A number of Frost's poems come to mind in this regard, though "Mending Wall" exists so consistently as an aural emblem of its theme that I want to walk through passages of it line by line. Everyone will, of course, know the famous first line of the poem ("Something there is that doesn't love a wall"), and, indeed, the poem's familiarity is a considerable challenge to its just appreciation—much as the folky familiarity of Frost's farmer-poet persona once hid the "terrible" Frost from view. If one were to stage the little scene of two men repairing a stone wall in the woods, the mise en scène would look roughly like this: x | y. One man stands stage left, the other stage right, with the wall between them ("We keep the wall between us as we go"). The poem is about division and the impulse to bridge this division, though it's important to note that the speaker who questions the necessity of the wall does so only to himself and not out loud to his neighbor. He is in this way complicit in the wall's perpetuation.

Each spring the two men meet to perform their yearly ritual of repairing the wall, which, due to unknown reasons, falls into disrepair each winter. How many men are in the poem? Two. How many times does the line "Something there is that doesn't love a wall" occur in the poem? Twice. How many times does "Good fences make good neighbors" occur? Again, twice. The first of these lines begins the poem; the other ends it, highlighting the two poles of the argument. Looking closer, the poem is a relentless dividing into two, rhetorically and on the level of diction. Here is the opening:

> Something there is *that* doesn't love a wall,
> *That* sends the frozen-ground-swell under it,
> *And* spills the upper boulders in the sun;
> *And* makes gaps even *two* can pass abreast.

A pair of "thats" and a pair of "ands" divide the sentence into twinned elements. (The gaps are wide enough for "two" to pass abreast.) The next sentence extends the twinning, first with "work" = "thing" and then the doubled verbs of "come after" and "made repair."

> The *work* of hunters is another *thing*:
> I have *come* after them and *made* repair
> Where they have left not *one stone on a stone*,

Not "one stone on another," mind you, but one stone on a stone. The repetition is percussive. The doubling (which continues throughout) is enacted upon the ear. Then there are Frost's clausal repetitions:

> The gaps I mean,
> No one has *seen them made* or *heard them made*,

And:

> And *set the wall between us* once again.
> We *keep the wall between us* as we go.

One hears these repetitions and divisions as a bodily rocking, back and forth, to and fro, as the rhetorical stresses mount up in twos; Frost has created a verbal music one can almost dance to. Again, the poem expresses division into two:

> To *each* the boulders that have fallen to *each*.

And a further doubling:

> And *some are loaves* and *some so nearly balls*

Frost reiterates the situation:

> Oh, just another kind of outdoor game, *One on a side*.

He then points out that the two men do not need the wall to keep their properties distinct:

> *He is all pine* and *I am apple orchard*.

The terms are then redoubled as a chiasmus:

> My *apple trees* will never get across
> And eat the cones under his *pines*, I tell him.

We then get the first instance of the poem's closing line, which itself contains a doubling:

> He only says, "*Good fences* make *good neighbors*."

By this point in the poem the pattern is so fully established that it becomes the very music though which the poem moves:

> "Why do they make *good neighbors*? Isn't it
> Where there are *cows*? But here there are no *cows*.
> Before I built a wall I'd ask to know
> What I was *walling in* or *walling out*, . . . "

Then the opening line returns, with a twinning on "elves":

> Something there is that doesn't love a wall,
> That wants it down. I could say *"Elves"* to him,
> But it's not *elves* exactly . . .

"Stone" is doubled a second time, here in a decidedly minor key:

> I see him there
> Bringing a *stone* grasped firmly by the top
> In each hand, like an old *stone* savage armed.

The pairing continues through to the end:

> He moves in darkness as it seems to me,
> Not of *woods* only and the shade of *trees*.
> He will not go behind his father's *saying*,
> And he likes having thought of it so well
> He *says* again, "*Good fences* make *good neighbors*."

In his second book of poems, *North of Boston* (1914), Frost includes this note on the verso across from "Mending Wall," which begins the collection: "*Mending Wall* takes up the theme where *A Tuft of Flowers* in *A Boy's Will* laid it down." That earlier poem, from Frost's debut collection, is worked out in rhymed couplets. It concludes:

> And dreaming, as it were, held brotherly speech
> With one whose thought I had not hoped to reach.
> "Men work together," I told him from the heart,
> "Whether they work together or apart."

The end of "Mending Wall" is wonderfully ambiguous—not the clear-cut sentiment one is tempted to construe, in which the speaker's vision of a world where clear divisions are unnecessary trumps the need for amicable separation. Yet the two men "work together" as good neighbors, despite their difference of opinion about the wall, a difference that, as noted above, the speaker keeps to himself. Perhaps this is the theme that the poem "takes up," or one of them at least.

In the music of the poem, Frost engages the abstract vitality of our speech. Much as George Herbert is able to create, in Joseph Summers's term, a "hieroglyph" of his subject though its pattern of lines and letters on the page, Frost creates an aural analog of the poem's meaning, in which the sound is the sense. The compulsive divisions in the language (included by Frost either consciously or un-) work out that division in the ear. I'm not sure if this fundamental structural principle in the poem has been elaborated previously; if it has, I am unaware of it. All I can say is that I first heard it before I saw it. I own a recording of Frost reading the poem, which I listened to repeatedly as an aid to committing the poem to memory. To hear Frost growling out "one stone on a stone" is to get the music of the whole argument of the poem in one's head. I think Frost would be the first to agree that one cannot fully understand a poem, its inmost sense, until one hears it read aloud.

For several years now I have taught a course for poets in reading poetry aloud. It's not only that poetry readings have become one of the most common ways in which readers come across new work. Reading aloud is an integral part of composition. Almost immediately the students realize that the audible reading of poetry leads to revision: some part of the expression is awkward or infelicitous and needs reworking. As poets gain experience in presenting their work to an audience, they begin to compose with that audience in mind, hewing close to the way that sound conveys meaning to an audience. As in "Mending Wall," it is the bars to such intimate communication that poetry is meant to bridge.

April 2014

Building the Gilded Age

Michael J. Lewis

ONE DESIGN PROBLEM that the American architect has never satisfactorily resolved is that of the great house. In comparison, the invention of the skyscraper was child's play. We lack the settled pattern of life that produced the English country house or the Italian villa, those fully rounded building types, whose rooms and amenities ripened over centuries and which express a distinct economic and social order. Here the tendency is either to inflate middle-class forms into the gargantuan, as Elvis did at Graceland, or to contrive self-indulgent fantasies, as Michael Jackson did at his Neverland Ranch.

The antebellum world did not know the problem. Most fortunes were created by making or selling something (one thinks of John Jacob Astor's fur-trapping empire) and grew incrementally. But after the Civil War, a new national railroad system opened another path to wealth. Through collusion and preferential fee schedules, one company could be favored and others discouraged, leading to absolute control over the production and distribution of a single product. So were born the monopolies, oligopolies, and trusts of the Gilded Age, as well as the robber barons who controlled them.

Their prototype was Cornelius Vanderbilt, the transportation tycoon, whose children lined Fifth Avenue with their mansions. But his successors achieved wealth at an even greater order of magnitude, such as J. D. Rockefeller, who formed the Standard Oil Trust in 1882, or Henry O. Havemeyer, who founded the American Sugar Refining Company in 1891 and came to control 98 percent of American sugar production. But once in possession of such a fortune, how was one to live?—like an English lord, a Medici banker, a Bourbon king? There was no single logical answer. One could only make an architectural hypothesis and see if it fit, like the various Petit Trianons, Loire Valley chateaux, and English

Palladian imitations that saturated Newport during the 1880s. Yet none had anything like the intimate relation to the land of its European prototype (one did not sally forth to inspect the vineyards or to summon the hounds). This is the incongruity that McKim, Mead & White, the principal architects of Gilded Age America, challenged.

McKim, Mead & White are celebrated for their lovely civic architecture: Columbia University, with its sovereign spatial order, or the Boston Public Library, that cult temple of literacy in pink granite. All show the "order and movement" that Buffon tells us is the wellspring of style. But however brilliant these performances, they were at bottom derivative, applying characteristically French solutions to characteristically French problems. It is rather in their houses where the imagination of the partnership blossomed. They devised two domestic types, each superbly gauged to its setting, and each crystallized in a single building. The suburban type was perfected in 1880 with the brilliant Victor Newcomb house at Elberon, New Jersey, a relaxed shingled affair, open in plan and informal in character. Two years later, they perfected the city type with the Villard Houses in New York: a dignified Renaissance palace that did not strut or swagger like its Fifth Avenue predecessors. One can scarcely think of two buildings that so swiftly and decisively changed the direction of American architecture.

This story is admirably told in Leland Roth's *McKim, Mead & White, Architects* (1983), the most important study of the firm. But Roth focused on the buildings, and touched only lightly on the thicket of social, financial, legal, and religious ties that connected architect to client. Even *Stanny* (1989), Paul Baker's splendid portrait of the wayward Stanford White, only treated this intricate subject impressionistically. Mosette Broderick's sprawling *Triumvirate* is the first comprehensive social history of McKim, Mead & White. A sprawling epic of interlocking lives, fortunes, and tragedies, it has a kind of grand momentum that at times suggests a Gilded-Age *Brothers Karamazov*. But at other times it wobbles under the sheer mass of genealogical information and family history and reads rather like a novelization of the social register (albeit a delightfully freewheeling novelization).

The bare bones of the story are familiar. The architect Charles Follen McKim (1847–1909) trained at Harvard and Paris and went to work for the mighty H. H. Richardson, another product of Harvard and Paris. In the office he met White (1853–1906), who was not academically trained but had a natural genius for the artistic and decorative side of architecture. After a series of false starts, the firm of McKim, Mead & White was formed in 1879, with William Rutherford Mead (1846–1928) serving as business partner. As partnerships go, it was an unusually stable vessel, White acting as sail, McKim as rudder, and Mead as anchor.

The firm never had to endure lean years. Success came early and was constant; by the time of McKim's death, some 940 buildings had already been completed. As its fame grew, it became prestigious simply to work in the office. The partners exploited this shamelessly, insisting on a probationary period of six to twelve month of unpaid work before draftsmen would receive a salary. The exploitation was mutual: an inordinate number of architects used them as the launching pad for their own careers, including Cass Gilbert, Whitney Warren, Grosvenor Atterbury, and Henry Bacon. Their own buildings carried the high standards of the firm throughout the country, so much so that by the 1920s its style had become something of an American civic vernacular.

As Broderick shows, it was the marriage of talent and social connections that proved decisive. McKim came from a prominent Abolitionist family, and he mined a network that ran from Unitarian Harvard to Quaker Philadelphia. Mead's connections were literary, his sister having married the novelist and editor William Dean Howells. But the chief rainmaker was the irresistibly convivial White. An office canard (which Broderick does not repeat) claims that the ratio of jobs brought in by the three partners was eight to two to ninety. And White was restlessly inventive when it came to the cultivation of clients, devising such flourishes as his color-coordinated dinner parties, where redheads served red wine and blondes white. One can see why the clientele came back for more.

In one instance, Robert and Ogden Goelet, the New York real estate speculators, ordered nine buildings from White during a single decade. One is the elegant office tower on the corner of Twentieth and Broadway in which *The New Criterion* is published, which Lewis Mumford singled out for praise in 1931 in *The Brown Decades* ("Nothing so fresh was done in New York for a whole generation.") Even from beyond the grave, his clients were loyal: after Robert Goelet's death in 1899, White built his white marble mausoleum at Woodlawn Cemetery.

A profile of a characteristic McKim, Mead & White client emerges from among Broderick's innumerable capsule biographies. They were typically successful entrepreneurs of undistinguished pedigree, such as James Gordon Bennett, the publisher of the sensationalist *New York Herald* (still remembered for his "Doctor Livingstone, I presume" scoop), or

Henry Villard, the self-made railroad tycoon whose self-invention included even his own name (he was born in Germany as Ferdinand Hilgard). McKim had a gift for papering over the blank spots and question marks in the family tree with architecture. He did so not with nervous verbosity, as had previously been the rule—as at P. T. Barnum's minaret-crowned "Iranistan" or Mark Twain's Gothic fantasia at West Hartford—but with reserve and understatement. Here perhaps his Quaker upbringing came into play. Or it was the fruit of his 1877 study tour of New England's colonial architecture, the first such investigation by an architect of note.

Whatever the cause, the result was the architectural mode that Vincent Scully has called the Shingle Style. A colonial revival in spirit but not in form, it drew freely on the wood forms of early colonial houses, before they hardened into Georgian rigidity. Elastic in planning and abstract in form, the style was endlessly flexible, and could be inflected to absorb stylistic elements from sources as diverse as the English Queen Anne Revival or provincial Normandy. It was also capable of expansion to any scale, which was not true of the more formal historical styles. Finally, in its use of local materials and ground-hugging form, it was the first style to have an organic relationship to the American landscape. It remains one of America's durable architectural successes, and the mode is still very much alive today (as a drive to East Hampton will confirm).

Broderick shows how McKim's domestic architecture flowed naturally into his clubhouses, another building type to which he gave definitive form. For Bennett, he built the Newport Casino (1879), the building that established the Shingle Style as the fashionable language of resort architecture. His urban clubhouses, in turn, followed the model of the Villard houses, in which a gracious Italian Renaissance palazzo evoked a sense of unhurried, leisurely urbanity. Of these he built a great many. It is almost as if McKim set out singlehandedly to house all of New York's clubmen, his projects including the Century Club (1889), the Metropolitan Club (1891), the Harvard Club (1893), and the University Club (1896), to name only the most prominent. (Here, at another remove, was also the stylistic source for New York's grand hotels, whose modern character was established in 1908 with the Ritz-Carlton, by White's protégé Whitney Warren).

Some architects take personal pride in shaping every aspect of the building's visible envelope and would no more think of delegating design responsibility than a sculptor would let an assistant carve a hand. Louis Sullivan and Frank Lloyd Wright fall into that category. But McKim, Mead & White did not see a building as a vessel of personal expression. Because of the thumping pace of work, in which a dozen or so buildings might simultaneously be in the course of design, this was hardly possible. They happily delegated the development of their preliminary sketches to their assistants, leaving themselves free to make site visits and cultivate clients. Broderick brings to life this aspect of the firm, showing the crucial role played by the silent partners in the drafting room.

One was extraordinary: the tragic Joseph Morrill Wells, the firm's chief designer from its earliest days until his untimely death in 1890. His works include the celebrated Villard Houses, and Broderick makes a convincing case that he pushed the firm to embrace classicism and to turn away from the robust Richardsonian Romanesque of the early years. But Wells seems to have been one of those immense talents utterly lacking in business sense. This is not so critical in literature or painting, where one is not responsible for meeting the office payroll, but it is fatal in architecture. Once offered a partnership by McKim, he flung it back with a sneer, saying he could never be on the masthead of an office that did "so much damn bad work." One imagines that the responsibility terrified him.

In lively vignettes like this, *Triumvirate* is at its best, but in two respects it falls short. Throughout the book, Broderick speculates infelicitously about the sexual lives of the partners, their friends, and their clients. In fact, much is based on negative evidence—she takes the destruction of many letters by White's son as conclusive proof of something disgraceful. As to what this was, she has no doubt—although she tells us at the outset that "the sexual orientation of White is of no importance to the work he did," she takes for granted that he was bisexual. So, apparently, was his friend Augustus Saint-Gaudens (like White, another compulsive seducer of artist's models), and "probably Mead" as well. When McKim's first wife divorced him in 1878 and accused him of "unnatural acts against the bounds of Christian behavior," Broderick declares that this must be a barely veiled reference to homosexual acts. Likewise, their disciple Whitney Warren (who had both a wife and a French mistress) is to have played a prominent part of the architects' "circle of bisexual and homosexual entertainment." Were there no heterosexuals at all, one is tempted to ask, in McKim, Mead & White's world?

This willful and credulous misreading of fragmentary evidence is of a piece with *Triumvirate*'s other flaw, which is its distractedly uneven writing. While some of its forty-nine chapters are delightfully written and explore their subjects at a leisurely pace, a few perfunctory four-page chapters are mere sketches. The most charitable interpretation is that Broderick was well into her project before she fully realized its magnitude, and flogged it quickly to the finish. This must account for otherwise inexplicable passages where the same proper noun is used repeatedly instead of pronouns (with which Broderick is stingy). The problem was unknown before there were word processors; when one had to type a chapter from beginning to end, sentences necessarily had to follow in sequence. Too often here one has the distinct feeling that sentences have been parachuted into paragraphs, without looking to see what was already there. In the end, Broderick has given us a book that is finished in some parts and roughly blocked out in others, an incomplete torso that barely does justice to its extraordinary subjects.

From 1915 to 1920, a lavish *Monograph of the Work of McKim, Mead & White* was published in regular installments, illustrated with newly commissioned photographs and large-scale drawings, ideal for reference or study; it was the definitive presentation of their work. That the firm would want to highlight their most recent, almost exclusively classical buildings was understandable, but by utterly omitting their earlier Shingle Style work, with its abstract freedom of form and plan, it gave a woefully distorted impression. Modernists could now scoff that McKim and his partners were simply copybook impresarios who did not actually design, but merely rifled through the pages of Paul Letarouilly's 1840 *Édifices de Rome moderne* until they found the Renaissance façade that best suited the job at hand. It was just this sort of facile argumentation that justified the demolition of Pennsylvania Station.

But the paradox of that demolition was that the most vehement protesters against the demolition in 1963 were themselves modern architects, and of the most prominent stripe, including Louis I. Kahn and Philip Johnson. Why this should be so *Triumvirate* does not explain; instead, one must turn back to the monograph for guidance. In studying the floor plans, one is immediately struck by how thoroughly the various aspects of each building are *resolved*. Its various interlocking spaces, its mode of construction, its outward appearance, all seem the concentrated expression of a single impulse, capable of no further refinement. For modern architects, who themselves sought to give their own designs a Platonic order (for example, the Seagram Building), it was possible to recognize in McKim, Mead & White a similar high-minded will that aspired to merge function and expression into a single compact unity.

Today, of course, it is no longer high praise to say of a design that it is resolved: open-endedness, contradiction, and irresolution are far more fashionable. It was once the case that rambling, fragmentary layouts were limited to awkward alterations, as when, for example, loft apartments were inserted into an old brewery, where new walls had to accommodate existing beams, and bathrooms and kitchens had to shoehorn themselves where they could. But one now finds such provisional layouts even in new construction, like the new Museum of Modern Art, with its tortuous paths of circulation and inconsistently expressed construction. Oddly enough, we may have arrived at a historical point where the situation prevailing in 1963 is exactly reversed: we are no longer affronted by the rhetorical classicism of McKim, Mead & White (indeed, we find it charming). It is, rather their abstract values of clarity and order that are hopelessly dated.

Such are the thoughtful lessons that Broderick's *Triumvirate* offers, which only make its flaws all the more lamentable. With a longer gestation, it would easily have been a classic study of American culture in convulsive change, in which the quivering energy of social insecurity paradoxically resulted in some of the most serene and refined buildings ever to grace this country.

October 2010

Mozart's Linnaeus

James F. Penrose

In 1801, some ten years after Mozart's death, *The Magic Flute* was performed in Paris as *Les Mystères d'Isis* (The Mysteries of Isis). It bore little resemblance to the *Flute* we know today: it was spiced up with arrangements of arias and ensemble pieces from *The Marriage of Figaro*, *Don Giovanni*, and, for good measure, bits of a Haydn symphony. Far from being shunned by a critical and discerning public, *Les Mystères* was wildly successful, so much so that a quarter century passed before Parisian audiences got to hear the real thing.

Across the Channel, *The Abduction from the Seraglio* and other Mozart operas fared little better in high-spirited mutilations by conductor-impresarios like Sir Henry Bishop. Despite outraged shrieks from the likes of Berlioz, musical vivisection was popular during much of the early nineteenth century; Mozart, revered as he was, was no exception. Musical tastes had moved away from the classical ideals. Giacomo Meyerbeer's pageants captivated the popular imagination while the music of Wagner, Schumann, Chopin, and Verdi (all Mozart worshippers) shaped more serious tastes. It was ironic that the composers who revered Mozart the most were the ones who moved public opinion away from his style of music. So it may not have been altogether surprising that in 1851 an obscure physician named Franz Lorenz published a little monograph called *In Sachen Mozarts* (In the Matter of Mozart). It was both an alarm and a call to action.

The monograph described the poor state of Mozart's *Nachlass* or musical estate. Only a portion of Mozart's works had been published, Lorenz wrote, the remainder being scattered across Europe in private collections or stored in a common warehouse where they were at risk of being destroyed by fire. As for Mozart's published works, these suffered from all number of errors, insertions, and "shocking mutilations and transformations" to the extent that their "original godlike form" had been distorted to an "unrecognizable caricature." It was a crisis for which Lorenz could see but one solution—a "young talent ... equipped with knowledge and eagerness, could seize for himself high honor ... and atone for our fathers' sins of neglect" by bringing forward accurate and complete copies of Mozart's works for publication. The "young talent" would require a sufficient musical knowledge, an "organized mind," large amounts of time and money, and complete devotion to the task.

Man proposes, God disposes. Ludwig Alois Friedrich Ritter von Köchel, an old schoolmate of Dr. Lorenz, read the monograph and was startled to find that he satisfied many of Lorenz's requirements. Musical knowledge? He was an excellent cellist! Organizational skills? He was a distinguished mineralogist and sufficiently regarded as a botanist that he had flora named in his honor. A frugal, financially comfortable bachelor, he had been pensioned off from the Austrian royal household staff. Moreover, he was a published scholar and poet, well connected socially, and acquainted with Otto Jahn—classicist, archaeologist, and the greatest Mozart scholar of the time. As for age, the fifty-one-year-old Köchel was of the view that "youth is wasted on the young" and almost immediately started to think about Lorenz's challenge.

The task was enormous. Even by 1851, little was known of Mozart's life and work. How much music he wrote, where it all was, and whether it was all genuine were issues that had defeated three generations of scholars. Clearly, the first step was to locate these works by retracing Mozart's life, travels, and correspondence. These compositions would then be systematically examined, described, classified, and published in a format allowing readers to gain a sense of both the entire *Nachlass* and individual compositions.

Some eleven years later, one of Mozart's own publishers, Breitkopf & Härtel, issued Köchel's forbiddingly titled *Chronologisch-thematisches Verzeichnis sämtlicher Tonwerke Wolfgang Amadé Mozarts* (Chronological and Thematic Catalogue of the Collected Works of Wolfgang Amadé Mozart). From its appearance in March 1862, the *Köchelverzeichnis* (Köchel Catalogue), as it is known, was considered a monument of the age. Some 551 pages long (later editions exceeded a thousand pages), with an eighteen-page introduction, the *Köchelverzeichnis* chronologically lists, numbers, and classifies Mozart's extant works from the earliest—a minuet for piano written by the five year-old prodigy—to the last—the Requiem, left incomplete at Mozart's death. It also provided a wealth of other information including a three-to-six bar musical theme or *incipit* for each movement of each work in the catalogue. Köchel assigned 626 numbers to Mozart's works, though occasionally several small compositions appeared under one number. Other works, not assigned a chronological "Köchel number," appeared in an appendix.

Historically, the first musical catalogues were sales brochures that listed thousands of compositions. Other catalogues were created for research or record-keeping purposes. Köchel relied on various proto-catalogues, one prepared by Mozart himself, in completing the *Köchelverzeichnis.* Köchel's work was not merely a more complete thematic study, however. Through its use of historical evidence, musical analysis, and scientific method, it pioneered a taxonomic approach, much like that used in classifying rocks and plants, to the cataloguing of musical works. Just at the time when musicology was gaining acceptance as an academic subject, Köchel offered a fundamental analytical technique that allows the study of a composer's creative life from the perspective of his work. Indeed, the *Köchelverzeichnis* was so sensible, yet so revolutionary, that its author might well be considered as one of the founders of modern musicology.

Köchel had little in common with Mozart. Unlike our impression of the composer as one of music's highest-octane personalities, Köchel emerges as an endearingly donnish, somewhat stolid figure who kept friends all his life and whom his contemporaries regarded with affection and respect. But the contrast made for a marvelous pairing, as Köchel's forensic gifts were well suited to resolving the disarray that plagued the Mozart *Nachlass.*

Köchel was born in Stein, Lower Austria, some fifty miles up the Danube from Vienna, in January 1800. His father, the local tax collector and an accomplished amateur musician, lived near Mozart's grandmother. In 1816, young Köchel enrolled at the University of Vienna where he studied philosophy for several years before reading law. His finances were affected by his father's death in 1820, and he took leave from his studies to tutor the children of a local official.

To his surprise, Köchel found that he was a superb teacher. His reputation was such that, in 1827, he was retained as private tutor to the four sons of the Archduke of Austria. While in imperial service, he spent much of his free time pursuing his botanical and mineralogical interests. Köchel met the mineralogist Friedrich Mohs (originator of the Mohs scale of hardness) who encouraged Köchel's original and sophisticated approaches to mineral classification. In his 1859 study of Salzburg mineralogy, Köchel used an innovative array of geographical, geological, and mineralogical references to describe, categorize, and cross-index, a technique he adapted to the classification of Mozart's compositions.

Köchel retired from imperial service at forty-two when the last of his charges attained majority. Ennobled and financially independent, he spent the next seven years collecting and classifying plants and minerals throughout Europe. Köchel's circumstances were in stark contrast to those of Friedrich Chrysander, friend of Brahms and biographer and cataloguer of Handel, who supported his studies by growing and selling fruits and vegetables from his garden.

As a botanist, Köchel was sufficiently respected that several species, including *bupleurum koechelii* (a medicinal herb used in Chinese traditional medicine), were named after him in the Linnaean manner. His scholarly travels were briefly interrupted for an appointment as school inspector in the Upper Austria region near Salzburg around the time of the 1849 revolutions. Köchel quickly fell out with the educational establishment and resigned, one biographer tells us, as his "enlightened views differed from the prevailing tendency." Köchel kept Salzburg as his base, however, and it was there in early 1851 that he came across *In Sachen Mozarts*. Despite Dr. Lorenz's anxious views about the Mozart *Nachlass*, the situation may not have been quite as dire as he thought. By the time Breitkopf & Härtel published the *Köchelverzeichnis*, somewhere from half to two-thirds of Mozart's works had been published in one form or another, a relatively high proportion compared, say, to the equivalent fortunes of J. S. Bach. Moreover, the *Nachlass* was not quite terra incognita, as its terrain had been partially surveyed by music publishers and amateur scholars.

The reputation of the Mozart family hit a low when, in 1771, the Empress Maria Theresa advised her son not to take the family into service because "*ce gens courent le monde comme des gueux*" ("these people go around the world like beggers"). Throughout his life, Mozart was a musical vagrant. In his youth, he constantly toured, composing as he traveled. Even later in life when he was established in Vienna, Mozart moved houses over a dozen times. All the while, he kept composing and writing out instrumental parts. To say the least, conditions were not good for keeping a well-ordered system of his compositions, let alone keeping fair copies of manuscripts and parts. It was this combination of fecundity and wandering, as well as publishers' willingness to issue corrupted works, that led to the disarray of the Mozart *Nachlass.*

Following Mozart's death, his widow Constanze supported the family by selling his manuscripts to publishers. During the 1790s, Breitkopf & Härtel published a number of works acquired from Constanze. Indeed, the company planned a complete Mozart edition for which it had drawn up a preliminary catalogue.

It seems, however, that Breitkopf & Härtel found the project too daunting. In late 1799, Constanze changed publishers and sold all of her remaining manuscripts to Johann Anton André of Offenbach, near Frankfurt. Constanze and André agreed that in addition to publishing Mozart's manuscripts, André's firm would also issue the first "chronological and thematic catalogue" of all Mozart's works, not just the compositions André had just purchased.

To help André along, Constanze gave him an example of such a catalogue: the priceless, handwritten *Verzeichnüss aller meiner werke* (Catalogue of my works) in which the composer listed the works composed between February 1784 until November 1791, three weeks before his death. This forty-four-page notebook (now in the British Museum) shows the date, description, scoring, and opening measures of 145 works written during Mozart's most profoundly creative period. Like Breitkopf & Härtel, André soon realized that preparing a complete catalogue was a nightmarish undertaking. To give an example of just one task that awaited Mozart's cataloguer, Mozart had been composing from age five, and there were hundreds of undated compositions predating his first notebook entry that had to be exhumed, ordered, and classified.

While André published a version of Mozart's notebook in 1805, he never printed the complete catalogue so desired by Constanze. Late in life, however, André prepared a thirty-six-page list of the early works. This 1833 list (also in the British Museum) provided much information about the early manuscripts as well as André's theory about the evolution of Mozart's handwriting, the means by which he dated the early works. In 1841, André published a catalogue of all the Mozart manuscripts he owned. After André's death in 1842, no collector, library, or conservatory appeared interested in acquiring his extraordinary collection of 173 manuscripts. Over the ensuing years, André's heirs began to sell the collection piecemeal. For the moment, the path to the *Köchelverzeichnis* had come to a halt.

The inventory of the 1799 sale, André's editions of Mozart's notebook, his 1833 list of early works, and the 1841 inventory would form the basis of much of Köchel's research. Additionally, a Viennese civil servant and collector named Aloys Fuchs amassed a large collection of Mozart's manuscripts and printed scores. Köchel also used this collection and the catalogues Fuchs prepared between 1830 and 1837. A large piece of the puzzle was still missing, however. Köchel still lacked the essential biographical information about Mozart to date much of the composer's work.

Providence acted again. In November 1847, while returning from the funeral of Felix Mendelssohn, the classicist Otto Jahn resolved to begin collecting background material for a life of Mozart. As a respite from his teaching and classical research (he wrote over sixty books on archaeology and philology), Jahn had spent several years working on a life of Beethoven. He concluded that to do justice to his subject, he would first have to understand the effect of Haydn and Mozart on Beethoven's music. Over the next twelve years, Jahn produced a four-volume biography of Mozart which, like the *Köchelverzeichnis*, was the first of its kind: a massive detailed work that drew from correspondence, contemporaneous sources, and Mozart's music to form a scholarly work so significant and so readable it stayed in print for over sixty years.

As part of his biographical research, Jahn started compiling a comprehensive catalogue of Mozart's works. In an extraordinary act of generosity, he abandoned his cataloguing research and donated his work to Köchel when he realized the value of Köchel's approach. (Jahn would similarly donate all his Beethoven research to E. W. Thayer for his *Life of Beethoven*). Jahn's biography and his catalogue research were the final pieces that Köchel needed to define and rationalize the Mozart *Nachlass*.

The *Köchelverzeichnis* begins with an affectionate dedication to Jahn before moving to a long and intensely interesting introduction about Köchel's sources and processes. The catalogue proper begins with a "Summary of Completed Works by Category and Number" (*Übersicht der vollständigen Kompositionen nach Gattung und Zahl*). It is here that we see the first actual examples of his organizational genius.

Köchel's scientific training is apparent in his cataloguing method. For centuries, botanists grouped plants based on resemblances of character and type. Classification of plants and animals reached the level of a science with Carl Linnaeus, whose systems were accepted by botanists and zoologists as the foundation for naming plants and animals. One characteristic of Linnaeus's presentation, the so-called "protologue" that summarizes everything associated with a new species—"description, illustrations, references, geographical data, citation of specimens, discussion and comments"—seemed to be adopted whole cloth in the *Köchelverzeichnis.*

Köchel classified Mozart's works into twenty-three categories ranging from the sacred to the secular. Readers are quick to see implicit family groupings: sacred works occupy categories I–IV, songs and choruses categories V–IX, piano works occupy categories X–XIII, chamber music XIV–XVIII, and orchestral works occupy categories XIX–XXIII. Köchel takes the first twenty-three pages of this section to categorize all Mozart's works that he illustrates by *incipit*, occasionally by title, and by chronological listing—the famous "Köchel number."

The numbers themselves come from the second part, and heart, of the *Köchelverzeichnis*, the "Chronological Catalogue of Completed Works" (*Chronologisches Verzeichnis der vollständen Kompositionen*). Köchel divided Mozart's creative life into five periods ranging from the juvenile through the final. From the evidence provided by Mozart's own notebook, it was relatively easy for Köchel to chronologize most of the 179 works in the notebook. For the remaining 447 numbers, presumably written before February 1784, however, there was considerable uncertainty. But within the framework of these five periods, Köchel assigned works as best he could, based on his fieldwork and evaluation of manuscripts over eleven years, and with the assistance of Jahn's, Fuchs's, and André's conclusions. Once a chronology had been established (even though, as Köchel admitted, occasionally based on conjecture), Köchel's sequential numbering followed.

The mass of factual detail assembled by Köchel was unprecedented and is arranged in a Linnaean spirit. On the top left-hand corner of each page in the chronology is the relevant year or years of Mozart's life; on the right the Köchel numbers. Each work begins with its Köchel number, then its title, instrumentation or vocal register, date and place of composition (asterisked if in doubt), a cross-reference to Jahn's biography and André or Fuchs's catalogue, a double-staffed 3–6 bar *incipit* for each movement (showing key, time signature, tempo indication, and volume), and number of measures. Under the heading "Autograph" (a term for the manuscript original), Köchel comments on the location of the manuscript. For example, for the E-flat Quartet K. 428, the autograph is described as being "In the possession of Mrs. Plowden in London." Köchel says the autograph bears the heading "Quartetto IV," is on eleven pages, and has twenty handwritten sides.

Under the heading *Ausgaben* (Editions), Köchel traces as many printed editions as he can find. Finally, under *Anmerkung* (Remarks), Köchel contributes observations about the history of the work. In the *Anmerkung* section of the analysis of the Piano Concerto in F, K. 459, for example, he notes that the title page of the old André concert edition is inscribed thus: "This concerto was performed by the author in Frankfurt-am-Main on the occasion of the coronation of Emperor Léopold II." Köchel concludes that because the Concerto in D, K. 537 is separately called the "Coronation Concerto," Mozart played both works in Frankfurt as part of the coronation festivities. Similarly, in the Recitative and Aria for Soprano "Alcandro, lo confesso" and "Non sò d'ondo viene," K. 294 (a version for bass voice appears as K. 512), Köchel notes that it was composed for Aloysia Weber (Constanze's sister), whom Mozart then admired (the German word is "glowed"). He goes on to quote from a letter that Mozart wrote in 1778:

> For practice I have also set to music the aria *Non sò d'ondo viene* etc. which has been so beautifully composed by Bach. Just because I know Bach's setting so well and like it so much, and because it is always ringing in my ears I wished to try and see whether in spite of all this I could not write an aria totally unlike his. When it was finished I said to Mlle. Weber, "Learn the aria yourself. Sing it as you think it ought to go; then let me hear it and afterwards I will tell you candidly what pleases me and what displeases me." After a couple of days I went to the Webers and she sang it for me, accompanying herself. I was obliged to confess that she had sung it exactly as I wished and as I should have taught it to her myself. This is now the best aria she has.

The *Köchelverzeichnis* is crammed full of these fascinating stories, so much so that the musicologist Alfred Einstein, the editor of the 1936 third edition and no fan of Köchel, praised him for doing for Mozart what nobody by then had done for Bach or Haydn, and in a manner that actually made the result enjoyable. Indeed, read *seriatim*, Köchel's ordering of the *Nachlass* is a biography of the composer through the medium of his work. Writers like C. M. Girdlestone in his great *Mozart and his Piano Concertos* used Köchel's protologue as the point of departure for further analysis. Generations of concert-note writers are equally in Köchel's debt.

The 1862 edition ended with an Appendix (*Anhang*), grouping lost, incomplete, transcribed, doubtful, and misattributed works. The second edition contains a Supplement (*Nachtrag*), an index, a list of first lines of songs, and an introduction containing a short biography of Köchel. These latter two sections have grown and shrunk appreciably over the years, depending on the approach taken by successive editors.

For all its significance, however, the *Köchelverzeichnis* was still only the first step in realizing Dr. Lorenz's ambition of a complete edition. While the state of the *Nachlass* had surely improved, many of the autographs and manuscripts that Köchel had so painstakingly tracked down and analyzed for his catalogue were still diffused over Europe—uncollected, unstudied, and unpublished. Scholars and artists may have known about the existence of these works, but their ready availability was another matter. Two years before the end of his life, the opportunity arose for Köchel to perform his last services to Mozart scholarship.

In April 1874, Breitkopf & Härtel announced the publication of a uniform edition of Mozart's operas. Köchel approached Hermann Härtel, the head of the firm, who agreed to expand the project to include the other 603 non-operatic numbers. Expenses were considerable due to the massive collecting, editing, and typesetting costs, and unlikely to be defrayed by sales. When Härtel died in 1875, he lamented that the business could not possibly sustain the project.

But Köchel was offering Breitkopf more than just ideas. In April 1876, when the publisher announced the Mozart *Ausgabe* (Edition) and invited subscriptions for the project it credited an anonymous "admirer of Mozart" whose financial support allowed it to "approach this . . . concept [which would otherwise be] remote from customary publishing economics." That anonymous admirer was, of course, Köchel himself, whose patronage would only be posthumously revealed. To ease the financial burden further, Köchel arranged for a number of imperial patrons and sponsors as subscribers, and supplied Breitkopf & Härtel with manuscripts and scores. The Mozart *Ausgabe* (the editors of which included the royalty of late nineteenth-century music: Brahms, Reinecke, Spitta, and Joachim) was published from 1877 until 1883, with supplements appearing until 1910.

Before he died in June 1877, Köchel published a number of other works including collections of Beethoven's letters, musicological research on early performance practice, a catalogue of the works of the seventeenth-century composer J. J. Fuchs, more botanical works, and even a volume of poetry. In no other work, however, was he as successful in capturing the attention and admiration of his time as he did with the publication of the *Köchelverzeichnis.*

While the *Köchelverzeichnis* resulted in other works coming to light, no attempt was made to order them into Köchel's system for many years. The 1905 second edition was edited by another musical amateur, Paul Graf von Waldersee, who made few modifications to the 1862 version, though he added references to the Mozart *Ausgabe* and expanded the *Anhang* and *Nachtrag* to take account of works that had come to light. Thus, the ballet *Les Petits Riens* found its way into the "Lost Compositions" section of the *Anhang* instead of the chronological listing.

But this just postponed the inevitable. As modest as he was, Köchel never dreamed that his work would have the enormous, almost gospel-like influence it did. His system made no provision for new works coming to light, and was unable to absorb them when they did. Alfred Einstein had the problem of inserting new discoveries as well as changing the chronology in those instances where he believed Köchel got it wrong. His solution was to insert letters after the relevant Köchel numbers to allow for the insertion of new discoveries. Sometimes this was easy, as in cases where Einstein moved a work from the appendix to the chronology, as in the case of K. 426a, the Allegro for Two Pianos, which Einstein believed was composed right after the Fugue in C minor for Two Pianos, K. 426. Matters get more cumbersome when Einstein redated a work already assigned a Köchel number where the new work would bear both the old and the revised listing. The 1963 sixth edition (the fourth and fifth editions were mere reprints) continued this practice with some works now bearing three numbers. *Der neue Köchel*, soon to be published, may resolve some of these issues.

Einstein once commented that "Köchel was a dilettante.... The more delicate and profound interrelations in Mozart's output were beyond him." Einstein himself, however, dated many of the works based on a subjective, almost holistic, interpretation of how they sounded and felt in their chronological order. In this, he was influenced by the French musicologists Theodore de Wyzewa and Georges de Saint-Foix, whose approach has not enjoyed unanimous scholarly approval following the rise of paper and handwriting dating techniques. Indeed, subsequent analysis suggests that Köchel was closer to the mark than his primary critic in various tricky date allocations.

Köchel, of course, realized the weaknesses of his system and begged readers to provide the information he knew was missing. "Nobody is more convinced than the author that much of the date ordering was unsatisfactory as no further sources wanted to reveal themselves," he wrote.

Other important issues have come to light over the years. The basic premise of Köchel's approach was that Mozart started and finished works in roughly chronological order. The scholar Alan Tyson has demonstrated that a number of works were begun and then put on hold for several months or even years before completion. Mozart also appears to have created variants of a number of his works. In short, recent evidence suggests the picture of Mozart neatly completing works like some sort of divinely inspired composing machine is flawed. In reality, Mozart's compositional process can be described as occasionally opportunistic, often restless, sometimes even chaotic. What it was not, it seems, was strictly chronological.

For its time and place, however, Köchel's work was a miraculous synthesis of scientific method and artistic judgment. That, perhaps, is why from the very beginning it has been called the *Köchelverzeichnis* rather than the *Mozartverzeichnis*. The effect of the *Köchelverzeichnis* and the five-and-a-half-linear-foot Mozart *Ausgabe* on nineteenth-century music was nothing short of momentous. "Conductors, composers, scholars and writers all hastened to book their tickets, as it were, for excursions along the quiet branch lines of classicism, away from the terminus of late romanticism," wrote the Mozart scholar Alec Hyatt King. "'The name of the engine that drew us,' they might have said with Samuel Butler, 'was Mozart.'"

October 2007

Let's tickle the ivories

David Dubal

THERE IS AN OLD PROVERB that goes "Play the piano daily and stay sane." For me, the main word of this proverb is daily. Playing the piano daily means inevitable accomplishment, and, without a sense of accomplishment, life is an impoverished journey.

Machines have taken us away from our hands. In his last days, Rachmaninoff continually practiced a composition he never performed. One of his last statements was: "Farewell, my dear hands." Today, we are starved for a deep contact with our hands. The poet Edward Dahlberg felt "our hands are already very stupid and morose. What can we do with them? What do we do with them?" Let's get back to our hands—they are craving good work. At one time, the terms "handmade" and "handcrafted" meant a great deal. In schools, the young are no longer taught to write in script. Handwriting provided the first glimpse of individuality. What a thrill to see our beloved's handwriting in a letter. And what of drawing, once an essential form of education? Painting and drawing are no longer common practice. Goethe, sickened by the Babel of words, counseled, "Let us draw, instead of talk."

There is wisdom, so I say, let us play the piano. Non-verbal music reaches into the depths of the unconscious. There is nothing so satisfactory for our hands—physically, sensuously, and artistically—as playing the piano. Nothing compares to the satisfaction of playing a small piece of Bach or Schumann. If you can't play a Bach invention perfectly, or even imperfectly, try to do it, and you will come to agree with me. The path to such an achievement asks for focus, discipline, attention, a delicate sense of touch, musical feeling, and more. Good practicing is meditation without the mantra. When you commune with Bach or Schubert, you can reach the heights of Mount Parnassus, where the atmosphere is rarified.

Almost everyone is musical. Music is an actual bodily need. Another saying goes "If something is worth doing, it is worth doing well," but I disagree. Like Chesterton, I feel that if something is worth doing, it is worth doing even badly. Playing the piano is not something to be graded. Adults should take it up the moment they feel the need to play music. As a matter of course, children should be given lessons without pressure. Playing the piano should be an act without material value. It must be a road of discovery, a trackless territory, and never a means of showing off. The piano won't serve the ego's craving for recognition.

When I was a student, I had an adult who studied with me. The man was gifted in a number of ways. He took his lessons seriously and worked hard. After about two years, when he thought he had mastered a group of compositions, he could not resist showing off. He rented a small hall and a Steinway and invited a large group of friends. I told him that this was a mistake, as he had no idea what kind of super-mastery was needed to play in public. He was a self-absorbed, flamboyant character who thought he could pull it off with his usual flair, as he did with his acting and dancing.

In the green room before the little concert, he was stunned to find his legs and hands shaking beyond control. Still, he went out to face his audience and made a complete fool of himself, flailing in every piece. The next day, he called me angrily, saying that he was quitting; he didn't love the piano, he told me. I told him I thought that was a good idea. I never saw him again. His narcissism excluded the possibility of properly loving music. The piano is not only a severe taskmaster, it asks that you possess character. If you have the temerity to play publicly, you are all alone, and the way you perform and your preparation tells a great deal about who you are. In a clash of wills, the piano will always win. Robert Schumann wrote, "The hearing of masterworks of different epochs will speediest of all cure you of vanity and self-adoration." Playing the piano teaches one much, especially humility.

The piano offers a variety of avenues for musical growth. The novelist E. M. Forster says of his own performances upon the piano that they

> grow worse yearly, but never will I give them up. For one thing ... they teach me a little bit about construction. I see what becomes of a phrase, how it is transformed or returned.... This gives me a

> physical approach ... which cannot be gained through the slough of "appreciation." Even when people play as badly as I do, they should continue; it will help them to listen.

To listen acutely is something that few achieve. Artur Schnabel put it bluntly, writing, "The intimacy created by listening to a piece of music (even repeatedly) is superficial compared with the result of repeated playing or even reading of the music. The aptitude for reading music as one reads words should be cultivated by everybody who is fond of music." The fact is that, today, reading music, an elementary form of musical literacy, has become rare, and many music critics do not possess this ability.

One of the most wonderful aspects of piano playing is learning and developing the ability to sight-read (score-read). What an adventure it is! As this skill develops, all of music becomes available to the pianist. If one is really curious musically, this is the greatest of feasts. The amateur probably doesn't have the time, patience, or even the desire to hone a piece to high technical polish. Who cares! That's for people who play in public, those who deal with the professional and commercial apparatus of music. Over time, I have realized that the amateur who constantly sight-reads is often a more cultivated musician than the performer who slaves away polishing and shining every phrase. The fine sight-reader may not be a concert pianist, but he knows how to *use* a piano.

In orchestral music, good piano arrangements will bring out clearly a score's roots. In the process of discovering them, one learns to be a conductor. Really getting to know Mahler in piano reductions gives us a real appreciation of his orchestral mastery. If opera is one's passion, piano reductions on many levels are ideal in developing a deeper understanding of the operas of all epochs. If one is serious about internalizing the depths and complexities of Wagner's *Ring Cycle*, there is no better way than slowly plodding through the arrangements of Karl Klindworth (an important pupil of Franz Liszt). Nothing could reveal Wagner's stupendous mind better. All the performances on all the stages of the world cannot bring one closer to these "music-dramas" than one's own two hands.

Another enchantment is the endless piano reductions of music for four hands, including the original duet literature itself. In Robert Musil's classic novel *The Man Without Qualities*, Clarisse and Walter play four-hand piano, "unloosed like two locomotives hurtling along side by side. Seated on their small stools, they were irritated, amorous, or sad about nothing, or perhaps each of them about something separate, only the authority of the music joined them together." During the Civil War, a Union general and his troops marched into Holly Springs, Mississippi, with the intention of destroying the little Confederate town. Looking at a beautiful mansion, the general walked in, saw a fine grand in the parlor, and began playing. Upon hearing the music, a beautiful young woman descended the long staircase. After a few minutes of conversation, the pair discovered that they had both studied in New York with the same teacher. The very next day, he again came to her home and they played duets. On taking his leave he said, "You and your piano take the credit for saving Holly Springs."

The invention of the piano was the greatest event in the history of music. As a cultural artifact, it is peerless. Through its existence, music expanded into many unexplored regions of feeling and form.

The arts are spiritually and emotionally interconnected. Nowhere is this heard more clearly than in the song literature of the world. The piano's developement in the last quarter of the eighteenth century was accompanied by an unprecedented burst of lyric poetry in England, Europe, and Russia. The new verse captured personal feeling through a rediscovery of the vernacular. The nineteenth-century Romantic composers were nurtured on this literature, and, from Schubert onward, dozens of them set their national poetry to voice and piano. With the piano, poetry found a new and expanded life. Such composers as Schumann, Brahms, Wolf, Liszt, Grieg, Tchaikovsky, Fauré, Debussy, Strauss, Borodin, and Rachmaninoff used the piano with an uncanny sense of description and detail. Just imagine any of these "art songs" being sung with harpsichord. It would provoke laughter.

The piano is also without equal as an artistic and social medium. It is found everywhere, from taverns to the White House, in churches and houses of ill repute. Wherever it is, it always beckons to us. One day, while visiting a nursing home, I encountered a shiny ebony grand in the cheerful sitting room. I asked the attendant if anyone played it. She responded that a few people strummed on it occasionally. Why, I asked, was the piano here? Her response told much. "Sir, the piano is here because it makes everyone happier just to see it. Most people have grown up with a piano." Indeed, many families strove to keep up with the Joneses in purchasing this expensive object, hoping to enrich their lives with music while watching their children grapple with the magic box, being brought to beauty and culture as they progressed through the classic purity of Clementi's time-honored sonatinas.

The piano represents a sense of continuity which lives on today in dozens of subtle ways. Discarding a piano feels so sacrilegious. Recently, I saw an old upright degraded on the street. I looked at it wistfully, knowing there is still a lot of music in those old keys. While I was standing there, others also stopped, looking sadly at the lonely instrument. One woman exclaimed, "How can anyone throw a piano away? A child should have it to begin piano lessons."

Emerson wrote: "'Tis wonderful to see how quickly a piano gets into a log-hut." When Oscar Wilde made his lecture tour in the wild and woolly mining towns of the American West, he was touched when he saw on the wall of a saloon a big sign reading "Don't shoot the piano player, he is doing his best." Growing up in Texarkana, Texas, Scott Joplin was taught the piano for pennies by one of the many poor immigrant musicians pouring into the United States. In Joplin's case, his teacher was a German Jew. Later, the creator of classic ragtime made his living by playing on uprights in the brothel parlors of the Missouri Valley region. Those rickety instruments spawned a generation of African-American ragtime virtuosi. When a client entered, the working girls hallooed for the professor to set the mood for their daily (and nightly) labors.

Alas, there are too many pianos that go unplayed. The world has changed drastically since the days when the piano was the centerpiece of a home. Few people now play instruments other than their CD players or iPods. Silence doesn't exist. Homes are flooded with the odious noises of television. The internet has robbed us of time and life itself, becoming the world's major addiction.

Once parents bought a piano to give their children the "finer things in life"—a middle-class phrase that now sounds quaint. George Gershwin, living a rough-and-tumble life on the streets of New York City, would say: "The piano made a good boy out of a bad one." The moment he had heard Anton Rubinstein's *Melody in F* played at a penny arcade, he was mesmerized. A piano would never leave his sight. Today, the piano is seldom in the living room. Children now play video games instead of Mozart.

We can no longer quite grasp what the piano meant to society in its heyday just before World War I. The instrument was almost deified while a mighty race of piano virtuosi round the world played the classics. Paderewski and many others were celebrities of the first magnitude. At the height of piano production in 1911, 310 piano manufacturers produced 376,000 pianos in the United States alone. It was no coincidence that 1911 was also the peak year for immigrants streaming into the country.

In 1915, Irving Berlin, who grew up with his piano, wrote the song "I Love a Piano." Popular music was changing American culture just as was Henry Ford's Model T automobile. Years after "I Love a Piano" was composed, Judy Garland sang it with Fred Astaire at the upright in the movie *Easter Parade*. The song is a delight:

> I love a piano, I love a piano.
> I love to hear somebody play
> Upon a piano, a grand piano.
> It simply carries me away.
> I know a fine way to treat a Steinway.
> I love to run my fingers o'er the keys, the ivories.
> And with the pedal I love to meddle,
> When Paderewski comes this way.
> I'm so delighted if I'm invited
> To hear a long-haired genius play.
> So you can keep your fiddle and your bow
> Give me a p-i-a-n-o, oh, oh,
> I love to stop right beside an upright
> Or a high-toned baby grand.

By the time World War I had started, however, phonograph sales pulled ahead of piano sales for the first time, and piano sales began to decline. Consumer culture was replacing the do-it-yourself ethic. When the Great Depression hit, the piano industry was a fragment of its former, glorious self. From hundreds of firms of piano-builders, only three dozen or so survived.

Once a house could not be considered a home without its piano. The psychological warmth of the piano in the parlor had a profound effect on family life, which was now beginning to slowly deteriorate. I am amused by present-day politicians who mourn the death of what they call "family values." I would tell them to call for the return of the piano in the home. Before the endless proliferation of canned music, mothers played for family and friends a variety of music, from hymns to sentimental popular songs, while feet moved to the current dance craze, and many a romance began near a piano. There may even have been flashes of radiant beauty when mother played the first movement of the *Moonlight Sonata.* D. H. Lawrence describes almost unbearable nostalgia for a mother playing to her child in his magnificent poem "Piano":

> Softly in the dusk, a woman is singing to me;
> Taking me back down the vista of years, till I see
> A child sitting under the piano, in the boom of the
> tingling strings
> And pressing the small, poised feet of a mother who smiles
> as she sings

The piano still exudes an aura of allure and romance. I was delighted with Joe Queenan's 2009 essay in *The New York Times Book Review,* "Play It Again. And Again." He wrote,

> For the past few years, whenever I've found myself down in the dumps, I have turned to books that contain the word "piano" in the title. Immediately, the dark clouds fade.... The very fact that I am reading a book that has something to do with the glorious old 88s invariably lifts me out of the engulfing gloom.
>
> Perhaps this is because of the elegance and majesty of the instrument itself, or because the very word "piano" is reassuringly beautiful. Or perhaps it is because I, like so many other baby boomers, have long dreamed of playing the piano but have had to settle for being able to strum a few primitive Neil Young songs on the guitar. Whatever the reason, "piano" is evocative in a way no other word for a musical instrument is. I do not get the same emotional payoff when I read *Come Blow Your Horn, The Advancing Clarinetist, Drums Along the Mohawk, The Tin Drum, The Cello Player, The Vanishing Violin, The Little Drummer Girl, The Soloist, Gideon's Trumpet, Young Man With a Horn* or even *Corelli's Mandolin.* The word "piano" itself possesses an ethereal charm that the nomenclature for other musical instruments lacks. Words like "harp," "English horn" and even "viola da gamba" do nothing for me. Literature pertaining to the banjo or the flugelhorn isn't even in the ballpark. And just forget about books like *Accordion Crimes.* The accordion *is* a crime.

Let's tickle the ivories

My least favorite name for an instrument is "organ." But the name is not the thing, and the central fact is that Beethoven did not compose his thirty-two sonatas for the bassoon. This greatest celebration of music could only have been created for the piano, or if you prefer, the pianoforte—it can, after all, play very loud indeed. Truly, the piano is "the king of instruments."

Writing in 1946, the art historian Bernard Berenson noted that "man seems to have begun as an artist and only in the last hundred years has he succeeded in emancipating himself from art completely, exchanging the possible Phidias in him for a Ford." In the intervening years, the population has become greatly alienated from art. Fewer and fewer know who Phidias was. When did you last meet a sculptor? In his 1897 novel *The Nigger of the "Narcissus"* Joseph Conrad writes of the artist who "binds men to each other, which binds together all humanity—the dead to the living and the living to the unborn."

All of us, consciously or not, crave art. The novelist Jeanette Winterson wrote,

> Art is central to all our lives, not just the better-off and educated. I know that from my own story, and from the evidence of every child ever born—they all want to hear and to tell stories, to sing, to make music, to act out little dramas, to paint pictures, to make sculptures. This is born in and we breed it out. And then, when we have bred it out, we say that art is elitist, and at the same time we either fetishize art—the high prices, the jargon, the inaccessibility—or we ignore it. The truth is, artists or not, we are all born on the creative continuum, and that is a heritage and a birthright of all of our lives.

Almost everyone who played the piano as a child and quit wishes they had stuck with it. But the present is here. Take charge. Go to concerts. Buy recordings. The great pianists each have different traits beyond their own specific tone. Rubinstein's noble simplicity, Horowitz's eroticism, Lipatti's purity and elegance, Gieseking's lavish color wheel, Kapell's scalding temperament, Cortot's visionary imagination, and Gould's asceticism are waiting to be revealed to you.

The piano recital is still a singular and exciting event. Keyboard virtuosity in itself remains a glamorous thing: the nimble muscularity of scales and arpeggios dashing down and cascading up the keyboard; octaves coruscating through the great concertos; the lid of the grand opened, the feet quivering on the pedals—the sheer danger of it all is breathtaking. And is there anything more rewarding than mastering a Bach fugue or conquering the exhilarating pitfalls in one of Liszt's transcendental études?

The piano is a shrine to the human spirit, an instrument so perfect that it has permeated the lives of the great composers. In its literature are compositions for every level of attainment. It is said that in China thirty million people study the piano. That's quite a good start. Let's go country by country. I actually believe that playing the piano may save the world. But forget about the world and save yourself.

February 2012

Operatic precocity

Heather Mac Donald

A TWELVE-YEAR-OLD British girl has written an opera of astounding wit, craft, and musical beauty. It received a theatrically riveting production by California's Opera San José this December, with the composer, Alma Deutscher, playing the violin, piano, and organ. Given the current cultural imperative to champion "strong women" and "girl power," you would think that Deutscher's accomplishments would be widely known. They are not, however, because Deutscher and her opera pose a conscious challenge to contemporary values in classical music and art.

The phrase "child prodigy" produces revulsion in many people, conjuring images of trained human seals being exploited by greedy parents for financial gain. So let's simply say that Deutscher is a phenomenal musical talent and that her parents are anything but exploitative, instead working zealously to protect her innocence. Since age five, she has been studying composition via Skype with a teacher in a Swiss village, who uses a method of training from eighteenth-century Naples. Young boys in a Neapolitan orphanage were efficiently turned into court and chapel musicians by improvising contrapuntal harmonies over bass lines. A third of the music in colonial Williamsburg was composed by products of the Naples school. Deutscher and her teacher, Tobias Cramm, improvise together across the Channel on their respective keyboards, turning phrases from Bach's *Well-Tempered Clavier*, say, upside-down and inside-out, experimenting with harmonies and modulations. Robert Gjerdingen, a Northwestern University musicologist, wrote the book on Neapolitan improvisation that inspired Deutscher's father to seek out the same training for his musically precocious daughter. Gjerdingen has been offering advice on her compositions since then. "At five you could say that her music was childlike but showed promise," he says. "At seven, she came back with something gorgeous. At ten, she started learning orchestration. Now she can improvise complex stuff beyond what music Ph.D.'s can do."

Deutscher's ear vacuums up musical languages from the eighteenth to the mid-twentieth century. Her piano concerto, which she premiered at the keyboard with the Vienna Chamber Orchestra in 2017, sounds like an amalgam of Muzio Clementi and Chopin, with some Donizetti thrown in for good measure. Her opera, *Cinderella*, is a massive step forward in terms of musical and psychological complexity. Deutscher has been fascinated with the Cinderella story since age three; a fantastically Fauvist drawing she made in 2011 depicts Cinderella and her two stepsisters with elongated limbs and torsos, swaying like exotic insects. Showing a "you go, girl!" streak herself, she objected to the fact that Cinderella's defining attribute was her small foot. When she started collecting musical ideas in 2013 for an opera, she modified the story to make the title character a composer. The Prince, rather than seeking her out via her lost slipper, would track her down after the ball with one of her melodies.

Deutscher's Cinderella is an alter ego for the composer; like Deutscher, she is assailed by tunes that keep pouring into her head. And the work is a send-up of the operatic genre itself, satirizing its conventions and singers' foibles. Deutscher and her parents conceived the ingenious plot; it is tauter and more dramatically compelling than many a Verdian story. (Alma's father, Guy Deutscher, is a linguist at Oxford University.) The libretto was a joint effort between her parents and various poets and dramaturgs. It started out in Hebrew, was translated into German for a Viennese performance in 2016, and ended up in English for the San Jose production. The text is both down-to-earth and literary, with a predilection for Shakespearean couplets that end scenes.

Cinderella lives with her stepmother and stepsisters in an opera house formerly run by her late father; she spends her days drearily copying out scores for their stage performances. The court minister arrives at the opera house to announce a royal ball whereat the Prince will choose a bride, but instead of leaving the family with the invitation, he mistakenly delivers a pharmacy prescription just given the king for his many ailments. The stepmother and stepsisters puzzle over the gruesome references to "ulcerations," "fungal inflammations," and "red and itchy boils," before deciding that they have before them an example of "modern poetry," written by the Prince to express his romantic pain. Since the ball will feature a singing competition for the amusement of the guests, they conclude that this is the text they are to set to music and perform. The tuneless stepsisters are unable to come up with a melody, but the stepmother finds a lilting song composed by Cinderella and steals it for her daughter to use when singing the medical prescription at the ball.

The stolen melody idea was inspired by Walther's stolen poem in Wagner's *Die Meistersinger*. Unlike Wagner, however, Deutscher has an effervescent sense of musical humor. The resulting complications from the switched medical prescription are musically and dramatically hilarious. Deutscher has been steeped in the *buffa* tradition; she estimates that she has seen "all of the happy operas," certainly all of Rossini's comedies. Guy Deutscher has been more careful doling out tragedies. *Tosca* was playing at the San Francisco Opera during *Cinderella*'s run, but the family did not attend it because the story is too dark. "I grew up in Israel," he said before a matinee performance of *Cinderella*. "I know that an early exposure to ugliness can scar your soul." *Rigoletto* has also been off limits, though Deutscher has seen *La Traviata* (her "first sad opera" she says), and she loves *Eugene Onegin*.

The *Cinderella* score is melody-driven; leitmotifs pour forth in profusion, melding into each other. Its musical language is a pleasing hybrid of opera, operetta, and the American musical. The overture opens with a shimmering Wagnerian diminished chord that blooms into sunlight and the opera's main themes. Schubert's Ländler and rippling song accompaniments are a pervasive influence. Though it is unlikely Deutscher has heard Schubert's operatic rarity *Fierrabras*, certain passages recall its harmonic progressions. She turns the opening of Dvořák's bittersweet A-major waltz, Op. 54, into a love duet between the Prince and Cinderella. *Der Rosenkavalier*'s galumphing music for Baron Ochs and John Corigliano's bumptious Figaro aria in *The Ghosts of Versailles* echo here in the comic ball and court scenes, though the connection with Corigliano likely represents a coincidental mining of musical possibilities rather than direct influence. Some of the wind writing—passing a motif from clarinet to oboe to bassoon—recalls Tchaikovsky. The Prince has the most thrilling melody of the opera—a passionate outcry of yearning, accompanied by a pounding pulse in the low strings and brass. Unfortunately, the theme, "Burn for me, flame of love," doesn't go anywhere after its first few modulations upwards, but is always cut off by another singer's interjection.

Deutscher's favorite musicals are *My Fair Lady* and *The Sound of Music*; here, the Fairy's soaring invocation of a star called Hope is a pure Rodgers and Hammerstein paean to the power of positive thinking. A syncopated outburst from the King in response to his son's romantic intransigence could come right out of *Sweeney Todd*, though there is no chance that Deutscher has heard that work, if *Rigoletto* is too sinister. Here, again, it turns out that there are different paths to similar musical discoveries.

To call up these comparisons is not to suggest that the opera sounds derivative. It is a unique work that speaks the language of a long musical tradition. To be sure, there are some pedestrian tunes and times when the orchestra merely parrots the vocal line. But the sheer amount of orchestral and vocal invention is stunning. Deutscher's most impressive accomplishment is her mastery of the classical tradition's rich resources for expressing dramatic conflict. After the ball, the Prince has a despairing minor-key soliloquy, trying to understand why the masked composer, whose song captivated him, ran off from their encounter without giving her name. The King enters in a rambunctious mood, believing that his son has finally found a mate. He tries to tease out the details of his son's conquest. When the Prince pensively reveals that he not only went outside with a woman but went to the balcony with her, the King draws a prolonged, delighted breath: "Oh, the *balcony*!" and gives a knowing wink to his minister. The rapid alternations in their music—the Prince's plaintive and introspective, the King's rollicking and extroverted—vividly delineates their opposing mental states. The King's joviality turns to exasperation when he learns that his son knows neither the name, face, nor social position of his balcony companion. The Prince interrupts at full tenorial bray, in an indistinct key: "And she is the girl I will maaaaarry!" The King and the minister wince and stick their fingers in their ears, one of the production's many self-referential digs. The Prince draws an even more disgusted response from his father when he retorts that he knows everything that matters about the mystery woman: he knows the "melody of her soul." "'The melody of her soul!'" the King spits out in disbelief. "I've heard enough of this nonsense. Life is not an opera!"

Wit is an adult trait, entailing irony and distance. Comedy is harder to write than tragedy, which is why there are—sadly—so comparatively few of them. When a ten-year-old pianist captures the pathos of a Mozart minor-key concerto, the question arises whether a child can possibly understand the emotional depths that he is conveying, or if he is simply an unwitting mouthpiece for the music. Here, too, one wonders whether Deutscher is as wise about human foibles as her score suggests, or whether she has simply absorbed certain musical tropes which do the work on their own. It is hard to say, but her intellectual precocity suggests that she may be a quick learner in matters beyond music.

The inevitable benchmark presents itself: the young Amadeus. It is an impossible comparison, yet it worms its way in. Mozart, too, composed an opera at age twelve—more precisely, a *Singspiel* (a comedy in German with spoken dialogue). The bravura momentum of the orchestral music in *Bastien und Bastienne*, written at the height of the galant period, has no counterpart in *Cinderella*. But the psychological characterizations in the latter are far more acute; the characters in Mozart's *Singspiel* remain bland pastoral stereotypes, despite Mozart's music. He was likely hindered by the generic qualities of the text, which was a parody of Rousseau's influential court entertainment *Le devin du village*. But Deutscher also has the resources of another 150 years of musical expression to draw upon.

The San Jose production was literally a labor of love. "Without exception, everyone adores her," says the conductor, Jane Glover, a highly regarded Mozart specialist. "We all wanted to make it the best for her." And they did. The baritone Nathan Stark as the King and the soprano Mary Dunleavy as the Stepmother stood out for their theatrical charisma. I spoke with a friend of Stark's before the curtain rose. "She's a genius," he had told her. "It was amazing to be ordered around by a twelve-year-old." Stark, whose voice is richly grained and resonant, exploited the comic delights of gestural exaggeration to the hilt, playing his emotions broadly and for maximal comic effect. Though young, he touchingly conveyed the wobbles and bluster of an old man.

Deutscher's father may be trying to protect her from premature knowledge of evil, but the cruelty of Mary Dunleavy's Stepmother was almost unbearable. Dunleavy's clear soprano could switch instantaneously from hypocritical syrup to a full-throated shriek. Deutscher phonetically memorized in German "Der Hölle Rache," the Queen of the Night's show stopping aria from *The Magic Flute*, when she was four. The Stepmother's rage-filled coloratura passages were part of the opera's self-referential satire; Dunleavy furled them out with power and precision.

Stacey Tappan and Karin Mushegain as the two stepsisters uninhibitedly turned themselves into childish shrews, unafraid to distort their faces and voices in impotent jealousy. Jonas Hacker as the Prince enunciated his spoken lines with rounded aristocratic syllables reminiscent of the baritone Thomas Hampson; his tenor was warm and dignified. Vanessa Beccera had a more mature soprano and wide vibrato than might be ideal for the title role, but she nevertheless winningly conveyed Cinderella's sweetness. The director, Brad Dalton, kept the stage action dynamic without gratuitous fussiness. The sets by Steven Kemp and the costumes by Johann Stegmeir were lovely recreations, in sky blue, dusty rose, and lemon yellow, of a Baroque theater and palace interiors. Glover led the Opera San José orchestra in a tight, windswept performance, clearly delineating the quicksilver changes of mood.

Deutscher is fully aware of the challenge her music poses to the classical composing establishment, as I discovered when we met. She has just bounced into the living room of a modest bungalow in San Jose, where she and her family are living for the duration of the run. She is in pigtails, pink socks, and a red crocheted tunic over red leggings; she radiates enthusiasm and good cheer, giving me a broad, happy smile and speaking breathlessly but precisely. "Quite a few people tell me this is not the kind of music that is allowed to be written now," she says. "I have to find my own musical voice, they say. But I never lost my voice, I don't need to find a new one. I'm writing in the language of music." Deutscher rejects the idea that musical development is teleological and one-way. "I'm not going back," she says emphatically. "I just want to write beautiful music that people want to listen to. This is the music that is performed everywhere. My music is therefore very modern. I'm alive, I'm a child, I'm not going back to the past." She has been told that people search in vain for dissonance in her music. She counters that dissonance and its resolution inheres in the very structure of classical form.

Deutscher is not exaggerating the reaction to her music. Every composer I spoke to was dismissive at best, though their responses were undoubtedly driven by suspicion of the child prodigy phenomenon as well. None had heard the opera, but only clips of earlier works on the web.

An American music professor who teaches out West advised me: "Were I you, I would not dignify [her opera] by writing about it." A British composer who has consulted for American orchestras said that he was barely able to sit still while listening to the web excerpts of Deutscher's music. "I found the interviews pretty disturbing, too," he said. "In fact very disturbing. The overall effect is, I think, thoroughly creepy. I just don't hear her working the material, and I suppose that's what I mean by composing. There's so little sense of contradiction."

Boris Zelkin, a film and TV composer living in Los Angeles, acknowledged her "tremendous talent," but cautioned that "her ability to organize sounds in ways they have been organized before ... says nothing about her abilities to create things that are new. She's working with anachronisms.... Her choice to find her voice in the works of the past makes me less excited about her and it makes me question the current state of Serious Music," he wrote in an email.

William Bolcom, best known for his piano rags and his cabaret collaborations with his wife Joan Morris, was the most tolerant. Her music is "uncanny," he said. "But I don't feel as if I'd heard from her so much as her near-perfect channeling of whatever obscure composer she has 'contacted.'" Bolcom said he can easily empathize with someone who finds music today too discordant, because, as a product of our discordant world, it is. But his own writing, he said, though skirting many old styles, is "always transformed by the fact I'm here in this moment."

Jane Glover was unequivocal about Deutscher's accomplishments, but she, too, applied a teleological framework to them. Glover first encountered Deutscher's music when a retired British music agent sent her a video of the less ambitious *Cinderella* production from Vienna. "I thought it was something extraordinary," she says, sitting in the lobby of the Westin San Jose during an afternoon off. "I continue to be as startled by her gift as when I first looked at it. The craft of it is utterly remarkable." Deutscher has a phenomenally good ear for instrumentation, Glover says. The orchestration (on which Deutscher has admittedly had advice) is "remarkably, incredibly competent," if her vocal writing is still awkward at times.

But Glover was just as insistent that Deutscher was not yet speaking in her "own voice." "She can't go on writing like this for the rest of her life," she said. "What is remarkable for a twelve-year-old wouldn't be for an adult. The language of music has moved on." And the sign that Deutscher has reached her own voice will be increasing dissonance in her music. Glover found the "moments of chaos" in the score most compelling. A theme associated with Cinderella is taken up by the orchestra and "distorted"—such passages provide a "glimpse of what might be," Glover said.

Of course, if Deutscher were writing in a post-Reichian idiom, no one would accuse her of needing to find her voice. It was once taken for granted that artists would learn their craft by imitating the masters of the past. Few young composers today, however, have had an immersion in Classical theory and music. They draw instead on pop, film music, jazz, and hip-hop. It is no wonder that their writing is so remote from the tradition that Deutscher naturally breathes.

Admittedly, there is something intuitively persuasive about the teleological argument. We have become used to the ideas that artistic style moves in one direction only and that the artistic past is off limits for anything other than brief archaeological visits. Deutscher, however, presents a natural experiment in the evolution of musical expression. As she inhales more and more music, will she point the way towards a path not taken in the Western classical tradition, one that avoids going off the cliff of atonality? Perhaps she will reveal that the language of thematic development was not in fact exhausted, contrary to received wisdom. The predominant characteristic of today's serious music is no longer even atonality; it is the substitution of mere sound for harmonic structure. Kaija Saariaho's *L'Amour de loin*, with its mysterious soundscapes, is a prime example. Perhaps, however, music still remains to be written that allows a listener to enter the movement of a composer's mind.

And yet, Deutscher may end up recreating the history of twentieth-century music, in an ontogeny-recapitulates-phylogeny moment, whether because the earlier harmonic language was in fact spent or because the influence of contemporary style is simply overwhelming.

Deutscher herself is not immune to the lure of novelty. She thought that she had found a new harmony, but then heard it in Bruckner's Seventh Symphony. "I was annoyed," she says. "He stole my chord." She may find that twentieth-century musical history is always one step ahead of her own experiments. Or she may discover an alternative musical universe.

Many people are waiting with bated breath to see what happens next. "Professional musicians are asking themselves: 'What is this and where does this go?'" says Gjerdingen. The conductor Simon Rattle was taken aback, Gjerdingen reports, when Deutscher came backstage after a performance of Rameau's *Les Boréades* to inquire about a chord, which she played on the piano. "I haven't seen anything like" her inborn sense of harmony, Rattle said in 2017.

There is still an enormous amount of music to be absorbed. She has not yet experienced the complete *St. Matthew Passion*. Glover would like her to listen to Janáček, in particular *The Cunning Little Vixen*. Deutscher said that after the San Jose run of *Cinderella*, she was planning to spend more time with *Tristan und Isolde*. Any work that you pour into her may change the output, so deeply does she synthesize musical influence.

What is clear is that it is premature to expect a twelve-year-old to have a defined artistic voice. It is enough to have mastered the structures of the past. The fact that she is a highly competent violinist and pianist also unites her to a bygone composing tradition. Most of today's young composers can barely play any instrument, certainly not well, says Andrew Balio, the principal trumpet in the Baltimore Symphony Orchestra and the founder of the Future Symphony Institute.

Deutscher's current projects include a musical, for which she has been gathering melodies, though she doesn't have a plot. Inevitably, she wants to write film music. She has composed a first movement for a symphony and some movements for a string quartet. "I love starting something but I get bored and it's more difficult to finish," she says, showing something in common with the rest of us.

The arts funding world is going to be painfully conflicted. On the one hand, she is female: Good! On the other hand, she writes in a traditional idiom and her imagination resonates to the West's heroic narratives: Bad! Despite her girl-power revision, Deutscher's Cinderella story rests on powerful archetypes of chivalry and romance. The Prince still kneels to put Cinderella's slipper back on, though nothing in the plot hangs on the gesture, because the image embodies the ideal of masculine strength humbling itself before feminine grace.

Here, by contrast, are some of the contemporary operas that were staged around the time of *Cinderella*'s American premiere: Opera Philadelphia presented *We Shall Not Be Moved*, which explored persistent structural injustices, such as the marginalization of the gender-fluid, inflicted on Philadelphia's communities of color. John Adams's *Girls of the Golden West* premiered in San Francisco. *The American Conservative*'s Bradley Anderson described it as "peak identity politics." The white males were all evil, responsible for the plot's racial violence, environmental destruction, and capitalist predation. Pittsburgh Opera gave *As One*, a story of a transgender woman, earlier in 2017. Not surprisingly, its 2014 premiere at the Brooklyn Academy of Music was a magnet for foundation and government grants, receiving funding from OPERA America's Opera Discovery Grants for Female Composers Program, the Virginia B. Toulmin Foundation, the New York State Council on the Arts, the New York State Legislature, and the National Endowment for the Arts.

Besides the Packard Humanities Institute, which underwrote the San Jose production, it is hard to think of many foundations that would be interested in funding an unironic fairy tale of love at first sight with a handsome prince. But Deutscher may not need much philanthropic support. In November 2017, *60 Minutes* ran a profile of her in advance of the *Cinderella* premiere. As the segment traveled across U.S. time zones, tickets started selling out. By the time the profile aired on the West Coast, the entire run was booked. The company hurriedly added additional performances to accommodate local patrons. This customer demand is almost unheard of for a new work. A smart producer would mount *Cinderella* on Broadway. In addition to its comedic force, its score puts recent musicals to shame, whether from the Disney franchise or Andrew Lloyd Webber.

A large part of the public's advance response to *Cinderella* was the enduring fascination exerted by child prodigies. But another part was the desire for music that marshals harmony and melody to create beauty. Deutscher is, as usual, one step ahead of her critics. In a 2017 video made for the Carinthian Summer Music Festival in Austria, she again responded to the claims that she needs to "discover the complexity of the modern world" and that the point of music is to show that complexity. "Well, let me tell you a huge secret," she said. "I already know that the world is complex, and can be very ugly, but I think that these people have just got a little bit confused. If the world is so ugly, then what's the point of making it even uglier, with ugly music?"

It will be a fascinating test of music and of our culture to see what Deutscher is composing in fifteen years.

May 2018

Bernstein at 100: a personal look

Jay Nordlinger

CONCERT HALLS are filled with the music of Leonard Bernstein this season, for we are in an "anniversary year": the centennial of Bernstein's birth. He was born on August 25, 1918, and died on October 14, 1990 (at seventy-two). Anniversaries are virtually the organizing principle of the music business. I have long complained of "anniversaryitis"—but there are worse afflictions, true.

New York is especially Bernstein-mad. The composer spent his career in this city, though he was born and raised in Massachusetts. He wrote, among many other things, "New York, New York," that catchy song from *On the Town* (you know which town). It's practically an anthem of the city. The New York Philharmonic asserts particular ownership of Bernstein, as well it might: he was the orchestra's music director from 1958 to 1969, and regularly conducted the orchestra thereafter. A few years ago—peeved at some expression of idolatry—I wrote that Bernstein was "kind of a god and mascot of the Philharmonic, and of New York." The subject of Bernstein provokes peevishness in some people.

On New Year's Eve, the Philharmonic had a Bernstein gala, conducted by Bramwell Tovey, an Englishman. In remarks to the audience, he said many over-the-top things about Bernstein—things he might have reconsidered in the cold light of day. But he also said this: Bern stein "was the most famous American musician of the twentieth century." When I heard this, I thought it was wrong. Then, in thinking about it for a few seconds, I could not contradict it.

It would be unfair to count Rachmaninoff (who obtained U.S. citizenship). Same with Horowitz (who in any case was probably not more famous than Bernstein). Gershwin? Copland? Barber, with his *Adagio for Strings*? Maria Callas (who was American-born, but later took Greek citizenship)? Philip Glass? No, Maestro Tovey was right: it must be Bernstein. (And we are talking about classical musicians, of course, not Elvis.)

Shortly after Bernstein died, his friend Isaac Stern, the violinist, made a good point: Bernstein's "multifaceted talents came to full flower" just as television became the dominant medium in America, and just as the recording industry took off. Bernstein was everywhere. He was on television—primetime network television—often. Today, classical music barely has a foothold in television, even at odd hours and on odd channels.

"He hated it when someone said, 'You're really the Renaissance man,' but, damn it, he was. He had more than music in him." So said Marilyn Horne, the great American mezzo-soprano, to me in an interview some years ago. She went on, "One could learn so much from Lenny, just by having a meal with him. He had so much to give." I asked her, "Did he like singing?" "I think he did," she answered. "I never rehearsed anything with him—even something I thought I knew rather well—that he didn't put a whole new insight into. I learned a lot from him." Other musicians, at the top tier, give this same testimony.

Bernstein wrote classical music and Broadway music. He played the piano and conducted. He gave lectures and wrote—wrote prose, I mean. Donal Henahan, the late critic, once spoke of Bernstein's "bewildering versatility." Have we had anyone else like him? Yes, André Previn comes to mind. He writes music, of various sorts. He is a pianist (classical and jazz). He is a major conductor. And he writes like a dream—prose. (Try *No Minor Chords*, his memoir of Hollywood. It was edited by Jacqueline Kennedy Onassis, who was also close to Bernstein.)

Throughout Bernstein's life, there was a debate: Should he narrow down and do less, so that he could do one or two things better, or *even* better? Should he write classical music, only? Musical theater, only? Should he concentrate on conducting? Should he throw himself into piano playing, and be an actual concert pianist? I am one of those who believe that he needed to do it all. That he needed the blizzard of activity. I'm not sure he would have done any one thing better, had he focused on just that.

Bernstein reminds me of William F. Buckley Jr., different as they were in their politics. Buckley edited a magazine, wrote a syndicated column, hosted a television show, lectured widely, wrote spy novels, etc. *When will he knuckle down and write a serious book?*, many said. *Why do we need another sailing journal or a hundred more columns on the news of the day when he could give us some summa?* I believe that Buckley needed his blizzard of activity, needed outlets for his various talents, needed to scratch a variety of itches. Both Buckley and Bernstein were dedicated workers. They got a lot done. Each worked until his final breath (and kept going, I bet).

In preparation for this piece, I spent a few days bingeing on Bernstein: his music, his conducting, his piano playing, and more. I do not propose a complete survey here, far from it. Rather, I have some comments to make, in this season of Bernstein-bingeing. If you sample Bernstein recordings, bear this in mind: he made more than four hundred of them. Not all of them are gems, as how can they be? Even Homer nods, especially when he makes more than four hundred recordings. But Bernstein's record (no pun intended) is impressive.

Our opinions of Bernstein probably say as much about us as about him. When I was younger, I was a bit allergic to Bernstein, though I always acknowledged his talent (and thought *West Side Story* a masterpiece). You perhaps know the rap on him: trashy, vulgar, shlocky; needy, showy, mannered; bathetic, self-indulgent, egotistical. Bernstein is guilty of some of that, I think, but my allergy has largely vanished. I have become more "latitudinarian" in my musical judgments (to use a Buckley word). Young people, as a rule, are strict. They insist on right and wrong, and their conception usually comes from their teachers. When you get older, you accept that there's more than one way to skin a cat—although there are still right ways and wrong ways.

For me, the key questions, certainly about performance, are: Is it musical? Is it reasonably faithful to the composer? Does the performer have a case? Almost never was Leonard Bernstein without a case.

A lot of conductors have played the piano, in public. Furtwängler, Walter, and Szell come to mind. Sawallisch, too. We should not count Eschenbach, because he was a famous pianist who then emerged as a conductor. Levine is a very good pianist. So is Previn, of course. Bernstein, too, was a very good pianist—a real pianist, not just a conductor who dabbled in piano playing—and he could probably have had a career, if he had wanted. We can see this in his earlier recordings especially.

In 1946, he recorded Ravel's Concerto in G (with the Philharmonia Orchestra of London, which he conducted from the keyboard). He plays beautifully and shrewdly. He observes French cool and American jazz (also cool). In 1947, he recorded Copland's Piano Sonata, in a commanding way. In 1959 came an enduring seller: Bernstein in *Rhapsody in Blue*, the Gershwin hit. Less famous but equally good is his 1966 recording of Mozart's Concerto No. 15 in B flat, K. 450, with the Vienna Philharmonic (which he also conducts). This performance is full of Mozartean character.

I will make two or three general remarks about Bernstein at the keyboard: He played with a big, fat tone. And his playing was masculine. Virile. The pianist he most reminds me of is Daniel Barenboim, who, as you know, has made a big career as a conductor, too.

Bernstein's later recordings, I find, are less good than his earlier ones. This is especially noticeable in the same repertory. Bernstein has practiced less, I imagine, and his fingers are sluggish. I once interviewed Eschenbach, who, that very morning, had resumed playing the piano after a long layoff. "My fingers felt like sausages," he said. Bernstein, in his later years, sometimes had sausage fingers. Also, the videos show us that his posture was poor: he sat close to the keyboard and hunched his shoulders, just as he did when he conducted, which was no hindrance. Bernstein looks restricted at the keyboard, and he was. His passagework is clumsy.

While he may have lost facility, he never lost boldness. He just bulls his way through, heedless of any obstacles. And even when he is at his worst, he shows you something musical. There is always some spark in his playing. The same is true of his conducting.

He loved Haydn, and conducted a lot of him. Try Bernstein in a 1984 recording—a film, actually—of Haydn's Symphony No. 92 in G, the "Oxford," with the Vienna Philharmonic. Bernstein is so alive. That is what Isaac Stern said about him and his music-making: above all, he was "so alive." In the Haydn symphony, Bernstein is free yet tasteful. He gets Haydn's humor. He lets the man have his flair. In these hands, the music swings.

"I got rhythm," the Gershwins wrote. American musicians are expected to have rhythm, and Bernstein was a leading example of this.

In my recent binge, I wanted to hear him in Brahms's Symphony No. 2, because a conductor must really know how to breathe in this symphony, and he should keep himself out of the way. I was worried that Bernstein would be all too present, and that Brahms would be distorted. I need not have worried—at least about a performance that

Bernstein gave with the Boston Symphony Orchestra in 1972. On the podium, Bernstein speaks like Brahms, or rather, he lets Brahms speak. It is a beautiful, Brahmsian performance.

At the top of his game, Bernstein had extraordinary communicative powers, and extraordinary leadership ability. He felt that he belonged on the podium, and that the music came through him. He was its advocate, and others needed merely to follow. You can see this in a 1979 performance of Beethoven's Ninth Symphony with the Vienna Philharmonic. (Kurt Moll, incidentally, is stunningly good as the bass soloist.) The music is incisive, uplifting, and right. And no one is having a better time in the auditorium than the conductor.

He bothered a lot of us with his podium style: his leaps and swoons and so on. But I like to say, "No fair lookin'." Music is an aural art, and if you don't like what you see, look away and listen. Moreover, a conductor must do whatever is necessary—stand on his head, if that's what it takes—to get from the orchestra what he desires.

Bernstein had a big appetite for music, as for other things, and he conducted almost everything. Curiously, he did not conduct much Bruckner. One of the Bruckner symphonies he *did* conduct was the Sixth, which almost no one conducts. For a famous man of the musical theater, he conducted only a modest amount of opera. He and Callas teamed for *Medea* and *La sonnambula*. He teamed with Marilyn Horne for *Carmen*. He teamed with Fischer-Dieskau for *Falstaff*.

A couple of years ago, I was writing about *Falstaff*, and I was positively drunk on the closing fugue. I think I listened to every recording of it—and none was better than Bernstein's. None was as good, actually.

In the concert hall, he championed his fellow American, Charles Ives, and indeed gave the premiere of Ives's Symphony No. 2—a full fifty years after it was written. He also championed Nielsen, the Dane, and Mahler and Sibelius, who are staples now, but who were not so established then. (Ives and Nielsen remain on the fringes.)

I wish to note, too, that Bernstein could conduct his own music, very well. In Bernstein, there is no one better than Bernstein. But doesn't that go without saying? Not necessarily. Some composers are less than ideal interpreters of their own music. I would rather hear Copland conducted by Bernstein than by Copland. And Stravinsky conducted by Bernstein than by Stravinsky.

The great Russian—actually, he became an American, like Rachmaninoff and others—was Bernstein's guest on television one night. The year was 1960. Bernstein called Stravinsky—as he did more than once, unambiguously—"the greatest composer of our time." (Remember that Shostakovich and Britten were also at work.) He said that a composer, in a recording, can show people for all time how his music should go. He then had Stravinsky conduct scenes from *The Firebird* (Stravinsky's magnificent ballet). I must admit, this conducting is awfully good, whether the last word or not.

Starting in 1954, Bernstein gave concert-lectures for the *Omnibus* program on CBS. In 1958, he gave the first of his Young People's Concerts, also carried by CBS. He did fifty-three of those concerts. The first of them was called "What Does Music Mean?" The last of them, aired in 1972, was on Holst's *Planets.* Over these fifty-three programs, Bernstein set an example in music appreciation. These days, almost every musician talks from the stage, whether asked to or not. Bernstein was really good at it. His thoughts were well organized, and he expressed them in excellent English. He also had a very good voice: a very good speaking voice. He could communicate in more than musical ways.

He spoke to the children at an amazingly high level. He spoke to them at a higher level than musicians today speak to adult audiences. He also assumed more knowledge (probably because he could). In his own day, Bernstein was regarded by many as low-brow, or at least a popularizer. Today, he would be considered the height of sophistication, maybe a snob. It's hard to watch Bernstein's Young People's Concerts now and not think that our culture has gotten markedly dumber.

In February 1960, he presented a program called "Who Is Gustav Mahler?" He tells the children that Mahler was one of the greatest conductors who ever lived. He then notes a criticism made by many people: Mahler may have been a great conductor, but he was not that good a composer, probably because his head was filled with the music of others—the music that he conducted—making it hard to compose music genuinely his own. Of course, this same criticism was made of Bernstein himself.

He then says, "I admit it's a problem to be both a conductor and a composer: there never seems to be enough time and energy to be both things.... That's one of the reasons I'm so sympathetic to Mahler: I understand his problem. It's like being two different men locked up in the same body.... It's like being a double man."

Bernstein has the orchestra—his New York Philharmonic—play some happy music from Mahler's Symphony No. 4. He then tells the children, "You might not believe it, but the man who wrote all that jolly stuff was one of the most *unhappy* people in history!" He further says, "When Mahler is sad, it's a complete sadness. Nothing can comfort him. It's like a weeping child. And when he's happy, he's happy the way a child is—all the way. And that's one of the keys to the Mahler puzzle: he is like a child. His feelings are extreme, exaggerated, like young people's feelings." Mahler was "half man, half child," says Bernstein. And, of course, that is said about Bernstein, with reason.

Years ago, I was talking with a musician friend of mine—a conductor—about Mahler. My friend did not care for Mahler. Explaining why, he said, "You know how young people say 'TMI'? 'Too much information'? That's how I feel about Mahler. The music is grossly personal." Leaving Mahler aside, that is a problem some of us have had with Bernstein, both as composer and as conductor.

Here is an interesting fact, slightly macabre: Bernstein lies buried with a copy of a Mahler score—that to the Symphony No. 5—lying across his heart.

When I looked at the catalogue of Bernstein's classical music, I was surprised by several things. First, there is less of it than I would have thought. Yes, Bernstein was busy as a conductor—extremely busy—but I somehow thought he had written more. Second, most of his writing was done in the first half of his career. There is a petering off. Third, he did not write very much piano music, especially for a composer who was so good a pianist. There is no concerto, for example. (There is no concerto for any instrument, except the violin, and he called that piece "Serenade.") Fourth, there are not that many art songs, for so famous a songwriter—for the composer of dozens of memorable Broadway tunes. But then, there is a fine line between his art songs and his Broadway songs, if any. Is "Somewhere" Broadway or "art"?

A radical in his politics, Bernstein might be seen as a conservative in his music. He clung to tonality when the fashion was the other way. He was willing to be simple when complexity was in style. He wrote for audiences and he wanted them to like it. He cared whether you listened. (Here, I allude to the famous, or infamous, title of a 1958 essay by Milton Babbitt: "Who Cares if You Listen?") Bernstein was attached to the old forms, including the medieval. Virtually his last work was *Missa Brevis.*

One of his best pieces, I have always thought, is the first one he ever published: his Sonata for Clarinet and Piano (1942). It is both French, as so many woodwind pieces were, and American. It is lovely and intelligent—with just enough jazz to make you grin. This sonata will likely remain in the clarinet repertoire.

Chichester Psalms (1965) has much beauty and power in it. (Have you ever thought of Bernstein as a religious composer? In addition to *Chichester Psalms* and *Missa Brevis,* he wrote a "Jeremiah" Symphony, a "Kaddish" Symphony, *MASS,* and more.) The second movement of the *Chichester* piece treats the Twenty-third Psalm, using a boy soprano. I find this music cloying. I am allergic to it. But I will also grant that there is an ingenuousness about it. Bernstein could be amazingly ingenuous or innocent, for such a sensualist and hedonist. The "Kaddish" Symphony (1963) I admit to being allergic to, even if my general Bernstein allergy has faded. The symphony strikes me as pretentious or pseudo-deep. It makes me cringe. I find parts of it emotionalist, rather than emotional. I can hardly listen. At the same time, I understand why other people respond to this piece. It is heart-on-sleeve. One man's pretentiousness or emotionalism may be another man's honest feeling.

I have said that the early sonata is lodged in the clarinet repertoire. What else of Bernstein will last? He himself feared that he would be remembered as a conductor, not as a composer. This may happen to Pierre Boulez, I believe. I wonder whether any of his music will be played, generations hence. This is impossible to tell. But I believe that Bernstein's Serenade (1954)—formally, "Serenade (after Plato's *Symposium*) for violin, strings, and percussion"—will last. When future generations want an American violin concerto from the middle of the twentieth century, they will turn to the Serenade, I wager. It is a beautiful, intelligent, and inspired work. More and more, I love it. I have always regarded it as Bernstein's best piece, in the classical field.

And I smiled when reading some New York Philharmonic program notes last October. It was almost a smile of vindication. Joshua Bell was playing the Serenade, and the program notes told a story: Late in his life, Bernstein was rehearsing the Serenade, and he turned to the soloist, Glenn Dicterow, to make a statement: "This is the best fuckin' piece I ever wrote."

Before leaving the subject of Bernstein's classical music, I should say this, too: he had an influence on other composers, especially Americans. Over the years, I have frequently described a new piece as "Bernsteinian," as regular readers can no doubt attest.

In 1954—the same year as the Serenade—he wrote a film score: that to *On the Waterfront*, Elia Kazan's masterpiece. The music enhances the movie. Later, Bernstein fashioned a suite from his score. He was nominated for an Oscar, but lost to Dimitri Tiomkin, who had written the music for *The High and the Mighty*. (Other nominees included two famous composers: Max Steiner, for *The Caine Mutiny*, and Franz Waxman, for *The Silver Chalice*.) Bernstein did not take his loss graciously. Not for him was "It's an honor just to be nominated." "I am furious about the Academy Awards," he wrote to his secretary. "It is obviously politics, and I don't care, except that it would have jacked up my price for the next picture to double. And that is important. Oh well." Bernstein, celebrated for his leftist ideals, sounds pretty money-grubbing in this note. I will also point out a curious fact: Bernstein wrote the music for what is many anti-communists' favorite movie of all time.

Opening Carnegie Hall's season in 2008, Michael Tilson Thomas gave a little talk. He was conducting his San Francisco Symphony in a Bernstein gala. Bernstein, he said—no, yelled—was a "lib-er-al." That's how he pronounced that word: with three distinct, fist-shaking syllables. The crowd erupted in applause and cheers. Was Bernstein a liberal? Only in the sense that the UC Santa Cruz faculty is. Bernstein was on the left, with such friends as Marc Blitzstein and Lillian Hellman. It was Bernstein who inspired Tom Wolfe's coinage "radical chic." Wolfe was writing about the fundraising party in 1970 that Bernstein and his wife, Felicia, had thrown for the Black Panthers. In 1989, the first President Bush wanted to give Bernstein the National Medal of the Arts. Bernstein refused, because of a controversy over federal funding of an art exhibit having to do with AIDS. In any case, Bernstein was involved in politics throughout his life.

I have no doubt that politics used to influence what people thought about Bernstein, musically. But that has largely burned away . . .

He wrote many pieces that are neither quite classical nor quite popular. Take his ballet *Fancy Free* (1944). Is it classical or popular? It is in between, I think, like Gershwin's *American in Paris.* What would you call *MASS*, Bernstein's "Theatre Piece for Singers, Players, and Dancers" (1971)? (I have quoted the subtitle.) The singers in the *Gloria in excelsis Deo* section sound like the Sharks and the Jets (gang members from *West Side Story*). What is *Candide* (1956)? Bernstein himself, on television one night, described it as "my operetta or musical or whatever you want to call it." He then conducted the overture. This overture, in all likelihood, will never leave the repertoire. Speaking to his audience of children, Bernstein said *Candide* had run only about two months on Broadway. Sadly, "the show is temporarily over, but the overture lingers on, I hope." The children may not have known it, but their parents probably did: Bernstein was adapting a lyric from a popular song—Irving Berlin's "The Song Is Ended (But the Melody Lingers On)."

The overture is fizzy and funny and fine (to quote a *West Side Story* song). Churchill once said of FDR, "Being with Franklin is like opening a bottle of champagne." The overture to *Candide* is that way too. So is the aria that the overture quotes, "Glitter and Be Gay." Another song from the show, "I Am So Easily Assimilated," is a funny one about the Jewish experience. *Candide* ends with "Make Our Garden Grow," which I refer to as a "secular hymn." It is a common gala-ender. In fact, the New York Philharmonic ended its recent New Year's Eve concert with it. Some audience members sang along with the professionals, unbidden: it is a hymn for the Church of the Upper West Side. As you might suspect, I'm not crazy about this song, having a slight allergy to it. Indeed, I react as to fingers on a chalkboard. But I should also say that "Make Our Garden Grow" is often performed in a treacly fashion, and it need not be.

Bernstein wrote two musicals—musicals that are obviously musicals, and not anything else—whose titles sound alike, confusing many of us. One is *On the Town* (1944) and the other is *Wonderful Town* (1953). Both musicals have lyrics by Comden & Green. *On the Town* is stocked with songs that endure: "New York, New York," "Lonely Town," "I Can Cook Too," "Lucky to Be Me," "Ya Got Me," "Some Other Time." *Wonderful Town*, not so much. ("Ohio"?) Also not enduring is *1600 Pennsylvania Avenue*, which Bernstein wrote in the American bicentennial year of 1976, with no less than Alan Jay Lerner. Almost nothing from it lingers on. On New Year's Eve in Berlin, Joyce DiDonato, the

American mezzo-soprano, sang "Take Care of This House" with the Berlin Philharmonic, under Sir Simon Rattle. I suspect a political point was being made, more than anything.

Finally, we come to *West Side Story* (1957). Bernstein dreaded being remembered as a conductor, not as a composer, but he also dreaded being remembered as the man who wrote *West Side Story*, period. Even if he *were* remembered that way—so what? *West Side Story* is enough for one lifetime, or ten. Years ago, record companies would put out box sets of complete operas, and also a single LP of highlights. I once described Handel's *Giulio Cesare* as a long, continuous highlights album. Every number in that show is a winner, one after the other. *Giulio Cesare* is an extended, historic bolt of inspiration (like the same composer's *Messiah*, in fact). Well, *West Side Story* is one big highlights album too. There is hardly a weak note, a weak moment, in the show. That goes for moments instrumental and vocal alike. "One Hand, One Heart" can be a little treacly—but it need not be performed that way.

"Something's Coming" is a model of anticipation. "Maria" is an outstanding tenor aria. "Tonight" is a rhapsodic duet. "America" is eternally hot. "I Feel Pretty" is an outstanding waltz-song, something that Brahms would have admired. "Gee, Officer Krupke" is comedy gold. "I Have a Love" is another duet, with Straussian intervals. And let me say about "Somewhere"—that Schubert wouldn't have minded putting his name to it.

As long as there is anything like musical theater, there will be *West Side Story*. As long as people want to sing and play and dance, there will be *West Side Story*. Those proverbial cockroaches that will survive a nuclear holocaust? They will have *West Side Story* to enjoy.

When *The New Criterion* asked me to write about Bernstein at 100, I sort of groaned. I was Lenny'd out a long time ago. But I much appreciated my immersion, my bath, my binge on Bernstein. When I was younger, I think I resented all the attention that Bernstein got, especially when others were ignored. (Attention often seems to be a zero-sum game.) *Why doesn't anyone care about Eugen Jochum?*, I would think. *Not sexy enough, not weird enough, not publicity-seeking enough?* I was nauseated by Bernstein's celebrity. I was repulsed by his obvious neediness and egotism, and by the Cult of Bernstein.

I understand my former views, and can still get peeved from time to time. But the Bernstein wars are long past, even if the melody, or smoke, lingers a little. The record is clear, for anyone to examine, whenever he wants: Bernstein was a great musician—a total musician—and a genius. In his vast and varied output, he made a big contribution to the cultural heritage of his country, and beyond.

February 2018

Contributors

J. CHRISTIAN ADAMS is President of the Public Interest Legal Foundation and a former attorney in the Department of Justice Civil Rights Division.

BROOKE ALLEN writes frequently for *The New Criterion* and other publications. A former Professor of Literature at Bennington College, she now teaches in its Prison Education Initiative.

BRUCE BAWER's latest book is *That Year: Dispatches from 2020* (Swamp Fox Editions).

PETER COLLIER (1939–2019), a novelist and biographer, was the co-founder of the Center for the Study of Popular Culture and founding publisher of Encounter Books.

ANTHONY DANIELS is the author of many books and is a contributing editor of *City Journal.*

PAUL DEAN is a freelance critic living in Oxford, U.K.

JOHN DERBYSHIRE is the author of *We Are Doomed* (Crown Forum) and several books on mathematics. He lives on Long Island.

DENIS DONOGHUE (1928–2021) was a literary critic and the Henry James Chair of English and American Letters at New York University.

DAVID DUBAL is an American pianist, teacher, author, broadcaster, and painter.

JOSEPH EPSTEIN is the author, most recently, of *Gallimaufry: A Collection of Essays, Reviews, Bits* (Axios Press).

JAMES FRANKLIN is Honorary Professor at the School of Mathematics and Statistics, University of New South Wales, and the author of *What Science Is* (Encounter Books).

Contributors

JOHN STEELE GORDON is the author of *An Empire of Wealth: The Epic History of American Economic Power* (Harper Perennial).

MARCO GRASSI is a private paintings conservator and dealer in New York. He is the author of *In the Kitchen of Art* (Criterion Books).

DOMINIC GREEN is Deputy Editor of *The Spectator*'s World Edition.

JAMES HANKINS is a Professor of History at Harvard University.

VICTOR DAVIS HANSON, a classicist and historian, is the author of many books and is a Senior Fellow at the Hoover Institution, Stanford University.

CHARLES HILL (1936–2021) was a research fellow at the Hoover Institution and the Brady-Johnson Distinguished Fellow at Yale.

JACOB HOWLAND is a Senior Fellow at the Tikvah Fund.

LAURA JACOBS's *Landscape with Moving Figures* is available from Dance & Movement Press.

DONALD KAGAN is Sterling Professor Emeritus of Classics and History at Yale University and the author of the four-volume *History of the Peloponnesian War* (Cornell University Press).

ROGER KIMBALL is Editor and Publisher of *The New Criterion* and President and Publisher of Encounter Books.

ADAM KIRSCH, a poet, is Poetry Editor of *The New Criterion.*

JOHN BYRON KUHNER is the former president of the North American Institute of Living Latin Studies (SALVI).

MICHAEL J. LEWIS teaches American art at Williams College and reviews architecture for *The Wall Street Journal.*

WILLIAM LOGAN's newest collection of criticism, *Broken Ground: Poetry and the Demon of History*, was published by Columbia University Press.

HEATHER MAC DONALD, the author of *The Diversity Delusion* (St. Martin's Press), is the Thomas W. Smith Fellow at the Manhattan Institute.

MYRON MAGNET's latest book is *Clarence Thomas and the Lost Constitution* (Encounter Books). He served as the 2020–21 Visiting Critic for *The New Criterion* and is Editor-at-Large of *City Journal.*

Contributors

HARVEY MANSFIELD is author of *Manliness* (Yale University Press) and is the William R. Kenan, Jr., Professor of Government at Harvard University.

ANDREW C. MCCARTHY, the author of *Ball of Collusion: The Plot to Rig an Election and Destroy a Presidency* (Encounter Books), is a contributing editor at *National Review* and a Fox News contributor.

ROBERT MESSENGER has worked at *The Wall Street Journal*, *The Weekly Standard*, *The Atlantic*, *The New York Sun*, and *The New Criterion*.

KENNETH MINOGUE (1930–2013) was the author of many books and Professor of Political Science at the London School of Economics.

GARY SAUL MORSON is the co-author of *Minds Wide Shut: How the New Fundamentalisms Divide Us* (Princeton University Press) and the Lawrence B. Dumas Professor of the Arts and Humanities at Northwestern University.

ALEXANDRA MULLEN is an advisory editor at *The Hudson Review*.

JAY NORDLINGER, the author of *The Children of Monsters* (Encounter Books), is a senior editor of *National Review*.

ERIC ORMSBY is the author of *The Baboons of Hada*, a selection of his poems (Carcanet), and *Ghazali* (Oneworld).

JAMES PANERO is Executive Editor of *The New Criterion*.

JAMES F. PENROSE is a lawyer living in Paris.

JAMES PIERESON, the author of *Shattered Consensus: The Rise and Decline of America's Postwar Political Order* (Encounter Books), is a Senior Fellow at the Manhattan Institute.

DAVID PRYCE-JONES is the author, most recently, of *Signatures: Literary Encounters of a Lifetime* (Encounter Books).

BENJAMIN RILEY is Managing Editor of *The New Criterion*.

ANDREW ROBERTS is the author, most recently, of *Churchill: Walking with Destiny* (Viking).

ANDREW L. SHEA is Associate Editor of *The New Criterion*.

Contributors

Alexander McCall Smith is the author of the No. 1 Ladies' Detective Agency series.

Kyle Smith is critic-at-large for *National Review.*

Aleksandr Solzhenitsyn (1918–2008), a Nobel laureate in literature, was the author of novels, short stories, and poems, as well as works of nonfiction and memoir.

Mark Steyn is the author of *After America* (Regnery), which was a top five bestseller in the United States and a number one bestseller in Canada.

Andrew Stuttaford is the editor of *National Review*'s Capital Matters.

Alexander Suebsaeng works as a doctor in England but has previously lived and traveled extensively in southern Africa.

Karen Wilkin is an independent curator and critic.

Keith Windschuttle is the author of *The Killing of History* (Encounter Books) and the editor of *Quadrant.*

David Yezzi, a poet, is Chair of the Writing Seminars at Johns Hopkins University.

Index

Index

Index

Index

Index

Index

Index

Index

Index

Index

Index

Index

Index

Index

Index

Index

Index

A NOTE ON THE TYPE

THE CRITICAL TEMPER *has been set in Galliard, Matthew Carter's interpretation of the types of Robert Granjon. Originally created for photocomposition and later updated and reintroduced in digital form, Galliard has enjoyed continuous success among book designers since its first release in 1978. Strongly influenced by the chancery hands of the sixteenth century, Galliard – and particularly the italic face – possesses a liveliness rarely seen in text types. Despite an august lineage that counts Granjon and Claude Garamond among its progenitors, Galliard retains a lightness and gaiety that readily recalls the dance after which it is named.*

DESIGN & COMPOSITION BY CARL W. SCARBROUGH